A YEAR AND A DAY
IN
MAGICK

A YEAR AND A DAY IN MAGICK

A complete week-by-week course
to a lifetime in magick

CASSANDRA EASON

quantum

LONDON • NEW YORK • TORONTO • SYDNEY

quantum
foulsham

The Publishing House, Bennetts Close, Cippenham, Slough,
Berkshire, SL1 5AP, England

Foulsham books can be found in all good bookshops and direct from
www.foulsham.com

ISBN-13: 978-0-572-03281-4
ISBN-10: 0-572-03281-1

Copyright © 2007 Cassandra Eason

Cover photograph © Jurgen Ziewe

Illustrations by Hayley Francesconi, Karen Perrins and Ruth Murray

A CIP record for this book is available from the British Library

The moral right of the author has been asserted

Printed in Great Britain by Mackays of Chatham plc, Chatham, Kent

CONTENTS

Starting the Journey   7

Week 1   What is a Witch?   13

Week 2   History of the Craft   25

Week 3   The Roots of Witchcraft   37

Week 4   What is Magick?   50

Week 5   The Wheel of the Year   64

Week 6   Festivals of the Wheel of the Year   73

Week 7   The Multicultural Wheel of the Year   85

Week 8   The Basic Tools of Magick   99

Week 9   Egyptian and Norse Tools of Magick   116

Week 10   The Four Elements and Four Directions   134

Week 11   The Elements as a Cohesive Force   147

Week 12   The Altar   157

Week 13   Transforming Your Altar for Special Rites   169

Week 14   Spellcasting   177

Week 15   Magickal Timings   192

Week 16   Magickal Timings in the Cosmos   202

Week 17   The God and Goddess in Magick   220

Week 18   Creating and Using the Charge of the God and Goddess   229

Week 19   The Magick Circle and Mystic Square   246

Week 20   The Book of Shadows   259

Week 21   Magickal Names   268

Week 22   Psychic Protection and Magick   281

Week 23   Writing and Using Chants   293

Week 24   The Power of Symbols in Magick   303

Week 25   The Power of the Earth   316

Week 26   The Power of the Air   328

Week 27   The Power of Fire   341

Week 28 The Power of Water   354
Week 29 The Many Faces of the Goddess   363
Week 30 The Triple Goddess   374
Week 31 More About the Gods   384
Week 32 Amulets, Talismans and Charms   398
Week 33 Spell, Charm and Mojo Bags   412
Week 34 Native American, Isis, Celtic Spell and Charm Bags
         and Witch Bottles   422

Week 35 An Introduction to Magickal Alphabets: The Runes   431
Week 36 Magickal Alphabets: Hieroglyphs and Witchcraft   451
Week 37 Magickal Alphabets of the Alchemists and Angels   466
Week 38 The Moon   475
Week 39 The Sun   490

Week 40 The Dark Sun   501
Week 41 Colours in Magick   510
Week 42 Candles, Crystals and Colour   527
Week 43 Herb and Fragrance Magick   550
Week 44 Angel and Archangel Magick   574

Week 45 Magick and Psychic Development   595
Week 46 Psychic Development and Scrying   607
Week 47 Rituals and Ceremonies   620
Week 48 Festivals: Oimelc to Litha   636
Week 49 Festivals: Lughnassadh to Yule   648

Week 50 Using Knot Magick   661
Week 51 Making Your Own Tools   674
Week 52 Preparing For Your Year and a Day Ceremony   687
Week 53 The End of the Journey, the Beginning of the Adventure   699
         Index   703

STARTING THE JOURNEY

W(+ ⚬) elcome to this year and a day course in magick and witchcraft. Whether you are a total beginner in magick, an experienced solitary practitioner or a coven looking for inspiration and additional teaching material, you can take each of the 52 weekly modules of this course as far as you decide to go.

For beginners, by the end of the course you will have achieved the first level or stage of your magickal journey. At this point, a year and a day from now, you may feel ready to make a personal initiation or dedication as a Wise Man or Woman (my preferred terms for priest and priestess). Mark the date in your diary now as a goal.

Experienced witches can undertake a personal journey to expand familiar concepts and look behind and beyond existing knowledge to become truly wise people and teachers of others. They can also enhance their current psychic and healing powers, connecting with and channelling higher powers of inspiration and wisdom.

However, you can use this book not only as a course, but also as a magick reference work to supplement your own training or magickal practice by using it as a source rather than a course, without following all the modules. The book reflects my own growing knowledge and often changing perspective, as I explore in more depth different magickal cultures and research new books. What is more, I am constantly learning from other witches and those whose newness to the Craft brings fresh and welcome viewpoints and questions about established practice.

The magick I teach

I believe that even the most complex magick should be accessible, described in clear terms, focused on spreading light and goodness, should reduce negativity in the world and above all be used to serve others. This is the message running through this course and through my own practices. Because of this wish to be inclusive, I have been described as 'fluffy', a 'crushed velvet witch', and even a 'good warm-up act' by a purist at a witchcraft conference.

My approach to witchcraft is, I know, unusual, based on a firm belief that everyone needs to develop a unique approach within whatever structure is right for them. My methods offer one such structure. Your personal path will evolve over the years, whether you are a solitary practitioner, a coven member or someone interested in casting spells to maintain balance in your life and to help others. In this way, magickal traditions, both individual and collective, grow and adapt to the needs of each new generation while maintaining the universal truths I describe in the early modules.

My core beliefs are primarily Wiccan, but I do not practise within a coven. I draw from the magick of the Ancient Egyptian, Norse, Celtic and, above all, the folk tradition, and emphasise the central, continuing and, to me, necessary connection with the natural world. For me, ceremonial practices are different from the magick of the home and the natural world by degree of formality, not in essence. How formal the magick you weave is may depend on the occasion and your own views of what works best.

My own background is working-class folk magick. In my blood are the traditions of the canal people of the West Midlands of England who practised their own form of water witchery to cope with the privations and dangers of living in a confined barge with many children. Child mortality was high among boat people – my uncle drowned in a canal lock one foggy night as a child, while visiting his grandfather, who had become a lock keeper after the family left the waterways – so protective magick would have been a priority.

I am also a trained Druidess, though again more solitary than a grove member, and so have come to emphasise magick in the eye of the sun and power of the Sun Goddesses, as well as the more traditionally based lunar wisdom. Just as much coven magick has three levels, so does Druidry, with its Bards, Ovates and Druids. Because Druidesses and Druids hold their formal and informal ceremonies within a circle or grove of trees or ancient stones, my own favourite magick relies heavily on natural settings.

A year and a day in witchcraft

The aim of the course is to help you to become a Wise Man or Woman. Even newcomers can reach the first stages in a minimum of a year and a day. Solitary practitioners may choose to structure their spiritual development into three broad stages with dedications at the completion of each stage. Thereafter you can progress year by year in what is a lifetime's work to follow in the path of the village Wise Women. This can run side by side with coven progression, but for solitaries it offers a structure in a tradition of Wise Women and Men found in almost all cultures throughout history.

I believe that in the modern world magickal practitioners have a vital role in acting as wise guides to those beyond the magickal community as well as within it. This could be at work, at home or in the wider community, to bring healing and harmony to others. Of course, your beliefs will often have to stay in the background, as there is still so much misunderstanding about magick. But there are many ways in which we can help to spread wisdom based on magickal principles. You will find that people gravitate to you for advice, even if they do not know your magickal background, because your aura or energy field radiates kindness, understanding and quiet authority the more you learn. This applies even if you only practise magick occasionally.

Finding your own magickal framework

Later in the course I have described creating informal magickal groups, if you do not want or are not able to find a local coven. Individuals within such a group assume roles according to their gifts and interests; some will be good at organising, creating and leading ceremonies, while others prefer to teach new members or become robe-makers or artists of the group. As they evolve magickally, members may write for publications within witchcraft circles or, more widely, lecture, create beautiful artefacts for sale or become experienced healers and diviners.

Solitaries take on all these roles and so become very powerful magickally and if they wish often work very easily with wise ancestors, spirit guides, angels and nature spirits to create a very spiritual circle of positive energy.

Using the course

The basic order of the modules offers a progression for beginners. Indeed, the core modules are topics that make an essential starting point for the course not only for relatively inexperienced practitioners but also for anyone interested in expanding or reassessing what might be familiar topics, especially if they hope to teach others.

However, each module can also be studied in isolation if you are using the book as a reference, and will work even if you choose not to develop a topic. Start at any point in the book and gradually build up your knowledge. Depending on what time of year you start the course, you can work with the relevant seasonal festivals by using the index.

Some modules are double, allowing for two weeks of study where topics are complex or there is a lot of information. Each module has a learning element and a practical element. These include an optional further research element, usually pointing you in other directions for personal research and often based on your local area or facilities or well-loved locations. At other times, this section will suggest ways of developing the week's material: for example, writing your own elemental chants based on a particular ancient site or a beautiful place while you are there. This might involve organising a chant-making workshop and recording the best. Even though there are many familiar and well-loved chants that circulate and strengthen the witchcraft community, there is always room for new material. I have suggested my favourite sources for the traditional chants for anyone unfamiliar with them.

You will not necessarily complete the practical assignments within a week, but you can start making basic notes that you can add to, refine or revise over the period ahead or when you have some free time. Write or reassess your personal contract with the date in your Book of Shadows. Then set yourself realistic targets. You could decide to learn the major elemental correspondences or some basic herb lore in a month and how this might be possible: for example, while you are travelling on trains to work.

By the end of the book, I hope that whatever your entry point you will have clarified what you believe and have decided whether your current practices are valid for you or if they need to be adapted. For example, having explored working in the modules with a Norse or Ancient Egyptian altar form, you might want to develop new ways of structuring your personal as well as ceremonial altar.

Timings

Although you should initially mark your first dedication a year and a day from now as a goal and guide, you might need to be fluid and move the day further away. Sometimes a module will take longer than a week if it covers an area you have found difficult in the past or if magick is unfamiliar. You might also, as I often do, become excited with a concept and want to dig deep. For example, you might want to experiment with the colours in the natural world as the focus for a ritual or spell, rather than using candles. There are thousands of years and countless traditions we all have to explore, and I know there are so many areas I have still to experience.

A year and a day is the minimum it will take most people to complete this course, though experienced practitioners will move faster through basic information. Take your time, enjoy the course and spend longer on areas that interest you most. As you progress, you might even choose a particular festival for your dedication ceremony.

Most people have to fit magick into the everyday world. Sometimes you will have a week or more when you can do little towards the course; there may be a deadline at work, a family celebration to organise or you may feel tired, unwell or just want a break. Unlike some courses, you can take breaks from this one whenever you need to. But however busy or stressed you are, try to spend a few minutes each day with your indoor or outdoor altar, sitting by candle, sun or moonlight or close to nature, even in the local city square. You can return to full power when you feel ready. Even the most experienced witches get jaded, but studying magick should never be a chore.

Make sure you prioritise your magickal time and space. Chores are always there, as are the demands of family and friends; but that magickal sunset or meteor shower is rare and so precious. The more you learn and practise, the more harmonious and focused you make your life. The problems are still there, but you are much more able to deal with them in an earthly as well as spiritual way, as your power and confidence increases.

Some modules you can save for a special holiday, a weekend away or even a day at the seashore or lakeside. Indeed, the practical component gives your recreation time a spiritual lift and ensures it remains memorable and significant – and trips to the forest are far cheaper and offer more family togetherness than a theme park or simulated experience.

The Book of Shadows

In Week 20 we will work with the all-important Book of Shadows, your own personal magickal book for recording just about everything you discover. This is a wonderful legacy for future generations as an online or published resource.

If you do not already have a Book of Shadows, for now start a notebook that you can copy over later and/or keep notes on your computer with back ups (skim through Week 20 if you wish). Keep a section for book references and page references from this and other books, and briefly summarise the main points. So many times I have searched through books I have read for a particular paragraph or list of associations. As you gather more and more source material, precise notes save so much time.

Above all, from the start, record your personal impressions, feelings and any spontaneous words or chants you created. I still regret that I cannot re-create the best every labyrinth chant I created in a huge turf labyrinth in Northamptonshire. I cannot recall what came to me on that perfect sunny day as I walked the labyrinth coils, though years later I still write frustrating approximations.

Extending your knowledge

There is a reading list at the end of each chapter of general and specialised books. I have suggested some of my own earlier books where these extend topics, but you can of course get these from the library and I recommend that you read widely from a variety of authors. I have included titles with very different approaches from my own so you can get an overall picture of what people believe and practise.

There is also a great deal of information online, including online Books of Shadows that may be helpful. I have suggested sites that I consider to be good. The rule I use is that if a site doesn't feel right I don't use it, no matter how apparently learned the authority. Note that complexity and obscurity are not the same as profundity; most true experts I have met in any field can talk in terms that we can all understand.

PRACTICAL ASSIGNMENT

What does magick mean to you?

What characters can you think of from myth, literature, fairy story or more generalised images?

* Even if you are very experienced, suspend your knowledge of magick and go back to your roots when you waved your tinsel wand and believed anything was possible. For even the highest forms of magick to work, you need to recapture that childhood wonder that emerges at special moments throughout our lives and keeps us going in the grey and the difficult parts.

* Really bringing those moments back to life is much harder than learning the techniques of magick and how to direct it. So that is why I want you to spend time rekindling that spark of wonder, the spark that ignites any spell and ritual and instantly converts words, actions and tools into living energy.

* List between 10 and 20 magickal or mythological characters or scenes from your personal history, at whatever age, when you felt pure wonder and connection.

* Develop one or two of these scenarios by sitting by candlelight in a quiet place or near your indoor or outdoor altar.

* Visualise or imagine (the power behind all effective magick) that you are walking into a jewel-coloured illustration in a storybook scene that becomes real as you re-create in your mind the sensations, the sounds, the fragrances, the anticipation and wonder.

* Now draw the scene round you and shake your fingers so you can feel it as real.

* Relax and let images and words just flow from the cosmic well of magick that contains everything from our first childhood concepts to the Wisdom of Solomon. Whether you are experienced or not, you might be surprised just how much new information comes that can be verified later from books and online.

* Record your visions and impressions afterwards by the light of an extra candle, so you can read them for inspiration.

* Keep the list and when you have a few moments and feel jaded, cynical or overwhelmed, make another magickal moment live again.

My list included:

* Santa Claus and childhood Christmases that started in the almost deserted city market where my father used to take me late on Christmas Eve to buy the Christmas tree (invariably the last scrawny specimen). After standing on the bus platform all the way home with the tree sticking out as we whizzed along, it was transformed with coloured lights that worked on the tenth attempt.

* Merlin, whose tomb I saw in the ancient Breton forest of Broceliande where he had been enchanted in nine magickal rings by his love Vivien, the Lady of the Lake, until the return of King Arthur.

* The Fairy Godmother from Disney's Cinderella, with her magickal wand that when circled scattered stars and transformed rags into a ball-gown, at least until midnight – and came into my dreams last night as I tossed and worried all night.

* Leaving the shimmer of the Sahara desert to climb down into a dark pyramid that was not claustrophobic but filled with light and from which I seemed to fly.

* Tramping through powdery snow dragging my bag, the weight of a dead elephant, to meet the car that would take me for an early morning train, in the middle of Sweden. This helped me to understand suddenly a little of the world of the Viking Wise Women who, in their animal skins, arrived at dark halls after travelling vast distances through what must have seemed a surreal world of winter white and glittering stars.

* Standing within a near perfect circle of moonlight on a deserted beach and creating an altar from what I found on the beach, shells, a hollow goblet-like stone filled with seawater and a perfect driftwood wand.

* Splashing through the path of sunlight in the same sea as the sun rose on the Solstice morning, singing my head off and making my friends charm bags from the flowers warmed by the dawn sunlight.

* Outside my old caravan, lying flat on a sunlounger at three in the morning, trying to catch falling stars from a meteor shower.

* Crouching in a partially open Neolithic long barrow on the hills overlooking the sea in Jersey, chanting with a bemused taxi driver who had agreed to drive me round the ancient and deserted sites.

* Walking behind a waterfall in the Lowlands of Scotland and looking out at a rainbow of light.

* Mist clearing as I drove towards Glastonbury on my first visit. Seeing the Tor hill rising up like an island out of the sea and understanding the mystical isle of Avalon for the first time.

WHAT IS A WITCH?

(*A*)witch is the name adopted by men and women who practise magick within a broadly agreed belief system or code of ethics. This code of ethics permits the manipulation, concentration, focus and release of magickal power, to bring about or accelerate change or to maintain stability and protect the wellbeing of the planet and all its creatures.

Most witches are Wiccan, one of the most popular forms of witchcraft worldwide today, though not all Wiccans are witches. The word witch is derived from the Anglo-Saxon wiccwe (masculine) and wicca (feminine) and Old Norse vitki and vitka.

Not all people who work with magick, the practice of witchcraft, call themselves witches. For many, the very act of practising good magick does imply an acceptance of the witchcraft beliefs and faith. Indeed, casting spells and carrying out rituals in isolation from the principles behind them, as advocated in a number of popular spell books, is limiting both magickally and spiritually. But just as people who haven't been to church since childhood say prayers in times of crisis, so spellcasting in isolation may act as a connection to the wider moral implications and obligations of magick, rather than serve merely as a psychic shopping list.

What do witches believe?

As in any faith, there are many variations in emphasis, but the majority of witches acknowledge a higher creative force in the person of the Goddess.

I am convinced we are all spiritual beings in a physical body. This spiritual form made of light, a perfected version of the physical body at its peak, can be seen clairvoyantly as the rainbow aura or energy field extending beyond the physical body. It enters the infant some time before birth (or some say at conception) and has been reported by numerous observers as leaving the body after death as spheres of light or as a being made of light.

This spiritual entity or energy contains a divine spark, part of what in witchcraft is called the Goddess. Indeed in the Charge of the Goddess, attributed to Doreen Valiente (see page 24), the Goddess speaking through her High Priestess says:

> From me all things proceed, and unto me all things must return. Before my face, beloved of
> Gods and of men, let thine innermost divine self be enfolded in the rapture of the infinite.

Some picture the Goddess as a force or energy, who is manifest in terms within human understanding, as the Great Goddess who appears in the mythology of many lands. For example, the Hindu Mahadevi, creator of the universe, oversees the main cosmic functions, creation, preservation and destruction. The three supreme Gods of modern Hinduism, Brahma the Creator, Vishnu the Preserver and Shiva the Destroyer, assume these functions, it is said, by her will.

From the all-encompassing undifferentiated Goddess force that contains both male and female energies emanates all creation. In mythology, from Australian Aboriginal to the Ancient Babylonian and Classical Greek and Roman, the Goddess is seen giving birth to creation and sometimes dying during the process, so that all that is created is made from her body. In this form, the Cosmic Goddess is also equated with Mother Earth herself from whom life came and to which it returns, for she embraces birth, death and rebirth: sound ecology as well as spirituality.

Some of these Goddess figures gave birth to the male who was to become her consort. Gaia is the most famous of the creating Earth Mothers who has given her name to modern green spirituality. She was called variously the deep breasted one, she from whom everything comes, and the first and the last, since she was the daughter of Chaos or swirling darkness. Gaia, it is told, created every living thing, plants, animals, hills, mountains, waters. She did this by embracing the other primordial being that was part of her, Uranus (Ur means to envelop). Gaia then separated herself from Uranus by birthing him and mated with him as Goddess to God. Myth tells he was not the best of fathers or husbands and was eventually castrated by his son Saturn, an equally bad father figure.

The God and Goddess are now separated and she is given a persona, sometimes as Moon Goddess, Earth Goddess and even Sun Goddess in lands as widespread as Scandinavia, the Celtic world and Japan. The male acts as the balancing animus or yang force and in early myths takes on aspects of the hunter, the God of vegetation and the protector/avenger. As Neolithic farming developed, he assumed the role of barley and grain sacrifice God.

In this differentiated or more personalised form, the Goddess gradually became the Sumerian fertility Goddess Innana, the Ancient Egyptian Isis, the Greco-Roman Diana and all the other maiden, mother and crone forms of myth that we will explore in later modules in the book. However, the Goddess still retains her greater role, as well as the anima or yin aspects that form the alter ego of the God: for example, Isis to Osiris the Ancient Egyptian resurrection and vegetation God. Therefore in many forms of witchcraft, the Goddess remains supreme in ritual and more powerful than the God power that emanates from her.

I believe that through magick in its widest senses, as a spiritual pathway, we can increase the size and power of our divine spark within us all whether we practise alone as a solitary witch or in a group, and maximise the effect of our spiritual body. In this way we can occasionally and perhaps after many years link in with the supreme Goddess form, as we call the power of a named Moon Goddess within us at full moon.

Witchcraft and evil

Good and evil both exist, as do night and day, darkness and light, creation and destruction. We might almost always aim to do good; but the existence of malice, deliberate harm and physical, emotional and psychic attack from external sources, as well as our own natural negative feelings at times, are issues that every witch has to deal with. We need to protect ourselves and our loved ones against global and more personally aimed injustices and evil in a way that does not compromise our own integrity but nevertheless is effective. More of this later. Equally, magick, like any other power, is neutral and can be used for good or evil or the grey areas in between.

Evil is not something that can be totally eradicated and we all contain negative as well as positive aspects as part of our personality. Though we strive to develop the good parts of our character aspects of ourselves, even the mildest mannered person can get angry over injustice: Jesus was furious with the temple moneylenders, according to the Gospels. Despair, resentment and jealousy are normal reactions if we or our loved ones are being abused, disregarded or mistreated; they are part of our survival mechanisms.

Destruction is the other side of creation and part of the cycle of existence. As witches we need to wrestle with the mainstream moral dilemmas of the world around and decide if and how we need effectively to respond practically as well as magically. For instance, we need to do some hard thinking about the terrible havoc wreaked by the South East Asian Tsunami of 24 December 2004 and wars in the name of saving nations like Iraq from tyranny that can bring their own evils. I have tried to work more with this theme: see The Wiccan Rede on page 18.

If you are angry, resentful or strongly dislike someone who has done you or a loved one harm precisely because you can use magick, this is a time to hold back. Just as after a blazing argument you should not jump in a fast car and roar off down a motorway, so it is not a safe time to cast spells, precisely because with all that negative emotional power you are generating you might do psychological harm, not least to yourself, that you will regret in calmer moment. So talk to a good friend, dig the garden or scrub the inside of the cooker until you feel calmer. Cry, yell and yell some more, then when you are calm think about an appropriate practical and magickal response. Wise Men and Women aren't wise 24/7, but wisdom can bring restraint from unwise action.

I have recently undertaken research at London's Natural History Museum on the cycles of death/decay, decomposition and transformation in the animal, plant and mineral kingdom, and this has helped me to understand the cycles of life, death and rebirth in the physical world spiritually and magically, as well as mentally. I would highly recommend a visit to a natural history museum, if such topics as the food chain and the formation of crystals and decomposition of rock into soil and sand are unfamiliar to you.

Witchcraft and the devil

The worst accusation against witchcraft is that witches worship the Devil in the person of the Horned God. Though such accusations should have been left behind in the dreadful three centuries of witch persecutions (see page 42), this dangerous nonsense still occasionally rears its ugly head in sensationalist, unsubstantiated media reports of infant sacrifices and upside-down crosses.

The word devil comes from the Ancient Greek word diabolos, which means accuser. Some have traced the origins of the Judeo-Christian Devil to the Persian Fire religion Zoroastrianism, central to which was the constant war between the spirits of good and evil, Ahuramazda and Angramainyu. Others associate his creation to the demonisation of earlier Gods when the great monotheistic religion Judaism was created.

This is in contrast to the Oriental and some pre-Christian Western philosophies that see evil as the other polarity of good. Gods of evil, such as Loki in the Viking tradition, were a necessary facet of creation and destruction, both of which are necessary for evolution.

The Devil evolved as a Christian concept that became crystallised by the Romanised early Church Fathers, including Jerome. They were familiar with the pre-Christian Graeco-Roman goat-footed God Pan, who symbolised wildness, and the Celtic antlered Cernunnos, Lord of Animals and the Hunt.

The organised military prowess of the Greeks and Romans and growth of the city states altered the emphasis of the God to a supreme Sky God who was a good soldier and statesman, with the hunter relegated in importance. The Judeo-Christian God was likewise a warrior king and judge with hosts of warrior angels.

It was argued that if God was good, he could not have created evil. Conversely, if he was absolute, no one else could have created it and therefore demons must be angels who became too proud, refused to praise God or insisted on keeping their free will, rather than surrendering it to God. Lucifer, once supreme Angel of Light and Lord of the Seraphim, the highest rank of angels, became fallen leader of the rebel angels. His image subsequently blended over the centuries with the downgraded and demonised horned and hoofed Gods such as Pan and Cernunnos.

The Horned deity is a symbol of male power and sexual potency but without the aggressiveness of the warrior image. The God was probably the earliest tribal sacrifice icon of the hunter-gatherer peoples, at the time the deer were rutting. Freud's Id or instinctive powers are inherent in the Horned God and, like other pre-Christian deities of challenge, wildness and courage, will defend the herd even at the loss of his own life. Therefore this aspect of the God of witches is a very positive dynamic and essential one.

Witchcraft in modern-day life

Though in many lands witchcraft is now accepted more openly, there are still places where clairvoyance and magick are forbidden or certainly disapproved of, especially if a practitioner has children. In Jersey, parts of America and even that most liberal of countries, Sweden, I have encountered mothers whose Wiccan beliefs have caused serious problems with educational and social services. All the parents I know who practise magick have environmentally conscious, incredibly gentle and kind children who have been brought up to respect every living creature.

You may find that some employers, acquaintances and neighbours do have problems with the idea of witches, mainly because of the numerous misconceptions of sensational films and lack of knowledge.

The problem with secrecy and taboos about magick is that it encourages less responsible, power-hungry people to set up more dangerous practices in the name of witchcraft. Young people may buy unsuitable books on mediaeval demonology on the internet, fascinated because of cult television series and frightening films on the occult. This fuels popular prejudice, as well as sending floods of letters to my website from concerned parents and teenagers who have become terrified after corresponding with less reputable so-called witches and mediums who tell them they are cursed and ask for money to remove the curse.

All we can do personally is to try to encourage awareness of responsible practices of magick. Invite friends and neighbours to share seasonal celebrations and take every opportunity to introduce alternative ideas and to dispel offbeat rumours with gentle humour. Write to the local paper giving the sensible viewpoint when silly stories emerge. Start websites or contribute to forums online. Talk on local radio or to organisations and groups in your locality about the pre-Christian origins of festivals such as Christmas and Easter, and raise awareness of the need to conserve ancient sites.

In conservative or traditionally religious areas this can be an uphill struggle, so don't put yourself in the firing line if it will make things hard for you, if you will lose your job or if it make it difficult for your children to be accepted in the local community. As a solitary witch, I could fill a book with horror stories on those topics! Bit by bit, explain factually and simply and by your own life show how wise and responsible witchcraft is. Find gatherings and groups where you can share ideas and organise events and make friends with like-minded people. Use the internet and go online if you work alone.

Things are getting better and witches such as Kate West and the witchcraft organisation Children of Artemis (see page 24) do a great deal of positive media liaison work to dispel rumours that we drink murdered baby's blood and sacrifice animals. Magazines and newspapers are also increasingly printing serious responsible articles about witchcraft, and pagan festivals attract many interested newcomers who are keen to learn more.

Each one of us, solitary or as part of a coven, is a teacher of tomorrow's witches and can one day make magick, if not mainstream, at least an acknowledged form of spirituality.

Witchcraft and Christianity

A number of practitioners do have problems reconciling witchcraft with Christianity or other orthodox religions. There is no doubt that conventional religion does frown on witchcraft, in spite of increasing acceptance of the Goddess in Christianity and Shekinah in Judaism. Of course, we know that Christian festivals were grafted on to pre-Christian celebrations and that Jesus was not born on 25 December. We also are aware that almost every healing ancient well, dedicated once to the Mother Goddess under her many names, to the ancient Irish Mother Anu or Brighid the Celtic Triple Goddess, was Christianised and rededicated. The Mother Goddess wells became Lady Wells for the Virgin Mary, Anu wells became St Anne, the grandmother of Christ, and Brighid waters became Bride wells, sacred to St Brigit or St Bride. They usually also acquired a brand-new Christian miracle to explain the apparently sudden appearance of water that had in fact been used for rituals and healing for hundreds or even thousands of years.

In many ways, witchcraft is more morally accountable than Christianity because you can't just confess and be absolved, but must carry and where possible put right your bad deeds and words in this lifetime (and some believe in subsequent lifetimes). The Wiccan Rede or rules below demonstrate what high standards of behaviour witchcraft demands.

I have no problem reconciling witchcraft with my being a Quaker, a faith that believes there is good or God/the Goddess in everyone. Personally I think that if a rule in a religion is not right for you and you are living as a good witch, then of course you can be a good Christian or belong to any religion as well. Sadly, it may not be possible to tell the local Christian organisation of your magickal activities, but whatever or whoever you call your God or Goddess, all are the same source of goodness and light.

The Wiccan Rede

These are the rules that apply not only to those who call themselves witches but also to anyone practising positive magick. The following are fundamental, though only the first is actually called the Wiccan Rede. If you are an experienced witch, you might find that your own interpretation of ethics varies and this section can act as a checklist for spring-cleaning some preconceptions or verifying and defining your own beliefs.

Rule 1: If it harms no one, do what you will

What is harm?

This rule is the hardest to keep. A magickal practitioner cannot carry out spells for personal advantage or on behalf of others if that spell will affect another person adversely, whether or not that individual is considered at fault. So to me this means you can't curse or hex anyone even if they are doing wrong to the vulnerable or hurting your family. (There are other legitimate magickal means such as binding and banishing that can be structured to avoid harming the perpetrator of malice while preventing the harmful effects of his or her actions or words.)

Some very good witches disagree and say that it is our duty to use whatever means necessary to restrain the wrongdoer. Would I curse or hex someone who was threatening my life or that of a loved one or someone vulnerable? Luckily I have never yet been in that position, so can maintain my moral stance. I think the problem is that when we start to act as judge and jury it is easy for the moral boundaries to melt a little and our own prejudices, which we all have, and sometimes blind spots will affect our judgement.

Influencing others

You should not mess with other people's minds or try to force them to leave someone else for you, even if they say they are in an unhappy relationship. When we are in love it is easy to believe the person we long for is living with an evil hag and her bloodsucking children, but people usually stay in relationships because they want to, however bizarre it seems from the outside. Often the evil hag is just neglected, aware her partner is straying and maybe trying to cope with everything on a reduced budget while he or she is wining and dining you. Similarly, the evil-tempered boss might be struggling with an illness or fraught with worry about a family member.

As witches, we can draw love and success within limits. That is why we need always to have one foot in the magick circle and on terra firma when casting spells, because the effects – as I will bore you with saying a thousand times – are felt by real people in the real world. You may only know the side of the story told to you by the person requesting the spell and you might need to word the spell very carefully to bring them happiness without harming a third party who might not be wholly guilty.

You cannot win promotion at the expense of someone else, even if they are doing the job badly and cheating the firm. Nor can you draw or bind someone to you against his or her will, albeit in the name of love. Psychology is a close relation of magick and psychic work, and if you manipulate others, neither you nor they will be truly happy. Love should be based on freedom, and success on effort and talent, not on manoeuvring someone else out of a job or causing them to make mistakes.

But again, what if you need the job because without it you can't pay your mortgage or feed your family? Adding 'if it is right to be for all concerned' can be a good provision to add to spells, so leaving judgements to cosmic laws.

On the whole, wrongdoers do tend to bring about their own destruction. The man or woman who takes your partner (with their full encouragement), robbing your children of a parent and perhaps bringing financial hardship, usually finds a year or so down the road that the cheating partner cheats again or shows those traits that made them an unpleasant person to live with, once the honeymoon period is over. Corrupt or inefficient officials who ruin your life or that of a loved one generally get found out somewhere along the road.

This is no consolation at the time and, like you, I know people who behaved terribly and flourished while their victims foundered. I never said the choices were easy and the wiser you get, the more black and white merge into shades of grey and certainties are replaced by complexities. If in doubt, I would advise caution rather than unleashing something you can't control or whose effects you can't fully anticipate. I do try to throw lots of healing and protective spells at injustices of which I have suffered so many. And I don't always feel better for doing so.

Ecological preservation

Harming none is a sound ecological principle. This law also prohibits any human or animal ritual sacrifices. I personally believe that any form of bloodletting is not helpful in ceremonies and I do not use human blood or body fluids. Locks of hair, yes; nail clippings, maybe. But this is for you to decide and to judge what is right for you and what you would be happy to talk about to a sympathetic friend. Many excellent witches do use menstrual blood and semen or vaginal fluids in marking runes and urine in protective home bottles in the age-old style. But there are substitutes. Above all, it is important not to harm your own private standards, even if others tell you that you are fluffy or not a real witch.

Rule 2: What you send out returns threefold

This rule means that whatever energies you send out in your magick will return to you with three times the intensity. Send out in love and generosity and good things will come bouncing back. Carry out healing spells for others and you will find yourself healed in the ways you most need. Send out with malice or anger and the vibes will likewise return in unexpected but potent ways, three times as powerful as the original emotions.

This brings us back to the issue of curses and of doing positive magick for the sake of your own health and harmony as well as for others. Not only witches and sorcerers, but also ordinary people and even priests have in all cultures and all times inflicted what might be termed deliberate psychic attack on enemies. In the case of professional magicians and bad witches, this could be on behalf of someone else for a fee. Malevolent attack is different from the evil eye, which tends to stem from unconscious envy or jealousy. I have been cursed or hexed many times and even for an experienced witch it is unnerving, if you are feeling unwell or anxious at the time. The unanswered question is whether cursing only works if the victim knows of it, thereby activating the self-fulfilling prophecy or making the psychic connection. Invariably, someone will phone me up or mail to say their 'friend' has cursed me and they are just warning me. Pointing, whether with a bone as in some African nations, or in Malaysia where a kris or dagger is used, can make a person lose the will to live and he or she may even be shunned by his or her companions in these societies.

Psychic defence

Ill wishing comes in many forms and the majority from non-witches, and almost as disturbing is the negative intent from spiteful neighbours, colleagues, love rivals and even so-called friends and relatives. My research suggests that real curses cannot be activated unless known and that you can send it back if you do know (see page 281 for effective methods).

However, you can feel the effects of more free-flowing, deliberate or unconsciously directed anger or spite directed towards you and later I will discuss how to identify these bad vibes without becoming over anxious about non-existent attack.

In fact, the threefold law offers one of the most powerful forms of mental and psychic defence against malice. You aren't harming the perpetrator because the ill intent they receive back is their own, magnified threefold, as if hitting a springboard.

Rule 3: Enough for your needs and a little more

I am often asked, if you are a real witch, why aren't you aren't you a multi-million-pound lottery winner or another J K Rowling? Why can't you magick up a fabulous lover and the house of your dreams?

On a practical level, if every witch did a spell to win the lottery we would all get a very small payout; besides which, that wouldn't be fair to all the people who bought tickets in good faith and took a chance.

The modern world generally encourages the idea that we can instantly have what we want. To give one example, celebrities are created from perfectly nice, ordinary people overnight for appearing on a TV reality show. Books tell us we have just to wish and can walk away from everything that bothers us and that we have a right to a permanently exciting relationship with no down or dull patches and perfect children who whistle and sing their way through to the white wedding and job as a lawyer or pop idol. Dreams are important and can come true, but most that are fulfilled involved a lot of hard work. The quality that underpins magick is, as any witch or would-be witch knows, more than writing a psychic shopping list.

This rule of magick reinforces the idea of service and responsibility and says that personally you can ask enough for your needs and a little more. It is, of course, valid to ask in spells for what you and your family need. If you are worried sick about money, you can't focus on the needs of the planet or the health of your friend's dog. Generally, if you ask for help through a spell, you will get a little more than you asked for, as long as your requests are reasonable.

Again, you might be given what you weren't expecting or, more likely, the opportunity to earn or obtain the money you need. But we are all governed by forces and interconnections we do not understand and if a spell doesn't work there may be factors behind the scenes that only become clear weeks later. That is why such clauses as *when and if it is right to be* and *in the way that will bring the happiness, fulfilment or healing sought*, do allow the spell energies to be used in the way that ultimately will bring the best results. That can be hard to trust when you are sad, worried or confused.

Rule 4: Keep the balance

This fourth rule is often forgotten, but is the essence of good and successful magick. We do not spellcast in a vacuum and the good things we ask for ourselves and others come from a cosmic resource pool. Think of magick as a credit card. We can draw on blessings when we need them, but although your cosmic credit limit may be high, you have to pay back something at some time.

I am not including the libations or offerings we make magically, though they are of great worth. This additional cosmic payback is on a practical and emotional level. If you ask for something in a spell, you should always give a little kindness or encouragement in return to a person, animal or place in need. This doesn't have to be immediate or monetary, but when you do have the spare time and energy this could be in the form of time or help. By doing this you will increase the positive energies at large in the cosmos, so ensuring that they are there for you if you have a problem in the future – and for everyone else.

You can relate it to the elemental nature of the spell if you wish (see page 134). For example, if you asked for love (water), you could teach a young relative to swim, take your old crotchety aunt to the sea or river for the day or go out when it is cold and foggy to feed the ducks.

PRACTICAL ASSIGNMENT

Exploring the Wiccan Rede

Any magick group or coven, even if it belongs to an existing tradition, can decide democratically what are areas of morality, good taste, the needs of working with different people in such a deep way and the boundaries that must be established. But your private contract with the cosmos is very different and should be drawn up by every solitary witch or group practitioner for their own personal work. Experienced practitioners should regularly revise and update this contract, especially at major personal, family or global upheavals and initiate discussions with other witches (online or with friends if you are a solitary) about moral dilemmas.

What matters to me? Write/rewrite your own Wiccan Rede (rules) and give examples of each rule from your past experience or create scenarios when each would apply. For example, if someone is leading your teenager into experimenting with drugs or bullying a family member, is it your duty morally to bind them from doing harm or are you interfering with free will? How does free will equate with the obligation to protect the vulnerable?

Supposing you lover is being unfaithful and there are children involved that are going to be hurt. Can you use magick to break the hold of someone you know is just playing on your partner's mid-life insecurities and whom you know has a habit of dropping people when someone more interesting comes along? What about terrorists? Should they be bound or hexed? Work out your own basic boundaries.

Can curses ever be justified?

Then you need to consider what you seek in the short and long term from your magickal work. Is it primarily to become more tuned into nature, to perform occasional spells when you need some extra help or power in your life?

Do you want to become or develop as a serious practitioner, to lead or teach others or to write about your newfound knowledge? Or is there another direction you would like to move towards? Do you want to develop through magick in other ways, such as healing or divination or mediumship or shamanism?

Does witchcraft in any way conflict with other beliefs you hold or other forms of spirituality or your daily world? Can you reconcile the two without compromising your own basic principles?

Define your power source. How do you regard the higher sources of energy: as God, the Goddess, or as a general more abstract source of goodness and creativity? Do you believe in angels and guides for healing work and to protect you or would you work more comfortably with nature essences or your wise ancestors? Perhaps you would prefer to call your own inner powers for inspiration and strength or maybe a mix.

All responses are valid and this is an area that may change over the months and years. But define your initial focus now and if lately as an experienced practitioner you have felt less connected, what changes do you need to make in approach to feel at one with a higher source?

Are you happy to work as a solitary or in a coven for now? What are your long-term aims regarding the structure of your magickal practice? These may change over the months or years, but if you are frantically searching in vain for a good coven, examine if you could for now work primarily as a solitary or create a group.

* What are your specific gifts? Poetry? Robe-making? Don't be modest. Have you the time and scope to develop these talents? If a solitary, could you use pagan gatherings or the internet to share your talents and even make money or a career from them? This is an old and respected tradition, as good craftspeople and creators are needed to keep the old skills alive and to act as a resource for those who do not have the time, inclination or talent to create beautiful things or to work with words. You are making money from hard work.

* Can you further the positive image of witchcraft or is now not a good time in your life or career? It may not be, so don't feel guilty. The time will come.

* Do you want to set up or join a cyber coven or perhaps a forum?

* Could you talk or demonstrate in a workshop a particular gift or area of expertise at gatherings?

* Do you want to dedicate particular times of the week to your magick work, even if you can't stick to them always? This could be 10 minutes every day or an hour or two a week or you might want to study for much longer. This will depend on your lifestyle and commitments and you can practise magick no matter how little time you can give. Whatever is right for you without making you feel pressurised or stifled is the key.

* Can we eradicate evil once and for all? What, if anything, could constitute a necessary evil or out of evil coming good?

* Write an article on witchcraft and aim some day to get it published.

* Think of ways in which you as an individual can improve the image of witchcraft in the community.

Further research

Try to locate one or two of the following suggested books if you do not have them already and aim to read or reread a favourite.

Go online and enter Witchcraft Ethics and Wiccan Rede in your web browser search tool. See especially what forums are saying about morals and ethics and contribute your ideas to the cyber covens.

Further information

You aren't expected to read the suggested books weekly. Rather they are books you should study over weeks and months, as they are good core material.

Background reading for those unfamiliar with witchcraft

* Farrar, Janet and Stewart, *A Witches' Bible*, Robert Hale, 2002
  Janet and the late Stewart were initiated into the Alexandrian tradition, but have drawn valuable material and insights from the late Doreen Valiente. She clarified and reworked a lot of the material of Gerald Gardner, the father of Wicca and modern witchcraft. For background on the Goddess in many ages and cultures and modern perspectives.

  The second part has excellent chapters on the ethics of witchcraft and I would recommend the whole book as reading through the course to give a different and very important perspective on traditional witchcraft practices.
* Gadon, Elinor W, *The Once and Future Goddess, Symbol for our Times*, Harper San Francisco
  Highly recommended as it mixes archaeology with spiritual insight.
* Starhawk, *The Spiral Dance, Rebirth of the Ancient Religion of the Great Goddess*, Harper San Francisco, 1999
  A classic from the feminist and political perspective, and well worth rereading. I think this is the best of Starhawk's books and a great work to set the context of modern witchcraft.

More advanced reading or for anyone who wants to read more widely

* Rabonivich, Shelley, *An Ye Harm None, Magic, Morality and Modern Ethics*, Citadel, New York, 2005

  Thought-provoking for examining or re-examining your own magickal principles and starting discussions with others who have read the book
* Stein, Philip and Rebecca, *Anthropology of Religion, Magic and Witchcraft*, Allyn and Bacon, 2004
  Another thought-provoking book, a good basis for group or coven discussions and solitary musings and for reference

Websites

* *Children of Artemis*
  Probably the best UK-based witchcraft organisation with many international connections and excellent source material, gatherings, information on covens, books etc. Very good for newcomers and experienced witches alike.
  www.witchcraft.org
* *The Pagan Federation*
  The Pagan Federation for people who want to attend ecological events, seasonal celebrations, conferences and workshops and explore all aspects of paganism. Offers access to its worldwide connections.
  www.paganfed.org
* *Witches' Voice*
  US-based international site with just about everything, including political commentary, resources and knowledge.
  www.witchvox.com

Music

* Listen to Kate West's excellent and upbeat *Chants* CD for her song that describes 'Cernunnos, Horned One, Cernunnos King of the Sun the hunter and hunted too'

HISTORY OF THE CRAFT

This module forms the first part of a double module offering an overview of the influences of different magickal traditions upon modern witchcraft. After beginning with the common roots of all magick, I have listed the periods by historical date, both for natural magick and ceremonial magick and for each suggested some of the wisdom that we as witches have gained from them. Read through this module and note any areas that have specially influenced you in your magickal practice or ones you would like to know more about.

If you intend to teach others or become adept in a branch of ancient wisdom, such as Ancient Egyptian magick, this is an area of study in which you will benefit greatly from visits to relevant sites and personal channelling from your Witch Guardian or Spirit Guide, more of which more later (see page 34).

Working with ancient wisdom

The collective wisdom of witchcraft today draws on the knowledge and experiences of many ages and cultures. Magick is like different streams and rivers from all over the world and ages that gather together in a single delta or estuary. The rich silt formed from this accumulated wisdom provides insights different from and greater than the original separate strands of knowledge, and creates the material seed bed for future magickal growth. This growth occurs for the individual practitioner as well as witchcraft generally, as we develop our own unique basis for magick.

Because of the easy access via the internet to historical source books and resources from many cultures and the ability to record, edit, save and modify our knowledge base in electronic form, we are very fortunate as modern witches in being able to collate and hand on our discoveries and insights.

Accessing the collective well of wisdom

With cheaper and faster air travel, some of us can visit locations where magick had its roots, such as Greece or Egypt. We can stand in a ruined temple facing the sunrise, creating our personal Hymn to the Sun (see page 495). You may find you are spiritually drawn to particular places and cultures. But even if you cannot easily travel in person, there are quality television programmes, videos and DVDs and online interactive clips of the sights and sounds of ancient places.

What is more, we are all very distantly related through the first humans. This genetic seed seems to be sufficient to connect us with the collective well of ancient wisdom of all times and places. This occurs spontaneously as we meditate or practise different forms of ancient divination, such as runes or crystals, after or during ritual. Connection also comes on deep levels if we hold old artefacts in museums or visit old sites. This is amplified by carrying out personal or group ceremonies in these timeless places where people have worshipped for hundreds or even thousands of years and left imprints of their rites.

But in favour of the exotic, do not overlook your own location and those of your immediate ancestors for the magick and folk customs practised in your own area. Even the most heavily urbanised areas have place names recalling old wells, ancient oaks or fairy glades, and local folk history books will often reveal nuggets of the older rituals behind local customs and celebrations.

What is more, we each have Spirit Guides, one of whom will help you with positive magick work as your Witch Guardian. This wise man or woman from a tradition with whom you have spiritual and maybe historical affinity helps you to overcome intuitively those gaps where older practices are not known or there is disagreement about what rituals were practised. Your coven may also have a Guardian whose name is related to the coven name.

Cave magick

Many aspects of witchcraft have common roots, and many experts believe it dates back to Palaeolithic times. From 35,000 BCE, the first recognisable modern human society emerged. After this time until about 10,000 years ago, communities created hidden worlds in caves by drawing, painting and engraving animals and humans in animal masks dancing in rituals on the walls. The caves of Lascaux near Montignak in the Dordogne, France, contain more than 2,000 pictures of horses, bison, deer and bulls. Because they follow the contour of the rocks, the images appear to be three-dimensional and full of life. Against this backdrop, cave dwellers could carry out rituals to increase animal and human fertility, the latter necessary for the survival of the tribe in hazardous times of incredibly high mortality.

The practice of cave art has continued in hunter gatherer societies and there are many fine examples of still used African and Australian rock sculptures.

Understanding cave art magick

These animal images were not just representations of what the hunters saw. The original act of painting, for example, antelopes galloping across cave walls, with some fallen and pierced with spears, was also believed to call real antelopes magickally to the hunting grounds and to guide the hunters to where the animals would be.

As clay lamps flickered on the cave walls and animated the images, hunters would, in ritual, be telepathically drawn to the place where the animals were feeding, in a two-way process that remains at the heart of modern spellcasting, though the second part is sometimes forgotten. We will work with magick and psychic development later in the course.

When repainted or touched in ritual, it was believed that the power was released from the earth, a belief that continues, for example, among indigenous people in Africa. Indeed, the Australian Aboriginals and many African people believe that the human artists were acting as mediums for the true creators, the spirits.

Many of these indigenous images have been identified as being originally created between 10,000 and 40,000 years ago. For example, in Kimberley in Western Australia may be found paintings of the Wandjinas, the spirits of rain. The Wandjinas are depicted with spots around their heads for thunder and lightning to bring ran, but without mouths so that the seasonal waters will not flood the earth. They are still repainted at the appropriate times before the rainy season, so that they will retain their power.

The development of ritual

From 14000 BCE comes evidence of the first recorded magickal rituals with images like the Dancing Sorcerer of Les Trois Freres, in the French Pyrenees. Painted in black on the cave walls, this shamanic figure, which may be wearing animal skins, stands high above the animals that are painted across the walls. Only his feet are human; he possesses the large, round eyes of an owl or lion, the antlers and ears of a stag, the front paws of a lion or bear, the genitals of a cat and the tail of a horse or wolf.

Talismans such as a wounded bison engraved on a stone that is 12,500 years old have been found in the Tarn et Garonne region of France. There are diagonal lines on the animal's side of red ochre to represent wounds and wavy lines indicating spears. Similar artefacts have been found from Siberia right through Eastern and Western Europe and Scandinavia. Such charms were probably empowered ritually and then carried to release the magickal energies over what may have been a long and dangerous trek.

Gifts to modern magick

The principle of sympathetic or attracting magick comes from this early time, as does the rudimentary concept of psychokinesis. This is the psychic mind power that enables us to draw what we want to us whether a thought, a person or the herds, and to find the person or situation we need by automatically being guided there in the days and weeks after the ritual.

Women and early magick

There is a strong female tradition in early magick. Pregnant and at first featureless Mother Goddess stone statuettes were probably the first fertility symbols, invoking the fecundity of earth and humankind over thousands of years. These statuettes have been found worldwide, with prominent breasts and hips. In later periods, they were carved with a girdle and necklaces and wore a head-dress or had coiled hair like the earlier forms. They are frequently stained by smoke, suggesting that they had been worshipped by the hearth as household Gods. The earliest known fertility figurine, found in Willendorf in Austria, dates from 24,000 to around 22,000 BCE or perhaps even earlier. She is made of limestone tinted with red ochre. The figure is just 11.5 cm (4^1/$_2$ in) high, with full, voluptuous breasts, buttocks and thighs, a deliberately emphasised genital area and a swollen stomach.

A particular characteristic of Palaeolithic Mother Goddess figurines is the lack of feet. It may have been such images were private icons held in the hand by women as a fertility icon during lovemaking to conceive a child and also during labour.

Alternatively, they may have served as a focus for fertility rites for the herds, as well as for humans, placed in Mother Earth herself by the pointed end and carried from place to place as the tribes followed the herds.

Gifts to modern magick

The Earth Mother still retains a central role in natural magick. In formal and seasonal rituals, libations or offerings are poured on to the Earth in her honour. The first amulets and talismans, both the Venus figurines and images of wounded bison, created the concept that power can be stored in a symbol or charm and released when needed.

The Moon Mother

There was a natural early association between the Earth Mother and the moon because the moon month coincided with the female reproductive cycle. The full moon became the time of the Moon Mother and was considered the ideal night for conception. In places where there is no artificial light, women still menstruate by the moon. In early myths, the Moon Mother gave birth to her Moon Daughter every month.

The Goddess of Laussel was found in the entrance to an Ice Age cave in the Dordogne region in central France. She dates from around 23000 BCE and is important because she is the first representation of the Earth Mother as a lunar deity. In her right hand, she holds a bison horn, shaped like the crescent moon. It is divided with 13 marks probably representing the 13 moons in a lunar year. Her other hand touches her womb.

Gifts to modern magick

The moon, especially the full moon, has from early times been a source of wonder and offered light for outdoor rituals, the origin of modern Esbats or monthly gatherings. This early beginning of lunar awareness evolved into the personalised Moon Goddesses, the three stages of Maiden, Mother and Grandmother or Crone, and the central role of the moon in magick, especially fertility and women's rites.

Evolution of the Fertility Mothers and the Union of God and Goddess

Fertility rituals remained at the heart of the relationship between humans and Mother Earth as they turned to farming, for it was believed that the fertility of the land, the animals and people were inextricably linked. Many of the seasonal festivals were originally fertility rites and vestiges remain today in May Day processions and Midsummer dances.

Once the Earth Mother became linked with the fertility of the crops in Neolithic times, from around 8000 BCE onwards, she took on distinct names and personality as Grain Goddess. Some of these most ancient Goddesses have survived in the Scandinavian and Eastern European folk traditions: for example, Nerthus, the original Scandinavian Earth Mother. Fertility rites took place in her honour at sowing, May or midsummer and at the harvest. Making love in the fields at these times was believed to awaken the fertility of the land and the people.

The first sacred marriage or Heiros Gamos, as it was called by the Ancient Greeks, was celebrated around 3300 BCE in rituals marking the annual renewal of love between the Sumerian Goddess Innana, the Earth and Fertility Goddess and Queen of Heaven to the shepherd king Dumuzi in the Middle East area of modern Iraq. However, paintings on an ancient vase suggest there may have been earlier rites, perhaps to more localised fertility Goddesses in the fourth millennium BCE. Dumuzi was banished to the Underworld for the barren half of the year when nothing flourished and on his return the marriage vows was renewed.

In other cultures, the Lord of the Hunt had became associated with care of the flocks and gradually with the growth of the grain. The sacrifice of the Lord of the Hunt who died for the herd at the beginning of the hunting season, often around the Autumn Equinox, was replaced by the annual willing sacrifice of the God of the Grain, with the first harvest. I have written much more of this in the modules on the Wheel of the Year and on seasonal celebrations (see page 73).

In Ancient Greece are vestiges of very old cycles of the Grain Mother and Daughter, Demeter and Persephone or Kore, whose worship was central to the Eleusian Mystery Religion.

Gifts to modern magick

From this development, magickally we derive the concept of the Goddess and God interacting and the two energies fusing together in formal magick ritual in symbolic (the athame or ritual knife and the chalice) or actual sacred sex of Priest and Priestess.

Also comes the present Wheel of the Year structure that is influenced by the agrarian and the slaughter or cleansing of the cattle at the beginning of winter, rather than the hunting calendar.

Formal magickal systems

Formal magick is not as old as the natural magick led by the shamans, the magickal priest/healers that are still powerful in indigenous societies. However, formal magickal systems are important in the organisation, development and transmission of magick knowledge. These systems elevated words, consistent order and structured ritual over spontaneous actions.

They first appear in societies where civilisation and literacy among the priestly castes came unusually early. The origins of formal ceremonial modern magick can be dated from the Magi, the wise men from the Assyro-Babylonian culture more than 5,000 years ago. They manipulated fire and lightning and were said to have been the first to discover electricity. It was the same priestly caste that took gold, frankincense and myrrh centuries later to the infant Jesus after following the star that it had been predicted would lead to a new prophet and saviour. The Magi also invented the zodiac with its 12 signs and the 360-degree circle that is still used in horoscopes in modern astrology.

During the 7th and 6th centuries BCE, the legendary prophet Zarathustra, called Zoroaster in Greek, taught that Fire or Asha Vahishta was the Divine Energy of Ahura Mazda, the God of Goodness or the Sage God, and that the rotation of the celestial bodies, the waxing and the waning of the moon, the seasons, the rise and fall of tides, are all due to the Law of Asha (Cosmic Fire) through which the universe is being slowly refined towards perfection.

Zoroaster's writings have given him the title of the Father of Magic. In the rituals he set forth, in his concepts of duality of an evil, as well as a force for good, that were almost equally matched in strength, and the central role of Fire in magick lie one of the alchemists' and magicians' most powerful tools.

Gifts to modern magick
From these times we have taken the use of ritual fires in the great Wheel of the Year, Fire festivals of Sabbats, such as Beltane, named after Belinus, God of fire, at the beginning of May, all forms of fire and candle magick, as well as the collation of magickal rituals, often in the form of poetry, such as the Hymn to Innana.

Magick of Ancient Egypt

Ancient Egypt is probably the most influential culture of formal magick and according to the Ancient Egyptians, heka or hike, old words for magickal power, was a gift from the deities to humankind to improve their lives and protect themselves and their families. Christian Jacq, a French scholar who has written a number of works on the magick of the old world, has defined Ancient Egyptian magick as 'the essential energy which circulates in the Universe of the Gods, as well as in that of humans'. See useful reading at the end of this section (page 36).

Religion and magick were not separated as they are now and healing was also part of the whole spiritual concept, with prayers, rituals and spells being an integral part of remarkably advanced medical knowledge. Today, we are increasingly learning that these old physician priests and priestesses who practised in the Temple of Sekhmet, the Lion Goddess, and under the protection of other deities, understood what modern doctors are only just rediscovering: that the mind and spirit are crucial to the healing even of the most apparently physically based problem.

The Ancient Egyptians were influenced by the Babylonians, but some believe their own supreme deities came from the heavens or, some say, Sirius B to bring the wisdom and civilisation that transformed Egypt in a little over 500 years from a simple farming society to the greatest and most advanced ancient civilisation the world has ever known. They were: Thoth, God of wisdom and writing; Isis, the Mother, Mistress of magick and Moon Goddess; Osiris, her consort and the vegetation and resurrection God; Seth, God of disruption and change, like the Norse Loki, and his wife Nephythys, Goddess of Twilight, silence and hidden mysteries.

The Ancient Egyptians left detailed documents and spells engraved on tomb walls from around 3000 BCE that form the basis for much modern ceremonial practice. You can find much information on Ancient Egyptian practices in the books of the Egyptologist E Wallis Budge, some of which – for example, The Book of the Dead – are online. I have also written about them in detail throughout the course and indeed describe how to set up an Ancient Egyptian altar (see page 171).

Gifts to modern magick
Ancient Egypt has taught us a great deal about the power of words to bring thoughts and wishes into actuality and to use images in formal ritual empowered by

words, to transfer concentrated power from the symbol. They also made the connection between healing and ritual and magick and the power of using crystal and clay talismans and amulets and perfected the Middle Eastern practice of burning incense. Above all, they introduced a variety of Gods and Goddesses, not least Isis who is still central in ritual and Goddess spirituality. They offer a way of calling on different focal powers for specific energies in ritual and, by the association of the deities with animals, the animal power that is an important source of strength and nobility.

The Hermetic tradition

Formal magick became increasingly male centred as the centuries progressed, although the female power, as with the Shakti or Goddess energy in Hindu spirituality, was always recognised as the power necessary to animate magick. The Hermetic tradition of Western magick was itself strongly influenced by early Ancient Egyptian magick as it joined with that of the Greek conquerors led by Alexander the Great from 332 BCE onwards.

Hermetic magick is named after the semi-divine first century Egyptian sorcerer Hermes Trismesgistos whose name means Thrice Blessed Hermes. His Emerald Tablet, carved in pure emerald is the cornerstone of Hermetic tradition. One of the surviving parts of the 42 original books, translated into Latin in 1200, was said to contain the secrets of all magick, told to him by the Greek messenger God Hermes or the Egyptian God of Wisdom Thoth. Its key principle, *As above, so below*, stated that through the connection between cosmic and earthly realms, by mind power and ritual, thoughts could be brought into reality. It also formalises the idea of sympathetic or attracting magick, and became central to astrology and alchemy.

From Hermetic magick, too, in the tradition of Ancient Egypt comes the concept that everyone, human, spirit and deity, had a true but secret name. If a magician could discover this name, he or she could command the entity to obey every command. This belief lay behind mediaeval and Renaissance angelology and demonology.

Gifts to modern magick

Hermetic magick was very influential upon later magickal traditions, such as the Hermetic Order of the Golden Dawn. For witchcraft, it has survived in modern incantations to the deities and use of the deity names in Wiccan ritual, not to command a deity, but to tap into the archetypal power. What is more, every magickal practitioner chooses between one and five magick names that contain personal power, often selected numerologically. We will work with these in week 21 (see page 268) if you have not yet chosen your magick name or names.

Hebrew magick

Another source of modern formal magickal practices comes from the Hebrew tradition. One source of this magickal wisdom was probably Ancient Egypt. The greatest Hebrew mystical system the Kabbalah was said to have been dictated by God to Moses who grew up in Egypt, of course. This was the secret or esoteric wisdom that was subsequently encoded in the early books of the Bible.

The second major Hebrew magickal influence is attributed to Solomon, the son of David. Solomon was a powerful magician, who, it is said, possessed a ring that enabled him to summon and control every spirit in the cosmos. His name was given to the magickal books known as Solomonic Magic. Much of the magickal knowledge of Solomon came, according to myth from Raziel, the archangel of divine mysteries and of magickal secrets. This mystical knowledge, given originally to Adam as consolation for losing Eden, inspired occult magicians through the ages right up to today. The most famous magickal work bearing his name is called the *Key of Solomon*. This gives details of magickal hours, summoning spirits, ritual tools, invisibility, binding incantations, talismans, archangels, colours and metals. It formed the main source of mediaeval ceremonial magick.

The *Key of Solomon* was regarded by A. E. Waite as the ultimate source of magickal knowledge. Waite was creator of the influential Waite tarot system and a prominent member of the Order of the Golden Dawn, a magick society formed in the UK in the late 1800s.

Gifts to modern magick

Solomonic magick is the source of many of the magickal lists and associations we have today, knowledge of ritual tools and the framework of much ritual magick.

The Hebrew alphabet with its numerological associations is one of the more powerful magickal writing systems that we will encounter briefly later in the course and develop in future courses.

Enochian magick

Though Enochian magick was at its height at the time of the earlier witch persecutions, its practitioners, like male ceremonial magicians generally, were not greatly affected (see witch persecutions, page 42).

Enochian magick is a very high and complicated form of angel magic, and also involved astral travelling through different mystical planes. It was first created by John Dee, Court Astrologer of Elizabeth I, under whose protection he lived. He successfully predicted the date of the Spanish Armada. He recorded the secrets of this angel and spirit conjuration that was told him by his medium assistant Edward Kelley, by the angels who appeared in their obsidian crystal or shew stone.

Dee's notebooks still form the main guide to Enochian magick. He said there were Nineteen Keys, incantations or angelic calls, central to the conjurations of angels and spirits and binding of demons and elementals to do the magician's will. After Dee's death, Enochian magick was not much used until it was revived by the Hermetic Order of the Golden Dawn. Aleister Crowley devoted a great deal of attention to this form of magick.

Gifts to modern magick

Angel magick is still popular, though usually in a less complex and far more spiritual way. Much knowledge of the elementals, spirits and archangels and the necessary incantations is inspired by Enochian wisdom. Archangels are commonly used to guard the watchtowers.

We have also derived the angelic script from these times and the concept of progressively higher doorways to planes of evolved magick.

The Golden Dawn and modern magick

However, the birth of modern magick is often calculated from the creation in 1887 of the mystical and secret Order of the Golden Dawn. Though it was not a magickal order itself, the Golden Dawn was responsible for the collation and teaching of ancient magickal practices.

The society is said to have been initiated when Dr William Wynn Westcott, a London coroner and a Rosicrucian, a member of the secret German mystical order, in 1887 discovered part of an ancient manuscript, written in brown-ink cipher. This revealed fragments of mystical rituals of the Golden Dawn, a mysterious organisation that, unusually for the time, admitted women as well as men. Westcott contacted Fraulein Anna Sprengel, a Rosicrucian adept living in Germany, whose name was found with the manuscript, and she gave permission for the establishment of the society in England. The aim of the Golden Dawn was: 'to prosecute the Great Work: which is to obtain control of the nature and power of [one's] own being'. It has been suggested that Westcott created the mysterious German woman to authenticate the projected secret society.

Although the Golden Dawn exists today in various forms on both sides of the Atlantic, the original society lasted for less than 20 years. However, the way was prepared for the New Age movement by the dissemination by Alistair Crowley of what was hitherto secret and elitist knowledge. On his defection, he published many of the Golden Dawn rituals and its knowledge in his own journal *Equinox*.

The society taught through a series of progressive degrees or stages many of the subjects that now form the core of New Age wisdom: alchemy, astral projection, astrology, clairvoyance and scrying, geomancy, the Hebrew alphabet, Kabbalistic correspondences and practice, tarot divination and after the initial stages of learning, ceremonial magick and ritual.

Occultists from this tradition, such as the late Dion Fortune who founded her own order, the Community (later the Fraternity) of the Inner Light, originally part of the Golden Dawn movement, have contributed a great deal of knowledge on ceremonial magick.

Dion Fortune who lived from 1881 until 1946 wrote a number of excellent fiction (as well as non-fiction) books about ceremonial magick, including, *The Goat Foot God* and *The Sea Priestess*, that give many insights and the base for creating magickal temples of power. I highly recommend them.

Gifts to modern magick

A great deal of ritual magick today is based on the Golden Dawn practices, as well as magickal correspondences and elemental associations. Dion Fortune has left a legacy of creating a mystical temple around your altar, of male/female polarities energised by the female, psychic protection, Kabbalistic magick and descriptions of beautiful rituals on moon and sea magick.

PRACTICAL ASSIGNMENT

Finding your Witch Guardian

Those who practise magick have at least one wise Spirit Guide who protects them as they work and brings knowledge in dreams, meditation and during communication with him or her. Usually the guide is someone wise who was once connected with a tradition that interests you or that is your main inspiration. If you work mainly at home, you may have a wise grandmother who held the family magickal secrets and transmitted them to her daughters or female relatives. If you are connected with the Ancient Egyptian tradition, your guide may well have been a temple priest or priestess.

Those of you who are experienced may be aware of this benign presence, but some newcomers to magick may be hesitant at the concept. If so, you do not need to connect with this Guardian now and they will certainly never intrude on your magick without your permission. We will work with Angel Guardians in magick later, using a similar method that is effective for any angelic or Spirit Guide contact.

Making contact

You will need a clear quartz pendulum or a crystal pendant.

Work in the evening or early morning. If you have time, have a bath by candlelight or soft natural light in lavender or rose foam or oils.

* You don't need psychic protection as such. But before beginning, splash a little natural mineral water from a dish into the centre of your hairline, to open and protect your Crown chakra or highest psychic energy centre.

* Then splash a few drops of water in the middle of your brow for the Brow chakra, then the centre of your throat for the Throat chakra and finally on the pulse points on your left and right wrist pulse points for the Heart chakra. This will cleanse and protect your aura or energy field.

* At the Crown say as you splash the water:

Above me the light.

* At the Brow:

Within me the radiance.

* At the Throat say:

That I may speak wisely.

* At the left wrist pulse point say:

The truth in my heart.

* As you anoint the right pulse point, say:

Beloved Guardian of the magickal realm come to me and protect me now and always.

* Light a white candle and from it a sandalwood or frankincense incense stick or powdered incense. Have the pendulum close by. Breathe regularly and gently, asking softly that your magickal Guardian will move close and make their presence felt.

* You may after a minute or so sense or see your Witch Guardian clairvoyantly with your psychic vision in your mind's eye. You may perceive the background of the world your Guardian inhabited on earth.

* You may alternatively or as well hear a deep melodious voice in your ear or just sense the presence and feel a light touch on your hair or brow.

Developing communication

At first you may not experience a clear connection but continue anyway.

Hold the pendulum in your power hand, the one you write with. We are not going to use it in the yes/no way but as a channel, like a radio or television aerial to strengthen the connection.

* Ask your Witch Guardian a question, for example:

What is your name?

* Then put your other hand close to but not touching the pendulum so you will feel the vibrations in your fingers.

* The pendulum may or may not move but you will feel and maybe see it vibrating or pulsating and the answer will come into your mind often at first as your own inner voice. In time, you may hear the Guardian's voice clearly.

* Ask another question, such as:

When were you first with me?
How did you first learn magick?

* Ask as many or as few questions as you want. At first the answers may be short, but in time you can establish this inner dialogue as any other communication with someone you love. There is no hurry.

* The inner picture of your Guardian will become clearer over time and communication deeper until you no longer need the pendulum.

Closing the communication

* Touch the four higher chakra or energy points with your index finger of your power hand and visualise each closing so you are quite peaceful. Move downwards from the Crown.

* By the candlelight write in your Book of Shadows or on paper the information you received during the encounter.

* Then when you are ready blow out the candle, sending the light to your Guardian with thanks and sit quietly in the fragrance.

* Plunge the pendulum into clear water nine times and leave it to dry naturally.

Developing the relationship

We will work much more with your Guardian over the coming weeks. Just by lighting a single white candle a few minutes before a spell or ritual and softly calling your Guardian's name, you can ask them to move close, protect you and empower you. You can also call on him or her before beginning study, writing chants or before sleep using the white candle to bring you answers in dreams or to take you to ancient magickal places.

Further research

Visit a museum or use an online source to find artefacts from the Palaeolithic times or study the magickal practices of contemporary indigenous hunting societies, such as the Sami Reindeer people of Lapland or the Inuit peoples of North America and Canada.

Try to locate one of the historical sources of modern magick as a book or on the internet so you can learn about a root of magick that interests you. Record any insights in your Book of Shadows. If you belong to a particular tradition, work with an unfamiliar historical root or one you have found hard to understand.

Does your region or indeed family have any ancient folk magickal customs or Midsummer spells you know? Look in local libraries and ask old relatives. By recording them you are preserving your local heritage.

Further information

Further reading

* Guiley, Rosemary Ellen, *The Encyclopaedia of Witches and Witchcraft*, 1989, Facts on File, New York
* Jacq, Christian, *Magic and Mystery in Ancient Egypt*, Editions du Rocher, Monaco, 1983. Translation, Souvenir Press and Janet M. Davis, 1998
* Levack, Brian, *The Witchcraft Source Book*, Routledge, 2003
* Murray, Margaret Alice, *The God of the Witches*, Oxford University Press, 1992
* Murray, Margaret Alice, *Witchcraft in Western Europe, a Study in Anthropology*, (1921), R. A. Kessinger Publications 2003

Websites

* *The Museum de la Sorcellerie* Museum of witchcraft in the Central Loire Valley of France. Website has English language information www.musee-sorcellerie.fr
* *The Museum of Witchcraft, Boscastle, Cornwall* Reopened after bad floods in the town; an excellent website with online artefacts and descriptions www.museumofwitchcraft.com
* *Salem, Massachusetts* There are a number of very good museums in Salem www.salemwichmuseum.com www.salem-ma.wprldweb.com

THE ROOTS OF WITCHCRAFT

In the previous module we explored the ancient roots of witchcraft and how formal and ceremonial magick contributed to the way we practise magick today, whether as a solitary witch or a coven member. In this module, I will write about folk and natural magick and how all the strands have joined in modern Wicca. I also refer to the times of persecutions that I have researched in Scandinavia, as well as the UK and America. These are part of any witch's heritage. While I have not dwelled on distressing details, I believe that in our work, by sending blessings through the ages and regularly remembering our wise men and women ancestors on our altars, we can work to heal the past.

Magick of the seasons

Now let us return to the less formal system of what we call witchcraft or pagan traditions. Pagan comes from the Latin word paganus, country dweller, and has come to mean anyone, city or rural dweller, who follows the cycles of the seasons, the moon and the sun.

Folk witchcraft and natural magick have preserved much from the northern tradition of Northern France, England, the Netherlands and Germany through Scandinavia, Eastern Europe and Russia to the Baltic. It embraces both Celtic magick, akin to Druidry, and Scandinavian magick, which has much in common with Saxon magick, which gave us magickal alphabets.

Seasonal celebrations

Seasonal celebrations can be and are practised within formal ritual settings, and the Sacred Marriage forms an integral role in the story of the Wheel of the Year.

However, primarily the Wheel of the Year follows the agricultural year and the principal deities are those of the sun and the grain, and involve the battle between the deities of darkness (in the sense of night) and light (in the sense of day). Deities of vegetation, the woodland, flowers and the abundant harvest of fruit and vegetables also play their part, even when in Christian times they became folk characters, such as Robin Hood, associated with the Green Man, and Maid Marian, the pre-Christian maiden Goddess.

Seasonal magick and rituals celebrating the passing of the year formed a focus for celebrations and offerings for good hunting seasons and good harvests, long before records were kept.

Gifts to modern magick

It would be hard to find a seasonal celebration not influenced by these traditions, as well as modern customs such as crowning the May Queen and Jack o' the Green celebrations throughout Europe. It also keeps magick close to power sources in the natural world and preserves the joys of spontaneous spellcasting and rites.

Celtic magick

Celtic magick has formed a major strain of the folk practices and natural magick of people throughout Western Europe and is especially influential still among those of Scottish, Welsh or Irish descent in America, Australia, New Zealand and South Africa. We know that the Celts swept across Europe in two waves from about 800 BCE, conquering and spreading their spirituality based on a love of and reverence for nature and a belief that the deities were part of nature, and not remote figures on mountain tops or in the heavens.

Druids and Druidesses, the Celtic priesthood, were officially wiped out in England by the Roman general Suetonius Paulinus around 60 CE. Those who survived fled to Brittany, Ireland, Scotland, Wales, Iona and the Isle of Man. In Wales, the Bardic tradition continued to flourish and the wandering musicians, known as the Derwydds or oak seers, were believed to have preserved the Druidic tradition in their songs and poems that were recorded much later by secular folklorists during the Middle Ages. It was not until 1700 that the last Druidesses came ashore from the Isle de Sene in Brittany to join a convent.

Celtic Christianity was greatly influenced by Druids. Saint Columba who founded the monastery on Iona, is said to have regularly prayed, 'My Druid, Son of God' or 'My Christ my Druid.' In Celtic lands the myths and poetry have survived orally and the myths are contained in such works as *The Welsh Mabinogion*. But because Celtic culture was preserved untainted in Ireland for far longer than other Celtic lands, this has proved the richest source for Celtic mythology. Here, the four chief myth cycles are the Ulster Cycle, the Fionn Cycle, the Invasion Races and the Cycle of the Kings.

Because these accounts were recorded by Christian scribes, inevitably the tales have become biased and patriarchal, but many regard the myths as containing the kernel of the hidden teachings of Druidry and their ceremonies. The heroes and heroines of song and story may have been Druids and Druidesses, just as the Gods and Goddesses became the fairies of folklore.

The modern revival of Druidry from the 18th century initially by academics and those influenced by the thriving Welsh Bardic schools, brought a much more ceremonial form of the craft. But at its heart, Celtic spirituality remains simple, revering the triple realms of Earth, Sea and Sky, and, with the fourth element of Fire, is seen as the central generative principle, as signified by the ritual or Nyd fires, kindled from wood with no external fuel.

Celtic influences

The Celtic emphasis on the Sun is a good counterbalance in modern magick. Druidry is regarded as a sister religion to magick and in both practice and principle they share many common factors, not least the Wheel of the Year that is principally related to Celtic myths.

Like more formal witchcraft, Druidry has three degrees or levels of initiation. Strabo, a Greek geographer (64 BCE–21 CE) writes at the end of the 1st century BCE of three kinds of Druids: the Bards, the Vates (Ovates) and the Druids:

> *The Bards are singers and poets; the Vates, diviners and natural philosophers; while the Druids, in addition to natural philosophy, study also moral philosophy.*

With the coming of the Anglo-Saxons and Vikings to the former Celtic world, the tradition grew of village or community wise women who worked as healers, diviners and casters of spells in every settlement, a tradition that was destroyed by the witch persecutions.

Gifts to modern magick

These are many and include: shape-shifting; weather magick; intermingling of the solar and lunar calendars in the eight festivals; working with elements within the natural world; herb and tree craft; reverence for ancient places; using wands; power animals; and incorporation of nature essences.

Scandinavian magick

Scandinavian magick, where even formal rituals are quite spontaneous and nature based, is said to have come originally from a mysterious ancient tribe known as the Volsungr who came south from the far north of Scandinavia with or just after the final Ice Age.

A priest/magician tribe said to guard the ancient forests and trackways, helping any in need, they introduced an early form of runes known as the Ur runes. The Volsungr spread their wisdom, including the sacred incantations and spells associated with each magickal runic symbol, but eventually disappeared back into the northern forests. It has been claimed that the Aesir deities such as Odin came from these people and were deified after their individual death/disappearance. Others say that Scandinavian magick derives mainly from Finnish shamanism.

Because the Vikings invaded and colonised so many lands in the northern hemisphere, their magick and the culturally related Saxon magick from the same Germanic root, has become the mainstay of the northern magickal tradition. This magick spread with colonisation and migration, and now influences practitioners in lands as far away from Scandinavia as Australia, North America, South Africa and New Zealand.

Scandinavian magickal practices

Accounts of Scandinavian magickal practices come from Denmark, France, England, Scotland, the Isle of Man and Belgium. The home or homestead has always been considered important in Viking magick and indeed magick was a force used in everyday life for good and regrettably sometimes for ill wishing. Though there were male practitioners, the art was primarily a female one at every level.

Much of the detailed knowledge of rituals comes from the Eddas, the mythical accounts of the old heroes and deities that nevertheless contained a great deal of information about magickal practices and actual events. They were recorded by Christian scholars some time after the events occurred. One example is the *Prose Edda* written by the Icelandic Christian historian and statesman Snorri Sturluson (1179–1241). He wanted to preserve the ancient tradition. In modern Scandinavia and also in America, Astaru or Odinhism and Seidr have revived these ancient Norse traditions.

The first Scandinavian country to be officially converted to Christianity was Denmark around 965 CE. King Olaf Tryggvasson converted Norway and Iceland during the first century of the new millennium. But in Sweden, paganism persisted and Viking wise women held sway certainly into the 1300s in Scandinavia, albeit unofficially. Many a farmer or chief went to church on Sunday but also made offerings on his personal harrow or stone altar to Thor and Odin, often roofed over among the farm buildings.

Domestic magick

Viking women using spindles and distaffs containing amber and jet or clear quartz wove power and protection into the thread by chanting spells as they spun and sewed. Magickal shirts and cloaks gave protection again wounding.

Most famous were the raven banners, the icon of Odin, that were carried into battle by Vikings. The magickal banner would be woven by the mother, sister or a virgin daughter of the warrior. The ground beneath it would turn black or the raven was seen to flap its wings. Sometimes the banner would be pure white and the raven would appear on it only in the heat of battle.

Norse witches

There were a number of different kinds of witches described in old literature, but in practice one person probably occupied more than one of the roles and may have combined them all, especially in later times.

The Seið was a senior magickal woman in the clan who lived apart or perhaps with a sister. She would cast spells on behalf of the tribe and important individuals, some good, some for revenge, and would travel in trance in the spirit or astral body to obtain healing or fertility for the people and animals from the deities and ancestral spirits. Like modern mediums, she would channel messages from the ancestors and the deities.

She was famed for raising winds or causing snows, landslides or high seas against enemies and invaders, and so these practitioners were tolerated even in early Christian times as a necessity for people still at war among one another.

The Viking Goddess Freyja, whose chariot was pulled by two huge black cats or lynxes, was mistress of Seiðr and she taught the Craft to Father God Odin.

Spá-kona or Völva interpreted Ørlög, the natural laws of the universe as expressed through the Wyrd or fate of individuals or whole clans. The name comes from the word for magickal staff, because these prophetesses would bang a staff on the ground to induce the necessary altered or trance state to interpret the runes. A Varðlokur, a rhythmic, soft chant, was also used to induce trance.

The Völva would predict military victories, as well as personal matters. Her mistress was Frigg, the Mother Goddess, who could see into the future, but would not reveal her visions, not even to her husband, the great Odin.

Galor or Galdr were chanters, men and women who sang or chanted over herbs and potions to be drunk to attract love, to bring victory or, in harsher times, to do harm to enemies. Like other Viking wise men and women, they were knowledgeable in the ways of trees and holy waters, especially wells that it was believed flowed from with the Norns or sisters of fate's well of the Wyrd, that nourished the roots of the World Tree.

They were hands-on Wise Women or Men who might be employed to change the luck of a farm or tribe by chanting and were often also the Vitki.

Some believe the word vitki/vitka is related to the Anglo-Saxon term Wicca (feminine) and Wiccwe (male) and over time it came more to refer to a male practitioner of the magickal arts.

The Vitki specialised in casting spells on the family stone altar or harrow, using a two-edged knife similar to the modern witch's athame but sharper, with a basic pot or iron cauldron. They crafted talismans and amulets, and would heal, bless land and people, and banish earthly and paranormal malevolence. They also used divination, such as wax on water, another parallel with the Völva.

Gifts to modern magick

Scandinavia gave us rune magick, writing, speaking or making the runic symbol with the body in ritual to release the stored power of each symbol (see page 431). It also introduced: the concept of trance, divination and psychic powers being integral to and not separate from magickal energies; spellcasting; knowledge of harnessing forces of nature and especially the weather; outdoor altar work; and the importance of raising power and inducing magickal states of awareness through chanting.

Christianity and the old ways in Europe and Scandinavia

After the establishment of the Christian church, the worship of the old deities and old ways were officially banned and the nature festivals supplanted by religious ones. Pope Gregory, who sent St Augustine to England in 597 CE, acknowledged that it was better to try to graft the new festivals on to the existing Solstices and Equinoxes: for example, Easter instead of the Spring Equinox. Churches and abbeys were erected on the sites of the old pagan temples and rededicated with holy water.

For centuries, however, the old and new religions co-existed, and people still consulted the wise women healers, who also acted as midwives and offered effective herbal pain relief. In the fields, on the seasonal festivals people would still dance and make love to bring fertility to cattle and corn, and leap high over fires, riding staves, staffs and broomsticks, to show how high the corn would grow.

A number of early churches had their mother altars that eventually became Lady Chapels dedicated to the Virgin Mary. Images of the head of the Green Man were adopted in numerous mediaeval churches and cathedrals as an icon of protection. The graphically portrayed Celtic fertility and birth Goddess Sheelagh na Gig images were put in churches in Ireland and in parts of England, as late as the 16th century, sometimes over the entrance to the church itself, symbolising the entry into the womb of the Mother. One example of this was at Killinaboy in Ireland, a church that is now ruined.

The village wise women/herbalists/counsellors/seers/midwives were the acknowledged centre of the community, handing down their craft from mother to daughter. Every family, too, had its own secret recipes for herbal remedies that they would also pass through the generations. The priests and nobles had no problems with the wise women, as they acted as the cohesive force of traditional society.

But this coexistence of belief could not remain, as both church and state became increasingly political and the place of women in society deteriorated further. In the 12th century, the German female mystic Hildegard von Bingen corresponded with kings, nobles, senior churchmen and even the Pope, advising and admonishing them. But by 1220, the holy fire at the saint's shrine in Kildare, dedicated originally to the Goddess and then to Saint Bridget or Brigit, believed to have burned unquenched for more than 1,000 years, was banned by the local bishop. In common with other lands, he also brought nuns under the control of a male priest, and women were no longer able to rule over monks or dual-sex abbeys.

The Burning Times

From the 15th century, political issues brought about the widespread persecution of witches who were mainly women. Throughout Northern Europe and Scandinavia, at least 100,000 people were executed as witches between 1460 and 1700. Some sources put the number as high as a quarter of a million people. Many more were lynched or hanged by mobs eager to blame bad harvests or dying cattle on witchcraft; others died in prison during torture. About three-quarters of those killed during this period were women, mainly older and lower class. But anyone who was different, eccentric, senile or physically deformed could be accused.

By December 1484, the Bull of Pope Innocent VII was published, appointing Heinrich Kramer and Jakob Sprenge, two clerics, as chief inquisitors in a crusade against witchcraft. In 1487, in their book *Malleus Maleficarum* or *Häxhammaren (The Witch Hammer)*, they described in lurid detail the tortures that could and should morally be used to obtain confessions from suspected witches. They stated that it was better to kill an innocent person who would be rewarded in heaven by God than to allow a guilty person to remain unpunished:

> *All witchcraft comes from carnal lust which is in women insatiable. Wherefore, for the sake of fulfilling their lusts they consort even with devils.*
> *Blessed be the Highest who has so far preserved the male sex from so great a crime: for since He was willing to be born and to suffer for us therefore He has granted to men this privilege. There was a defect in the formation of the first woman, since she was formed from a bent rib, that is, a rib of the breast, — she is an imperfect anima, she always deceives.*

Possible reasons for the persecutions

The emphasis on the sin of Eve and the inferiority of women had existed since the time of St Paul, but with the rise of an organised male medical profession, women healers became a threat, not least because their skills ensured less painful childbirth. According to the 15th century Fundamentalist Church fathers, this was contrary to the curse of God that the daughters of Eve should bear children in sorrow. So the midwives were a prime target for the new persecutions, being accused of sacrificing babies to the Devil, an accusation that was seemingly confirmed by 'evidence' gathered by the authors of *The Witch Hammer*. Given the high rate of mortality, a grieving mother might easily blame the midwife.

What is more, this time saw the beginning of the appropriation of common land and the enclosure of smallholdings that almost all peasants possessed round their homes. Accusations of witchcraft carried the penalty of the seizure of land, so this was an easy and legitimate way of removing a peasant reluctant to give up his or her land rights. By condemning the wife as a witch, the whole family would be implicated and disgraced. In the case of an elderly, childless widow or middle-aged spinster, a common victim of the witch hunts who perhaps had inherited land from her father, or a younger widow who refused to remarry, there would be none to speak out on her behalf.

The majority of men accused of witchcraft were the husbands, sons or father of accused women.

The witch hunts

The witch hunts started in the European Southern Alps and over the next 200 years spread throughout Britain, Western Europe and Scandinavia. The *Malleus Maleficarum* became the handbook of inquisitors throughout Europe, and Protestant and Catholic churches alike persecuted witches with viciousness and a zeal bordering on paranoia

The seasonal gatherings often held at full moon now were translated into wild tales of female covens meeting and copulating with the Devil. (Men very conveniently forgot their own leading roles and unbridled sexuality at these celebrations.) In the hysteria that followed, even cats, legitimately kept to reduce the risk of infection from vermin, were believed to be witches in animal form, a demonic spirit or familiar, and were hanged or burned with their owners.

Most confessions that were extracted under torture and published were remarkably similar in their content to the vile practices listed in graphic detail in *The Witch Hammer*. It is obvious that the poor women were told exactly what they should say, in order for the torture to stop. Although torture to obtain a confession was not allowed in some countries, except by royal assent, many inquisitors were very cruel to even young victims who would confess in the hope of having their interrogation brought to an end. Sexual abuse was rife. Inquisitors excused their own behaviour towards captives as evidence of the evil of the women whom the Devil forced them to assault, unwillingly.

Young children were regarded as a legitimate source for intimidation in order that they might incriminate their mothers and grandmothers. The child's evidence was in many lands considered enough to condemn and execute a witch and afterwards the children of condemned witches were equally cruelly treated by the religious authorities. I read of one young boy in Sweden who was beaten for a year every Sunday after church to drive the Devil from him. How could he ever have grown up to experience or show love after having watched his mother, like so many others, being beheaded and her body immediately burned, and then been hurt himself for a whole year afterwards?

Swedish witchcraft trials

Though relatively few people were killed for being witches in Sweden compared with countries like Germany or Scotland, there were horrific incidents of torture and executions between 1668 and 1676. There was burning and beheading, and women were buried alive in pits, often though they had committed no crime. Many innocent women were identified as witches by Visgossar, young orphan boys who were paid with food and money by the priests and inquisitors to identify women as witches as they left church.

In the first witchcraft trial in Lillhärdal, in the province of Härjedalen, 30 women were executed and their own children were tortured into making confessions that their mothers had taken themselves and other children to Blåkulla, the place of the devil, and subjected them to hideous atrocities.

There is a mountain now called Häxberget or Bålberget, the Mountain of the Witches or Bonfires where 71 people, all women except six, from Torsåker and two nearby parishes, were beheaded and burned on 1 June 1675, after being given communion. The place still is said to echo with the screams, and some have described that on the anniversary the streams run red.

Witchcraft in America

In the colonies of America, the most notorious trials were those at Salem, Massachusetts, between 1692 and 1693. During this mass hysteria, 141 people from the town and immediate area were arrested. Many accused were model citizens and devout churchgoers who knew nothing of the old ways. Nineteen were hanged. Even a dog was hanged.

The hysteria began with accusations by teenage girls who had been dabbling with the occult and whose experiments went wrong. A four-year-old child, Dorcas Good, was the youngest victim to be accused of witchcraft and imprisoned. She was released on bail after her mother was hanged, but her younger sibling died in prison. Dorcas was driven insane by her experience.

Some researchers have suggested that the desire to appropriate land was behind at least some of the mass accusations as well as rampant superstition and overzealous investigators. A landowner, Giles Corey, apparently originally an innocent witness of the trials, was pressed to death, a torture that took three days, rather than confess, which would have seen his property taken from his descendants.

The end of the story and the beginning of modern witchcraft

Although the last execution for witchcraft in England was Alice Molland at Exeter in 1712, it was not until 1951 that the Witchcraft Act of 1736 was repealed and replaced with the Fraudulent Mediums Act.

By the late 20th century in the USA, witchcraft was recognised as a valid religion by the Supreme Court and accepted by the US army. However, that is not to say that in traditionally religious areas it is easy for witches in the US or elsewhere.

The birth of Wicca

Wicca has been defined in a variety of ways. Most commonly it is described as the major organised religion of neopagan witchcraft, formally established by Gerald Gardner in the years after the Repeal of the Witchcraft Act in the UK in 1951.

Wiccan takes the Wiccan Rede as a central principle and regards the divine life source as a part of nature, not a force beyond creation as with the Judeo-Christian God. This divine source of life is manifest as the God and Goddess within everything living, male and female, animal, bird, tree and flower (see page 14). Wicca is sometimes regarded as the oldest religion on the world.

Neopaganism has been defined as modern polytheistic (many deities) religion, practised by contemporary followers of pre-Christian religions such as Ancient Egyptian, Greek, Norse and Celtic. These followers are often divided into two distinct groups: those who are nature orientated and those who are part of magickal groups practising formal rituals, derived from ancient and secret traditions.

Wiccans, of course, embrace both categories with the variations between different kinds of Wicca depending on the degree of formality and the nature of the ancient sources of religion on those rites. That is, of course, a generalisation, but it gives a starting point for your own definitions of your own kind of magickal heritage. Some witches do not call themselves Wiccans. Others work primarily as healers and ecologists, and celebrate the eightfold years and revere nature, rather than focusing on magick.

Can anyone be a Wiccan?

I believe that if you follow the Wiccan Rede and observe the eight seasonal festivals and the full moons, then you can if you wish call yourself a Wiccan, whether you work alone or undertake formal training and initiation within a coven.

As I said earlier, the word witch is derived from the Anglo Saxon wiccwe (masculine) and wicca (feminine) and Old Norse vitki and vitka. But the origins of the name witch also carry the connotation of wise, and so Wicca is the craft of those who seek and hopefully attain wisdom.

There is a vast amount of information about more formal Wiccan practices in books and on the internet. At the end of this chapter, I have suggested a number of excellent books on the foundation and development of Wicca, written by and about those who created and developed it.

Rae Beth, a contemporary witch, coined the title hedge witch to describe solitary practitioners. This name is derived from the old idea that a witch walks between worlds or along the hedges of reality. Solitary practitioners and wise men and women traditionally planted hawthorn hedges round their homes both to offer magickal protection and to act as a physical shield from the idly curious.

Can you practise magick without being a witch and can you be a witch without practising magick? Are healing and celebrating the Wheel of the Year magick in themselves? Is, as Aleister Crowley said, every intentional act an act of magick? By the end of the course I hope you will have your own answers to these chicken-and-egg questions.

The seeds of modern witchcraft and magick

Witchcraft never really disappeared, in spite of the persecutions. The last notable prosecution under the revised but still prohibitive Witchcraft Act of 1735 was of Helen Duncan, who was imprisoned under the Act in 1944. In fact, she was a medium who was channelling messages from dead soldiers and sailors and so was considered a risk to national security by the authorities, since she apparently knew information they were withholding.

Many wise great-grandmothers carried on magickal practices secretly in their homes, handing on the old rituals and remedies until the mid-1900s and they still do in remote places. These family covens would pass the traditions down through the matriarchal line and, for those that could write, the Books of Shadows, so-called partly because of the secrecy needed, were usually buried or burned with the witch on her death. But inevitably before widespread literacy as late as the mid to late 1800s in the UK, much knowledge remained oral among the ordinary people who practised the old ways.

From the late 1800s, a spate of influential books opened the way for general magickal knowledge and interest. There is no doubt that they gave inspiration to Gardner and other modern founding witchcraft fathers and mothers. Foremost were the writings of the American Geoffrey Leland. It is said that Leland's knowledge dated back to the cult in Ancient Greece of Diana and her daughter Aradia, established around 500 BCE. This cult had spread to Italy and was transmitted to present-day witchcraft in fairly formal format, giving many beautiful ceremonies.

In 1886, Leland wrote his famous *Aradia, Gospel of the Witches*, based on the teachings of Maddalena who claimed to be an Etruscan hereditary witch and whose traditions went back to the early nature traditions. His was the first book ever to publish incantations and spells. He told how, according to Tuscan legend, Aradia, silver daughter of Diana, was sent to earth by her mother to teach witchcraft. There's much more of Aradia later (see pages 241 and 366).

Sir James Frazer's *The Golden Bough* written in 1890 also provided a valuable source of knowledge on magick and ritual throughout the world. Frazer showed how folk magick among indigenous peoples followed formal magickal stages and principles (see below) and wrote about sympathetic and contagious or attracting magick with actual examples from different cultures. In recent years, some people have disputed its accuracy, but it still remains a valuable classic, as well as source book in the principles of magick. Ironically Frazer believed that the concept of magick was false, because he said it could never be used to manipulate the physical universe. He believed science explains magick, but without meaning to he argued a powerful case for it.

In 1921, Dr Margaret Alice Murray wrote *The Witch Cult in Western Europe* and in 1931 *The God of the Witches*, linking witchcraft with Palaeolithic religions, and this was a great influence on Gardner.

In 1951 after the repeal of the Witchcraft Act, witches gradually felt able to come out of hiding. Gardner claimed connections with one of these hereditary covens in the New Forest, being initiated just before the Second World War by a witch called Dorothy Clutterbuck. He was a retired civil servant when he established modern Wicca. As well as the hereditary coven knowledge, Gardner had for years been fascinated by spirituality, archaeology and ritual magick. During his time in Malaysia, he became interested in the use of ritual knives and daggers, and wrote a book on this craft. He became influenced by a secret occult Rosicrucian Order and by Aleister Crowley, who ordained him as an Honorary Member of the Ordo Templi Orientis. Crowley's religious doctrines became collected as the *Holy Law of Thelema*.

In 1954, Gardner wrote his first non-fiction magick treatise, *Witchcraft Today*, which opened the way for people who had no family connections to learn about the practices of witchcraft.

Growth and diversification of Wicca

Doreen Valiente, Mother of Wicca and one of the most famous and greatest modern day witches, Gardner's High Priestess, reworked much of Gardner's material especially the Book of Shadows (see page 260). She removed a lot of the early Crowley influences on Gardner and gave us the present form of the Charge of the Goddess still used, not only in Gardnerian and Alexandrian covens but also by solitaries and groups everywhere.

The Alexandrian tradition was founded by Alex Sanders and his first wife Maxine in the 1960s, and they became known as the King and Queen of the Witches. Alex named the movement after Alexandria, the city on the Nile Delta in Egypt, whose library was said to contain the wisdom of the whole world (as well as it relating to his own name). It is often described as an eclectic tradition, taking the best from a number of sources, including Gardnerian and Enochian magick.

Alex Sanders claimed to have been initiated as a witch by his grandmother Mary Bibby, who allowed him to copy her Book of Shadows. A gifted clairvoyant and with mesmeric mind powers, he and Maxine brought coven witchcraft into even greater media awareness and expanded its popularity. They trained many fine witches and you can still sometimes occasionally hear Maxine lecture. Many of their writings are out of print, but they are well worth reading.

Since the 1970s, many branches of Wicca have been established, organised and less formal. Raymond Buckland was the first US witch openly to practise his Craft and after being a Gardnerian witch for more than 10 years, he formed the influential Seax or Saxon Wicca Tradition. His book *The Complete Book of Witchcraft*, written after he became a solitary, is still among the best for teaching how to make tools. It includes detailed instructions for witchcraft techniques not revealed in print before. His chief contribution has been to make understanding of witchcraft practice more open and accessible, especially for solitary practitioners.

PRACTICAL ASSIGNMENT

Making a place of the wise ancestors

You might find it helpful to have a small table or shelf in your altar room to recall the wise witch ancestors of the past, especially those who suffered persecution. This need not be a gloomy place, but a small shrine of love and blessings through which you can send blessings and connect spiritually with witches throughout the world. I have found this symbolic centre of wisdom to be spiritually empowering as a solitary practitioner.

Making your shrine

* Keep a single white or pink rose in water in the place of the wise ancestors and an unpolished piece of rose quartz.

* Place a white or beeswax candle there also. Light this on the first day of each new month after dusk or as near to the beginning of the month as possible or the beginning of the new moon cycle, if you prefer.

* Hold the rose quartz to the candle light to remember those wise people and others who knew nothing of magick or Herbalism who were accused centuries ago and also anyone in the world who is persecuted for their beliefs.

* Speak a few words of healing to them through the crystal and say:

We shall not forget you.

* Then send and ask for blessings from all those who practise witchcraft in a loving way today throughout the world, your spiritual brothers and sisters.

* Blow three times softly into the flame and whisper:

Be at peace and in the light of love.

* Finally, ask the protection and blessings of your Witch Guardian or Guardian Angel.

* Blow out the candle and send the light to the past, the present and to those who one day will carry on the tradition.

Further research

Research the witch persecutions in your own region and if possible lay flowers on the scenes of the worst tragedies in other places you visit.

Further information

Further reading

* Briggs, Robin, *Witches and Neighbours, The Social and Cultural Context of European Witchcraft*, Blackwell, 2002
* Broedel, Hans Peter, *Malleus Maleficarum and the Constraints of Witchcraft*, Manchester University Press, 2003
* Peters, Edward, *Magic, the Witch and the Law*, University of Massachusetts Press, 1982
* Ruikbie, Leo, *Witchcraft out of the Shadows*, Robert Hale, 2004

Websites

* Museum de la Sorcellerie
  Museum of witchcraft in the Central Loire Valley of France. Website has English language information
  www.musee-sorcellerie.fr
* Museum of Witchcraft, Boscastle, Cornwall
  Reopened after bad floods in the town, an excellent website with online artefacts and descriptions
  www.museumofwitchcraft.com
* Salem, Massachusetts
  There are a number of very good museums in Salem
  www.salemwichmuseum.com
  www.salem-ma.wprldweb.com

WHAT IS MAGICK?

In this module we will study the meaning of magick and the natural laws behind it to understand more about how magick works. We will also examine the structure of different kinds of magick we practise. By understanding the underlying processes when we cast spells to attract, bind or banish, we can direct the required energies in the most positive, effective and focused way. We can also combine different magickal energies to create balance and replace with new growth what has been lost or we are taking away.

What is magick?

The word magick comes from the same root as Magi, the wise and learned Persian priests of Zoroaster (see page 29). A Mage is someone who has a great deal of knowledge and wisdom about magick.

According to the late occultist Aleister Crowley, magick is, *the science and art of causing change to occur in conformity to the will*. Crowley believed that we need to access the higher part of ourselves to understand our true will as well as to gain the power and self-control to act upon it. As you work with magick and the ongoing spiritual and psychic development that is intertwined, so this higher self or our divine spark/inner spiritual being is able to guide you into ever more effective and positive practices. Your Witch Guardian will also offer protection and wisdom, as well as reminders of the responsibility that comes with increased power.

Another colourful modern day icon is Isaac Bonewits, an American Arch Druid who believes that Wicca is not an ancient religion and that there should be a full-time paid neopagan clergy. In his extensive and thought-provoking writings, he has given one definition of magick as:

A system of concepts and methods for the build-up of human emotion – to concentrate and focus this emotional energy – usually to affect other energy patterns, whether animate or inanimate, but occasionally to affect the personal energy systems.

These definitions bring together the concepts of willpower, emotion and wisdom as central tenets of magick and the ability through ritual, words and actions to bring about desired changes, both in the external world and what is sometimes forgotten within the spellcaster. By making an internal change, the spellcaster has the willpower, focus and confidence after the rite to make the desired result occur in the earthly world.

Emotion generated during and by a ritual is sometimes considered the true offering made to the cosmos/deities in exchange for blessings (more of this later).

We know that psychic powers don't operate in a vacuum. If telepathic communication, a power implicated in successful magick, is with a loved one or concerns something that really matters to the people transmitting the message, it is far more successful than a telepathy experiment in a laboratory. Equally, if the spell means something to us and we feel deeply as we cast it, even the simplest magick is more powerful than an elaborate rite where the meaning and feeling is secondary to the format.

My own definition of magick

Magick is the deliberate amplification, concentration and focus of our own innate psychic powers. These magickal energies are amplified by the natural energies of the earth and cosmos and of any who are sharing the ritual whether human, angelic or nature essences. It involves the focused release of that concentrated and amplified energy to bring about external and internal change, and to transfer desires and needs from the thought to the plane of actuality. The magick can be either released outwards into the cosmos and earth or poured within us or an animate symbol, such as herbs in a charm bag, that will act as a lucky talisman or protective amulet.

Magick is a source of personal and sometimes collective power when a number of people work together, a source of protection. Above all, each act of magick is renewal of our connection with the natural world, the cosmos and the earth.

The power of belief

Back to the cave pictures and the hunters throwing spears at the images of a wounded antelope or bear on the cave wall, chanting and dancing. In animating the spirit of the bear to release living animals and to increase their own hunting skills, hunters take from the ritual the strength and information (telepathically) for a successful hunt. Because they believed in the power of the ritual (and the shamanic figure conducting it), that belief and the released positive emotions added to the likelihood of success. Any talismans they carried, like the wounded bison image etched on a rib I described in the previous module would store and release the power of the ritual and the positive emotions generated at times when the hunter was feeling dispirited. This would offer the hunter renewed energy and hope when things were not going well or it was cold and wet and the hunters lost heart.

So belief is another strand that I would like to add to the definition of magick. If you believe that the purpose of the magick is attainable, then you make (or will) it so and often spells end with *So mote* or *So shall it be* for this reason.

Of course, some goals are more immediately and easily attainable then others (a good case sometimes for divination before a ritual). But given the infinite nature of the universe and the interconnection of all things (more on that later), in theory almost anything is possible magickally and in the ensuing efforts made may also be attained in actuality.

Exchange in magick

Magick involves exchange between the petitioner and the energy or deity being petitioned or, more abstractly, the cosmos or earth.

Once, ritual offerings were directly related to the blessings asked for. Offerings to the bear or antelope spirit and later to the Mistress or Goddess of wild things as thanks for allowing one of its creatures to be captured were and are common in hunting societies. The hunter would return the bones of the slain animals to the forest or of fish or seals to the sea. This still happens in societies like the Inuit and Sami. Modern Swedish hunters leave the entrails of the slain moose or deer in the forest before taking the carcass home, though few know the symbolic reasons for this action.

Offerings of the finest of the meat at a feast to the deities being invoked played an important part in Norse magick right into Christian times and underpins many ancient sacrifice rites. In farming communities the sacrifice of the grain spirit in the cutting down of the crops had to be honoured, formerly by the sacrifice of the blood of criminals or prisoners of war sprinkled on the fields or, in times of hardship, by the offering of a willing human sacrifice who might be of noble blood.

Sacrifice of blood was also made for safety against invasion. In the British Museum in London may be seen the figure known as the Lindow man, found in a peat bog at Lindow near Manchester. It has been suggested by the eminent Celtic archaeologist and historian Anne Ross that the man was a senior Druid or king who had died ritually around 60 CE, possibly as a willing sacrifice at Beltane, on 1 May, the beginning of Summer. This sacrifice may have been to ask the gods to intervene on behalf of the Celts against the Romans who were threatening their existence at that time.

The man had undergone a triple ritual death, with a cord tightly knotted round the neck, twisted by a stick at the back. His throat was then slashed and his blood drained and finally he was drowned in the marshland. In his gut was found mistletoe pollen, the sacred plant of the Druids, suggesting he had been given a ritual drink shortly before his death. The triple death invoked the Celtic gods Taranis, the thunder God Esus, deity of the underworld, and Teutates, lord of the tribe, who each demanded a particular kind of death from the victim. In more recent times, a figure made of the last grain to be cut, symbolising the grain spirit, would be ritually burned and the ashes scattered on the fields.

In parts of Germany in modern folk custom, a child wrapped in a thick roll of straw is rolled across the fields in spring and aferwards the straw burned. The Easter fires in parts of Europe, on which the straw Judas man is burned, recall the earlier pagan rites of the human spring/summer sacrifice of a traitor or criminal.

Price of the ritual or spell success

This primitive exchange underpins modern magick and accounts for the failure of some modern instant spells carried out just to ask for good things without any thought of returning the favour to others or the cosmos. Indeed, in old folk spells this bargaining is sometimes recalled in the words and actions. In the love spells of St Andrew's Eve (29 November), or on the night of St Andrew's Day itself, at midnight girls would pull one hair from their heads for each year of their life, saying during the ensuing spell:

I offer this my sacrifice
To him most precious in my eyes.

As we offer food, incense or flowers, especially if we burn or cast the offering into water, we are symbolically releasing the life force to carry our petition. At the same time, we need to be promising in our hearts or aloud what service we can offer to others or the planet as our part of the ongoing bargain. Offerings and libations feature in later modules in detail.

Spells and rituals

There is a great deal of overlap between spells and rituals depending on their length, organisation and purpose.

A spell tends to be a less formal kind of magick, usually cast for a specific purpose or need, and with the results required within a specific stated time frame. For example you might cast a spell for a loved one attending an interview the day after the spell, so that they may speak coherently and persuasively and those interviewing them to be receptive. You could specify the spell energies to be activated for an hour before the interview and continue while the interviewing panel were considering their decision. The energies are raised and then released, so they will bounce back to activate the purpose of the spell. The interview success could have been represented during the spellcasting by a symbol, perhaps a crystal that once empowered in the spell could be carried by the interviewee to release the success energies if last minute-nerves appeared.

Some define a spell as the actual charm or incantation made. In contrast, a ritual is usually based on a more general or long-lasting focus that may or may not be specific, like drawing down the moon and channelling the wisdom of the Goddess, acting out some stage of the God and Goddess cycle, or a general wish for abundance. Specific spells can be cast during a ritual.

A handfasting ceremony joins a couple in love so long as they both desire it, so long as the sun shines and the water flows, or through many lifetimes. An Autumn Equinox ritual would give thanks for the harvest and the offerings symbolise the petition for abundance in whatever way is appropriate, on all present and the community throughout the coming winter days. What is more, whereas a spell builds up to a climax and release of energy, the ritual releases energy more evenly throughout the weeks and months ahead.

Spontaneous versus structured magick

Some of the best magick can be spontaneous, cast on a windy shore or when you wake to a truly golden dawn. On such an occasion, words tumble out, your movements seem guided by the energies of the place and time and the right flower, leaf, stone or shell are at hand to serve as the symbol and driftwood or a time-smoothed twig as an impromptu wand.

However, even spontaneous magick follows basic magick laws or operational principles. These principles can be been observed generally in life, but are concentrated in magick and their effects amplified by the spell or ritual itself. Indeed, Isaac Bonewits says all actions that are done under the same conditions are usually associated with the same results. The more similar the structure of events, the more similar the outcome. Therefore if you are using the similar tools, words and actions as previous rituals for the same purpose and follow the basic structure of spellcasting (see page 177), the more precisely the likely results can be defined in advance.

Even in folk magick, the same incantations and spells for love and healing were used over the centuries on particular festivals. For example, the same St Agnes' Eve love spell was certainly cast at 10 pm on the evening of 20 January from the 11th century and is still used. By a dim light, a young girl would stick rows of pins from a pincushion lightly into the sleeve of her nightgown and recite:

> Sweet Agnes, work thy fast.
> If ever I be to marry man
> Or ever man to marry me,
> I hope this night him to see.

This promised to give dreams of a lover known or unknown and marriage by the following May Day. Over the centuries, the spell acquired the collective love energies of girls everywhere who spoke the words at precisely the same time and date and followed the simple action with the pins. It continues to do so, as long as someone somewhere continues the tradition.

But because magick is essentially a living growing craft, this does not mean that you cannot or should not devise your own words, tools and actions and vary rituals within the basic format to suit your unique needs. We all find new ways that work better that we use until an even better way is discovered by us, in a book or by a fellow witch who shares her wisdom. Recording the new insights or elemental associations in your Book of Shadows helps to establish new traditions. By the principle of Morphic resonance, which basically means when one person does or discovers something new, the new insights seem to filter into the deep consciousness of others – each of us is responsible for the growth of magickal wisdom.

Nor does this imply that you have always to carry out a spell externally in a particular setting. Successful witches learn to use visualisation to build and release power in the mind, even in the most crowded or unmagickal setting.

How does magick work?

Basically magick operates through our innate psychic powers and the higher divine spark we contain that develops the more we work spiritually. Psychokinesis, or the power of the mind to draw to you mentally what you want or send away what you do not, is a power we all possess. In later units I have written about the strong links between psychic development, magick and divinatory processes.

A magickal spell or ritual with its build-up of power amplifies the psychokinetic energy of the participants and also enables you to draw energy into the symbol and yourself from the natural world. Magick in any positive form is essentially a self-empowering process that fills the personal aura or rainbow psychic energy field round you with determination and confidence. As your aura expands, so your personal range of possibility increases.

Telepathy is another important psychic power, especially in love, success, binding and banishing magick. It enables us to call to a known lover or to connect with the person who would make us happy, wherever they are. An example would be reciting:

Near and far, o'er land and sea,
A lover true I call to me,

while looking into a candle flame. The candle is blown out and the light used like a beacon to make the telepathic connection with the potential lover, whether on another continent or working in the same office.

Telepathy also enables us to align our minds with different deity qualities, whether we draw these into ourselves (invoking) and speak as though we were the deity (much more of this later, as in the drawing down the Moon Goddess ceremony at full moon (see page 475) or calling upon the protection and power from beyond us, for example the Archangels (evoking), to guard the four quarters of a circle.

Different kinds of magick

Anthropologist Bronislaw Malinowski (1884–1942), whose books are well worth reading, said that magick has a triple purpose: to produce, protect or destroy. These are parallel to the common magickal terms to attract, to bind and to banish. The latter two could also be called protective or defensive magick. I would suggest that there is also balancing magick, which I describe later (see page 60) and much healing magick relies on this balancing of what is to be removed such as pain, with the infusion of new energies, to redress the balance in the sick person or animal.

Sympathetic magick
Most magick works on the principles of what is called sympathetic magick, based on the interaction of similarities.

James Frazer, like many other magickal researchers and philosophers, including Isaac Bonewits, recognised the powerful law of like attracting like and the principle that all things are linked together on a psychic level by invisible bonds. These bonds are activated and strengthened magickally through establishing a physical link based on the external similarity. Frazer divided sympathetic magick into homeopathic magick and contagious magick and these are very useful divisions, though homeopathic magick is sometimes just called sympathetic magick.

Homeopathic magick
This is the kind of magick where there is a direct connection between actions or words carried out to empower a representative symbol (for example, a coin to bring money) and the transference of those effects to a person or situation that the symbol represents. The symbol might be a doll or dolls tied together for love magick, a gold jewellery to attract prosperity, herbs to attract health, a lucky charm or spell bag to bring good luck or a beeswax image that can be fashioned into any relevant form for any purpose, such as the model of a lion to bring courage.

Take, for example, the old attracting or calling magick candle spell, where a lover lit a candle and called her known but maybe inattentive or undemonstrative lover in the flame, saying:

As the wax melts,
So melts my lover's heart.

The more the symbol is linked to the person or strength desired, whether visually, in sounds, fragrance, texture or a more abstract association, like the melting process of the wax, the stronger and more lasting the effect of the spell or ritual. This is especially powerful where the symbol is carried or worn after the spell as a talisman.

For example, the ancient Egyptian frog-shaped amulet represented the frog-headed fertility Goddess Heket and the frogs that appeared at the time of the Nile flood, which restored fertility to the land. The amulet would often be made of green malachite to signify growth and once empowered would attract fertility to the wearer or prosperity. The frog was also a symbol of rebirth, because of the transformation from egg to frog. Alternatively, the frog hieroglyph or symbol of the frog, believed to release the power, could be etched on the clay from the dried Nile mud.

Homeopathic magick can also be used for banishing. An example would be to hold a dark cord in a candle flame until it broke, saying:

As this cord breaks,
So the link is cut between me and xxx,

perhaps someone who was causing you pain or a relationship or addiction you could not give up. You would then bury the remaining cord.

Contagious magick

This involves direct contact between the symbol and what is to be empowered. The earlier example of the child rolled in straw across the fields is contagious magick. The straw was burned afterwards and the ashes dug into the fields to make them fertile. The outward actions symbolised the story of the sacrifice of the grain God whose essence was present in the last sheaf of grain to be cut down at the first harvest. This rite formed a sort of magickal shorthand for the sacrifice and future fertility saga. In some societies, this grain from the last sheaf was preserved in the form of a figure to be burned and scattered on the fields the next spring or made into small corn dollies or grain mothers to signify the transference of power to the Goddess. These corn dollies were kept to protect the home throughout the winter.

Another example of contagious magick is the old custom of making love in the fields on May Eve to fertilise the crops – and the couple, if they wanted a child – by a two-way transference of fertility. The connection continued even after the ritual had ended though the effects did diminish over time (but lasting long enough for the fertility to take root).

Another example would be rubbing meat on warts to transfer the virus from the person and then burying the meat in the earth to decay, along with the warts.

Attracting magick

Attracting magick embraces both homeopathic and contagious magick to bring you something you (or the person for whom you are casting the spell) need or desire. The accumulated power of the ritual when released creates sufficient energy to call to you what is it you asked for, whether externally as you project it outwards – for example, a new job opportunity after a period of unemployment – or within you for confidence, entering through the upper stomach or belly area via the solar plexus energy centre, as you direct the energy at the end of the rite.

You can, of course, attract good things for others by proxy and perhaps send them the symbol you used to transfer the accumulated power to the person needing it. You could also leave the symbol in a place that needed healing or with a map of an overseas area in trouble. The focus may be tangible or less specific, such as good health, happiness, good luck or increased psychic awareness.

Attracting magick may be best repeated over several nights, especially if you are working on the nights leading up to the full moon. More of this in the module on the Moon and magickal timings (see page 202). Indeed the waxing or increasing moon from the crescent to the night before the full moon is the best time for attracting magick of any kind. An example would be moving two candles closer each night of the spell, lighting one from the other. This would bring reconciliation and restore good feelings between two family members who have quarrelled or two warring factions overseas, as represented by the candles.

For restoring health, set a dish of salt, a universal symbol of healing and well-being, in the light of a blue or purple candle until the candle is burned. This fills it with light as symbolised by the healing colours and the fire power. Then tip the salt into running water with such words as:

> Go, flow to the rivers and the sea,
> Bring back, I ask good health to me.

This casts the petition, in the form of the salt, for an inflow of health into water symbolising flow, to be swelled by the rivers and the sea and to flow back symbolically, amplified on the incoming tide (even if you live far from the sea) as an inrush of renewed energy or to kick start the immune system.

Complex magick uses precisely the same principles.

Working with the energies of attraction

A lot of attracting magick involves setting things in motion, like bump-starting a car with a flat battery and then using natural momentum by pushing the car downhill to ignite the necessary spark. Once you have set the spell energies in action, let nature use the initial energies to amplify natural growth. An example of this using contagious magick can be seen in an Eastern European spell that involves a woman scooping up the earth in which a lover's footstep is imprinted and planting marigolds, a love and marriage flower, in the soil. As the flowers grow, so will the love, it is said, which lead to marriage.

However, you could either weekly or monthly top up the magickal energies by empowering a moss agate (a growth crystal) by setting it in front of a green candle, calling love to grow and blowing out the candle. The light would be transferred to the crystal that would then be planted in the soil, thus regularly topping up the original magickal input.

Protective magick

Protective magick operates on two levels. The first is by repelling danger or fears of harm, whether actual or perceived perhaps through the empowerment of a protective amulet, which we can carry with us into hazardous situations. On a more subtle level, protective magick enables us to build up a psychological and psychic shield round our aura over time, so that we are less vulnerable to spite and other negative influences. This can be helpful in enabling sensitive children and adolescents (as well as adults) to develop coping strategies towards, for example, bullying, because you can enclose someone else in protection.

Protective magick includes binding and banishing magick. Both operate through sympathetic homeopathic or contagious magick using similarities to offer protection: for example, a spiky plant, however small.

Binding magick

This blocks harmful effects for a specified time, like quietening a noisy neighbour who is affecting your sleep and so making you ill. You might make a beeswax image and place a tiny rose quartz crystal in the mouth with the words:

Speak and move around softly and with thoughtfulness.

You would need to take great care of the image so it came to no harm and after a specified time roll it back into a ball.

Banishing magick

This actively repels harm or danger whether immediately or as ongoing protection, for example creating a psychic barrier using smudge (see page 284) or planting protecting plants such as bamboo, cactus or rosemary indoors or out round a home or property to prevent burglary or vandalism.

The fusion of polarities or negative attraction

However, sometimes protective magick can work on the principle of negative attraction, that opposites attract and contain the seeds of the other. In medical homeopathy, remedies contain small quantities of substances that induce the condition that is to be cured, and conventional immunisation often does, too.

According to the Norse myths, creation occurred as a result of the fusion of Fire and Ice. You can also use opposites in magick: for example, fusing Goddess and God energies by plunging the athame (male) into the chalice (female). It is known with all forms of magick that the combination of the four elements creates a dynamism that generates in their synthesis a force greater than the separate elements.

But let's focus on protection for now. One sample of banishing protective magick using the fusing of polarities is where a fire is lit close to the sea just before high tide. As the tide washes over it the dynamic force of the opposing Fire and Water creates a magickal surge manifest as a physical hiss. This can cast effective protection against the raging or physical abuse of a bully, an overpowering addiction or debt problem, or against dangers of fire (for example, if a loved one is a fire-fighter or you worry about fire because you live in a high rise flat).

I write more of polarities and the God and Goddess powers later (see page 71).

Binding magick

Binding magick is a very valid form of positive magick. However, you need to be very sure of your motives and that you are not interfering with the free will of the person whom you are binding. Binding magick can be practised both for positive and protective purposes. For example, you could bind your partner to you in fidelity (given the constraints of free will I mentioned in Module I). You could temporarily bind a small child to you if you were going on a long journey, so he or she doesn't get lost or wander off. You could also bind a known or unknown person from harming yourself, your family, your home or your animals or from exerting a destructive influence over a vulnerable teenager, if he or she was trying to persuade your child to experiment with harmful drugs.

I believe (some disagree) that you cannot stop people from going about their daily life, even if you consider them to be doing harm to themselves or others. But you can forbid their destructive behaviour from affecting you or anyone you have taken under your care for the purpose of the magick; and yes, you can work magick to protect all the young vulnerable members of the club where you know the drug-pusher secretly operates. The harm none rule really necessarily kicks in here and as your magick becomes more complex, as do the moral issues.

Binding spells often involve the use of images, such as small fabric dolls or ones made from beeswax or clay that you then tie with knots in ribbons or cord. (Of course, you do not harm the image.) You then gently wrap the figure in soft cloth and put it in a safe place until the specified time for the binding spell is through. Afterwards you return the wax or clay into a ball and bury it.

You can also cast protection round your home by burying iron nails in the ground, washing the doorstep regularly with an empowered mixture of salt, pepper and water or placing amethyst crystals on indoor window ledges, like a defensive psychic wall, to bind anyone from entering the psychic barrier to do you, your family or property damage. Make a charm bag to hide near the front door or a traditional witch bottle buried in the earth (see page 426).

You do not have to be specific about the attackers, though there may be a particular person who has threatened you. You can ask for protection against all who come with ill intent or hate in their heart. In a time of increasing car crimes and muggings, the car can be protected with an empowered crystal like haematite or sodalite or a herb bag containing basil in the glove box.

Obviously you cannot always physically bar certain people from your home. However, you can bind their harmful effects: for example, a relative or ex-partner from speaking vicious words that might upset children, or debt collectors from intimidating you, as less scrupulous ones may do. You could use crystals, such as blue lace agate, which softens words.

Binding magick is good on the full moon where you get powerful opposing lunar and solar energies pushing to create a fusion, as the sun and moon are on opposite sides of the earth.

For more urgent matters, you also need to specify the timescale of the binding and then repeat the spells as necessary. Ongoing protective charm bags need to be replaced every three months or when they have lost their fragrance. Witch bottles or jars, if buried, have a very long life of many years.

Banishing magick

Banishing magick is also very positive, since you can banish sorrow, sadness, pain and sickness, bad habits or people who make you unhappy. It is good for ending a relationship, especially if you have been betrayed or badly treated, so you can quickly recover your self-esteem and self-confidence and live and love again. It can remove any ongoing negativity, psychic attack or physical threats to you, your home or loved ones, such as bullying at home, at school or in the workplace.

Banishing magick can also help you to end in your own mind the ties of a destructive relationship, especially if you have been betrayed or badly treated but blame yourself or cannot let go. It can involve burying a symbol of what you wish to banish, for example a rotting fruit, so that new good life will grow from it, casting dead leaves or flowers into water, lighting a white candle from a dark one and blowing out the dark candle or using the splayed hand gesture outwards to send back pain or malevolence with such words as:

I return the malice and pain.
Send it not again.

For faster results you could leave a small branch of dead leaves on the top of a windy hill or drop dying petals into a fast-flowing stream. Again this is an area where you need to be sure of your motives and banishing magick should always be carried out when you are calm.

Curses are one issue that arises. From my experience, unless you know you have been cursed then the curse will just bounce back on the sender three times and leave you unharmed. But usually the person or a friend of theirs tells you, in which case with your free will you don't have to accept the curse, but can send it back without adding anything.

Balancing magick

If you need instant action or ongoing relief, attracting and banishing magick is perfect alone. However, sometimes in spite of the spell a situation can remain unresolved in the long term.

Psychologically and psychically, if you do a spell to get instant money but don't resolve what it is that caused the crisis, then the magickal solution is only temporary. Of course, you can repeat the spell. But it may be better to work magickally with the source or cause of the problem that prompted the magick in the first place. If you cast a spell to call back a lover after a parting but don't resolve the issue that caused it, or are filled with unvoiced and justifiable resentment, the effects of the original spell are not going to be long lasting.

In balancing spells, as well as removing pain or sickness or stopping cravings for an unwise addiction, you need to build up the underlying energy and immune system. This might mean initiating a change in lifestyle to ensures the problem does not return or, if chronic, that the body and mind are more prepared to minimise debilitating effects.

Balancing magick is usually quite slow, as is the resolution of long-standing problems in the everyday world. For example, you could bury a decaying fruit with a stone, so that new shoots will grow as a long standing family rift is repaired slowly. Or, you could bury a symbol of what is to be banished; for example, a pack of cigarettes beneath a growing plant, such as lavender. Its increasing fragrance is a reminder of good intentions. After dropping dead petals into flowing water and naming for each what has been lost that holds you back, maybe anger after an unfair job loss, you could then cast petals from a living flower after them. You then name the new plans you have: for example, to launch a new creative venture after redundancy or to travel for a while to fulfil dreams that were cast aside. Similarly, with a candle spell to bring a fast infusion of money, a cleansing herb such as sage could be dropped in the candle flame to signify the shedding of responsibility for a person or situation that drains your resources and a new long-term financial strategy.

Restoring the balance magickally

There are many situations where moderation is the aim of the magick, whether at home to calm arguing family members, at work in an over competitive business, or in personal restoring health and optimism, or in world events.

You can use it to balance the conflicting demands of different family members or members of a work team, to resolve rivalries and jealousies among friends and neighbours, pets who hate a newcomer or to bring together a new step family. You could join cords representing each person in a continuous circle, hanging it behind the front door or keeping it in a desk at work, regularly smudging over each knot with sweetgrass to keep the loving (or at least tolerant) connection.

Balancing magick can also be employed to tip the balance in a relationship where you or a loved one are being bullied, emotionally blackmailed or ignored, or where unfair competition or favouritism is blocking deserved promotion. It also works to balance money when more is going out than coming in, to ensure you sell your present home and buy a new house in synchronicity and to get the balance right in your life between the demands of work and chores and love and happiness.

You can do this by having two bowls, one overfilled with seeds or nuts and the other empty, and making them equal as you chant words to restore fairness or balance. Or you can buy some of those old-fashioned metal scales with pans on either side that often are on sale in house or gift stores more as kitchen decorations. The seeds and nuts are then mixed in a cake that is eaten by you, a piece a day or by all concerned at the same time —or in the case of property matters left in the kitchen when prospective buyers come (and a few carried in a charm bag when you are negotiating a house purchase where there is a chain or obstacles).

Any transition time like tide turn, the first day of the week or the month or the day after a major moon change, such as the first day after the full moon, are good for balancing magick.

PRACTICAL ASSIGNMENT

Write and record your personal definition of magick

Make a note in your diary or Book of Shadows of your responses to the following questions. Check in six months' time to see if your definition has changed in the light of any events in your life, as well as your growing skill with magick.

* How do you define yourself right now in terms of Wicca, hedge witchery or organised witchcraft? Do you desire a change and if so what steps would you take over the next few months?

* For each kind of magick – attracting, binding, banishing (protective) and balancing – list ways each could be used in your present everyday world or that of loved ones to bring about an improvement.

* Look back at my suggestions for rituals for each or, if you are an experienced witch, ways you already use them and try and find at least three new ways of using each kind of magick.

* What do you consider valid exchanges with the cosmos/earth symbolically and practically in return for blessings or protection you or loved ones need now?

* Think of examples of homeopathic and contagious magick that you have used or would like to use.

* Work with the idea of the fusion of polarities: Fire and Water, Fire and Ice. Name some more.

Further research

Find out more about one or more different modern witchcraft traditions online or in books that interest you, what they believe, how they differ and, most importantly, how they define and practise magick.

* Research any festivals or moots in your area where you can hear lectures or perhaps attend a different tradition's open meeting.

* If you know a lot about magick already, take a tradition you have perhaps dismissed and see if you can find positive qualities in it that could enhance your own work.

* Start your own list of useful terms. Read book and online definitions and then explain them as if to someone who knows nothing about magick. Make this an ongoing task for your existing/future Book of Shadows.

Further information

Further reading

* Bonewits, Isaac, *Real Magic, an Introductory Treatise or Basic Primer of Yellow Magic,* Weiser, 1989
* Buckland, Raymond, *Complete Book of Witchcraft,* Llewellyn, 2002
* Crowley, Aleister, *Magick in Theory and Practice,* Castle Books, New York, 1989
* Crowley, Aleister, *The Holy Books of Thelema,* Red Wheel/Weiser, 1989
* Crowley, Vivienne, *Wicca, The Old Religion in the New Age,* 1989, Aquarian/Thorsons
* Deutch, Richard, *The Ecstatic Mother, the Path of Maxine, Witch Queen,* Rachman and Turner, 1977
* Fortune, Dion, and Knight, Gareth, *Applied Magick,* Red Wheel/Weiser, 2000
* Frazer, Sir James, *The Golden Bough,* Penguin, 1996
* Gardner, Gerald B, *The Meaning of Witchcraft,* Magickal Childe Inc 1982
* Gardner, Gerald B, *Witchcraft Today,* Citadel/Kensington, 2004,
* Leland, Charles G, Aradia, *Gospel of the Witches,* Phoenix Publishing, 1990
* Malinowski, Bronislaw, *Magic, Science and Religion and other essays,* 1948, Kessinger, 2004

* Sanders, Alex, *Alex Sanders Lectures,* Pemton Overseas Inc, 1971
* Valiente, Doreen, *ABC of Witchcraft,* Phoenix (WA) 1988
* Valiente, Doreen, *Witchcraft for Tomorrow,* Robert Hale, 1993
* Wilson, Colin, *Aleister Crowley, The Nature of the Beast,* Aeon Books, 2005

Websites

* *Covenant of the Goddess*
  One of the oldest and best US Wiccan organisations with excellent international resources and links
  www.cog.org
* *Isaac Bonewits*
  Fascinating and sometimes controversial site
  www.neopagan.net
* *The Realm of White Magic*
  Excellent Australian website resource with web links to sites with information about witchcraft in Australia
  www.magic.com.au
* *Witchweb/The White Goddess*
  Community of Wiccans, witches and pagans, on line forums for exchange of information and resources
  www.witchweb.org.uk

THE WHEEL OF THE YEAR

This is in fact a triple module as it is such a vital and detailed topic. In this first module and the following two, I will give you an overview of the seasonal Wheel of the Year in different cultures and its importance in magick. I have also devoted two weeks later in the course to examining each festival in detail and to describe Norse, Mediterranean, Christian and Eastern European variations of the eight festivals, as well as the usual Celtic associations.

For experienced practitioners, these modules will enable you to develop your seasonal attunements more creatively and to work with alternative Wheel of the Year structures from Ancient Egypt and Australian Aboriginal spirituality (see page 85). You can move ahead to the relevant week if a major festival is approaching and you would like some extra information or inspiration.

In this module, we will examine the significance of the Wheel of the Year in witchcraft and neopaganism, based mainly on the Celtic structure. It also studies how the seasonal celebrations and offerings were seen as a necessary part of life from early times and have continued to be so, even in modern urban life It is quite short because I would like you to spend more time on the written assignment, so that you have planned your personal Wheel of the Year based on the Wheel dates below before moving on to studying the magickal festivals. Often, because the traditions are so strong, the personal daily life relevance is not given the pre-eminence it should. Yet we turn the Wheel of the Year as surely as our agricultural ancestors did and, as it was for them, it is part of our whole ongoing lives and not just special magickal days.

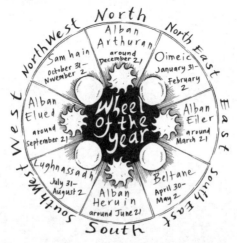

The significance of the eightfold year

The Wheel of the Year with its eight divisions is central to many magickal traditions, not only formal but also neopagan and in the folk world. The eight festivals are known as the sabbats and are the sacred days of Wicca, Druidry, neopaganism and personal forms of nature spirituality. The Wheel divides the year equally into six-week periods, according to the European and Celtic agricultural and domesticated animal husbandry cycles.

Some witches in the southern hemisphere move everything round six months and celebrate the Midsummer Solstice on or around 21 December (see page 644 for more information). In Scandinavia and parts of North America and Canada, it may still be cold on May Day, the ritual beginning of summer. For this reason, dancing around the Midsummer Tree, the Scandinavian equivalent of the maypole, takes place at the Summer Solstice. What is more, celebrations can be adapted to suit the climate. For example, in Scandinavia and around the Baltic, young men traditionally skated the spirals of labyrinths made of ice and snow to celebrate the Midwinter Solstice around 21 December to release the sun maiden or daughter in the centre so that she could be reborn.

The structure of the wheel

The four solar festivals, the quarter days or the lesser sabbats, the Equinoxes and Solstices that fall midpoint through the four seasons, provide astronomical marker points of the high and lows and two stable points of cosmic and earth energies. They can vary each year by a day or two because of the tilt of the earth. They must have been significant throughout history because builders of passages graves and stone circles from the 4th millennium BCE aligned entrances and marker stones with the rising and setting of the sun on these days.

Magickally and ritually, they are often calculated like the other four points on the Wheel, the cross-quarter days or greater sabbats, from sunset the evening before, the beginning of the Celtic and Norse day, until sunset on the day after the festival day giving a 48-hour period. These cross-quarter days fall midway between each of these solar festivals and are traditionally the four annual Great Fire Festivals that form the major rites in the Wiccan and neopagan calendar.

In Japan, the traditional lunar calendar uses the cross-quarter days as markers for the season, so that, for example, the first day of spring, called Risshun, falls on the first cross-quarter day of the year on 3 or 4 February. Formerly, this festival marked the beginning of the New Year in Japan.

Early seasonal magick

Seasonal celebrations were originally prompted not by calendars but by the changes in light, warmth, rainfall and the natural growth cycle. The celebrations may have been marked in hunter-gatherer times when particular trees blossomed, snow retreated from particular landmarks or migratory birds flew overhead, the appearance of the herds with their young and when nuts or berries ripened in the forests. This we can see among indigenous peoples today whose lifestyles have been relatively unchanged for hundreds or thousands of years.

Once moon times were calculated, as marks on bone, wood or stone, people could anticipate from one year to the next the coming of the rainy season or when the reindeer herds might be returning. The full moon names reflected the naturally occurring phenomena: for example, when the geese first lay full moon in Native North America, which occurred in February or March. These festivals centred on asking the deities and the ancestors for good hunting and often involved ritually sacrificing the first slain animal as offering to the archetypal or spirit animal, and returning the bones to the place of killing or, in the case of a seal, to the sea.

Rituals also reflected growing awareness of the changing yearly light and natural cyclical patterns of vegetation or foliage. The modern pagan Midwinter Solstice rituals when the sun reached its lowest point in the sky and the trees were stripped of leaves took the form of sympathetic magick. Fires were lit and evergreen branches hung with torches to give power to the sun and to cause new life to stir within the bare trees by magickal transference from the evergreens. No one knows how old these seasonal celebrations are, but midwinter and midsummer feature in the rites of lands as far apart as the formal cults of Ancient China, where the Emperor symbolically broke the soil and made offerings at midwinter, to the Summer Solstice in Lapland, when sun rings or grass garlands are woven and butter is rubbed into the doorposts by the indigenous Sami people to honour Baiwe, the Sun Goddess. A special sun porridge, rich in dairy foods, is the centre of a family feast during which the father of the family would pray for bright sunshine over the birch forests and that the reindeer would give milk.

Because these celebrations seemed generally to work, the forms became entrenched as rituals and ordinary people took responsibility for the turning of the year. By their ritual recognition of the change points, they aligned their energies with those of the seasons to their mutual advantage. Whether in coven or privately, we can connect with these energies and so empower and enliven our own celebrations.

Through the common seeds of early humans from whom we are all very distantly descended, we can draw power from the magick of ancient cultures and their seasonal rites, both those belonging to our region and physical heritage and those to which we are spiritually attracted. We can also access this ancient wisdom via morphic resonance whereby members of the species connect with learning of other humans (I believe especially from those cultures to which we are spiritually drawn).

Seasonal rituals take form

Once the hunter-gather way of life had been replaced in more temperate regions by the farmers of the Neolithic period from around 8000 BCE, the ritual year became inextricably linked with the annual sowing and reaping cycle. The Father of the Hunt, who was Lord of the Winter, and Mistress of the Animals, who was Lady of the Summer, were succeeded by Grain Goddesses and Gods. The Gods were also regarded as the spirit within the grain and sacrificed their life annually for the fertility of the soil with the harvesting of the crops. Blessings were asked at the time of sowing and again at high summer to bring plentiful sun and rain to ensure an abundant harvest.

From about 3500 BCE, a number of these agricultural rituals centred on long barrows and passage graves to ask the blessings of the ancestors. I would recommend visiting La Hogue Bie in Jersey, a large passage grave you can still enter and at quiet times make private dedications. It is aligned with the Spring Equinox sunrise. If you get the chance to chant in the inner sanctum as I did (much to the embarrassment of my teenage son Bill), you will discover the sound rolls over the roof and echoes to enclose you in a sphere of sound. There are also a number of passage graves and long barrows open to the elements around the island, usually high up overlooking the sea (where in Druidic tradition earth, sea and sky meet) and sometimes with farming land round.

We know that bones from West Kennet Long Barrow in Wiltshire (another site that is very quiet and worth visiting) were carried in procession to nearby Windmill Hill in the north-east for ritual and when I visited after a long climb up the hill there was a place inside where you can make offerings and where a candle often burns. The barrow is on the ley line to Silbury Hill (see Lughnassadh, below) and links with the ley wheel around Stonehenge and Avebury.

The Hunebedden or long barrows in Holland, all also sited along ley lines, were guarded by the White Ladies (probably priestesses and now land spirits) who also protect ancient tombs in Germany. Though chosen by Woden, the Anglo-Saxon Father God, the priestesses' most important function, according to myth, was to carry out rituals in honour of the Earth Mother to ensure the crops and fruit would be plentiful. In this way people's lives were practically as well as ritually linked to the turning of the year – and still are, even in towns, if we work with the Wheel.

Seasons and the rituals

Throughout the ages, harvests and the accompanying festivals were still primarily ruled by what was happening with weather and growth in the external world. For example, the Mother Goddess monolith at Silbury Hill near to the Avebury stone circles, the tallest prehistoric monument in Europe and one of the world's largest man-made mounds, built in 2600 BCE, was a ritual centre at the Celtic festival of Lughnassadh.

The festival of the first grain harvest Lughnassadh in this area began when the first full Moon in August shone in the water of the moat, said to represent the mother's milk. But of course the physical harvest was also dictated by the real weather. We cannot always celebrate a festival at the appointed day or hour, especially as a solitary practitioner, and since the new energies begin before the ritual date and remain strong for some days afterwards you should have the confidence to celebrate your harvest when it feels right, or you have cleared an urgent business commitment that is taking your attention.

Don't ever feel you have missed out. The best Summer Solstice celebration I ever had was the day after the Solstice during which I had been travelling the ultimate nightmare journey. This followed an equally horrendous marathon television show; I waited four hours for my appearance for which I had spent many days researching, only to be pulled off at the last moment because the show ran out of time. During that late celebrated Solstice, I vowed I would never dance to the media circus tune again, even for promised high-profile publicity coverage, and so I took back my own power.

Others will move all the festivals to the nearest weekend to allow for time and space to celebrate, and since the energies are powerful for the days after the festival then this is no problem.

In the modern world, people live and travel far from the small closed communities of the past. Many live and work in towns rather than on the land, with 24/7 heating and lighting, and this can lead to psychological and spiritual burnout. The Wheel of the Year is one of the most natural ways to get back in touch with your natural ebbs and flows, and with natural cycles of cold and heat, light and darkness. By working with the fruits, trees and flowers of your own region, you can connect with the slower cycle rather than linear A to Z dash of the modern world.

Different kinds of seasonal magick

Seasonal magick draws on sympathetic forces in both homeopathic and contagious rites to attract the new energies of the season and to banish darkness, by lighting fires to strengthen the power of the sun as I described at the Midwinter Solstice.

Contagious magick is central to the Wheel of the Year where people physically align with the earth: for example, by baking and eating bread at Lughnassadh, the first grain harvest at the beginning of August or making love in the woods and fields at Beltane on May Eve to link the fertility of humans, animals and crops.

Balancing magick is vital at the Equinoxes, to hold the Wheel steady at the balance of light and darkness, so that it will turn smoothly and bring the increase or decrease of light harmoniously and not tip or lurch.

Celebration versus ritual

In the previous unit I described some differences between a spell and a ritual (see page 53). Seasonal rituals are derived from the open-ended celebrations of the passing of the year. Celebrations are by their nature spontaneous and there will be times when you want to take perhaps the central facet of a ritual, for example the traditional Beltane fire and then open it up to your own inspiration in a place of beauty or at your own private altar, surrounded by the seasonal fruits and flowers of your own locality. This allows the energies of the rising or falling year to carry you.

By doing this, our own natural ebbs and flows can be harmonised and we can draw spiritually and emotionally directly on the seasonal powers. In the modern world, we find vestiges of these old festivals and some of their old customs, such as at Christmas and Easter. For those practitioners who do live in very narrow communities or encounter family opposition, you can often apply the principles and nature-based aspects of the older festivals to make the modern commercialised ones more spiritual.

Solar and lunar energies

The Solstices and Equinoxes are solar in their focus and timings. However, the other four the cross-quarter days are traditionally regarded as lunar orientated in terms of their underlying energies.

The four solar festivals, the Solstices and Equinoxes, can be calculated accurately each year. The other four festivals are calculated by some modern practitioners as the day upon which the sun enters 15 degrees of Scorpio for Samhain (end of October/beginning of November), 15 degrees of Aquarius for Oimelc (end of January/beginning of February), 15 degrees of Taurus for Beltane (end of April/beginning of May) and 15 degrees of Leo for Lughnassadh (end of July beginning of August).

In yet another tradition these four festivals are celebrated at the first full moon of the four star sign periods or the first full moon around the festival date. The full moons of the different months were also ritually important, as well as markers of what was happening to the crops, fruit and the migrating birds and animals. We will work with the Celtic and Native North American moons in the module on moon magick.

But the eightfold year can also be regarded for magickal purposes as the eight stages of the moon that it passes through each month, but writ large. Imagine the moon as passing just once through the whole year in a gigantic cycle. For example, the full moon phase and the Midsummer Solstice are both times of maximum power (more on this in the separate festivals below).

If this aspect interests you, you can mark the festival twice, first using the actual date of the festival, but then also on the evening of its nearest related moon phase to the festival. Sometimes, as in 2005, you get an actual correlation: for example, the full moon on the Summer Solstice, as a double surge of power.

The Triple Goddess

One of the key concepts is that of the Triple Goddess, who was pictured in many cultures as the Maiden, Mother and Crone or Wise Woman aspects of existence. This progression mirrored the cycles of the Moon. But the Triple Goddess also reflects the passage of the Earth Mother through the seasons.

Among the Navajo, Changing Woman or White Shell Woman came from the first medicine corn bundle, held up by first man. In this ritual action, Sky and Earth, White Shell Woman's parents, came together in her creation. Each year she mirrors the seasons, growing older throughout the year from spring. In the summer she is the fertile Corn Mother. By midwinter, Changing Woman has become old and wise and enters the altar room within her shining home. She undergoes rebirth so that she is once more a beautiful young maiden when spring arrives. Changing Woman ensures the seasons revolve, controls the weather and grants abundant harvests if her people remain in harmony.

The changeover was not always peaceful. There are legends of how at the Celtic early spring festival Oimelc (31 January eve for three days) and in Christian times on St Bridget's (Bride's) day on 1 February the Maiden Goddess's lamb fought against and defeated the dragon of the Old Hag of winter, the Cailleach. Before the battle between Winter and Spring was over, the leader of the Celtic tribe in legend had to mate with the Old Hag who became transformed as he lay with her into the lovely maiden Goddess through the power of sacred sex.

The Mother became the Hag at Samhain, 31 October at sunset, when she stripped off her beautiful adornments and descended into the Underworld to encounter death in order to try to bring back her love. But at the same time she is the pregnant mother, heavy with the sun child. Sometimes again the roles overlap and so the midwife of the Sun God, the crone or the triple midwives, the Madrones (see page 380) and the Mother of the God exist together. In some midwinter rites a single midwife is transformed into the mother as the new sun is born on or around 21 December, the Midwinter Solstice.

Indeed, the Crone does not finally concede her hold over the year until at midnight on May Eve, Beltane on 30 April, the Old Hag of winter, finally casts her staff under a holly bush and turns to stone until six months later at Halloween. We will follow all these cycles in more detail in the next module.

This aspect of the Wheel links with the progress of our life through different ages and stages. It brings us face to face with issues of resistance and surrender, and how we can become wise at any time if man or woman we embrace the Crone.

The deities of the eightfold wheel

Some people get very confused by the mythological circle of the Celtic Wheel of the Year with good reason, because there are two separate factors or myth cycles in operation that sometimes overlap.

The light/darkness cycle is represented by an ongoing annual battle for supremacy between the two brothers Llew or Lugh and Goronwy. They are not strictly twins (though they are often called this) since they are born six months apart, but each is the alter ego of the other. At the Spring Equinox (around 21 March) Llew/Lugh is supreme, but his decline begins with the birth of his brother at the Summer Solstice and he dies at the Autumn Equinox when Goronwy is supreme. But Goronwy grows weaker from the rebirth of Lugh/Llew at Midwinter that begins the new light cycle. So throughout there is loss and gain, strengths and weakness, to be balanced briefly on the days of equal light and darkness at Spring and Autumn Equinoxes.

Personally, these are vital brief days of balance and equilibrium for us all and we have much we can learn from each brother on these days. We should listen as they briefly meet in unity and then continue the dynamic but cruel struggle necessary for life and the Wheel to continue turning.

In an even older tree myth saga they are the Oak King (the light brother), who ruled from Midwinter, and the Holly King (dark), whose reign was from Midsummer to Midwinter. Neither brother was bad, nor could be overcome forever (back to the concept of polarities). The dark, quiet times, when the land lies fallow and people are also supposed to rest more, are as essential as the bright, active, growth times. In Christianity, these two are mirrored in Christ who was born at Midwinter and his cousin John the Baptist who was born around the Midsummer Solstice, and whose name was adopted for the Christian Midsummer, as St John's Day on 24 June.

God and Goddess of the Wheel

Interwoven and sometimes overlapping the story is the love and union/parting of the Sun/Grain God and Earth Goddess and the annual rebirth of the Sun King at the Midwinter Solstice. For the God/Goddess, progression through the year is also vital to the Wheel's turning, with each taking predominance at different festivals or coming together equally as in a sacred dance or ritual coupling, the Great Rite of Witchcraft, when male and female (signified in ritual chalice and blade) are joined and become one.

The God celebrates his birth and the triumphal return of the sun, though weak, at Midwinter. The Goddess nurtures him as the infant at Oimelc, the festival of milk, at the beginning of February. At the Spring Equinox, he is her suitor and impregnates her so that the Sun King can be born in the continuing Wheel turn on the following Midwinter Solstice.

On Beltane, May Day, they celebrate the woodland wedding but he is not yet ready to become the God King and she is still the maiden crowned with flowers. By Midsummer he is her equal, but for one brief day only before his power declines. As God King and Goddess Queen, they celebrate the sacred marriage, the Great Rite. By Lughnassadh, the beginning of August, he transfers his remaining power to her because he is old and sick, and he offers himself for the land in sacrifice.

By the Autumn Equinox the widow is alone, but the dark brother claims her as his bride and impregnates her so that he, too, may be reborn at the next Midsummer. So the Wheel turns. At Samhain, the modern Halloween and most important date in the ritual calendar, the widow descends to the Underworld to be with her true love. Chaos reigns until her return three days later, having encountered and submitted to death herself and accepted that it is a part of life and even she cannot defeat it or stop it taking her children. The Goddess created death as well as birth and so the witch comes to terms with mortality in this and the Descent of the Goddess (see page 394).

Then at Midwinter, around 21 December. the infant Sun King is reborn and the cycle begins anew as his mother protects her new infant. In some myths she hides him with her until she can safely emerge as the Maiden/Mother at Oimelc and present her child to the world. This cycle mirrors the agricultural year and also the older hunter-gatherer traditions, when the God of Winter died at the start of the hunting season, still around the Autumn Equinox in many lands. It is also a personal journey for witches of both sexes, as different facets of themselves, anima and animus, and their relationships with others enter new cycles and the power balance constantly but subtly alters. Occasionally the two cycles overlap: for example, at Lughnassadh at the beginning of August when Lugh or Llew as both Sun King and Barley King is cut down in the last sheaf of grain at the first harvest, though his death in the role of light brother is not until the Autumn Equinox.

In the annual celebrations of Europe and Scandinavia, women from the village or town or, in earlier times, priestesses would represent the Goddess in her different forms. It was believed that she was present in spirit and might be seen leading the processions by those with clairvoyant sight, children or virgins. The Goddess also appears in different aspects as the Maiden, the Mother and the Wise Old Grandmother of Winter, linking us with the Moon Goddess, sometimes in more than one guise at a single festival.

PRACTICAL ASSIGNMENT

Plan your personal Wheel of the Year

* Plan your personal magickal seasonal year ahead in terms of how it fits into what is going on externally in your everyday life, as well as the call of the seasons.

* Which are going to be your personal ebb and flow periods and what are your milestones, personally as well as magickally?

* Look initially at Midwinter Solstice/Christmas, the Spring Equinox/Easter, the Summer Solstice/Midsummer and the Autumn Equinox/harvest time in later September. Do any of your planned holidays/milestones coincide with these and what do you anticipate celebrating/dread about spring, summer, autumn and winter in the year ahead?

* Can you express these ritually or use the seasons to give you personal strength?

* Is your Wheel going to be different this year from last? How can you turn the Wheel magickally and personally to take control of the energies, or at least ride the highs and lows and not be submerged by them?

* Now look at the other four ritual and magickally more important dates as well and see how your own life mirrors the light/dark brother and God/Goddess patterns of movement described above. What issues do they raise for you and what opportunities?

* Is one of the eight festival times *your* festival this year, or, if not, is there one that most summarises your aspirations for the 12 months ahead? Could you go somewhere or plan an event to make this festival a real catalyst for the future?

* Are you turning the Wheel or are events spinning it out of control or slowing it, with the stagnation stopping you moving forward?

Further research

How the society we live in and our religious and cultural background shapes our concept of the Wheel. Find out about festivals that interest you: for example, Divali or Hanukkah from other cultures. See if and how they can add to your own future Wheel of the Year celebrations and perceptions.

Further information

Further reading
* Nichols, Mike, *Witches' Sabbats*, Acorn Guild Press, 2005
* Pennick, Nigel, *The Pagan Book of Days, a Guide to the Festivals, Traditions and Sacred Days of the Year*, Destiny Books, 2001

Websites
* *Cassandra Eason*
  Detailed section on the eightfold year, including suggested rituals
  www.cassandraeason.co.uk

FESTIVALS OF THE WHEEL OF THE YEAR

In this Module we will study in more detail the eight festivals that make up the Wheel of the Year. I have outlined the magickal framework of each festival and suggested preparatory spiritual activities to tune into the different festival energies as you read about them. You will find a lot more information later in the course to help you structure your own festival rituals and learn how they were practised in different cultures.

You will not want to try all of the suggested activities in a single week, but they are something you can work on around the festival times or whenever you need the energy of the particular festival any time of the year.

Oimelc or Imbolc

31 January–2 February, a cross-quarter day

* **Focus:** New ideas, for the promise that winter will end; for planning the future and for putting out the first shoots of new love and the growth or regrowth of trust; for taking the first steps to launch any projects that start in a small way; for rituals to regenerate any areas devastated by neglect or pollution in your life or more globally; for melting rigid attitudes that may have led to conflicts between families and work colleagues or the isolation and alienation of disadvantaged groups through prejudice; and rituals for newborn infants, babies and young animals

* **Keywords:** Trust, germination

* **Element:** Fire/Earth

* **Direction:** North-east

* **Deity forms:** The Maiden Goddesses who will soon replace the Old Women of winter (see page 234 on Gods and Goddesses for examples of these and other seasonal deities)

* **Nature of festival:** Light/candles

* **Energies:** Rising

* **Angel:** Raguel, Archangel of ice and snow who melts the winter snows with his fiery sword. He wears dark grey and silver robes with a halo flashing with icicles.

* **Moon phase:** Crescent

Cycle of the year

Imbolc means in the belly of the mother. The first festival of spring often when the land is still frozen, it is a reminder that new life stirs within the Earth. This was the all-important time when sheep and cattle had their young and so fresh milk and dairy products were first available to the community.

Though it is the time of the Maiden, the other aspects of the Goddess also overshadow her, the newly delivered mother of the Sun King whose milk is mirrored by the milk of the ewes who gave this festival its name of Oimelc or ewe's milk. The dark brother still holds sway, but the young God of light is growing in power as he is nursed by the Goddess. The Maiden Goddess melts the frozen land with her wand of fire (see page 637 for much more on this festival).

One of the Celtic names for the pagan festival was Brigantia, after Brighid, the Celtic Triple Goddess, here in her maiden aspect replacing the Old Hag of Winter's rule. She was Christianised as St Bridget, Brigit of Kildare or St Bride in Wales and Scotland, whose day is 1 February. Brigantia was also the name of a Gallic Earth Goddess.

In myth, the Maiden Goddess Brighid mated with Llew/Lugh, the young God of light, and a virgin was chosen to likewise mate with the chief of the tribe to ensure the coming of new life to the land. It is said that, like Llew, he embraced Cailleach, the Old Hag of Winter who was transformed in his arms to the lovely virgin Goddess.

The Christian Candlemas, the festival of candles, took place on 2 February, the day of the Purification of the Virgin Mary on which she took Jesus to the temple for the first time.

Tasks

* Personal purification, using smudge sticks, spiritual and, if you wish, physical detoxifying.

* Candle meditations or just quiet times sitting by candlelight talking to your Guardian Angels and Spirit Guides as you hold a clear quartz crystal sphere as a focus (it need only be small).

* Creating a candle web with friends or relatives for healing or peace. Choose an evening when you are all at home and agree in advance a time when you will all focus on the same person, animal or place, sending healing through the candle. You can adapt the web for people who live in nearby time zones: for example, France and Scandinavia are one hour ahead of the UK.

* Leave the candle to burn through.

* Unless you live in a warm land, plant seeds indoors or under glass, naming for each handful what you wish to bring into your life in the months ahead. You can plant the seeds on the Spring Equinox.

Alban Eiler, Ostara or the Spring Equinox

From around 20 March–22 March, a quarter day

* **Focus:** Fertility and positive life changes, new beginnings and opportunities, for new flowering love; for initiating creative ventures, travel, house moves, clearing what is no longer needed in your life; anything to do with conception and pregnancy, children and young people, mothers; for healing, spring-cleaning and casting out what is no longer of worth, welcoming the winds of change; rituals to cleanse the seas and air of pollution, for new peacemaking initiatives of all kinds, and to encourage major attitude changes towards, international, national and local issues
* **Keywords:** Initiation, signs of growth
* **Element:** Air
* **Direction:** East
* **Deity forms:** All Dawn and Spring Goddesses
* **Nature of festival:** Rebirth/eggs
* **Energies:** Balanced
* **Angel:** Raphael, Archangel of the Dawn, the East, the spring and of healing. He carries a golden vial of medicine, with a traveller's staff, food to nourish travellers and is dressed in the colours of early morning sunlight, with a beautiful green healing ray emanating from his halo.
* **Moon phase:** First quarter or waxing (increasing) half moon

Cycle of the year

In Gaelic, Alban Eiler means the light of the earth that returns after the winter and the time of sowing begins in earnest. Young animals are thriving and the early spring flowers are in bloom.

Bonfires were lit and the corn dolly from the previous year was burned or the effigy of a straw sacrifice man – in Christian times, the Judas man – to ensure that the fertility of the previous year is passed on into the new crops. It was a reminder, too, of the sacrifice of the Grain God, because the corn dolly, symbol of Mother Earth, was made from the last sheaf of grain cut down, in which his essence resided.

Ostara, the Norse Maiden Goddess opens the doors of spring and mates with the young virile triumphal God of light (in earlier times the lord of the hunt) to conceive the child of light who will be born on the Midwinter Solstice the following December. The light and dark brothers fight and the light twin kills his brother, so henceforward the days will be longer than the night. The dark twin descends to the Underworld or the womb of the mother, like the seeds planted in the earth, to await rebirth.

Eggs from hens laying for the first time as light returns were painted and set on the shrine of Ostara and later to the Virgin Mary.

Tasks

* Plant the seedlings outdoors grown from the seeds you planted at Imbolc. If they did not thrive, plant seedlings rather than seeds, naming again or adapting the earlier plans.

* Spring-clean your home, your paperwork and your emotions.
* If only for one day, make a spiritual pilgrimage to a sacred place, either unfamiliar or well loved. Allow words and actions to come, using only tools and materials you find there.
* Make a clay or beeswax egg and plant it beneath a fragrant herb, naming a new beginning or change of attitude you know will take a while to achieve but that will be worth it.
* Also plant a crystal in a marked spot, naming something you will achieve in six months. You can dig it up at the Autumn Equinox.

Beltane or Beltaine

30 April–2 May, the second most important cross-quarter day of the year and the beginning of the Celtic summer

* **Focus:** Fertility whether for conceiving a child or improvement in career, business or financial matters; for increasing commitment in love, for passion and the consummation of love; for creative inspiration, improving health and increasing energy; for optimism and self-confidence; for abundance in every way and for generosity; for people in their 20s and 30s; for giving up bad habits; and rituals to send strength for freedom of speech, action and beliefs everywhere
* **Keywords:** Passion, fertility
* **Element:** Fire/Earth
* **Direction:** South-east
* **Deity forms:** Fire and blacksmith Gods, the Green Man
* **Nature of festival:** Fire/flowers
* **Energies:** Rising
* **Angel:** Camael or Chamuel, Archangel of courage, divine love and justice who wears a deep red tunic with dark green armour, a halo of dark ruby flames and rich green wings.
* **Moon phase:** the gibbous moon (bulging almost full moon)

Cycle of the year

Beltane or Beltane is named after the Irish Bealtaine meaning Bel-fire, the fire of the Celtic god of light, known as Bel, Beli or Belinus. Sundown on May Eve heralded the signal for Druids to kindle the great Bel-fires from nine different kinds of wood. It is also called Walpurgis Night, after the nine-day Anglo-Saxon festival held for the Fertility Goddess Walpurgis or Walpurga. She was Christianised as St Walpurga.

Beltane, of which the modern May Day has survived, marked the beginning of the Celtic summer, when cattle were released from barns and driven between twin fires to cleanse them and to invoke fertility as they were released into the fields. It also marks the marriage of the Goddess as May Queen, the flower maiden, to the Sun King, here in his woodland form as the Green Man, lord of the forest and of vegetation, and the last appearance of the Maiden Goddess at a time when flowers were covering the earth as a sign of the ever increasing warmth and light.

On I May, the magicians Math and Gwydion, created the Goddess Blodeuwedd, the Celtic Maiden Flower, from nine flowers – primrose, broom, meadowsweet, cockle, bean, nettle, hawthorn, oak and chestnut blossom – to be the wife of Llew, the Welsh Sun God. The God moves forward to take his place as equal, giving up his wild ways and his lifetime in the forest. He marries her in a woodland wedding and crowns her with flowers, promising her a crown of gold one day.

The Light God becomes ever stronger as light and warmth increases and the two myths merge for a while. Winter was finally dead as at midnight on May Eve Cailleach Bhuer, the Old Hag of Winter, cast her staff under a holly bush and turned to stone until six months later on Halloween.

Beltane is a time of great fairy activity, especially around standing stones and stone circles. Sacred wells are also very potent on I May both for healing and for fertility. Traditionally, the ritual should be finished by sunrise, but any May morning energies will work as well.

Tasks

* Light your own Bel bonfire or use a fire dish or huge candle embedded in sand. Burn pieces of wood or thread to signify what you wish to grow in your life. Also, burn dead wood or darker threads to signify what stands in the way of your future success or happiness.

* Make a garland or a basket of nine different flowers to decorate your home as a reminder of good times ahead and for each flower make a wish for something that will need all your power and optimism to fulfil.

* Visit a labyrinth or a maze, or just spiral over grass, earth or sand in bare feet, connecting with the earth energies.

Alban Heruin, Litha, Midsummer or Summer Solstice

From around 20–22 June, a major quarter day

* **Focus:** Power, joy and courage; male potency; success, marriage, fertility of all kinds, especially for older women, for people approaching middle age; strength, energy, self-confidence, health, wealth and career; maximising opportunities, seizing chances and enjoying the present; tackling seemingly insoluble problems, bringing light and life and hope, also for tackling major global problems such as global warming, famine, disease and preventing cruelty to people under oppressive regimes and intensive farming methods where livestock suffer

* **Keywords:** Power, achievement

* **Element:** Fire

* **Direction:** South

* **Deity forms:** All Sun Gods and Goddesses

* **Nature of festival:** Sun/gold

* **Energies:** The turning point as full power begins to wane from this day

* **Angel:** Michael, Archangel of the sun, noon, fire and summer; also sometimes associated with Beltane. He holds a golden sword and the scales of justice.

* **Moon phase:** Full

Cycle of the year

In Gaelic, Alban Heruin means the light of the shore. It is the height of the light year, and hence the festival of power and triumph. Druid ceremonies are held at dawn and noon on the Summer Solstice at sacred stone circles such as Stonehenge. Some Druids and Druidesses keep vigil from sunset on the previous evening.

The God is seated on twin thrones with the Goddess and they crown one another with gold. This is the sacred marriage of the earth and sky or the land/king and the Goddess/priestess in which the Goddess or her representative – in later times a married woman of rank from the local settlement – casts the wedding bouquet made of brilliantly coloured flowers and fragrant flowering herbs on a hilltop fire, to add her power to the sun.

The God reaches his full power and maturity, but knows that after the festival he will begin to lose this vitality. Even at the height of joy is an awareness that even he is subject to the powers of the changing seasons. Because the Goddess loved him so deeply, bonfires were lit and sun wheels thrown down the hillsides to delay the moment when his power must wane and he must leave her.

Just as the Midwinter Solstice became Christmas with the spread of Christianity, so was the Summer Solstice linked with the feast of St John the Baptist, who was born on 24 June, as the alter ego of Christ.

In the Light God cycle, the dark twin is reborn, but cannot yet challenge the Light God even though the power is starting to drain from him. In some myths they do fight, but the dark brother backs off, having made the first small wound in his glorious brother that will prove fatal.

Tasks

* Make sun water by leaving out still mineral water in a bowl covered with film or mesh from dawn until noon (or for up to eight hours on a darker day). Add clear quartz or citrine crystals to the water when you put it out (the previous evening if you prefer) and remove these at noon. Use the water as an energiser in baths and drinks and to splash on the centre of your hairline to open and clear your Crown chakra and your aura.

* Light a gold candle and set any small gold items of jewellery round it or in the sunlight for a few hours to transfer the power of the sun into your life as you wear the jewellery.

* At any opportunity, open your arms and legs wide, palms outstretched and uppermost and breathe in sunlight, drawing it upwards through your whole body. Sigh out though your mouth any darkness, sorrow or fear. When you feel full of sunshine, say nine times slowly, *I am filled with the light. I am pure light.*

Lughnassadh/Lammas

31 July- 2 August, a cross-quarter day

* **Focus:** Justice, human rights, freedom from abuse of any kind; for partnerships, both personal and legal or business, for signing contracts or property matters; promotion and career advancement and regularising personal finances; journeys to see friends and family or on business; the renewal of promises and fidelity; willing sacrifice for the greater good, natural justice and karma, trusting the cosmos to provide by giving without seeking immediate return; for people in their 40s and 50s; globally, rituals for fighting through legal redress for injustice for oppressed people or creatures, especially making sure that workers in Third World countries are not exploited financially; for teaching new skills so that people in poor lands and deprived areas may have a chance to create their own prosperity; and for all acts of unpublicised charity.

* **Keywords:** Generosity, commitment

* **Element:** Earth

* **Direction:** South-west

* **Deity forms:** All grain and sacrifice gods, Earth Mothers

* **Nature of festival:** Transformation/bread

* **Energies:** Waning

* **Angel:** Sachiel, Archangel of the grain harvest and of abundance. He wears robes of deep blue and purple, carries sheaves of corn and baskets of food, with a rich purple and golden halo and blue and purple wings.

* **Moon phase:** Disseminating moon (the waning or decreasing full moon)

Cycle of the year

This is the festival of the first grain harvest and the funeral games of Lugh the Sun God or, in an earlier tradition, the funeral games of the Earth Mother Talitiu, foster mother of Lugh and one of the three Celtic Mothers. She was said to have died preparing the fields.

The God renews (or in some myths makes for the first time) the sacred contract with the Goddess in the Celtic form of Eriu/Nass. He promises to defend and die for the land, a ceremony undertaken by king/leader and priestess of the Goddess. Eriu was the Irish Earth and Sovereign Goddess. In one of the magickal transformations from Maiden/Mother/Crone, Eriu was pictured as a hag who was thus made lovely by the golden light of the sun. The Sun/Grain God transfers his remaining light and warmth to the Goddess for the continuing growth of the crops. He willingly sacrifices himself for the growth of the rest of the crops and his spirit enters the grain. He descends to the Underworld, back into her womb, to be reborn on the Midwinter celebration as the infant Sun King.

The final battle of the light and dark twin cannot take place until the Autumn Equinox six weeks later and so the myths divide again. In the straightforward light/dark saga, the light brother grows weaker as his dark brother grows in strength, but his dark twin cannot yet challenge him and win. Some practitioners fix the sacrifice of the God as the Autumn Equinox, the second harvest or see the Barley God as fatally wounded, but lingering until the second harvest is home and thus allowing the dark twin to deliver the death blow in the autumn.

Tasks

* Bake your own bread in the shape of a figure that can either be the Grain Spirit or the Grain Mother. Eat or share it and name the transformations you seek in your life/the world.

* Cut down an area of weeds or overgrown grass or spend a day on an organised project clearing a local wilderness, to clear your own way ahead spiritually.

* Light an orange candle every evening if possible for a week as a reminder of blessings you have received, especially any you might not have deserved. At the end of the week, make a practical or spoken small blessing to the life of someone who does not merit it.

Alban Elued, Autumn Equinox

About 21 September–23 September, a quarter day

* **Focus:** The completion of tasks, the fruition of long-term goals; for mending quarrels and forgiving yourself for past mistakes; for money owed, for assessing gain and loss; for family relationships and friendships; for material security for the months ahead; for abundance in all aspects of your life; for issues of job security or the need to consolidate finances; all matters concerning retirement and older people; the resolution or management of chronic heath problems; rituals to ensure enough food, shelter and resources for vulnerable communities and individuals; relief from flood and famine; protection of endangered water creatures, dolphin, whales and fish, whose death involves great suffering; and for peace, especially where initiatives are already in motion

* **Keywords:** Balance, forgiveness

* **Element:** Water

* **Direction:** West

* **Deity forms:** All river and freshwater deities, also the mistresses of the animals and lords of the hunt

* **Nature of festival:** Reconciliation/fruit and nuts

* **Energies:** Balanced

* **Angel:** Rismuch, angel of agriculture and cultivated land, wearing every imaginable shade of brown, carrying a scythe and a hoe as symbol that he is conserver of the land and the crops. His symbols are sheaves of wheat and ears of corn, dishes of seeds and nuts, and straw animals or knots tied with red ribbon that are part of the very ancient folklore of many regions (linked also with Lughnassadh).

* **Moon phase:** Waning half moon or last quarter moon

Cycle of the year

The gathering of the second or green harvest of fruit, nuts and vegetables; also the final grain harvest, the storing of resources for the winter and barter for goods not available or scarce. Feasts of abundance and the offering of the finest of the harvest to the deities was a practical as well as magickal gesture, part of the bargain between humans and deities. Rotten fruit and vegetables were where possible fed to animals or discarded. Barley wine was brewed from the earlier crop.

Alban Elued means in Gaelic, light on the Water and so the sun is moving away over the water to shine on the Isles of the Blest, leaving the world with encroaching darkness.

Ancient tales tell of the death of the old Horned God at the hands of his successor or by offering himself to the huntsmen

The God is in the Underworld, the womb of the Mother awaiting rebirth.

While the Goddess mourns for her love she must prepare for the harvest over which she presides. But she is tired herself and getting heavier with the Light child. The Dark twin challenges and kills the Light brother who returns to the Earth/the womb and the two legends temporarily merge again. The Dark Twin ritually mates with the Goddess to ensure his successor.

Some myths blame Llew the Welsh God of Light's faithless wife Blodeuwedd or Arthur's Queen Guinevere for transferring their attention to the dark twin. But even these treachery myths reflect the need for the new dark twin to be born at the Summer Solstice, so the Wheel continues to turn.

Tasks

* Make a list of what needs to be done urgently, a second list of less pressing but necessary tasks, and a third list of matters that are best left (some of which may be things you did not want to do anyway). Throw away the third list and draw up a realistic timescale for the completion of the other tasks.

* Contact an old friend or a family member with whom you have lost touch and decide if there is anyone with whom you would like to reduce or cease communication.

* Buy or make seasonal fruit jam and hold an old-fashioned tea party to bring different generations together.

* Dig up the crystal you buried at the Spring Equinox, wash it and carry it as a reminder of spring to come.

Samhain

From 31 October to 2 November, the major cross-quarter day of the year and the beginning of the Celtic winter and New Year

* **Focus:** Remembering the family ancestors; for looking both backwards to the past and into the future; for psychic and physical protection; for overcoming fears, especially of ageing and mortality; for retired people and those in their 70s and 80s; for marking the natural transition between one stage of life and the next and, for laying old ghosts, psychological as well as psychic; globally this is a time for rituals to aid charities and initiatives to help families and the elderly, the sick and terminally ill; also for the preservation of ancient sacred sites and the cultural heritage of the world, including the wisdom of indigenous peoples

* **Keywords:** Tradition, preservation

* **Element:** Air/Fire

* **Direction:** North-west

* **Deity forms:** The Crone Goddesses, The Gods and Goddesses of Winter, snow and ice

- **Nature of festival:** Past worlds/nature spirits/fey energies
- **Energies:** Waning
- **Angel:** Cassiel, Archangel of compassion and silence. He is pictured as bearded, riding a dragon and wearing dark robes, with indigo flames sparking from his halo.
- **Moon phase:** The balsamic or waning crescent moon

Cycle of the year

Samhain means summer's end and the acceptance that the nights would get longer and the weather colder at a time when the herds were brought down from the hills and family members returned to the homestead for the winter. The animals that were to be kept during the winter were driven through fires, so that they might be cleansed of disease and parasites. Others were slaughtered with reverence and salted to be preserved for food.

At this time of no time, the family spirits returned shivering to seek warmth at the family hearth and the fairies were on the move to their winter quarters. The Goddess descends into the Underworld to visit her lost love, the Sun King and the world is in mourning. Meanwhile in her absence, timelessness rules spirits, fairies roam free and other ancestors come to visit families.

The Cailleach, the Crone Goddess of the Celtic World, moves to the fore at this festival. She is the winter sun, which shines from All Hallows to Beltane Eve, and Grainne or Dia Greine, the Celtic Sun Goddess, ruled the rest of the year. They are mother and daughter in a revolving cycle.

The dark brother rejoices at his supremacy and takes the throne alongside the Goddess, who is forced to marry him.

In pre-Christian times, the fires of Ireland were extinguished at sunset on Samhain. A fire was kindled by the Arch Druid/Druidess on the hill of Tlachtga in Ireland, and every great family carried home torches to rekindle their hearth fires, which were kept burning thereafter.

Tasks

- Explore or develop a form of divination that interests you.
- Spend time outdoors, listening to the wind in the trees, the sound of the sea, water running over stones or bird song. See if you can spontaneously hear any messages.
- Find out about a family ancestor or visit a place where your family used to live to connect with your roots.

Alban Arthuran, Yule or Midwinter Solstice

From around 20–22 December, a major quarter day

- **Focus:** The rebirth of light and hope; for domestic happiness and security, family togetherness, anything to do with the home and property and for financial security; for long-term money plans; for patience and for accepting that which cannot be changed; for very old people, for carers, for welcoming home travellers or estranged people and for restoring enthusiasm and health in those who are worn down by illness or lack of hope; globally this is a time for rituals of renewed faith in the face of despair and cynicism; for work to provide homes and shelter for people, birds and animals, and more efficient and humane welfare services; the regeneration of famine or war-torn lands; improving conditions in all institutions

* **Keywords:** Hope, trust
* **Element:** Fire/Air
* **Direction:** North
* **Deity forms:** All Sun Kings, Sun Goddesses and Mother and Crone Goddesses
* **Nature of festival:** Rekindling extinguished flames/light in the darkness
* **Energies:** Turning point as the energies begin to rise again
* **Angel:** Gabriel, Archangel of the moon, who took the news to Mary that she would have a son Jesus. Picture him in silver or clothed in the blue of the night sky with a mantle of stars and a crescent moon for his halo, with a golden horn, a white lily, alternatively with a lantern in his right hand and with a mirror made of jasper in his left.
* **Moon phase:** The new moon, when it is not visible in the sky but the energies have turned

Cycle of the year

There was a natural fear about food supplies not lasting the rest of the winter, especially if the weeks ahead were hard. The sun had reached the lowest point in the sky. After the Midwinter Solstice, when the physical and psychic crisis point was passed, people held feasts as a magickal gesture to attract abundance. They hung lights from evergreen branches to encourage the trees and vegetation to sprout green again and to give power to the sun.

In Gaelic, Alban Arthuran means the light of Arthur, and refers to the rebirth of Arthur as the Divine Child called the Mabon; the festival of the restoration of the power of the Sun and the Sun Gods and the almost imperceptible return of the light and with it hope.

The Sun God is reborn after the fear that the world will be overwhelmed by darkness on the Shortest Day. The Crone Goddess or sometimes the three Mothers act as midwife. In some legends, the maiden Goddess Brighid acts as midwife.

The light twin returns and the dark twin knows his power is on the wane. He watches jealously the attention being paid to his newborn brother.

In passage graves throughout the world, such as Newgrange in Ireland, people waited in darkness for the first shaft of light on the Solstice morning to illuminate the inner shrine. Then their lanterns were relit from a single flint.

Tasks

* Light a dark candle to represent the past or matters that now must be accepted. From it, light a white candle for the future and then extinguish the dark candle. Let the white candle burn, allowing the cosmos to send what you most need.
* Make or buy small dried herb sachets or bath products for friends and family as a gift for no special occasion except to say, *I appreciate you.*
* Hold a party and let each person present light a candle from a central one and in turn name someone or a place to which they wish to send light.

PRACTICAL ASSIGNMENT

Creating your Wheel of the Year

* Start the Wheel of the Year section in your Book of Shadows.
* Note any of the spiritual preparations that I have suggested that would be helpful for you. You may like to choose one to explore that is connected with the closest festival time wise.

Further research

Begin using online resources and books to note any myths and folk customs that enrich your own understanding of the Wheel.

Further information

Further reading
* Hutton, Ronald, *Stations of the Sun, a History of the Ritual Year in Britain*, Oxford Paperbacks, 2004

Websites
* *Mike Nichols*
  Probably the most comprehensive Wheel of the Year site
  www.geocities.com/Athens/Forum/7280

THE MULTICULTURAL WHEEL OF THE YEAR

(★A★)s witches, I believe it is important that we draw inspiration from a variety of sources to enrich our work. Though this is not a module you might expect to find, I am including the Egyptian Three-Spoke Wheel of the Year and the Two-Spoke Wheel of the Norse, Andean and Australian Aboriginal tradition. In teaching witchcraft I have discovered that especially for a relatively familiar topic, such as the Wheel of the Year, that tends to be rooted in the Celtic tradition, personal and coven ritual really expand when different kinds of inspiration are introduced. The Egyptian world especially links with modern Wicca and can help structure more formal festival ceremonies.

Connecting with other cycles of nature

Whether you are a solitary practitioner or work magickally mainly with others, you can draw from the energies of different seasonal wheels through the spiritual connection we have with other cultures and ages, even if they are on the other side of the world.

As well as using these ideas to inspire your Eightfold Year, you can also adopt the different wheels for magickal energies when your needs (or indeed the place you live) are out of synchronicity with the eight Celtic festival order. For example, you might need a new beginning in September, the time of harvest in the Celtic Wheel, which should traditionally bring resolution and assessment of what has been gained and lost. In this case you could use the flood seasonal new beginnings ritual from the first season of the three-spoke Ancient Egyptian Wheel of the Year given below.

Egyptian Wheel of the Year

In Ancient Egypt there were only three seasons: Akhet, the time of the flood/water from early July-October/November; Peret, the time of growth, sun and water mixed, from October/November to March/April; and Shemu, the time of harvest, the dry of the sun/fire alone from March/April to July. Magickally, this three-spoke wheel is important because it offers, between the extremes of the water/flood season and the fire/sun/harvest season, a long, stable, balancing season where water/the Nile/chaos, which represents chaos and sun/fire/order, ruled equally.

Moon wise you would regard the flood as the waxing moon, the time of balance as the full moon, and the time of fire as the waning moon.

Three-spoke Egyptian Wheel of the Year as the basis for ritual

In Egypt today, as it has been for thousands of years, the land is dominated by the power of the sun and by the waters of the Nile (now via irrigation canals). These two contrasting forces formed the central core of Egyptian magick. The sun represented order and time, as the rising and setting of the sun marked the parameters of day and night and the passing of the year. The Nile was chaos, but also the fertilising power that still is responsible for the fertility of the land around the Nile, as the desert stretches vast and arid on either side. It has been not much more than 35 years since the creation of the Aswan Dam in Southern Egypt stopped the annual flooding of the Nile.

Balance between fire and water so that both would manifest their creative not destructive aspects fell under the control of Ma'at, the cosmic principle of balance, personified as the Goddess Ma'at, the Goddess of order, truth, justice and goodness in this world and the next. This balance was the responsibility on earth of the Pharaoh, manifestation of Horus, the Sky God, son of Ra, the Sun God. But though balance is necessary sometimes the extreme forces, whether water or fire, are equally essential to bring change (water) or prolonged, intense power (fire/the sun).

Inundation (Akhet)

When water predominates, July to October/November

At this time the rising of the brilliant Sirius associated with Isis, heralded the coming of the flood and the beginning of the Egyptian New Year.

Use the time of water: for rituals for change, and new beginnings, for fertility, for washing away what you no longer need in your life, for emotional matters, love and family, for a major sudden inrush of money or power, for travel, for career or home moves, for protection against attack and for taking steps into the unknown and the unpredictable.

Work outdoors near water, the sea, a river, canal, lake or pond when possible. Initially I have suggested an almost instantly set up indoor ritual, but it can be easily adapted for a watery location when you have time and opportunity.

Use the symbol above and those of the other two seasons as talismans after the ritual (see the module on Talismans, Amulets and charms for ways to make your own).

Focal deities

* **Hapy:** The Nile God, portrayed as fat and male with female breasts, with a papyrus plant on his head, to whom prayers and offerings were made for a good flood. A good flood was one that was not too deep to wash away the soil but enough to fertilise the land along the Nile.

- **Heket:** The frog-headed fertility Goddess who brings prosperity and protection to the home, as well as fertility. She breathed life into the clay figures made by her husband Khnum, the Potter God.

- **Isis:** Known to the Romans as Stella Maris, Star of the Sea who carries the full moon disk on her headdress, in her magickal role of hidden Isis or Isis Veiled.

- **Osiris:** Consort of Isis and the rebirth God who caused the Nile to rise from the Underworld and is often associated with the flood itself. He is portrayed as a mummified figure wearing the crowns of Egypt and carrying the ceremonial crook and flail, and with the curved beard that denotes a pharaoh who has become divine in death.

- **Satis:** Lady of the waterfalls who poured the waters of the Nile to cool the parched earth. She is a beautiful woman with the white crown of Upper Egypt and two gazelle horns.

- **Sobek:** The Crocodile God Sobek was pictured as either a crocodile or crocodile-headed human, who brings protection against spite, attack and malice, as well as potency and prosperity.

- **Tauret:** The Hippopotamus Goddess, a variation of the Mother Goddess Mut. She is shown as a pregnant hippopotamus with huge breasts and sometimes the tail and back of a crocodile. She brings fertility, happiness and security to the home and is a fierce protector.

A water ritual to bring new energies into your life

- You will need:
  A bowl of water
  A white flower, preferably a lotus, water lily or any flower that grows near water
  A bowl of seeds
  A tray of sand or soil
  A twig, if possible from a tree that grows near water

- Work in the late afternoon. Set the tools for the ritual on a white, rectangular cloth with the bowl of water to the west, seeds to the east and the flower in the south and the tray of earth set in the north of the altar. Many people working with Egyptian magick face south.

- Using your twig, draw the hieroglyph for water in the tray of earth.

- As you draw your Water symbol, say:

    Kings of the Flood, fertile Queens of the blue water, I am the fertile Nile and would flow
    with you.

- Face the water (or set the bowl of water in front of you) and take your flower between your hands. Say:

I am the flower of the sacred waters, child of the Sun. The time of the Flood is near and I ask to be carried to new places/new opportunities, to seed new life.

❋ Cast the flower on the waters or set it in the bowl of water.

❋ Cast next your seeds on the water, saying:

Flow, grow, swell as the water and bring the change/opportunity I desire.
[Name your purpose and the fruition of that desire.]

❋ Stir the water with your twig and name the focal deity/deities of the ritual, which can be entirely of your choice, saying, for example:

Isis, Heket, Tauret, and Hapy, carry this prayer and this ritual on the waters
and accept my offerings.

❋ Gaze into the water and half close your eyes and you may see an image of the nature of the future change or how you will be helped or protected.

❋ Wash away the image in the tray with the bowl of water and tip the contents of the tray outdoors.

❋ You can of course carry out the whole ritual using a lake or pool and draw the hieroglyph in the sand or earth near the water, using a long branch to stir the water source. In this case drop the flower and seeds into the water and take water from the source in a bowl to erase the image.

The growing season (Peret)
The balance of water and fire, November to March

Once the flood had receded around October or November, the season of planting and sowing came, using the sheep and goats to tread in the seeds into the narrow fertile strip along the Nile. (This method is still used by modern farmers along the Nile.) The water was still important to irrigate the fields through the canal system and by drawing water using the ancient shaduf, a bucket and pulley, devices still in use 5,000 years later. But the sun was also of prime importance in causing the crops to grow and so this period represents the balance of water and fire, river and sun.

As with the inundation magick, you can invoke these energies whenever you need them.

Use the time of balanced water and fire for: rituals and empowerments for growth and improved fortune in any area of your life, for stability, for harmony and for balancing different needs, relationships, priorities or responsibilities; use it also to learn new skills or psychic arts, to carry through a creative project, for fidelity and commitment in love and for health; good for second careers or turning hobbies into careers and for home improvements. Work in a garden, park or open green space or on a balcony or patio with green plants.

Focal deities

* **Geb:** The Earth God, often pictured as a red or brown prone figure with erect phallus and vegetation growing from his body, lying beneath Nut, his wife, the Sky Goddess, who is arched above him.

* **Khnum:** The Potter God, who created humans from clay, is also associated with this balance, because he was said to release the waters of the Nile at the first cataract to keep the waters flowing throughout the year. He was depicted in the form of a ram and was worshipped as a creator god in Upper Egypt from predynastic times. Over time, he acquired a human form with a ram's head.

* **Nefertum:** The young beautiful God who emerged from a lotus as it opened in the morning. Nefertum is depicted either as a beautiful head rising from a lotus flower, a child with a side lock sucking his thumb, sitting inside the lotus or as a youth with a lotus headdress.

* **Osiris:** In his role as God of vegetation with a green face.

* **Isis:** In her earth or unveiled form as opposed to her lunar form is seen often on a throne with the infant Horus on her knee. The sun disk on her headdress between two cow horns, was a representation of the nurturing Earth Mother, Christianised as the Black Madonna.

A fire and water ritual for balance in your life

* You will need:
  A smooth area of soil large enough to stand in
  A jug of water (in the north of the area in this ritual)
  Herbs such as lavender that grows profusely in Egypt, basil, mint, parsley or thyme that were popular herbs in Ancient Egypt (in the east of the area)
  An outdoor torch or large garden candle (in the south of the area); you can buy oil-fuelled ones at garden centres and these are especially suitable for Ancient Egyptian magick

* Begin as the sun is setting. Light your torch and stand on the earth so you are facing the light.

* In the centre of the earth plot with a stick draw or trace in a row from left to right the symbols for water, for Nefer or harmony and the sun (see below). Leave spaces between them and make them large enough to walk round.

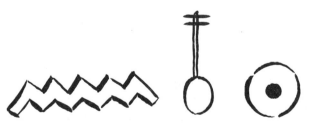

* With great care, take the torch and circle the water symbol clockwise, saying:

  As Fire joins to Water, so shall the land flourish. I am the land and the crops that will grow tall. Geb [or one or more of the deities named] hold my course straight and true.

- Return the torch to its place and taking the jug, circle the sun hieroglyph clockwise and sprinkle a few drops of water in a circle round it as you do so. Say:

  As Water joins Fire, so shall the land flourish. I am the land and the crops that will grow tall.
  Geb [or one or more of the deities named] hold my course straight and true.

- Set the jug back in its place.

- Taking the herbs, with a small trowel, dig a hole over the hieroglyph Nefer for harmony and place the herbs in the ground. Say:

  So do I plant the roots of my future harmony deep within me. I am Geb
  [or name your focus deity or deities. You can take in the power of as many as you wish].
  I receive the offering of life thus planted.

- Water the herbs from the jug and then pass the torch clockwise around the herbs, saying:

  As Water joins Fire, so they are harmonised in the fertile soil. I am the fertile soil and the
  crops I have planted will grow as harmony within and from me towards others.
  For I am Geb [or your focus deity or deities] and I hold the course straight and true.

- Tend the herbs regularly and as they grow with sun and water, so will you feel the harmony extending through every part of your being.

Harvest (Shemu)

The dry season when fire predominates, from March/April to early July

By March or April, the river was at its lowest point and the canals, too, were increasingly dry. But the water has done its work and in this time when fire predominates, the crops can be harvested. If the original flood had been high enough to spill over into desert lands, flowers blossomed at this time. It is said that Nephthys, sister of Isis and Goddess of twilight, who represented the desert, made love with Osiris when such a flood overwhelmed her. He was symbol of the flood. She conceived and gave birth during the season of harvest to Anubis, jackal-headed God of Mummification and the Underworld and the alter ego of Horus, son of Osiris with his true wife Isis. Horus is also considered the son of Ra, the Sun God, as mentioned earlier.

The desert had fierce sandstorms and also in times of drought might encroach on the once fertile land. At the time of the harvest, the rebirth of Osiris as the ripened grain was celebrated and thanks given to Isis as Corn Mother who used her magick to give him life. Part of the rite was a ceremonial burial of the grain Osiris. This was a small, flat, hollow, clay model of the Osirian mummy or Osiris himself that had a compartment filled with grain. These were also placed in tombs.

Use the time of fire: for rituals to bring success, power, the fruition of plans and hard work, for the restoration of heath and energy, for self confidence, courage, for justice and abundance; for overcoming obstacles, for wearing away opposition, for major ambitions and dreams, for fame, creative and artistic fulfilment and recognition.

Focal deities

* **Isis and Osiris**
* **Min:** The phallic fertility god depicted as human, with his right arm holding a whip or flail raised high behind his body. He wears two tall plumes on his head with a cord hanging down and has an erect phallus.
* **Nephthys:** As the desert flower, a beautiful woman with protective wings of gold or in a more shadowy form with a very high headdress.
* **Ra:** The Sun God, identified as the sun at its full power. He is depicted by the symbol of the sun and also in his solar boat. Ra is shown variously as a man with a curved beard and the sacred serpent coiled around a sun disk or a hawk-headed man, crowned with the sun disk and sacred Uraeus serpent.
* **Sekhmet:** Goddess of fire and healing, pictured with the head of a lioness with the sun disc on her head and the sacred cobra, protector of the pharaohs, on her brow. She can take the form of a lioness. In her more usual lioness-headed form she carries an ankh or sistrum.
* **Thoth:** whose sacred birds, the ibis, came to eat the corn in huge droves at this time. Depicted with an ibis or baboon head or as these creatures with a crescent or full moon disk on his head, Thoth is also seen as a scribe with his magickal palate, recording the words and commands of the deities and writing the laws for humankind.

A fire ritual for personal power

* You will need:
  A square yellow, orange or red cloth to serve outdoors as an altar
  A dish of seeds such as sunflower, poppy, cumin or caraway (in the east on the cloth)
  A ball of clay or dough (in the north on the cloth)
  Dried grasses or ears of wheat and barley (also in the east on the cloth)
  Red cord to tie them (in the south on the cloth)
  Four large red flowers, which can be silk or paper (at the four corners of the cloth)
  A large incense stick or incense dish, of orange, poppy, sandalwood or frankincense (or mixed in a powdered incense) or sagebrush smudge (to the south-east of the cloth but not on it)
* Work in sunlight, preferably at noon. Set the cloth on grass or on a large rock where the sun or at least the noon light shines on it.
* Set all your tools on the cloth except for the incense torch.
* Light the incense torch to the south-east of the cloth.
* Around the cloth, set the four flowers at each of the main compass points, beginning in the south and moving clockwise.
* At each point say:

So blooms the desert flower. So blossoms my life. So shall I reap the harvest even of desert places.

✽ Sit facing south, close to the cloth. Taking the clay, hollow out the shape of a man just deep enough to contain seeds. Say:

Grow, be fertile, man of clay, you who are reborn.

✽ Set the seeds within it, saying:

I have within me also the seeds of the harvest grain. I take in the power to be born anew and ever reborn in assuredness of success and power, but only with good intent.

✽ Leave the figure in the centre of the cloth and then weave round it still on the cloth a circle of the knotted dried grasses, using the red wool to secure them.

✽ Chant as you create the circle:

Mother Isis, I make the magickal knots. I weave and bind the power only for good and the highest purpose. Fill me with power. I am the knot. I am the power.

✽ Carry the incense just beyond the four flowers, outside the cloth beginning in the South and moving clockwise around the four compass points, making a square trail of smoke. Say:

Desert flowers, blossoms of the sun, I ask the blessings of the harvest.
I am the harvest and will bring abundance into my life and to others.

✽ Return and sit facing south just beyond the cloth, allowing the sun or the light to enter and fill you with confidence. You might like to make a private invocation to one of the harvest/solar deities or visualise the image of one or more of them in your mind.

✽ When you are ready, take the clay figure and dig a hole within sight of the cloth to the south.

✽ Bury the figure in silence, facing the east that it may be reborn.

✽ Gather the flowers, beginning with the one in the south and moving clockwise. Leave them as an offering on top of the earth where you buried the figure.

✽ If you do not have suitable earth, use a large pot with growing flowers and bury it there, still facing east.

✽ Extinguish the incense torch in a dish of sand or soil or an earth plot if it is available and dispose of it in an environmentally friendly way.

✽ Use your cloth at home on your altar for a while and add a vase or pot of red flowers.

The two-spoke Wheel

Other lands have two seasons, winter and summer. This was once the way of dividing the year in the Celtic and Norse world where hunting and animal husbandry were as important as crop growing. Indeed, even in the Eightfold Wheel, Samhain and Beltaine that mark the beginning of the Celtic winter and summer are still regarded as the main fire festivals and the central axis of the Wheel.

Samhain was the time when animals were slaughtered for the winter food and breeding animals put in barns. It was the time of the ancestors when they, too, returned to the warmth of the family hearth, as the dimensions parted on the Celtic New Year. The purification of the animals and their release into the fields with their young was celebrated ritually at Beltane, the beginning of the Celtic summer, around our May Day. This was also the major fertility festival for people, cattle and grain.

In the Old Norse world, where hunting remained an important way of life (and still does, even in cities), these two seasons were called sumar (summer) and vetr (winter). Until about 1700, when the new Gregorian calendar replaced the old Roman one, winter for the Vikings of Scandinavia and in Denmark extended from 14 October to 14 April and the summer ran from 14 April to 14 October. The change points from summer to winter and winter to summer were the cause of major religious rites (see weeks 44 and 45, pages 574 and 595).

Wet and dry seasons

Another important dual Wheel of the Year formation is the wet and dry seasonal contrast. Wet and dry seasons rotate at different times throughout the globe in the southern and northern hemispheres, so you can use this kind of magick at any time to act as a catalyst for major change. Wet and dry seasons occur in more tropical areas: for example, in the Andes even today and in Australian Aboriginal spirituality in the southern hemisphere, the seasonal changes dominate magickal rituals.

Unlike the Three-Spoke Egyptian wheel, there is not the season of balance between the extremes. Rather as with the Oriental Yang, the masculine/positive, hot, dry element, and Yin, the female, negative (in the sense of electrical current), cold, wet element, when one force or season reaches excess, it tips over into the other. Therefore you can use the huge surge of power created by the Two-Spoke Wheel to move your personal world forward and to bring major changes spiritually, emotionally or externally.

In my book on natural magick (see page 98), in the chapter on sound magick I have written in detail about the Andean Indian peoples, descendants of the Incas, who live and farm in accordance with the energy flows of Pachamama, the Earth Mother. Because the Andean mountain climate has alternately dry and wet seasons, the intense cold of the nights and the sunny days of the dry season caused the drying of the earth. To generate new life, water must be coaxed ritually from the underground world of the ancestors, to flow through the landscape as springs, rivers and lakes, fed by the natural cycle of rainwater and snowmelt high in the mountains. Music is integral to these ceremonies. Disequilibrium that is strongest at the transition of the seasons is also necessary to generate this flow. This is a form of polarity magick.

The following section on the Australian Aboriginal Wheel of the Year follows similar principles though the climate differs from the Andes.

Australian Aboriginal seasonal magick

Australian Aboriginal traditions are at last being revived in Australia. For many people worldwide these traditions offer powerful magickal principles as an antidote to modern living, and for witches they are a source of pure, undiluted ancient wisdom.

The Aborigines have lived in Australia for at least 40,000 years. One of the most important rituals in the Aboriginal ceremonial year was the annual sacred sex ceremony of Kunapipi, the Earth Mother, and Jarapiri, the male form of the Rainbow Snake in Northern Australia. According to myth, he still slumbers in sacred waterholes, under waterfalls or in caves, and manifests himself in ritual through the dance, ceremony and sacred lovemaking by the individual Aboriginal male.

Kunapipi is the symbol of the reproductive qualities of the earth, the eternal replenisher of human, animal and plants. She is represented in the rites by the female Aborigine and together male and female annually re-enact the sacred marriage with the earth to ensure fertility of land and people and to bring the rains The ceremony is held just before the monsoons are due to begin. The male ejaculation is imitated and, it was believed, stimulates the rain to fall and the monsoons to be released. Sometimes Kunapipi appears as two sisters or as her own two daughters.

As male/female polarities combine and fuse, the Wiccan Great Rite mirrors the release of energy in vibrant form.

Working with the separate polarities using words and images

The male/female polarities signify the Two-Spoke Wheel of the Year. Just as winter contains the seeds of summer, the Goddess the seeds of the God and yang, when it reached a height, tips over into its polarity yin, so in Australian Aboriginal spirituality the two energies share common roots. The following rituals will work with these dual energies, using the ancient rock art tradition and the male/female sets of twins who symbolise the two seasons, though, of course, the dry season is much longer. The dual images coming together creates the necessary force to precipitate the change.

I have written much more about the use of words and images in magick in week 14 (page 177). The principle is that by creating an image and speaking words of power over it or touching the image in ritual, the energy stored in the image is released by the words/actions. Early hunters threw spears at the pictures of the animals painted on the cave walls to bring a successful hunt. The image, especially painted or drawn on a natural and relatively permanent medium like rock, remains one of the most powerful forms of magick.

Rock art and magick

Rock paintings go back at least 40,000 years and in some places among indigenous peoples, for example, in Africa and among Australian Aboriginals, this form of spirituality continues as part of their sacred contract with the earth and their ancestors. Many of the images, especially those depicting deities or ancestors, were more than pictures and were considered to contain the essence and magickal power of the deity form represented in the painting. Indeed, it was often believed that the form depicted in the rock emerged spontaneously from the rock as the creator of the painting worked on it, rather than being a form the artist externally imposed on the stone.

When repainted or made offerings in ritual, the image was and still is believed to release the power of the earth. Though the rituals I suggest are quite passive, they are profoundly spiritual and can make a good contrast to the general active nature of seasonal rites.

The bringers of rain

In Kimberley in Western Australia may be found paintings of the Wandjinas the spirits of rain akin to the Lightning Brothers (see right). The Wandjinas are depicted with spots around their heads for thunder and lightning to bring rain, but without mouths so that the seasonal waters will not flood the earth. They are repainted at the appropriate times before the rainy season, so that they will retain their power.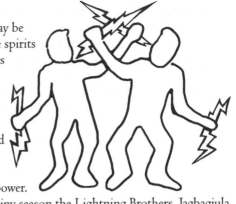

In other legends, just before the rainy season the Lightning Brothers, Jagbagjula and Jabarringa, of Wardaman spirit lore are said to fight over a wife. They are depicted in rock art at Delamere in the Northern Territory. Their struggles bring lightning and the resulting rain that is vital for the world's renewal. They have axes to split the storm clouds.

These sky heroes form the focus of great ceremonial rituals prior to the end of each dry season, some centred on the ancient paintings. Their effects seem truly magickal, because even the day after the first monsoon rain, greenery is springing up everywhere.

In magick ritual, the rainy season will bring the release of stagnation, an impasse or lack of creativity or fertility, the flowing or restoration of, love, power and spiritual connection as well as hastening major positive house or career change, travel and an infusion of fast or urgent money.

The Earth Sisters to stop the 2ains

The Waugeluk sisters emerged at the time of dreaming from the sea with their mother, Kunapipi. They then travelled north, carrying with them knowledge of ritual and fertility. They were eaten by the rainbow snake and henceforward he spoke with their voice. There are numerous other sister legends among different Australian Aboriginal people, including the perpetually pregnant Djannwul sisters, dual manifestations of the Earth Mother. They followed the path of the Morning Star to the Place of the Sun with their brother and wherever their yam stick touched trees sprang up. They were eaten by the rainbow serpent Galeru.

Then there are the Wawalaz or Walawag sisters of North East Arnhemland, again symbols of fertility, who live in a whirlpool. They came from the south, one carrying a baby boy, and they named the animals and set the different dialects and languages. The youngest gave birth to a girl. These sisters are daughters of the Djannwul. They were eaten by Yurlungu the Copper or Rainbow snake who regurgitated them and their rebirth forms part of the initiation rites from boyhood to manhood. They come from the North Central Arnhemland and are often depicted on bark paintings.

In magick ritual, the dry season will bring the restoration of stability and good fortune after a turbulent period, peace and stability at home, gradual growth of health, stable finances, the building or rebuilding of a relationship on firm foundations, absorption and arrest of any excesses, such as debt, sorrow, illness, exhaustion, and will soothe excessive emotions, anger, jealousy, addictions or fears.

Making your mark on the seasons

It was believed that jiva or seed power was deposited in the earth by every event or action and left a vibrational residue in the same way that plants deposit seeds. Therefore these rituals have not only an immediate effect but also, by marking over the images you create and speaking the appropriate words regularly, you can reactivate the power you generated, like flicking on a light switch, without needing to repeat the whole ritual.

To bring the rains

* You will need:
  A flat dark rock or slate about the size of your hand
  An outdoor place near water if possible
  Coloured chalks or poster, masonry or acrylic paint in red, green, blue, black, white and yellow and a brush.
  Alternatively a pointed screwdriver, awl or any hand tool to etch the design in the stone (you can then paint the grooves)and paint grooves with masonry paint in traditional Aboriginal colours yellow, red, black, blue, green and white
  A small spade to dig a hole in sand or soil or a deep bowl containing a little soil or sand and a large jug of water
  A blanket to sit on if you wish

* As dusk falls, especially on a cloudy day, set your rock or slate on the ground (soil or sand is best but you can also work on grass). It should be directly to the north of you as you face north.

* Dig a hole to the east of your slate as you face north or set the bowl of soil to the east. The water source or jug of water should be to the west.

* Create your own sacred power picture, based approximately on the Lightning Brothers (see page 95) or create your own based on any online images you find.

* Draw spots or zigzags and diagonal lines to indicate thunder, lightning and clouds if you wish. Add axes to break open the clouds and do not give the figures mouths, so the flood will not overwhelm the earth.

* As you draw, paint or etch create a soft rhythmic rain chant: for example, say:

  Brothers bring the fertile rain, making green the barren earth.

* Endow the picture with your own hopes and dreams for a better world for yourself and your descendants.

✳ When you have finished hold the image on your outstretched palms and say:

I call . . . into my life. May it be so and may life flow anew.

✳ Ask for any special need. Put the image down and collect water from the source or take up the jug and pour into the hole or on top of the soil or sand, continuing until you have created even the smallest pool, however muddy, as earth and water mix. Say:

The rain has fallen and softened the earth. I give thanks to the Lightning Brothers and their Father Jarapiri. Blessings be.

✳ Keep your rock art in a recess in your house. When the colours fade, repaint or retouch the images, repeating the words. When you no longer need it, return it to the elements to fade in its own time.

✳ You can make the creation of the image as elaborate as you wish with circle casting, lighting smudge sticks (now made in Australia as well as America), drumming and chanting. You could work on a large image with a group of people and dedicate it for a global collective purpose.

To stop the rains

✳ You will need:
The same materials as for creating rain, except that this time you need a bowl a quarter filled with water and a container of sand or earth. In the ritual you will pour the sand or earth into the water till you have absorbed it. Otherwise use a small hole dug in the earth filled with a little water that you can fill in to signify stopping the rains.

✳ This time, as you create the Earth Sisters picture ask that floods dry up and the sun shines, so that the land may absorb the rains, crops grow and the animals and people have safe homes.

✳ Ask that security and growth occur (for your chosen purpose or generally) as the earth absorbs the excess moisture.

✳ When you have buried the water, thank the Earth Sisters and their generic Mother Kunapipi.

✳ Again, you can create a large-scale ceremony

PRACTICAL ASSIGNMENT

Combining the images

❋ For a moment of fusion in your life when you need a sudden change, commitment, to conceive a child, a burst of power or determination for a survival issue or to overcome obstacles, abuse or attack, you would draw a Lightning Brother and an Earth Sister facing each other and holding hands. More graphically if you wish and can work privately and keep the image unseen portray the couple making love as the rain falls and the lightning flashes. This is one of the most powerful fertility icons you can have.

❋ Creating the dual energy image is enough and you need no empowerment except to name the purpose of the drawing and ask the blessings of the Lightning Brother and Jarapiri and the Earth Sister and Kunapipi.

❋ Smudge it clean regularly after each use and when you no longer need it return it to the earth where it will not be uncovered.

Further research

Explore one of the cultures in this module and find out all you can about its geography and climate, as well as its history and religious practices. Often large city museums are a good source of artefacts and exhibits.

Further information

Further reading

❋ Budge, E Wallis, *Egyptian Magick*, Dover Books, 1985

❋ Cowan, James, *Aboriginal Dreaming, An Introduction to the Magical Wisdom and Thoughts of the Aboriginal Traditions of Australia*, Harper Collins, 2002

❋ Eason, Cassandra, *Cassandra Eason's Complete Book of Natural Magick*, Quantum, 2005

Websites

❋ *Aboriginal Art*
Inspiration about Aboriginal art and plenty of information
http://aboriginalart.com.au/culture/dreamtime.html

❋ *Australian Museum Online*
Good background on Australian Aboriginal wisdom
www.dreamtime.net.au/indigenous/spirituality.cfm

❋ *Guardian's Egypt*
Comprehensive links site on Ancient Egypt
http://guardians.net/egypt/religion.htm

THE BASIC TOOLS OF MAGICK

This is another dual module and it contains a great deal of background information on the traditions of magickal tools. In this part, I have focused on tools that are set on a Wiccan altar. I have also described the four sacred treasures of magick that almost every Wiccan altar will contain and given suggestions on how to empower and cleanse your tools. Within a coven you will, of course, learn particular ways of setting an altar based on their traditions. But for personal altars and for solitary practitioners you can be as creative as you wish in the tools you use.

Magickal tools are essentially no different from any other tools, whether chisel, paint brushes, computers or a telescope to look at the stars. They may be the finest available or improvised. The hammer was known as the Birmingham screwdriver in my childhood Midlands home, because my mother (the DIY expert of the family) believed anything could be made to fit with a good smack! Essentially, all tools, magickal, mundane or technological, are only as good as the person using them. You might prefer to keep everything simple for your everyday magick and, like your best china, keep your ceremonial artefacts for special occasions.

Making your own tools

In week 51 (see page 674), I will describe ways of making your own wands, staffs and pentacles, and sources for creating and engraving a personal athame. You might want to move forward immediately after reading this module if you are interested in creating your own tools.

Many covens encourage members to make and engrave their own tools, as this is a powerful way of filling them with your personal power. But if, like me, you are technically inept, there are many rituals for making ready-crafted tools just as much a part of your essence. If you go to country fairs or magickal or pagan festivals, you will often meet craftspeople who will create special tools for you at reasonable prices in natural materials, or you might have a friend or family member who is skilled with wood or metalwork. In some Wiccan traditions, it is a requirement you make your own tools and wand-making, for example, is relatively easy. But personally, I do not equate the ability to create something in crafts with magickal ability.

Altars

The altar is the surface on which you set your most magickal tools and substances. The more time you can spend in your altar space, the more endowed it becomes with your own unique magickal essences; the same is true of tools, however acquired.

I have seen altars that vary from a piece of slate on stones, an adapted metal toolbox that when unfolded revealed a full-blown miniature altar with grooves for a tiny chalice etc, windblown stone harrow altars on Scandinavian hillsides, to an elaborately constructed Golden Dawn ceremonial setting and a shimmering perfumed Egyptian altar in a reconstructed temple outside Cairo. I will discuss all these and more, but at the end of the day, the altar you create will be enhanced by the astral or spiritual altar that overlays it, whether a temple open to the stars or an enchanted woodland glade.

For key tools, like the athame and knife, I have given a list of their different functions and for others a more general, less detailed overview.

The Four Sacred Altar Treasures

These will be present on almost every indoor or outdoor altar, even ones you create spontaneously on a beach or lakeside using the materials in situ. Each of these treasures emanates from the Grail tradition and before that from the treasures of the Tuatha de Danaan, the old gods of Ireland, who in later times became the opalescent fairy folk. These tools are enshrined in the four tarot suits that can be used to represent them (see pages 595–606 for more on scrying, psychic powers and divination).

Each tool is related to other special magickal tools: for example, the Athame to the Sword and the sacred dish to the Pentacle; so there are several tools that by their symbolism hold deep and ancient magickal significance.

The Four Treasures of the Tuatha da Danaan and the Grail

The chalice

* **Element:** Water
* **Direction:** West
* **Energies:** Goddess
* **Tarot symbol:** Cups
* **Qualities:** Feelings, initiation and rebirth

The chalice is the symbol of the mystical Holy Grail. That used for rituals is traditionally made of silver, but you can also use one of crystal, glass, stainless steel, wood, clay or pewter.

The Grail itself is most usually represented as the chalice that Christ used at the Last Supper, in which His blood was collected after the Crucifixion. As such, it not only signifies a source of healing and spiritual sustenance, but also offers direct access to the Godhead through the sacred blood it once contained. According to Roman Catholic doctrine, the wine in the chalice is transformed into the blood of Christ during Mass through the mystical process of transubstantiation. In other Christian denominations, the sacrament is seen as a symbolic representation of the holiness of Christ. The Grail legend is then an allegory for humankind's spiritual quest for enlightenment, a pathway to reach the heart of divinity.

Some legends identify the Grail as a small stone, drinking vessel, others as a larger silver cup. The most popular tradition says that the original Grail cup was incorporated by Roman craftsmen into a gold and jewelled chalice called the Marian chalice, named after Mary Magdalene. There is the possibility that there were two Grail cups, one obtained by Mary Magdalene and one by Joseph of Arimathea, the wealthy merchant who cared for Christ's body after death.

In magick, the chalice or ritual cup represents the Water element and is placed in the west of the altar. Water is the symbol of the Great Mother and so the chalice signifies the womb of the Goddess. In ritual, when either the wand or the athame is plunged into the chalice, it represents the symbolic union of Goddess and God. In many modern covens, this rite has replaced an actual sexual union, which tends to occur more rarely now and in privacy between established couples only.

The chalice is also central to the sacred cakes and ale rite that occurs at the end of formal ceremonies as the pagan equivalent and much older version of the Christian Holy Communion. The offering of the body of the Grain God is signified in the honey cakes set on the pentacle or sacred dish. The beer or wine in the chalice was traditionally fermented from the sacrificed barley/vine cut down as the harvest at Lughnassadh (more of this on page 648). The rite goes back thousands of years. The chalice is filled with wine, fruit juice or water, depending on the needs and preferences of the group. The cakes and ale as well as the male/female chalice rite can easily be incorporated into a solitary practitioner's ritual.

Additionally, the chalice may be presented at the western quarter or Watchtower when the west is being opened after the circle has been cast.

In the other tradition, the Grail or Graal was the Cauldron of Annwyn, one of the four treasures of the Irish Father God, the Dagda. It is also linked with the Cauldron of Cerridwen, the symbol of rebirth and initiation, loved by Druids and Druidesses. I have written more about cauldrons in the next section (see page 118).

The dish/pentacle

* **Element:** Earth
* **Direction:** North
* **Energies:** Goddess
* **Tarot symbol:** Pentacles, coins or discs
* **Qualities:** Sensations, stability, nourishment

The dish or pentacle symbolises the dish from which Jesus ate the paschal lamb. In Celtic tradition, it represented the ancient Stone of Fal on which the High Kings of Ireland stood to be crowned. The Stone was on Tara, the sacred Hill of the High Kings of Ireland, and before that it was the palace of the hero Gods. In the 7th century the stone was taken to Scotland, where it became the much-disputed Stone of Scone, for many years in the English coronation chair. I have written more about the guardian stone elsewhere (see page 121).

Accounts from the 13th century of the Grail procession speak of a silver dish that was always filled with food. It is also linked with the Dish of Rhydderch, a Scottish 6th century King, which gave whatever food was desired.

The pentacle is often a round, flat plate or dish engraved with an Earth pentagram within a circle (see below, the next module, page 129) and week 51, page

681, for the different elemental pentagrams and how to draw them). It is set in the centre of the altar or, if you prefer, towards the north and is used for consecrating the salt and water and other tools. It may be carried to the north watchtower when greeting the guardians of the quarter.

Like the pentagram, the pentacle has been a magickal sign for thousands of years. The five-pointed star is a sacred symbol of Isis and modern witches often regard the single top point as representing union of the Triple Goddess aspects.

Pentacles can be made of clay or beeswax, etched or painted on slate, or bought ready made as metal, wooden or pottery dishes. Wax ones were originally made during the times of persecution so that they could be thrown on the fire if unwelcome visitors came. (Wax pentacles can be used until they crumble and then replaced.) You will also see upright, freestanding pentacles that are set in the north of the altar are made of silver, copper, brass, bronze or wood or any metal that can be engraved.

The magickal significance of the pentagram/pentacle

The circle round the pentagram that makes up the pentacle signifies the human frame enclosed by the everlasting protection of Goddess and God as the circle without beginning or end. The circle touches all points so uniting the elements.

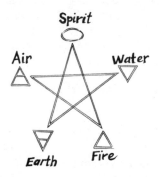

The open pentagram without the circle is more proactive, while in the encircled form it is protective.

To the Ancient Greek mathematician and philosopher Pythagoras, the five elements made up a person. They were energy (Fire), fluid (Water), breath (Air), matter, (Earth) and mind (Spirit), or, put another way, liquid, gas, solid, plasma and aether. The pentacle was of significance in alchemy, Kabbalah, and ceremonial magick. By sympathetic magick, the pentacle linked the human and divine as well as the unity of mankind with the earth.

Generally in magick the single point is at the top of the pentagram, symbolising rising into Spirit, though the point down can represent the Wiccan Horned God. The star-like shape shared by the hexagram that I describe at the end of the next module (see page 129) links with the mystical heavens.

Pentagrams and pentacles can also be used to banish harm and to call the Earth elementals, personified as gnomes. Some witches wear pentacle or pentagram necklaces as a symbol of their craft.

The sword

* **Element:** Air

* **Direction:** East

* **Energies:** God

* **Tarot symbol:** Swords

* **Qualities:** Thinking, power, wise authority

The sword symbolises the sword of King David. The magick sword was also the most prized treasure of King Arthur. Excalibur was entrusted to Arthur by Morgan le Fey or Vivien (or one of the other Ladies of the Lake who occupy the same role in different legends) as the person who was sufficiently noble to pull it from the stone in which it was embedded. Excalibur was originally one of the 13 sacred Celtic treasures, the sword of Nuada of the Silver Hand whose sword hand was cut off in battle. With a new hand fashioned of silver, he went on to lead his people to victory.

This magickal sword identified Arthur as hero king, a reincarnated solar deity with his Round Table as a gigantic sun wheel. Morgan le Fey wove Arthur an enchanted scabbard that would protect him from serious wounding in battle as long as he possessed it. She later took back this gift and so it is said he lost his power Excalibur was returned to the Lake Lady by Sir Bedivere after Arthur's death.

In some versions of the Grail legends, it was the sword, rather than the lance, that injured Bron (see below), the wounded King (linked to Bran the Celtic hero God) that caused the land to waste away.

Swords are not at all hard to obtain. I bought one very reasonably in the Breton Arthurian forest of Broceliande. However, some modern peace-loving witches do not like the concept of using swords, even though they are pretty spectacular for drawing out a circle in a forest floor or symbolically in the air when making a spiritual circle. They are also used in coven magick as a way the priest symbolically lays his authority and power before the priestess, by setting down his sword before her as he kneels. She then uses it to draw the circle.

The sword is male to the female cauldron and can be used in love rituals and for the union of male and female, God and Goddess energies in any rite, by plunging the sword into the waters of the cauldron, as the culmination of a rite. Generally, however, the chalice and the knife or the wand tend to be used for the same purpose, unless it is a very grand ceremony. In practice, most witches use their athame or ritual knife as a substitute for the sword and so the athame properly thereby assumes its place as one of the four key tools. However, I have written about the athame as the first and most important altar tool later in the module (see page 106) to avoid diverting from the final treasure.

The spear/lance/wand

* **Element:** Fire
* **Direction:** South
* **Energies:** God
* **Tarot symbol:** Wands, staves or rods
* **Qualities:** Inspiration, intuition, passion (in every way)

Wands symbolise the sacred lance of Longinus that pierced Jesus's side. In Celtic tradition it is the spear of Lugh, who slew his grandfather, the old solar God Balor with it and so brought about the new order.

The bleeding lance has magickal connotations and in a number of myths the lance continued to bleed until the true heir of the old King, who was pure in heart, came to the Grail castle. In Norse mythology, the Father God Odin hung nine days and nine nights on the World Tree as a form of initiation/ritual death and rebirth pierced by his own spear.

The bleeding lance is also a common motif of the Grail legends. In one of the many versions of the Grail, Bron the Fisher King and guardian of the Grail, was wounded in the side by a spear, but could not die or his barren land be restored to life except by one who could ask the correct questions about the Grail. There are many versions of the legend that has fascinated countless generations, in which the correct but secret question the woman must ask is:

Whom does the lance serve?

The answer here should be:

You, my lady, for evermore, its power and its protection.

The question concerning the chalice or Grail Cup is:

Whom does the grail heal?

The answer is:

You, my wounded Lord, in joy and in fertility.

This underpins much of the ceremony of the wand (the blade/athame) and the chalice in ceremonial magick. I think the wand is the better correspondence because it is the tool of Fire mingling with Water, God with Goddess in total unity.

Some people have different wands for different needs and a special one for major outdoor ceremonies or for a boost of power. You can also find or buy a small twig wand for travel. My miniature one is less than 30 cm (12 in) long. You can use any small smooth branch as a temporary wand by asking the blessings of the forest where you find it. Hazel is the most usual wand wood, a symbol of wise authority, justice and fertility. I have listed other wood meanings in module 51 (see page 675). These meanings are also useful when buying or making a staff or staves.

Using a wand

* Make ever increasing clockwise circles to attract whatever or whoever is needed, in your life, anticlockwise in decreasing circles to banish sorrow, illness, bad luck and anything negative.

* Circling your wand continuously clockwise in small regular circles (using the power hand, the one you write with as is customary for wand use) will enchant any symbol that represents a need. Chant as you work and move your other hand in similar sized circles, at the same time anticlockwise, all the while softly chanting the purpose of the spell. By association you are sending power to whomever or whatever is represented by the symbol. You can empower herbs or crystals by the same method.

* Write in the air with your wand your magickal intentions or any secret magickal names you use, faster and faster. When you reach a peak of power, raise your wand to the air vertically and then bring it down behind you and back up again to waist height to release the power.

* Cast a small circle of protection about an arm span all around yourself in the morning before work or in the evening when you get home if you feel afraid, unwell or under attack. Alternatively, hold the wand in front of your face while speaking banishing words. You can hold your other hand upright palm outwards. This is a good way of banishing anxiety, pain or physical weakness albeit temporarily.

* Direct power generated through magickal words towards a place or person by holding the wand horizontally in the right direction, whether a mile or a thousand, and reciting the place name nine times saying:

May it be healed / restored / saved.

(Nine is the number of completion perfection.)

* Draw a circle of power and light before a spell within which to carry out magick by walking round the visualised circle, Point your wand diagonally downwards from waist height in front of you, seeing light coming from it to protect above and below in the circle. You can close a circle in the same way (see page 247 for circle casting and uncasting).

* Open the four directions of your circle by drawing elemental pentagrams in the air in the four directions in the air, face high, as you welcome the four guardians. You can likewise in reverse order close the circle with banishing pentagrams drawn in the air in the four directions. A number of practitioners do close the circle in the same direction as they opened it and also the watch towers.

- Draw down the moon or sun by holding the wand in a sharp angle to the sky and turning in rapid clockwise circles for the sun (and the reverse for the moon) physically to create the psychic sensation of the heavenly body rushing down towards you.

- Fill the wand with power by leaving it on the outdoor altar for brief periods during storms for courage, rain for healing or banishing, under a rainbow for granting wishes and in winds for change. Hold it soon afterwards and feel the energies passing through it and you can top up your own energies and determination. As a personal power channeller, amplifying your own power to give you daily strength, hold it at a 45-degree angle facing the morning sky, noon, dusk and midnight, filling you with cosmic and earth power.

- When your wand becomes weathered you can keep it near the altar until it shatters. Empower a new one meanwhile, as the old one's work is done.

Altar tools

As well as the four sacred tools that have a central place on any formal magickal altar, there are tools that are frequently part of a formal altar in a number of witchcraft traditions. I have also listed tools that are useful, some of which will stand around rather than on the indoor altar or be used primarily for outdoor ceremonies. I have written about constructing an outdoor altar in the module on altars. I have also listed tools used in ancient Egyptian magick and in Norse magick that share much with Anglo Saxon magick, both of which were influential in the UK.

All the tools in the chapter are suitable for solitary practitioners and often you can improvise until you find or make the piece that is right for you.

Athame

- **Element:** Air
- **Direction:** East
- **Energies:** God
- **Qualities:** Thinking, focus, directed personal power

The athame is a central tool of ceremonial magick and has a long tradition of formal usage. Indeed, it is said that knowledge of the athame, along with the ceremonial sword and other formal tools, passed into ritual magick through the writings of Raziel, Archangel of divine mysteries and of secrets. Raziel is credited with writing the esoteric Book of the Angel that passed finally to King Solomon who derived from its pages his own magickal powers and wisdom. Solomon's writings did categorise the ritual knife as a tool of Fire.

The athame or ritual knife is usually double edged with a black handle and sheath (black to absorb power) so that it can be hung off the waist cord or a belt. However, some witches prefer handles made of bone, antler or grained wood. Black originally denoted the otherworldly nature of the knife.

The athame is held in your power hand (the one you write with) and kept sheathed, except when in use. The blade is usually made of iron or steel, since it is regarded as a magickal metal that originally came from meteorites and so believed to be a gift from the deities. However, the blade can also be bronze, wood, bone, stone copper (the metal of Venus), brass, gold (metal of the Sun) or silver (metal of the Moon). The blade of mine is slate, good for practitioners who do not like using metal.

It is blunt with a dull blade and not intended for cutting anything physical, apart from maybe a handfasting cake. (There is a belief that fairies and nature essences hate and fear metal. For this reason a number of practitioners believe that herbs should not be cut with metal.) Rather it is used to attract, channel and direct energy in magickal work and rituals. A coven will have a larger athame for use by the High Priestess in ceremonies.

The two edges of the blade signify the balance of the mind and spirit with the body or handle of the knife. It may be magnetic and magickal symbols are inscribed on the hilt. It may be presented to a new witch on the evening of her first initiation, but if you are new to magick you will want to use yours from early on in the course. The blades or handles of the ritual knife are traditionally decorated with magickal symbols. For example, the Anglo Saxon rune tiwaz shown below is the rune of the powerful warrior God and also emblem of the Pole Star Tiu and is a popular magickal symbol for swords. Runes as I describe later (see page 432) release the protective power they contain when you paint, etch or touch them or even write them in incense smoke over a tool.

Tiwaz, the swordsman deity

Thurisaz, the hammer of Thor

The Hammer of Thor shown above is a very protective rune symbol of the Norse Thunder God. These runes are also used to engrave the Seax, the sharp Norse ritual knife and the sacred ritual tool representative of the mythical Hammer of Thor (see page 436).

Ritual functions

Apart from the wand, the athame is magickally the most essential magickal tool.

Empowering other tools: Touch them with your empowered athame and speak words created by yourself for this purpose or given by your coven to draw down power and upwards protection.

Making sacred water: Pre-ritual and at other times, having empowered your athame (or you may keep it ready charged in its sheath,) use it to stir sea salt three times clockwise when preparing your magickal water. Make the cross on the surface three times with the athame, trying not to disturb the water. You can likewise mark water that has been left in full moonlight for healing purposes with your athame with nine moonwise or anticlockwise circles.

Circle measuring: You can if accurately measuring a circle in soft earth, sand or grass, set the athame in the centre of your projected circle and attach the measuring rope to estimate the radius.

Circle casting: Point the athame diagonally towards the ground, and walk round the circumference, tracing the circumference in the air with extended arm about level with your hip bone. Alternatively stand in the centre, slowly turning and projecting a circle of light around your desired circumference from the extended blade to create a circle of light on the ground. At such times, you may find even a dull blade shimmers as the light rises from the light circle, unless you close clockwise.

Opening the four quarters of the circle: Invoke the elemental Guardian Spirits by drawing the appropriate pentagram in the air in the four main directions with your athame. Reverse after the ritual to close the elemental energies.

Power raising: Use the athame as an extension of your power hand as a conductor of energy, especially in solitary rituals. Hold it above the head with both hands to draw down light and energy into the body and the athame.

Releasing power: One method of releasing power is to bring the vertically extended athame down with a swift cutting movement, horizontally at waist level, thrust it away from the body and upwards once more to release this power into the cosmos.

Grounding: After a ritual, you can drain excess energies by pointing the athame to the ground.

Storing the power: Direct the concentrated athame energies directly into a dish of herbs or crystals for healing, rather than skywards. You may also pour the accumulated power of the spell directly back into the earth to heal the planet.

Making gateways: Use the athame for entering and leaving the circle to open and close your gateway any time during the rite.

Protection: As part of any banishing/protective spell, you can direct the blade downwards to Mother Earth or outwards horizontally (for example, through an open doorway) to send back negative energies directed at you. You can also draw a defensive circle barrier of light by holding the athame towards sun/ moon/star or candlelight and drawing a visualised barrier round your home/land/loved ones. Stand in the centre of the visualised area and project the light circle.

Empowerment: Before an important meeting or event in your life or when you need courage, spin round nine times deosil (which means clockwise; widdershins is anticlockwise) with blade extended; then raise the blade to the sky, down to the earth and then skywards again asking for strength and courage. Finally, trace round your outline with the athame power saying: *I am complete in courage and integrity. I fear nothing and offer all.*

In some traditions the sword and wand change positions with the sword/athame signifying Fire, but this association works well for me.

Bell

* **Element:** Earth
* **Direction:** North
* **Energies:** Goddess
* **Qualities:** Calling, awakening, harmonising

The bell is traditionally rung nine times at the beginning and close of each ritual while standing in the south of the circle facing north. It is also rung to invoke the protection of angels or the power of a deity and in ceremonies to welcome departed members to the circle. It is also good for cleansing a ritual space.

You can sound the bell in each of the four elemental quadrants before creating the invoking pentagram to request the presence of each elemental guardian, to mark different phases in a ritual, or to invite the presence of nature spirits and elementals or the ancestors. You can ring the bell as much or as little as you wish. It is a good way for a solitary practitioner to create a sense of ceremony.

Traditionally a hollow metal or crystal bell was used, but more recently Tibetan bells or a singing bowl are sometime substituted. Tibetan singing bowls, although associated primarily with meditation and healing, are a perfect way to start and end a ritual, so that the sound vibrations are raised and the spell carried into the cosmos on the sound.

The singing bowl vibrations are long lasting after each touch or strike. You can harmonise a chant to be released at the climax of the spell, at the same time as the final singing bowl sound fades into cosmic silence. The rounded, wooden striker (puja) or wand resembles a mixing pestle and sometimes has a padded or leather striking end. The striker is usually sold with the bowl. Some bowls have a mallet as well, purely for striking the side of the bowl.

Bowl

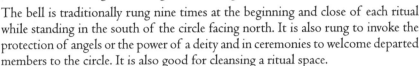

* **Elements:** Earth and Water
* **Directions:** Mainly north and west but can also be
  used for incense in the east and a small candle in the south
* **Energies:** Goddess
* **Qualities:** Container/shaper of energies, nourishment,
  offering gifts or blessings

The bowl is related to both the cauldron and the chalice and is integral to ritual, both as a central libations/offerings dish and for holding elemental substances, most usually salt in the north and water in the west. Coarse sea salt is kept in a bowl in the north, both to purify the circle in its own right as part of the casting ceremony and as the Earth element, to empower a symbol and to cleanse tools during ritual. Soil may be substituted for salt in outdoor ceremonies.

Matching ceramic deep bowls can often be bought at cookware stalls and are set side by side on the pentacle when sacred salt water is made for purifying the circle and for healing. Deep shells can also be used. Wooden bowls are traditionally placed upon a harrow or outdoor northern tradition altar to contain offerings used for blessings or to gift.

Candles

* **Elements:** Fire
* **Directions:** South (though candles can be used in different colours to signify all the directions)
* **Energies:** God and Goddess
* **Qualities:** Illumination, power, inspiration

These are the elemental substance of Fire and since they burn down in ritual are arguably not tools. I have written more on them in the modules on the four elements (see pages 316–362) and on setting up an altar where I have also written about robes, jewellery and God and Goddess statues (see page 159). Candles are also an integral part of many other modules. There is specific information in week 42 covering colours and candles, since they are such an essential part of magick (see page 527).

Cords

* **Element:** Earth/Air
* **Direction:** Centre/north-east
* **Energies:** Goddess
* **Qualities:** Stored power, release, loyalty/commitment

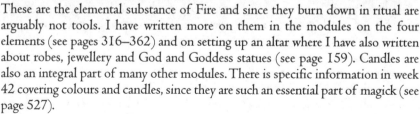

Cord magick dates back certainly to the Ancient Egyptians who practised red cord love magick, calling upon the seven daughters of Hathor and tying a knot for each. The idea of power being bound and released in knots is almost universal, from Africa through to Ancient Greece and Mediaeval Europe, where witches would sell knotted cords with winds tied up in them.

Practitioners may have a single 2.75-metre (9-foot) cord in red plus a series of shorter cords in different colours, which you plait yourself. or you can buy ordinary curtain cord. They can be used in binding spells and to hold and release stored energy in a controlled way: for example, undoing a knot once a day for nine days, if you tie nine knots. They are also used in covens in initiations and in coven rituals to form a collective wheel to raise power.

The length of cord you wear as a girdle will depend on your girth, but should be long enough for knot tying and to hold your athame. Over time it takes on the essence of the wearer. For the solitary practitioner, it can be a personal declaration of commitment to the Craft when worn in ritual. This personal worn cord that you can empower regularly is a version of the cord measure taken of the size of a witch during a first initiation that is sometimes kept by the coven as a measure of loyalty.

When it frays you can burn the old one on the last night of the old moon, and empower and wear the new one the next day. (Unusually, I like to empower personal cords for the first time at the private time of the dawn of the first day of the new Moon when it is not visible in the sky.)

There are various knot chants I have described in week 50 (see page 661), and there are also different orders of knot tying. The following are the most popular. Generally knots are tied in an increasing single chant of power and then released daily (or hourly or whatever). If the knots were important or long lasting, you could tie one a day, repeating the cumulative chant on successive days up to the relevant knot number and on the last day of tying reciting the whole chant.

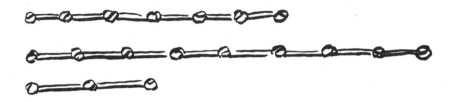

For seven knots, most often used for love or healing

6——2——4——1——5——3——7

Or:

6——4——2——1——3——5——7

For nine knots for success or power

8——4——2——5——1——6——3——7——9

Or:

8——6——4——2——1——3——5——7——9

Thurible or censer

* **Element:** Air
* **Direction:** East
* **Energies:** God
* **Qualities:** Thinking, spiritual connection, uplifting

A thurible or censer is a metal dish or more ornate burner used to hold charcoal and incense throughout ceremonies and for private incense burning to clear space and raise consciousness, even in a simple spell. Ceramic dishes or abalone shells are used for burning herbs or smudge either alone or on charcoal. Sand may be added to an open, flat, heatproof dish used for charcoal burning.

PRACTICAL ASSIGNMENT

Empowering tools

Magickal tools, whether bought or made, need to cleansed and charged with the energy of the user or on behalf of the coven if a coven tool. The tools can then regularly be recleansed or recharged in a shortened version of the original rituals.

The concept behind cleansing and empowering is to first remove any influences (not necessarily bad but just not yours) from the energy field or aura of the tool. Then you energise the aura or energy field or spirit form of the tool and imprint on this the energy field of the owner or group aura of the coven. Some believe that these processes are ways of reawakening the original creative processes of the wood or metal that forms the tools.

There are numerous ways of doing this and throughout this course you will discover your own ways of cleansing and empowering tools. I have suggested a method I find effective that you can adapt to your own style of magick. You can also empower tools at the same time as you dedicate and rededicate your altar. Moon and sunlight are great for empowering, especially the full moon, a traditional time for cleansing and consecrating new tools.

Dedicating your tools

Though you may well obtain or make your tools separately, you can cleanse and empower more than one tool (or indeed all of them) in the same ritual.

Cleansing

Fire and smoke (incense) are the most effective ways of purification. I have recently combined this with the concept of the three ancient Cosmic Mothers who constantly bring new creation to life. One is the Earth Mother, one the Moon and one the Sun Woman. You can cleanse each artefact separately or put them together and circle round them in turn with the incense and candles.

* Indoors or out, light three candles: first a green one for the Earth Mother; from the green candle, light a silver one for the Moon Mother; and finally from that, a gold one for the Sun Mother.

* Then hold a large, firm incense or smudge in sage, pine or lemon briefly in each of the three candles in turn so it flares.

* Cleanse your tool/tools by circling the artefact/s nine times anticlockwise with the smoke of the smudge or an incense stick. Then hold and turn the tool three times above each of the candles in order of lighting, in every instance anticlockwise. If it is a large artefact or a group, you can instead pass each of the candles three times round it in turn after the nine incense swirls, still anticlockwise. Whichever method you choose, move your body with the candle or smudge rhythmically. Use broad-based, heat-resistant candleholders.

* Chanting, in the Norse tradition known as creating a Galdr (sometimes but not always based on rune names) is an effective way of raising the power and harmonising your energies with that of the artefact. Combine it with the incense

and fire (though for re-empowering and recleansing you can just chant and visualise the actions if you prefer). Repeat this chant continuously and slowly as you move, as though soothing a baby:

Three by three, three by three, Mother Earth I call on thee.
May this [name tool] be purified by Mother Earth, she who gives to all life birth.
Be cleansed likewise by Mother Moon, who grows all in her starry womb.
Three by three, Sun Mother too, in thy warm arms life leaps anew.
Be purified and blessed be. Creation waits midwifery.

Empowerment

Once cleansed, you need to empower and dedicate each tool separately for positive purpose using its own elemental power (see above). So, for the wand you need Fire, the staff Air, and so on. If you are dedicating more than one tool, work through them in groups in order, Earth tools first, then Air, then Fire and finally Water.

* Leave the Mother candles burning, but in addition light a tall dark blue one to the right of them to represent the Sky Father energies. You should do this whatever the element of the tool being empowered. You can also use this Father candle to empower any Fire tools and to light the incense for your Air tool empowerment.

* For Earth tools, using sea salt, make three clockwise circles of salt round the tool, continuing to make circles of three, intertwining if you wish. Create an empowering Earth chant as you do so, incorporating the power of the element and the qualities of the tool being empowered (see list above). Again, you can just use the words for re-empowering. If you are not yet experienced in the associations of the four elements, either read the list starting on page 136 or visualise aspects of the Earth that are important to you: green forests, tall rocks, old stone circles. As you chant not only picture the natural setting of the element, but also hear the sounds and create the fragrances.

* Continue chanting and sprinkling circles of salt, just a few grains at a time. Either go over the same circle line or move in and out with an overlapping circle pattern, whatever feels right until you feel and see the outline of light round the artefacts so that they appear to glow green or golden brown.

* For Air tools, use incense. Weave sets of nine clockwise smoke spirals round the artefact, so that you make a kind of knot or web pattern. Visualise and chant about what Air means to you, winds, clouds, and the top of a favourite hill. Continue to chant and weave the smoke until the tool or tools being empowered have a pale yellow or pearly grey aura round it.

* For Fire tools, pass the blue Father candle either round the artefact/s or vice versa in sets of three clockwise fire circles. Picture fire, whether a bonfire, ritual fire, the sun or a huge flickering flame that dances like a figure. (You may see a Fire elemental, like a wand of flame, the least human like of the elementals.) Continue until you see a golden, red or orange glow around the tools.

* For Water tools, use water from a sacred source or in which nine tiny clear quartz crystals have been soaked for eight hours from first light or when you wake, whichever is sooner. Make a series of three clockwise or spiralling circles of

water droplets, while chanting. Visualise a river, the sea, a waterfall or the falling rain. Continue words and actions until you can see the soft blue aura round the tools.

✺ When all is done, recite three times softly:

Thanks be to the Mothers, so shall it be three by three. I give thanks also to the Father of all. As this tool/these tools are filled with his creative light, so shall that power rise to star filled skies. Here on earth likewise may the light of the Father and the love of the Mothers be used only for the greatest good and the purest intent as I use my tools in ritual. So mote [may/shall] it be.

As you empower any of your tools you may enter a gentle, trance-like state as your brainwaves dip into the deeper, slower, theta rhythms. These are most usually experienced when dreaming, but are a common response in magick.

Regular cleansing and empowering

As I said, you can repeat just the words of the original cleansing and empowerment over the tools to re-empower them. If you use this method record any elemental chants you created in your Book of Shadows. You can cleanse your tools after a ceremony if you wish by passing them through, round or above a candle flame and this will also re-empower them.

Some, like the athame, are suitable for standing blade down in the earth or, like the pentacle, resting uppermost on the earth and sprinkling with an infusion of hyssop that can be used to cleanse absolutely anything sacred (see page 572 for more on herb magick for infusions). The Earth will re-empower and running water has a similar effect, though, of course, it is not suitable for all tools.

If a tool feels dull or lifeless, you can almost instantly re-empower it using a pentacle and a wand or athame, depending on whether you feel it needs a sudden inspirational infusion of Fire/wand energy or a more assertive focused burst of Air/athame power. The pentacle acts as the grounding element and ensures the charge remains within the tool. A pentacle will re-empower a wand or athame and either of these can re-empower the pentacle.

✺ Set the tool so it is touching the pentacle. If the tool is large you can draw an invoking pentagram on the ground beneath it.

✺ Touch the artefact with the tip of the wand or athame and picture sparks of light for the athame or coiling golden flames for the wand entering the tool. Say softly as a chant:

Grow light and grow bright, be radiant and filled with life once more in the name of She who is our Mother and He who fathers all [name your favourite deities if you wish].

Further information

Further reading

* Cicero, Chico and Cicero, Sandra Tabatha, *Secrets of a Golden Dawn Temple, Book 1 Creating Magickal Tools*, Thoth Publishing, 2005
* Eason, Cassandra, *Cassandra Eason's Complete Book of Natural Magick*, Quantum, 2005
* Fortune, Dion and Knight, Gareth, *Introduction to Ritual Magick*, Thoth Publications, 1997

Websites

* *Blessings Cornucopia*
Comprehensive overview
www.blessingscornucopia.com

Egyptian and Norse Tools

of Magick

Not all tools that we use belong on the altar but may nevertheless have an important part to play in spells and rituals. A cauldron, for example, can serve as the centrepiece of a ritual, especially in outdoor rituals where it may stand in the place of the altar.

In this module I have described these additional tools and also some from the Ancient Egyptian and Norse traditions. The ones I have chosen from the older worlds are those that work well with and on a Wiccan altar, as well as part of their own traditional altars that I will describe in a later module (see page 171). Finally, I have included a practical section on inscribing tools with magickal symbols to endow them with your personal essence and to make them more powerful.

Non-altar tools

The altar is the sacred focus of magick. The area around it, especially within a cast magick circle, is also empowered and protected and some of a witch's most prized treasures may be set within this space as additional sources of power. A few, such as the broom and staff, may be kept beyond the circle to act as protection during ritual and to guard the home and garden at all times.

Asperge

* **Element:** Water
* **Direction:** Any, though it is associated with the West
* **Energies:** Goddess
* **Qualities:** Cleansing, awakening, restoring

An asperge is an alternative or additional space cleansing method to the broom, especially outdoors. It is popular in the Druid and Norse traditions, but can be adapted to any ritual.

At its most basic an asperge can be a bundle of evergreen twigs tied together and dipped in salt or pure water. The water is then sprinkled around the area to be purified with appropriate words of blessings. Alternatively, you can add to the water a few drops of a cleansing flower essence such as Glastonbury thorn. You can also buy silver or brass aspergilla used for sprinkling holy water in formal religions.

Boline

* **Element:** Air
* **Direction:** Any
* **Energies:** God
* **Qualities:** Application, shaping, dedication

A boline is a white-handled knife with a curved blade. It can be used for carving runes and symbols on pieces of wood or clay for spells, on candles, to cut cords and if you use metal (which I do not) for harvesting herbs. A sharp engraving tool is also sometimes called a burin.

Some bolines are like the legendary Druidic small scythe, with a blade like a crescent moon. (A gold one was apparently used for harvesting mistletoe.) In Druidry, the scything action signifies the release of energies into the cosmos, a reminder that all tools are ultimately sacred if used in ritual, whether they are for altar or ceremonial use or are more practical in nature.

The letters inscribed on the knife handle are often painted with red ochre (see page 132).

Broomstick/besom

* **Element:** Earth
* **Direction:** South of the altar lying horizontally at the foot of the altar with the bristles east to west or, if leaned upright, with the bristles uppermost; a vertical broom is set outside the circle to the south-west
* **Energies:** God and Goddess united
* **Qualities:** Unity, cleansing, watchfulness

The broomstick is used for cleansing the ritual area, especially outdoors, or can be used before asperging in a formal ceremony. Occasionally for a spring-cleaning ritual, a circle is made by a group of people holding brooms horizontally, waist high. It may have originally been called a broom because the bristles were made from dried broom or bracken. Besoms are traditionally made from ash for the handle with birch twigs for cleansing and with willow, the moon tree, to bind it.

In Wiccan handfasting, jumping the broom by the couple indicates the physical and spiritual joining of the two people as the bristles (female) are united with the handle (male). It is also used in fertility rites and for protection of the home. The broom can also be used to raise storms. Some witches carve or paint a crescent moon at the top of the handle; others use their personal ruling planetary and birth sign glyph.

You might like to scatter dried lavender or dried herbs in the area to be cleansed and sweep it in anticlockwise circles, saying:

Cleansed be of all harm, of all sadness and all that is not of loveliness and value.

Cauldron

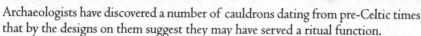

* **Element:** Earth and Water, but can also be used as a vessel for the other two elements
* **Position:** North-west
* **Energies:** Goddess
* **Qualities:** Nourishment, rebirth, initiation

Archaeologists have discovered a number of cauldrons dating from pre-Celtic times that by the designs on them suggest they may have served a ritual function.

Associated with the womb of the Great Mother, mythological cauldrons of the pre-Christian world were owned or tended by female guardians. Like the more homely versions in later times, the cauldron of legend would contain food that always magickally restored itself, a brew endowing wisdom and inspiration or the power to heal even mortal wounds.

Because it is such an ancient tool and linked with the Grail, I will describe the main myths. In Celtic lore, the Three Mothers, the Matronae or Madronae/ Madrones, kept the Magick Cauldron of Regeneration at the bottom of a lake (or the land beneath the waves) until it was appropriated by the Celtic hero God Bran the Blessed to restore slain warriors. The Matronae were triple Fate and Fertility Goddesses and in Romano-Celtic statues held children or corn and fruit on their knees. Bran was in mediaeval myth himself transformed into Bron, keeper of the Holy Grail Cup, the Christianised version of the cauldron that was guarded by a Grail maiden.

The Cauldron of Cerridwen

According to legend, the late 5th century Celtic bard Taliesin received his bardic gifts and great knowledge from the Cauldron of Cerridwen through the process of death, transformation and rebirth.

Legend tells that as Gwion, Taliesin was the foster son or servant boy to Cerridwen, the Crone Goddess of prophecy and keeper of the cauldron in which inspiration and divine knowledge were brewed. Gwion stole three drops of the brew of wisdom, made from the ingredients of every season. The mixture was intended for Cerridwen's son Avagdu to compensate for his ugliness. More favourable versions say that some of the liquid splashed Gwion and he licked his fingers.

The often-quoted shape-shifting sequel took place in which Gwion escaped from Cerridwen by turning into a hare, a fish, a bird and a grain of wheat. Cerridwen pursued him as a greyhound, an otter, a hawk and a finally a hen who ate the grain, so conceiving Gwion as her child. These transformations happened on the magickal festival of Lughnassadh, 1 August, when the Corn God sacrificed himself for the fertility of the land. Nine months later on May Eve, Taliesin was born and was cast in a leather bag into the sea, itself a symbol of the womb of the Great Mother. A bard called Elphin found him in the weir of salmon, the fish of wisdom and prophecy, and cared for him.

The Pentre Ifan Cromlech in Pembrokeshire is a former Druidic sacred site of initiation. Initiates would remain in total darkness for several days awaiting rebirth. Nine virgins would stir and breathe the pure life force on a cauldron in which a brew of barley, flowers, herbs and seawater foam was created. The would-be bards each drank three drops to represent Gwion's three drops of inspiration and the rest was poured away to symbolise casting off the former life of the initiate.

The Cauldron of Annwyn

As well as being a historical poet and seer, Taliesin attracted many stories of his magickal origins and nature. According to an early Welsh poem, *Preiddeu Annwyn*, often credited to Taliesin himself, the bard sailed to Annwyn, the Celtic Otherworld with King Arthur, who was regarded as the reborn Sun God/King, to find the Graal or the Cauldron of Regeneration. This Cauldron, known as the Undry, provided an endless supply of nourishment, had great healing powers and could restore the dead to life, either to their former existence or a new life form in the Otherworld. The cauldron would not boil the food of the coward.

The Cauldron was one of the 13 Celtic treasures owned by the Father God Dagda, but was originally the cauldron of the Great Mother Anu or Danu.

The cauldron in modern magick

The iron cauldron really comes into its own as an outdoor natural magickal tool, but if you have a small one it can also fit in your altar room to the north-west of the altar. I have four cauldrons in varying sizes, one small enough to stand in the north-west of my table top altar.

Uses for a cauldron

* Half-filled with water on the full moon so that you and anyone present can look into the silvery water and scry (look for images). You can interpret these images as you would dreams to answer questions or to receive wisdom from the Moon Mother (and your wise inner self) through the symbols you perceive in the cauldron water (see page 203 for more on moon magick).
* Scry also in bright sunlight on water or by candlelight and drop a handful of dried chopped cooking herbs on to the water to give you moving images to answer questions.
* With a candle in the centre embedded in sand or a small fire in a fire basket to make a Fire element cauldron. Make sure your cauldron is cast iron not a replica and put a heatproof fire basket or metal liner for a real fire. In this you can burn wishes, scatter herbs or incense.
* Burning incense inside as charcoal or as sticks or cones embedded in sand (as an Air cauldron).
* To dance and chant round the cauldron.
* As an Earth cauldron, in the centre of a ritual area (with or without an altar) to receive offerings such as flowers, fruits and crystals in a seasonal celebration or abundance ritual.
* Filled with earth and planted during a ceremony with growing herbs, and flowers; also buried coins, crystals as part on an ongoing celebration rite. This indicates prosperity/love/healing will grow as the plants grow.

The staff

* **Element:** Air
* **Direction:** North or east outside the circle as
  a guardian, always north for the stang (see page 121)
* **Energies:** God
* **Qualities:** Guardianship, strength, protection

The staff is the tool of travellers from the Archangel Raphael and St Christopher to the huge chalk figure of the Long Man of Wilmington who was first etched on the side of Windover Hill in East Sussex, around 700 BCE. He is a tall figure without genitals with an even longer stave on either side indicating perhaps a doorway into other worlds, his dods or measuring sticks also used for marking ancient ley track ways in this world.

The staff is longer than the wand, usually heart height or the same height as the user, and carried in the power hand. Some practitioners prefer shoulder height, tall enough for support but still manageable. Staffs or staves are used vertically in magick. It is another important tool, not in ritual magick but in natural magick and all forms of nature religions and Druidry.

Uses for a staff

* Marking the centre of a visualised circle and hanging a lantern on if it is dark or during midwinter celebrations (see page 657).

* Set to the direct north or east just outside a visualised or actual circle with an empowerment, to act as guardian or watcher and keep away all harm. In earlier times of persecution, there would be an actual watcher who stood on high ground, holding the staff, looking for any who might intrude or be hostile to a gathering.

* Knocking on the ground three times in the centre of a magickal circle to draw upwards the power of the earth; also to ask for the presence of the wise ancestors and the nature essences in a ritual or when you are carrying out personal meditation or past life work.

* Marking out a physical as opposed to visualised circle outdoors if you want to make one in earth or sand, Afterwards the markings can be rubbed out with the end of the staff.

* Directing healing sky energies into the earth with a downward movement.

* As a psychic as well as a physical strengthener as you walk up hills or over rough terrain.

* As a prayer tree in the centre of a circle on which you and others can hang feathers to represent petitions and then release them to carry the prayers.

* To set behind your bedroom or house door at night with a night-time blessing and request to invoke the protection of the protective land guardians. You could engrave it with protective runes (see page 431).

* As a representation of the world tree axis that was supposed to link earth with heaven. As such, it naturally conducts power between earth and the skies when

set in the ground. You will be energised by the union of power when you take your staff up again, even if you were just having a rest or picnic.

Bell staff

The bell staff or bell branch comes from the Druidic tradition. It was traditionally made of apple or willow, a moon tree and sometimes had three clefts or small branches.

The branch was decorated with three or nine silver bells, also sometimes with apples, nuts and sea shells. It is used especially in moon ceremonies. The bells are rung to stir the air and so make the link with higher energies and to create harmony in the ritual. It can also be used to purify an indoor place where there are bad earth energies or negative feelings. It is carried rather than set down.

Stang

A stang is a cleft staff usually of ash that is set to the north instead of the east of the altar to signify the Horned God and to act as protector of the circle. It can sometimes be topped with antlers or horns. On certain festivals a candle can be set in the cleft to offer passage of light into other dimensions, especially, but not exclusively, at Samhain.

Alternatively a scarecrow may be substituted, with an animal skull on top and dressed in white linen, and, like the staff, put beyond the circle. Though this is not Wiccan, it is a lovely old custom, especially for outdoor rites of winter.

Guardian/doorkeeper stone

* **Element:** Earth
* **Direction:** North or to the south of the altar so you stand on it and face north during the ritual
* **Energies:** Goddess
* **Qualities:** Grounding, stability, protection

This is linked with the sacred stone of Fal, one of the four treasures of the Dagda. If it is an actual stone slab or slate, it may be set on the ground to the south of the altar so that you stand on it during ritual as you face north. Alternatively, it can be a small representative pointed rock or a crystal standing on the ground to the north, just outside the circle (or within, if you prefer it).

It signifies and acts as a focus for your Witch Guardian. In this guise, he or she is a gatekeeper against anything harmful from the spirit or human world approaching you, like the protective staff.

You do not have to use a crystal to activate your doorkeeper. However, keeping one of the following crystals permanently just inside the room will act as a temporary home for your doorkeeper while you work and store and accumulate the guardian energies. Place it so that you can see it when the door is open or closed or near the tree or bush in the garden that forms an entrance to your working space.

* The following are good doorkeeper crystals (it only needs to be very small):
* Phantom quartz: a clear quartz crystal in which a phantom crystal appears. Phantom quartz occurs when the growth of the crystal is interrupted and it

leaves a shadowy smaller crystal like a veil within the larger host crystal. Sometimes another coloured crystal can grow around it: for example, rose quartz or green chlorite Often the phantom quartz is in a pyramid shape.

* A channelling or laser crystal, clear crystal quartz with seven edges surrounding the large sloping face.
* An Isis crystal, named after the Ancient Egyptian Mother Goddess: clear quartz with five edges surrounding the largest sloping face.
* Smoky or rutilated quartz.
* Some practitioners bring back a stone from a favourite mountain.
* Any crystal pyramid or small crystal sphere.
* Meteorites are good as they are filled with cosmic energies.

As you set the crystal or stone in place (or if it is a permanent fixture, touch it before the ritual), ask:

Be for me, guardian, guide and protection.

Afterwards, when you have closed the circle, tip a little of the remaining consecrated water on it or any clear water and say:

I give you thanks for your wise guidance.

Depending on the nature and location of your main altar, you may leave it permanently in place, which is what I prefer; but if not, wrap it in a dark natural fabric cloth to store.

Drum

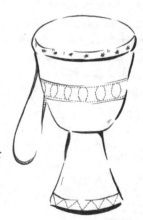

* **Element:** Air
* **Direction:** Everywhere in and outside the circle
* **Energies:** God
* **Qualities:** Rhythm, ecstasy, altered consciousness

The drum is probably one of the greatest mood creators and consciousness raisers in magick. Even if you have never played a note of music, I would advise everyone, solitary and coven member alike, to buy their own and use it regularly. Drums can be bought easily and very reasonably from craft fairs or ethnic stores. Among such people as the Inuits, drums were painted with symbols and used for divination.

For accompanying rituals and chants or raising and release of power, you might like to use a hand-held tambour-type drum, so you can beat time with a stick. For more intense drumming for personal empowerments and shamanic work, use your thumbs and the side of your hand until you have a steady rhythm. Increase the rhythm until you can feel it in every part of your body. You may find that you are swaying as you drum and that you may start to move naturally.

Combine drumming and the chanting and feel the energy flooding through you in formal and informal rites or just for connection. There is more on chanting on page 293.

Ancient Egyptian magickal tools

Not surprisingly, many of these correspond to the tools on a conventional witchcraft altar. However, there were different emphases in Ancient Egypt: for example, perfume was used to cleanse and empower the altar, and daily offerings were of central importance. On page 171, I have described setting up and using an Egyptian altar in greater detail. Here I propose to describe tools that can enhance modern magickal ritual in any tradition and that are potent additions to any witch's magickal treasures.

The Egyptian Wand

* **Element:** Air
* **Direction:** East
* **Energies:** God
* **Qualities:** Seeking, sending out, restoring order

This is very different in focus from the more fiery inspirational wand and can form a bridge with traditions in magick that regard the wand as an Air tool. It is held in the power hand to amplify power, either by sending energies into the universe as you circle it as if to throw or when flicked away from you as a defensive device to fend off malevolence.

The most common kind of Ancient Egyptian wand resembled an Australian Aboriginal boomerang. This was no coincidence, because it was based on the throw stick used by Ancient Egyptian wild fowlers. Both they and the original Australians realised – although separated by 10,000 miles of ocean – that if you were trying to knock down a wild bird with a thrown stick, it was far more accurate if the stick was slightly curved. The Australians took it one stage further and developed the tricky stick that would come back when thrown (rather like the magickal hammer of Thor in the entirely different culture of the Vikings, see page 126). The Ancient Egyptian wild fowlers would hide in the reeds of the Nile waiting for passing ducks and geese. In Egyptian art, flocks of wild birds were used to represent the forces of chaos. So by extension, the throwing stick and wand was seen as a force for bringing chaos back under control.

The throw stick was so highly regarded by the Egyptians that it is used as a hieroglyph meaning throwing.

The wand based on the throw stick – the device that brought order from chaos – was used to protect the home and especially women who were pregnant or in labour. It was decorated with various protective amulets or charms and deities. Early examples of these wands dating back to 2800 BCE have little decoration and have points that end in the heads of animals.

Seven hundred years later there was a change in style. Wands began to be decorated with elaborate carvings on one or both sides, often of protective deities such as Tauret, the Hippopotamus Goddess, and Bes, the lion-headed dwarf.

You can buy these wands on the internet or easily make your own from environmentally friendly balsa wood. They have the virtue of being easily obtainable from craft shops; light and easily cut into a boomerang shape with a craft knife. See page 679 for detailed instruction of this fun activity.

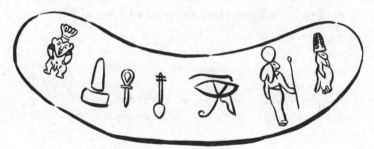

Illustrations 1 and 7, looking left to right (not the Eygptian way) show Bes, the protective dwarf, and the defensive Tauret, the hippopotamus

The sistrum

* Element: Air
* Direction: North-west
* Energies: Goddess
* Qualities: Joy, fertility, female authority

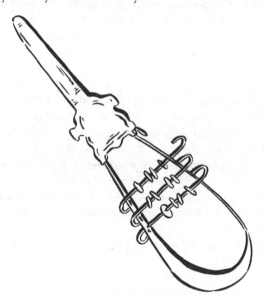

Sistrum decorated with the head of Hathor

The sistrum is a metal rattle that is used to begin and end ceremonies and to enhance power through sound. It was often seen in Egyptian art in the hand of the goddesses Isis, Hathor or Bastet, the cat-headed Goddess of women and children. Temples would have a senior priestess, sometimes a royal person, who would play the sistrum at ceremonies. The instrument is meant to resemble the cow horns on the headdress of Hathor, bent round to form a loop. Threaded through three holes on each horn were three thin metal rods. It was used to drive away harm and chaos and to build up power.

The sistrum is very different from a shamanic rattle, because it always retains dignity and joy, rather than unbridled ecstasy of shamanic rattling (at least that is the way I use it). It is an excellent magickal tool in any magickal tradition.

You can buy sistrums, but on page 684 I have suggested a very simple method of creating your own, even for a handicraft inept like myself! Alternatively, you can improvise with a hoop of bells wound around a bent and twisted metal coat hanger. When cleansing a space, you can ring the sistrum clockwise around a room or artefact, to drive away negative energies psychically. Ringing the Sistrum around your own aura or energy field will also remove the tensions of the day and other people's negativity.

Norse tools

Pre-Christian Norse religion was generally practised in ordinary homes rather than special temples, though there are some elaborate structures: for example, a temple dedicated to Thor at the foot of Helgafell, the holy mountain in Iceland. Around 1060 CE, the German Christian historian Adam of Bremen writes of the gilded heathen temple at Uppsala, not far from Stockholm, that was sacred to Thor the Thunder God, Odin the Father God, Freyr, God of fertility, and one of the more ancient Vanir native gods. Near the temple was a sacred spring where offerings were cast into the waters, often of gold arm rings (torcs) dedicated to the gods, asking for success in battle or prosperity. There were also priest chieftains called Godar. The Uppsala spring was later Christianised as the spring of St Erik, the patron saint of Sweden.

Ceremonies were generally conducted in open consecrated space, called the vé that could be triangular or, often, square. The harrow was the outdoor altar close to a guardian tree representing the World Tree. It was made of a stack of stones with a flat one on top or a series of tiered flat stones (see page 174).

The following artefacts differ from the modern westernised Witchcraft tradition, though they are still common in East Anglian magick. However, they can be adapted to enhance the magick of any tradition and sit comfortably with Wicca.

The arm ring

* **Element:** Spirit (all four elements united)
* **Direction:** Centre, usually set in a special indentation
* **Energies:** God or Goddess according to whose powers are being invoked or to whom the arm ring is dedicated
* **Qualities:** Dedication, loyalty, principles of magick

This was the most important item on the Norse altar, sometimes called a torque (which is also the word for a broad, metallic neck ring). It is a broad silver or copper bracelet that does not meet or fasten around the wrist. Traditionally, it might be dedicated to Thor, God of thunder, Freyr, the ancient Fertility God of the older order of nature deities, or Odin, the All Father. Copper ones are often named for the female deities, such as Frigg, Goddess of women and prophecy and wife of Odin, and Freyja, the Fertility and Love Goddess who was the sister of Freyr.

The arm ring can be a personal as well as a collective focus for dedication. Traditionally oaths of loyalty or promises were made to the deities while touching it, in return for the blessings of help or victory being sought. As a solitary practitioner for personal power you can wear the arm ring during a ceremony to empower it and touch or hold it (or even wear it) before a special event in your life. Some practitioners like to keep a permanent arm ring in the centre of the altar and empower another one to wear for a special purpose or as another private symbol of practice.

Hammer

* **Element:** Fire
* **Direction:** South
* **Energies:** God
* **Qualities:** Defence, healing, fertility

In myth, the symmetrical hammer of Thor, Mjolnir or Mjollnir, was thrown by the Thunder God against the frost giants and the trolls. Its sparks caused lightning and the hammer sound of thunder.

An actual hammer is used or the Thor rune (see page 436) drawn in the air or on the ground to empower and sanctify a magickal area. The hammer is a power and defensive symbol banged (with care) on an outdoor altar, along with chanting, to raise the power. It can be banged on the altar three times to open a rite instead of blowing a horn (or raising and lowering the Seax or ritual knife, another initial Norse altar greeting). Others present can move their power hands in a hammer movement. The hammer is also used lightly to bless another tool, and in fertility and love magick.

Small ornamental hammers are easily obtainable and are effective for solitary practitioners, as a way of raising personal energies by banging and chanting at the same time, getting faster and faster. The word Mjolnir signifies the storm and, as a miniature amulet, represents protection against all danger.

This hammer image above is quite a complex design but you need only trace the outline in smoke or etch it on a tool, unless you are skilled as an artist. Alternatively, you can simply use the rune of Thor's hammer, Thurisaz (see below), which is ideal for empowering a hammer.

Horn

* **Element:** Earth/air or water, the latter if it takes the form of the drinking horn, the Norse equivalent of the chalice
* **Direction:** North for the former, west for the latter
* **Energies:** God
* **Qualities:** Summoning, wildness, connection with earth

A feature of northern magickal traditions, the horn may also be found as the Horn of Bran the Blessed, the Celtic giant hero God whose head is said to be buried under the Tower of London protecting England. This was obviously a drinking horn, since it was said never to be empty. The drinking horn can also be a cup made of bone or horn. It is also used in seasonal celebrations to make toasts to the deities and spirits of the season and as part of the libations/offerings. It is an excellent artefact for outdoor and woodland rituals.

You can if even vaguely musical blow a traditional curved hunting horn (often sold with a mouthpiece) at the beginning of a ceremony, facing north to invite the wise ancestors, and once to close the ceremony. You can also use it as a focus in Horned God rites.

The Triple Horn of Odin is shown below. These were three interlocking drinking horns that were a symbol of dedication to Odin and a sumbol of toasting the Gods as a way of sharing a feast with them.

Spear

I have already mentioned the spear of Odin under wands. Actual spears or sheathed spearheads are part of the wands tradition, with the same associations. The ash spear Gungnir was one of Odin's most prized weapons, fashioned by the Svartalfs or earth elves to hit its mark always. Traditionally, battles were started by throwing a spear with the declaration, *May Odin declare for righteous*, i.e. by choosing the worthy victor.

A sharp, pointed, long ash wand or one tipped with an elf arrow, a flint, is a good substitute in any magickal tradition for a wand and can be used for Grail rituals or symbolically in releasing energies into the cosmos. In Anglo-Saxon magick, the fire rune Gar seen below signifies the spear of Odin and can be engraved or painted on a spear or of course on wands.

The Gungnir symbol is the Ingwaz fertility rune combined with the image of the spear of Odin

Seax or ritual knife

The Norse ritual knife and tool in Seax or Saxon Wicca shares the qualities of the athame or sword. The real difference is that it is sharp and so is used for carving runes or cutting wands, as well as for drawing and releasing power athame style. Some have hollow handles that can be filled with talismans and protective amulets.

The Seax can be raised to the heavens and down to the earth in the opening greeting of the ritual, facing first north and then south. If others are present and have knives, they can raise and lower them at the same time. Of course, the athame can be substituted for this greeting and may be safer than waving sharp blades. It is set horizontally, blade to the east, to the south of the arm ring.

Symbols

I have already given some signs associated with particular tools, such as the rune of Tyr or Tiwaz with the sword and there is more on magick symbols later (page 303). A number can be used on different tools. The following are magickal glyphs or signs that are particularly useful for marking magickal tools, either physically or as secret signs in smoke. Each releases the qualities in its meaning.

Runic symbols can be used on any magickal tools, with the exception of Ancient Egyptian ones, which tend only to work with hieroglyphs. Egyptian hieroglyphs can be used with any form of magickal tool except Norse ones (with the exception of the arm ring) or physically heavy tools, such as the cauldron or staff. Celtic symbols are resistant to Egyptian tools, but other wise work anywhere. For each of the symbols that follow, I have listed tools on which they work particularly well.

The Sun
Symbol of light, life, inspiration and power

This is the Celtic Awen and consists of the three rays of the sun. At the time of the midsummer sunrise, the sun casts three spreading rays of light, which open the gates of Annwyn, the doorway to the Celtic Otherworld.

The Sun/gold in Alchemy

Use on all God and Fire tools, as well as on any tool used for healing or to bring abundance.

The waxing moon

The Moon

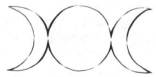

The Triple Goddess

Use on all Goddess tools along with the symbol of the three phases of the Moon that signifies the Triple Goddess: Maiden, Mother and Wise Woman/Crone. Also good for bowls used for water, chalices and drinking horns, all Water element tools and the broomstick.

Invoking Earth pentagram

This is the form of pentagram that you can use for inscribing tools unless you wish to use the relevant elemental pentagram, for example the Fire Pentagram for your wand (see page 627 for different elemental pentagrams).

Banishing Earth pentagram

Banishing is for protection. Use on absolutely any tool.

The Hexagram or Solomon's Seal

The Solomon's Seal is perhaps the most magickal symbol of all because it is based on the sacred triangle. The triangle represents the number three that is associated with many religions and cultures: the Triple Goddess; the Christian Father, Son and Holy Spirit; even earlier, the Egyptian Isis, Osiris the Father God and Horus their son; as well as human inner triplicity of mind, body and spirit. The two triangles of the seal are the triangle of the Water element descending and the triangle of Fire ascending. With the mingling of these elements are also formed the triangles of Air and Earth. The triangles of the four elements, Earth, Air, Fire and Water, fuse into the middle quintessential shape of five, and the six external points give the magickal seven spaces, seven being a sacred number of perfection.

This perfectly balanced symbol is ideal for use on all tools used to achieve balance or harmony. Like the pentagram, it is effective inside bowls for helping the contents to merge with other elements of the ritual or spell.

Spirals

Spirals are ancient Mother Goddess symbols that from Palaeolithic times have signified the fertile womb, rebirth and inner spiritual mysteries. Double and triple spirals of the Mother Goddess are etched on the stones of a number of passage graves in Western Europe. Their purpose was to protect the dead and to lead them to rebirth. The most famous spirals are at Newgrange in the Boyne Valley, not far from Dublin in Ireland. Lying on a small hillock, which is said to represent the Mother, the huge passage grave was originally built about 3100 BCE.

The Triple Spiral is another symbol of the Triple Goddess, Maiden, Mother and Crone or in Celtic lore three sisters. Use either symbol on any Goddess tools, especially womb images like cauldrons and bowls, and as a dedication to the Goddess on arm rings or on the guardian/grounding stone.

Ouroboros

Mediaeval alchemists portrayed the ouroboros, the snake swallowing its own tail, a symbol of endless cycles of time, birth and rebirth unbroken. Because of the shape, it promises long life and protects against infidelity and all destructive, divisive forces.

Use on all Goddess tools, such as cauldrons, chalices, bowls, especially for water, and on healing wands and staffs.

The Healing Caduceus

The double entwined snake of the classical Hermes and Mercury's caduceus, often a living, growing staff, is a symbol of both healing and powerful communication. The snake forms two circles, the interlinked cycles of good and evil, life and death, light and darkness. The wings on the caduceus are for wisdom. It can guard against gossip and malicious words, as well as illness, and by association with Mercury, who was among his many patronages God of moneylenders and thieves, against poverty and trickery.

Circle of Light

Circle of Darkness

Use on healing wands or protective staffs or any tool used in healing.

The Horned God

A witch symbol suitable for all God tools, such as stangs, staffs, spears, wands, horns and athames and for any assertive tools, such as the hammer or spear, and arm rings concerned with the Gods. Good for any natural magick tools.

Elhaz or Algiz

Elhaz or Algiz is the rune of eelgrass (sharp marsh grass) or the elk and is the rune of the evolving spirit and higher self. Use for Air tools and also any where dedication and spiritual aestheticism or Spirit Guides are involved, such as arm rings, the grounding stone or staffs.

Naudhiz

The rune of need and the ancient ritual Nyd Fire. As a Fire rune symbol of abundance, seasonal rites, passion and magick, it can be used on all Fire tools, such as the wand, and also assertive tools, such as the athame. Associated with the burning of nine sacred woods, it is effective for any wooden artefacts.

Ankh

The Ankh, meaning the key, is an Ancient Egyptian hieroglyph and symbol of eternal life. This is the special amulet of Isis, representing her union with Osiris.

It is the symbol of life, eternal life and the life force that runs through all creation. Use on a tool such as the besom that unites male and female, but also on any symbol of rebirth, such as the chalice or cauldron, and as a protective symbol on the athame. It is linked to the sistrum and the Ancient Egyptian wand.

The Eye of Horus

A symbol of inspiration associated particularly with the Summer Solstice. The Eye of Horus has retained its traditional significance as a bringer of good fortune, health and energy and against all forms of malice. Use it on any tool, especially if you face opposition to your Craft or feel that your powers are developing very fast.

PRACTICAL ASSIGNMENT

Inscribing tools and the third optional stage for the initial dedication

In the previous module I described how you could dedicate and empower your tools. You might have become aware that as you empower different elemental tools your own aura temporarily takes on the same predominant elemental colour: for example, green or golden brown for Earth tools.

Whether or not you decide to engrave or paint physical symbols on to your tools (or already have, if you are an experienced practitioner), you can inscribe your tools magickally on the astral plane. This is possible by drawing the symbols over the tools in incense smoke. For precision use a large firm incense stick in frankincense, nag champa, dragon's blood or sandalwood, as you would a pen. Secret symbols are doubly powerful because they are written on the aether.

❋ Replace any of the mother or father candles that have burned down.

❋ Light your incense by holding it in all four candles in turn, Earth, Moon, Sun, and Father/Sky left to right.

❋ Hold the cleansed and empowered tool in your receptive hand, the one you do not write with. You can only empower one tool at a time, unless you decide for any reason that you have a particular personal icon (for example, the Hammer of Thor) that represents your magickal approach for every tool. In this case, it would not matter about the elemental nature of each tool. You would just draw a huge smoke symbol over all of the tools collected together with the smoke of the incense stick, held in your power hand.

❋ Choose one astral or hidden symbol for your individual tool initially. As you use the tool over the weeks and months, you may add others or slightly change its energies, perhaps related to a particular need: for example, protection. There are no limits to the number of symbols you can add over time to a single tool and the most recently added energies will remain the most powerful. If you do not add a new symbol at re-empowering, the original symbols will be reactivated by the re-empowerment and will not be affected by any prior cleansing.

❋ Depending on the shape and size of the tool, either make a large symbol above it or repeat the same symbol two or three times along the length.

❋ As you do so state the name symbol and the purpose of the empowerment. For example:

I empower this wand with the healing Caduceus of Hermes that my wand may always be filled with healing powers and directed for whatever purpose ultimately to heal, reconcile and integrate.

❋ Leave the incense and candles to burn through after you have psychically engraved your tool or tools.

Further research

Now is the time to take stock of what for you are essential tools and what can be improvised or left for when you have more free money. Ask around other witches and join some forums that I have suggested in previous modules and others you will easily find on the internet. Find out what they consider essential tools and any unusual items they have on their altars. Then you will be ready to plan or maybe reorganise your personal indoor and outdoor altars.

Further information

Recommended reading

* Fries, Jan, *Seidways Shaking Swaying and Serpent Mysteries*, Mandrake Press, 1996
* Harris, Eleanor L, *Ancient Egyptian Magic and Divination*, Samuel Weiser, 1998
* Harvey, Ralph, *The Last Bastion*, Zambezi Publications, 2005
* Matthews, Caitlin and John, *Encyclopaedia of Celtic Wisdom*, Element, 1994
* Pennick, Nigel, *Secrets of East Anglian Magic*, Robert Hale, 1985

Websites

* *The Odinist Fellowship*
Information and illustrations of Norse tools
www.odinistfellowship.co.uk
* *The Order of Bards, Ovates and Druids*
Huge amount of information on nature spirituality
www.druidry.org

THE FOUR ELEMENTS AND FOUR DIRECTIONS

Though we are primarily going to work with the four elements that are the core of both traditional and modern witchcraft, we will be taking our field of vision even wider. We will be exploring alternative ways of working with the elements: for example, the Celtic triple system of earth, sea and sky; the five Chinese elements; and the five Norse elements.

The actual physical elements that shape our magickal practices depend on the climate, the land vs the sea mass and the cultural background in which we work. For those who, for example, practise magick in Northern Australia, Earth, the main land mass, may be to the south and questions arise about how physical and symbolic elements and directions can best be synthesised.

Both the Chinese and Norse systems have Earth as the stabilising central element, while the Celts have Fire as the central creative principle and energising spark for Earth, Air and Water. In contrast, in the traditional westernised system that comes from Ancient Greece, the fifth central element forms the synthesis of the others and in its formation generates the energy necessary for magick to take place. By looking at different elemental perspectives, I have found that the four element system becomes much more dynamic and open to creative magickal development.

The four elements in traditional magick

The system used in witchcraft today is rooted in the world of Ancient Greece, where a number of philosophers created a system of the Four Elements – Earth, Air, Fire and Water – that they believed were present and the building blocks of all creation, including humans. Magick practitioners believe that the synthesis or fusion of these elements creates spiritual energy called aether, akasha or spirit in which thoughts and desires can be animated and transferred (or, rather, catapulted) into material reality.

The history of the western elemental system

The Greek philosopher Empedocles lived in Sicily in the 5th century BCE and is credited with being the first person to put forward the theory that all matter consists of Earth, Air, Fire and Water, spiritually as well as materially. He linked Zeus, the Greek Father God with Air, Hera, his consort with Earth, Hades his brother and God of the Underworld with Fire and Persephone or Nestia, the maiden goddess daughter of Demeter the Grain Goddess with Water. Persephone was abducted and forced to spend part of the each year with Hades, so causing winter, as her mother grieved. The Water symbolised Persephone's tears at being parted from her mother.

In the 1st century BCE, the Greek philosopher Plato tried to explain the four elements mathematically.

The Greek doctor Hippocrates and the philosopher Aristotle regarded the elements as interplay of hotness and coldness, and dryness and wetness. Fire (dry and hot) and Water (wet and cold) are opposites, as are Earth (dry and cold) and Air (wet and hot). This concept continued right through the Middle Ages until the 18th century with the belief that the elements were reflected as bodily fluids or humours in people, imbalances of which explained illnesses and mental disorders. The psychotherapist Carl Gustav Jung was fascinated by the elements, alchemy and the spiritual world, and he gave the elements a modern psychological spin. He hypothesised that everyone had a predominant elemental trait, a secondary one, a shadow element that we find difficult and identify as a fault in those we dislike, and a fourth element that is generally undeveloped. In his theory, Earth is the sensations mode, Air thinking (logic), Fire intuition and Water feeling (emotions).

Magickally as well as psychologically we tend to be attracted to a particular element and may find one really hard to relate to and work with. For this reason, the elements are important to understand from the inside out. As witches, as we explore them on different levels, so our personalities spontaneously integrate.

The elements in magick

Each element stands not only as a cardinal direction point on the Wheel of the Year, but also has myriad associations radiating from it. Elements are the foundations that form magick and the folk tradition, and unlock a whole treasure-chest of symbols, some of which I have listed below.

Magickal practitioners call upon the elemental quarters of a circle and their guardians not only for protection but also to add their various powers to energise and give life and form to the symbolic elemental work to be carried out within the circle.

The colour associations I give are those most frequently used in magick and that have always worked for me in different traditions: golden brown or green for Earth and the north; yellow or grey for Air and east; red, orange or gold for Fire; and blue or silver for Water. Vivienne Crowley gives yellow for Earth, blue for Air, red for Fire and sea green for Water. Moon River Wicca, a relatively new but growing Wiccan training order based in the south-east of England, uses green, brown or black for Earth, white, blue or yellow for Air, different shades of red, orange and gold for Fire and purple or silver for Water.

Earth

Qualities

Astrological signs: Capricorn, Virgo, Taurus

Character: The facilitator/carer

Energy: Receptive/passive

Energy raiser: Drumming

Function: Solid form, manifestation, law giving, binding

Keywords: I accept and nurture all

Nature: Cold and dry, heavy

Negative qualities: Over-caution, rigidity, unwillingness to adapt, blinkered vision, stubbornness, laziness, greed, inertia, materialistic

Planets: Venus, Saturn

Polarity: Goddess

Positive qualities: Patience, stability, generosity, reliability, endurance, perseverance, respect for others and traditions, protectiveness, fertility (also water) acceptance of others as they are and of self, groundedness, tolerance, caretaker of the environment

Psychic gift: Psychometry/clairsentience

Associations

Colour: Green or golden brown

Elemental creature: Gnome

Elemental tool: Pentacle

Point of the pentagram: Lower left

Sacred elemental substance: Salt

Season: Winter

Senses: Touch and taste, also common sense

Tarot suit: Pentacles, discs or coins

Time of day: Midnight

Time of life: Old age

Deities

Archangel: Uriel, Archangel of protection

Deities: All Earth Mothers, Creator Goddesses, Mistress of Animals and Crone Goddesses, also Earth Fathers, Horned God and Gods of the hunt (see Module on Gods and Goddesses, page 220)

Guardian of north wind: Boreas

Ruler: Geb or Ghob, an elemental king whose throne is covered with crystals, silver and gold. He is guardian of miners and others who work within the earth and of those nature spirits who live or work in the Earth.

Correspondences

Animals and birds: Antelope, badger, bear, boar, cow, bull, dog, stag, sheep, squirrel, rabbit, chipmunk, serpent, snake, bee, spider, wolf

Body parts: Legs, feet, spine, skeleton, bowels

Crystals: Most agates, especially moss and tree agate, amazonite, aventurine, emerald, fossils, jet, malachite, petrified or fossilised wood, rose quartz, rutilated quartz, smoky quartz, red and gold tiger's eye, all stones with holes in the centre

Earth places: Caves, crypts, ley lines, forests, ice, snow, rocks, mountains, gardens, also temples, old stone circles, homes

Fragrances: Cypress, fern, geranium, heather, hibiscus, honeysuckle, magnolia, oakmoss, patchouli, sagebrush, sweetgrass, vervain, vetivert

Materials, substances and phenomena: Salt, herbs, flowers, trees, coins, bread, corn and wheat, fabrics, nuts, clay, grass, soil, sand, berries, potpourri, herbs, crystals and gems, plants, soil, clay and sand

Natural associations: Earth lights, crop circles, fields of grain, sand storms, earthquakes and tremors, land guardians or Landvaettir, the ancestors

Use in magick

For protection, property, the home and all domestic matters; for stability in any area of your life; for a steady infusion of money and banishing debt; official matters; for families and animals; for crystal, herb and all environmental magick; for spells concerning institutions such as the law, politics, finance, health and education; also a focus for all rituals against famine, deforestation and land pollution and devastation through unwise building or industrialisation and for caring for animals and their natural habitats

Air

Qualities

Astrological signs: Aquarius, Libra, Gemini

Character: The initiator, planner

Energy: Active

Energy raiser: Music, song

Function: Movement, initiation, change

Keywords: I investigate and communicate

Nature: Warm and moist

Negative qualities: Sarcasm, spite, gossip, fickleness, superficiality, emotional coldness, dishonesty, pedantry, unwise speculation or gambling

Planets: Mercury, Jupiter, Uranus

Polarity: God

Positive qualities: Communication skills, persuasiveness, joy, focus, intelligence, fair mindedness, logic, independence, clarity, good memory, mental dexterity, optimism, teaching abilities, poetic and musical gifts, concentration, commercial and technological acumen, versatility, healing gifts through orthodox medicine or from higher sources

Psychic gift: Clairaudience

Associations

Colour: Yellow or grey

Elemental creature: Sylph

Elemental tool: Sword

Point of the pentagram: Upper left

Sacred elemental substance: Incense or smudge

Season: Spring

Senses: Smell, hearing

Tarot suit: Swords

Time of day: Dawn

Time of life: Birth, childhood

Deities

Archangel: Raphael, Archangel of healing

Deities: Maiden, spring and flower goddesses, Gods of light, Sky Father Gods, messenger and healing deities, star deities

Guardian of the east wind: Eolus

Ruler: Paralda, winged queen of the sylphs, who lives on the highest mountain on earth

Correspondences

Air places: Mountain tops, hills, towers, steeples and spires, the sky, pyramids, open plains, tall buildings, balconies, roof gardens, the sky

Animals and birds: Eagle, hawk, nightingale, birds of prey, white doves, winged insects, butterflies

Body parts: Breasts/chest, lungs, throat, brain

Crystals: Amethyst, angelite, blue lace agate, clear crystal quartz, citrine, diamond, herkimer diamond, danburite, lapis lazuli, sodalite, sugilite, sapphire, turquoise

Fragrances: Acacia, almond, anise, benzoin, bergamot, dill, fennel, lavender, lemongrass, lemon verbena, lily of the valley, marjoram, meadowsweet, papyrus flower, peppermint, sage

Materials, substances and phenomena: Fragrance oils, flowers, wind chimes, feathers, four winds, clouds, balloons, kites, feathers, airborne seeds and spores, smoke, winds, whirlwinds, hurricanes, storms, boats with sails billowing in the wind, weather vanes

Natural associations: Clouds, light, the life force, spirits, ghosts (believed to enfold themselves in the wind to travel), angels, elves, fairies

Use in magick

For passing tests and examinations, for learning; for travel, for changes and improvements in career, for house moves, for money spinning ventures; for anything to do with science, technology or the media; for healing the ozone layer and slowing down global warming; to recover lost or stolen items; to uncover the truth; for new beginnings; for feather magick

Fire

Qualities

Astrological signs: Aries, Leo, Sagittarius

Character: The creator/action man or woman

Energy: Active and projective

Energy raiser: Dance, ritual fires

Function: Ascending, transforming, urgency

Keywords: I inspire and I make my mark

Nature: Warm and dry

Negative qualities: Addiction, anger, aggressiveness, cruelty, domination, hatred, jealousy, rebellion, passion led, flirtatiousness and unfaithfulness, violence

Planets: Sun, Mars

Polarity: God

Positive qualities: Courage, inspiration, idealism and altruism, fidelity, striving for perfection, defence of the weak, intuition, imagination, creativity, leadership, good health, transformation, fertility in all aspects of life, transformation, courage, mysticism, clairvoyance, prophecy, determination to overcome any obstacle, energy, living spirit, abundance

Psychic gift: Clairvoyance

Associations

Colour: Red, orange or gold

Elemental creature: Salamander

Elemental tool: Wand

Point of the pentagram: Lower right

Sacred elemental substance: Candle

Season: Summer

Senses: Vision, survival

Tarot suit: Wands, rods or staves

Time of day: Noon

Time of life: Young adulthood, finding a partner, producing offspring

Deities

Archangel: Michael, Archangel of the sun

Deities: All Fire Gods and Goddesses, deities of passion and seduction, blacksmith and metal deities, deities of the sun

Guardian of the south wind: Notus

Ruler: Djinn, a being made of pure Fire

Correspondences

Animals and birds: Cat, lion, cougar, stag, dragons, fireflies, dragonflies and the legendary golden phoenix (symbol of transformation and rebirth, which burned itself on a funeral pyre every 500 years, only to rise again golden from the ashes)

Body parts: Heart, liver, spleen, stomach

Crystals: Amber, bloodstone, boji stones, carnelian, garnet, lava, iron pyrites, obsidian, ruby, topaz

Fire places: The family hearth, deserts, shimmering sand, hill-top beacons, red rock formations, altars with candles

Fragrances: Allspice, angelica, basil, bay, carnation, cedarwood, chamomile, cinnamon, cloves, copal, dragon's blood, frankincense, heliotrope, juniper, lime, marigold, nutmeg, orange, rosemary, tangerine

Materials, substances and phenomena: Candles, beeswax, flames, ash, fibre optic lamps, lightning, Jack o'lanterns, clear crystal spheres, anything gold, mirrors, oranges, sun-catchers, sunflowers and all golden flowers, volcanoes, forest fires, and solar eclipses

Natural associations: Blood, the sun, ritual and hearth fires, stars, bonfires, comets, rainbows, meteors, lightning torches (wood was believed to contain fire that could be released by friction), djinns (genies) and fire fairies

Use in magick

For fulfilling ambitions; for wise power and leadership; for all creative and artistic ventures; for religion and spirituality; for success in sports and competitive games; for courage; to increase psychic powers, especially higher ones such as channelling; for pleasure, passion and the consummation of love; for sacred sex; for the removal of what is no longer needed; for binding and banishing, for protection against a vicious attack or threats; for candle magick; against drought, all pollution caused by burning fuels or chemicals, forest fires and the 'slash and burn' policy in rainforests

Water

▽

Qualities

Astrological signs: Pisces, Cancer, Scorpio

Character: The integrator/peacemaker

Energy: Passive and moving

Energy raiser: Rattles, prayer and chanting

Function: Merging, integrating, dissolution

Keywords: I love and I bring peace

Nature: Cold and moist

Negative qualities: Possessiveness, sentimentality, excesses in any area of life, manipulation, lack of motivation, instability

Planets: Neptune, the Moon, Pluto

Polarity: Goddess

Positive qualities: Beauty, compassion, empathy, peacemaking, harmony, sympathy, love, forgiveness, unconscious wisdom, purity, ability to merge and interconnect with nature, the cycles of the seasons and of life

Psychic gift: Healing/telepathy, scrying

Associations

Colour: Blue, silver

Elemental creature: Nymph

Elemental tool: Chalice

Point of the pentagram: Upper right

Sacred elemental substance: Water

Season: Autumn

Sense: Sixth sense

Tarot suit: Cups or chalices

Time of day: Sunset, twilight

Time of life: Middle years right through retirement and the third age

Deities

Archangel: Gabriel, Archangel of the moon

Deities: Moon and love deities, sea, sacred well and water Gods and Goddesses, Goddesses of initiation and the mystery religions

Guardian of the west wind: Zephyrus

Ruler: Niksa, beautiful rainbow coloured ruler of the undines, the water spirits

Correspondences

Animals and birds: Frogs, dolphins, otters, beavers, herons, ducks, seals, whales, swans and all water birds, all fish, especially the salmon, starfish, crabs, sea horses, crocodiles, alligators

Body parts: Womb and genitals, hormones and glands, hands

Crystals: Aquamarine, calcite, coral, fluorite, jade, moonstone, fluorite, pearl, opal, tourmaline

Fragrances: Apple blossom, apricot, coconut, eucalyptus, feverfew, heather, hyacinth, jasmine, lemon, lemon balm, lilac, lily, myrrh, orchid, passionflower, peach, strawberry, sweet pea, thyme, valerian, vanilla, violet

Materials, substances and phenomena: Milk, wine, sea shells, crystal spheres, scrying bowls, dark mirrors, reflections in water, tides, floods, tsunamis

Natural associations: The moon, rain, ritual baths, mists, fog, dreams, mermaids, water sprites

Water places: Pools, streams, estuaries, waterfalls, sacred wells and springs, whirlpools, rivers, the sea, marshland, flood plains, aquariums, water parks

Use in magick

For love, relationships, friendship, the mending of quarrels; for astral travel; for protection of those far away; for dreams; for purification rites, healing using the powers of nature and particularly water, especially sacred water; for scrying and divination, all water, sea and moon magick; for travel by sea; for fighting floods, cleansing sea, lake and river pollution, in campaigns for fresh water to parts of the world where there is none; for world health initiatives; for care of whales, dolphins, seals and all endangered sea creatures

PRACTICAL ASSIGNMENT

Walking the four elements

This is a method I first used while training as a Druidess. I then adapted it in my other tradition as a solitary white witch and using it encountered the elements on a very personal level by walking and weaving them, not as a circle but as a cross formation within a circle. Some Native North Americans practise a similar walk using the Medicine Wheel.

I would recommend working outdoors. Ideally, you should find a place with trees to the north for Earth, a hill to the east for Air, a shimmering plain with the sun directly over it or ascending or descending, according to the time of day for Fire and a body of water to the west. Since most magick is practised in more mundane settings, you can endow the four direction points with their own ideal qualities in your imagination.

* Plan your elemental quarters in advance, as elaborate or as simple as you wish, with animal, crystal, fragrance and deity associations. Read through the lists above. Then let the ideas merge and push them back into your unconscious to weave their own connections and focus on the physical walking.

* Either draw the design below in earth or sand or mark the centre and four main directions with five stones. It should be large enough for you to walk the visualised pathways.

* Alternatively, find a place where you can stand in the centre of four main markers (stones), perhaps in a stone circle or where there are four focal trees.

* Leave the circle entirely empty of tools. You are working through the chakras or energy centres on the soles of your feet (more of drawing and directing magickal energy through your chakra system later, see page 178). These are connected to your Root chakra and through that with the earth.

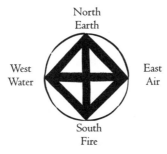

North
Earth

West   East
Water   Air

South
Fire

* If you wish to cast a circle (which you do not have to do for this exercise), stand in the centre facing north and, as you turn on the spot clockwise, with your index finger of your power hand draw a circle of light that spirals outwards to enclose you in a complete circle.

* Now, using your mind, project the light to illuminate the invisible pathways between the quadrants, beginning in the north as though someone were lighting them.

- Go to the northernmost point of your circle following the vertical pathway of light ahead, raise your arms high and wide and greet the Guardian of the North.

- Ask that he or she may take the form most helpful and protective for you on the journey ahead. Close your eyes then open them and in your mind or externally you may see a wise ancestor, a Land Guardian, one of the ancient Crone Goddesses or perhaps an Earth Angel in all the colours of the land and forests. You may feel snow or ice. Ask for protection and blessing on your spiritual journey.

- Walk now, not round the circumference of the circle but on the visualised diagonal north to east pathway of light.

- Face the east and as you greet the Guardian, ask that you may see him or her in the form that will be most challenging and exciting on this journey.

- Close and open your eyes and you may see a winged messenger, a spring or flower maiden Goddess, a shimmering yellow angel or a tall sky being. Ask for knowledge and for blessing on your spiritual journey.

- Move next along the south-eastern diagonal pathway of light and face the south. As at the east, raise and extend your arms wide and greet the Guardian asking that you may see the Guardian form who will most inspire your spiritual journey.

- Close and open your eyes and before you either in your mind's vision or externally may be a God or Goddess of the sun or of fire or a magnificent red and gold angel. Ask for enlightenment and for blessings.

- Walk next along the diagonal visualised south-west path until you reach the west. Face outwards and with arms raised, greet this Guardian and ask again that you may see the Guardian form that will fill your heart with peace and with love. Close your eyes, then open them. You may see a water deity or a silver Moon Goddess or silver Angel. Ask that the path ahead will be healing and lead you to harmony.

- Return on the path to the north and face inwards towards the centre of the circle. Where will you walk? What will you learn and see? Allow your feet to guide you.

Weaving the elements

You can move round the pathways of your circle in different ways. Since all the elements are part of the same whole, you can weave the elements into a pattern by walking direct pathways diagonally between the different elements (see picture on page 143). The first time you might only try one or two and may want to sit down part of the way and let the impressions and insights flow within you. As you try this exercise again, note in your Book of Shadows those combinations that gave you particularly meaningful walks. This may be expressed by a sense of peace or meaningful dreams or divination after the ritual that answers questions you had not realised you needed to ask.

Some paths may seem more difficult or less fruitful. Afterwards, ask yourself why. You can work in a cross formation unless elements are next to each other, in which case move in a clockwise direction. You might not want to start your walk in the north, in which case follow the pathways to what is for you the starting point of a particular journey.

See the lighted paths as an energy grid. Allow your feet to take you to the starting point, which may not be the one you anticipated. The following are connections that may be helpful initially, but you will develop your own personal connections and associations. Imagine the effect, for example, of Water on Fire or Air on Fire. This might cast images as you walk that in turn evoke memories and feelings related to your own life. Increasingly, it will also connect with the rich mythology, often unconsciously recalled, of the different elemental symbols and their interconnections:

* North to south, Earth to Fire, for an increase in power, joy and illumination; good if you need a sudden surge or energy to act or clarify matters

* South to north, Fire to Earth, for moving from the outer to the inner world, allowing plans and ideas to lie fallow and to relieve a sense of urgency that is wearing you out rather than achieving results

* West to east, Water to Air, towards the rising light, the direction of rebirth, new beginnings and regeneration after illness or sorrow

* East to west, Air to Water, to reap what has been sown, to lay down old burdens and to allow time to heal

* North to east, Earth to Air, for bringing the seeds of plans and dreams into the outer world, for learning to trust and love again

* East to north, Air to Earth, for moving away from malice, destructive situations and relationships and keeping one's own counsel for a while

* South to east, Fire to Air, increasing the impetus for any endeavour, seeking substance through which to channel dreams and energies

* East to south, Air to Fire, for maximum increase, a natural progression for fulfilling any goals that also demands maximum effort

* North to west, Earth to Water, for seeking wisdom from the past, reassessing mistakes and missed opportunities and letting them go

* West to north, Water to Earth, for letting go of the desire for control and walking trustfully into the darkness knowing light will return

* South to west, Fire to Water, for allowing events to run their course and for attaining balance in your emotions

* West to south, Water to Fire, tempering anger and desire with altruism and compassion

If you have room, you might decide to make elemental pathways marked with stones in your garden.

Further information

Recommended reading

* Crowley, Vivienne, *Wicca, The Old Religion in the New Age*, Aquarian/ Thorsons, 1989
* Eason, Cassandra, *Alchemy in the Workplace*, Crossing Press, 2004
* Lipp, Deborah, *The Way of Four, Create Elemental Balance in your Life*, Llewellyn, 2004
* McArthur, Margie, *The Wisdom of the Elements, the Sacred Wheel of Earth, Air, Fire and Water*, Crossing Press, 1998
* Rupp, Rebecca, *The Four Elements, Water, Air, Fire and Earth*, Profile Books, 2005

Websites

* *Astrology and the four elements*
  Interesting astrological perspective to the elements
  http://accessnewage.com/articles/ astro/higelems.htm
* *The four elements*
  Site with plenty of ideas for personal work as well as information
  www.thedance.com/wicca101/ 4elem.htm
* *Moon River Wicca*
  An old path in the modern world
  www.moonriverwicca.co.uk
* *WebWinds*
  Good history and background
  www.webwinds.com/thalassa/ elemental.htm

THE ELEMENTS AS A COHESIVE FORCE

The elements are also central to the magick and spirituality of other cultures. To the Celts, the Chinese and the Vikings, they were living forces, rather than abstract powers, manifest as: wind, soil, rocks; the sun and lightning; hearth or ritual fires; and the sea, rivers and still lakes. We will work more with this aspect of the separate elements later, but for now we'll examine how the different elemental systems worked as a cohesive force to generate the mystic element that was the synthesis of and greater than them all.

The Celtic tradition

Though the Celts acknowledged four elements, they focused mainly on three: Earth or Land, Sea (Water) and Sky (Air). Three is a very important number in Druidry. The Celts believed that fire was the unifying generative/cleansing force behind existence, set in the centre of a triple spiral or three concentric circles moving outwards, from earth, through sea to the outermost sky. These realms are not abstract concepts, but the earth beneath our feet, the sky above and the vast oceans that mark the limits of the land. That everyday physical connection is the core of the Celtic elemental system.

So highly regarded were the three realms by the Druids and Druidesses that oaths were pledged by Celtic leaders, saying if they broke their promises the sky could fall upon them, the ocean swallow up the land and the land fall beneath them. This acknowledged the power of the whirlwind and hurricane, the tidal wave and the earthquakes that were believed to reflect the anger of the deities.

The magick of the place where earth, sky and sea meet was used for burials of the ancestors long before the Druids, and many long barrow graves and stone circles are set overlooking the sea or another water source. I would recommend a visit to Jersey in the Channel Islands, where, in spite of its small size, there are several beautiful long barrows dating as early as 3400 BCE that are still totally accessible but often deserted.

I believe that as witches we are caretakers of the elements, one of the conditions of our being able to use them magickally. Though I am the least militant and most idle of souls, I know that it's no use singing *The river is flowing* and expecting a passing water deity to send me blessings if the local canal is clogged up with supermarket trolleys and more than a third of the world doesn't have clean drinking water!

The Land and Earth

This is the natural home of people, animals, insects, plants, trees, crystals and stones and since it is the one with which we are most familiar, it may be the easiest with which to relate if you are unfamiliar with magick.

The land is generally relatively stable, although earthquakes and erosion can bring change. My own island suffers badly from erosion and each year parts of the cliff – and sometimes houses – fall into the sea and what were once steep walks down to the sea become a little less steep each year.

The Sea and Water

The sea is wild and constantly changing, ebbing and flowing, affected by the pull of the moon as water is sucked up from it into the sky, being returned in the endless cycle of rain and rivers. It, too, has a rich life of fish, seals and seabirds, as well as myriad plants. In some Celtic cosmologies, the sea is linked with the Otherworld, the Isles of the Blest, and it is no accident that flesh and blood Druidesses made their home on islands where land and sea meet so dramatically.

The Sky and Air

The sky is the realm of light and shadow, of sun, moon and stars, of the winds and the rain, the clouds and the vastness of endless sky over a treeless plain. Its emptiness can be frightening or liberating and when it is illuminated by a sheet of lightning or a brilliant sunset, we can understand why it was so readily associated with deities.

The three realms in ritual

These are my favourite rituals from the Druid tradition that are equally valid in Wicca and a good way of understanding the Celtic elemental system. Celtic magick faces east, the direction of the rising sun.

The Celtic Triskele or sacred spiral is symbol of the three realms. The central triangle within it is Fire.

* Choose a place where you can see water if not the sea and the sky is open above. Wide grassy cliff tops are very good for this kind of ritual and you can use a small fire dish (see outdoor altars, page 166) for a safe fire element.

* Draw a life-size Triskele in sand or on earth, or make one of stones or shells on grass or chalk on a paved area. Light a fire in a fire dish or a cauldron in the centre or a huge candle embedded in sand.

* Walk the spirals in and out to develop a light trance state. As you do so, chant your own needs from the Earth, Sea and Sky in turn or making blessings to them.

* End by casting offerings of herbs from the other three elements on to the fire to integrate and release the powers personally and ritually.

* Occasionally work by drawing three concentric circles round your fire, the outermost representing earth, the middle one water and the inner one the sky, with your fire in the centre of all three. Leave small gateways between the realms.

* Draw an entrance like a processional route from the west where you will enter, cutting through the three realms/circles as a straight pathway to the central fire.

- In the outermost circle of the Earth, place symbols of the Earth, a dish of small fruits, nuts and flowers.

- In the middle circle of the Sea, set a dish of seaweed, sea salt or a pot of water plants, such a water lily.

- In the innermost circle of Air, have a dish of feathers, seeds or small mirrors to reflect the light.

- Make sure for each realm you have one item that will burn easily and quickly. Have your dishes near the entrance to each realm so you can easily pick up symbols as you begin to circle each realm. Begin in the realm of Earth and carry with you a small dish in which to collect your flammable offerings.

- Facing east at the entrance of the Earth realm looking towards the centre and the Fire, state what you regard precious about the Earth. As you do so, begin to walk clockwise around the Earth circle.

- When you have completed the circuit, pick up a flammable Earth symbol, place it in your offerings dish and move into the middle circle of the Sea.

- Again, face east and the central fire, describing what you value most about the Sea or water and begin your Sea walk. If you allow words to flow as you tread the realms, you may be surprised at your own eloquence.

- Collect a flammable tribute before you leave the Sea realm and place it in your offerings dish.

- Proceed to the third realm, the Sky. Once more, describe your feelings about the Sky realm, while walking round the circle. Add your final flammable tribute.

- Enter the Fire centre, facing east. Make an offering to the Guardian of the Fire from the gifts of each realm in turn, asking for healing to the three realms and anyone who may be ill or troubled. The less you ask for yourself, the more you will receive under cosmic blessings. This ritual is a good one for sending healing to species and places, as well as people and specific animals. You might choose an example for each realm. Take as long as you need and do not rehearse your words as you may find what you ask was not what you thought you needed to ask.

- When the tributes are burned, thank the Guardian of Fire. Walk back round each circle in turn, still clockwise or sun wise, thanking the Guardians of the three realms in turn.

- When you are outside the circle, face the four directions in turn, working from the north to the west, then south, then east, asking:

  May there be peace in the north, may there be peace in the south, may there be peace in the west and may there be peace in the east.

- Finally, facing the centre, ask that there may be peace throughout the whole world. This common Druidic blessing, though perhaps not a Celtic one, is a good way of bringing any ritual to a close. I have also used it in a later module.

- You can carry out this ritual with other people, asking them to represent the different realms (as many as you like for each element) and perhaps one to act as Guardian of the Fire, to receive the blessings and burn them, adding personal prayers and blessings.

The Five Chinese elements

These are the most remote from Westernised magick, but their value is in the concept of balancing the elements and that each has its own time and season that mirrors human ebbs and flows.

Though this is inevitably a very brief overview, Chinese elements are very instinctive. They make a lot of sense spiritually and magickally, if you meditate on some of the concepts in a quiet still place of natural beauty or work with wind chimes, mirrors, green plants and goldfish in tanks to find your own harmonious balance. Indeed, in my book on natural magick I have described how you can create your own Oriental garden haven.

You can use any of the associations listed to below give you balance, such as different colours. I have listed some practical forms of each element you can add to your magick place or your home or workplace to get an elemental balance or to infuse the energies you need.

Yang and Yin

The fundamental concept behind much Chinese philosophy and indeed medical practice is expressed as the duality of the forces or essences of yang and yin. These represent the positive and negative energies that are present in all things and govern all human existence. They are in constant ebb and flow, causing continual changes and depending on each other, and together they form a balanced whole. There can be no light without darkness, no life without death.

The yin/yang symbol is two interlocked curved shapes within a circle, one white, one black, with a spot of the contrasting colour within the head of each. Think of Yang as God energies and Yin as Goddess and it all becomes more relevant. The five Chinese elements can be thought of as ways of expressing different aspects of those God and Goddess energies.

The 24-hour cycle expresses itself as day and night. Day belongs to Yang but after reaching its peak at midday, the Yin gradually begins to unfold until it is night. In turn, when Yin reaches its peak at midnight, Yang gradually unfolds until it is day again. This cycle is true for all opposites. Thus, any phenomenon may belong to either Yin or Yang but contains the seed of its opposite.

Yang represents masculine, light, activity, heat, strength and energy. Yang is inherent in the vital functions of the growth of an organism, metabolism and circulation, which promote action and energy. Yin represents the feminine essence, passive and cold. Darkness, calm and weakness, Earth, weather and sorrow are examples of Yin. It is inherent in the blood and all vital body fluids of reproduction, which have the ability to moisten and ease natural functioning.

The transformation of energies

According to Chinese tradition, the universe is composed of five elements: Metal, Wood, Water, Fire, Earth. Their interactions are controlled by Yang and Yin. An integral part of the Chinese holistic system is the transformation of energies between these elements, either in a creative or destructive sense (both creation and destruction are seen as a necessary part of the process of change). Each element has its own characteristics and properties, and harmony depends on their interaction. This is a fascinating area of study and I believe even rudimentary knowledge helps us to work more effectively within the westernised elemental system.

The core of Feng Shui, as with other ancient Chinese systems for looking at the world, including the Chinese horoscope, revolves around the interaction of these Five Elements. There is a natural creative order of the Five Elements that if followed naturally leads to harmony, prosperity, health and happiness. The productive sequence is illustrated below:

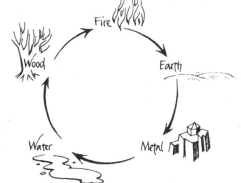

* Water nourishes plants and trees, so producing Wood
* Wood fuels Fire
* Fire burns into ashes to form Earth
* Earth is the source of Metal from which it is extracted
* Metal can be condensed to Water or can be melted from liquid

When this cycle flows harmoniously within our lives we are well, content and creative. Therefore it is known as the productive cycle. But there is also a destructive order:

* Water extinguishes Fire
* Fire melts Metal
* Metal breaks Wood
* Wood, as the roots of plants or trees or the wooden spades and ploughs used by ancient farmers, splits open Earth
* Earth is absorbed by Water

As in all magick it is necessary to take away the old for new growth and life:

* Earth helps Metal, is helped by Fire, hinders Water and is hindered by Wood
* Fire helps Earth, is helped by Wood, hinders Metal and is hindered by Water
* Water helps Wood, is helped by Metal, hinders Fire and is hindered by Earth
* Metal helps Water, is helped by Earth, hinders Wood and is hindered by Fire
* Wood helps Fire, is helped by Water, hinders Earth and is hindered by Metal

Wood

Animals: Scaly
Body organs: Liver, eyes, ligaments, gall bladder
Colour: Blue/green
Creature: Dragon
Day: Thursday
Direction: East
Metal: Iron
Quality: Benevolence
Season: Spring
Sense: Vision:
Significance: New beginnings, creativity, fresh growth, connections
Sound: Calling
Time of life: Birth
Ways of using Wood: As green or woody plants, anything made of wood, such as bamboo wind chimes (yang) and more supple wood (yin), miniature trees, vegetables, anything green
Weather: Rain

Mù

Fire

Animals: Winged
Body organs: Heart, ears, arteries
Colour: Red
Creature: Phoenix
Day: Tuesday
Direction: South
Metal: Copper
Quality: Prudent action
Season: Summer
Sense: Taste:
Significance: Activity, joy, enthusiasm, energy
Sound: Laughter
Time of life: Adolescence
Ways of using Fire: As lights, candles, lanterns, anything red, such as hanging banners or ribbons, anything pointed
Weather: Heat

Huǒ

Earth

Animals: Smooth skinned

Body organs: Spleen, nose, stomach, muscles

Colour: Yellow

Creature: The Ting, sacred Chinese symbol of cauldron, abundance and nourishment

Day: Saturday

Direction: Centre

Metal: Gold

Quality: Belief

Season: Late summer

Sense: Touch

Significance: Stability, honesty, inherited prosperity, patience

Sound: Singing

Time of life: The first part of adulthood

Ways of using Earth: Ceramics, anything square, pottery, statues of all kinds, clay, rocks and plants, yellow fabrics or anything yellow

Weather: Wind

Tǔ

Metal

Animals: Furry

Body organs: Lungs, large intestine, hair, skin

Colour: White

Creature: Tiger

Day: Friday

Direction: West

Metal: Silver

Quality: Righteousness

Season: Autumn

Sense: Smell

Significance: Success in business, the harvest, cutting through (symbol of knife or cutting through metal)

Sound: Wailing

Time of life: Adulthood/Maturity

Ways of using Metal: Dome shapes, arches, circles, metallic objects (especially silver), jewellery, metal wind chimes, coins, knives, anything white

Weather: Clear

Jīn

Water

Animals: Shelled

Body organs: Kidneys, lower orifices, bladder, bones

Colour: Black

Creature: Tortoise

Day: Wednesday

Direction: North

Metal: Tin

Quality: Knowledge

Season: Winter

Sense: Hearing

Significance: Communication, travel, learning, arts, media

Sound: Moaning

Time of life: Old age

Ways of using water in your life: Goldfish in tanks, wind chimes, water features, musical instruments such as flutes, glass, mirrors, pictures of water, anything black

Weather: Cold

水

Shuǐ

The five Norse elements

Like the Celtic elements, the five Norse elements – Ice, Fire, Air, Water, Earth – are firmly rooted in the real world of the colder Northern regions.

The mythology very much reflects the actual hardships of this often frozen world. For example, the Frost Giants represent the monumental struggles experienced by ordinary people, especially in the north of Scandinavia, to survive the long, cold winters before modern heating systems were invented. It was believed in folk custom that the Frost Giants sent the freezing winds and the snow into Midgard, the world of humans. Midgard is a central world on Yggdrasil, the World Tree, and signifies the element of Earth.

In Norse cosmology, four of the strongest dwarves, Norðri, Suðri, Austri and Vestr, held the four corners of the heavens on their shoulders and gave their names to the four compass points. The stars were made of sparks from the world of Fire in Muspellheim.

Ice/north

To the north of Midgard and below it on the tree was Nifleheim, the region of mist and ice. This was the place from which the ice in the north spanned the Abyss, Gunnungar-gap and fused with the Fire from the south to bring forth life.

Nifleheim was the home of the older Frost Giants or Thursar, most of whom were wiped out by the Aesir, the new order of gods (though Ymir the Frost Giant and first being was their ancestor). They were related to the Frost Giants of Jotunheim, but were less evolved.

Fire/south

This is Muspellheim, the region of Fire and home of the Fire giants. From here came the creative Fire that fused with Ice. It is the balance for Fire and Ice that is regarded as vital for the survival of Midgard, the land of men, and also of Asgard and Vanahaeim, the realms of the Gods on the higher levels of the tree and indeed all the worlds of Yggdrasil, the World Tree. The Fire Giants were ruled by the mighty Surt, with his iron hammer forged from Fire.

Ragnarok, the end of the world of the old gods and men, was said to come when Ice and Fire once more overwhelmed creation.

Air/east

In the east is an eagle-like entity that creates winds in Jotunheim, the realm of the Giants against whom Thor the Thunder God constantly waged war. The continuing power struggle was a threat to the established order, but was necessary cosmically to keep the dynamic balance. The capital of Jotunheim was Utgard, the citadel of the Frost Giants. Sometimes the Aesir Gods would enter into an uneasy alliance with the Jotunheim Giants, but would trick them when possible.

Water/west

Vanahaeim, the land of the old nature and fertility Gods and Goddesses, entered into a truce with the Aesir, whose chief deity was Odin. Most famous of the Vanir were Freyr, the Fertility God and Freyja, Goddesses of beauty and love. This realm was described as watery and very green.

Earth/centre

Midgard, the stable centre of the Norse elements and realm of humans, was between the realms of the Aesir and the light elves' realm Lojossalheimr above them. Below was Svartalfheimr, world of the dark elves that were famed for their metalwork, and also of the dwarves who guarded the treasures of the earth.

PRACTICAL ASSIGNMENT

Using the Norse elements

The following ritual incorporates the five Norse elements and synthesises them. Using either the five Norse elements, the five Chinese elements or the three Celtic ones, weave your own spell or ritual to bring them all together.

* Drop Ice into boiling water on a hob (Fire) and as it hisses (Air) call aloud nine times your particular creation you wish to bring into being.

* Leave the Ice to melt to Water. Then take the water off the hob, leave it to cool and use the Water to plant a fragrant herb in the Earth.

* As the herb grows (Earth) and its fragrance is released (Air), so will your creation likewise take shape, empowered by the five elements.

Further research

Follow one of the strands of the elements in a culture that interests you, because inevitably this module only gives an overview.

Further information

Recommended reading

* Aswynn, Freya, *Northern Mysteries and Magick*, Llewellyn, 1998
* Hobson, Wendy, *Simply Feng Shui*, Quantum, 1999
* Parsons, Sandra, *Seeking Spirit, A Quest through Druidry and the Four Elements*, Capall Bann, 2000
* Spence, Lewis, *The Magic Arts in Celtic Britain*, Constable, 1995
* Twicken, David, *The Four Pillars and Oriental Medicine – Celestial Stems, Terrestrial Branches and the Five Elements for Health*, Writers Club Press, 2000

Websites

The Druid Network
On line Druidry and resources
www.druidnetwork.org/index.html
Feng Shui Times
Articles and resources
www.fengshuitimes.com
Miercinga Ríce
Good for all things Norse
www.ealdriht.org

THE ALTAR

The altar is the heart of a witch's home and also of the coven. There are many kinds of altars, influenced by different traditions. However, the altar is ultimately an expression of how the individual witch and coven define the nature of their magickal practices and their beliefs. It also acts as a repository of power that increases over the weeks and months.

For a solitary practitioner, altars indoors and out are of great significance and power because ritual work is carried out within or near the home. This ensures the home will be blessed by a sense of peace and sanctity. For a solitary witch or coven member, there is no doubt that the personal home altar is always a sanctuary and healing source. A few minutes by candle light holding a favourite crystal and burning incense will restore the personal still inner centre and connection with the divine core within and the Goddess energies, no matter how chaotic or stressful external events may be.

What is an altar?

The word altar is derived from the Latin word for a high place. Altars are dedicated spaces raised off the ground on a table or plinth. They are also raised symbolically as the place where divine and human can meet through ritual.

The altar may be:

* permanent, kept in a particular place and regularly dedicated

* semi-permanent, set up for ritual in a space used regularly but not left set; or a table or stone slab adapted for magickal use

* temporary, set up for rituals often outdoors or in a special place

Some practitioners who work with others also have a semi-permanent or permanent altar at home for personal use.

Purpose of the altar

For less formal spells you might decide not to use an altar. Even so, it is useful as a focus for private contemplation, prayer or meditation. Five or ten minutes sitting by the light of a candle or with moon or sunlight flooding the altar, burning a fragrance a ceremonial oil or incense such as sandalwood, frankincense or myrrh will over weeks and months build up the energies of the altar. It will restore harmony and fill you with quiet joy and confidence.

You can adapt your altar for different seasons and needs by changing the candle, colours, fragrances, flowers, herbs, crystals and symbols to alter the emphasis subtly. For example, with herbs and wildflowers it is possible to create an indoor nature altar to bring freshness to a frantic urban lifestyle.

Altars can be as elaborate or as simple as you wish, depending on the kind of spell or ritual you are carrying out and your own preferences.

Permanent indoor altar

This is the most usual form of altar used by Wiccans and other witches in the western magickal tradition.

If you belong to a coven the form of the altar, what is set permanently on it and how it is prepared for ritual will be already established, but your private altar is a reflection of what matters to you. This may change as you explore different magickal traditions or your own spiritual priorities change.

Just as our homes are a reflection of our personality, so your altar will reflect your spiritual nature and potential. Over time you can collect treasures, not necessary of monetary worth, but statues, crystals, dishes and tools. The walls of the room can also reflect in pictures, papyri and artefacts facets of your magickal self. Gifts, too, add love of the giver to the altar. Keep your scrying and divinatory tools here, as well as your Book of Shadows, if necessary in small boxes and chests so each facet of your spiritual work amplifies and is empowered by the others.

Value your altar space and demand that others do, too, just as you respect your children's dens and your partner's precious collections.

Choosing the right altar

An altar is traditionally circular or square, but the size is not important. However, it is essential to have a space, however small, where you can sit, kneel or stand in front of your altar and work with it. If you cannot have a room, shed or wooden chalet in the garden for your altar space, you can improvise with a table in your bedroom or conservatory. If space really is at a premium, create an altar with bricks and a large piece of slate. Slide it under your bed when not in use and keep the artefacts in a cupboard.

You can paint the directions on a smaller altar and perhaps the Earth-invoking or calling/attracting pentagram in the centre (see page 129). The pentagram is a symbol of spirit or aether, the synthesis of the four elements. If you draw the equal-armed cross of the elements on a circular altar, you form the solar cross, another ancient sign for spirit and synthesis.

It is often easier to site a permanent indoor altar in the centre of the room or at least move it there for rituals so you can move all round it (push furniture back if necessary). If you have a large rug, you could paint a circle underneath it on the floor big enough for the required one and a half tall adults lying on the floor (traditionally counted as 9 ft).

Crystals, herbs and fragrances are the best ways to keep natural energies flowing into your altar when it is not in use, so have these around the altar room. When you have time, light a single white candle on the altar to purify the energies.

Use natural wood for your altar. Add an altar cloth adorned with moon, suns, zodiac signs and images of nature, made of natural materials such as silk or cotton.

Alternatively, buy a large scarf with designs of nature or hem your own fabric square. You may like to change the colours of the cloth according to the season.

Align the direction of the altar with a compass or if this just won't fit your room use approximations. Indeed, magick north is magnetic rather than true north. As long as you always use the same direction for magickal north it will accumulate those energies, even in more formal magick.

Setting up the altar

Think of the altar as four segments and decide if, for example, the north segment is the 12–3 o'clock position from north to east or if north is better served as north-west to north-east as shown below. These inter-directional segments correspond to the main festivals on the Wheel of the Year.

* Shadow time spans Samhain to Oimelc (north-west to north-east with north, 12 o'clock, as the centre point)
* East or dawning time (Oimelc to Beltane) is north-east to south-east with true east 3 o'clock as the mid point
* South, the time of light (Beltane to Lughnassadh) is south-east to south-west with true south, 6 o'clock, at the mid point)
* Finally the time of harvest (Lughnassadh to Samhain) is south-west to north-west, with the true west, 9 o'clock, as the mid point

Circle casting, opening the directions and empowering the symbol at the four directions, is precisely the same however you divide or imagine your quadrants divided. I like this method as it enables the ritual tools and other artefacts to fan out as you work for the central cardinal point in each direction.

Rather than trying to give you precise positioning of tools, which will vary according to the number of tools in each area and the nature of the ritual, I have left you to decide which is most useful nearer the edge or easily accessible in its segment in a particular ritual. Think how you would lay a table: cutlery is set in the order it is to be used, from the outside moving in.

Once you are experienced, this setting will become instinctive. However, you might need to rethink and reorder the placing on your private altar, so that the energies flow as your words and actions become effortless. For each quadrant, you may have any or all of the items listed below.

North, direction of midnight, earth and winter

* A green or silver directional candle
* A bell
* A flat pentacle dish on which you will set your salt and water bowls when you are making sacred water; alternatively draw an invisible attracting or invoking pentagram once in incense smoke over a plain dark ceramic plate or dish and redraw it monthly in smoke
* A small bowl of sea salt
* An optional earth crystal. such as red jasper, tiger's eye or red tiger's eye, moss or tree agate or garnet, rose quartz or smoky quartz; elemental crystals balance the energies and on mini-altars they can serve to signify the directions
* If you are having a cakes and ale ceremony (see page 633), the cakes can be on a dish in the north or in the centre of the altar

East, dawn, air and spring

* The directional candle in yellow or pearly grey
* Incense holder and incense (see page 569 for making your own incense); alternatively or for certain ceremonies you may need a couple of holders and incense sticks for using to enchant or empower the symbol (see page 186) or for writing your magickal names (see page 268)
* Smudge sticks for cleansing the space and maybe an abalone shell for holding the lighted smudge
* The athame or ritual knife unless worn on the belt, possibly set on the altar to empower it; a sword may be used for more formal group or coven rituals
* An air crystal. such as amethyst, citrine, lapis lazuli, blue lace agate or sodalite

South for noon, fire and summer

* The elemental and/or directional candle in red, orange or gold; if using two candles, red is the best elemental colour or undyed beeswax
* A deep candle holder that should have a heatproof lip or handle of a substance that will not burn you as you carry it, with either a metal dish beneath it or a broad base so you can burn grains or salt, herbs, cords or paper wishes and empowerments in the flame, and a heatproof surface to catch the ashes
* The wand
* Fire crystal, such as amber, carnelian, clear crystal quartz, obsidian, sun stone or aragonite

West for twilight, water and autumn

* Chalice
* Bowl of pure water to signify the water element; this can be mineral water, tap water or rainwater that has not touched the ground (i.e. from a barrel or bowl on a low roof)
* Water crystal, such as aquamarine, fluorite, green jasper, jade or green tourmaline

* In rituals where fragrance is important, oil burner and fragrance oil to match the dry fragrance of its alter ego the incense in the east

North-east

* Cords, if being used, or you can tie round your waist
* Pottery offerings/libation bowl to hold offerings during the ceremony or for any bread/wine that outdoors you would pour directly on to the ground

North-west

* Mini cauldron or on ground (this can be in the centre of a circle without a main altar)

The centre of the altar

* Matching tall slender altar candles, Goddess candle to the left and God candle to the right (or yin and yang, anima and animus, female and male) with a wide space between them; some practitioners reverse the order
* Alternatively, a single larger white candle right in the centre to signify the undifferentiated divine energy
* An optional Goddess statue from your favourite tradition or a God/Goddess pairing from your favourite culture (it is permissible magickally to mix cultures; God on the right is my preferred positioning) or a round amber crystal for the Goddess and a pointed jet crystal for the God (some practitioners attribute jet to the Goddess, but since in the Scandinavian tradition amber is called the tears of Freyja, the goddess of magick, this seems a stronger association for me)
* A dish or flat pentacle to hold the symbol that will act as the focus of the ritual

Dedicating your indoor altar

Work in the morning when you wake. In this dedication you will use all six candles (the Goddess, God and the four elemental ones), the bowl of salt (Earth), the athame (Air), the wand (Fire) and the bowl of water (Water) to signify the four elements. You will also need the pentacle plate in the north and incense in the east. (If you are using loose incense on charcoal, heat the charcoal before you start, so that it will be hot when you come to use it.)

* Stand facing the north just south of the altar. Begin by stating your purpose:

> *I dedicate this altar as my special space of sanctity and of positive power.*

* First light the left Goddess candle and from that the right God candle and say:

> *I ask that the Lord and Lady bless this altar and my work that it and I may be through your light instruments of the greatest good and the highest intent.*

* Next you are going to incorporate the powers of the four directional and elemental Guardians, to protect the altar and to join their powers to create the fifth element within the altar. Light each directional candle, first the north from the Goddess candle, the east from the north, and so on clockwise, asking at each quarter beginning in the north that each of the Guardian powers will grant you

its special blessing on the altar and your work. Look into each candle flame and even if you are experienced you may see each Guardian in a new way.

* When you have lit all four directional candles, take the bowl of salt in your left hand and set it partly on the flat pentacle plate in the north and to its right, and partially on the pentacle plate the bowl of water.

* Taking your athame in your power hand, touch the surface of the salt and then the surface of the water with the blade, saying for each:

May you be blessed and purified, empowered and sanctified, Earth, Air and Water as now you are united.

The athame is the Air input.

* Return the knife to its place and take nine pinches of salt from the bowl and one by one add them to the water bowl.

* Replace the salt bowl in the north and swirl the water bowl clockwise with both hands saying:

Be joined in power and in purity. Empower and purify this altar and my work.

* Now for the Fire. Holding the saltwater bowl in your receptive hand, take the wand (Fire) in your power hand. Circle a few centimetres above the bowl containing the salt/water mix with your wand nine times clockwise and say:

Three by three the power I raise, three by three may the elements mingle, fuse and call wise power and healing to my altar and my work.

* Return the wand to its place and sprinkle with your power hand the salt water droplets in three circles clockwise on the ground, beginning in the north to enclose the whole altar and then in spirals between the artefacts and candles on the altar. Repeat softly three times:

Life ,light , love and loveliness enter here, the love of the Lady, the life of the Lord, the loveliness and light of the Guardians.

* Return the water bowl to the west, saying:

Blessed by Earth and Water, safe from all harm. So I dedicate this sacred space and my endeavours.

* Light your loose incense on the preheated charcoal or a single incense stick. Pass it round the edge of the altar in three clockwise circles and say:

So may all be sacred and of worth.

* Return the incense to its place and finally pass the candle of the south round the entire circle, clockwise three times, beginning in the north, saying:

Flame and flare that my altar and my work may be filled with inspiration, creativity, vitality and above all be cleansed of all that is not of worth or worthy in me. Blessings be on all.

* Finally, facing north and standing to the south of the altar, with your wand held in the air in front of you just higher than your head, make the invoking or

opening pentagram of power shown on the left, below. This symbolises the connection of your own power amplified through the altar.

* Raise your arms above your head in a V to allow the power to merge with that of the sky, rising upwards through your energy centres and flowing downwards through your feet towards the earth and up again so that you are filled with rainbow light. I have written more about your chakras or energy centres on page 179, because these are a vital source of power raising in spell casting and ritual.

* Even if you are unfamiliar with these ideas, think of your body as filled with whirling rainbow spheres: red at the base (the root of your spine and the soles of your feet); rising up orange at your navel; yellow, the stomach area; green, radiating from your heart, down your arms to your hands; blue around your throat; rising as indigo/purple round the centre of your brow; and finally rising as violet, gold and white from the crown of your head.

* Think of your altar likewise filled with the rainbow light, flowing from you as you now hold your hands fingers downwards over the centre. You and the altar are momentarily one, joined with the white light of the lord and lady, the four elemental coloured lights emanating from the four Guardians and the rich red light rising for the earth (and when you work outdoors the greens of the different nature essences).

* Make the banishing or closing pentagram in front of you facing the north of the altar and say:

The dedication is complete. Blessings be.

* Leave the candles and incense to burn through.

Smudge over the altar weekly using a smudge stick or incense if you have not used it and before setting it for a ritual with anticlockwise and clockwise spirals alternately, or use a lighted sage, lemon or pine incense stick. You can do this if you need to put the altar away.

If you already have an altar, you can use the above ritual to rededicate it and give it fresh impetus.

The inner temple

Your physical altar is the connection between you and the spiritual or astral planes. The more easily you can transform the visible by the invisible, the actual into the potential, the more powerfully you can connect your words and actions with the almost limitless source of magickal energy from whatever time and place calls you.

Spend time in your indoor magickal place and allow the images and sensations to build up, carried on incense fragrance and soft candlelight. Eventually, you'll only have to light your candle and incense to be in your marble temple open to the stars, the dark cool sanctuary deep in the earth belonging to a mystery religion, Egyptian inner sanctum or an enclosed silk walled room with a jewelled vaulted ceiling and pillars of pure gold. This is more than fantasy, because you are connecting your own individual power to that of different ages and places that have left their aura or imprint.

If you believe in past lives, you may well have followed other magickal traditions and may recall dimly some of these earlier settings as you allow your altar to connect you with the collective magickal well of wisdom. A group or coven can create a joint vision that takes on form and spiritual reality, and helps to strengthen the collective group psyche, a wonderful preparation for when you try to draw down the power of the Goddess and God either individually or as a group. Above all, you can invite your Witch Guardian to teach and inspire you in these quiet times.

The outdoor altar

Covens sometimes have a special place where they can meet, perhaps an area of woodland or a private large garden. There may be a focal point where the altar is set up. If you are a solitary practitioner, you might have a special spot used regularly for rituals by you and anyone you work with. In both cases, the tools and formation of the altar may not be very different from your indoor altar, apart from the addition of outdoor tools, such as a fire dish and a larger cauldron.

If possible, try to make a small, permanent, private, outdoor altar. As a bonus of an outdoor altar, you will discover that your garden flourishes, that all manner of wild birds and small animals are attracted to it, and that the atmosphere is always one of vitality mixed with tranquillity.

Creating a permanent outdoor altar

Try to find a spot that is relatively sheltered so you don't get too buffeted in inclement weather. Gazebos are good for wet-day outdoor rituals. It is very easy to mark out a permanent area round an outdoor altar using stones trees or bushes. You can have a protective square and then cast a circle within that as part of the ritual (see week 19).

You need a small table to serve as your altar, either circular or square. Choose natural wood (you can weatherproof it), but not metal or plastic. Alternatively, use a large piece of slate or flat stone raised on bricks or stones. Garden centres often sell boulders and you may find one flat and wide enough to make an altar; or make a stone pile or harrow, like the Vikings did.

You do not need a cloth, but a small piece of slate in the centre is useful on which to set your symbol dish and other small pieces, and you can use other pieces of slate to put under anything hot, such as your candle and incense.

How much you leave in place will depend on how private the altar is, but if possible hold the energies between rituals with the four main elemental symbols below and also a central God/Goddess focus. Their weathering and decaying is part of the process and makes your altar part of the changing year. Below I have only listed the altar tools and substances that differ from the indoor altar.

North/Earth/midnight

* A dark pillar stone of about 15-23 cm (6-9 in) high, rounded on top, square or diamond shaped
* A pot of growing herbs or a flowering plant in an Earth fragrance, such as heather or vervain; optional, but they offer a focus for nature energies and essences, especially if you live in a town or are working on a patio or balcony (you will need to trim and replace them regularly)
* A bowl of dried herbs, fresh or dried petals or soil instead of salt in suitable rituals, added before the ritual (salt should not be scattered on grass or cultivated soil); cast your circle round the altar space with a bowl of dark earth if it is soft and dry, then use incense and water as the other two circles – see page 250)

East/Air/dawn

* A tall narrow ceramic container with several feathers in black, white or grey
* A pot of growing herbs or flowers in an Air fragrance, such as fennel or dill
* For rituals, a large smudge stick in sagebrush or cedar to the east; this is sometimes substituted for incense in outdoor rituals, but of course you can burn incense as well (you may be able to get an abalone shell with natural holes to hold the smudge as it burns or burn large dried herbs like sagebrush without charcoal in the shell or a flat heatproof dish)

South/Fire/noon

* A tall, thin, pointed pillar-type red stone rock, like an obelisk, of similar size to the Earth one
* A Fire fragrance herb or flower, such as chamomile or rosemary

- An outdoor wand: for example, a natural twisted piece of wood or wand-shaped twig (you can weatherproof it)
- For rituals, use an undyed beeswax candle for Fire and similar for God/Goddess altar candles; you can buy naturally dyed beeswax candles for elemental candles

West/Water/twilight

- An unglazed ceramic bowl to catch rainwater
- A Water fragrance herb or flowering plant, such as lemon balm or feverfew
- For rituals, add a pottery or wooden chalice if possible

The centre

- Natural God and Goddess representations; for example, one or two small branches of wood or rock with a face and shape of deities naturally etched within; alternatively, carve out a rough shape from two pieces of wood or make your own pottery representations (you can buy clay that does not need firing); when the wood or clay crumbles, you know that it is time to bury the old artefacts and create new
- A large conch-like shell for the female/Goddess and a bone horn or small antler for the male/God
- Small stone statues or a single female one to signify the united divinity forces

Around the altar

- Asperge, often associated with the west (see page 116)
- Broomstick or besom (comes into its own with an outdoor altar), south of the altar lying horizontally at the foot of the altar bristles east to west or, if leaned upright, with bristles uppermost; a vertical broom is set outside the circle to the south west (see page 117)
- Cauldron, north to west or in the centre, depending on the nature of the ritual; cover in inclement weather or bring outdoors when needed (see page 118)
- Fire dish (the single most valuable outdoor tool) set on the ground to the south of the altar or used as the centre of rituals, either a specially crafted one of copper or iron, or any large, fireproof, metal dish either with metal legs or raised on heat-resistant bricks to avoid scorching; this can be a very large cast iron wok or the bottom half of a domed iron barbecue, again the kind with legs (a chiminea is also a good source of fire)
- You can also create a less permanent ring of fire round the altar with outdoor torches and garden incense
- Staff or stang, north or east outside the circle as a Guardian (always north for the stang, see page 121); set in place before a ritual or at significant times when you need extra protection of the area.

PRACTICAL ASSIGNMENT

Dedicating the outdoor altar

Your outdoor altar will be naturally cleansed and empowered by the physical elements manifest in rain, wind, as well as the sun and moon. Because of these flowing natural powers, the dedication will also be less formal. Dedicate it with the light of morning.

You will be working with your outdoor wand and a smudge stick in sagebrush or cedar or a large incense stick in a tree fragrance, such as pine or eucalyptus. You will also need a bowl of soil or petals in the north and a bowl of rain or bubbling tap water in the west.

* The first time you set up the altar (or when you rededicate it), sweep the area in anticlockwise circles with your besom or broomstick and then asperge or ritually cleanse it with water it by using a bundle of evergreen twigs tied together dipped in a large bowl of rain or bubbling tap. Ask that only goodness and light shall remain.

* Stand at the west side of the altar facing east; this is a light dedication, even if the sun is not shining. Light the incense stick or smudge and hold it in your power hand.

* Move round the altar clockwise and stop at the east side of the altar. Face inwards and over the centre of the altar raise the smudge skywards and then down towards the centre saying:

> *By sky and wind, may this altar and my work be blessed and empowered by the light of the morning.*

* Then face outwards east so your back is to the altar and repeat the empowerment, ending by extending the smudge at a 45-degree eastwards with the words:

> *So far as the eye can see and my words be heard, may my heart extend in love.*

* Replace the smudge and continue to the south. Raise the wand skywards and to the Earth, facing inwards towards the centre of the altar as with the smudge.

* Repeat the actions facing outwards to the south with your back touching the altar, again ending by extending the wand outwards to the south. This time change the words slightly to begin:

> *By Fire and Sun may this altar...*

* Walk to the west and raise and lower the water bowl over the altar to Sky and Earth facing inwards (looking east), then outwards to the west, and in outstretched hands at chest height, offering the water outwards to the west. This time alter the beginning to:

> *By Moon and Sea may this altar...*

Go to the north and taking the bowl of soil raise and lower it first facing inwards (looking south) and the outwards north back against the altar, finally offering it at chest height with both hands to the north. This time begin:

By Angels and by Mother Earth may this altar...

❋ Finally, take the smudge and beginning in the east walk in three clockwise circles round the altar, saying:

So grows light in the east, the south, the west and north. Blessed be you guardians who stand watch at the four quarters, kind angels, devas, elemental spirits and nature essences and not least the wise ancestors. I greet also my Witch Guardian and ask for her continuing counsel and her guardianship.

❋ This might be a good time to set down the smudge and put in place your outdoor guardian stone or crystal to the north of the altar parallel with where you will set your staff (see page 121).

❋ If you wish, you can also plant seeds in the bowl of soil and water it from the bowl in the west. Smudge over the bowl of seeds and finally pass the wand over it three times. You could use another bowl in the north and keep the seeds in the centre as a symbol of the life of the altar. (If they do not thrive, you can plant some more.)

❋ Whether or not you plant the seeds, end the ritual by sitting quietly in the south facing the altar so that you are touching the ground. Raise your arms high and wide and say:

You are all welcome. I offer you honour and give reverence to all that is created in sky, sea, flowing waters and that lives above and within the earth. Blessings be. The dedication is complete.

❋ You can smudge the altar occasionally if there has been a long dry period or you sense the power is not as great as usual.

Further information

Recommended reading

❋ Duffy, Eamonn, *The Stripping of the Altars ,Traditional Religion in England from 1400–1580* ,Yale University Press, 2005 (Nothing to do with altars as such, but a good insight into what happened in conventional religion as background to the Witchcraft persecutions)

❋ Linn, Denise, *Altars, Bringing Sacred Shrines into your Everyday Life*, Rider, 1998

❋ MacGregor Mathers, S. L., and others, *Ritual Magic of the Golden Dawn*, Destiny Books, 1997

❋ Streep, Peg, *Altars Made Easy, a Complete Guide to Creating and Using your Personal Altar*, Harper San Francisco, 1998

Websites

❋ *Occult 100*
Good index of altar topics and information, as well as other magick info
www.occult100.com/bos/

❋ *Magic Rituals*
Good for solitary practitioner altars
www.magicrituals.com/bosaltar.htm

❋ *Paisley Magick*
Nice pictures, ideas and links to other altar pages
http://paisleyblue.bravepages.com/altar.html

TRANSFORMING YOUR ALTAR FOR SPECIAL RITES

In this module I will first describe how to transform your altar into a night-focused altar for special rites and for work at night with the stars and moon. Night altars are excellent for bringing out the clairvoyance of a witch and for developing magickal abilities on a deep level. Then we will work with an Egyptian altar formation, ideal for indoor and formal work and an outdoor natural magick-based Norse altar. There is more about working with the sun and on Egyptian altar rituals later (see page 501).

Though you may not adopt these different traditions, each has features that will enrich Wiccan altar work.

Preparing a night altar

If you live in an area where there is bright street lighting, you may wish to put heavy dark curtains at the window of your altar room and perhaps one over the door to enclose your night space. Outdoors you should work away from any light.

Cover the altar with a dark blue cloth. Position candles chosen from the colours listed below, to the left and right of the centre of the altar. You can have a set of night altar artefacts, either of silver, glass or dark wood or stone.

In the centre of the altar, some people have a statue of one of the moon deities in dark wood or plaster. You can get some beautiful Egyptian Goddess figurines or a Black Madonna and child, the Virgin Mary in her winter, earth aspect modelled on the Egyptian Isis and her son Horus. Circle this statue with your favourite small, dark crystals. However, you may prefer to have a vase of white flowers, the colour of the Moon, as your focus or a large crystal (see below).

Set a large dark crystal sphere in the centre of your night altar, either in front of or as a substitute for a statue. Amethyst or purple fluorite are particularly powerful, or use an uncut piece of amethyst or an amethyst geode. Amethyst is the single most healing and protective night stone and need not be expensive if you use the unpolished kind.

A night wand need not be long, but should be pointed at one end and made of a dark crystal. Often you can buy a smoky quartz crystal point quite cheaply. Use it for casting circles in formal night rituals, for stirring salt into water to create circles of protection and for directing healing rays. You can also improvise with a long, twisted corkscrew twig from a moon tree, such as alder, sycamore or willow.

Have either a dark witch's mirror or a smoked glass bowl half filled with water in the centre of your altar to use as a scrying bowl or dark mirror.

* **Night candle colours:** dark red, silver, rich dark green, grey, deep purple, midnight blue, burnished gold
* **Night incenses and oils:** jasmine, patchouli, pine, sandalwood, myrrh, mimosa, rose
* **Night crystals:** apache tear/obsidian, angelite/celestite, smoky quartz, purple and green fluorite rutilated quartz, jet, blue beryl, rose quartz, moonstone/selenite, garnet, jade, pearl, opal, onyx, sodalite, dark agates

Working with your night altar

Sometimes you will want just to sit in front of the night altar, having lit your candles and incense, holding your crystal or gazing into the scrying bowl or mirror lit by candlelight. Allow chants and empowerments to form in your mind. This inner magick is very powerful. At other times you may weave rituals in the usual way, but either outdoors beneath the moon and stars or indoors by candlelight.

Any release of night power is softer, like a hiss made by a snake, very smooth and with sinuous rhythmic movements. This can be absorbed by the darkness, the stars or mother moon and transformed into healing or positive effect in the morning like dew. Dew was once believed to be the discarded dreams and tears of humans transformed by the moon into new hope and that sums up night magick.

Seeing the night rainbow

We think of the night as black, but once you become familiar with using it magickally you may become aware of its essential colours, even when it is pitch dark and no candles are lit. You may see any or all of deep inky blues, smoky grey, ruby red, rich deep emerald, amethyst and silver, even faint burnished gold.

Persevere with the technique below as once you can see the night rainbow you are opening powerful channels of your mind and spirit that can be used for healing and for channelling goddess wisdom. Try to work for seven consecutive nights or if not, leave as few gaps as possible.

* You will need all seven of the night rainbow candle colours, dark red, silver, grey, rich dark green, deep purple, midnight blue and burnished gold. On night one, light the first of your night-coloured candles, beginning with your favourite colour and adding one more colour each night, until by the seventh night you have lit them all.
* Each night sit by the light for about five minutes, visualising the colour(s) extending as a halo round the flames.
* After about five minutes blow out the candles in reverse order of lighting and you may see the after glow of colours for a minute or two.
* Each night you will see the aura of the colours on the darkness for a little longer after the candles are extinguished.
* By the seventh night you have all seven colours. Half close your eyes and the colours will merge and dance. As you extinguish them, imagine the colours merging into your night rainbow.

* On the eighth night, light only the first colour candle you chose. Picture the other colours emerging from the darkness. If you persevere, if necessary repeating the eight night cycle, in time you will see your night rainbow spontaneously whenever you enter your special place or work outdoors, even in pitch blackness.

The Ancient Egyptian altar

Why should the altars of a long dead civilisation be of value in modern magick? Partly because Egypt was so influential on ritual magick. What is more, this graceful and timeless form of spirituality offers a way in which solitary practitioners especially can link into the power of ancient ceremony wherever they practise magick.

The temple was the house of the God or deities and where the ka or soul of the god dwelled. Its form and rituals were considered a reflection of the universe and the way or maintaining order over chaos. Though we no longer literally believe that the spirit of the Gods dwells within the statues or altars we set up, nevertheless they can act as a way of making the link for us.

In timeless rituals using water, perfume and incense, we can establish a harmonious rhythm to bring order and serenity in our lives that can stand against the frantic activity of the modern world. You may only want to use this form of altar on certain occasions or perhaps adapt some of the features to your Wiccan altar, so although I give a full system simply take whatever you want from it.

The Egyptian altar is traditionally a square or rectangular table or large piece of stone supported on bricks. If you want a cloth, use a square of white linen or cotton that does not quite cover the tabletop.

The tools and substances of Egyptian magick

Egyptian altars and practitioners face south, the direction of the source of the Nile. All you have to remember is that when you stand in the north facing south, Water and the west is on your right hand (though, of course, in exactly the same position). The elements are the same as for Wicca, with Earth in the north and so on.

* **South:** A simple oil lamp with a wick or a beeswax candle to represent the element of Fire
* **North:** A small tray with soft yellow sand, some heaped in the centre to form a pyramid mound representing the first earth that rose from the waters; alternatively, a small squat pyramid in crystal, such as white or yellow calcite
* **East:** An incense burner and incense; traditionally, frankincense was burned at dawn, myrrh at noon and Cyphi, Kyphi or Kapet at dusk, but you can substitute sandalwood for Cyphi if you cannot obtain it
* **West:** A small ceramic bowl for water; no temple is compete without its lake to represent the primal waters from which life came
* **Centre:** A statue or a picture of one or more of your favourite deities or a pottery or stone animal to represent their animal form, if they have one; Hathor or Bastet the cat-headed Goddess was popular on family altars; or a deep pottery bowl in which to place daily fragrant offerings such as flowers, potpourri, incense, herbs or spices

- **North-west:** Sistrum; wand (see page 123)
- **South-east:** A round or oval hand mirror, sacred to the goddess Hathor, patroness of women, music and dance, often decorated with Hathor or the eye of Ra or Re, the sun God from which the first Hathor mirror was formed; used to catch the light on your altar (traditionally the rays of sunset) and to reflect the power into an amulet or charm or to remove pain and for divination; used for scrying
- **South-west:** Perfume in a small bottle with a stopper to which you can add fragrances; since Egyptian perfume is alcohol free and pure oil, an essential oil is a good substitute (Lotus and papyrus are traditional but you can use rose, sandalwood, chamomile, frankincense or myrrh and dilute it with a carrier oil such as almond or virgin olive oil – 7-10 drops of essential oil to 30 ml of carrier oils, slightly less essential oil if using for personal anointing); alternatively, use a rose or lavender water
- Four very tiny dishes to hold the perfume for anointing one at each of the main directions on your altar

Dedicating your Egyptian altar

Rather than a once-and-for-all dedication, each time you begin a ritual using your Ancient Egyptian altar you can purify the altar. Indeed, in ancient tradition it was purified three or four times a day as part of the daily temple life. Few of us would have the time to do that, but the triple purification is a powerful method for making a particular day sacred: perhaps a birthday or a milestone in your life, just to halt the rush of days or when sharing a spiritual weekend with good friends. I have written about the triple/quadruple ceremonies at dawn, noon, sunset and midnight on page 496.

The following is a more general triple dedication that can be used not only when you set up/use an Egyptian altar but also whenever you wish to mark a significant private or group altar time, whatever form of altar you are working with. It can be incorporated into other rituals. Face south and move round the altar sunwise.

Purification by water

- Walking from the north of the altar as you stand facing south, pass round directly to the west.
- Take the bowl of water from the altar and holding it in your receptive hand continue round the altar through the south then the east and finally back to the north. As you walk, scatter a few drops of water at each of the four corners of the altar, beginning in the north-west corner and proceeding to the south-west, the south-east and finally the north-east corner.
- At each corner say:

  With the waters of the celestial Nile, I purify this altar and this ritual/my work. Satis and Anukis, Goddesses of the Nile waters who pour cooling waters on the parched land, I call your wisdom and your healing into this place of sanctity.

- Return the water to its place, return to the north of the altar and stand facing south.

Perfume purification

* From the centre of the altar, pick up the perfume bottle and remove the stopper. Holding the bottle in your hands as you stand in the north, facing south, walk round to the south of the altar via the west and pour a little of the fragrance into the small dish.

* Inhale the scent and place a single drop on your brow with the index finger of your power hand. (If you are sensitive to the oil, do it symbolically.)

* Do this at all four directions saying:

> *With the fragrance of the sacred lotus of Egypt I purify this altar and my work. Nefertum, young God of perfume, youth and beauty who rose from the lotus at the dawning of the first day, I call your vitality and your life giving powers into this place of sanctity.*

* Return to the north and face south.

Purification by fire and incense

* Walk round to the south via the west and light the candle or lamp.

* Proceed to the east where you will add the first incense to preheated charcoal. As you do this, say:

> *With Air and Fire, with Fire and Air, I purify this altar and my work. Horus, hawk of dawn and Lord of the Sky and you mighty Ra, Master of the noonday sun, as together you soar golden. I call your light and inspiration into this place of sanctity.*

The altar is now ready and you can place offerings of flowers or loose incense and tiny fresh fruits in the offerings dish, giving thanks first for the blessings of your life, however small, and then asking blessings on your altar and on any who need power and healing, including you.

PRACTICAL ASSIGNMENT

The Norse altar

I wrote on page 125 about the stone Norse altar called the harrow that was either a pile of stones with a flat top or large black stone with an indentation in the centre. Much natural magick in the UK and America has been influenced by the Viking magickal tradition. You may not want to use a full Norse altar setting, but a number of artefacts, such as the arm ring, are excellent tools in modern witchcraft.

Tools in the Norse tradition

Centre

* **The Arm Ring:** The most important item on the altar (see page 125) and a focus for personal empowerment; many contained a large proportion of silver
* **Offerings Bowl:** A large wooden or copper offerings dish or bowl on which some of the cooked food from the feast that is central to the Norse blöt or ritual (or token food) is offered to the deities; traditionally set to the north of the arm ring
* **Seax or ritual knife:** Set horizontally, west to east, blade to the east, to the south of the arm ring

North

* **Horn:** Curved hunting horn blown at the beginning and end of a ceremony; you can substitute a rattle

East

* **Incense:** Dried herbs were burned in a small fire pot often stone and flat with a handle like a mini frying pan, called in some traditions a recels; buy smudge sticks or use large dried leaves of sagebrush in an open heatproof ceramic or metal pot; alternatively burn leafy or woody incense fragrances rather than floral or ceremonial

South

* **Hammer:** Banged on the altar three times to open a rite or raise power, set vertically, handle to south, on south to north line of the harrow
* **Spear (optional):** To direct power, in which case it will stand to the south of the altar, point to the east horizontally on an east-west line (you can use a long, pointed ash wand but wands as such are not part of the tradition)
* **Large red candle or fire torch**

West

* **Drinking horn or horn or bone cup or bowl:** Made of wood or copper, equivalent to the chalice, this also serves as the blessings bowl and used to contain mead or water for drinking and blessing the altar during the ritual

- **Asperge:** A fresh leafy branch is used every time, usually of ash, oak or pine, dipped into the drinking horn; some practitioners have a separate drinking horn/cup and blessings bowl

South of the altar

- **Cooking pot:** Traditionally made of iron or stone, the fire over which it hung also gave light (or substitute a kettle-type domed barbecue); feasts in which humans and deities shared were a feature of the major Norse rites and for this reason the cooking pot was considered a ritual tool; it can be set just outside the sacred area for a group seasonal celebration to the south (or if alone you can have a dish of bread and hard Scandinavian cheese); some of the feast or token food was offered to the deities mixed with mead in the offerings bowl

Dedicating the Norse altar

- Set the harrow with a minimum of the arm ring, candle, incense, blessing bowl/ drinking horn half filled with mead or water, the offerings bowl containing crumbled bread or food cooked from the feast and the seax or hammer.
- Light the central candle and the incense and leave them in place.
- Standing at the south of the altar, face the north, the direction of Ice, and raise the seax to the skies and then down to the earth three times or bang the hammer three times on the altar calling on the Sky Father Odin and Frigg the Earth Mother or Freyr the fertility Father and Nerthus the ancient Grain Mother to bless the altar and grant you power and wisdom as you work.
- Repeat facing south, the direction of Fire, standing at the north of the altar.
- Next make the Thurisaz Hammer of Thor rune sign in the air first to the north (from the south) and then south (from the north), asking for the protection of Thor on the altar and on your work.

The offerings

- Facing north, standing in front of the harrow in the south, raise the goblet or drinking horn/bowl upwards to the skies and drink from it saying:

Blessings.

- Return it to its place.
- Next raise the offerings bowl and take some bread or cooked food from it to eat, saying:

Abundance.

- Lift the drinking horn/bowl again and tip some of the mead into the offerings bowl and say:

Strength and unity, health and stability.

- Return them to their places.

* Take the asperging twig and dip it into the drinking vessel. Sprinkle the liquid clockwise around the harrow, beginning in the north, and make a complete circle of liquid drops, saying:

Bless all who come in peace and kinship, gods and humans, ancestors and land wights and all you hidden beings of earth, land and sea. You are welcome to share these offerings and this rite and in return I ask your blessing and protection on my altar.

* Return the drinking vessel and asperge to the altar.
* Tip the offerings bowl on the ground to the north of the altar, saying:

I offer this to Father Odin, to Lady Frigg his consort, wise Spinner of Fate, to Freyr of the hunt and grain, to golden Freyja loveliest of all and thee wise Mother Nerthus of the Earth. I offer you my altar in good service.

* Bang the hammer or raise the seax three times as at the beginning of the rite and then say:

The bargain is sealed, the dedication complete. Thor is satisfied.

* Leave the candle and incense to burn through.
* You can re-empower the altar before or during rituals.

Further research

Recommended reading

* Clark, Rosemary, *Sacred Magick of Ancient Egypt, Spiritual Practice Restored*, Llewellyn, 2003
* Thorsson, Edred, *Northern Magick, Mysteries of the Norse, Germans and English*, Llewellyn, 1998

Websites

* *Alternative Religions*
  Excellent links to information about the Norse religion and its revival
  http://altreligion.about.com/od/astaru/
* *Tour Egypt*
  Extensive overview of Egyptian religion
  www.touregypt.net/featurestories/religion.htm

SPELLCASTING

("**A**")leister Crowley said that every intentional act is a magickal act. Or put another way every magickal act is an intentional act, in the same way that a beam of energy deliberately focused on one spot is far more powerful than if it was dispersed randomly and over a wide area.

Think of the *Some day my prince will come* scenario. All a bit vague and ineffectual as the Goose Girl or dispossessed princess dreams about her prince as she washes a never-ending pile of dishes. But then she sings the words and the bluebirds join in — and that stirs the energies sufficiently to attract a Fairy Godmother who can wave her wand and generally get things moving. Of course, if the princess had cast a spell in the first place, that would have set matters in motion rather faster. The released energies would have directed the prince telepathically towards her scullery and stirred up her own inner energies to tell the Wicked Stepmother (or Ugly Sisters, depending on the script) that she wasn't scouring the pots and pans any more and was off to the ball, if necessary in her designer rags. Her energy field would have been so radiant no one would have noticed her frock anyway, least of all the enamoured prince.

Spellcasting is all about focusing, raising and releasing power so that we, or the person on whom the energies are focused, are empowered to bring the thoughts into reality. This module explores ways in which we can use our personal energy system and that of the earth, nature, the cosmos and other people to amplify our inner powers to effect positive change through magick.

How do spells work?

Psychology

Most witches know that magick and psychology are sisters. If you cast a spell, you psyche yourself up and fill yourself with enough self-confidence and determination to take a much more proactive approach to life. For example, you apply for jobs you might have thought out of your league or demand of a lover the considerate treatment everyone else tells you that you deserve. The placebo effect should not be underestimated and like many witches I have been thanked for the brilliant results of a spell before I have cast it. The same applies when people feel the effects of a hex as soon as someone informs them of the ill intent, whether or not they have actually been cursed.

However, spells are so much more than psychology. Psychology doesn't cover, for example, the magick arrival of precisely the required amount of money from a totally unpredicted source to the caster of a money spell, at the time it is most urgently needed. Processes like visualisation and empowerments that are good psychological tools can be made even more effective within the concentrated structure of a spell. In this way, the imagined results are manifest more quickly and powerfully than could have been anticipated by a change in attitude and positive thinking alone. What is more, if you believe in yourself/the spellcaster (the psychology part), then changes can be made on the thought plane that are translated into positive tangible results (the magickal component).

Raising the level of awareness/consciousness by the spellcaster

Changes made on one level can effect changes at another: a sound scientific principle. Energy raising within a spell lifts the awareness of the spellcaster/s to a level beyond that accessible by and to the conscious mind.

In spellcasting, we can move beyond the material and logical levels restricted by measured clock time and the sequential ordering of events and the manipulation of matter on a physical level. It becomes possible to operate on the spiritual or non-tangible level where such restrictions do not apply. Every symbol used as the focus of a spell contains an energy field round it, made up of magickal and mythological associations as well as personal ones, if the object belongs to the spellcaster or the person for whom the spell is being cast.

In the spell, we can activate the inherent power of the symbol by raising our own level of energy to access the higher levels of our spiritual aura or energy fields. At this higher level, we can access the power necessary to transform the need or desire represented by the symbol into tangible results on the material or Earth plane.

Concentrated energy sources

Obviously you are going to need to generate and then release a lot of energy to accomplish that transference, which is the reason spellcasting is tiring. Energy comes from your personal rainbow-coloured energy system or chakras, combined with that of anyone you are working with, hence the release of power is often described as a cone of coloured stars that cascade into the sky.

The forces of nature are also energy sources. These may be actual, such as the earth, from trees, flowers, herbs and crystals, either in the place you are working or concentrated within the circle or on the altar. They are also kindled through the elemental substances of the four elements: salt for Earth; incense for Air; candle for Fire; and Water.

Energy also comes from higher sources: the four Guardians of the Watchtowers, Devas or higher nature essences, your Witch Guardian, the wise ancestors, Angels and Archangels, especially the four who traditionally protect the circle, Uriel in the North, Raphael in the East, Michael in the South and Gabriel in the West, and finally the God and Goddess in whatever form you name and call them within the spell or ritual.

For spellcasting the personal energy system is the most important.

The chakra system

Chakras (Sanskrit for wheel) are energy vortices, sometimes called padmas or lotuses, because they have been described as jewels surrounded by whirling lotus petals. These psychic centres that have also been likened to whirling discs, spheres or spinning coloured discs, are the channels through which the life force flows from the sky and earth, from animals, trees, plants, crystals and other people.

This core energy is processed and filtered via the cone-like seal in the centre of each chakra, forming a channel from the seven layers of the aetheric or rainbow spirit body to the physical body. These layers are woven into and influence the steps of spellcasting and the process becomes largely spontaneous as you develop your magickal abilities. The light and influence of each sphere merges with the one above and below.

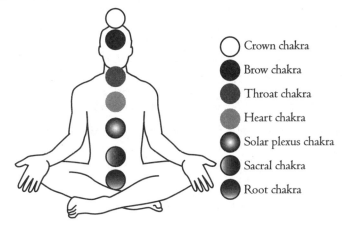

As well as the chakra or aura colours that you can visualise and may see as you move outwards and upwards through the levels, so each spiritual plane that exists independent of this system has its own ray colour. As you are able to connect with the different and progressively more ethereal layers of your aura, so your awareness of these spiritual planes increases. For this reason each plane is associated with a particular aura level and the chakra that fuels it.

The following explains how each energy centre is involved, its psychic senses and the higher levels of the aura and the corresponding planes that allow you to activate and perform magick.

The Root or Base chakra or Maladhara, linked with the etheric layer/earth or etheric plane

* **Fragrance:** Lilac, patchouli or strawberry

* **Ray:** Violet

* **Magickal energy:** The source of magick

This first aura level is powered by the red Base or Root chakra or psychic body energy centre that is located around the perineum as you sit on the ground, the base of the spine and the minor chakras in the soles of your feet. The Earth plane is the one closest to Mother Earth on which we walk and so it is linked with the physical form of the spell, the symbol you use, the elemental substances, your tools and the energies of crystals, flowers, herbs and trees though these also affect the more spiritual levels.

This also is the level of the Root or driving energy of the spell power. At this stage as you perhaps make the symbol from wax or clay and state aloud the purpose of the spell, you activate your own raw, red, Root energy, linked with an energy called Kundalini. This can be envisaged as a serpent coiled around the base of your spine, and is named after an ancient Hindu serpent and Earth goddess who empowered the gods.

Here as you begin you will become aware of your Witch Guardian who will guide you from the Earth plane upwards. It is the level at which you cast the circle (whether visualised or actual, for this is a realm that links with meditative powers and dreams, and so is the gateway to the spiritual). In this way, you mark the protected and empowered space in which you will weave your magick and imprint the physical space with psychic power. This level gives you earthing, grounding, protection and is also where you return to after the spell energies are released. Having travelled upwards through your chakras, the released power bounces back into you and the symbol so it can act as a charm.

Picture the red Root energy rising from the earth and your energy uncoiling, so that as you touch the symbol it vibrates with potential.

The Sacral chakra or Svadisthana linked with the emotional layer/ astral plane

* **Fragrance:** Carnation or myrrh
* **Ray:** Rose
* **Magick energy:** Warmth and emotion

The second layer of the aura is powered by the orange Sacral chakra. It is located around the top of your genitals/womb and radiates to just below the navel.

Astral comes from the Latin word for star and this is the plane in which imagination or visualisation lifts the physical spell and endows it with the all-important emotion, the belief in the spell and the desire for it to succeed. This is a vital stage in spellcasting and from this plane you can draw energy if outdoors from nature essences and from the Guardians of the Watchtowers. In Native North American spirituality, this is the level of the wise clan animals located at the points around the Medicine Wheel. This is also the level of mythological archetypes or universal symbols. As you endow your symbol with the elemental qualities through the elemental substances, the symbol will become animate and the words you speak are likewise animated with power (more of this in later modules on writing chants and the power of words, see page 293). The Sacral chakra is also linked with the moon and so this inner sphere may be pictured flecked with silver stars.

Visualise the red Root energy now mingling with the orange and silver of this sphere that is specially activated by moonlight (or silver candles). The orange in your aura will become brighter and, like the symbol, draw power from the elemental substances and the Guardians of the Elements. As the light pours into the symbol you may sense the symbol beginning to glow and to feel warmer and lighter if you hold it or pass it round a group.

The Solar Plexus chakra or Manipura, linked with the mental layer/rainbow plane

* **Fragrance:** Lily or mint
* **Ray:** Orange
* **Magick energy:** Raising power

The third level of the aura is powered by the golden yellow Solar Plexus chakra. It is located around the stomach area or slightly higher in the upper stomach.

This is the layer of power and of the beginning of the transformation of the purpose of the spell on to a higher plane. This is where the spiritual template or form of the symbol is manipulated magickally on a more abstract level, and all kinds of insights may come to you as you chant or move. You receive extra energy from your Spirit Guides and those guides of any people whom you are working with, as well as the wise ancestors, if called upon.

Visualise the Sacral orange energy now spiralling and growing, pushing the yellow Solar Plexus energies upwards and also outwards into the symbol. As the yellow in your aura becomes brighter so you move into alignment with magickal energies. As you start to raise the power through words and actions, so you become less aware of the physical surroundings and of the planned structure of the spell. Words and actions become spontaneous as your own personal boundaries become more fluid.

The Solar Plexus is also linked with the sun and so the inner sphere may be touched with rays of gold. It is especially activated by sunlight.

The Heart chakra or Anahata, the astral layer/Buddhic plane

* **Fragrance:** Rose or thyme
* **Ray:** Yellow
* **Magick energy:** Merging with focus of spell; integration

The fourth layer of the aura is ruled by the green Heart chakra and links the three lower and personally orientated chakras and aura levels with those that connect to higher dimensions. It is located in the centre of the chest or breasts and radiates over heart and lungs down the arms to the minor chakras in the palms of the hands.

This is the level at which you can draw power from higher sources and any crystals, herbs or greenery bring in healing and higher powers will amplify the energies of the Devas and higher nature essences. Your own innate healing powers will also be activated. Any polarity or gender magick involving the mingling of God/Goddess interchange energies in more formal ritual, for example uniting the chalice and the athame will begin once you reach this stage of energy connection. Angelic power will add to the increasing spiritual power and any seasonal, lunar or solar energies you timed the spell to coincide with, will add their forces.

See the yellow of the Solar plexus light rising to swirl round the Heart chakra, making you feel momentarily dizzy as you now encounter higher light pouring inwards and downwards. As you merge with the rising rhythms of the spell so the symbol's spirit double will be ready to absorb the necessary forces to bring the required changes to the actual situation. This spiritually charged force enters your personal energy field as you allow the spell to carry you.

Sending healing through crystals or herbs will be effective once you are using this level of your aura and your Heart chakra in magick, a level that is accessible through the spell or ritual structure to any spellcaster of good intent.

The Throat chakra or Vishuddha, the etheric template/ Atmic plane

* **Fragrance:** Lavender or mimosa
* **Ray:** Green
* **Magickal energy:** Release

The fifth layer of the aura is ruled by the blue Throat chakra and is associated with sound. It is situated close to the Adam's apple in the centre of the neck.

The Throat chakra is the gateway from a personal to a more global perspective. This is the level at which your higher self is able to reach towards the Archangels and towards Beings of Light. You may see your personal God and Goddess in specific forms in the distance and, as you call out the release of the spell energies, ask for their power to send the spell energies into the cosmos. Now the green Heart light is temporarily constricted, like water being forced up a narrow pipe, and then opens out again into blue chakra light.

As you receive even more light from above and around as well as below, you call out the words of release This is the stage, too, when you are able to reach out and access the higher part of your own potential and send out your own power into the spell release in pure trust that all will be resolved. Now you may see rainbow stars, even from planes and aura levels you have not yet reached, cascading around you.

Because you and the spell are now one, the release of the power will be immensely intense and the symbol may become momentarily brilliant.

The Brow chakra, Third Eye or Savikalpa Samadhi, the celestial body link with the Anapudaka plane

* **Fragrance:** Sandalwood or sage
* **Ray:** Indigo/blue
* **Magickal energy:** Awareness and connection

The sixth layer of the aura is ruled by the indigo Third Eye or Brow chakra and is the realm of light. It is located in the centre of your brow between and above your eyes and radiates into the lower cavities of the brain.

At first, these precious moments at the height of a spell or more prolonged in ritual will enable you to connect with the God and Goddess and to draw down their wisdom. In ceremonies such as drawing down the moon or speaking as though you were the God or Goddess, this level can be reached without spell energies being released, but this takes time and patience. It can also be developed by working with divinatory tools or scrying with your cauldron or another water surface by candle or moonlight. This is a good time after release to allow prophetic insights about future action to flow within you. In spellcasting, the amplified energies flow back smoothly and slowly into the actual symbol and into you and anyone for whom the spell is being cast.

Visualise the rainbow stars of the previous stage merging and swirling and falling as coloured mists or warm rain, flowing in and out of your aura and chakras leaving you feeling connected, aware and relaxed. In ritual, this would be at the stage where you might share cakes and ale or make offerings to the deities.

The Crown chakra or Nirvakelpa Samadhi, the ketheric template or the Adi plane

* **Fragrances:** Frankincense and lotus
* **Rays:** Red and gold
* **Magickal energy:** Unity with all things, connection with divinity

The seventh and outermost layer of the aura that merges with the cosmos is ruled by the violet/white/gold Crown chakra and is located at the crown of the head, beginning at the hairline and moving upwards and outwards to join the cosmic powers at this highest level. It connects with the higher parts of the brain and integrates the whole mind, body and spirit.

If you are new to this concept, you will perhaps be surprised that the violet ray was the ray of the Earth plane. But of course though we describe the upward ascent of planes and chakras, in fact everything is linked and as T S Eliot said, the end of any journey is the place we first started, but totally transformed by the journey as we know it for the first time.

Spiritually, this level is not part of the spell process except that the symbol, the spellcaster and any person for whom the spell is cast are now transformed and inspired by the cosmic powers that strengthens the spiritual connection with divinity made at the Brow level. Your spells and rituals are blessed by the downward-flowing energies from and via the Crown, even though you may not be fully aware of this super-conscious connection.

Since this is the level of the undifferentiated Godhead/god and goddess as one, even an experienced witch will achieve it only rarely when he or she enters a sensation of total unity with all things, earthly and cosmic (very different from thinking you are the daily confidante and messenger of the Godhead – and we all meet those people often enough). Mystics attain this state if they are lucky after many years of contemplation and study and then only by letting go of all that painstakingly acquired knowledge and expectations. The Adi plane may be experienced during an initiation, whether personal and private, of the kind you may wish to enter after the theoretical year and a day or in coven. In moments, too, when you call down the Goddess, just for a moment you may have a fleeting sense of being overlaid by the Goddess energies (very different from being possessed) and glimpse for a moment the whole picture of illumination and peace.

This level of aura awareness has been described as attainable occasionally through sacred sex or peak experiences. But, it is as likely to come in the supermarket queue or while digging the garden and you will think: Oh, yes that is the point of it all.

After the first aware contact with this highest level, comes the sheer responsibility of witchcraft and the hard work of doing good and being wise really begins. In the meantime, keep activating the Crown chakra in ritual and meditation, for the cosmic energies are filtered through it and will bless the spells and rituals even of the most inexperienced practitioners, if you relax and trust.

The chakras and spellcasting

Personal spiritual energy is vital in spellcasting and magick generally since it helps us to raise energy through progressively higher spiritual levels. The more magick and or psychic work and divination you do, the more easily these higher levels are activated. In time this greater awareness will filter into your daily life making you ever wiser and more harmonious

Your chakra or bodily psychic energy centres draw in energy from the other sources (such as nature) and during spellcasting, absorb the power inherent in the symbol you use, the elemental substances and the process of energy raising within the spell. The result of this energy raising is to channel the spell through our own minds and bodies so that the amplified power is released through our aura or energy field round the body, to enable the spell energy transference to take place. In this way, the desired result is manifest in the material world or at least the means given to the spellcaster by which the desire can be more easily attained

As the spellcaster you are filled with light and if you looked in a mirror straight after a spell you would see how much clearer and brighter your aura is. This ongoing energy makes personal spellcasting so effective, because as well as releasing the power that comes boomeranging back to make the spell succeed, you carry the stored power within you in the day and weeks ahead. A further positive benefit of casting spells for others is that you absorb some of the blessings (under the threefold law) and even if the subject is absent, they will receive the light and power from the spell. What is more, the symbol can act as a charm to release the stored power over a specified period of time.

We all have a rainbow coloured spiritual energy body within us that is an ideal form of ourselves at the peak of physical, mental and spiritual development. It is hypothesised that this is the form in which we travel astrally or in out of body experiences, when our double or doppelganger is seen miles away perhaps in a place we were thinking of strongly. It may also be the part of us that survives death.

The rainbow energies radiate out beyond the physical body and enclose it in a seven-layered ellipse. This is perceived most strongly around the head and shoulders as the aura or energy field, about an extended arm span all round us. The aura is energised by our chakra or psychic energy system, the psychic power centres or spheres that are located within the spiritual body but whose energies penetrate the physical body three-dimensionally.

We have many invisible but powerful chakras or energy centres within us, linked by spiralling pathways of energy called nadis. But the seven described above are the most significant in healing, psychic development and magick.

Bringing chakras into magick

If you are new to spellcasting, you may not at first be aware of the background ray colour as you enter each plane of awareness and these planes become progressively mistier the more ethereal they are. But in time you will see them clearly as you cast spells, so that your personal rainbow, the aura and chakras are seen against the plane's own predominant colour. By seen, I mean clairvoyantly with your inner psychic eye, though some people do perceive them as external colours, especially as power is raised in a spell. The colours of the lower planes remain as background, rather than completely fading as the spell progresses.

This awareness of the planes occurs in its own time and you may become aware of them as the spell energies are released, as coloured lights or stars and your personal and the plane colours flare together.

Though I talk about drawing up the energies from the Root to Crown chakra as though a deliberate process or action, in fact this happens within a spell or ritual structure as you raise power. However, by connecting with your chakras in quiet times, for example by lighting candles in all seven chakra colours and focusing on them in meditation, spellcasting becomes more effective and natural as you flow with it.

If you work with a group or coven as you move into familiarity with one another so your chakras will synchronise and you will be able to pass the energies among you spontaneously during group chant or dance that will create a collective chakra energy source.

The five stages of spellcasting

You will identify these stages in rituals and ceremonies, as well as spellcasting. Spells come in many forms, from a simple empowerment involving visualisation to a formal structure where you cast a circle, welcome Guardians and incorporate different tools. However, I would recommend that even for the simplest spell you visualise a clockwise circle of light around you and ask for Angelic/deity/Guardian protection in a formal or informal opening blessing as part of Stage 1 of spellcasting as described below. After Stage 4 you can thank the Guardians, especially your Witch Guardian, and picture the circle light fading and returning to the ground.

Stage 1 Defining the purpose of the spell formally and creating/choosing the symbol to be empowered

This is the most vital part of the spell. You might have a definite purpose for a spell, but sometimes you wish to allow your wise, unconscious mind and your Witch Guardian or Guardian Angels to fill in the details, and you ask simply for love, happiness etc, *to come into my life/the life (name person) in the way most appropriate.*

Next you need to decide on the focus or symbol of the spell. Natural materials are always best and if you craft the image yourself from clay, dough or beeswax, then you are able to endow it with your own personal essence from the start (see more of this later, page 303). Beeswax melted over a candle or a softened beeswax sheet is perfect because you can fashion any image, such as a heart for love or a baby in a cradle for fertility. Equally every herb and crystal has magickal meanings and so can be a focus for a spell, especially if you intend afterwards to carry them as a talisman or as part of a lucky bag. In theory, there is no limit to what you use as a symbol, as long as there is a clear visual or mental connection to bind it to the spell purpose. (I have suggested numerous symbols later, so if you are new to magick you can look ahead to page 307 for ideas.)

Once you have the symbol/image, and you have carried out any circle casting, opening blessing, candle lighting and so on, you need to establish formally the purpose of the spell, aloud if possible. You should do this while holding the symbol or passing it round if in a group, so that each person can verbally define the purpose. This verbalisation of intent dates back to the Ancient Egyptian belief that words equal power. They considered that words used to define rituals re-created the first creation, when Heka, God of Magick, spoke the thoughts of the Creator God Ptah. Through these words Heka created the vibrations necessary for the mound of earth to rise from the primal waters. When working alone, if you wish you can start with I am... and then state your secret magickal names of power. You would also define any Angels' or deity names whose energies you were seeking to help your magickal endeavour. I have developed this theme in the module on chanting and the power of words in ritual (see page 294). I have also given information on choosing your magickal names (see page 274).

Stage 2: Setting the energies in motion

Now you are ready to begin endowing the symbol and spoken intention of the spell with elemental power.

One of the most common methods of empowering a symbol is to pass the symbol round or through the four elemental substances in turn, salt, incense, candle flame and water, so the power builds up within it and within you, and any spoken elemental empowerments cause the energies to stir. Begin with the salt in the north, then the incense in the east, the candle in the south and the water in the west.

In a more complex spell, you could also incorporate the main elemental tools, the pentacle in the north, the athame or knife in the east, the wand in the south and the chalice in the west, or you could add these to the raising the power stage. Again, the principle is to name the tool and what powers you are endowing your symbol with. For example, for the athame or knife in the east, as you touch the symbol with the blade you might say:

> *I endow you with the power of steel to cut through all obstacles...*

Stage 3 Raising or increasing the power

This is the most active and powerful part of the spell, and involves building up the speed and intensity of the action you started in Stage 2. Whatever method you use, the aim is to merge your own spiritual energies via your physical actions and words with the symbol, the elements, and the time and place energies. As you empower the symbol so you are further empowering yourself. Raising the power is especially easy out of doors as you connect, especially if barefoot or wearing thin-soled shoes with the natural spiralling energies or straighter ley flows beneath the earth.

There are many ways of raising power, limited only by your imagination. You can dance, drum, chant or all of these, use your wand or athame to accumulate power, tie knots in a cord. All of these are potent, whether you work alone or with others. In a group you can pass the symbol faster and faster round the circle with a *Pass the magick on* type chant. Best is a combination of words or sound and movement in such a way that the conscious mind is carried along by the power, like riding a carousel, as everything blurs except for the music.

The prime purpose of this stage, as I said, is to empower not only the symbol but also yourself, since you are the vehicle to carry the magickal energies from the material through thought and progressively higher spiritual planes as I described above in chakra raising.

If working alone, you can remain at the altar and enchant the symbol by moving the palms of both hands a few centimetres above the symbol in the centre of the altar. Alternatively, use a pair of lighted incense sticks, one held in each hand, a few centimetres above the symbol, the right incense stick or hand moving clockwise and the left one anti-clockwise. Move them faster and faster and create a chant to draw in all four elemental powers, sung or spoken faster and faster. Increase the speed and intensity so the incense sticks cross and uncross over the symbol. As you move the sticks rhythmically, recite your elemental chant continuously, louder and quicker until the words are no longer separate. Or, keep moving your hands in the same way as you did the sticks, faster and faster over the symbol as you chant.

Another method is to move your wand or athame clockwise over the symbol in flourishes in the power hand. You can move the other hand anticlockwise in rhythm if you want. (Swords are a bit dangerous for power raising.) You can also spiral a smudge in huge circles over the altar allowing it to dictate its own pathway and shapes. A very simple chant is:

Air, Water, Fire, Earth, bring I ask, this wish to birth, followed by Earth [pause], Air, [pause], Fire, [pause], Water [pause].
The power of the earth [clap and stamp], the power of the Air [clap and stamp], the power of the Fire [clap and stamp], the power of Water [clap and stamp].

You can continue over and over again at increasing intensity and speed, adding variants or weaving your own simple four or five-word elemental chants round the natural surroundings and the elemental associations.

Other spell chants include Goddess names, the most popular sung from Northern Scandinavia to Central London being: **Isis**, the Ancient Egyptian Mother Goddess; **Astarte**, the supreme female divinity of the Phoenicians, Goddess of love and fertility, associated with the moon and all nature; **Diana**, the Graeco-Roman Goddess of the moon and hunt and Queen of the Witches; **Hecate**, the Ancient Greek Crone Goddess of the Underworld and Waning Moon; **Demeter**, the ancient Greek Grain Mother; **Kali**, the Hindu creatrix/destroyer and fierce Goddess; **Innana**, the Sumerian fertility Queen of Heaven and Earth goddess in the Middle East area that is now modern Iraq. You can substitute your own Goddesses/Gods from any tradition. Chant or sing them as a continuing list: Isis, Astarte, Diana, Hecate, Demeter, Kali, Innana, Isis, Astarte, and so on. Others include part or all of the witches' rune or chant (see page 300) that has long moved out of any specific magickal tradition.

You could move round and round the altar or circle, chanting and clapping, while stepping, stamping or whirling and twirling. Sufi spiritual whirling dancing has been eagerly adopted by the New Age as a way of altering consciousness. Trust your feet to follow the spirals of the earth energies. You can add the beat of a drum or a tambourine. We can all play these, without training or a natural ear for more formal music. Just let your hands and feet set the beat and if you chant alone they all harmonise. The simpler and more repetitive words and actions the better. Drumming the different elemental rhythms at the four quarters is an excellent power raiser (for example slow and smooth for Water, regular and measured for Earth), and then gradually the four rhythms can merge into one as you move round the quarters very fast. Move the drum until you feel that the power has reached its height, like revving a car with the hand brake on or a plane whose wheels are starting to lift off the tarmac.

Stage 4 Release of power

This stage will blur and merge naturally into the previous one, if you trust yourself.

When the moment is right, raise the incense sticks and hold them upright above your head, calling for the power to fly. Then plunge the incense sticks simultaneously into a bowl of sand to extinguish them. Do the same with a smudge with a final spiralling above your head (as though you are using a lasso). The secret is to put out the flame at the precise moment you release the power vocally into the cosmos.

Alternatively, lift your hands and outstretched arms, high either side of your head, swing them behind you and forward waist high in a slashing movement and down again. Do the same with a wand or athame, upwards and down, slashing in front of you, behind the power side of your body and coming to rest in front of you, pointing downwards.

End a song with a final shout, dance with a final clap and leap, or a final drum roll, as you call out:

The power is free / the wish is mine or the spell is done

to express the culmination of the spell.

During Stage 3, you might have become aware of a spiralling rainbow vortex, often called a cone of power. This is light from your aura/charkas, the rays of the different planes you access, colours from nature, the earth and the symbol, especially if made of a natural substance like herbs, which will glow green, or crystals that when empowered are filled with brilliant white light and rainbows, as well as their own crystalline colour. This now will explode round you in a glorious firework display, complete, if you are lucky, with music, like the climax of a rock concert, the moments when choral music fades into harmony and silence or the crescendo of a symphony orchestra, depending on what to you is musical bliss.

It now seems that anything is possible and you can recall this glorious moment if carrying through the intention in the real world becomes daunting.

An alternative Stage 4

If you are carrying out a healing spell or one for gentle love or letting go of sorrow or indeed in a balancing or house blessing ritual, setting off psychic fireworks may seem too fierce. You may decide instead to steadily infuse a healing herb mix with the power to relieve pain or exhaustion or so they can afterwards to be buried for peace in four directions. You can use gently directed power psychically to steer away someone that is making you unhappy and release the symbol afterwards into water.

You build up the power in Stages 2 and 3, but steadily and rhythmically. When the power in your spell has built up to almost a climax, instead of releasing it, hold it for a moment, keeping your voice and your movements steady. Then begin to recite the words slower and more softly. Make your movements even slower and gentler until your words fade through a whisper to silence as your feet become still. The incense sticks, your hands or wand will likewise become still.

Point downwards with smudge, incense sticks, wand or your hands towards the symbol at a 45-degree angle (slightly away if necessary so no ash falls on it). Athames seem to me less effective for this kind of magick.

Push very gently in your mind, holding your hands with your fingers pointing downwards or incense sticks or wand motionless a few centimetres above the symbol, picturing power and light flowing into the symbol. You may detect a rainbow aura or green light round the symbol. End by saying softly:

May this power bring peace/healing. Blessings be on all.

When you feel the power ebbing, stand motionless or silent for a moment and then replace the wand, smudge or incense sticks in their place or holders or put your hands in front of you downwards so any residual power can flow into the symbol or to heal the Earth. With either form of climax you and any present may sink to the ground or stand quietly.

Stage 5 Moving to a conclusion/grounding or internalising the power
Now you need to need to ground yourself and create the space and stillness for the amplified cosmic energies to flow gently back and empower the symbol and you/the person for whom the spell is intended. If the subject is absent, you can visualise them holding the symbol, if you are not sending it as a gift after the spell.

Hold the symbol quietly and allow the energies to synthesise and flow between you and the symbol. If you are working as a group pass it round quietly for each person to hold and endow it with silent or quietly spoken final blessings. Then hand it to the person for whom it is intended (or if absent return it to the centre of the altar). In a ritual or a more complex spell, now would be a good time for the cakes and ale ceremony and/or any divination or channelling, using the residual psychic energies.

Then you can say farewell to the guardians of your quarters if you opened them and uncast the circle, picture the light fading, extinguish any candles and make a spoken farewell blessing, if the spell was informal. Don't be in too much of a hurry to get back to the world; it will turn for another five minutes without your intervention. Even the shortest spell with virtually no ceremony should provide a space away from the mundane.

Close your chakras by touching each chakra point, starting with the centre of your hairline for the Crown chakra and picture the light fading and the chakra turning slowly and harmoniously. Continue down until your touch the soles of each foot, right and then left. This is like drawing the blinds at your windows in the evening so the light remains within.

Finally, sit on the ground and press down with your hands and feet on to the earth to let excess unfocused energy drain out. Alternatively, stand with your feet apart and your hands by your side, fingers pointing downwards and feel yourself gradually slowing down and your body and mind relaxing.

Tidy away and when ready to leave, whisper softly or say in your mind:

The rite is finished. Blessings be on all.

If the symbol was only temporary and does not need to be kept for a specified time or sent/carried as a talisman, roll any wax or clay into a ball. If it is to be used again, for example, a tarot card, smudge it to remove spell energies. Otherwise bury the symbol, saying:

Return with blessings to the Mother of All.

PRACTICAL ASSIGNMENT

Creating a nature spell

* Choose as your spell focus a current need, personal, for a friend or family member, for the community or more globally.

* Create a natural symbol using dough, clay or beeswax. As you form it, formulate the words that will summarise the spell purpose clearly and precisely to avoid ambiguities and to comply with the moral laws of magick. If you prefer, wait to create it until you are at the spell place.

* Take your symbol to an open-air setting (or maybe find clay or sand in situ to fashion an image).

* Look for an impromptu altar.

* Now find the tools and substances you will need also in situ or nearby. Use leaves or petals for the Earth element, a feather or leafy twig for Air, a pure white stone held up to the light for Fire and perhaps rainwater collected in a rock indentation for Water. Find a wand made of a twig or driftwood.

* Improvise and use the chakras in your palms and the soles of your feet to raise and release the energy.

* Create a blessing and cast light round yourself and then follow the spell stages.

* Afterwards bury the image and return the materials/impromptu tools to where you found them, having passed your hands over them palms down nine times and asked for the energies to be released.

Further research

In Module 2 I suggested you found out if there were any folk spells or rituals in your region, perhaps centred around a local well or saint (see page 36).

Whether or not you discovered any, research the history of a sacred site or building near to you and create a spell or ritual to transfer its particular energies to a symbol or to release healing or positive powers into the cosmos.

Add this rite to your Book of Shadows and perhaps post it on the internet to create a new custom in your area that may take root over time.

Further information

Recommended reading

* Davies, Brenda, *The Seven Healing Chakras*, Ulysses Press, 2000
* Eason, Cassandra, *Chakra Power*, Quantum/Foulsham, 2001
* Farrar, Janet and Stewart, *Spellcasting, Spells and how they Work*, Robert Hale, 1992
* Farrell, Nick, *Magical Pathworking, Techniques of Active Imagination*, Llewellyn, 2003
* Karagulla, Shafica and Van Gelder Kunz, Dora, *Chakras and the Human Energy Field*, Theosophical University Press, 1994
* Regardie, Israel, *The Middle Pillar, Balance between Mind and Magic*, Llewellyn, 1998
* Rivers, W. H. P., *Medicine, Magic and Religion*, Routledge, 2001
* Some Malidama, Patrice, *Of Water and Spirit, Ritual Magic and Initiation in the life of an African Shaman*, Penguin Arkana, 1994

Websites

* *Kheper*
Comprehensive background into chakras
www.kheper.net/topics/chakras/chakras.htm

* *Chakra Balancing*
Very detailed site on all aspects of magick
http://healing.about.com/od/chakras

MAGICKAL TIMINGS

he timing of a spell or ritual helps to attune your spellcasting to the prevailing natural and cosmic powers. Of course, you can carry out a spell at any time if the need is immediate. However, if you can work when the most appropriate background energies are naturally strongest, your spell flows more easily and your magick is amplified by these natural forces.

Over the centuries measured time such as days or months has absorbed the magickal properties of different deities and planets by association. I have written in detail about lunar and solar magick later (see page 202). Here I will give an overview of the essential information.

You can decide which criteria to use in a spell: for example the phase of the moon, the sun time such as dawn, plus perhaps the best day of the week for your spell or ritual purpose. If the spell needs more precise timings, you can also calculate the best planetary or Archangel hours (see page 216). Slower seasonal energies (see page 64) form background energies that can be woven into general spellcasting.

You can also establish your own timeframe for the successful result of a spell or ritual. This can affect when and how often you need to cast a particular spell: for example, the three days before and the night of the full moon for a concentrated build up of power to bring love. You also have to decide what would be a realistic timeframe for fulfilment of the spell need. This may be quite specific: for example, success in a particular interview or test; or something more open ended, like getting a book published, which might not happen overnight and might have other conditions attached. I recently cast a spell for someone who wanted to find a reputable publisher with good overseas connections and a reliable sales record from a series of books, and such matters that are not so time specific.

Days of the week

The easiest timeframe to calculate is the day of the week on which a spell is cast. This can be further fine tuned by choosing an hour that synchronises with the power of the ruling Archangel/planet of the day (see page 212).

Seven days in a week became fixed in a number of cultures because of the seven ancient planets (including the Sun and moon) that were believed to influence their particular days. Each day has its own planet, Archangel, colour, crystals etc that can be used to strengthen a spell carried out on that day. I have given the planetary glyph at the beginning of each day, so that you can if you wish draw it in incense smoke or on paper on the appropriate day as part of the spell.

The system is an interlocking one, so that the planetary associations you will encounter on page 212 are very similar to the day of the week they rule. The same is true of the magickal correspondences of the seven Archangels who are linked with the days. So if you know the crystals and fragrances of Sunday, you also know them for the sun and Archangel Michael. However, I have repeated them where relevant to save you constantly having to refer forwards or backwards; in some cases, too, there may be additional associations.

Sunday ☉

Sunday is called *dies solis* in Latin named after the Graeco-Roman Sol who was God of the sun and also the sun itself. If you prefer a female focus, the Norse Goddess of the sun was Sunna, sister of the Moon God Mannaz. In Old English the day was called Sunnandæg.

* **Archangel:** Michael
* **Colour:** Gold
* **Crystals:** Amber, carnelian, diamond, clear crystal quartz, tiger's eye, topaz
* **Deities:** Apollo, the golden Roman God of the solar light; the Welsh Llew or Irish Lugh; Ra, the Ancient Egyptian Sun God, linked with the full power of the sun, Helios, the Ancient Greek God; Saule, the Baltic Sun Goddess; Grainne, the Celtic solar crone Goddess
* **Element:** Fire
* **Herbs and oils:** Juniper, rosemary, saffron, St John's Wort
* **Incense:** Cloves, cinnamon, chamomile, frankincense
* **Metal:** Gold
* **Planet:** Sun
* **Spells:** For personal fulfilment and ambition, power and success, fathers and mature men, for new beginnings, creativity, energy, joy, improving health, prosperity and self-confidence; overcomes bad luck
* **Trees:** Bay, birch, laurel

Monday ☽

Monday is the day of the moon, called *dies lunae* in Latin, the day of the moon goddess Luna who ordered the passage of the moon through the year. In Norse myth, the moon god was Mani; in Old Norse, the day was Manidagar and in Anglo-Saxon Monandaeg.

* **Archangel:** Gabriel
* **Colour:** Silver
* **Crystals:** Moonstone, mother of pearl, pearl, selenite, opal
* **Deities:** Selene, Greek full moon goddess and twin sister of Helios, the older Greek Sun Goddess; Diana, Goddess of the witches, who took on all aspects of the moon; the Ancient Egyptian Isis, as Goddess of the moon and sea and mistress of magick and enchantment; Myesyats, the Slavic Moon God, who represented the three stages of the lifecycle like the lunar goddesses

- **Element:** Water
- **Herbs and oils:** Chamomile, lotus, poppy, wintergreen
- **Incense:** Jasmine, lemon, myrrh
- **Metal:** Silver
- **Planet:** Moon
- **Spells:** For home and family matters, women especially mothers and grandmothers, children and animals, fertility, protection, especially while travelling, clairvoyance and psychic dreams, for sea and gardening rituals, herb magick and healing and keeping secrets
- **Trees:** Willow, alder, eucalyptus

Tuesday ♂

Tuesday is the day of Tiu or Tiw, in Anglo-Saxon called Tiwesdaeg. The Norse name was Tysdagr, after the Norse Tyr, the God of war, and associated with the Pole Star and also altruism, being called the Spirit Warrior. In Latin it was *dies Martis*, the day of Mars.

- **Archangel:** Samael
- **Colour:** Red
- **Crystals:** Garnet, bloodstone, ruby, jasper
- **Deities:** Ares, Ancient Greek God of war; Mars, Roman God of war; Bellona Roman Goddess of war, the female counterpart of Mars whose chariot she drove into battle; the Morrigu Irish Crow battle Goddess sisters; Tyr, the Norse God who sacrificed his sword arm to save the other gods from Fenris wolf
- **Element:** Fire
- **Herbs and oils:** Basil, coriander, garlic, pepper, tarragon
- **Incense:** Dragon's blood, ginger, mint, thyme
- **Metal:** Iron, steel
- **Planet:** Mars
- **Spells:** For courage, change, taking the initiative, independence and separateness from others, resisting injustice and protecting loved ones under threat, overcoming seemingly impossible odds, for health and vitality, for passion, the consummation of love, young men and all in the armed forces or services
- **Trees:** Cypress, holly, pine

Wednesday ☿

Wednesday is the day of the Norse Odin or Woden/Wotan, called Wodnesdaegr in the Anglo-Saxon, the Norse Odinsdagr. Odin was the Norse Father God who was also associated with travellers and with wisdom, poetry and inspiration. In Latin it was *dies Mercuris*, the day of Mercury, the messenger God.

- **Archangel:** Raphael
- **Colour:** Yellow
- **Crystals:** Agate, citrine, falcon's eye, jasper, malachite, onyx
- **Deities:** Thoth, the Ancient Egyptian God of wisdom, writing and medicine;

Hermes, the Greek messenger god and counterpart of the Roman Mercury, both of whom carried healing staffs; Heimdall, in Viking myth, the gold-toothed Guardian of the Rainbow Bridge between the realms of the gods and mortals; Iris, the Greek Goddess and later Angel of the rainbow

* **Element:** Air
* **Herbs and oils:** Dill, fennel, parsley, valerian
* **Incense:** Lavender, lemongrass, lemon balm, lily of the valley
* **Metal:** Mercury, aluminium
* **Planet:** Mercury
* **Spells:** For money-making ventures, clear communication, persuasion, adaptability and versatility, improving memory and sharpening logic, for any teenagers, for study, examinations and tests, mastering new technology, short-distance travel, house moves and short breaks, conventional methods of healing, especially surgery, for business negotiations, overcoming debt, and repelling envy, malice, spite and deceit
* **Trees:** Hazel, ash, silver birch

Thursday ♃

Thursday is named after Thor, the gigantic Norse Thunder God, whose hammer Mjollnir he threw against the frost giants and trolls. He was Thunor or Donar to the Anglo-Saxons. Thursday is called Thursdaeg, the day of Thor, in Old English and Thorsdagr in Ancient Norse. The Romans gave it the name *dies Iovis*, the day of Jupiter, their supreme God.

* **Archangel:** Sachiel
* **Colour:** Blue, purple
* **Crystals:** Azurite, lapis lazuli, sodalite, turquoise
* **Deities:** Zeus, the Ancient Greek supreme God who like Jupiter ruled the weather and wielded thunderbolts at those who angered him; Perun, the Slavic God of thunder and lightning, dark-haired with a beard of gold; Raiden, Japanese God of thunder and lightning whose huge drum causes thunder
* **Element:** Air
* **Herbs:** Clove, honeysuckle hyssop, meadowsweet, mistletoe
* **Incense:** Agrimony, cedar, sandalwood, sage
* **Metal:** Tin
* **Planet:** Jupiter
* **Spells:** For increase and expansion, for career, leadership, learned wisdom, long distance travel and house moves, justice and the law, authority and altruism, marriage, permanent relationships, business partnerships, middle aged people, fidelity, loyalty and male potency and for banishing excesses and addictions
* **Trees:** Beech, oak, redwood

Friday ♀

Friday is named after Frigg, the Norse mother Goddess of women and marriage and wife of Odin; alternatively it belongs to Freyja, Norse Goddess of love, beauty and fertility. It is also linked with the old word for freedom; Frigedæg is the Old English and the Old Norse Freyjasdagr. The Latin was *dies Veneris*, the day of Venus, Goddess of love.

* **Archangel:** Anael
* **Colour:** Green, pink
* **Crystals:** Amethyst, emerald, jade, moss agate, rose quartz
* **Deities:** Aphrodite, Ancient Greek Goddess of love and the sea; Innana, Sumerian Goddess of beauty, abundance, fertility and passion (Venus, Aphrodite and Innana are closely linked); Juno, Roman Goddess of committed love and marriage, wife of Jupiter
* **Element:** Earth
* **Herbs and oils:** Feverfew, heather, hibiscus, lemon verbena, yarrow
* **Incense:** Geranium, rose, strawberry, vervain
* **Metal:** Copper
* **Planet:** Venus
* **Spells:** For all forms of love magic (especially to attract love), for young women, beauty, the arts, crafts, relationships, friendships, for marriage and fidelity, blossoming sexuality, the acquisition of beautiful possessions, mending quarrels, peace, for the environment, fertility and women's health matters; also for reducing the influence of destructive lovers and possessiveness
* **Trees:** Almond, apple, cherry

Saturday ♄

Saturday comes from the Latin *dies Saturni*, the day of Saturn or Seater. He was the God of fate and of agriculture and was said to have ruled over a golden age of peace and plenty after he was dethroned by his son Jupiter. In Old English, the day was called Sæteræg.

* **Archangel:** Cassiel
* **Colour:** Brown, black, grey
* **Crystals:** Hematite, jet, lodestone, obsidian, smoky quartz
* **Deities:** Cronos, the Ancient Greek god of time and fate who was deposed by his son Zeus; Horus, Ancient Egyptian God of sky and time, who represented the passage of the sun through the sky at different times; Fate Goddesses in various cultures, such as the Roman Parcae, three very old women who spun the fate of mortal destiny
* **Element:** Earth
* **Herbs and oils:** Aspen, comfrey, Solomon's seal, starflower, tea tree
* **Incense:** Carnation, mimosa, pansy, patchouli
* **Metal:** Lead, pewter

* **Planet:** Saturn
* **Spells:** For unfinished business, with endings that lead to beginnings, for slow-moving matters and for accepting limitations, as well as for overcoming obstacles that are long standing, for easing depression or doubts, official matters, psychic protection, binding spells, locating lost objects, animals and older people, regaining self-control over bad habits or emotions.; also for repayment of money owed and banishing pain, guilt or illness
* **Trees:** Blackthorn, cypress, yew

Months of the year

Each month has its own energies and favours particular kinds of spells. Though you cannot necessarily postpone a spell for the required month, you may find it empowering to carry out for example at least one January-related spell during that month and so on through the year as a focus for your month's work. Often, too, if the month seems wrong for a specific spell you may be able to find a quality the month possesses that does at least loosely fit with your spell need. But months are not a vital factor.

January

* Ruled by Janus, the Roman God of gates and doorways who has two faces looking in opposite directions.
* Good for spells for new beginnings but also to leave behind the past; also for spells to reconcile two different people or areas of life pulling different ways; for mending quarrels.

February

* Named after the Roman festival of fertility and purification, held on 15 February from which we get St Valentine's Day on 14 February.
* Good for spells for awakening new love and trust, for increasing good luck, melting coldness or indifference and planting the seeds of future success; also for any cleansing/purification spells and also for driving away what is destructive or redundant.

March

* Named after Mars the Roman God of war, for this was when war resumed after winter and the start of the Roman year.
* Good for spells for courage, action, passion, overcoming obstacles, new business ventures, for physical strength and independence.

April

* Named after Aphrodite, Greek goddess of love, the sea and beauty and also Aprilis, a Goddess of the Etruscans, the people who once inhabited central Italy.
* Good for spells for love and fertility, creativity, increase in any aspect of life, especially health and money, for beauty, healing and happiness.

May

* Named after the Roman Maia who was a maiden Goddess of flowers who had a festival at the beginning of May.
* Good for spells for increase in every way, for travel, for growing love and family happiness, for additions to circle of family or friends, investments and house plans; also for flower and herb spells and for blossoming love.

June

* Named after Juno, Roman Goddess of marriage, women and mothers.
* Good for spells for marriage and love commitment, fidelity, partnerships of all kinds, fertility, peace and prosperity and all women's magick.

July

* Named after the birth month of Roman Emperor Julius Caesar who linked emperors with the God Jupiter and so became an icon of power.
* Good for spells for power, career, ambitions of any kind, leadership, acquiring knowledge, justice, travel or house moves.

August

* Named after Augustus, the first of the Roman emperors, because a number of lucky events of his life happened in August.
* Good for spells for reversing bad luck or loss, for opportunities previously denied and the opening of doors, for the fulfilment of earlier plans and projects, for getting what is owed and finding or recovering what is lost.

September

* Named after Septem, seven because it was the seventh month after the New Year in March and is associated with wisdom, knowledge and truth and in Ancient Egypt with eternal life.
* Good for spells for uncovering secrets, resolving injustices, for increased psychic powers, for all forms of training, retraining, and tests and for finding solutions for difficult questions.

October

* Named after Octo, the eighth Roman month after New Year and associated with financial advantage, called the way of the serpent in ancient law.

* Good for spells for success in competitions and games of chance, for reaping rewards of earlier efforts, for all money and property matters, speculation and learning new skills and technology.

November

* Named after Novem, the ninth Roman month after New Year and the number of initiation and perfection in many religions.

* Good for spells for making dreams come true, for completion of creative efforts that have taken time to perfect, for aiming high, for binding others from harm and banishing fear of failure, for success in official matters and for relocation or a second career.

December

* Named after Decem, the tenth month after New Year and the number of unity of the ancient Egyptian Isis and Osiris deities who promised immortality to ordinary people.

* Good for spells for uniting people and business expansion, for getting creative ventures into the public eye (for example, a book published), for a major life change or turning things around.

Days of the month

For these I have given the prevailing energy of each day that may aid particular kinds of spells. The numbers also apply to months: for example, the first hour of the first day of the first month (popular for New Year magick and celebrations) will be good for new beginnings. The first day of any month especially if it is a Sunday, the first day of the week, will contain a lot of innovative power. The 11th hour of the 11th day of the 11th month is a signal for two minutes' silence still in a number of countries to remember those lost or injured in war. You can make all kinds of combinations if you use the months.

I refers to the 1st of the month, 2 as the 2nd and so on.

1 New beginnings, 2 Balance, 3 Expansion, 4 Caution, 5 Communication, 6 Peace, 7 The unknown, 8 Calculated risk, 9 Fulfilment, 10 Attracting, 11 Health, 12 Expanding possibility, 13 Secrets, 14 Moderation, 15 Letting go, 16 Rebuilding, 17 Limitless potential, 18 Binding, 19 Resolution, 20 Banishing, 21 Travel, 22 Power, 23 Family, 24 Prosperity, 25 Fidelity and loyalty, 26 What is lost returned, 27 Taking risks, 28 Home, 29 Creative success, 30 Celebrations, 31 Fertility.

Aetts or day tides

Days began at different times in different traditions and for the Ancient Greeks and Romans the day ran from sunrise to sunrise. In contrast in the Celtic, Germanic and Norse traditions the new day began at sunset of what would be the previous day to us, and this is reflected in the celebrations of the Wheel of the Year.

The Aetts or day tides come from the northern tradition and survived as a way of dividing the day for country dwellers especially in eastern and north-east England until the 1800s. Starting with the early morning tide this fits better with modern life. If you wish, you can use the traditional sunset to sunset timeframe for your magickal work.

Aetts are effective for magick because in town or countryside they reflect slower broader divisions of ebb and flow energies and can be woven into moon and sun times. What is more, if it is winter and dark and dawn is not coming until you are on the way to work, you can use a morning tide to launch a new beginning. Each three-hour period has special strengths, qualities and areas of focus.

O'clock times are a powerful moment to release energy in a spell. Even more potent for magickal workings are the chime hours and the minutes before and just after them, i.e., 03.00, 06.00, 09.00, 12.00, 15.00, 18.00, 21.00 and 24.00. It is said that those born on a chime hour are especially psychic and intuitive and able to look backwards and forwards into time.

If you need a special energy or are worried about an aspect of your life, you can identify the best aett for your need and if possible cast a spell to coincide with the chime hour. Alternatively, spend the chime hour either looking into a candle flame or into still water in sunlight and letting pictures filter into your mind that will offer wisdom.

The Power of the Aetts

* **04.30–07.30:** Morningtide is the time of awakening, fertility and new beginnings. The Chime Hour begins at 06.00. Use its energies for new beginnings and on all matters concerning infertility, conception, pregnancy and birth of both babies and projects.

* **07.30–10.30:** Daytide is the time of work and money-making. The chime hour begins at 09.00. Use its energies for solving money problems, money spinning ventures and for success.

* **10.30–13.30:** Midday is the time of endurance and perseverance. 12.00 is the chime hour. Use its energies for matters that are proving wearisome or long in bearing fruit and for difficult people.

* **13.30–16.30:** Undorne is the time for change, transformation and illumination. 15.00 is the start of the chime hour. Use its energies for exploring new horizons and travel plans.

* **16.30–19.30:** Eventide is the time of the family, of home and reconciliation. 18.00 begins the chime hour. Use the energies for questions concerning children of all ages, domestic matters, marriage and partnerships.

* **19.30–22.30:** Nighttide is the time for love, passion and learning. The chime hour begins at 21.00. Use its energies for love relationships, close friendships and acquiring formal knowledge.

* **22.30–01.30:** Midnight is for healing and restoration of mind, body and spirit. The chime hour is midnight, 00.00. Use its energies for insight into illness, especially the chronic kind, for mending of quarrels and the world of the spirit.

* **01.30–04.30:** Uht is the time of sleep and old age. The chime hour begins at 03.00. Use its energies for concerns over elderly relatives and about ageing and for calm sleep.

PRACTICAL ASSIGNMENT

Timing in your magickal day

❋ Begin to look at your daily and magickal life in terms of the different timeframes given above and see how, for example, the aetts could fit into your own lifestyle. If you are a shift worker or commute you can perhaps tune into the tides in a modified way: for example, a night worker could use the 19.30–22.30 for any mind/problem-solving tasks and also for dynamic people encounters and the next period, 22.30–01.30. for resolving disputes and difficulties and formalising any matters or agreements in writing or by mail. Alternatively, we can kick into aetts mode at the weekend or on days of leisure and carry out rituals at the ideal time, rather than when we have a free slot.

❋ Look also at your future diary in terms of optimal days and months for particular magickal and personal projects and decide to make your first of the month a mini New Year.

Further research

There are many fascinating calendars that have become associated with myth and magick, such as the Chinese, the Ancient Egyptian and the Mayan. Go online or to the library if you have time and see what you can find about measuring time in societies with strong magickal or ancient spiritual traditions. Do days named after animals (Mayan), animal-based years (Chinese) or deities (Egyptian) add anything to our understanding of the magick inherent in the structure of time?

Alternatively explore an indigenous culture that measures time in sleeps or by natural omens and phenomena like the Native North American and Australian Aboriginal traditions. Does this make for better magick?

Further information

Recommended reading

❋ Bruce, Marie, *The Witches' Almanack*, Quantum, 2007

❋ Duggan, Eileen, *7 Days of Magick*, Llewellyn, 2004

❋ Ellwood, Taylor, et al, *Space/Time Magick*, Immanion Press, 2005

❋ Hawking, Stephen, *A Brief History of Time*, Bantam, 1995

Website

❋ *Calendars Through The Ages*
A comprehensive site into the history and methods of calculating time in different ages and cultures
http://webexhibits.org/calendars/

MAGICKAL TIMINGS IN THE COSMOS

In the previous module, I wrote about day, month and the aett tides of the day and night in magickal workings. These are in a sense the earth or root times of magick. Now, we'll go cosmic, looking at the moon, sun and planets as a source of magickal energies. Because these energies change according to the hour, time of day or period of the month, they can not only give spell timings greater accuracy but also add their power to that of the spell and ritual.

Moon times

The moon is undoubtedly the most important time structure in magick. In week 38 I have written about the moon deities in detail (see page 236), but here I have started by listing associations that you can use in any moon phase if you are focusing on a moon time in ritual or in ceremonies to call down the moon.

Moon correspondences

* **Animals/birds:** Bat, heron, moth, owl, snake, wolf
* **Archangel:** Gabriel
* **Colour:** Silver or white
* **Crystals:** Moonstone, pearl, mother of pearl, pearl, selenite, opal (unpolished green or pink ones are very cheap); also white or pearly sea shells, especially double ones
* **Day of the week:** Monday
* **Element:** Water
* **Flowers:** Any with small white flowers or that are especially fragrant at night
* **Herbs incenses and oils:** Coconut, eucalyptus, lemon, lemon balm, jasmine, myrrh, mimosa, lotus, poppy, lemon verbena, wintergreen
* **Metal:** Silver
* **Trees:** Alder, eucalyptus, mimosa, willow

The phases of the moon in magick

The phases of the moon offer differing energies that can help not only the timing of a spell, but also add power to strengthen a wish (waxing) or can bind or banish sorrow or bad luck (waning). The full moon is the most powerful force of all for change, for consummation or supreme effort of any kind, for polarity/gender magick and for action. I also use the full moon for binding if the problem is difficult and the perpetrator powerful in the world's terms.

You can follow the different moon phases in the weather section of the paper or a diary. But always what you see in the sky and what you feel are your best guides to using moon energies in spellcasting. The best way to follow the monthly journey of the moon is to watch it in the sky, not just for one month but for several. Even in town you can use buildings as markers and will note slight variations in position on ensuing months, because of the moon's irregular path.

Catherine Yyronwrode on her excellent and extensive site, one of the best on the net (see page 219) says if the moon is shining in the sky in the evening when the sun sets, it is waxing and each night rises a little later in the day and gets a little fatter. The full moon rises almost at the same time as the sun sets. If the moon is not in the sky when the sun sets, she says, but rises long after sunset or you see it faintly during the day the following day, rising again a little later and looking thinner each day, you know it is waning.

Each day in your Book of Shadows write just a line or two of the way you feel and over the months you may detect a pattern that explains hitherto seemingly random mood patterns and energy flows. Men as well as women are affected by the moon emotionally and perhaps also physically in our daily lives. If we can tune in with the ebbs and flows, then we become more harmonious and able to use natural energy surges as the moon waxes, and not try to force ourselves more than necessary or to take risks when the moon is waning.

Calculating the moon phases

In magick, there are three main divisions. The triple divisions accord with the maiden, mother and wise woman mythology and I have described the Goddesses (and Gods) associated with the different moon phases in the module on the Triple Goddess (see page 374).

The waxing or increasing period

This waxing period is usually calculated from the crescent moon to the night before the full moon. Use the waxing moon for:

* Making a new beginning
* Working towards a longer-term goal
* Improving health
* Gradually increasing prosperity
* Attracting good luck
* Enhancing fertility
* Finding friendship, new love and romance
* Hunting for a job

* Making plans for the future
* Increasing psychic awareness

Full moon

The time of the full moon is calculated as anything from the second of the full moon by purists, the day of the full moon and the period until the next day or even the week of the full moon. Use the full moon for:

* Fulfilling an immediate need
* Boosting power or courage immediately
* Changing career or location
* Travelling
* Protecting yourself psychically
* Healing acute medical conditions
* Raising a large sum of money needed urgently
* Consummating love
* Making a permanent love commitment
* Ensuring fidelity, especially in a relationship that is looking shaky
* Bringing about justice
* Fulfilling ambition
* Gaining promotion

Waning moon

The waning period extends until the waning moon crescent disappears from the sky. Use the waning moon for:

* Removing pain and sickness
* Removing obstacles to success and happiness
* Lessening negative influences
* Reducing the hold of addictions and compulsions
* Banishing negative thoughts, grief, guilt, anxiety and destructive anger
* Banishing the envy and malice of others
* Ending relationships gently

There are also more subtle divisions and these I will describe as well, so you can decide the best way of relating to the lunar energies. Other practitioners work with the dual waxing and waning periods with the full moon in the centre as the waxing reaches a climax of power and then tips over into the wane.

The dark of the moon

The intervening two and a half to three days are called the dark of the moon, when the moon is so close to the sun that it is invisible.

The Eight Phases of the Moon

This is the division pattern I work with as it allows you to time moon spells more precisely according to the need. I have also listed the angels of each period so that you can incorporate them into spells.

First, however, is a chart of the 28 moon angels so you can work each day with just one of the angels if you prefer, rather than as I have suggested the three or four associated with that phase.

As you work with moon angels you will starts to visualise them more clearly and find that you relate to one or two special ones and may channel their wisdom. Though I have described how I picture these moon angels, you may see them entirely differently. Count I from the first day of the new moon, marked in diaries as a black circle. If there are 29 days, use Angel 28 Amnixiel twice.

I	Geniel	8	Amnediel	15	Atliel	22	Geliel
2	Enediel	9	Barbiel	16	Azeruel	23	Requiel
3	Anixiel	10	Ardifiel	17	Adriel	24	Abrimael
4	Azariel	11	Neciel	18	Egibiel	25	Aziel
5	Gabriel	12	Abdizuel	19	Amutiel	26	Tagriel
6	Dirachiel	13	Jazariel	20	Kyriel	27	Atheniel
7	Scheliel	14	Ergediel	21	Bethnael	28/29	Amnixiel

First period: the new or dark moon, days 1, 2 and 3 of the cycle

Angels: Geniel, Enediel and Anixiel

Picture these angels as black shadowy forms with pale silver wings and a pale silver halo.

The new moon (or dark moon) rises at dawn and sets at dusk. Because the sun and moon are in the same part of the sky, the sunlight obscures the moon in the day. At night, the moon is on the other side of the earth with the sun and you will see nothing.

While this period generally is not used for magick, it is a powerful period for divination and meditation and for allowing the seeds of the future to grow. I have also recently discovered the power of the dark of the moon for balancing magick, especially if you carry the spell over the moon changeover period. You would banish on the last day of the old moon, do holding/healing magick on the dark phase and as soon as that crescent appears you introduce the new to replace the old.

Day 1 is good for meditation.

Some months you may glimpse the crescent moon on day 3, in which case you can merge the two energies of the new and crescent.

Second period: the waxing moon, days 4–14

From when the crescent first appears in the sky to the day the full moon rises. The light increases from right to left during this period. The closer to the full moon, the more intense the energies and the larger the moon disc.

Crescent moon: days 4–7

Angels: Azariel, Gabriel, Dirachiel and Scheliel; crescent moon angels with the exception of Archangel Gabriel who is tall and silver, have crescent moon haloes and a soft shimmering light all round them and are very delicate and feminine.

The first crescent is very slender and is most easily seen at sunset close to the place the sun sets. The crescent moon rises mid-morning and sets some time after sunset. During these days, the moon can be seen on a clear day from moonrise to moonset.

Use its energies to set plans in motion, for matters concerning animals and small children, and for optimism and for new love, family joy, to make wishes and for the gradual growth of money.

First quarter or waxing (increasing), day 8–11

Angels: Amnediel, Barbiel, Ardifiel and Neciel

Waxing moon angels can be seen surrounded by radiant silver moonbeams with glowing golden wings. They are feminine in energy.

The moon rises about noon and sets about midnight, and can be seen from rise to set.

Use its energy for spells for improved health, good luck, courage, attracting or increasing love, for employment issues, house moves and faster finances. Day 8 is very good for healing. Day 10 is special for visions and spiritual insights.

The gibbous moon (bulging almost full moon), days 12–14

Angels: Abdizuel, Jazariel and Ergediel

Visualise these angels in flowing robes of silver and gold with long, white gold, flowing hair.

The gibbous moon rises in the middle of the afternoon and sets before dawn the next day. It can be seen soon after rising and then until it sets. It is easily recognisable by the bulge on the left side.

Use for spells for increased power or increasing commitment in love, for fertility, promotion, travel, also for patience, for the relief of long standing illnesses and problems. Days 13 and 14 are good for all purification and cleansing rites.

Third period: the full moon, days 15–17

Angels: Atliel, Azeruel and Adriel

These are glorious silver and gold angels, studded with stars and with huge, full, starry haloes.

The moon is considered magically to be full from moonrise to moonset on the night of the full moon. The hours immediately around that period and also, to a lesser extent, the following day can also be counted. The full moon rises at sunset and sets at sunrise, so you can have a brief period when both sun and full moon are in the sky together: amazing energy.

Use these days to initiate sudden or dramatic change, for a surge of power, for success, the consummation of love, raising money urgently, for healing, for prophecy, for all matters concerning women and also motherhood, for conception and for granting small miracles, for artistic and creative success and all legal matters, for fidelity. Day 15 is good for meditation as well as channelling wisdom from the Moon Mother or Gabriel, Archangel of the moon.

Fourth period: the waning (or decreasing) moon, days 18–28 or 29

The moon decreases from right to left until finally the crescent disappears from the left. About two and a half days later, the crescent reappears on the right as a silver sliver again. Waning moon magick should not be thought of as dark or negative, but rather as a process of bidding farewell to what is no longer wanted or helpful.

The disseminating moon (the waning or decreasing full moon), days 18–21

Angels: Egibiel, Amutiel, Kyriel and Bethnael

Picture these as more mature angels, very female, with pure white robes and pale shimmering blue haloes and wings.

The full moon is shrinking and rises now in the mid-evening, setting in the middle of the next morning, being visible for much of the time.

Use the decreasing full moon for protection of home, self and loved ones, for banishing bad habits, phobias and fears, for ending a long-standing destructive or abusive relationship, for relieving acute pain and fighting viruses and for leaving behind the past that holds us back from happiness.

The waning half moon or last quarter moon, days 22–25

Angels: Geliel, Requiel, Abrimael and Aziel

These angels are mistier, but still shimmer silver and gold from their wings and haloes. They are dark haired and feminine in their energies.

This moon rises about midnight and sets around midday the next day. It is visible for the whole time it is in the sky.

Use for protection while travelling, especially at night, from fears that wake us in the night, from phantoms and nightmares, for reducing major debts, for concerns about older people, for mending quarrels and for avoiding intrusion of privacy, for peaceful divorce and for relieving stress. Day 23 is an important time for healing and the 25th for all women's needs.

The balsamic or waning crescent moon, days 26–28, (and day 29, where relevant)

Angels: Tagriel, Atheniel and Amnixiel

Her angels are almost transparent with a single star on their headdress and silver, grey hair, very female and slow in their movements.

The balsamic moon rises before dawn (after the midnight of its day) and sets at mid-afternoon of the following day. She is best seen in the eastern sky in the dawn and very early morning.

Use the waning crescent for quiet sleep if you are an insomniac, for peace of mind if you have been anxious or depressed, for protection from crime and harm, for the easing of addictions, for keeping secrets, for saying goodbye finally and for finding what is lost or has been stolen.

Moon void of course

This is not apparent in the sky, but is a brief time when spells tend to be less effective and, in everyday life, meetings or projects tend to get stuck and travel plans can go haywire. The void of course occurs as the moon leaves one astrological sign and travels to another. The moon spends about two and a half days each month in each zodiac sign. The void of course can last from a few minutes to almost a day.

You can check in any almanac, such as *Old Moore's* or, increasingly, horoscope pages in newspapers will alert you to this and the times. In an almanac it will be marked as v/c or even VOC next to the moon symbol and the time it begins. The next entry will tell you the time the moon enters the new zodiac sign, marking the ending of the void of course period. If you need to do spells at the void of course time, add extra incense, fresh flowers or herbs to counter the effect.

The sun in magick

In the Celtic and northern traditions, as well as among the Australian Aboriginals, there are sun mothers as well as sun fathers. They emphasise the nurturing power of the sun and often according to myth take a very active part in the ripening and harvesting of the crops (see page 239). For example, the Baltic Sun Goddess Saule would be seen in the summer walking among the growing crops, her golden hair streaming down her back.

I have written a whole module on sun magick including working with the three or four sun time divisions and the Ancient Egyptian altar. Though magick is rightly associated with the moon, nevertheless magick in daylight has a pure clear quality. If the sun is shining then the whole spell or ritual is energised and vitalised. As a Druidess I became fascinated by rituals in the eye of the sun and have noticed that the energy generated in me during daytime spellcasting lasts long after the spell. Without the Sun there could be no life and growth or fertility. Yet in excess it can be a destructive force. It affects winds, weather and like the moon the tides. The sun can be gentle, empowering, healing or beat down over parched deserts, burn skin or wither the crops.

Connecting with the sun

Sun magick is more instant than moon magick and each day offers a microcosmic form of the four main yearly solar festivals. Each dawn is a mini Spring Equinox, each noon a Summer Solstice writ small, each dusk an Autumn Equinox and midnight a Midwinter Solstice, promising that light will return with the new day – and how many of us have waited, unable to sleep, for that dawning.

Increasingly practitioners of magick are working with sundials and if they have the space creating a mini Stonehenge in the garden (you need an open vista), marking sunrises and sets on significant days like the Summer Solstice. But even in the centre of a town, you can note how the sun rises and sets over different buildings during the year. Within your home where a certain room regularly has sunlight, create a sun altar (see page 496).

Take time to stop and tune into a sunrise or sunset at work, as well as in ritual, and make an empowerment or blessing. There is more on this on page 210 and in my book on natural magick.

Sun and moon energies

The more you work with the sun and become aware of how it can enhance and empower lunar cycles in spellcasting, the more all embracing magick becomes. You can combine lunar and solar energies. For example, in balancing magick you can work with the full moon round about sunset in the brief time they are both in the sky. On the day of the full moon at noon when everything is buzzing, anything seems possible, and spells for power or energy need little input to fly high.

Synchronise your sun and moon days and times to have the initial impetus of the sun followed up by the slower lunar energies. On the morning the first crescent is due, begin a spell at dawn, and continue with empowerments at noon and sunset. Then watch for the first crescent of the month shining silver, just after sunset, to make your wishes so the day becomes truly one of new beginnings. Equally, twilight solar rituals on the waning moon, even though you can't see it in the sky, will start the tide of gentle banishment that you can then culminate in a final part of the ritual when late at night that waning moon finally appears.

Sun correspondences

The following associations can be used in spellcasting or when calling down the power of the sun (see page 491).

* **Animals/birds:** Eagle, hawk, jaguar (the dark sun), lion, macaw, raven, salmon, stag, sometimes the bear
* **Archangel:** Michael
* **Colour:** Gold
* **Crystals:** Amber, carnelian, diamond, clear crystal quartz spheres and rainbow quartz, tiger's eye, topaz
* **Day of the week:** Sunday
* **Element:** Fire
* **Flowers:** Any yellow or golden ones, but especially sunflowers, marigolds and golden carnations
* **Herbs, incenses and oils:** Cloves, cinnamon, chamomile, frankincense, olive, rosemary, saffron, St John's wort
* **Metal:** Gold
* **Trees:** Bay, birch, laurel, palm

The sun and time

The apparent motion of the sun across the sky formed the basis for measuring time from early days and at any locality. When the sun reaches the highest point in the sky during any given day, it is noon. This point is called the meridian. Since the length of the day according to solar time is not the same throughout the year, mean solar time was invented, based on the motion of a hypothetical sun travelling at an even rate throughout the year. The difference in the length of the 24-hour day at different seasons of the year can be as much as 16 minutes.

Standard time, which is based on solar time, was introduced in 1883 by international agreement and the earth was divided into 24 time zones. The base position is the zero meridian of longitude that passes through the Royal Greenwich Observatory, Greenwich, England, and time zones are described by their distance east or west of Greenwich. Within each time zone, all clocks are set to the same time. In 1966, the US Congress passed the Uniform Time Act, which established eight standard time zones for the US and its possessions. In 1983, several time zone boundaries were altered so that Alaska, which had formerly spanned four zones, could be nearly unified at less than one time zone.

Modern magick recognises the 24-hour clock and uses the current time in the time zone in which the practitioner is working.

Magick and measuring the sun

In winter, dawn is far later than in summer and dusk is far earlier. This also means that except on the Equinoxes you do not get equal divisions between the four daily solar change points, dawn, noon, dusk/twilight and midnight (the time of the invisible sun, when it is at full height on the other side of the world). Depending on where you live, you might have almost continuous daylight at the height of summer and a true midnight sun (as opposed to the magickal dark sun or sun that is visualised at midnight shining through a hole in the dark sky from the other hemisphere of the world, see page 502).

Myth recognised this magickal dark sun. In Ancient Egypt, the Sun God Ra sailed his boat through the Duat, the dark womb of the Mother, at night and had to fight Apep the chaos serpent. Among the Mayans, Kinich Ahau, the Sun God whose name meant face of the sun, took the form of a macaw by day. He became a jaguar at night to fight the fierce nightly battle in the Underworld that the sun might rise again in the morning.

For everyday spells, as opposed to special rituals where you want to greet the actual dawn and the rising sun, you can work with the timeframe suggested below and use candles where necessary to supplement the absence of daylight.

Dawn: the time you wake or begin your day

Noon: when you break for lunch

Dusk/twilight: when you go home from work

Midnight: before you go to bed

That way even if you just mark the four divisions when you have time with simple blessings, you can harmonise your working day/a day of leisure with spiritual marker points and so make each day more sacred. Picture the angels of the sun in your own way and in time you will connect with their power, health bringing and inspirational qualities and hear their messages.

Dawn/waking

Every dawn is a Spring Equinox written small, a resurrection, the birth of new hope. Today is the day you anticipated or feared in many sleepless nights or anxious moments. So walk into the dawn with courage, knowing that this day will be absolutely the best one ever, because you will make it so. For dawn spells or any during the morning, face east.

Angels

Raphael Archangel of dawn, is also the healer Archangel and protector of travellers (more of him on page 577). Picture him carrying a golden vial of medicine, with a traveller's staff, dressed in the colours of early morning sunlight, with a beautiful green healing ray emanating from his halo.

Och is also angel of alchemy and minerals and is a bringer of health and long life. He is a misty yellow with tiny sparkling yellow gems round the hem of his robe.

Gazardiel is the angel appointed to guard the east and oversees the rising and setting of the sun. He is a yellow and green angel with a sparkling halo with the colours of sunrise and sunset.

Use dawn magick for spells for: travel; initiating a project or new beginnings in any aspect of your life; optimism; reversing bad luck; improving health; improving career prospects; house moves; improving financial matters; finding new love and trust.

Noon

Be not sad, be as the sun at midday says a passage in the *I Ching*. Whether the sun is beating down or hiding behind sullen clouds, the noon energies are powerful, like the Summer Solstice whose microcosm or mini-version it is. The sun king rose in triumph and so you will overcome any obstacle to fulfilment. For noon spells or any around the middle of the day or early afternoon face south.

Angels

Michael Archangel of the sun is pictured with golden wings in red and gold armour with sword, shield, a green date branch and carrying the scales of justice or a white banner with a red cross.

Oranir is the chief angel of the Summer Solstice or Midsummer Day and protects us against all harm, if we speak his name. He is brilliant gold.

Galgaliel governs the wheel of the sun as it turns in the sky. His halo is like the rays emanating from the sun disc.

Use noon magick for spells for: creating a sudden burst of power or confidence; bringing a fast or large infusion of money; for major promotion or career advancement; for consummation of love; for a permanent commitment in love or to ensure fidelity; sending absent healing for serious or acute conditions; successful resolution of a court case or official matter; to send urgent or major healing; for joy.

Dusk/going home

My late mother used to say, *Never let the sun go down on anger.* This is the daily message of dusk, writ large in the Autumn Equinox. What is gained and what is lost all merge into the darkness and with them we can drain resentment, regrets and also be pleased with ourselves for what we have achieved during the day, however small. For dusk or twilight spells face east.

Angels

Scachlil is the angel of the sun's dying rays and governor of the ninth hour. He flares golden for the last time each night as the sun sinks.

Aftiel, angel of twilight, is a shadowy angel, best seen outdoors as the last rays of the sun are disappearing, with silvery grey wings and a halo containing the purple of sunset.

Jeduthun is leading angel of the evening choirs in heaven. As a result, it is said, the world is blessed because God is pleased with the singing and so dawn will break again. Visualise him with his scrolls of music in the evening light, a faint rainbow formed from the harmony of the notes around his head.

Use dusk magick for spells for: letting go of regrets. anger or guilt; psychic and physical protection; reducing pain and illness; reducing debt; justice and just reward; love in maturity; home and family matters.

Midnight

Midnight corresponds with the Midwinter Solstice, the rebirth of light. Just as sunset began a new day for the Celts, so in the modern world midnight is the transition. *The darkest hour is before the dawn* is another popular saying that rings of truth. But in another time zone the sun is shining brightly and we know, unlike our distant forebears, that the sun does not disappear into the sea or back into the womb of the earth mother to sleep until morning. But nevertheless each morning when it reappears is a small miracle and affirmation of hope. For midnight spells face north.

Angels

Uriel is a regent or guardian of the sun who brought alchemy to humankind. Guardian of midnight, Uriel is a pure pillar of fire, dressed in rich burnished gold and ruby red with a bright flame-like halo (see page 290).

Leliel/Lailah, angel of the night, has deep midnight blue robes and a halo and wings flecked with stars.

Use midnight spells for: sending healing (10 pm is the healing hour), especially chronic conditions and pain; forgiving self and others; accepting what cannot be changed chronic pain; contacting absent family members and friends; connecting with wise ancestors, Guardian Angels and Spirit Guides; bindings and banishing of all kinds.

The planets

Each of the planets rules a day of the week and two hours every day, one after dawn and the other after dusk. You can use its associated metals, incense and so on to strengthen a spell worked on that day. The associations are the same as those of the days of the week listed in pages 193–196. However, I will give more information on each of the planets and the glyph that you can use on charms or talismans to invoke its powers. For example, for a Venus love charm you would make it on a Friday, her day, at the first hour after dawn, her hour (or her other hour, which varies after sunset), perhaps painting her glyph on rose quartz, her crystal, and naming the purpose by writing over the crystal in rose or vervain incense smoke, her fragrances.

The spell purposes also apply to the hours the planet rules each day. You will notice that to correspond with the days of the week only the seven ancient planets that could be seen with the human eye that include the sun and moon are used.

I would suggest you use star maps online to see when various planets are visible in the night sky. Connecting with the actual planet is very empowering magickally and then when you work on a planetary day or hour you can clearly picture the heavenly body and its deity.

The sun ☉

All cultures have worshipped the sun. In Ancient Greece, the Solar God, Helios, was praised each dawn as he emerged in the east and drove his chariot of winged horses around the sky. In myth, Saule, the Baltic Sun Goddess, at the beginning of December began her long journey of return and on the feast of St Lucia, on 13 December once the Northern Goddess of Light Saule danced with her daughters, the planets (see page 239).

The Sun intensifies the influence of any sun sign in which it appears on a *natal* chart. It spends approximately a month in each sign.

Rules: Leo and Sunday and the first hour after dawn on a Sunday

Astrologically represents: The essential self, identity; personality and unique qualities

Use the sun in spells: for innovation of all kinds and new beginnings. It is also potent for energy, joy, health, prosperity, spiritual awareness and self-confidence. It will bring wealth and prosperity where there is poverty and failure and will help to break a run of bad luck. The sun is for all matters concerning fathers.

The moon ☽

The moon has traditionally been regarded as the consort of the sun, her silver to his gold, Queen Luna to King Sol in alchemy. The Goddess Diana (sister of the Sun God, Apollo) was worshipped as the moon in all her aspects.

Since the moon spends only two and a half days in each sign each month, its influence is relatively transient and so its position is an important calculation in daily or weekly horoscopes and short-term predictions. This also means that its spell energies vary according to which sign it is in the month (see page 484 in the module on the moon for more on this).

The Moon influences the tides and there is also a hypothesis that it affects the flow of energies in women and to a lesser degree men.

Rules: Cancer, Monday and the first hour after dawn on Monday

Astrologically represents: the emotional and unconscious aspects of the personality and was in earlier times the most important planet in a chart

Use the moon in spells: for the home and family matters, especially the mother, children and animals. Its prime focus is fertility, and it rules over all the ebbs and flows of the human body, mind and psyche. The moon will provide protection, especially while travelling, and will aid psychic development, clairvoyance and meaningful dreams. It is potent for all sea and gardening rituals and for herb magick and healing, as well as for keeping secrets.

Mars ♂

Mars is the planet with a reddish tinge. Red being seen as a warlike colour, it ended up with the name of the Roman God of War. Mars, son of Jupiter, was the father of Romulus and Remus who founded Rome and as God of both agriculture and war, very much represented the ideal Roman, first as farmer and then as conqueror in ancient times. Mars is still regarded as the bringer of wars.

It takes nearly two years for Mars to complete its orbit through the zodiac and so its influence is slower and longer lasting than the planets that are closer to the sun than the Earth, a factor that can be crucial in negotiations of peace in trouble spots where fighting can go on for months.

Rules: Aries and is the co-ruler of Scorpio, Tuesday and the first hour after dawn on Tuesday

Astrologically represents: initiative, independent action and maintaining a sense of separateness from other people, at home or work in a small group situation

Use Mars in spells: for courage, change, taking the initiative, independence and separateness from others, also to overcome seemingly impossible odds, to defeat opposition and to enhance health, strength and vitality; use also for passion and the consummation of love.

Mercury ☿

Mercury was the Roman winged messenger of the gods (known as Hermes to the Greeks), the son of Jupiter. Carrying a rod entwined with two serpents that could induce sleep, he travelled between the heavens, Earth and the Underworld. Through his skill and dexterity, he came to rule over commerce and medicine and thieves.

Mercury takes about 88 days to complete its orbit of the sun, and so is a swift-moving planet in charts and may therefore be crucial for calculating the timing of affairs regarding communication or financial wheeling and dealing.

Rules: Gemini and Virgo, Wednesday and the first hour of Wednesday after dawn

Astrologically represents: the way the basic character is communicated or expressed in the everyday world

Use Mercury in spells: for money-making ventures, clear communication, persuasion, adaptability and versatility, improving memory and sharpening logic, learning, examinations and tests, mastering new technology, short-distance travel and short breaks, and conventional methods of healing, especially surgery. It is also potent for business negotiations, overcoming debt, and repelling envy, malice, spite and deceit.

Jupiter ♃

Jupiter, known as the sky father, was the supreme Roman God, ruler of the universe. Like his Greek counterpart Zeus, he controlled the thunderbolts, which were carried by his eagle, the king of the birds. He ruled not despotically, but as the chief of a triumvirate of deities, the others being his consort Juno and Minerva, Goddess of Wisdom. Jupiter is known as the joy-bringer and is associated with all forms of good fortune and prosperity.

Because Jupiter takes about 12 years to circle the zodiac, the effects of this planet tend to be more pervasive and gradual, bringing periods of renewed optimism and economic growth, when it is favourably inspected. As a natal position, it coincides in personal charts with major change points in the lifecycle: for example, from birth to adolescence.

Rules: Sagittarius, is co-ruler of Pisces and also Thursday and the first hour after dawn on a Thursday

Astrologically represents: expression of the personality in the context of wider society and culture

Use Jupiter in spells: for all forms of increase and expansion, be it in the realm of money, career, power or joy, leadership, conscious wisdom, creativity, extending one's influence in the wider world, idealism, justice and the law, authority and altruism, marriage, permanent relationships (business and personal), fidelity, loyalty and male potency; also for overcoming any excesses.

Venus ♀

Venus is sometimes known as the Morning or Evening Star, because she shines with brilliant silvery hue. At her brightest, she is the most brilliant object in the sky other than the sun and moon. She is also the nearest planet to Earth and the closest in size. For this reason she is sometimes regarded as Earth's twin although, in fact, Mars is more like Earth. Venus takes 225 days to travel round the sun and so can be influential in the progress of a love affair or business partnerships.

Venus, whose Greek name was Aphrodite (born of the foam), was beauty incarnate, the Roman Goddess of love and seduction.

Rules: Taurus and Libra, Friday and the first hour after dawn on a Friday

Astrologically represents: the way an individual interacts with significant others, such as lovers, parents, families, business partners and friends

Use Venus in spells: for love and all forms of love magick (especially to attract love), for beauty, the arts, crafts, relationships, friendships, blossoming sexuality, the acquisition of beautiful possessions, and the slow but sure growth of prosperity (Venus rules all matters of growth). Like the moon, she can be invoked for horticulture, the environment, fertility and women's health matters. Since she can be associated with excessive and unwise love affairs, her spells can, paradoxically, be used to reduce the influence of destructive lovers and possessiveness.

Saturn ♄

Saturn, the ringed planet and another giant, is even further out in space than Jupiter. In mythology, Saturnus, the Roman form of Cronos, God of Time, was Jupiter's father who was deposed by his son. Saturnus had devoured all his children except for Jupiter (Air), Neptune (Water) and Pluto (the Underworld), the three powers it is said time cannot destroy. Saturnus therefore had to bow to the inevitable.

Because it takes Saturn 28–30 years to complete its orbit of the zodiac, this is the longest planetary cycle that will occur more than once in an average lifetime and so in a natal chart, it represents the major stages of human life, as well as affecting more global affairs by spending more than two and a half years in each sign: long enough to be felt as a recession.

Rules: Capricorn and is co-ruler of Aquarius, Saturday and the first hour after dawn on a Saturday

Astrologically represents: the expression of the individual's personality and interactions within the restrictions imposed by society and the constraints of space and time

Use Saturn in spells: concerned with unfinished business, with endings that lead to beginnings, for resolving all slow-moving matters and for accepting limitations, as well as for overcoming obstacles that are long-standing or need careful handling.

It can also be used for lifting depression or doubts, meditation, long-term psychic protection, locating lost objects (as well as animals and people) and regaining self-control over bad habits or emotions, to slow down the outward flow of money and to encourage those who owe you favours or money to repay; also to banish pain and illness and bring acceptance of what cannot be changed.

Planetary hours of the day and night

The planetary hours are used to give particular power to spells and rituals by reflecting the planetary energies that are strong at certain periods every day. So the sun hours in a particular day would, like the day Sunday, give a huge infusion of power and be good for success or new beginning rituals.

Therefore the sun hours on a Sunday would give you double sun power or you might choose to cast your spell on a Mars hour on Sunday to add some assertiveness and determination to the ambition you were seeking to fulfil by working on Sunday. In this case you would mix the associated colours, so maybe using one gold candle for the sun and a red one for Mars (whose associations are identical to Tuesday).

Reread the days of the week (see page 193) to remind yourself and maybe write them as planetary associations in your Book of Shadows with the appropriate planetary glyph.

Sunrise to sunset

The first hour period each day at sunrise is ruled by its day planet. As you will see, the planetary order has a regular pattern. So the first hour of Sunday after dawn is ruled by the sun, and so on.

Hour	Sunday	Monday	Tuesday	Wednesday	Thursday	Friday	Saturday
I	Sun	Moon	Mars	Mercury	Jupiter	Venus	Saturn
2	Venus	Saturn	Sun	Moon	Mars	Mercury	Jupiter
3	Mercury	Jupiter	Venus	Saturn	Sun	Moon	Mars
4	Moon	Mars	Mercury	Jupiter	Venus	Saturn	Sun
5	Saturn	Sun	Moon	Mars	Mercury	Jupiter	Venus
6	Jupiter	Venus	Saturn	Sun	Moon	Mars	Mercury
7	Mars	Mercury	Jupiter	Venus	Saturn	Sun	Moon
8	Sun	Moon	Mars	Mercury	Jupiter	Venus	Saturn
9	Venus	Saturn	Sun	Moon	Mars	Mercury	Jupiter
10	Mercury	Jupiter	Venus	Saturn	Sun	Moon	Mars
11	Moon	Mars	Mercury	Jupiter	Venus	Saturn	Sun
12	Saturn	Sun	Moon	Mars	Mercury	Jupiter	Venus

Sunset

Hour	Sunday	Monday	Tuesday	Wednesday	Thursday	Friday	Saturday
I	Jupiter	Venus	Saturn	Sun	Moon	Mars	Mercury
2	Mars	Mercury	Jupiter	Venus	Saturn	Sun	Moon
3	Sun	Moon	Mars	Mercury	Jupiter	Venus	Saturn
4	Venus	Saturn	Sun	Moon	Mars	Mercury	Jupiter
5	Mercury	Jupiter	Venus	Saturn	Sun	Moon	Mars
6	Moon	Mars	Mercury	Jupiter	Venus	Saturn	Sun
7	Saturn	Sun	Moon	Mars	Mercury	Jupiter	Venus
8	Jupiter	Venus	Saturn	Sun	Moon	Mars	Mercury
9	Mars	Mercury	Jupiter	Venus	Saturn	Sun	Moon
I0	Sun	Moon	Mars	Mercury	Jupiter	Venus	Saturn
II	Venus	Saturn	Sun	Moon	Mars	Mercury	Jupiter
I2	Mercury	Jupiter	Venus	Saturn	Sun	Moon	Mars

Calculating the planetary hours

Read the following once or twice and then practise calculating the sunrise to sunset and sunset to sunrise planetary times for the day ahead.

* Because the times of sunrise and sunset are different each day, the first planetary hour begins at sunrise and you can then calculate the 60-minute segments from this all the way to sunset for the individual day.

* The first 15 minutes of any planetary hour are always the most potent.

* Allow one hour for each of the planetary hours. So if sunrise was at 06.13 on a Sunday that would be the Sun's hour until 07.13 and Venus's hour would be 07.13–08.13, Mercury 08.13–09.13, and so on.

* At the height of summer, the days are much longer than the nights, so you will need more than the 12 hours given on the sunrise to sunset list given above. In this case, go back to the start of the list. From Hour I on that day continue down the list until you hit sunset.

* The last hour after sunrise will be incomplete since it is unlikely that, say, a 06.13 sunrise would be followed in the evening by a precisely 20.13 sunset. That does not matter at all. The only time you get precisely the 12 hours are on the Equinoxes on 21 March and 21 September or thereabouts.

* Start the sunset first hour at the precise hour and minute of sunset as given in the newspaper or your diary, regardless of the fact your sunrise period hour before may not be quite complete or even that you have run into another before sunset hour begins, for just a few minutes.

* So if sunset was 20.22 on the Sunday, Hour I after sunset would be Jupiter until 21.22 and then Mars as Hour 2 after sunset at 21.22 until 22.22, and so on, regardless of the sunrise start time earlier in the day.

* It doesn't matter that there are fewer than 12 hours of sunset to sunrise in summer. Just keep going hour-by-hour through the night, then start again with the next-day sunrise.

* There is a more accurate but complex method of measuring to the second that experienced witches might know and is in my *Practical Guide to Witchcraft*. However, the method here is near enough to work well, especially if you say, for example, *This is my Mercury hour after sunset as I begin this spell*. Much easier is to use an online site to give you the accurate times, and concentrate on the magick not the mathematics.

* In contrast, in winter you will have more sunset hours than the 12 listed. Again, for longer winter sunsets to sunrise periods you can start the 12-hour cycle again when you have been through it once.

PRACTICAL ASSIGNMENT

Adapting spells

Recently I created what I considered an excellent three-part sea spell to bring the tides of change into the life of a woman living in Malibu, whose career seemed for no good reason to be blocked at every turn. I calculated the moon, tides, etc. Then she emailed me to say all the Los Angeles area beaches were suddenly closed for several days for environmental reasons. Since the spell was going from the end of the waning period, which we had almost reached, through the dark to crescent moon, it involved a swift and serious rethink. Sometimes you will not get the ideal circumstances, especially if a spell is cast over a period of days of even weeks.

Being able to adapt, substitute and find short cuts to overcome hitches comes with experience and ensures you can practise magick under even the least ideal circumstances. Build in contingency plans when planning spells and you will find it easier to be flexible.

If you are experienced in magick and know about planetary/Archangel hours and the influence of the moon on particular zodiac signs as it passes through all 12 each month (see page 484), you can add as many factors as you like to the background energies, but note which are crucial and which just beneficial.

* Without writing whole spells, plan the outline of a spell for yourself/people you know and calculate:

  * The external factors, trying to get in at least three in place, moon, sun, day etc

  * The ideal setting

  * The timeframe: three days before the full moon, every Friday, the first of the month, every full moon; and for how long: weeks or months or until it works? Is that realistic, given the constraints of everyday life and other magickal commitments

* If it is a long-term spell, how can you get round the wrong moon phase on some of the occasions or if you/the person has to be away on one of the Fridays and can't do the spell?

- When is the anticipated fulfilment? By the time the next moon is full? Within three moons? If for love, should the love last through this lifetime/through many lifetimes, as long as the sun shines or the waters flow/so long as we/they both shall will it?
- If the romance sought by the spell doesn't last, should you build in an empowerment to find someone else who will make him/her/me happy?
- Should you leave some spells open ended, as when the time is right/when it is right to be or is that sometimes a let out clause? Is an open-ended spell fraught with hazards or advisable in many cases, unless there is a specific date, such as a driving test?
- Once you have the spell outline, check for possible hazards caused by people/weather/circumstances. Can the spell be adapted easily if circumstances or the weather changes? (Some cannot and should not be cast unless everything is right.) If you can adapt to possible hazards what candles, crystal, herbs could balance the missing factor?
- Keep the spell and in future modules you can add to it.

Further research

Either explore planetary timings further or look up the current planetary positions and go stargazing.

Further information

Recommended reading
- *Llewellyn's Almanac*, Llewellyn
- *Llewellyn's Pocket Planner and Ephemeris*, Llewellyn
- *Old Moore's Almanack*, Foulsham
- Pepper Elizabeth, *Witch's Almanac*, Witch's Almanac Press, 2007
- *Tybol Astrological Almanac*, 27 Heversham Avenue, Fulwood, Preston PR2 9TD
- *We' Moon 07*, Mother Tongue Ink, Oregon (my favourite)
- Eason, Cassandra, *Cassandra Eason's Complete Book of Natural Magick*, Quantum, 2005
- Eason, Cassandra, *A Practical Guide to Witchcraft and Magick Spells*, Foulsham, 2001

Websites
- *Farmers Almanac*
  Good website, also in journal form; excellent, especially on moons
  www.farmersalmanac.com
- *Catherine Yronwode*
  Also very good on talismans and amulets
  www.luckymojo.com/moonphases.html

See also Week 38 for good moon sites.

THE GOD AND GODDESS IN MAGICK

Deity energies in magick represent a higher or idealised form of particular strengths and qualities. We already possess the seeds of these evolved qualities within us. When we call either on the God or Goddess or different named deities from traditions around the world, we are awakening our own inner divine or higher spiritual core I believe we all possess.

This is a dual module and I have given a comprehensive list of gods and goddesses from different traditions in the next module. I have not separated them because in different cultures the same deity energies: for example, the moon and sun can be represented by male or female deities. But first, we will focus on bringing the God and Goddess energies into magick and our lives, working specifically with the Charge of the Goddess.

The Divine Force

The undivided Divine Force is the Great Goddess in the mythology of many lands. From the all encompassing, undifferentiated Goddess force that contains both male and female energies emanates all creation. In mythology from Australian Aboriginal to the Ancient Babylonian people and that of Classical Greece and Rome, the Goddess is seen giving birth to creation and sometimes dying during the process so that all that is created (including the God form) is made of and from her body. In her life-giving role, the Cosmic Goddess is also equated with Mother Earth from whom all life comes and to which it returns, because she embraces birth, death and rebirth: sound ecology as well as spirituality.

But in ritual and myth, the Goddess power becomes even more personalised and differentiated as a separate God and Goddess, representing the polarities of animus and anima, male and female, each containing within the other the seeds or potential and aspects of the other energy like yang and yin pictured right.

In witchcraft, the Goddess still retains her greater role, as well as the more specific anima or yin aspects that form the alter ego of the God. Therefore in many traditions the Goddess remains supreme in ritual and more powerful than the God power that emanates from her.

Finding your own God and Goddess path

Can we carry out magick and believe in the principles of witchcraft without reference to specific Gods and Goddesses? Yes, but you would find it hard not to refer to and draw energy from some higher power, whether an undifferentiated source of light and goodness or nature at her most evolved, some creative principle that is both external and at the same time contained as the spiritual core within us, our own inner God or Goddess. We can aspire to develop and draw down higher energies into ourselves whatever we call them or from whoever we derive them, and the more you work with magick the more active your own divine centre becomes.

In Witchcraft we are lucky, because there are a huge range of deity focuses from many ages and cultures, so that we can connect a God and Goddess that is right for us ritually and personally. Even experienced witches may find their personal deity focus changing at different life stages, crises and challenges, as well as for different rituals and seasons. But there may be a special Goddess or God who is always central, no matter how many deities you work with.

Though variations of the Horned God, Diana or her daughter Aradia are a traditional pairing in rites, you may find you relate most readily to Ancient Egyptian or Celtic deities, perhaps because of some past life connection. Let your God and Goddess polarity and the Great Goddess (the latter may become one and the same in ceremonies like drawing down the moon) take the form and names that are right for you, even if they are different from conventional descriptions of the deity. For some practitioners, the names God and Goddess are used whatever the deity quality or power is being invoked (more of this in the practical assignment at the end of this module).

You may prefer to use names outside those traditionally applied to deities. This is also fine. I knew one witch who called the Great Goddess Esme and her God form David and for her this worked well. If you do this, you are not making up deities but channelling the energies within terms of your own frame of reference. This is ultimately what even the wisest writer from the past or spiritual organisation has done when trying to describe forces beyond a single physical form or human comprehension.

How to talk to the God and Goddess

Statues on your altar, candles, pictures, a jet and amber crystal, a shell and horn/antler or wooden or clay representations are ways I have suggested of representing the God and Goddess on your altar. Representations of the deities are a good focus for linking our personal spells and rituals with Cosmic and Earth Mother powers. Especially for solitary practitioners they also provide a connection between all practitioners in all times and ages who reach out to something greater to illuminate their lives.

Isis is called the Goddess of 10,000 names and the same is true of Gods, because whatever you call them, however you visualise them, they are all the same energy source and force, and will help us to move closer to fulfilling our own spiritual blueprint.

The following method is a way you can connect with the Goddess and God energies at your indoor or outdoor altar or in a place of beauty, whether as part of a formal spell or ritual or privately.

Purification

This involves preparing yourself spiritually to remove connections with the outside and material world. You will carry out the first five stages before rituals, as well.

* Have a bath using rose or lavender fragrance and then when you are dry, anoint each of your four higher chakras, Crown, Brow, Throat and Heart, with a single drop of pure water, rose or lavender water or essential oil diluted in a carrier oil.

* Say as you touch the centre of your hairline,

Above me the Light.

* Then at the Brow,

Within me the radiance.

* Then at the Throat,

That I may speak wisely.

* Finally at the left and then the right wrist pulse points for the Heart chakra,

The Love in my Heart.

* Light a white Goddess candle (left) and from it the God candle and then either light frankincense, myrrh or sandalwood incense sticks or put incense based on one of those fragrances on preheated charcoal.

* Ring a bell or strike a Tibetan singing bowl three times.

* Then sit in silence looking at a Goddess/God stature representation or both or close your eyes and visualise the deity form you need. You can speak to both the Goddess and the God if you wish, addressing first one then the other, or you can choose the focus you prefer.

Prayer or invocations

Prayer does have a place in witchcraft as in any other religion or even if you just use magick in your everyday world. It acknowledges the sacredness of the Craft and the willingness to open your heart and spirit to higher forces. It is not a substitute for spellcasting, but this slower, gentler connection is good if you are new to Goddess/God work or find the concept of working with higher powers difficult. It also adds another dimension to magick for solitary practitioners and coven members alike who could create a group prayer, each adding a line of the prayer as they sit in circle.

Prayer is different from spellcasting since it is a dialogue with the chosen God or Goddess when you talk to the Mother and/or Father from your heart. Sit or kneel and say,

I am within the God/the Goddess and He/She within me. So am I blessed and ever shall be.

Unlike channelling you do the talking, either aloud or in your head not a cosmic shopping list, but about yourself as you truly are and would like to be. You can, of course, ask for your needs, but unlike spellcasting you are gently floating any request for blessings, in the knowledge that your prayers will be answered at the time and in the way most appropriate. This is quite difficult because suddenly we are the child again and in a sense we have to lay aside all we have learned. We have to go back to the beginning and cannot learn how to pray except by praying.

Receiving wisdom

The final stage is listening, sometimes to the silence and allowing the stillness to enter you.

Gaze into the candle flame and inhale the fragrance. You may not get immediate answers to your prayers but a sense of wellbeing and peace. Occasionally you may hear words in your mind or find that after prayer you can receive wisdom that afterwards you can record in your Book of Shadows. Some practitioners pick up a pen and let the words flow. But if channelling does not follow accept the experience for what it was, a moment of connection.

You may find it helpful afterwards to read short passages from traditional witchcraft writings, such as Doreen Valiente's Charge of the Great Goddess. You may prefer another ceremony from a traditional Book of Shadows or some favourite poetry that inspires and uplifts. Alternatively, write your own inspirational magickal words.

Assuming deity powers magically

I have already mentioned the power of words to animate spell energies and this we will work on further in later modules. In Ancient Egypt it was believed that by speaking as though you were a deity you could amplify the higher power in yourself.

In magick, a common technique when working with deity powers is to use *I am* to merge your own spiritual energies with those of the most positive aspects of earlier deities (for certainly pre-Christian deities had their moods and foul tempers). In Ancient Egyptian magick, for example, Sobek, the Crocodile God, was frequently invoked for protection by taking on his symbolic fierceness, in doing so changing the aura of the speaker to emit defensive vibes that would over the days ahead make those threatening the speaker back off without knowing why. One version of this protective spell was:

> *I Sobek outface thee. With my mighty jaws, swift slashing tail and my razor claws I fear none, mortal or immortal. Yet shall I not attack thee. Slide back into the Nile slime and hide thy face in shame.*

Excellent for outfacing workplace bullies or vicious-tongued relatives.

The Charge of the Goddess and the God

Calling down into ourselves the Goddess power, usually on the night of the full moon and the God at times of God power (for example, the eve or dawn of the Summer or Midwinter Solstice) opens channels whereby you are filled with an inrush of Goddess/God power. This instantly floods your whole being with light and over time increases your own spiritual capacity to do magick. While in coven magick it is the High Priest who calls down the Goddess into the High Priestess, and the High Priestess who channels the God power into her High Priest, even if you work alone you can safely and effectively invoke these energies into yourself and as a result receive profound insights into life and spirituality.

The Charge or Command of the Goddess is similar to a Christian creed, but acts as the vehicle for the Goddess power, so that the Priestess/Practitioner speaks the words as though she were the Goddess. In doing so the Priestess/practitioner is overlaid with the Goddess presence (as I said earlier, this is not the same as being possessed). Those watching have reported the speaker becoming transformed with radiance and their aura illuminated with gold, as the highest level of the aura and the highest plane of deity power are momentarily merged.

The God Charge, which tends either to be the Horned or Dark God, is less commonly used, but I believe it is an important part of ritual for both men and women. I have created my own version of both Charges and you may find it helpful as a basis for writing your personal Charges (or of course use it if you wish in your rituals). The Charge of the God is described in the next module, but much of the information regarding using both Charges is common to both and so I have included it here.

Writing your own Goddess Charge

You can create your own Charge of the Goddess, looking at the Doreen Valiente one and other forms including mine to get the basic structure. There are also the Mother of Mystery, Aradia, the Triple Mother (Earth, Moon and Spirit) and the Creation Goddess Charges and you can create many variations. Here I am focusing on the main Great Goddess Charge. You can then weave into your Charges any names of Goddesses that have meaning for you and refer to the aspects of the Goddess or the cultures that for you are the most significant.

For there is no right structure or content except what is right for you and you may adapt your Charge over months and years. However you may find it useful to work around the basic framework given below. You may decide to work on your Charge at quiet times sitting in your altar place and reworking the words until they resonate. It may be easier to speak rather than write words to allow inspiration to emerge spontaneously from your own divine core. If you prefer, allow the words of your Charge to flow either as you draw down the moon or call the Goddess power at other times in ritual. You can speak these inspired words aloud and record them on a tape or CD, and later transcribe and perhaps fine-tune them.

* If you are working alone, surround a clear bowl of water or crystal sphere with white candles or sit in bright moonlight and, looking into the water or crystal, begin to speak. Tape-record your words to make them easier to recall. If you do not consciously try to formulate poetic expressions, profound poetry and rich images will emerge almost from another place. This is the deep pool of collective wisdom speaking through you.

* If working with a coven or magical group you can create the Charge collectively by sitting in circle and passing the crystal sphere or bowl of water from person to person, adding lines as each gazes into the sphere or water by moonlight or a

circle of tea lights. This can be recorded and transcribed for the collective Book of Shadows.

- As each person gazes into the water or sphere, he or she should speak from the heart a series of images about what the Goddess represents to him or her.
- You can go round the group as many times as you wish and then end with the Isis Astarte chant below or one you have woven to include your favourite deities.
- Afterwards solitary practitioners and coven members may see the Goddess in the centre of the circle.
- Working on the Charge can be a fruitful activity every three months whether you work alone or in a coven/group. If you are a solitary practitioner, play the recording and join in if you wish looking into a candle flame or in a wild open place and feel the energies of women and men through the ages resounding beyond and within you.

Cassandra's Charge of the Goddess

The following is a version I have developed since the first writing to incorporate my favourite Goddesses, especially in the three forms of maiden, mother and wise woman that link with the phases of the moon. I have not created it so the power needs to be drawn by a male into the female, though the opening lines could be spoken by another individual of either sex or by the practitioner to centre herself. I have used the Celtic maiden Brighid (often pronounced Breed), the Ancient Egyptian Sky Mother Nut and the Norse grandmother Hulda. If you prefer you can keep your Goddesses within a single tradition or use a variety of Goddesses, as in the Valiente Charge.

The Mother in all her aspects

This opening section links the concept of the Mother of All to the three phases maiden, mother and crone and so centres all the different goddess powers into a single energy source to be drawn down into the speaker:

So spoke the Great Mother who has been known in many forms and by many names in countless ages, but is and always will be one and the same. As the Maiden, she is Brighid, Lady of the sacred wells whose white wand melts the frozen fields and restores fertility to land, animals and people.

As Mother she is Nut, Egyptian Sky Mother whose body was covered with stars as she arched over the whole world, she who received the Sun God Ra into her womb each night to be reborn with the new day. Finally she is you Hulda, kindly grandmother of the forests who covers the winter fields with snow that they may rest. Gently you gather the unborn children and those who have passed beyond earthly life, round the fire in your cave to keep them warm and wrap them in soft blankets you have woven from the stars. With the first light you are midwife to the young sun Vali the Light Bearer and so transform the old and outworn into new life to be yourself reborn as the Maiden in the Spring.

The Goddess speaks

This is the part where the practitioner begins to speak as though she were the Goddess and in doing do is able to merge her own individual self with the Goddess power:

When the moon is full or at any time of the day, night and in any season you can call on me, Goddess, mother, sister, friend, daughter, grandmother who has lived and loved and laughed and cried through all ages and all places, for I bring love, joy, health, healing and abundance.

You may bring me your hopes with the waxing moon, your dreams to bring to life as the moon is full blown and your sorrows and fears on the wane. You may rest when the moon is dark, knowing that there is a better tomorrow and that I will lift you up, dry your tears and hear your whispered hopes. For I am with you in all states and stages, in youth and in age, when you call and when you are silent, when you turn to me as an eager child and when you weep solitary tears in your pillow when your dreams have dissolved into ashes and all earthly comfort is gone.

I hold the key to the mysteries of existence and the universe, but these I will share with all who come with willing heart and open mind. For they are not hidden from you, but all round you in every season, every time and every place as they have always been and always will be to those who open their hearts to me.

I am in the moon as she passes through the sky, in the brilliant sun chariot of noon and summer, in the fertile earth and the mighty waters and in the stars. For I am them as I am part of you, and you of me and you too are of the same divine fabric as the moon and the fertile earth and the waters, the stars, the sunshine and the life-giving rain.

The gifts of the Goddess

This section is a reminder that the Goddess of witchcraft is mother of life and earth and should not be feared, but revered and approached with love and assurance of being welcomed as a beloved child:

I do not ask sacrifice or worship for I come to you in love as a gentle mother, with compassion and with understanding and forgiveness of those things in your heart that you fear to look on in yourself. Yes I am fierce, defending my young as any mother and my green places and creatures from all who would do them harm; but I would rather teach than avenge, restore and regenerate than destroy what can and will be mended given patience and endeavour.

I am the healer of sorrow, pain, loss and doubt. Through me and through my herbs, oils, crystals and sacred waters you can share and spread my healing wisdom, above all in gentle words and kind deeds.

As I give life, so in death all return to me to be transformed, renewed and born again. I was with you in the beginning and will be with you in the end.

The responsibilities and blessings of seeking connection with the Goddess

This section talks about continuing the Goddess connection through awakening and developing your own spark or core of divinity. Since the Goddess (or however you envisage this creative power) made us from herself, we are part of her and her children:

If you work with honour, love, humility and for the Highest Good, then you will awaken your own divine spark and spread light and goodness throughout the earth. For what you give, will I restore to you threefold and more, time without time and for evermore.

You and I together were and are Isis of 10,000 names, Mother of Egypt and Enchantment, Astarte, golden Queen of beauty and fertility of the sun scorched places, Diana, brave huntress and mistress of the Moon, Hecate, wise grandmother of the crossroads of destiny and light in the darkness, Demeter, mother of the ripening grain and teacher of the mysteries of the hidden subterranean places of the soul, dark Kali fierce avenger whose face few dare gaze upon, but who promises regeneration in the eternal dance; and finally you, Lady Innana, who upholds in sacred marriage the sanctity of the earth and offers abundance to all who pledge fidelity.

We are of the circle and we are the circle. May the circle that is cast in my name live forever in your hearts and in your lives, without beginning and without ending.

Isis, Astarte, Diana, Hecate, Demeter, Kali, Innana.

Repeat or sing the names faster and faster and louder until you are filled with power. They have their own rhythm if you let it come. Then let the names become slower and more quiet, fading back into the stillness, the silence of the Goddess. Finally, whisper:

Blessed be.

Using the Charge of the Goddess and the God in ritual

Though the Charge of the Goddess is frequently associated with the full moon Esbat or monthly coven gathering, you can use the Charge any time you wish, at times of personal or ritual significance. There are many occasions you may wish to incorporate the Charge of the Goddess or God into ceremonies or rituals: for example, into drawing down the sun and moon ceremonies (see pages 491 and 476). However, there are times when the Charge and the resulting insights are ceremony in themselves and you could substitute the Charge for the prayer stage above, which would then create a very powerful third stage of listening and channelling the wisdom of the Goddess. For the solitary practitioner, the Charge can form a monthly ceremony of rededication and connection.

* If you are a solitary practitioner, nothing can be more spiritual than to sit, kneel or stand in your altar place indoors or outdoors or at a place of natural beauty. Light candles and incense, raise your arms high and wide in a V over your head and then bring them out in front of you palms uppermost.

* Speak the words of the Goddess or God. It is best if you can to learn the Charges whether a prewritten one or your own creation. If you forget the words you can improvise and so add to the wisdom.

* Occasionally you may just allow words from the Goddess to come on a particularly beautiful moonlit night or shimmering sunlit day. Don't even try to recall or record it; just accept it as one of those moments in and out of time.

* As a group or alone, you might see an image of the Goddess in the centre of the circle.

* Even if one person speaks the words, all present will be overlaid by the presence of the God and Goddess and may be inspired to speak if a crystal sphere is passed round.

A male practitioner may be more comfortable speaking the Charge of the God and, of course, men can use the full moon to draw down the God power, since there are a number of moon Gods in the northern magickal tradition. Sometimes, however, a woman may wish to work with the Charge of the God and vice versa and this will help you to tap into all aspects of your personality and divine potential (see the next module for the Charge of the God, page 229).

PRACTICAL ASSIGNMENT

Creating your Goddess form

* Sit quietly by candlelight and burn ceremonial incense such as frankincense, myrrh, sandalwood or the Egyptian cyphi or kyphi.

* Allow your ideal Goddess form to evolve in your mind and if you wish give her a name that feels right, even if it is not one of a deity you know. We all experience divinity in our own way and if you can identify with those that seem right for you, then you can more easily absorb higher powers.

Further research

Use the internet, as well as the sources I have suggested, to discover different forms of the Charge of the Goddess. Either create your own Charges or begin to learn the Goddess Charge that most resonates with you.

Further information

Recommended reading

* Budapest, Zsuzsanna, *Holy Book of Women's Mysteries*, Wingbow, 1997
* Crowley, Vivianne, *Wicca, the Old Religion in the New Age*, Robert Hale, 1998
* Eason, Cassandra, *Complete Guide to Woman's Wisdom*, Piatkus, 2001
* Farrar, Janet and Stewart, *The Witches' Goddess, The Feminine Principle of Divinity*, 1987, Phoenix Publishing Inc., New York
* Forrest, M. *Isadora Isis Magic, Cultivating a Relationship with the Goddess of 10,000 names*, Llewellyn, 2001
* Graves, Robert, *The White Goddess*, Faber and Faber, 1988
* Starhawk, *Circle Round, Raising Children in the Goddess Tradition*, Bantam (US), 2000
* Trobe, Kala, *Invoke the Goddess, Visualisations of Hindu, Greek and Egyptian Goddesses*, Llewellyn, 2000
* Valiente, Doreen, *The Charge of the Goddess*, Hexagon Publishing, 2000

Websites

* *Fellowship of Isis* International, multi-faith organisation dedicated to honour the Goddess in all her forms; training programmes www.fellowshipofisis.com
* *Covenant of the Goddess* Confederation of covens and solitaries worldwide www.cog.org
* *Doreen Valiente Charge of Goddess* Good resource for Valiente Charge and links to other sacred texts http://paganwiccan.about.com/library/texts/blgoddesscharge.htm Another site for the Valiente charge – and the whole site is a huge resource http://sacred-pathways.com/Charge of the Goddess.html

CREATING AND USING THE CHARGE OF THE GOD AND GODDESS

In this module we are continuing the theme of God and Goddess energies and will work on creating and using the Charge of the God. The all-important God and Goddess theme is continued in later modules when we examine the different roles and faces of the Goddess and God in ritual. In this module I have also listed some of the most popular deity forms found in magick and spiritual work. You can discover more about ones with which you are unfamiliar, but who seem to represent deity aspects that resonate with your own magickal goals and current stage of exploration.

Creating and using the God Charge

You will find Charges of the God in traditional magick, but you can create your own in exactly the same way as you did for the Goddess.

If you work alone, create your Charge while sitting in an open place in bright noon sunlight and visualise a God form in the centre of the circle that seems relevant to you. In a group, pass a wand or athame from person to person, adding what God power means to you, drawing on in any culture or age including the 21st century (see page 232 for ideas). Different people can create/recite different parts of the whole during ceremonies, or one person speaks and the others visualise the God and draw his power within them.

Here I have focused on the Celtic Cernunnos, to incorporate the idea of the Horned God of Magick, the green-faced Osiris, the Resurrection and Grain Father God of Egypt, Dionysus, the Ancient Greek Sacrifice God of vegetation, ecstasy and the vine, Shiva, Hindu God of both creation and destruction, good and evil, fertility and abstinence for the Dark Lord aspect. He is the Lord of the Dance who, it is said, will one day bring about the end of the world. Dumuzi is the shepherd sacrifice Lord of Innana, the Great Mother. Finally I have invoked Lugh (Llew in the Welsh tradition), the Celtic God of Light who died as the Spirit of the Grain each year and was reborn as the sun at the Midwinter Solstice. But you can equally use your own favourite Gods.

In the end chant, I have called upon Ra, the Ancient Egyptian Sun God, the

Norse Odin, the All Father, also God of inspiration, wisdom and poetry, Agni, the Hindu Fire God of both lightning and the celestial sun, Pan, the Greek Goat God with his wild music who has become an icon of spontaneity in witchcraft, Poseidon, the Ancient Greek Sea God with his trident that could stir up storms, and Thor, the protective Norse Thunder God whose hammer emitted lightning as he threw it against the Frost Giants.

Wonderfully empowering at solar festivals, you can recite the God Charge at your altar or outdoors in bright sunlight. Whether alone or in a group, afterwards gaze into a clear crystal sphere and you will see many images of power and glory that can inspire you to follow your dreams.

Cassandra's Charge of the God

The Call to the God

This calls down the God as the first born of the Mother:

These are the words of the father, who is son and consort of the Great Mother, first born in the beginning from she who created the universe from her own body. From her smiles and tears and ever fertile womb he sprang, singing with joy, leaping high as he explored the wonders of creation and made them his own.

The Guardian of all

The God is seen as the generative and protective force, a very positive male power for men and women to relate to and absorb:

I am he, the antlered one, untamed power of the hunt, the charging horned beasts and the wild woodland who offers food, shelter and protection to all created creatures from the mightiest stag to the smallest butterfly. I was present at the making of humans of all races, clans and creeds equally, breathing life into the clay forms which the Mother fashioned from the earth.

I am Cernunnos, Horned Lord of Winter, also known as Herne of the Wild Wood. As Master of the Animals and Lord of the Grain I offer willing sacrifice of my life for the land and people.

Lord of rebirth

Here the God offers the hope of renewal of youth and vigour, together with recognition that we are all part of the seasonal cycles and the continuing increase and fall of light and darkness, of birth, growth, decay, life, death and rebirth:

As Lord of the Dark Places beneath the soil, Osiris, I who taught men how to sow and plant and reap, I am potent still, promising rebirth with the Nile Flood, my seed watered by the tears of my eternal love Isis; resting in the nurturing womb of the Mother, I grow strong again, like all creatures who enter the gentle earth, resting but never slumbering until I hear the call to life once more. Thus will I rise as Lugh, radiant son of light, at the darkest hour in the coldest of days, as the sun himself to shine glorious. From my loins spring future suns, in never ending cycle of birth and death and renewal as long as the sun shines and the waters flow which is forever and a day unto eternity — or until the thread of time is spun and the Mother takes all back into herself.

At that golden hour of my rebirth I bring the promise of lighter days, of warmth and pleasures as the Midwinter yoke is conquered once more. So do I turn the wheel and grow in strength and I take my Goddess for my bride. First will I crown her with flowers and then with gold.

I bring power, strength, and courage, nobility, to defend the weak, the vulnerable and to give of my life blood to maintain what is of worth and just and lovely.

The challenges of the God

Here the God offers not ease but challenge, excitement and glory to all who follow him and accept the price:

I am the All Father and you my beloved children need fear nothing, if you heed my wise words and accept my challenges.

Mine is not the path of ease, but of ecstasy in the wild wood where the untamed instincts bow only to natural law and natural justice; as Dionysus, fruit of the sacred vine, as Shiva, Lord of the dance trampled by black Kali and by her restored as she dances life back into my body, strapped in agony to the sacred wheel — to leap free and to dance ever to the point of stillness and release.

As the Shepherd Lord, Dumuzi, banished to the regions of despair by Innana the Golden and brought back by her by her sacrifice and submission to her need of me that the earth might not remain barren.

As Barley King, grown tall and ripe, I feast and laugh and sing of the spirit that never can be broken. I call increase and abundance, as fields and the animals and humankind are made fertile by the sacred coupling of God and Goddess, man and woman, stag and hind beneath the May bowers and blossoming trees and then in the full eye of the sun as for one brief long day of summer I am her equal, enthroned and crowning her in gold.

Birth follows death, plenty follows dearth, creation follows necessary destruction and so renewed, I dedicate myself to the sanctity of all life ruled by the highest of intent and in humility lies the hour of my greatest triumph.

We all are autumn leaves falling, green leaves budding, the sun at noon and the dark sun at midnight and so dance with me through the days, outfacing fear and mortality into glory never ending.

Cernunnos, Horned One, proud Hunter of the Sun, Agni, flame of hearth and lightning flash, Poseidon of the azure waters, Ra in your sun boat shimmering gold, Odin of the Wild Sky Chase, Pan of the Wild Wood, Thor of Thunder come to us, be with us, be in us, be as one, Cernunnos, Agni, Poseidon, Ra, Odin, Thor.

As with the Isis chant (see page 226), repeat or drum this last part of the chant louder and faster. With the God Charge, you end it on a high and fast note, then allow the energies to flow within you and subside.

Deities of magick

I have listed here the strengths and the kinds of magick for which the energies of the most significant Gods and Goddesses generate positive results. You may discover others. List in your Book of Shadows any of the deities that you do not already work with that you feel may be worth exploring in more depth mythologically and through meditation and ritual.

There are numerous online images of the deities that may inspire you, and I have written more about Gods and Goddesses in later modules (see pages 363, 374 and 384).

Earth Goddesses

For nurturing, for all mothers and children of any ages spells, fertility, abundance, home, family and animals, the environment.

Demeter: Greek Earth and Barley Mother, symbol of fertility and prosperity, pictured surrounded by baskets of apples, sheaves of grain, corn, garlands of flowers and grapes.

Gaia: The ancient Greek Earth and Healing Mother, whose name has been given in modern times to the Earth and Earth ecology. She was depicted as a well-rounded figure, rising from the earth to which she remained connected. Her first creation was her consort Uranus, the starry heavens whom she split in birthing from herself, as a separate male element.

Mati Syra-Zemlya: Also known as Moist Mother Earth, the Slavic Goddess who spins the web of life and death. In Christian times, she has become closely associated with the Virgin Mary and one of her most important days, on which none may dig or plough, coincides with the Assumption of the Virgin Mary on 15 August.

Nerthus: The ancient Viking Earth Mother, consort of Njord, (see Sea Gods, page 243) associated with the growth of the crops. Fertility rituals were practised in the fields in her honour at the time of sowing, even in Christian times and her statue was ritually washed in a lake and carried across the fields on a wagon.

Earth Gods

For financial security, practical skills, property, house sales or renovation, potency and waiting for the right time for action.

Freyr or Ingvi: Son of Njord and one of the old Vanir Nature Gods, associated with the fertility of the earth, animals and people. God of Yule, he was born on the Midwinter Solstice and was invoked to bring prosperity and protection to the home. Twin brother of Freyja, Goddess of beauty, he is also described as a Horned God of the Hunt.

Geb: The Ancient Egyptian Earth God and consort of Nut the Sky Goddess, associated with the sacred goose who laid the egg from which the world emerged. He is shown as green with papyrus flowers growing from his body, reclining on one arm, so that his body forms the undulating land.

The Green Man: The ancient God of vegetation, known as the Hidden One, or Wild Herdsman, still recalled in European May celebrations. He brings rain and the growth of plants.

Osiris: Son of Geb and consort of Isis, who, after his murder by his brother, became the embodiment of the annual growth of the corn, watered by the tears of Isis as the Nile Flood. Clay statues of Osiris planted with seeds were buried to symbolise the new life out of the body of the God.

Goddesses of the Hunt

Use for obtaining and freeing resources and finances, for all women's employment and business ventures, protection of the vulnerable and for seizing opportunities.

Arduinna or Ardwinna: French Gallic Maiden Goddess of the Wild Wood, who rode on a wild boar and demanded an offering for every animal she allowed to be hunted.

Artemis: Greek Virgin Huntress and Moon Goddess, who released animals for the hunt and protected pregnant creatures and their young, and human mothers in childbirth. Twin sister of the young Graeco-Roman Sun God Apollo, she travelled the night sky in a silver chariot pulled by white stags, shooting silver shafts of moonlight. As the Great She Bear, Artemis was worshipped by her virgin priestesses at the new moon, as well as at her festivals.

Bugady Musun: Siberian Mother Goddess of the Animals, an old but very physically powerful Goddess who sometimes assumed the form of a huge elk or a reindeer. She controlled all food supplies and even today is offered the finest part of the first animal killed.

Devana or Debena: Czechoslovakian Goddess of the forest and of the hunt, called Dziewanna in Poland. A beautiful young virgin, she rode accompanied by her maidens and hounds and, like the Graeco-Roman Diana, was also a Moon Goddess. Devana heralded in the spring and also controlled the weather.

Flidais: Ancient Irish Hunt Goddess who could shape-shift into any of her creatures. She rode in a chariot pulled by stags and possessed a cow who could give milk to 30 people at a time.

Zonget: A Siberian Mistress of the Herds, Zonget rules all birds, animals and the people who hunt them. Birds and animals would allow themselves to be trapped if she ordained it. Zonget is said to appear to mortals as a grey Arctic bird.

Lords of the Hunt and Gods of wild animals

For male power and animus energies, for courage, action, power, willing sacrifice and protection.

Cernunnos: The generic term, meaning Horned One given for the various Horned Gods of the Celtic tradition. Cernunnos was Lord of Winter, the Hunt, animals, death, male fertility and the underworld. He died at the beginning of the hunting season in autumn and was reborn in the spring. His importance is in his continuing role as the male principal in modern Wicca and other neopagan faiths.

Herne the Hunter: Another ancient form of the antlered God from the Germanic and specifically Anglo-Saxon world that has survived in the folk tradition of England. It is said his ghost is seen when there is a national emergency as a sign that he is still protecting his people.

Pan: The Greek herdsman's God of forests, flocks and fields. He was portrayed as half-goat, with horns and goat legs and feet. Too wild to be allowed on Mount Olympus with the other deities, he roamed the groves of Arcadia, playing his magickal pipes.

Ullr or Uller (Holler in Anglo-Saxon): Norse God of oaths, hunting, archery and winter sports, ice, frost and snow. He is sometimes called the Dark Odin because in some myths he ruled in Odin's stead for the five winter months with Frigg in her crone form of Hulda.

Svantovit: Slavic Horned God who was protector of the fields and was also invoked for the success of the harvest. Portrayed with four heads holding a horn of wine, his totem or power animal is the white horse.

Bird and insect Goddesses and Gods

For Air spells, travel, victory, protection, healing and new beginnings, wisdom and learning.

Hina: Polynesian Butterfly Goddess, called the creatrix of the world, Lady of the Moon and her spirit is said to be contained in every woman. Now Hina lives in the Moon, having travelled there on a rainbow pathway.

Garuda: Hindu God, king of the birds who can fly faster than light. He acts as steed for the preserver God Vishnu. Portrayed with the head, wings, talons, and beak of an eagle and the body and limbs of a man, his body is gold.

Horus: The Ancient Egyptian falcon or hawk-headed God, son of Isis and Osiris. He protected the pharaohs who were considered an embodiment of Horus on earth. His eyes were the sun and moon and his wings could extend across the entire heavens.

Morrigu: The three Irish raven sisters, Morrigan, Macha or Nass and Badbh or Nemainn. They flew over the battle fields as huge crows or ravens, warning of the enemy's approach and encouraging the chosen tribe to victory.

Valkyries: The Norse battle Goddess maidens whose name means in Old Norse choosers of the slain. In early times they were called the raven maidens and later described with cloaks of swan feathers. They prophesied who would win the battle and carried the noble slain to the heavenly halls of Valhalla.

Flower Goddesses

For spring and summer rituals, love, romance, friendship and self-esteem.

Antheia: Greek Goddess of new or young love, her name means blooming or blossoming. She is portrayed as a young girl carrying baskets of flowers.

Blodeuwedd, Blodwin, Blancheflor: Goddess of May Day, of the moon and the blossoming earth. She was created from nine different flowers as a bride for Llew, God of the increasing light.

Flora: Roman Goddess of flowers whose festival, Floralia, lasted from 26 April until 3 May. This was a major fertility festival throughout Eastern and Western Europe. Flowers came from her mouth and were scattered by the wind.

Weather deities

For protection of home and property against inclement weather, for bringing change and fresh energies, for moving obstacles and for energy and new beginnings; also for weather spells.

Hulda/Mother Holle: Also called Berchta, Goddess of winter and snow. In the Norse tradition, snow is said to fall when Hulda (or Mother Holle or Frau Holle in the myths of Germany and the Netherlands), shakes her bed and the feathers from the eiderdown fly. The crone/winter aspect of the Mother Goddess Frigg she cared for unborn children in her cave. She is considered a patron of magick, gave flax to mankind and taught them how to hunt.

Lei-King or Lei-Kung: Chinese lord of thunder and also justice, he is described as having a blue skin, wings and claws and would hurl thunderbolts upon the unrighteous who had escaped earthly justice.

Perun: Slavic God of thunder and lightning, dark-haired with a beard of gold whose sacred tree, like the majority of Thunder Gods, is the oak. Perun carries a huge axe or mace.

Raiden: Japanese God of thunder and lightning. He is portrayed as fierce and red, with sharp claw-like hands. He carries a huge drum and when he beats it, those on Earth hear the thunder and know he is angry.

Thor: Thunor in the Anglo Saxon, also known as Donar in Germany, he is the largest of the Germanic Thunder Gods. He controls the clouds, lightning and the rains, as well as justice and the crops. The wheels of Thor's gigantic wagon cause thunder as they roll across the sky. He probably preceded Odin or Woden the All Father mythologically, even though called Odin's son. Thor is a mountain top dweller, hurling thunderbolts and lightning flashes against the unrighteous, both Frost Giants and humans. Thor's magickal hammer Mjollnir aimed true and returned to his hand. When he threw it in the ongoing battles against the Frost Giants and trolls, sparks flew that caused lightning. Thursday is sacred to Thor.

Yuki-Onna: The Japanese Snow Goddess and also the Death Goddess. Her long, white hair merges with the snow and only part of her body clothed in white can be seen as she merges into the snowy landscape.

Moon Goddesses

For love and fertility, moon magick, women, beauty, marriage and healing.

Andraste: British Celtic Moon Goddess worshipped by Queen Boadicea. Her sacred animal was the hare. She is associated with the waxing moon and the Spring Equinox.

Ariadne: Cretan Goddess whose name means high fruitful mother. Images of her with snakes in her hands represent her oracular priestesses, who prophesied in her name, wreathed with snakes, especially on the night of the full moon.

Arianrhod: The Welsh Goddess of the full moon, time and destiny, who turns the wheel of the stars.

Candi: She is the female counterpart of Chandra. Lunar God and Goddess, they presided over the moon on alternate months.

Diana: Goddess of the witches and witchcraft, the moon and Huntress Goddess of the Romans. The ultimate Moon Goddess, Diana became official Goddess of the witches as early as 500 BCE in Italy. Though a maiden Goddess she is also worshipped as Goddess of all aspects of the moon and is linked to the Greek Artemis.

Isis: Ancient Egyptian Mother and Moon Goddess of enchantment, also Goddess of the sea and in her more earthy form, of nature, wife of Osiris and mother of Horus. Her headdress represented the full moon, held within the crescents of the waxing and waning moons. Loved also by the Romans, in modern magick Isis is a central figure in Goddess-focused spirituality.

Lucina: The Ancient Greek and Roman Moon Goddess whose name means she who brings the light. She represents the maiden aspect as part of the triple Goddess with Diana or Selene as the Full Moon Goddess and Hecate the wise one (see crone Goddesses, page 238, for Hecate)

Luna: The Roman Goddess, whose name in Latin means the moon that rules the months. She orders the passage of the moon through the year and her special time is the first day of the waning moon.

Nanna: Norse Moon Mother, called the selfless one who loved her husband the God of light Baldur so much she cast herself on his funeral pyre when he was killed.

Rhiannon: Welsh Goddess of the underworld and a Moon Goddess associated with the full moon and white horses and bringing prophetic dreams.

Selene (Luna to the Romans): Greek Goddess of the full moon, twin sister of Helios the Greek Sun God. She rose from the sea in her chariot drawn by white horses at night and rode high in the sky on the full moon.

Moon Gods

For getting back in touch with natural rhythms of life and the body, to restore health, keep away harm, for potency and fertility and for better times ahead.

Aningan: Inuit Moon God, brother of Seqinek, the sun girl. They were also called Akycha and Igaluk. He is a great hunter who can be seen standing in front of his igloo.

Chandra: Hindu God of the moon whose symbol was the hare.

Khonsu or Knensu: Ancient Egyptian Moon deity. His name means he who crosses the sky. He was alter ego of Horus as rising Sun God. He is depicted in human form with a crescent moon supporting the full moon disc.

Mani: Norse Moon God and brother of Sunna, Sol the Sun Goddess, who like his sister constantly runs from the wolf who will devour him at Ragnarok, the last battle.

Myesyats: The Slavic Moon God, represented the three stages of the lifecycle, like the lunar Goddesses. He was first worshipped as a young man until he reached maturity at the full moon. With the waning phase, Myesyats passed through old age and died with the old moon, being reborn three days later.

Sky Gods and Goddesses

For Air spells, for achieving ambitions, for logic, learning, justice, moves of all kinds, career and travel altruism, and attaining justice and for concerns relating to the planet and its creatures.

Hermes: The winged Ancient Greek messenger and healer God; who like his Roman counterpart Mercury, is also God of medicine, moneylenders, speculation and thieves.

Jupiter: The supreme Roman Sky God whose Greek counterpart was Zeus, cast thunderbolts upon the unrighteous. Known as the Sky Father, Jupiter was ruler of the universe, offering a role model for the ideal emperor who was general, statesman and spiritual leader. His consort was Juno.

Nut: The Ancient Egyptian Sky Goddess whose body arches over the earth, covered in stars and into whose womb Ra the Sun God enters to be reborn each night. She was wife of Geb. the Earth God.

Odin: (Anglo Saxon Woden or Wotan) the Norse father and king of the Aesir Gods and of all humans. He was God of inspiration, wisdom and poetry, as well as war. His two black ravens, Huginn (Thought) and Muninn (Memory), told him of events all over the world. A great shape-shifter, especially as an eagle, he is often described as a traveller with a grey beard, floppy hat, a blue grey cloak and staff or his magnificent winged helmet. Wednesday is sacred to him. To acquire wisdom, he hung from the World Tree for nine days and nights and traded an eye. He also led the wild hunt across the sky at yule. His consort was Frigg.

Zeus: Father of the Greek Gods, lord of justice and defender of all who were helpless. He was also God of rain and ensured that the rains would fertilise the crops and the fruit trees. His consort was Hera.

Crone/wise woman Goddesses

For issues of ageing, endings leading to beginnings, overcoming fear, sorrow and sickness, transformation, good fortune, older woman's magick and healing.

Cailleach: A generic name Cailleach meaning the veiled one in Scotland and Ireland. As the Scottish Cailleach Bhuer, the Blue Hag, she manifested herself as an old woman wearing black or dark blue rags with a crow on her left shoulder and a holly staff that could kill a mortal with a touch. She cared for the moorland animals in winter.

Cerridwen: The Welsh Great Mother, keeper of the cauldron of inspiration and rebirth. Crone Moon Goddess especially associated with Druidic initiation and mistress of shape-shifting and prophecy, she brings about death, which is followed by rebirth.

Hel: The most misunderstood of the Norse deities and enjoying a huge revival as the source of prophecy in modern Norse Seiorcraft where practitioners go into trance to communicate with the ancestors in her realm. Sometimes linked with Hulda, early legends tell how she received and restored all deities and human, except those slain in battle that in the Viking world were accorded special status. She gave shelter to the slain Solar God Baldur that he might be healed and reborn as the new Sun God. Hel was worshipped and loved by ordinary people, even after the coming of the missionaries, in deep caves symbolising the womb of the earth. Her shrines were places of prophecy. With the increasing predominance of the male Gods like Odin and later the coming of Christianity, she was linked to the realms of cold and darkness.

The Norns: Called Urd (past), Verdhandi (present) and Skuld (what is becoming), they are the Norse Sisters of Fate who constantly wove the destiny or wyrd of humans and the deities. According to Ørlög, they wove the eternal law of the universe. The sacred Well of Wyrd or Fate at the foot of Yggdrasil, the World Tree, was under the guardianship of the Norns. Each morning, the Norns read the fate of the deities in this well.

Hecate: Greek Crone Goddess of the Underworld, also Goddess of good fortune, especially for sailors and hunters and of the waning and dark of the moon, crossroads, secrets, witches and witchcraft and of midwives,

Sun and Fire Goddesses

For female power, courage success, fertility, creativity, psychic and physical defence, healing abundance and joy.

Amaterasu Omigami: The Japanese Sun Goddess whose name means great august spirit shining in heaven. She is very compassionate, but when the affairs of humanity make her temporarily despair she retires to her cave, causing an eclipse.

Brighid: The Celtic Triple (three sisters) Goddess of fire and of the hearth, patroness of healers, poets and blacksmiths. Her holy fire was tended first by 19 virgin priestesses called the Daughters of the Sacred Flame, and later by the nuns of St Brigit at the Abbey at Kildare on the site of the Goddess grove (see also the Wheel of the Year, page 638).

Gabija: The Lithuanian Goddess of the hearth fire, who was honoured by throwing salt on the fire each evening after the main meal.

Saule: Baltic Queen of the heavens and earth, dressed and crowned with gold. She drove her golden chariot across the skies, and danced with her daughters the planets on the festival of St Lucia, the light maiden, just before the Midwinter Solstice.

Sekhmet: The Ancient Egyptian lion-headed Solar Goddess of fire, magick and healing who is the patroness of modern businesswomen. One of the most powerful and ancient deities, Sekhmet was Goddess of both war and healing. Her husband was Ptah, the Creator God.

Sol: Norse shining sun maiden and sister of Mani, the Moon God. Her golden chariot was pulled by pure white horses called Aryakrr the early waker and Alavin the rapid goer.

Vesta: The Roman Goddess of fire, whose virgins tended the sacred fire in Rome, the guardian of Rome. For hundreds of years, her sacred fire was carried across oceans with colonists and soldiers and always kept tended.

Sun and Fire Gods

For leadership, authority, energy, fame, prosperity, career, a burst of power and fulfilment.

Agni: The Hindu God of fire, is said to be manifest in lightning, in celestial sun flares, in the sacred blaze rising from the altar and in household fires.

Apollo: The Graeco-Roman Sun God, twin brother of Artemis, the Moon and Huntress Goddess, was also God of prophecy, music, poetry, archery, healing and divination. Young golden God Apollo, most handsome of the Gods, was the ideal representation of a young emperor, cultured, wise but also warlike.

Baldur (Balder): The Norse God of pure love and light, was sacrificed at Midsummer by a dart of mistletoe at the hand of his blind brother Hodur who was tricked by Loki, God of disruption. It was said that after the destruction of the Aesir Gods, including Odin, at the last battle of Ragnarok, Baldur would be reborn at yule.

Helios: Ancient Greek Sun God, called Sol by the Romans. He was regarded an embodiment of the sun and wore a golden helmet from which the sun's rays radiated. He ascended the heavens in a chariot drawn by winged, snow-white horses to give light, and in the evening descended into the ocean.

Ra or Re: The Egyptian Sun God who rode his sun boat across the sky and at night fought and overcame the chaos serpent Apep in order to maintain stability and measured time. Ra was portrayed as the sun at its full power.

Lugh: Llew in Wales, the ancient Irish God of Light and the cycle of the year, born at the Midwinter Solstice, made king at the Summer Solstice and willingly sacrificed at Lughnassadh at the beginning of August, in order to maintain the fertility of the land and ensure the success of the harvest.

Yucatan: The Mayan Sun God, was also called Kinich-ahau, Lord of the Face of the Sun. He took the form of a macaw by day and a jaguar at night to fight the fierce nightly battle in the Underworld.

Ra, the Sun God

Goddesses of love, beauty, magick and fertility

For the coming of spring and new energies, for love, romance and fertility spells, commitment and marriage and passion for self-esteem and self love and all spells for radiance and beauty.

Aphrodite: The Greek virgin Goddess of idealised love, passion, romance and beauty. Her name means born of the foam and she is also a powerful Sea Goddess whose sacred creature the dolphin pulled her chariot across the waves.

Aradia: Daughter of the Moon Goddess Diana and called her silver daughter. She came to earth to teach her mother's wisdom and is often called upon as queen of the witches.

Freyja: Norse Goddess of love, magick, beauty and sexuality who leads the Valkyries (see above) and the Idises, the prophetesses who demanded sacrifice for success in battle. Like her twin brother Freyr, she comes from the old Nature Gods, the Vanir. She is described with either blonde or flaming red hair and drives a chariot pulled by black cats. She wears her magnificent cloak of swan or raven feathers that enables her to turn into a falcon and has a fabulous necklace of amber, the stone called the tears of Freyja, that are said to form the Milky Way.

Iduna: Norse Goddess of spring and eternal youth. She was guardian of the golden apples of immortality that kept the Gods and Goddesses young and occasionally favoured mortals with an apple to bring them a child. She was wife of Bragi, God of music and poetry.

Ostara: Oestre in Anglo-Saxon, a Goddess of fertility who is celebrated at the time of the Spring Equinox, when she flung open the gates of new life. She remained beloved even in Christian times. In Germany, altars made of stone were dedicated to her and coloured eggs and flowers set on them at Easter. She is sometimes thought to be the maiden form of Frigg and her symbols are the hare and the egg.

Sif: Norse Goddess called she of the golden hair. Her hair fell like a golden veil to her feet. It signified the growing crops and she was Goddess of the harvest and wife of Thor (see above).

Venus: Goddess of love and beauty and the Roman form of Aphrodite. By her liaison with Mercury, she gave birth to Cupid. She is symbolised by the planet Venus as the Morning Star. In her Evening Star aspect, Venus takes on warrior energies, good for fighting for love.

Women's and Mother Goddesses

For mothering, fertility, abundance, fidelity and marriage, mature sexuality and the sacred marriage, for women, the home, creativity and in the modern world icon of all women who whether they work in or out of the home have to multitask.

Astarte: Supreme female divinity of the Phoenicians, Goddess of love and fertility. She is associated with the moon and all nature, supreme female divinity of the Phoenician nations, the Goddess of love, abundance and fruitfulness.

Bast or Bastet: The cat or cat-headed Goddess of Ancient Egypt, Goddess of music, dance, women, fertility, the moon, young women and joy. She offered protection to homes and families against disease and vermin.

Frigg: Frigga, Frija, Fricka, Norse queen of the deities, Goddess of women, marriage, the home, childbirth and the wife of Odin. She is associated with the naming of children, spinning and weaving, as well as prophecy. As Goddess of the atmosphere and clouds, she wears white or dark garments that dictate the weather. She is tall and stately, with a crown of heron feathers and golden keys from her waist. Her spinning-wheel forms a constellation in the sky, known also as Orion's girdle. She invited to her heavenly hall couples who had lived virtuous and faithful lives together.

Hera: The wife/sister of Zeus is the supreme Greek Goddess of protection, marriage and childbirth, whose sacred bird is the peacock. She is a powerful deity of fidelity and women whose partners are faithless call upon her to avenge them.

Innana: Sumerian queen of heaven who evolved into the Babylonian Goddess Ishtar. Innana was Goddess of beauty, abundance, fertility and passion, famed for her loveliness and her lapis lazuli necklaces. She was linked with the annual sacred marriage between Goddess and God to bring fertility to the land and people.

Juno: Roman Queen of the Gods, the wife/sister of Jupiter. Protectress of women, marriage, childbirth, she is invoked in sacred sex magick.

Parvati: The beautiful young Hindu Goddess and alter ego of Kali who in some myths was formed from Parvati's skin. Her name means she who comes from the mountains. With her, the God Shiva is depicted as the ideal family man living in his sacred city Benares with their offspring Ganesh, the elephant-headed God of wisdom and prosperity, and Karttikeya/Skanda, God of war. Many statues depict the couple entwined with Shiva touching her breast and Parvati holding the mirror of destiny.

Sea and Water Goddesses

For change and increase in all things, for washing away pain, sorrow and what holds you to the past, for magick of the tides, attracting on the incoming and banishing on the outgoing, and for healing spells.

Benten or Benzai-ten: The Japanese Sea Goddess, who is described as being very beautiful. She rides a dragon while playing a harp-like instrument, for she is also the Goddess of music and dancing.

Cliodna of the Golden Hair: Celtic Sea Goddess and queen of the land of promise over the waves, where there was perpetual peace and harmony. Cast wishes on to the seventh or ninth wave for her (or the Norse Ran) using shells, pearls or white stones.

Ganga: Hindu healing Water Goddess who is manifest as the sacred river Ganges and was daughter of the Mountain God Himalaya.

Heket or Heqet: Ancient Egyptian frog-headed Goddess who breathed life into the clay figures made by her husband Khnum, the Potter God. She was Goddess of childbirth.

Ran: The Norse Sea Goddess, who it was said loved gold more than anything. Sailors would carry a piece of gold for safe passage. If they did drown then she would receive them into her halls where wine flowed. If angered she would cause storms or spread her nets over rocks and lure ships to their doom with sudden mists. She and her husband/brother Aegir had nine beautiful, golden-haired daughters called the waves or billow maidens.

Sedna: Inuit and Arctic Sea Mother, the old woman who lives under the sea. She is Goddess of sea animals and releases the shoals of fish to the people who make her offerings. Shamans dive down to comb her tangled hair to win her favour.

Sea and Water Gods

For change, travel, sudden wealth and for all creative and artistic ventures, for fertility and potency, for a surge of energy.

Aegir: Norse God of the deep seas, belonged to an older order of Gods than Odin and was answerable only to himself. He was an old man with a white beard. He caused storms and would drag ships with rich treasure beneath the waves. But he assisted the ventures of those he favoured.

Hapy or Hapi: The Ancient Egyptian God of the Nile flood, who wears flowing papyrus and lotus flowers on his head, carrying a loaded offering dish with wine, food and lotus blossoms.

Njord: Ruler of seas near to shore, the winds and safe harbours. He was a Vanir God and father of Freyr and Freyja and was exchanged as hostage with the Aesir. He calmed the storms of Aegir and protected commerce and fishing. He was also God of summer and so had problems when he married his second wife Skadi, Goddess of winter.

Poseidon: Greek God of the sea and brother of Zeus, who rode across the waves in a chariot pulled by giant sea horses and carried a trident. He became Neptune in the Roman tradition and was said to have drowned Atlantis because of the corruption of this golden race.

Gods and Goddesses of fate, justice and wisdom

For all matters of justice, neighbours and community affairs, authority, truth, officialdom, the acquisition of knowledge, balance and stability.

Athena or Athene: Daughter of Zeus, patron of the city of Athens, is Goddess patroness of all forms of the arts and literature, as well as justice and wisdom. The owl is her sacred bird and the olive her symbol.

Hathor: Ancient Egyptian Goddess of truth, wisdom, fertility, joy, love, music, art, dance and protectress of women. She is said to bring husbands/wives to those who call on her. She is frequently shown wearing a sun disc held between the horns of a cow as a crown. As a symbol, she nourished the pharaohs.

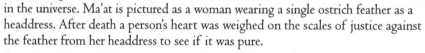

Ma'at: The Ancient Egyptian Goddess of truth and justice, was responsible for maintaining the correct balance and order in the universe. Ma'at is pictured as a woman wearing a single ostrich feather as a headdress. After death a person's heart was weighed on the scales of justice against the feather from her headdress to see if it was pure.

Tyr (Ziu, Tiu or Tiw): Norse God of war and courage, noblest of the Gods and the giver of the law and justice. He was called the spirit warrior and represented the Pole Star. He was once leader of the Aesir deities, but allowed Odin to take over. He sacrificed his sword hand so that the evil Fenris wolf could be bound and so he saved the other deities. His sword was a sacred symbol and hung so its blade reflected the first morning sunlight. His name is given to Tuesday.

Trickster Gods/Gods of change

For endings leading to beginnings, for asking questions, for challenging a corrupt or inefficient status quo, for accepting our own weaknesses, for necessary if disruptive change.

Loki: Norse Trickster deity of a very old order of the Ettin giants. He represented evil but often by leading the deities to reveal their own weaknesses. He challenged the structure and order of the Gods.

Maui of the Many Devices: The Maori Demi-God hero who brought necessary advances in civilisation to mankind, often by trickery. For example, it is told how Maui went to Mahuika, the ogress clan mother, who kept fire in her fingernails. Each time he asked she gave him one of her fingernails of fire, Maui deliberately extinguished the flames and it was not until he demanded the last nail that she created a huge conflagration, so bringing fire into the world. Then he was able to take enough fire for all his people, so they might be warm and cook their food.

Set or Seth: The Ancient Egyptian God who was originally defender of the solar boat against Apep the serpent, he became demonised as the evil uncle of Horus the younger brother and assassin of brother Osiris, associated with desert and the desert sandstorms.

PRACTICAL ASSIGNMENT

Deities

✳ Allow your ideal God form to evolve in your mind and if you wish give him a name that feel right, even if it not one of a deity you know.

✳ Start to work on Goddess and God pairings. Though they may be obvious ones, like the Roman Juno and Jupiter or Ancient Egyptian Nut and Geb, you can combine the deities of any culture that express for you the synthesised energies you need. These may vary from ritual to ritual.

Further research

Use the internet as well as the sources I have suggested to discover different forms of the Charge of the God.

Research any deity forms that interest you from the list above.

Further information

Recommended reading

✳ Jackson, Nigel, *Masks of Misrule, the Horned God and his Cult in Europe*, Capall Bann Publishing, 1998

✳ Richardson, Alan, *Earth God Rising, Return of the Male Mysteries*, Llewellyn, 1991

Websites

✳ *Charge of the God*
www.magicwicca.com/wicca/
charge-god.html
http://www.paganlibrary.com/
rituals_spells/index.php

THE MAGICK CIRCLE
AND MYSTIC SQUARE

The magick circle goes back to the earliest forms of ceremony and is central to modern witchcraft. The mystic square belongs to the folk tradition of northern magick and comes from the pre-Gardnerian years. It is still popular in Norse revivalist magick and in East Anglian magick, as well as among the few water witches of the English Midland canals still practising their arts.

I often cast a square of visualised light round the area where I will be working, especially for outdoor magick and particularly in a public place. Alternatively, I work within the ancient nine grid square formation (eight squares surrounding the central ninth square) for solitary rituals.

Some Druids and Druidesses believe that you do not have to create a separate circle for rites because all places are sacred. As long as you have at least four people to hold the four directions in a ceremony, then a circular grove can be left psychically open during ritual for people to enter or leave as they wish. However, in practice by standing in a circle with others and perhaps linking hands for the opening prayers/invocations, a circuit of power is created that is passed round continuously, even when the hands are no longer joined.

You might ask why you as a witch need to cast a circle since witches believe that the Goddess and God are immanent, that is, present within all creation, and so the ritual site should be already sacred. They are not purely transcendent i.e. above and separate from the imperfect world like the monotheistic God of Christianity and Judaism. In fact, many witches see the Goddess and God as both immanent and transcendent, present in nature but at the same time greater than what they have created. Since Wicca recognises the existence of both good and evil as polarities, with humans being given the choice, the circle is by definition a specially protected space where only good may enter at a time when practitioners are open and vulnerable, and so circle casting brings this extra safety.

This course is rooted in the Wiccan tradition, so circle casting will be the most important aspect of this module.

The magick circle

The circle has no beginning and no ending and serves as the temple for the practitioner/s to connect with the Goddess and God energies, regardless of the physical place it is cast. It is the bridge between the dimensions and creates in any working within it a higher state of awareness. This is unlike a Christian church or cathedral where the physical building acts as the meeting place of God and human. Whether physical or symbolic, the cast circle marks an Otherworld space within which the restrictions of time and space do not apply. Here the four elements combine to create the energy and magickal substance aether or akasha in which thoughts can be transformed into actuality in the material world. Within the circle, too, meet deities, angels, the four elemental Guardians of the directional watchtowers, the wise ancestors and nature essences in outdoor rituals as well as the Witch Guardians of any witches present.

The circle overlays the physical space with the spiritual and until it is activated by the opening casting and strengthening, the space is not sanctified or empowered. Within the circle, your spiritual higher self can more easily take control using knowledge not accessible to the conscious mind. No wonder the circle glows with rainbow light even before you have raised the power in spellcasting.

The seven directions of the circle

Some practitioners influenced by the Native North American medicine wheel add the centre as the point of unity to the four cardinal directions north, east, south and west (see below), plus upwards from the centre for the Sky Father/Great Goddess and directly downwards for Mother Earth/the Horned God. This can work well if the centre of the circle is clear for you to stand and extend a lighted smudge or incense stick in all six directions and finally spiral smoke around yourself for the seventh direction, the point of unity within yourself as you stand in the centre.

For this kind of ritual, the east or dawn is the first direction, then clockwise turning on the spot in a circle for south, west and north, then direction five downwards for Mother Earth/the Horned God and six upwards for the Father Sky/the Great Goddess (these two pairings are interchangeable). Finally comes unity or spirit, the still point of the ever turning circle of life and your magick circle, here centred within yourself, as you smudge. Honouring the directions is very powerful and often emotional.

Protection of the place and circle casting

As well as a place of power, the circle marks the boundaries between the magickal world of spirit and all the worries, demands and thoughts about the everyday world, as well as excluding any negative energy from the material sphere. Because you are working with spiritual powers, it also prevents anything less than benign entering the sacred space where you are spiritually open and vulnerable.

* Personally, your ritual bath and putting on special robes helps to leave the everyday world behind and removes the psychic clutter in your aura you have accumulated during the day.
* Physically and psychically cleanse the circle area beforehand if it is a formal spell or ritual using smudge, sweeping or asperging the area with water (see page 624). In a coven the maiden may sweep and the priest or priestess then asperge the area.
* Solitary practitioners can carry out both activities before bathing, or they should anoint the four higher chakras before casting the circle.
* Ringing a bell or striking a singing bowl will also cleanse an area.

- Find the centre of your planned circle, which may coincide with the centre of the altar (or a cauldron if you are not using an altar). The central altar is good if you are carrying out an altar-based ceremony, as you then receive the concentrated power of the central axis directly.

- If the altar is in the north, mark the centre of the planned circle with your staff or an equal-armed cross drawn on the ground with your athame or even a small pointed stone. These not only to help you cast an even circle but also will be the place of most concentrated power.

- In some formal magickal traditions, a candle or flame is lit in the centre of the altar (which in this case is sited in the centre of the circle) and the flame is kept burning throughout the ritual. A few practitioners have the facilities to keep a flame sheltered in glass burning all the time on the altar and use this to light all candles in a ritual. It remains alight when all other lights are extinguished during the Midwinter Solstice ritual.

What size should a circle be?

A circle, always cast clockwise, should enclose you, your altar and tools if you are using them and anyone working with you. Traditionally, circles are 9 ft in diameter, created with a 9 ft cord looped over and pulled taut over a central stake in the ground (the cord should be a bit longer to allow for the loop). You'll need a compass to identify magnetic north, unless you are using known places for an approximation.

Some traditions have a 5 ft or 6 ft diameter circle for an individual and 9 ft for a coven, but I think these are too constricting in size except for altar work, as I like to dance or stamp around. However, for quickness you can make an approximation of diameter. Estimation is useful if working alone. A tallish man is 6 ft, so imagine one lying down across the centre of the circle and add about half his height in your mind. This gives 9 ft for the circle. You can also set four smaller stones in advance around the circumference at the main directions to guide you when circle casting.

However, you may need a smaller circle in a confined space and some of the best magick I have practised has been with four people around an altar one at each cardinal direction. You can create a larger circle if you are inviting lots of people. Estimate in multiples or divisions of three, a sacred number for your required diameter from the 9 ft diameter concept.

Circle casting in spells and rituals

Though magickal protective circles were used by mediaeval ceremonial magicians, they come originally from the folk tradition as people for thousands of years danced in circles around a festival fire or ancient stone circles to celebrate the seasonal change points. There are so many variations in circle casting, so choose a system that feels right for you.

Unless you are practising high ceremonial magick that requires precise measurements and movements (for which I would advise joining a society that practises Golden Dawn or a similar formal magickal system), circle casting is symbolic. It ultimately depends on your own spiritual powers and good intent.

- In the northern magickal tradition circles are generally cast north to north, but you can start with the east if you prefer.

- Whatever form of circle is cast, even if you are not personally creating it, perhaps at a public ritual, visualise the circle of light spreading as the circle is cast and you will strengthen it, as well as making a personal connection.
- If you are casting the circle, whether actual or visualised, first raise light throughout your whole body from the Root chakra to the Crown.
- Picture light pouring in from all round, red upwards from the Earth through your feet for the Root, silver from the moon for the Sacral (even in daylight), yellow from the sun for the Solar Plexus (even at night), green from nature for the Heart (have plants around indoors), sky blue from the angels for the Throat, indigo or purple for the Brow chakra from the Archangels and Elemental Guardians, and white, gold or violet from the deities for the Crown.
- Visualise the rainbow colours merging into pure white light within you and radiating from you.
- Shake your fingers and you will sense, if not see, them glowing.
- If working with others, guide them through these stages before circle casting.
- Then make your opening blessing, sometimes referred to as the call to ritual, which might alternatively be a horn, a singing bowl or bell sound. Other people begin with a poetic piece from their own or a traditional Book of Shadows.

A physical circle

You can create a permanent circle to be empowered before a spell or ritual, made of stones or constructed before a ritual by those taking part. The stones you build it from don't have to join, but give an outline at the eight directions. The size of the materials will depend on the size of the circle. White stones are generally used.

You can also make a large temporary physical circle with fallen leafy branches, herbs or flowers set clockwise around your altar area or chalk a circle in a paved area. You could also make a temporary circle of crystals, small stones or shells, kept in a box between rituals for the purpose.

If you use tea lights, light them clockwise from inside the circle at the start of the ceremony. They can be lit by participants round the circle with a spoken blessing, if you have a number of people, or each person can light their own in turn, after making the body of light and the opening blessing. Alternatively, you could put a large green candle in the north for Earth, a yellow one in the east for Air, a red one in the south for Fire and a blue one in the west for Water and light these when you open the four quarters of the circle or early in the spell/ritual to open the circle and create tangible markers. You would cast a spiritual visualised light circle first to enclose them. Some practitioners use white candles.

Use a natural existing outdoor circle, such as a grove of trees or a ring of flowers or toadstools. Always ask permission of the natural essences of the place. You do not need to cast or uncast this kind of circle, as the natural energies will hold the power and protection, but always leave an offering.

Other ways to create a circle are to draw one clockwise in earth, snow or sand with a stick, or your staff or a sword. Try to do it in a single sweep. Best of all is the circle of people linking hands. Indoors you can paint a white circle beneath a large rug in an altar room.

Near the beginning of a ritual, you should empower a physical circle with any of the methods below, after evoking the light body within you and making the opening call, or you can cast a purely symbolic circle.

Symbolic circle casting

The most usually cast magick circle is a symbolic one, which may be physically cast by first walking round the visualised circle area clockwise with a sword, wand or athame. It is visible psychically as a circle of light, but not seen externally except by those with evolved clairvoyant sight and children. You can form this psychic light circle in the air about waist or knee high, whichever feels more natural, with a pointed crystal or wand, an athame, ritual knife or even a sword for formal magick, held in your power hand.

Direct the point at about 45 degrees, casting the circle in front of you so you step into the emerging light and become empowered. You can enclose the circle stepping in yourself and closing the circle afterwards (at the north). If others are present, complete the circle over the heads of those either side of the visualised doorway at the north-east/north, so the circle closes where you began (north-east if you cast from the east).

If you wish, make a circle casting chant that you repeat either aloud or in your mind as you walk: for example,

> May the circle be cast and remain unbroken. May the love of the Goddess be forever in my/our heart/s. Blessings be on this rite and all present.

If working alone the *all* would include the nature essences, your Witch Guardian, wise ancestors, etc.

Finally, you might wish to create a dome of light from inside over the circle with the wand or athame by moving it in an arch upwards and outwards in clockwise spirals or leave your temple open to the sun, moon or stars.

Making a triple elemental circle

* If using the elements to strengthen a circle, light any candles and consecrate the salt water for the circle casting (see page 162) after drawing your circle of light round a symbolic circle.

* If you are casting purely a triple elemental circle, consecrate the salt water after the opening call.

* If the circle is an existing physical one, empower it psychically by walking round the outline three times clockwise, once with each of the three elemental substances, sacred salt water, incense and candle flame or salt, incense and water. With a group, you can have three people walking clockwise round the circle in procession carrying the three substances.

* Make the circles one on top of the other and close the circle after the last person has entered.

* If you prefer, sprinkle the salt and water and waft the incense or pause with the candle flame at the four cardinal points still clockwise, north to north.

End the triple elemental casting by sprinkling each person present with a few drops of either the salt and water or the water alone saying:

> You are blessed and welcome.

* If you are working alone, end the triple circle casting by taking the water and sprinkling yourself and saying:

> May the Lord and Lady. Goddess and God bless me and my spell/ritual.

* I have worked in circles where the triple elements are used before sealing the circle by walking round with the sword, athame or wand.

Visualising the circle of light

You can do this when you want a quick spell or if you are in a place where it would not be appropriate to walk physically round a circle area (maybe you are in a park or on a beach and other people are around not connected with you). Visualise the circle appearing round you. It is also effective in a relatively confined space, such as a small garden, indoors, in your office or a lonely place if you feel vulnerable.

* Stand in the centre of your area facing where you think north is (or east if you prefer). You can keep a tiny compass in your bag for such moments.
* Holding a pointed quartz crystal, your wand where practical (I have a very tiny crystal one in my bag) or subtly extending the index finger of your power hand, waist high, turn your body and feet slowly in a circle, but remain on the same spot in the centre.
* Picture light flowing outwards, creating a circle round you and the space you are working at the required distance. Make the circle of visualised gold, white, silver or blue light in one sweeping continuous movement of your hand.
* You can also visualise a light circle emerging by turning with your hands in front of you, fingers horizontal, palms down and index fingers extended.
* Alternatively stand motionless and, with the index finger of your power hand extended, see light flowing from it and encircling you. Picture the light flowing upwards from the earth and downwards from the sky joining to form a reddish gold light circle of required circumference.
* If doing protective magick, you can cast your visualised circle as wide as you like beyond the physical room.

Uncasting the circle

Some people do not uncast a circle but consider closing the four elemental watchtowers at the four directions at the end of a ritual and snuffing or blowing out any directional/elemental candles sufficient. However, I feel that uncasting the circle after a ceremony is a way of restoring the ritual place to its earlier state though now blessed, which in the case of an altar room will be harmonious and peaceful rather than buzzing. It also helps to bring you and anyone else present back to earth and the everyday world, while absorbing some of the remaining ritual radiance into your aura as it gently fades.

The reason for uncasting an outdoor psychic light circle is to release any remaining energies after a ritual so that any animal or bird wouldn't get tangled up in the energies, and anyone entering the space will not pick up any vibes, however pleasant, that do not belong to them. Do this round a physical circle, too.

I uncast circles anticlockwise: I always have. Some practitioners say that is wrong, but moonwise or anticlockwise seems to me the completion of what was set up sunwise or clockwise, and goes with the natural flow. I do not believe one is undoing the spell or reversing energies. But I respect the traditions of those who uncast clockwise or not at all.

* To uncast, walk round anticlockwise from north back to north in the northern magickal tradition (or east to east) with the wand or athame etc behind this time, picturing the light returning to the source, finger, crystal or wand. Say a closing chant, such as:

> *May the circle be open yet remain unbroken in our hearts and in our lives. Blessed be.*

* Alternatively, stand in the centre facing north (or east) and turn anticlockwise on the spot, drawing the light back into the crystal, athame wand or finger, or picture the radiance sinking into the ground. This is a nice ending to a simple personal spell or ritual.

* You uncast a triple elemental circle just once by walking it with a wand etc or standing in the centre and turning anticlockwise.

* With tea lights, blow any still alight out in reverse order of lighting (sending a final blessing in each light). If in a group, the individuals who lit them can do this one by one. If a natural substance like herbs or flowers formed the circle, leave them to blow away.

* Uncast the spiritual circle round a more solid permanent physical circle to release the energies. Then make a gateway in the physical circle by removing a stone, for example, from the circle perimeter in the north-west and south-east for energies to blow in and out at will. The energies will soon dissipate and you can replace the stones after 24 hours.

* A collective stone or shell circle made on a beach can be dismantled after the ritual or one drawn in sand or earth rubbed out or left for the tide or rain (make an opening in the line north-west and south-east if leaving it to the elements).

* In any uncasting, even after a quickie spell, finish with a closing blessing to carry the magick into the everyday world and then say:

> *The rite is ended. Blessings be.*

or,

> *Merry meet and merry part and merry meet again.*

* Some practitioners use either the index finger of the receptive hand or the athame or wand to uncast the circle held in the opposite hand from that used in casting.

Doorways in circles

There are generally few reasons for leaving a circle during ritual, unless you are enacting a drama with friends or a coven and, for example, the crone is called into the circle, or at the Midwinter Solstice if the midwives leave after birthing the Sun King. Where possible, even they should remain within the circle and for any dramatic re-enactment, for example, the descent of the Goddess to the Underworld to seek her love (see page 654) or the return of Persephone, a larger than usual circle should be cast and the characters remaining within it head bowed or shrouded in a cloak until their entrance.

If anyone must leave, one method is to cut a doorway in the circle close to the ground with the athame in the north-east, piercing as though through an invisible membrane and tracing a sphere-shaped doorway anticlockwise just large enough for an individual to leave the circle. As you leave the circle, the accumulated energy rapidly and smoothly fills the hole made.

When you return, you can pierce the circle again near the ground at the same place in the north or north-east, depending where you cast the circle from, redraw the doorway clockwise and walk through it. The energy will seal the hole and enclose you within. The missing energy is considered to be contained in the athame and so you should not put it down while outside the circle. Someone waiting outside can enter the circle using the clockwise doorway action.

The tradition of the square

The square is a very powerful symbol of earthly power and protection that is represented in city and town squares, the centre or heart of the city where through history people gathered. All major Roman towns had their forum or square around which major buildings and monuments were grouped. Even today, throughout the world people come together in city squares to celebrate the New Year and major national or regional events.

Sacred and religious buildings were sometimes built on a square plot and the square formation was used to hold relics or enclose a particularly holy sanctuary. The square was symbol not only of earthly kingship but also of divine power invested in an earthly king. Mediaeval sorcerers would stand in a square within the magick circle when working with demons. Some squares were undoubtedly used to mark as sacred land where, for example, a former sacred Roman temple stood, just as a circle of stones or tree stumps beneath a church or cathedral might indicate a former sacred Druidic grove.

In magick, the square has served as a protective enclosure. The tradition of the mystic plot or square continued in areas of England where the Vikings settled until the late 1800s and even to this day in some remote places where folk magick remains strong. The water witches of the West Midlands used a magickal square for magick. They were people who came from the Netherlands to live and work on the Midland canals in the 1800s. They practised an ancient form of folk magick that did not die out until the mid-1900s (and in fact there are still a few practitioners). Rituals were practised on a square of land adjacent to the canal bank within a triple magickal square. Each square was joined by four lines and constructed from wood and was known as the mill. Only women entered the sacred area under the leadership of a senior female water witch, though the chief male, known as the master standing at the edge, summoned a spirit entity to assist in the ritual.

In modern Iceland, the Landvaettir or land guardians often have particularly sacred square fields that cannot be built on where offerings are left so they will protect the homes and farms around.

Like the circle, the magickal square is usually drawn directly into the earth as a way of connecting with earth power and wisdom, though often only the corners and midpoints are marked where a square is a permanent feature. It is empowered either by walking round it, sometimes with fire, or by visualising the boundary lines filled with light.

Working with the mystic square

The mystic square has two distinct magickal functions. The first is forming a permanent protective area around a temporarily empowered circle, especially in rural areas such as Sussex and East Anglia in the UK. The square was marked out with wooden agricultural implements, cornerstones or even naturally placed trees and bushes as an indication this was a designated magickal space. Offerings would be left there to the land spirits. These protective squares might also be drawn around homes to act as a barrier against all harm, earthly and paranormal.

The area chosen was invariably one of great ley power and there would often be a ley line crossing point in the centre of the marked square that would coincide with the temporarily erected circle. Wooden rather than iron implements were used at the corners and no iron permitted within the ritual circle space, as this was believed to impede the flow of ley power. The ritual circle would instead be marked with the staff, a horn or bone tool or a flint knife (if you can ever make or obtain one of these, treasure it).

You do not need to use a square at all in ritual. However, if you ever get the chance to work in an open space, whether alone or with others, I would recommend you try creating a square at least once, as it is one of the old magickal traditions that we are losing. Any rituals within it, whether or not you make an inner circle (see page 255), will be very potent and feel secure.

If you want the extra protection and concentration of power, for indoor or outdoor magick you can designate a protective square around the outside of your home, using four convenient markers such as trees or bushes, even if they are not on your property and, marking the four corners and midpoints if possible with dark stones. Since few of us have detached homes with a square of land round our homes, you might have to compromise by using boundary fences or indoor markers such as pot plants, crystals or candles at the four corners of your altar room to mark the boundaries, even if it is not quite square and cast the circle just inside it.

My square goes along my back fence to include my neighbour's fence, then down to his hen house and back along my front wall and along the other neighbour's fence. Even if it is not in your garden, the protective square will harm no one and indeed the area may become safer and feel friendlier as a result. Plants will flourish and birds and small wildlife increase. Outdoor magick is much easier for creating a square, especially if there is an open place where you regularly go to carry out rituals.

* The first time you make the protective square, walk the physical square round your home, your altar room or the designated area outdoors from the furthest away top left-hand corner in the north-west, walking clockwise round the boundaries to complete the square.

* If you physically can't walk the whole square, project your power arm, hand and index finger outstretched in the right direction to draw the invisible line, then walk to where you can physically pick up the line again and carry on walking. Modern urban magick is harder than when people were surrounded by fields,

but with ingenuity there is always a way. Draw the imaginary line in the air at about waist height.

✳ Chant softly and continuously (in your mind if necessary):

May all be safe within, house and human, animal and bird, butterfly and bee, flower and tree, protected and blessed by the lord and lady.

✳ You can assign the corners also to protective angels or the shadowy Landvaettir, the tall brown guardians who in Iceland, Finland, Sweden, Norway, Germany and eastern parts of the UK are recognised as protecting land and all who live on it. If you prefer and it is practical, protect the corners with traditional taller dark pointed stones or plant small thorny bushes.

✳ You could set your guardian stone near the centre of the square as protector.

✳ If the shape of your home really makes it impossible to make a physical square draw a plan of your home and any buildings round it (even if they do not belong to you) on white paper with black pen and mark in with pen the square boundaries clockwise, afterwards going over the perimeter with pointed clear quartz or your wand to symbolically enclose the actual area with light.

✳ Put small amethysts at the corners of the paper square and at midpoints and smudge it weekly, repeating the chant above as you do so.

✳ Before creating your actual circle for a spell, activate the square by picturing the boundary lines as white light forming along the top horizontal (west to east) line of the square.

✳ Extend your wand or power index finger and see light flowing from it to make the lines.

✳ Keep turning, making next the vertical north south line of light along the right east side as you face north (or the furthest distance directly in front of you in the approximate direction from a known place).

✳ Standing in the centre of the altar room or your ritual area, you can picture the boundaries even if they are not on your land or you only drew them on paper.

✳ Repeat the chant and keep visualising your light square getting brighter and brighter until you have all four lines of radiance in place and can see a shimmering outline square of light in your mind. You are now ready to cast the circle.

Working magick within the square

The square was also used directly as a magickal enclosure anciently on the great seasonal fire festivals, at Midwinter, Midsummer and Harvest. The square was made up of nine turf squares, etched in the earth. Eight were removed to reveal bare earth, leaving the middle one to form the centre of the ritual fire.

In lands conquered by the Vikings, the mystic square in folk magick became a substitute for the circle and the centre of the ninth inner square sometimes housed the stone pile altar, called the harrow in the Norse tradition or, as above, the ceremonial fire.

Certainly in the UK, the mystic square was measured in units of 3 ft or their multiples, depending on the number of the group of practitioners assembled. This is very easy to set up or draw. The corners were sometimes marked with holes ready for the squares to be created. If you want to know a precise method of measurement I recommend reading Nigel Pennick's *Secrets of East Anglian Magick*. Sometimes in common with the water witch tradition, a roped square was made about knee high with iron or wooden stakes to mark the sacred area, but this is not necessary. The northern boundary was traditionally left open, to allow psychic powers from the earth to flow within the square. Alternatively, outdoors a square of fire torches can be used to mark the corners and the midpoints of east, south and west, again leaving the north open.

Before use, the area within the boundaries was cleansed with water and twigs tied together or herbal smudge/incense in alternate anticlockwise and clockwise spirals while saying continuously, *Cleansed be, purified and sanctified.*

Magick squares really only work well as circle substitutes for outdoor spells and rites as the energies are very intense and need space to keep the energy flowing freely. I have written about using the square in ritual in the module on altars (see page 134), but I will repeat and expand the square casting technique here.

The making of sacred space

* If others are present for your rite they can assemble in a square formation (within ropes if you have preset them, adding the last stake to the north-west as you enter to close the square).

* Whether working alone or leading the ceremony, stand in the centre of the square in front of the harrow facing north.

* This can be a good occasion to have a source of flame in the centre of the altar.

* Taking up a fire torch, candle or other fire source from the altar, face the four directions clockwise in turn beginning facing north.

* Holding the fire source vertically in your power hand say:

   > *By Fire I call protection, by flame I kindle power, from the north, the east [face east], the south your home, great burning brand [face south[and west [face west]. I call you fiery Guardian of this sacred place and of the realms of fire, to bless, strengthen and purify my/our heart/s and this sacred rite.*

* Face the north again, the direction of Ice in the Norse tradition and raise the seax knife to the skies, then to the earth three times or bang the hammer three times on the altar, calling on the chosen deities or Odin for the Sky and his consort Frigg for the earth to bless the rite and protect those present.

* Make the Thurisaz rune sign in the air facing south, the direction of the realm of Fire asking for the protection of Thor at this ritual (name it and if you wish say a few words to sum up its purpose).

The calling

* If you have a musical horn or bell blow it facing north to open the ceremony.

* If not or afterwards make your opening blessing. Call any deities, Odin and Frigg or the Goddess and God as lord and lady in a slow chant three times. Frey the ancient Norse fertility and Horned God and his beautiful sister Freyja are sometimes considered the original lord and lady.

- If you have a musical horn or bell now face west and sound it three times to ask the presence and blessing of the ancestors. If not, face west and ask them if they will bless the occasion.

- See page 174 for continuing the rite.

The Scandinavian grid of nine

In Scandinavia, the mystic square formed the outline for an individual practitioner's grid of nine squares, three by three. These were made by the seio, the witch seer of the Norse world. Squares would be drawn either directly into the earth or in earth scattered on a raised wooden platform erected in a sacred place. She channelled wisdom from the spirit world, specifically from Helheim where the Crone Goddess Hel cared for the deceased.

The seio sat on a raised throne or raised platform within the central square of the grid and travelled astrally to Helheim to talk to the ancestors and receive advice for the living. Only later did the Goddess Hel get demonised and in recent years there has been a revival of seio craft.

A variation on the platform/earth was an ox hide divided into nine squares in the centre of which the practitioner sat. Lengths of wood were also used to form nine squares, again with the practitioner sitting or standing in the centre.

Working within nine squares can be very empowering if you are a solitary practitioner. Draw your nine squares with an external joining boundary line on all four sides and carry out the seven directions honouring ritual I described earlier in the chapter. Have a small altar on a flat rock so you sit on the ground in front of it in the central square or work without an altar. This may feel a bit intense for a new practitioner, but sitting with your smudge and wooden tools, perhaps on a windswept hill or plain in the centre of your grid, makes for powerful magick.

PRACTICAL ASSIGNMENT

Circle casting

❋ Plan your own form of circle casting for your private spells and rituals formal and informal or if you are an experienced witch assess if you would like to modify your present methods. Create your own casting and uncasting chants.

❋ Find an open space where it would be possible to empower a mystic square or find ways using candles and crystals that you could make one in a limited space indoors. Again, devise your own chants.

❋ If you feel ready, devise a simple ceremony using the individual grid of nine.

Further research

Explore the traditions of the Native North American medicine wheel with its four winds, four directions and 12 power animals. See how this could enhance magickal circle casting and use.

Further information

Recommended reading

❋ Bradley, Richard, *Archaeology of Natural Places*, Routledge, 2000

❋ Campanelli, Dan, and Campanelli, Pauline, *Circles, Groves and Sanctuaries, Sacred Spaces for Today's Pagans*, Llewellyn, 1993

❋ D'Este, Sorita and Rankine, David, *Circle of Fire, The Symbolism and Practice of Wiccan Ritual*, Avalonia, 2005

❋ Harvey, Ralph, *The Last Bastion, The Suppression and Remergence of Witchcraft, the Old Religion*, Zambezi Publishing, 2004

❋ Pennick, Nigel, *Secrets of East Anglian Magic*, Robert Hale, 1995

❋ Sun Bear, *Dancing with the Wheel*, Simon and Schuster Inc, 1991

❋ White, Kirk, *Adept Circle Magic*, Citadel, 2006

Websites

❋ *About Pagan / Wiccan Religion*
Series of articles on circle casting and rituals
www.paganwiccan.about.com/circle casting/
www.angelfire.com/realm2/ amethystsbt/circlecasting.html
Comprehensive information on circles

❋ *Medicine wheels*
Sun Bear Medicine Wheel diagram and link to other medicine wheel pages
www.ewebtribe.com/StarSpider Dancing/wheel.html

❋ *Breathless Noon*
Excellent site on sacred space and time
www.mothersmagic.net/theology/ sacredtime.php

❋ *How to construct and understand a Medicine Wheel*
www.spiritualnetwork.net/native/ medicine_ wheel.htm

THE BOOK OF SHADOWS

According to Gerald Gardner, a Book of Shadows had to be copied from another more experienced witch, so passing on a core of traditional wisdom and ensuring continuity. However, for many modern witches, their private as opposed to the coven Book of Shadows is an ongoing record of their own magickal journey. The biggest revolution has been the internet where traditional wisdom from many sources is suddenly available worldwide, allowing any witch to draw from a variety of sources to create magickal correspondences and ritual material that is right for them.

But personal experience will always be vital in the Book of Shadows and in that way we can all add to the evolution of the Craft by contributing our own insights. Sometimes a newcomer will ask a question about an established practice or offer a new alternative insight, and so from day one of their study, every witch has valuable material that should be recorded. This module will focus mainly on creating your own Book of Shadows, but most covens do welcome contributions to the collective Book of Shadows that keeps traditions constantly fresh and evolving. There is no one, definitive, set-in-stone source of wisdom. The witches' bible is made up of the experience of all witches past, present and future, and so is rather part of an ever-flowing and growing stream.

The old name for a private magickal book is a grimoire, but Book of Shadows is more commonly used. Shadows refers to the secrecy needed to keep the wisdom safe in times of persecution.

The origin of the Book of Shadows

Although in times before literacy was widespread most hereditary witches passed their knowledge orally, there are stories of written books of inherited knowledge of rituals and healing and magickal herbs. These are very different from the tomes of high magick that were often in Latin or Hebrew.

The Book of Shadows was kept by a magister, magus or local coven master who might be a literate local man, such as a teacher, a scholar or a squire who kept his identity secret. He was considered less likely to crack under persecution than a woman who had to protect her children from inquisitors. We know a little of these wise or cunning men from accounts of witchcraft trials of the 16th and 17th centuries, where they were sometimes described as fairy devils. Women told under torture how they were initiated by a grey or dark man, probably a coven master rather than an otherworldly demon.

Certainly in times of persecution and even afterwards, the information contained in such works was memorised, so that the book could be destroyed in times of danger. However, with widespread persecution, much of this oral and written knowledge, some in the UK dating back to the Anglo-Saxon wise women, was lost.

One of the earliest recorded Books of Shadows was *Aradia, or Gospel of the Witches*, transcribed from the Etruscan witch oral tradition and published in English in 1899 by Leland. The first official UK Book of Shadows that extended beyond individual families or covens was probably written by George Pickingill, the East Anglian witch father and keeper of the traditions of hereditary witchcraft. He was responsible for nine covens, including the New Forest Coven into which in 1939 Dorothy Clutterbuck was said to have first initiated Gerald Gardner.

Gardner's own Book of Shadows brought the concept into the public domain and has over the years in its revised form inspired many other Books of Shadows. He first published rituals from this in his novel *High Magic's Aid* in 1949 and drew on sources from many ages and cultures. His original Book of Shadows was influenced by Aleister Crowley.

From about 1954, Doreen Valiente was instrumental in rewriting the Book of Shadows, excluding Crowley's material, and her lovely rituals are available all over the internet. Alexander Sanders adapted the Gardnerian Book of Shadows in his own Alexandrian tradition, adding new material, and it is said the concept of writing your own Book of Shadows originated with the Alexandrian tradition.

Should the Book of Shadows be secret?

Though at one time coven Books of Shadows were kept in secrecy with only one coven copy, gradually rules relaxed so that after initiation coven members were permitted to copy material into their own Books of Shadows. With the technological revolution, an increasing number are published online as well as in books, and indeed, Gardner paved the way for this with his writings.

Copying out material by hand has the advantage of making the information valued and recalled. I think that every witch should have a handwritten Book of Shadows, even if for convenience and security material is passed and copies stored on a computer. I am in favour of openness and the sharing of information.

However, some witches argue that some of the more traditional rituals are open to misinterpretation by those who have not received the training in which such rites have a context: for example, those involving being sky clad, binding with cords, the scourge or the fivefold kiss that includes the genitals. Such aspects can be open to abuse by unscrupulous practitioners (I have met some) for whom intimate connections are used for power and sexual gratification over innocent and unwary would-be witches. However, since the floodgates did open, it is all the more essential that we as witches guide newcomers with advice and knowledge. The more open witchcraft can be, then the less the power of those who hide behind it for their own gratification.

In this course, I have given my own accessible form of witchcraft and offered sources for a variety of other opinions and practices. In writing your own Book of Shadows I suggest you study as many versions of other Books of Shadows as possible and then decide what is right for you and makes you feel spiritually and physically comfortable and sacred.

About the Book of Shadows

What should it contain?

The Book of Shadows should be a primer, a witch's bible and a resource for all the magickal correspondences and knowledge you acquire over the months and years.

Later I have suggested possible categories into which you could divide your Book of Shadows, a number of which follow the module subjects of this course. Basically, these can include your own beliefs and comments on the Wiccan Rede and also sources such as the principles of the Council of American Witches. It can also include: seasonal and Esbat rituals; colour and elemental correspondences; herb lore; chants, both created and taken from other traditions, dances and dramas; spells for all occasions; and divinatory wisdom. You can use a cross-referencing system for relevant linked material. Have a look at online resources for other ideas of topics.

When should you begin your Book of Shadows?

Whenever you begin to study witchcraft. For solitary practitioners especially, your book will become a reminder of what you have learned, a source of inspiration, a resource and a wise friend. From the first you can collect magickal knowledge and rituals from a variety of sources and gradually add your own.

If you already have a Book of Shadows, you can use the ideas in this module to add or rethink your present format, so that it is becomes even more valuable and you can instantly access the required information. Think about using it as a teaching resource for passing on the Craft and about developing your own creative ritual writing and poetry, as well as collating any channelled wisdom from Angels or Guides.

Creating Your Book of Shadows

Ideally every witch, whether solitary or a coven member, should have at least two personal Books of Shadows, plus some kind of basic filing/computer system.

You need an ongoing resource book. Use a notebook or journal that you update as you gain new information or try new methods, as well as good sources for candles, herbs etc. A loose-leaf version is ideal. Alternatively, date notebooks as they become full, list the contents and file safely.

Keep with you an even smaller notebook whenever you have a day out or a weekend or holiday for noting information about any new plants or herbs you see growing, legends of wells, ancient sites, museum visits, local rhymes and chants, churches and cathedrals that may contain Green Men or Angel lore. You can also write down information about statues of saints and see if they have any pre-Christian parallels. All kinds of unexpected people come out with fascinating information or experiences even as we go about our daily life, and it is easy to forget details and not be able to trace the source.

A cuttings folder for interesting articles, photographs or small pamphlets from places you visit is also a valuable source of knowledge. Also keep here your jottings from lectures or courses, and try to write these up regularly in your larger resource book. Also write comments about any books you read and anything new they teach you. I know there is nothing more infuriating than leafing through a book trying to find a relevant quote that seems to have disappeared into thin air.

You could also set up a computer version of your resources or an efficient card file index for cross-referencing and finding information quickly. Information stored on computer can be edited and rearranged and you can initially access online reference material or even old witchcraft books online and exchanges on forums. The internet is a good way of receiving a flow of knowledge as a solitary and you can find online forums to share your ideas.

For your hand written Book of Shadows you can buy velvet or leather-bound specially crafted Books of Shadows, try a stationer's (office superstores usually have a huge range of blank folders). Try to find the kind with a binder (not a ring binder, but where the pages slide into the spine). This will allow you to add to and revise material. If not, allow sufficient blank pages for each section so you do not run out of space. Alternatively, there is no rule that the Book of Shadows has to be a single volume. You could have slim blank leafed volumes for rituals, one for spells and another for chants and poetry, and keep them in a box or on a high shelf.

Black ink on white or cream paper is customary, though for Angel work green ink is used. A fountain pen is best. Keep this just for writing your Book of Shadows. Some practitioners write sections in runic or Angelic script (see weeks 35 and 37), but since there are not exact correspondences for all the sounds, you may choose to save magickal alphabets for spells or ceremonies.

Caring for your Book of Shadows

It is worth keeping computer floppy disks or copies of your most valuable work so that you can create a treasury of wisdom over the years, in spite of computer crashes, spillages and losses.

Keep your material in a safe place. A woman I know had her notebook seized by her ex husband who showed it to the presiding judge in a custody case. In fact this was counterproductive and the judge said the contents were fascinating, that the woman was obviously very ecologically aware and would bring the children up to love nature. However, in different circumstances or if disapproving relatives pry, you need to ensure information cannot be misunderstood and used against you by sometimes unsympathetic officials or employers, especially if you have children. If you share a home then even harmless curiosity can make you feel uneasy and intruded upon.

Put a password lock on this part of your computer: not because there is anything wrong with what you are doing, but because it represents a vulnerable spiritual part of yourself that you should share with those trusted friends or family you know will value your insights.

Should a Book of Shadows be destroyed on a witch's death?

In ancient traditions, a Book of Shadows is kept until the witch's death, when it is burned. However, generally I would advise keeping the book, especially if you are a solitary practitioner and this is the only record of your work, to hand down to an adult child who is interested in the arts, to another friend or relative who will treasure it, to an archive or for publication either in book form or online. That way we can carry on the living traditions to future generations and bring witchcraft back into the light of day as a viable more general religion.

For example, had Gerald Gardner's Book of Shadows not been inherited by Doreen Valiente, we would have lost a great treasure to the witchcraft community.

Can the knowledge be transmitted to other lifetimes?

Some witches believe that though their Book of Shadows is destroyed they will retain the knowledge in future incarnations or it will be given back to them in childhood by a spirit guide. In case you think these sounds fanciful I will tell you about Andrew, now 50, who is very logical and worked for a top London media agency until he decided to live a simpler life.

In my book *Psychic Power of Children*, I gave an account how Andrew had an invisible winged griffon-type friend he saw from the age of six, who apparently taught him the arts of magick at this very young age. Here is some of Andrew's experience:

When I was very young I was drawn to this strange place that was a long walk from my home for a young child. People called it the Place of the Dead. You stepped down into the woods and there were no birds and no wildlife.

Haimayne, my invisible friend, smelled strong like a lion and was brown and yellowy, velvety, but was skin and bone. Though he had wings he never flew.

Haimayne didn't hold conversations as such with me or talk about trivia. He would tell me what to do and how to pronounce words we needed for our rituals. I wrote these down in what I called my Glossary.

Before an adventure, Haimayne would tell me what we needed — salt, matches, something to write on — there was always slate around the area, chalk to write with on the slate and sometimes berries for the juice.

When we were going travelling we had to prepare a tablet the night before as a protective charm either of clay or wax. It took ages to prepare. I used my grandfather's old tobacco tin filled with clay and straw or wax. The following morning one side would still be soft and we could press into it the journey plan. A figure to represent me, a small person for Haimayne, a vertical line to indicate the path of the travel and equals signs for the time we would stay away. We would leave the tablet over the stile in the hawthorn tree where water came from the ground in the crown of the first hawthorn cleft.

It was like leaving a note saying when we could be found and as long as it was undisturbed we could come back safely. Afterwards we would get rid of the map by burning it.

From the age of about six when he came into my life, Haimayne was my teacher and best mate. Haimayne taught me spells and chants, water divination and woodcraft about the trees and what you could use the woods for. When I was 11, he taught me how to use candles and mirrors to look through time. Each had to be precisely aligned and as an adult, others have commented on the complex mathematical processes involved in my early diagrams that I have kept.

Looking back at these, we always used pictograms or strange marks when we were writing our spells though Haimayne did help me to read and write. There were special words in my Glossary book for the four directions and the stars, for ghosts and for saving lost souls. They weren't another language really, just written how I was told to pronounce them by Haimayne. Though I found formal learning difficult, Haimayne made me pronounce things over and over to get them right.

I found as an adult I knew all about trees, birds, herbs, flowers and old places. It was just the names I was taught were different from the ones I have seen as an adult. But the information was all true and far beyond the grasp of a young boy except I did learn it then.

Suggested contents of your formal Book of Shadows

These can be arranged in any order to suit you and you may wish to add categories of your own or leave out ones that are not appropriate for you.

* Your own statement of the ethics and purpose of your Craft and any formal rede you work by (we began this on page 62, but it will evolve over many years your own wisdom grows).

* Any definitions of magick or witchcraft you find helpful from your own experience or traditional sources. Note any you like as you read different books.

* Elemental correspondences and elemental pentagrams. The four elemental Guardians of the watchtowers, titles and invocations at the four quarters, your own and ones from other sources.

* Inspirational texts, such as the Valiente Charges, the witch's rune chant (see page 300); as well as other sources, such as poetry, the Bible, Celtic blessings, Hebrew or Buddhist literature; your own poems and inspirational writings. Also include your own Charges and relevant myths, such as the Descent of the Goddess (see page 394).

* Tools you use and those you would like to acquire; how to make them, cleansing and empowering tools, both your own methods and those you have seen/read about.

* Altars. Setting the altar for different occasions and from different traditions, such as Ancient Egyptian if relevant to you. Dedicating the altar.

* Magickal times, days of the week, tides of the day and planetary and Archangel hours, months, etc.

* Numerological values and meanings for calculating good magickal times, the number values of the names of people for whom you may cast spells, etc.

* Gods and Goddesses, names and significances.

* Colour significances.

* Crystal information for magick and healing.

* Herbs, magickal meanings, brews, lotions, baths and potions from a variety of sources, including your own.

* Magickal flowers and trees, especially magickal meanings of woods for wand making etc. Where and when flowers bloom locally, so you can remember to go to the bluebell wood.

- Spells. A large selection for all occasions, your own and those of others that seem effective. You can subdivide this into topics if you wish.

- The moon, phases and times, full moon names, moon magick through the month, lunar deities. Drawing down the moon rituals, your own and ones you have collected.

- The sun, the four divisions and rituals to honour them, drawing down the sun, solar deities.

- Sabbats, the seasonal rituals. Start a section for each of the eight festivals and include myths, magickal correspondences such as candle colours, fragrances etc and your own rituals, plus any you have found that you like.

- Esbats. An addition to the moon section as you may not always be able celebrate your Esbat on the full moon. Basic rituals and formats, also if you meet with others how you will celebrate the occasion.

- Chants. Ones you have written plus favourites from other cultures, such as Tibetan chants. Lists of suitable background music.

- Rituals for rites of passage, such as any private dedications to witchcraft, house blessing ceremonies, plus any special occasions such as baby blessings or handfasting. Note also any public ceremonies or handfastings you attend, what you liked or how you would do it differently. Long before I carried out these ceremonies for others I collected material from a variety of sources. If you record rituals for birthdays or anniversaries, you can develop a sacred personal year ritual calendar. Include here candle rituals and any occasions not marked by the Wheel of the Year, such as New Year.

- Incenses, magickal meanings and your favourite recipes, both your own and from different sources that work well for you.

- Fragrances, essential oils and perfumes that you use in ritual, magickal meanings and mixes of your own and from other sources.

- Angels and Archangels. Magickal correspondences, rituals and channelled wisdom.

- Witch Guardians, Spirit Guides and Wise Ancestors. You may encounter particular ancestors, whether historical, in your family or from a culture to which you have an affinity/past life. They will increasingly channel wisdom to you and fill in missing knowledge.

- Amulets, charms and talismans, ones you have made and relevant symbols and methods from other cultures.

- Magickal alphabets from any source that feels right for your magick writing, such as runes, Angelic alphabets or Egyptian hieroglyphs. Where there are missing correspondences to ordinary letters, compromises that will work for you.

- Scrying, dreams and divination work. You will find it helpful to create your own symbol system based on your own meditation and scrying work, such as reading clouds or wax on water; add meanings from other sources. Include also personal and traditional meanings of any specific form of divination you use, such as tarot cards.

- Nature essence and spirit work. Include here experiences with nature beings and also anything you discover about the myths of different nature spirits that correspond with your own personal contacts. Add information from holidays in other lands.
- Earth, Air, Fire and Water. Places where you have experienced these phenomena within nature, also your own Earth, Air, Fire and Water visualisation and those from other sources. In the Water section you can include magickal waters you have made.
- Healing. You may wish to have a separate healing book in which you write the names of anyone who is ill or any animals, species or places to which you regularly send healing. In your Book of Shadows record any healing rituals or charms you have created/learned.
- Psychic protection. Different ways of creating psychic shields, any binding or defensive spells and rituals that work for you.
- Psychic experiences of you and your family or friends or any you hear. Details can easily fade unless recorded with dates.
- Books that have inspired you, plus perhaps key quotes.

PRACTICAL ASSIGNMENT

Organising your Book of Shadows

Spend time collecting, collating and organising your material. Even if relatively new to witchcraft you will be surprised how much information you have already gathered. If you are experienced, add a completely new section to your existing Book of Shadows.

Further research

Locate other Books of Shadows either in book form or on line for inspiration and aim to find new material or slants to existing knowledge.

Further information

Recommended reading

* Eason, Cassandra, *Psychic Power of Children*, Foulsham, 1994
* Gardner, Gerald, *Witchcraft and the Book of Shadows, a definitive record of the practices of Wicca*, I-H-O books, 2002
* Graves, Robert, *Greek Gods and Heroes*, Laurel Leaf Books, 1995
* Green, Marian, *A Witch Alone – 13 Moons to make Natural Magic*, Harper Collins, 2002
* Jones, Evan John and Valiente Doreen, *Witchcraft: a Tradition Renewed*, Robert Hale, 1999
* Lady Raya, *Book of Dreams and Shadows, a Witch's Tool*, Red Wheel/Weiser, 2001
* Lady Sabrina, *A Witch's Master Grimoire, the Encyclopedia of Charms, Spells, Formulas and Magical Rites*, New Page, 2001
* Macgregor Mathers, S L, *The Grimoire of Armadel*, Red Wheel/Weiser, 2001
  17th century translation of popularised Christian magick.
* Morrison, Dorothy, *The Craft: A Witch's Book of Shadows*, Llewellyn, 2001
* Moura, Ann, *Book of Shadows, Grimoire for the Green Witch*, Llewellyn, 2003

Websites

* *Gardnerian Book of Shadows online* www.sacred-texts.com/pag/gbos/index.htm
* *Internet Book of Shadows* Huge collection of online articles on magick and neopaganism, by a variety of authors, including much traditional material www.sacred-texts.com/bos/index.htm
* *Magdalena's Online Book of Shadows* Interesting topics, an excellent basic online resource www.msu.edu/user/rohdemar/earth/bos.html

MAGICKAL NAMES

Every practitioner needs at least one magickal name for practising the Craft. This is used by other practitioners and may be sometimes adopted when writing about magick. In earlier times practitioners would never reveal this name except to other coven members and some witches still maintain this privacy. I think this is entirely a matter for choice.

The Ancient Egypt magickal tradition embraces five magickal names, as taken by the Goddess Isis, Mistress of Enchantment. These were all secret except to the practitioner. Though you may choose to be known in witchcraft circles by one particular magickal name, having four others that are entirely private does, I believe, create a repository of power especially for solitary practitioners.

The names can be chosen to reflect a particular deity power, a tree or star. However, since each letter of the alphabet has a numerical meaning that in itself has powerful magickal significance, you can in addition calculate the underlying qualities or vibrations of any chosen name.

The power of names

In some cultures, even the everyday name was filled with magickal significance. In the Native North American tradition, an adolescent boy or girl would go out into the wilderness and fast and meditate until a bird or animal came near whose name they would adopt as a power icon, such as Running Bear.

In Ancient Egypt, the ren or name was considered part of the soul and it was said that so long as your name was spoken or recalled so would you live spiritually. For this reason, the name of an Egyptian child was chosen with great care to reflect those qualities desired in the child. Sometimes a compound name would contain a deity name, indicating that the child was under the protection of the deity. The name was also important because it would appear on tombs and be used for eternity in the land of the blessed. The prefix Nefer as in Nefertiti, the beautiful wife of Akhenaton, was the hieroglyph for beauty and harmony. Tutankhamun's name contained ankh, the hieroglyph and symbol of eternal life, and Amun, the name of the supreme creator god. Tut is a form of Thoth, adding the wisdom of this senior god of knowledge to the young pharaoh. Kings, scribes and nobles were often blessed with the name Amenhotep, which means Amen or Amun is at peace.

Of course, the power of names could also be a terrible weapon in Ancient Egypt, since it was believed that every part of the body, soul and spirit was interdependent. To erase a name from a tomb was to destroy the spirit in the afterlife. For example, Thutmes or Thutmoses III, the son of Thutmoses II and a concubine, was proclaimed pharaoh on death of his father in 1478 BCE. However, the widow of the king, Hatshepsut, became regent for the young king and reigned as pharaoh herself for 29 years. She effectively excluded him from power. On her death, Thutmoses III had his revenge by disfiguring her statues and deleting her name from all her monuments. Those whose names were not spoken at the offerings table in mortuary chapels or shrines by relations would, it was believed, cease to exist in the afterlife and so a prayer was often set over the shrine so that passers by might also recite it. In life, too, inscribing the name of an enemy on a pot or wax image and then destroying it was thought to destroy the living person: not to be recommended, though you can legitimately write the name of a sorrow, fear or threat in wax and then roll the wax into a ball to make it formless, and then bury it.

Secret names

Right from Ancient Egyptian times, words have been recognised as containing magickal energy that is released when the words are spoken or written and this underpins modern spellcasting. One of the main sources of the use of secret magickal names is the Hermetic tradition that is based on Ancient Greek practices that were themselves influenced by Ancient Egypt. I mentioned this tradition in the module on the roots of witchcraft (see page 37).

From the Hermetic tradition comes the belief that everyone, human, spirit and deity had a true but secret inner name, as opposed to the one used in daily life. If a magician could discover the name of a spirit, he or she could command the entity to obey every command. This belief underpinned mediaeval and Renaissance angelology and demonology and has survived in modern incantations and use of the deity names in Wiccan ritual. It also appears in fairy tales such as the Brothers Grimm's Rumplestiltskin, where only by guessing the name of the bad elf could the girl be freed from having to give him her child in return for spinning straw into gold. Magicians addressed themselves by their own secret name as they began a magickal incantation, but would never write it down.

The power of Isis

The power of the secret name is demonstrated in an Ancient Egyptian myth that tells that Isis, the mother and Moon Goddess and wife of Osiris, won her great magickal power by tricking the Sun God Ra into revealing his secret names to her. When the God was old, she secretly collected some of his spittle and fashioned it into a serpent that she left in his path to bite him. The bite left him in intense agony and he called upon the other gods to cure him. But because the serpent had been created from Ra's own substance, none of the other deities could relieve his pain. Isis said that she could cure him if he would reveal his secret names to her. At first he tried to give her false names, but she persisted and as his agony grew worse, he agreed. She cured him, but because she knew his secret names, she gained all his magickal knowledge.

Some feminist researchers believe the myth was created or altered from an earlier version to discredit Isis when the Romans were so worried about her popularity overtaking their own deities. We know she was a powerful magician in her own right; for example, myth tells how she threatened to stop the sun's course when her infant son was stung by scorpions and none would aid her until at last the magician supreme Thoth brought healing. But the point of the myth is valid and so your magickal names signify the special private spiritual part of yourself that you may not want to reveal to the everyday world.

Creating magickal names

Every witch chooses, or some believe rediscovers, her secret name or names from a past world, which might be the name of a favourite deity, an angel name, a magickal creature or a beautiful flower or tree that has personal significance. Of course, you may be content with one magickal name and that is a very valid witchcraft tradition. However, you may like to create four additional names Ancient Egyptian style to add to your chosen name or if you are new to magick to select five power names that describe the person you are and also what you would like to become. You can then if you wish use the first openly in the Craft.

Adopt your name/s from any culture to which you feel drawn or choose a variety of deity or nature essence names from different cultures. Alternatively, you can base them purely in nature, animals or birds or magickal plants.

Method 1

* Begin by lighting a white or beeswax candle as soon after twilight as possible.
* Now light a divinatory incense stick such as sandalwood, jasmine, sage or rose from the candle and set it in a holder. Position the incense so the smoke curls behind the candle.
* Sprinkle a few granules of salt, the sacred substance of the element Earth, into the flame so it sparkles.
* Looking into the candle flame, say softly:

> *May this name I use [give nine times any current magick name you have] be blessed and purified. Blessed be.*

* If you don't have a magick name yet say instead after lighting the candle and incense and sprinkling the salt:

> *May the name/s that I am guided to be blessed and purified. Blessed be.*

* Now take a blue ink pen and white paper and write all the names you are attracted to or which have significance, in a long list and then allow others to flow spontaneously into your mind as you relax. Start the list with any current name you have. Some you may not recognise as they will come from the collective well of wisdom or some would say were names you carried in a past world you are now recalling. If you need inspiration, read the deity lists beginning on page 232.
* Take a clear crystal pendulum and pass it through the smoke of the incense and then the candle flame and say:

> *I ask that the Goddess, the wise ones, my Guides and Angels will guide my hand to find the name/s that is/are right for my magickal endeavours.*

- Pass the pendulum slowly in turn over and a few centimetres above each name below your present one and it will vibrate so you can feel it in your fingers. The pendulum will suddenly seem heavy as it is drawn downwards by gravity over up to five names. You need not hold it over your current magickal name unless you are having doubts about it.

- If there are fewer than five chosen names in total, wait and over the weeks or months others may come to you, perhaps a particular bird that sits outside your window or an unusual crystal you keep hearing about or seeing.

- Pass the pendulum now through the smoke and then the flame to cleanse it and set it down.

- Write the chosen names on a new piece of paper; recite them nine times in the order that feels right, first using any magickal name you already use. Then say:

> *When I speak these names in ritual or in times of need, so may their power and protection enfold me. I offer them now in humility to the Lord and Lady.*

- Then burn the paper in the candle flame. Place a large metal tray beneath the candle and holder to catch the burning paper or drop the paper in a deep bowl of sand or earth as it catches alight. You are not destroying your names, rather sending them into the cosmos to be blessed. Afterwards, say:

> *May my name/s live as long as the sun endures and the waters flow. Blessed be.*

- Allow the candle and incense to burn through. As you wait, visualise the different power names taking form as spirit guides round you and in the incense smoke. Perhaps you may spontaneously channel words from the archetypal or idealised forms of the names, either the original deity, the angel whose title you adopt, a star or constellation or the lord or lady or chief of the species of animals you chose.

- Afterwards bury the ash and dispose of any candle wax.

Method 2 Using numerology

In Ancient Egypt and among the Phoenicians the priest-scribe caste discovered the art of mathematics and made it intrinsic to magickal ritual. Numbers, mathematicians thought, held the key to everything. The Hebrews and later the Greeks gave each of the letters of their alphabet a numerical value. The Ancient Greek mathematician Pythagoras believed that each of the primary numbers had different vibrations and that these vibrations echoed throughout heaven and earth, including mankind. The music of the spheres expressed the harmony of the heavenly bodies that each had their own numerical vibration.

You can see what energies your present magickal name is vibrating and then choose or adapt spellings of any other chosen magickal names to give a balanced numerologically significant overall magickal vibration, each name reflecting different strengths. The hidden powers of your magickal names will be reflected in your aura and so will be conveyed in the messages you unconsciously send to others via your aura in your everyday as well as magickal life.

Often, too, secret names are our alter ego or shadow self and can make us a more integrated personality. Inexplicably in logical terms any magickal names you have previously chosen will be precisely the magickal meaning you intended.

Select up to five names as for Method I and then work adding or subtracting letters or titles to give the magickal meaning you desire. I have given the example of Freyja the Norse Goddess of Love and Beauty below.

The number meanings

I will first give the correspondences for the letters under the Pythagorean system and then I will describe both the background meanings and the magickal or witchwise significance of the different numbers. You can also use numerology when naming a magickal group or assigning secret names, as some practitioners do, to personally significant tools.

1	2	3	4	5	6	7	8	9
A	B	C	D	E	F	G	H	I
J	K	L	M	N	O	P	Q	R
S	T	U	V	W	X	Y	Z	

* Add together all the number values of the letters in each individual chosen name/s and reduce the number total again by adding, to a single number (1–9).

* If you do want a particular number meaning, keep experimenting. If, for example, you chose Owl, which is 14 and so 5, the communicator, and this does not feel right, you could add White Owl (7), Grey Owl (6) or Owl Woman (8), for the owl was a form the Celtic wise crone Goddesses.

* If you keep getting the same number no matter how you alter the spelling, that number is an important hidden aspect of your psyche and the name and should be adopted, even if wasn't the number you hoped for consciously.

Creating the energies you want

To make this clearer, let's use the example of Freyja, the young Norse Goddess of love, fertility and beauty whose chariot was pulled by black cats. Her tears were amber and she was mistress of the Valkyries, the swan maidens who carried the worthy slain from battle to the heavenly halls. It was Freyja who taught the art of magick to the Norse Father God Odin.

FREYJA
6 9 5 7 1 1 = 29,

which can be added up again to give 11, which can further be reduced to 1+1= 2.

2 is the number of the integrator and if you adopted this name would enable you to weave together different traditions and practices and make you skilled in healing magick and also balancing magick. This is the kind where within the same spell you first cast away what is no longer good and replace it with something new that will grow in your life.

Whether a solitary practitioner or a coven or group act, you would as the bridge between different ideas and people and find it easy to work with both the Goddess and God.

Freyja brought together the ideas of the different deity groups: the Vanir, her own people who were nature deities and healers, and the more warlike Aesir. But you might say, *Well that's not my idea of Freyja at all. My Freyja is that wild beautiful battle maiden in her cloak of swan or falcon feathers and flame coloured hair streaming behind her in the wind.*

So let's drop a letter.

FREYA

6 9 5 7 1, which gives us 28, which makes 10, which reduces to 1.

Freya as 1 is the Innovator of Magick, the leader of Odin's Valkyries, but nevertheless rides ahead alone. So if you are or would like to become a natural leader of others or an innovator who practises a unique form of magick alone, spell the goddess name Freya, if she is one of your choices.

Let's try another magickal name.

SUNFLOWER

1 3 5 6 3 6 5 5 9 = 43 = 7

7 is the number of the wise one and the mystic, perfect for magick. In Ancient Greek myth, the original sunflower was once the water nymph Clytie. She was so sad that her love for Helios, the Greek Sun God, was not returned that she sat on the ground day and night, watching his fiery chariot pass across the sky as the sun rose, reached his height and descended into the ocean. So long did she watch that her limbs became rooted in the Earth and she was transformed into a sunflower, symbol of constancy. Her gaze is forever fixed sunwards as she climbs towards her love. But she must die each year and let new seeds fall.

I saw field upon field of sunflowers lifting their heads to the sun when I was staying in Central France recently and realised what a powerful name this is.

The numbers
Number 1 contains all others numbers. The others 2–9 are alternately even, regarded as a female, anima or yin and receptive number pattern, and odd, male, animus, yang and an active number vibration,

Number 1
Number 1 is unity, the word or logos, the first manifestation of creative light that multiplies into millions of unique parts, each separate and yet containing the power of the first. It is associated with the one Goddess/God, the Mother of All or the All Father, depending on your beliefs, the oneness of all humankind and the separate self. One, all alone and the prime source of everything, stood for reason, which the Pythagoreans saw as the ultimate force.

Magickal qualities: The number of the innovator and the powerful solitary witch or group leader. A number 1 secret name signifies you are an initiator of action, one who is always devising new chants, incense combinations and original ceremonies.

You use books and teaching as a basis for developing your own unique style of witchcraft. You are a powerful raiser of energy, even in a forest with no tools but with only a small branch you have adapted as a wand. You can work alone and direct your energies to global as well as personal issues or you could if you wished become a wise leader of a coven one day.

The number of the rising sun.

Number 2

Number 2 is the symbol of duality, the separate mother/anima principle and the father animus. Number 2 contains both complementary and opposing forces of polarity, light and darkness, as symbolised by the Celtic oak and holly kings, the waxing and waning year, who fought at the equinoxes. Two – the first even and therefore female number – also stood for opinion.

Magickal qualities: The number of the negotiator and integrator. A number 2 secret name confirms you as someone who will by example make others aware within and maybe beyond the witchcraft community of your spiritual wisdom. You will weave together different traditions and merge easily in ritual with cosmic and natural sources of power. You can see the deeper meaning behind the magick and will be able to reconcile seemingly conflicting opinions within the Craft and come up with a wise compromise. Whether you work alone or in a group, you will help others to follow more natural spiritual ways of daily living.

The number of the Setting Sun or some attribute the Moon to this number.

Number 3

Number 3 is the number of a trinity – father, mother and son, Father, Son and Holy Spirit and the Triple Goddess maiden, mother and crone. The sacred triangle is a form representing the eternal, especially in Ancient Egypt. Three is a number of fertility and creation. Three – the first odd and therefore male number – stood for potency.

Magickal qualities: The number of the creator of ritual and the disseminator of knowledge. Whether you are a solitary witch or work in a coven, your Book of Shadows will be inspirational. You are a natural poet and can capture in words written and spoken the different elemental forces and the hidden energies of the seasons. You can chant and dance instinctively, even with little training, because you can feel the natural rhythms of the earth. You could become a teacher and help to counter the misinformation and prejudice against witchcraft by writing and maybe talking to local organisations.

The number of Jupiter.

Number 4

Number 4 is the number of the square, the physical and material world and is said to be the most stable of all numbers, with crosses having four arms symbolising spirit, the vertical line penetrating the horizontal matter. This is the Goddess and God or father and mother principle set and divided even further within time, space and matter. Four, the balanced, square number, stood for justice.

Magickal qualities: The number of the realist who can span the worlds and bring magick into daily life. You are the one who knows about hard work and that magick has to be practised within the constraints of daily life. You will not allow time limitations or other commitments take you from the Craft. Equally you won't neglect what needs doing in daily life. You have the perseverance to learn all the correspondences in magick and memorise chants so you can focus on the magick at key times – and not be worried about forgetting your words.

The number of Saturn.

Number 5

Number 5 is a very spiritual number, representing the quintessence, the fifth element created from the other four that unifies Earth, Air, Fire and Water and is itself greater. The pentagram is a magickal symbol of great spiritual and magickal power, like man or woman extending their head or single point upwards to the heavens. Five, which was created by the union of three, the first male number, and two, the first female number, stood for marriage.

Magickal qualities: You are the witch who time travels and shape-shifts easily, who may not recall precisely which herb or crystal you need usually because you have read and learned so much you have run out of mind slots – or are leaping six stages ahead. Nevertheless, you practise effective magick because you psychically tune into the ancient source of knowledge. Always inventive, you can also ensure your magick is relevant to the 21st Century world and constantly evolving. You love visiting different places for new ideas and materials.

The number of the Voyager and Mercury.

Number 6

Number 6 is of great mystical significance since it represents the six days taken to create the Earth and the six-pointed hexagram and the Seal of Solomon, a form with pagan as well as formal religious associations as a symbol of perfection and integration. Six held the secret of cold.

Magickal qualities: The number of the peacemaker and environmentalist. You will be the original green witch who loves nature deeply and is concerned for endangered species halfway across the globe, as well as the effect of mobile phone emissions on sensitive youngsters locally. You won't be a rich witch, at least not financially; but you will be loved for your concern for others, and your healing and protective magickal powers will grow daily.

The number of the planet Venus.

Number 7

Number 7 is the number of perfection, the most sacred of all numbers, a combination of the sacred three representing spirit and the four elements of nature, manifesting the Goddess in every aspect of creation. To the Ancient Egyptians, seven was a symbol of eternal life. The seventh day was holy because on this day the Goddess/God rested after creation, according to the Bible. There were also the seven ancient planets that were believed to endow humans with their qualities as they descended to Earth through the spheres. In seven could be found the secret of health (three – potency – together with the balanced number 4).

Magickal qualities: The number of the wise one and mystics. You may feel as though you were born a witch even though your parents may have been strict churchgoers or very logical. For you, witchcraft is more a question of remembering the old ways and you will have or develop great channelling abilities, especially from the Moon Goddesses and the Angels. You may develop strong past life recall, maybe even being a healer or seer in an earlier world. These you may well become in this life.

The number of the moon.

Number 8

The number 8 is sometimes called the way of the serpent as humans travel on the road to wisdom by weaving through different choices and polarities. This path is mirrored in the shape of the number. As the highest single even number, it represents balance and this path is also one associated with prosperity and authority, especially matters of justice with its emphasis on cause and effect. Eight held the secret of love (this time the potent three was added to five, the number of marriage).

Magickal qualities: The number of the entrepreneur and the organiser. A natural media witch, you have the power to make things happen right away, organise a successful midsummer celebration for 100 and celebrate the old ways while keeping more conventional members of the community singing along happily. You are the one to set up an online coven if you do not have any local contacts and to track down in translation the old sources of knowledge – or translate them yourself if necessary.

The number of the planet Earth.

Number 9

Number 9 is primarily the number of initiation, both in religion and magickal rituals where actions are carried out nine times as a sign of perfection and completion. As the last of the single numbers, it brings the sequence to a close. After it there are no new numbers, merely combinations. It is poised on the edge of the units and double figure numbers and is associated with walking between worlds. Number 9 held the secret of harmony (5 – marriage – together with 4 – justice).

Magickal qualities: The number of the crusader, the changer of history. Fortunately they no longer burn witches for you are a natural campaigner and crusader of tolerance and of free speech. This may be for more awareness of spirituality in the later stages of school life to counter the sensationalism of cult vampire series, for the acceptance of witchcraft as a valid faith and not a cranky alternative or for overcoming pockets of prejudice where witchcraft is still regarded in mediaeval terms as the spawn of Satan. You probably already visit sites of witch executions and leave flowers and maybe try to get their stories published.

The number of Mars.

Using your magickal names

Once you have your names you can weave them into a chant with which you can begin private rituals or use as a private empowerment in daily life whenever you need strength or feel vulnerable or that your identity is being eroded and your opinions ignored.

The following chant is an example of a practitioner who feels a strong connection with Ancient Egypt as a number of witches do and so might choose five Egyptian deity names, the first her overt or open Craft name:

I am Nephthys, lady of twilight, whose red flowers bloom in the parched desert. I am Nut, Sky Goddess, arched over the whole world, the woman covered all in stars. I am Sekhmet, lady of Fire, she who never turns from a challenge or danger but offers healing to those who love me. I am Sothis, star maiden, who heralds in the fertile Nile flood with my radiance and promises renewed abundance to land and people. I am Uajdet, the wise cobra, who stands guard over her young and those in need, she who stings the cruel and vicious and yet can cure the most fearsome bite in the innocent and who marks the appointed end of the mightiest Pharaoh.

* Speak your secret power chant with increasing speed and intensity or sung on a simple rising and falling tune (see page 299), at a deserted lakeside, a seashore or hillside into the wind or in the middle of a forest. Chant very softly in your mind on a crowded train, crammed in a lift or whenever you feel overwhelmed by noise or crowds.

* Recite your names also at dawn or when you wake and greet the light, at noon or when you break from work in the middle of the day to reassert your power and energise yourself; at twilight or when you go home to gather your psyche together after the demands of the day; and finally, whisper them at midnight or whenever you go to bed to bring peaceful, healing sleep.

* Write them in incense smoke over amulets, talismans and charms to endow them with your essence and also over spell symbols.

* The *I am* declaration, followed by your magickal name/names preceding any deity name used, is a potent way of beginning any personal spell or private ritual and marks the space between the spiritual and everyday world by raising the vibration level. You would say, for example, as you held and raised the focal symbol at the beginning of the spell:

I am [list name/s, silently except for the first name if others are present] and my magickal intention in this rite is [name purpose of the spell].

* Empower a crystal by writing your magick name/s over it nine times in incense stick smoke so that as you hold or carry the crystal in the days ahead the deep power of your secret names is activated even in the everyday world (good if your identity or security is under threat).

* Add up the total number significance of all your magickal names together and reduce the total to a single number, which is your overall magickal signature. You can then wear this number as a talisman: for example, as earrings or cufflinks for 2, a single pendant for I, a charm bracelet with five charms for 5, or eight

alternate jet and amber beads threaded on a necklace for the God and Goddess energies for 8, and so on.

* It can be useful for a very special spell to work out the numerological significance of the deity or Archangel whose name you are invoking. This is good in Archangel Rituals. Spend some time practising converting names to numbers so the process becomes fast and you memorise the number values of each letter.

PRACTICAL ASSIGNMENT

Creating a power name talisman

Using magickal number squares

From early times, mathematicians have been fascinated by magick squares in which numbers are laid out in grids three by three, four by four, etc, so that the rows, columns and diagonals all add up to the same number. Such squares were considered of mystical significance. Magickal number squares can be used in a variety of ways in conjunction with your main magickal name to create a talisman of power.

The square of Saturn that I have used has three rows, columns and diagonals that all add up to 15. Saturn is the planet of stability and is the most usual and potent form of number square. You can also make seals or number patterns for deities, angels or another person for whom you are making a talisman or charm using the method below.

Making your talismanic shape

Your special talismanic shape will be created by tracing the numbers of your name on the magick square. As an example I have given my ordinary rather than my magickal name. I have to keep something secret!

CASSEASON, which becomes 3 1 1 1 5 1 1 6 5

Traced out on a magick square (making a zigzag shape where a number, here the 1, is written three times consecutively and then twice more) it looks like this:

which gives the sign of

* You can carve or draw your own symbol on a piece of wood or pottery as your very own magick sign and use it on your altar dishes or tools. The shape can also be painted in colours or on crystals whose colours are associated with specific needs: for example, red for courage and pink for mending quarrels.
* The shape can be transferred to a thin scroll of paper and worn in a small silver tube on a chain round your neck.
* You can draw it in soft wax for special wishes or engrave it on the side of a candle that you burn to bring power or banish fear.
* You can mark the numbers on a drum or tambourine and memorise the number order. I have a tambourine marked with the square of Saturn, which I regularly use to tap out my name pattern.

further research

Explore the topic of numerology more extensively, either looking at the more complex Hebrew system or the applications of numerology in other areas of your life, in your magickal work or in divination.

Further information

Recommended reading

* Clodd, Edward, *Magic in Names and other things* (1920), R A Kessinger Publishing, 1987
* Decoz, Harris, and Monte, Tom, *Numerology*, Perigee Books, 2001
* Drury, Nevill, Watkins *Dictionary of Magick :Over 3000 entries on the World of Magical Formulas, Secret Symbols and the Occult*, Watkins Publishing, 2005
* Eason, Cassandra, *Complete Guide to the Tarot*, Piatkus, 2000
  Contains a section on numerology.
* Eason, Cassandra, *Alchemy at Work*, Crossing Press, 2004
  For using numerology in your work life.
* Forrest, M. Isidora, *Isis Magick, Cultivating a Relationship with the Goddess of 10,000 names*, Llewellyn, 2001
* Pennick, Nigel, *Magical Alphabets: The Secrets and Significance of Ancient Scripts — Including Runes, Greek, Hebrew and Alchemical Alphabets*, Weiser/Red Wheel, 1992
  For Hebrew numerical associations.
* Schimmel, Anne Marie, *The Mystery of Numbers*, Oxford University Press USA, 1994
* Vega, Phyllis, *Your Magickal Name*, New Page, 2004

Websites

* *The Inner Dimension*
  Not for the faint hearted but an excellent explanation of the intricacies of Hebrew numerology
  www.inner.org/gematria/geatria.htm
* *Avalonia*
  Good explanation of numerology and generally a very good site for magickal information
  www.avalonia.co.uk/book_of_shadows/numerology.htm
* *Information on magick squares and their use as talismans*
  http://mathworld.wolfram.com/MagicSquare.html

PSYCHIC PROTECTION AND MAGICK

Inevitably, psychic protection has already appeared in the course, in the form of asperging the site of a ritual, cleansing tools, circle casting, creating a protective square and anointing your chakras. We will also meet it in the module on making amulets, talismans and charms, on herbs, incense and crystals and on Angels, all of which can offer ongoing protection to a ritual space.

If you practise magick with good intent, then you are very safe and indeed. I add, *For the greatest good and with the purest intent* and *If it is right to be* if a spell is directed towards a third party. However, even within those criteria magick involves spiritual openness as your chakras open, to other dimensions and to others, especially, for example, during a healing or banishing spell. While the circle is an enclosed protected place, every witch brings with them the effects of the daily world, unless they have cleansed themselves psychically. Working without some form of ritual cleansing is like cleaning the carpet and then walking into the room with muddy shoes.

In everyday life witches tend to be sensitive, giving people who take on the troubles of the world. Their natural psychic abilities open them up to impressions from the world of the living and the world of spirit. These are not necessarily harmful, but can be emotionally and psychologically draining. Therefore this module focuses both on ritual and personal protection. On page 189 I described grounding yourself and closing the chakras or psychic energy centres after a spell. Chakra closing is an excellent way of stopping yourself buzzing with energies after magickal or divinatory work.

Protective magick

Protective magick works on two levels. The first is immediate and involves consciously creating a safe space round us and a personal enclosed energy field. Within these we can practise magick or in our daily life be insulated from psychic overload or negativity, however caused.

On a more subtle level, ongoing psychic protection builds up gradually and remains in the background day and night, offering an effective filter. When we do need extra instant or ritual protection, it is easily and swiftly activated to full power.

Once you are familiar with different protective rituals, you can create short cuts to evoke their defensive power. For example during smudging or working with the Archangels touch the centre of your brow and say, *When I touch my Brow/Third Eye chakra, I will instantly awaken the protection of the angels/the fragrance.*

Personal preparations

Many modern witches do not fast for 24 hours or abstain from sex for the same period before a ritual, as magick has to fit with the everyday world, even ceremonial magick. But try to slow down your activities in the hours before the ritual, eat a light meal and turn off all phones, faxes and computers if you are working from home.

Before any spell or ritual and when you have time before working at your altar, when channelling wisdom from angels or guides or meditating, it is good to prepare yourself with a ritual bath or shower and keep loose robes just for your magickal work (unless you work sky clad). Such cleansing has a symbolic as well as a physical effect, shedding the pollution and stresses of the everyday world and its negativity and distractions, and also casting round yourself the protection of the fragrances and the words you use: for example, to call on deity or angelic protection.

On page 34 I suggested a method of anointing your chakras when you do not have time for a bath or are away from home. Alternatively, you can half fill a small spray bottle of still mineral water to which three tiny pinches of sea salt have been added and shaken with a blessing, asking the Goddess to purify you in your ritual. Prior to the ritual, spray this mix on your four upper chakra points, repeating the blessing. It can also be protective if you feel under psychic or psychological attack in the everyday world and you can modify the blessing to the situation.

You can also use smudge or a herbal incense (see below) as an aura cleanser.

Ritual baths

Ritual baths are among the most ancient of magickal traditions and in temples throughout history the ritual bath house was an essential feature. The first ritual baths were probably pure water, either from the sea (the forerunner of salt baths) and under running water such as a sacred waterfall or spring (the modern shower is an excellent substitute).

Salt baths

These vary from adding nine pinches of magickally empowered salt to clear bath water, that you keep in a special sealed container, to an empowered bath salt mix. You can either use commercially but organically prepared salts in a pine, eucalyptus, lemon, tea tree, rose, rosemary or lavender fragrance (or a mixture) or make your own from three parts Epsom salts, two parts baking soda and one part sea salt with essential oils added (see weeek 43 for other purifying fragrances).

The secret of making your own salts is in the mixing and empowerment and you can save mixes you have created in a sealed container You can also by the oils you use add other qualities, such as eucalyptus for overcoming obstacles, lavender for mending quarrels and good luck, rose for love and healing, pine for new beginnings, creativity and fertility and rosemary for encouraging money to flow into your life (see page 551). Magick is multi-levelled and with practice can simultaneously serve a number of purposes. However, you can also empower ready-made bath salts.

* Remove prepared bath salts from their container and put them in a ceramic or glass bowl. If making your own, take the three basic ingredients listed above and add a few drops of cleansing essential oil such as pine, lavender, rose, rosemary (sparingly), tea tree or eucalyptus to the mix. These are good-tempered oils, and

should not be irritants, unless you have a very sensitive skin (in which case stick to rose or lavender). Experiment until the mix is fragrant.

* Mix your salts (whether your own or ready-made) with a ceramic or wooden spoon clockwise, chanting softly and regularly:

May the light and protection of the Mother enter here, dispelling darkness and fear. So mote it be.

* When you sense the mix is empowered, chant more softly and slowly and slowing your movements so all fades into silence and stillness.
* Fill the bath with warm water and when it is filled, make the sign of the banishing pentagram (see page 287) in the water. Some practitioners make an invoking pentagram (page 163). If the mix is to banish harm, the former seems to me more appropriate.
* Light scented candles in the bathroom, so the light shines in the water.
* Wash your body downwards, in anticlockwise circles. Rinse your hair.
* If you are using a shower, rub an essential oil shower mix into your body.
* When you are ready to get out of the water, swirl the reflected light three times anticlockwise and take out the plug saying:

Go in peace, flow in harmony, to the sea of eternity.

* You can do this after you have switched off the shower as the water drains away.
* If having a salt-based bath you may like to rinse your hair and body afterwards in pure water.
* Afterwards, shake yourself, especially your fingers, to remove any remaining energies of the day. Say:

So am I purified of the world and I enter my magickal space with anticipation and with a gentle and loving heart.

Keep your magickal robe if you wear one ready washed and pressed, either on the back of the door in your magick space or bedroom covered with a sheet or folded in a special drawer. A sleeveless kaftan type robe is useful to avoid trailing sleeves.

Some practitioners have special jet and amber jewellery (God and Goddess powers) that they wear for ritual, or you could wear a silver pentagram pendant or any silver jewellery decorated, for example, with a crescent moon. Copper is also very magickal, as is pure gold. When not in use, keep the jewellery in a box and smudge over it every week or so with a small herbal smudge or a pine or sage incense stick. Put it on an indoor window ledge on the night of the full moon if not wearing it for ritual.

If you wear the pentagram all the time, smudge it before ritual or sprinkle a circle of sacred salt water or a hyssop infusion (see page 559) round it before putting it on.

Don't be in too much of a hurry to start if you are working alone. Sit quietly by candle or natural light, allowing images to flow in and out of your mind, playing soft music if you wish, and lighting a fragrance oil or incense.

You can also have a protective bath after a bad day or if you feel under attack.

Using smudging or incense

One of the easiest and most effective methods both of cleansing your aura for ritual and casting ongoing protection round yourself as a psychic shield is to use smudge sticks or incense, either as sticks or in a dish wafted around you with a feather or your hands. You can also use this as a way of creating a psychic shield around yourself. You can learn more of psychic shields in my book *Psychic Protection Lifts the Spirit* or the other books I have listed or by following links on suggested websites. Another method of making a psychic shield is to visualise a bubble of light enclosing you, perhaps using a candle as a focus and breathing in the light. Use monthly smudging for ongoing protection or when you have had a stressful period and as a substitute for a ritual bath immediately before a ritual.

* Light a sage smudge stick or large firm leaves of grey or white sage of the sagebrush variety that you can obtain from many outlets. Grey sage, the Mother Goddess herb is especially effective. Small squat smudge sticks burn especially well and give out a steady but subtle stream of smoke. You can substitute a broad, firm incense stick or a dish of incense in pine, lemon, rosemary, juniper or any other cleansing and protective fragrance or a mix (see page 565).

* Swirl your smudge stick held in your power hand, in front of you and all round you clockwise and anticlockwise alternately so you establish a gentle rhythm as you stand. Alternatively, waft the smoke as you sit with the incense in front of you (not so close so it will make you cough). The smudging is symbolic rather than physical. You can use feathers or a fan to spread the smoke if you wish, held in your receptive hand.

* Place your smudge in a deep container so that the flow of smoke slows or move away from the incense dish.

* Sit quietly as you did when you were a child in your favourite hiding place when you did not want to be found, enjoying the enfolding stillness and calm.

* When you are ready, extinguish the smudge stick by tapping it against a ceramic container or in a bowl of sand and wait for the incense in the dish to die down.

* Shake yourself like a puppy in rain and your aura is bright again, but protected.

* When you are entering a difficult or potentially dangerous situation or carrying out a spell or ritual, visualise the smoke shielding you and hiding you from harm.

The power of blessings

Almost every Wiccan spell or ritual or indeed any encounter between witches usually ends with *Blessed be* or *Blessings be [on you]*. Likewise, all rituals and even short spells should where possible begin and end with a blessing. These can be very simple, taken from any tradition, adapted to suit your purpose or created and recorded in your Book of Shadows. The Celtic tradition is rich in blessings and there are numerous sites on the internet where you can find inspiration.

For ongoing protection at night, burn a candle and recite a blessing, then blow or snuff out the candle and send the light to someone who needs it. In the morning, splash your four upper chakras with water and recite a blessing. Here are my own favourite blessings:

The Druid prayer

Before or at the start of a spell or ritual, turn through the four directions starting in the east, raising your hands in front of you with arms extended chest high and palms uppermost and say:

> *May there be peace in the east,*
> *May there be peace in the south,*
> *May there be peace in the west,*
> *May there be peace in the north,*
> *May there be peace throughout the whole world.*

On the last line, extend your arms, still palms uppermost as far to the side as possible, still chest high, facing east again. Druidic ritual begins in the east. It also makes a good ending.

The Celtic circling prayer

There are numerous versions of this Celtic circling prayer where people would walk in a circle reciting it. When alone I stand with my wand facing north and make circles clockwise with the wand as I speak the blessing, rather than moving myself. I use this blessing not only in rituals, but also at the beginning and end of lectures as it is gentle and all embracing, and I face whoever is present while speaking or turn if people are in a circle. It is also wonderful for protecting an unfamiliar area chosen for ritual by walking round three times speaking the words as a soft continuous chant.

> *Circle this room/home/site/ritual, Mother, Father,*
> *Keep harm without, keep peace within.*
> *Circle this room/home [etc], Father, Mother.*
> *Bless all who gather here/bless and protect me here, this day/this night.*

Teresa of Avila

The 16th-century mystic St Teresa de Avila was a joyous figure, in spite of the intense austerity of her life. She likened dying to the process of a butterfly leaving the empty chrysalis behind. She created a number of lovely prayers. This is one that has often soothed me when I feel afraid or alone whether, waking in the night worrying or being in a dark or unfamiliar place as I travel.

> *Let nothing disturb you/me,*
> *Nothing dismay you/me.*
> *All things pass,*
> *But God/the Goddess never changes.*

Protective blessing rituals

More complex blessing rituals have a place both for the solitary practitioner and for a group in a circle. A group should first join hands to create a connection and then under the guidance of one of the members or the high priestess/priest, individually speak the words and carry out the actions before the formal circle casting. Some also close the rite with them. If alone, you could also use the light created to work within rather than making a separate circle casting.

The lesser banishing pentagram rite is a very complex and profound ritual, though not necessarily a number of researchers say, very ancient. It involves using names associated with Hebrew mysticism and the Kabbalah and below I have suggested two sites, one for the actual ritual, and one for a Wiccan version, where you can study the original if you wish.

If you are unfamiliar with this form of spirituality, I suggest that you read around the subject if you want to use the conventional form, in order that the rite is truly meaningful and not just names intoned and actions followed. Alternatively, get instruction from a more formal magickal tradition, unless your own coven is experienced in its teaching of the full lesser banishing pentagram rite.

My opinion is that in ritual we should always use deity and spiritual names and actions that have personal significance for us; magick does not depend on the complexity or the high status of words you use. The traditional version also does not recognise the Goddess, since it was created in the tradition of the monotheistic God, so I think my version is more Goddess friendly. For this reason, I have given adaptations of the different parts that are meaningful to me and seem to be helpful for others I have worked with and taught. As a solitary or as part of your coven or group teaching, you could use mine as a basis or interim step for creating your own more complex protection rituals if, and only if, you feel you would like to work with the more ceremonial versions of protection.

Part 1 The Kabbalistic Cross

The traditional version uses the names of the spheres of light or splendid sapphires on the mystical Hebrew Kabbalistic or Qabalistic Tree of Life, the bidirectional link via the 10 spheres and 22 pathways between the Godhead and the individual. It is based on the first part of the lesser banishing pentagram ritual. The second and third parts are the forming of the banishing pentagram followed by the Invocation of the Archangels, that I also describe in modified form. You can use any part entirely separately.

The Cross (or the Wiccan version here) can be used when you feel afraid or especially vulnerable, before a ritual after your bath or smudging, or as the first part of the ritual before circle casting. Perform it very slowly, enunciating each word and visualising the cross of light forming within you. The words address a single source of divinity or light. You can visualise your own personal source of goodness, perhaps as the undifferentiated Goddess.

* This first and top sphere, Kether or the Crown at the top of the Tree of Life, is described as an emanation of pure white light from the undifferentiated force that has no beginning and end. Face north. Stand straight and touch the top of your forehead (the centre of your hairline) with your right hand saying:

Great Mother of us all, thou art the divine light above and within me; so am I connected to the divine light and protection within myself through my own spark of Goddess divinity.

* Bring your hand down in a straight line, visualising this as a shaft of light to touch your genitals or womb, saying:

Thou art the Kingdom on Earth, Mother who brought forth life; so am I connected and rooted within my body as your child of the Earth.

* Touch your right shoulder and say:

Thou art Fierce, Wise Father [or Mother, if you prefer], the power beyond and within me, so am I protected from all harm by thy divine power and strength.

* Draw a line across with your right hand, to touch next your left shoulder and say:

Thou art compassionate mother the glory, beyond and within me, so am I illumined by thy glory and thy love.

* Clasp your hands in front of you over your heart and say:

For ever and ever, great mother, without beginning and without end.

* Finally, extend your hands and arms to form a cross in front of you or across your chest as you say either, *Aum* (the sound that according to Buddhists and Hindus brought the universe into being), *Amen* or *Blessed be.*

Part 2 The Banishing Pentagram Ritual

This is usually the second part of the above, but can be used separately, perhaps after a blessing prayer or whenever you feel afraid or vulnerable. Traditionally drawn with an athame, you can also create it in front of you between your head and solar plexus with your wand, a pointed crystal, the index finger of your power hand or visualised as appearing as a pentagram of light if you are in a place where you must create it internally.

* Facing the four directions in turn, starting with the north, make the banishing pentagram with your athame, your wand, a pointed crystal or the index finger of your power hand, at each of the four directions and say:

Goddess of the Earth, Mother of All, bless and protect (north), Goddess of the Sky, Mother of All, bless and protect (east), Goddess of the Sun, Mother of All, bless and protect (south), Goddess of the Moon, Mother of all, bless and protect (west).

* You are now ready to begin your rite or to face any fear or danger if you used this Part 2 separately.

Alternative Part 1 The Wiccan Cross — a template

I use this without mentioning specific deity names and allow the deity forms to appear in my mind, which can vary according to the ritual or occasion. However, you can assign your favourite deities, whether for general protection or as part of the ritual, when creating your own version or adapting this.

Because this version involves turning in a circle, you have the option of speaking it after the circle casting or, as I prefer, standing in the centre of the planned circle (or in your place on the perimeter, if part of a group). You can carry it out any place at any time as part of a separate ritual.

The cross is made within a circle, visualised or actual, by turning to face the four main directions, thus being doubly protective. In my version there is a balance between male and female energies, but you could equally make your protective cross by celebrating the growth of light the defeat by the God of light of his twin the Dark God at the Spring Equinox, the Sun King in all his glory at the Summer Solstice for the south, with the west as the time the God of darkness overcomes is twin the God of light on the Equinox, and the rebirth of the Sun God at the Midwinter Solstice through or the triumphant Horned God (see weeks 29–31 for details of different mythologies).

You could celebrate the life of the Goddess from maiden (east) to mother (south) to wise woman (west) and the ancient Bone Goddess of death and rebirth in the north who becomes the new maiden Goddess in the continuing cycle. I like the version that combines God/Goddess with creative/destructive elements, as it seems especially protective.

Another option is to start with the north, Midwinter, to keep in tune with the more traditional Kabbalistic Cross version that started in the north. Adapt the ritual below accordingly. It can also be incorporated into a slow dance and chant.

* Standing with your feet together and your arms by your side, begin by facing east, the direction of the Maiden Goddess who becomes pregnant at the Spring Equinox. Touch your forehead in the centre of your hairline with your right hand and say:

  Blessed are you holy maiden, untouched vessel of new life and fertility. Bless and protect me.

* Turn next to the south, here the direction of the Sun God who attains full potency on the Summer Solstice. Touch either your navel or the genitals/womb with your right hand and say:

  Blessed are you, golden father who crowns the mother with pure gold and takes your place her equal for this one brief day of glory. Lord of the sun who causes the crops to grow/land and sea to be bathed in light and fertility, bless and protect me.

* Turn next to the west, the direction here of the willing sacrifice, the Grain God who was cut down, sometimes recalled in the Grain Mother created from this sheaf. Touch your right shoulder with your right hand and say:

  Blessed are you who offered your body as the grain that there might be after a necessary period of fallow, new life once more, you who enter the dark womb in the certainty of rebirth. Bless and protect me.

- Turn finally to the north, the direction of the Earth Mother who brings forth the new Sun/Grain God on the Midwinter Solstice. Touch your left shoulder with your right hand and say:

Blessed are you, womb of the earth who gives and takes life, only to renew it in a never ending cycle of promise throughout eternity, bless and protect me.

- Finally turn in all four directions, clasping both hands over your heart, saying:

Protected and blessed in love and in fertility, in truth and in harmony, for now and for eternity. So mote it be.

Part 2 Wiccan version

You can adapt the banishing pentagram stage, using your chosen deities.

- Turn from the east in all four directions and make the banishing pentagram in all four directions, if using the ritual above substituting the maiden in the east and adding, *Bless and protect* as you make the first banishing pentagram in the east.
- In either version, the pentagrams are often visualised as four pentagrams of Fire or light that are joined in a circle of light with the Cross of Light extended through you as you stand in the centre.

Part 3 Invoking the Four Archangels

If you were using the first two parts of either the Kabbalistic or Wiccan Cross, you would repeat the Kabbalistic or Wiccan Cross after this angelic invocation. The four parts could form a ritual in themselves at a time you need protection or as the preliminary to a longer rite.

Now the Archangels are called to stand behind the four directional pentagrams. Their cross of light radiates in all directions and, most importantly, forms above your head, making a star of light above you, with you always in the centre. As you look upwards, you can picture its centre above your head, radiating directly down through your body into the earth as it revolves and shimmers.

Archangels of the Four Quarters

The four traditional directional protective Archangels (see page 576) are sometimes invoked as the Guardians of the Quarters or are represented by the four directional candles. They will fit with either version of the Cross. However, they are also one of the most powerful forms of protection for magick and everyday life. Therefore this part of the ritual is frequently used separately.

Before you begin this part, I would recommend lighting four candles, naming each Archangel as you do so, beginning with Uriel in the north. You can also light the relevant incense in the four quarters. If you do carry out all four parts, afterwards turn round several times fast clockwise or dance clockwise looking upwards. As you spin, you will see that star of light shimmering above you.

You can read more of the mystical formation and the more precise mystical and geometric creation of the star, but I believe nothing is more powerful than performing all four parts of the rite by candlelight or beneath a starry sky and then spinning in joy and weaving the light round you.

Uriel

Uriel, whose name means Fire of God, is the Archangel of transformation and alchemy and of the planet Mars. He is a pure pillar of fire that brings warmth to the winter and melts the snows with his flaming sword. Picture Uriel with an open hand holding a flame, dressed in rich burnished gold and ruby red with a bright flame-like halo like a bonfire blazing in the darkness and a fiery sword.

Direction: North

Colour: Ruby or dark red.

Incenses: Basil, copal, sandalwood and ginger

Raphael

Raphael, whose name means God has healed, is the Archangel of medicine and of all forms of healing and science and of the planet Mercury. Picture him carrying a golden vial of medicine, with a traveller's staff, food to nourish travellers in his wallet, dressed in the colours of early morning sunlight, with a beautiful green healing ray emanating from his halo.

Direction: East

Colour: Lemon yellow or misty grey, but often also perceived as green

Incenses: Lavender, lily of the valley, pine and thyme

Michael

Michael, whose name means who is like to God, is the supreme Archangel, Archangel of the sun. He is the leader of the great warrior angels and is one of the chief dragon-slaying Angels. Michael is pictured with golden wings in red and gold armour with sword, shield, a green date branch and carrying the scales of justice or a white banner with a red cross. He is the ideal young golden-haired warrior. In Muslim lore, Michael's wings are said to be the colour of green emeralds.

Direction: South

Colour: Gold

Incenses: Chamomile, frankincense, marigold, rosemary, sunflower and sage

Gabriel

Gabriel is Archangel of the moon and with Michael he forms the highest of the Archangels. His name means God has shown himself mightily. Archangel Gabriel carries God's messages. Picture him in silver or clothed in the blue of the night sky with a mantle of stars and a crescent moon for his halo, with a golden horn, a white lily; alternatively, with a lantern in his right hand and with a mirror made of jasper in his left.

Direction: West

Colour: Silver

Incenses: Eucalyptus, jasmine, lily, myrrh, lilac and rose

The Archangel invocation or calling

❋ Stand motionless facing east and looking upwards, with your arms wide chest high and your palms uppermost, saying:

> *Before me stands Raphael,*
> *Behind me Gabriel*
> *On my right hand Michael*
> *On my left Uriel*
> *The circle of light encloses me*
> *And above me is the shining star.*

❋ As you say each line, picture each Archangel, guarding one of the four fiery pentagrams, that are joined a circle of light and above a six rayed star whose light shimmers in all directions.

❋ Feel your body filled with white starlight, which joins with the red light of the earth and becomes pure gold within you.

PRACTICAL ASSIGNMENT

Self awareness

Examine your own magick work and everyday life and list any special stresses or areas of vulnerability and devise a personal ongoing psychic protection programme. Monitor yourself and the attitudes of others towards you and record how if at all you feel more protected/are practically less open to intrusion or unfriendliness.

Further research

Find out what you can about Celtic blessings and those from other faiths or, if you are interested in ritual magick, the lesser banishing pentagram ritual and the Tree of Life.

Further information

Recommended reading

* Eason, Cassandra, *Psychic Protection Lifts the Spirit*, Quantum/Foulsham, 2001
* Fortune, Dion, *Psychic Self Defense*, Thorsons, 1976
* Fortune, Dion, *The Mystical Qabalah*, 1979, Ernest Benn Ltd,
* Hansard, Christopher, *The Tibetan Book of Living*, Hodder and Stoughton, 2001
* Harlow, Dorothy, *Energy Vampires: A Practical Guide for Psychic Self-Protection*, Inner Traditions Bear and Company, 2003
* Matthews, Caitlin, *A Celtic Devotional*, Godsfield Press, 2003
* Matthews, Caitlin, *The Psychic Protection Handbook*, Piatkus, 2005
* Meckaharic, Draja, *Spiritual Cleansing, a Handbook of Psychic Protection*, Red Wheel/Weiser, 2003
* Morris, Desmond, *Body Guards, Protective Amulets and Charms*, Element, 1999
* Penczak, Christopher, *The Witch's Shield, Protection, Magical Awareness and Self Defense*, Llewellyn, 2004

Websites

* *The Cauldron*
  Comprehensive view of psychic protection
  www.ecauldron.com/protection.php
* *Inner Voice*
  A good Celtic blessings site
  www.innervoiceshaman.co.uk/celtbless.html
* *Less Banishing Pentagram ritual*
  www.kheper.net/topics/Hermeticsm/LBR.htm
* *Spirituals Baths*
  Informative site for ritual baths
  www.ladybridget.com/w/scbath.html
* *Synergy*
  Good for attunements and developing psychic shields
  http://synergy_2.tripod.com/psychic/intro_pd.html
* *Wiccan version of the Less Banishing Pentagram Ritual*
  www.sacred-texts.com/bos/bos025.htm

WRITING AND USING CHANTS

I have already written about the power of names, both our own magickal ones and using those of deities to absorb their powers. In magick, all words spoken in ritual or as part of a spell are intrinsically powerful and therefore it is important in devising ritual to use words wisely and to ask for what is needed. There is the example of a woman who asked me for a love spell to bring to her a man who shared her interests, was passionate, considerate and would be faithful forever. A year later, she came to see me again for another spell, this time for family harmony. She complained that the man of her dreams had indeed come into her life within weeks of the spell, but he had two teenage children who were being very difficult and ruining their love life. She had not specified that he must be childless.

In this module we will focus on using words in chants, rhythmic spoken or sung repetitive phrases to raise power or to increase the level of spiritual personal awareness sufficiently to make spellcasting effective.

Chants have the effect of organising words into a natural rhythm, compressing spell wishes into magickal rather than everyday language structures and so concentrating concepts. In this way, their meaning is powerfully impressed on the aether created by the spell and on our auras, which are likewise empowered by the repetitive and often increasing intensity of the sounds.

The power of words

In the module on spellcasting (see page 177), I described how in one of the major creation myths of Ancient Egypt the God Ptah thought the world in his mind and then created it by speaking magickal words or hekau. The power he used was called heka, which represents as well as the God of that name, the lifeforce. This power animates everything as it did at the first creation. In some versions of the myth, it was the God Heka himself who spoke creation into being.

So to the Ancient Egyptians, every act of magick was a recreation of that first act of creation. The concept has entered modern magick down the millennia and many witches know from experience that by using words powerfully and wisely, thoughts and desires can be brought into actuality through spells, invocations and ritual prayers.

Sacred sound

How then can words achieve this effect? From Ancient Greek times, harmonious sounds have been regarded as a microcosm or earthly expression of the harmony of the heavenly bodies. Since only a small proportion of the vibrations of the universe could be heard by the human ear, the purpose of chant and song was to attune the spirit of the chanter or musician to these more subtle spiritual sounds on higher levels. In doing so, the soul might move closer to harmony and unity with the cosmic rhythms.

Through this attunement, the disparate elements and energies of a spell are harmonised and raised to create the spiritual state and substance of aether, spirit or akasha. In this magickal state or energy force, our wishes are held beyond measured time, filled with power, transformed and bounced back into actuality. Mantras that originate in the Hindu and Buddhist traditions involve chanting sacred words or phrases aloud or in the mind. Mantras can be perfected by adepts as a means of developing and channelling psychic energies whether for healing, for positive power or astral, out-of-body travel.

You can therefore chant to great effect privately. What is more, when chanting is part of a ritual in which other voices are joined, great collective spiritual and psychic power is generated to launch a need, healing, blessing or empowerment. For this reason, solitary witches often join with friends, family or other witches and pagans at public celebrations or for special occasions such as seasonal ceremonies.

However, with the spread of the internet and good chanting CDs, solitary practitioners can collect a body of chants for every occasion and if they feel that they need extra power for a rite can sing along to prerecorded chants or use them as background. I can often be seen in traffic jams on the M3 chanting away to my Museum of Witchcraft chant CDs.

Chanting magick

Chanting, the art of saying or singing repetitive words or phrases rhythmically, has been used magickally and in religious and mystical ceremonies for thousands of years. Chanting involves a special thought mode, not just the logical left brain analysing and categorising in words, our conscious thoughts. Nor is it quite like the right brain clairvoyance or enhanced visualisation, where we work primarily through images and conjure up pictures of rushing rivers and mountain peaks as we describe them in our elemental chants.

Chanting at its most powerful synthesises left and right brain to evoke a spiritual out-of-body state that may seem to last for an hour or more though the chant may only be for five minutes. You will know this is happening when as you picture the rushing rivers to generate power, you are sailing on or swimming in the water, feeling the splashing cool sensation on your face and tasting the purity (cosmic rivers are never polluted).

Whether using voice alone or accompanied by dancing and or drumming, in isolation or with others, chanting increases the spell tempo and is the single most effective way of raising and releasing power. It also positively affects the chakras, the psychic energy centres and the aura of the chanter. For this reason, you can create a ritual just by chanting alone or by a very simple single action such as knot tying (see page 661). In contrast, soft chanting will soothe and harmonise the spirit, creating a light trance state in the chanter (and any listeners). This is excellent for becoming receptive to channelled wisdom, for healing spells, empowering herbs or charm bags and for creating personal harmony and stillness.

Sources of chants

Many of the favourite witchcraft chants appear on different CDs, with different words and are passed on orally at festivals or in different traditions over and over again. Sometimes no one is quite sure who originally created the original.

The evocative *Earth my Body, Water my Blood, Air my Breath and Fire my Spirit* as far as I know has no acknowledged author. But I would be pleased to know the source if any reader has this information. The *Isis, Astarte* chant I have mentioned several times is attributed to Deena Metza and Caitlin Mullin. My favourite,

The river is flowing, flowing and growing, the river is flowing down to the sea.
Mother, you carry me, your child I will always be. Mother you carry me down to the sea.

was, I understand, written by Diane Hildebrand-Hull.

The original chants get adapted by different covens or individuals who use them for inspiration. They may grow to several times their original size. For example:

We are an old people, we are a new people, we are the same people, stronger than before.

written by Morning Feather and Will Shephardson, often runs to many verses in rituals: for example, adding *wiser than before, younger than before.*

While there are copyright considerations for public or professional use for those chants whose authors are known, like any song you are free to sing them privately or in group activities or covens. A lot of the Doreen Valiente material is now in the public domain and even in a formal Book of Shadows like Gardner's, popular poetry appears in the Beltane rituals: for example, Rudyard Kipling's 'Oak and Ash and Thorn'. You may find inspiration in old folk songs or poetry you loved at school for your own chants and I would advise every witch to start a poetry section in his or her Book of Shadows.

How chanting works

The secret of any good chant is repetition, so that the conscious mind memorises it quickly and then switches off, leaving the wise unconscious mind to control the ritual and make spiritual connections. Chants vary generally from a few words or up to four lines, with some rhyme or resonance. If there are verses needed for a longer chant ritual that might involve variations on the same theme, for example a *Maiden, Mother, Wise One and Horned God*, with emphasis in different verses, a simple repetitive chorus will link them. Occasionally a longer chant, such as the Witch's Rune (see below), is used for dance or power raising.

It is important to learn chants by heart so you can forget them consciously, and this is where listening to CDs or MP3 recordings on journeys can be good. However, there is also a valid place in ritual for spontaneous chants: for example, when empowering herbs or a spell symbol or purpose. Some witches are gifted at creating the words in situ, but others may prefer to formulate root words beforehand around which your own chants can develop during the spell. Some witches prewrite or plan every chant, even for a basic spell or use those given in a spell book. Whatever *feels* right for the individual witch is right.

In groups or covens, eye and hand contact (for example, dancing in a spiral or moving rhythmically when you need someone to clap or sound the rhythm) can help to build up the collective power of the chant. Alone you can dance, drum or rattle as you chant. You don't have to worry about synthesising your own rhythm with others and can release the power when you are ready. If when working with others using or devising chants, anyone makes you feel inadequate or as though you are not chanting 'properly', you should not be intimidated. Usually this is someone who has followed instructions to the letter, but does not use their innate creativity.

Chanting should be pure joy, whether you are attending a chants workshop at a festival or singing or reciting with a coven or group. I was put off circle dancing for years because I joined a group whose members were technically very proficient. They were more concerned with learning complicated new dances than with experiencing the spirituality and connection, and certainly did not want an enthusiastic but clumsy newcomer. Sing and dance with your children or with friends on a moonlit shore and take your rhythm from the waves. Have fun!

Chanting is a gift to and from the Goddess and is for everyone. That said, if you get a good teacher then it all becomes easy much quicker. You can, of course, chant entirely in your mind and internalise a spell when it is not possible to say it aloud, or use a chant as a powerful personal empowerment at key moments in your everyday life.

Creating your own chants

Creating your own chants is best of all because they can be tailored to a particular need, person/people and occasion, and you can record your favourites in your Book of Shadows or on CD or tape. Most of us are inherently poetical, but the enthusiasm and confidence can get stifled at school. It can be rapidly rekindled.

Use nature as your inspiration. Compose chants to the moon, the sun, and the stars, to the winds, the trees and the ocean while you are experiencing their beauty or strength. Weave chants round the elements (see week 10 for ideas). The more natural energies you can call into your chants, the more you activate the energies of the actual forces around you.

Sometimes you will just need a few root words and let nature be the backdrop. My *Earth, Air, Water, Fire* chant repeated continuously faster and faster is an example of a basic but effective way of raising power. As the tempo becomes more upbeat and intense, you can change the rhythm to a louder definite beat: *Earth [pause], Air [pause], Fire [pause], Water[pause], Earth* – and so on until the power is so high you release it with actions such as raising your arms, leaping or slashing the air with your athame, as you call, *I am pure Spirit. Earth, Air, Water, Fire, bring to me what I desire,* is a variation and there are countless ways you can weave the element names into a chant.

An excellent time to write chants is at the end of a spell or ritual when you are inspired but need to wait for a candle or incense to burn away. If prewriting a chant for a particular spell or ritual, first decide whether there is an existing chant you could use or adapt or if it is better to write your own. Do you need more than one chant in the spell or ritual or can you vary the same words throughout at different stages? It is in many ways easier to stick to a root chant and build it up during the spell in logical phases and phrases.

You need to consider what (if any) will be the deity focus or if there will be a number of deities you invoke. Maybe you need a repetitive *Isis, Astarte* type chant with particular Gods and Goddesses: for example, different mistresses and lords of the hunt. Do you need the polarity God and Goddess or lord and lady, or one of the myth cycles of the sun?

Will the setting for the spell be integral to the chant? If you are carrying out your spell by the sea, the tides are the obvious energies to weave words round. However, you might want to include the other elements, for example Earth (sand) or Fire (a fire made on the beach to be carried away by the sea after the spell (see page 58). Will you include wind power for the Air element, as it lifts the foam? Picture your setting beforehand and be prepared to adapt a prewritten spell chant if the weather changes to take advantage of the bucketing rain.

What time will the spell or ritual be? Sunrise? Moonrise? If lunar, what phase? Is this timing integral enough to be included in the chant: for example, as Lady Moon or the Moon Maiden for the waxing? Or will this be reflected in the deity names? Are the seasons involved and if so what aspect? The dark days? the winter snows? Are these integral to a more complex chant?

Who will say or sing the chants: you, friends or your coven? If more than one person, is it a collective chant or will you take it in turns in the early part of the ritual and maybe join chant energies as you rise to a crescendo?

Are you planning any accompaniment, such as drumming, rattles or a singing bowl for a gentle healing rite? If so, will voices and music work in tandem or one succeed the other in subsequent waves?

Building up the chant

First write some words and ideas, as well as deity names that need to be included, to give you the bones of the chant. This initial information will probably be much longer than the finished chant. Then compress it and get rid of unnecessary phrases so the ideas are concise and the chant memorable.

Work on any phrases to add the essential power. This is where you would weave in natural forces and deities. Be descriptive, not just a silver moon but also one that dances through the skies or shimmers on the water creating a pathway. Add any identifying deity attributes: a cauldron for the Celtic Cerridwen, a bow and silver arrows for the Greek huntress Artemis of the woodland. Close your eyes and picture the deity, the natural forces and the setting of the spell to give you inspiration. If you are working indoors, light floral, ceremonial or woody incense as appropriate and work by candlelight.

When you have what seems a good format read it aloud. The words need not rhyme though many chants do have alternate rhyming lines, but they must flow if the chant is to have a natural rhythm. If it sounds awkward, turn a phrase around or substitute a word. Change the word order or use a word twice for emphasis.

Finally say the chant slowly and mesmerically or faster and intensely, whichever suits the purpose, tweaking words and taking out unnecessary ands and buts until you are satisfied.

Revising chants

The following are two chants that were good ideas but did not work out. Have a look at the original and changed versions and if you feel they are still not quite right do a complete rewrite. In the practical assignments at the end of this module, I have given you four more rudimentary chants to revise yourself. If you work with others or have an interested friend, get them to write their version of these and the chants at the end and you may be surprised how different but how effective they all are in their own way.

The Cauldron Chant intended for a cauldron abundance ritual

Mother, your cauldron gives all that we need, to nourish our souls and our spirits feed.
Cauldron of plenty, cauldron of birth, created to nurture all things on earth. Cauldron of
life, of gifts never ceasing, grant likewise to us, abundant blessing.

Improved version

The original version is too wordy and tries too hard to rhyme. It is also too complicated to learn. It needs a Cauldron Goddess like Cerridwen to focus it.

Cauldron of plenty, cauldron of birth, created to nourish all things on earth. Cauldron of life,
of gifts never ceasing, grant us. Cerridwen, abundance and blessing.

Let's try one more.

The Three Sisters of Fate Chant, intended for use before scrying with candlelight on water

Witches three, you weave for me, the web of my destiny; weave within your circle bright,
threads of gold and silver light. Witches three, by day and night, spin the thread of pure
moonlight, that I may see the pattern.

Improved version

I have left in the somewhat different last line as I feel this stops it becoming too trite. But the rest is far too repetitive and unoriginal.

Witches three, weave for me, web of my destiny; Witches three, day and night, spin threads of
gold and shimmering light, that I may see the pattern.

Singing chants

You can recite chants and never need to sing a note if you hate singing. But if you do want to sing your chants, picture golden and sky blue light emanating from the Throat chakra and begin with the lowest note you can comfortably make and then the highest without any undue strain. This is your natural range.

Traditional shamans and a number of witches use a pentatonic scale – one of five notes instead of the eight in today's standard notation. Try picking out melodies using only the black notes of the piano. A great deal of folk music is based on the pentatonic scale.

When you have the scale fixed in your mind, improvise melodies around it, allowing words and sounds to form faster and faster until they are entirely spontaneous and then create a regular rhythm, perhaps of three or four words or more that can be repeated.

Weave the words into a melody

Here is a very basic five-note rhythm, called a pentatonic scale - five notes instead of the eight in the octave. This is a good basis for setting chants to music.

The simple chanting tune given here is in the pentatonic scale (the numbers correspond to the marked piano notes).

Don't worry if they sound odd to you. The tunes are not meant for listening as you would to a song, but repeating over and over until you raise and release power or enter a state of heightened awareness akin to meditation or a light trance state. In this way the chanting frees the psychic part of the mind from the doubts and restraints of the conscious everyday world, so you can do magick more easily.

You can literally sing anything and can if you prefer use the eight notes of the middle C octave (doh, re, me etc).

Each of the rainbow colours has its own note and you can literally sing a rainbow to empower your chakras or as part of a colour or healing spell. You could create a chant by adding words to each note for example on middle C intone, *Red bring courage*, on D *Orange joy*, and so on (see week 41 for colour meanings). Top C, not shown, is white. Sung faster and faster, the ascending/descending scale is also potent for other words. However, you can also adapt any musical phrases to fit your chant.

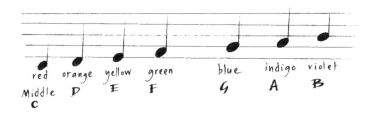

The Witch's Rune or Chant

Chants with or without drumming, spoken or sung, are excellent before rituals to create the magickal aura round the circle, and, if you are with others, to create collective energies. The Witch's Rune is one of the best examples of this. It has many versions and the original credit I have found for its creation is to Doreen Valiente. I am fairly certainly it is not copyright. Of course, anyone could use it in private or coven ritual even if it were, just as we can freely recite poetry or sing folk songs. (See further information listings for sources.)

In practice, many people have over a number of years adapted a version of the Witch's Rune that is right for them. Once you have chanted it and maybe danced and drummed as you chanted, you will understand why it is probably the most popular chant ever devised for solitary practitioners and coven members alike.

It is also chanted during spellcasting and as a ritual chant to lead a dance and so raise power by movement as well as words. The dance may be in a group as a spiral inward and then outwards, led by the coven maiden, or as an alternate circling three moonwise anticlockwise rounds then three clockwise circles, faster and faster. This continues until at a signal everyone rushes into the centre or towards a central fire, holding hands to release the spell as they call out the purpose. Solitary witches can have a brilliant time circling and spiralling round the altar, a fire or outdoors as they chant faster and faster to a final, *and all is won*.

What follows here is my version that I learned years ago, but enter it on any web server and a dozen more will appear.

Darksome night and shining moon,
East then south and west then north,
Hearken to the witches' rune.
As I come to call thee forth.

Earth and Water, Air and Fire,
Power of wand and witch's blade
Waken ye to my desire,
Weave ye as the web is made.

Queen of Heaven, Queen of Light,
Lend your power unto my spell,
Horned Hunter of the night,
Send incense, salt and pentacle.

By all the powers of land and sea,
By all the might of moon and sun,
As I do say, so shall it be.
The spell is cast and all is won.

PRACTICAL ASSIGNMENT

Rewriting chants

Now try rewriting these embryo chants. There are no right answers. Practise cutting back on the words and rearranging the ideas to come up with a sharper, more focused chant. Don't worry about offending the author. The originals come from my very early chant writing. We all have to start somewhere! If you wish, take the ideas and come up with an entirely new format. Do send your versions to my website www.cassandraeason.co.uk.

When you have finished, create a chant of your own for your next planned spell or ritual. Try to incorporate the spirit of the place where it will be held.

The Pipes of Pan Chant for a forest ritual to free the spellcaster from unfair restrictions

Wild as a child, you run through forest, fields and shore, freedom I ask, could I ask more? Freedom of winds, of rain and tide, freedom of waterfall and river wide; freedom to flow to the open sea, as true to myself as I can be, embracing joy spontaneously; come Pan with wildness, set me free.

The Triple Spiral Chant for fertility and protection

Womb of the Mother, from ancient days, bringing rebirth in myriad ways; rebirth of life and hope and light, from deepest rock to mountain height. Mother mine give life to me, for now and for eternity, dearest mother that is all, when you are close I cannot fall. Womb of the Mother me embrace, enfold and always give grace.

The Magick Wand Chant for a special wish

Three times three, for all to see, my wand will circled be, round, above and to the ground. Three times three, the blessings grow. It shall be so. Three times three the circle cast, the words are spoken, joy at last. The wish is free; it comes to me, fulfilled in actuality. Blessings are, to fall on me, three by three continuously.

The Healing Staff Chant for knowledge

Serpents wise, before my eyes, coil and turn, that I may learn, the secrets of your healing. Serpents wise before my eyes coil and turn that I may earn your gifts now revealing. Now do I coil before your eyes and I am wise.

Further information

Chants CDs

* Crow, Liz, and Robertson, Heike, *Chanting*, Museum of Witchcraft, 1998
* Crow, Liz, and Talboys, Carole, *Chanting II*, Museum of Witchcraft, 2001
* Reclaiming and Friends, *Chants: Ritual Music from Reclaiming and Friends*, Reclaiming Records, 1997
* Various Artists, *Best of Pagan Song*, Serpentine Music, 2004
* West, Kate, *Elements of Chants*, Mandrake Press, 2005

Recommended reading

* Andrews, Ted, *Sacred Sounds, Transformation through Music and Word*, Llewellyn, 1992
* Crowley, Brian, and Crowley, Esther, *Words of Power*, Llewellyn, 1990
* D'Argeto, James, *The Healing Power of Human Voices: Mantras, Chants and Seed Sounds for Health and Harmony*, Healing Arts Press, 2003
* Crocker, Richard L, *An Introduction to Gregorian Chants*, Yale University Press, 2000
* Phagan, Janval, *Wake the Flame. Pagan Chants and Songs*, Flying Witch Publications, 2004

Websites

* *EarthSpirit Web*
  Includes Pagan Chant Library, an excellent resource for chants.
  www.earthspirit.com/mtongue/chtlib/chyilfr.html
* *Dharma Haven*
  Most significant Tibetan chant plus access to other Tibetan pages
  www.dharma-haven.org/tibetan/meaning-of-om-mani-padme-hung.htm
* *Gardnerian Book of Shadows online*
  For Valiente's Witch's Chant or Rune
  www.sacred-texts.com/pag/gbos/index.htm
* *Chants, songs and MP3 recordings*
  www.geocities.com/firebornspirit/chants.html
  www.soulrebels.com/beth/chants.html
  www.seeliecourt.net/panpipe/oldchan.html

THE POWER OF SYMBOLS IN MAGICK

Every spell needs a symbol to act as a focus and receptacle for the magickal energies. If this symbol is kept as a talisman after the ritual or left on the altar, it becomes an ongoing focus for the gradual release of the power generated and stored in it during the ritual.

A more open-ended ritual may have a number of related symbols. For example, ears of grain at Lughnassadh both embody the essential nature of the harvest celebration and, if given to participants, continue to attract abundance over the weeks ahead into their lives. Even if a spell is just spoken or visualised, a token crystal may be held that acts as an external repository of the spell energies. Some symbols have intrinsic properties already, such as the colour or composition of a crystal that is used as a focus: for example, a green aventurine to attract luck. These inner qualities could be enhanced by speaking words to call good fortune into the crystal or by writing the intention in incense over it.

In this module, we will study different kinds of symbols and how they can be filled with power for different purposes. Look at page 185 for an examination of the role of the symbol in relation to the ongoing spell process, and pages 510–526 on crystals and colour will give extra background information.

How symbols work

The early 20th-century occultist Dion Fortune considered that symbols contained the stored power and mythological associations of all who had used the same symbol in other times and places: for example, a rose is a token of love from Ancient Egyptian rites to pink-covered contemporary teen spell books.

I would suggest you keep not only a collection of small actual symbols (see below), but also note in a section on spell symbols in your Book of Shadows any mythological or personal associations that build up, like the legends of the lucky horseshoe or green currency notes in money magick. This can also be useful when you are deciding the contents of charm bags.

I have already described different kinds of magick beginning on page 54. All symbols must have some resemblance to the spell purpose to establish the psychic pathway between the desire and the fulfilment of that desire. The likeness could be direct and tangible: for example placing an empowered tiny doll in a cradle by the bed of a couple making love, to encourage conception through the transference of fertility from the symbol to the couple. Equally, the association could be mythological or magickal: for example, a red candle for courage that might be engraved with the glyph of Mars, the God of war (right), or his magickal seal:

(see page 212 for more planetary associations and glyphs).

Red is the colour of Mars and if you used a scented candle in some spice fragrance that would add another layer of meaning, since spice is the scent of courage (and also passion). The candle could also be endowed with the name or situation for which the spell was being cast (the power of words). Since a lighted candle contains the four elements – Earth as the wax body of the candle, Air as the smoke, Fire as the flame and Water as the melting wax – as it burns, the courage will symbolically flow into the person for whom the spell is being cast.

Images and magickal power

Because wax and clay are essentially neutral materials, the emotions of the creator at the time of fashioning the image and the words and intentions spoken to animate it, will determine its purpose. As long as you always create an image with positive intention and do not hurt it, then image–making is very positive. Generally, after you have used a symbol I suggest that (unless keeping for so many days is part of the spell), you roll it back into a ball (see below).

Making actual images to resemble people or animals can be equally benign. An old tradition fills a featureless cloth doll with healing herbs to represent a sick person. You can also craft the image of a lover or family member with beeswax, dough or clay and send them protection, healing or courage through it. I personally do not use hair or any other personal nail clippings or bodily fluids from the person for or about whom the spell is being cast, because I believe creating an image and naming it is sufficient connection and avoids psychic intrusion.

Ill-wishing using images has persisted in negative magickal systems throughout the world right through to the present day, not least the infamous wax doll that was stuck with pins and melted. This practice undoubtedly originated in prehistoric magick, but was developed to a high level of sophistication in Ancient Babylon and Egypt, as figures of enemies were burned, drowned or beheaded to bring success or protection. Often these were devised as defensive measures in times of real danger rather than out of pure spite, but nevertheless have no place in modern magick, as images are beyond doubt a powerful tool. This is why it is important not to recite very ancient texts about smiting your enemies or grinding them underfoot over images (or indeed at all) or generally invoking demon or deity names from Ancient Egyptian, Hebrew or mediaeval magick or even saying words whose meanings you are not sure of.

Another problem with creating images of other people is that we have to be careful we are not overriding the free will of anyone else, even with the best intention. This is even more relevant than in pure spoken magick, because we are creating a representation of them and in doing so making a strong psychic connection with them.

We can legitimately morally bind an image of someone from harming our loved ones by turning their attention aside magickally or casting a screen of protection and psychic invisibility round the loved one, or indeed anyone who is vulnerable to the harm. However, we should not compel anyone to stop loving someone else, to desire only us or to compel a noisy neighbour or spiteful colleague to leave (more of this later). The more proficient we become at magick and the more we are asked to cast spells for others, the easier it is for boundaries to blur, especially if we have great sympathy with the person for who we are casting the spell.

You can create an image out of wax, clay or dough to represent an addiction or destructive emotional bond and then as part of the spell roll it into a formless ball to banish what you no longer want without doing any harm or releasing any negativity. Equally, in making an image of yourself for healing or to gain strength, you are endowing it with your essential self, your emotions, hopes and dreams and so it is a very powerful form of self-healing and determination. Coloured clay can reflect different purposes (see page 512 for colour meanings).

If you use dough, after the spell you can bake the symbol, eat it and so absorb the magick, if the purpose was to attract love or abundance. For wax, either melt a squat beeswax candle on a flat metal tray or holder or soften a sheet of beeswax. You can unroll an old beeswax candle, if you do not have any sheets. Undyed beeswax sheets are easily available from craft stores as well as New Age outlets. I pre-roll balls of beeswax and keep them in greaseproof paper, ready for spells.

Using natural symbols

The best symbols are those you make yourself because in crafting them, however simply, you are endowing your personal essence into the symbol. If spellcasting for others, you can ask them to make or finish the symbol.

It may be possible to find a natural source of clay. A beach near my home provides an abundant supply of dark red clay. After a ritual, you can return the clay to the soil if you find or buy natural untreated potters' material. Self-hardening clay can be bought for rituals where you want to keep the image for a long time for a slow-working spell. Ordinary clay is especially good in binding spells or banishing spells when the symbol of the actions to be bound or the destructive habit is to be reabsorbed by the earth. It is also excellent in group rituals, as a number of people can mould into it their collective energies.

Since it was believed by the Ancient Egyptians that part of the spirit, the ka or soul, resided in statues, make any figures with kindness and gentleness, even for banishing or binding. Create your symbol or figure on a white cloth on a wooden chopping or breadboard. Before you begin, first pass incense three times around the dough or the candle you use to soften the wax over the image (see also page 681 for making wax pentacles). Alternatively, you can form a circle of dough and in it draw a symbol: a flower for love or beauty, apples if you need health, a pile of loaves for abundance at home or for money, a bird for freedom or travel, or a tool for learning new skills or a book.

Then for whatever kind of image you intend to create, sprinkle a few drops of salt and then water on top of the unformed clay or dough or three times around the softened beeswax clockwise. Say three times:

> *I purify this clay/dough/wax and my heart from all negative intent. May only goodness reside within and may I work only for the highest good and with the purest intent. Blessed be.*

Chant the spell purpose softly and continuously as you make the desired shape.

With soft clay or dough you can push healing or empowering crystals into the image, whether at places of pain or the site of illness or tiny ones all over the face and body or symbol, such as clear quartz crystal chips for energy or a surge of power. On a beach or lakeside, make a sand image in the centre of your magick circle by piling it up or drawing it with a stick.

For nature spells, also obtain a variety of growing and dried herbs (see page 551 for magickal meanings) and store in small drawstring bags in different colours.

Draw a rune symbol (see page 431 on magickal alphabets) on a round stone, a crystal, clay, dough or beeswax or a small wooden disk to signify the spell purpose, such as Fehu for prosperity or successful house moves.

Runes are more than a magickal alphabet. They are believed to contain within each sign the energy to release the meaning of the specific rune into the life of the spellcaster. For a really important spell or ritual you can further empower any image or figure after you have created it as well as before. I make the image, then purify myself and finally re-empower the image. You could incorporate this post-creation empowering into an early part of your spell or ritual or can make the symbol as part of the ritual.

In this case, you would purify yourself beforehand and then use one of the quick methods of self purification after forming the image, again as part of the spell. Also do this with images or symbols you have collected (see below). Take your incense censer or stick, using a cleansing sacred fragrance such as cedar or myrrh and facing south pass the smoke in a cross from south to north, then east to west over the stick, then south-east to north-west, and south-west to north-east, to form a star in smoke, saying:

> *Be for me the strength/love/power/protection.*

The power of writing

Another method of symbol creation is to write the purpose of the spell reduced to three or four key words. There are a number of ways you can do this, with a paper knife or small screwdriver or metal nail in a circle of melted beeswax, dough or clay, in black or blue fountain pen ink on white paper (some practitioners use red) or in incense smoke over the symbol.

You can use your ordinary handwriting or printing, a magickal alphabet or not use any vowels. If missing out vowels, also either change any double letter in the word/s to a single letter or only write each letter once, even if it appears two or three times in the same phrase or word. Alternatively referring to the sigil formation on the Square of Saturn (see page 278) reduce the spell to a single word and etch or write the sigil shape created. Which is best? Whichever is right for you.

If writing the spell purpose in any form, recite it softly over and over again as you write it. Say it again, after saying, I am… and your magickal names, as you hold the symbol early in the spell.

Beginning a symbol collection

As part of your magickal collection, obtain a small wooden box to keep a set of symbols for a variety of instant spells and rituals. Market stalls and ethnic craft shops who share the profits fairly with indigenous workers are good sources of items such as small fabric dolls, baskets and statues. Specialist shops that sell dolls' house furniture are a source of miniature dishes of fruit or loaves of bread as well as cradles and beds. Suitable items include:

* A thimble for domestic happiness
* A tiny padlock for security at home
* A heart for love
* A phallic symbol for potency and fertility
* A key for a new home
* A wooden toy boat for travel
* A car or train or bus for safe commuting
* A plane for long distance travel
* A gold ring for marriage
* A silver ring or necklace for fidelity
* Coins especially with holes (such as Chinese divinatory or the old Spanish peseta) in copper, silver and gold and green currency notes for money magick
* Silk flowers for when you cannot obtain the right fresh flowers
* A key charm for a house move to a first home
* Tiny painted wooden eggs for fertility in any venture –you can paint your own
* Small fabric dolls, to represent people in, for example, a love spell and ribbons to tie them together
* Candles in zodiacal colours to act as a focus for different people and also coloured candles for different purposes, such as blue for justice or pink for reconciliation
* A variety of small crystals of different kinds and colours: for example, quartz for change, jasper for strength and any agate for balance; a rutilated quartz will help talents to be recognised and debts overcome, a yellow jasper will protect you against malice or gossip, and a moss or tree agate encourage prosperity or health to grow or return
* Tarot cards: for example, the King and Queen of Cups or the Lovers for love and marriage, the World for travel and the Wheel of Fortune for attracting good luck

Preserving the power of the symbol

I have already mentioned some ideas for after the spell, such as burying clay after rerolling and baking dough and eating it. As I said earlier, I have recently moved away from breaking or destroying an image after use it, even if, for example, the form represents a bad habit or destructive emotional hold someone has over you. Any destruction would seem to release negativity, but be guided by what you feel is right. If you feel that therapeutically it would be good for the image to be destroyed, a compromise is to let nature take her course and leave it open to the elements. You can leave dough outdoors rolled into a ball for birds or small animals.

If the symbol is for banishing, make your dough with less oil so that it is quite dry and will crumble naturally. Breaking off bits of ourselves, even symbolically by smashing an image, can be unbelievably painful. The crumbling method is especially good for removing chronic pain or a deep-seated sorrow. After a spell where the image is not to be kept as part of the ongoing release of power, roll clay or beeswax back into a ball. You do not need to throw it away unless you want to, in which case bury it or dispose of it in an environmentally friendly way.

If you do intend to recycle it for future spells, remove any lingering energies from the ball. Pass over it swirls of fresh incense or smudge (rather than what is still burning from the spell) and say:

May all be as it was before, cleansed and free. Blessings be.

You should keep clay in a damp cloth or plastic and put beeswax back in its greaseproof paper. You can smudge metal or ceramic images from your collection in the same way. Sprinkle crystals or living plants with water or pass a crystal pendulum rounds them nine times anticlockwise.

If you made or used an image to attract love, health or happiness, you may wish to leave it open on your altar, either for the allotted number of days stated in the spell or, if it was open-ended, as long as feels right, with fresh flowers to keep the energies moving. Anoint it regularly with a few drops of pure water or an appropriate fragrance or essential oil: for example, chamomile to attract prosperity or bring family happiness. Repeat the spell purpose as you do this and end by saying:

May this be achieved/completed in the fullness of time/by the time [specify the timeframe of the spell]. So mote it be.

If you created a figure for healing you could anoint it daily on your altar, with a few drops of a healing oil or fragrance such as lavender, myrrh or rose.

If you made two figures to gently end a relationship, move them apart a little each day, finally when you have reached the altar edge wrapping your hopefully now ex-lover's feelings in cloth. Keep their image in a drawer until it crumbles naturally, when it can be buried. Preserve your own image separately wrapped in silk. You can bury your own image of lost love when it crumbles, but remember before you do so to create and empower a new strong image of yourself to keep on the altar and stud it with clear quartz crystals for new vitality and joy (see page 538).

PRACTICAL ASSIGNMENT

Get to know tarot cards

The occultist Eliphas Levi who in 1856 made the first connections between the tarot and the Kabbalah, said that if you had a tarot pack you did not need anything else for magick and wisdom. Certainly a tarot pack with its 78 images offers a comprehensive symbol resource base for almost every kind of magick spell, especially if you use a richly illustrated pack like the Morgan Greer with its jewel-like colours.

Keep the pack wrapped in dark natural cloth such as silk just for magick spells. You can empower the cards used in spells as for permanent symbols.

The major arcana, the first numbered 22 cards in the pack, are generally used for magick, as these symbolise universal images such as the Magician the Creator/trickster, the Empress, the Mother, the Emperor, the Father and qualities such as Strength and Temperance (moderation). Arcana means hidden wisdom.

Packs such as the Rider Waite, The Universal Waite, the Morgan Greer and the Aquarian pack have illustrated minor cards (aces to tens). These can also become the focus of magick: for example, the eight of Wands, which shows eight wands flying through the air for travel, or the six of Swords with a women being ferried into calmer waters for bringing peace. In a love spell, the two chosen cards would be moved progressively closer during the spell or on subsequent days.

The court cards can signify people (see below for the characteristics). They can represent all kinds of family and business relationships in a spell. Some practitioners have one court card that they consider represents them that they keep in the middle of the altar during a spell, sometimes below the symbol being empowered. You can use as many or as few cards as you wish, putting them either in front of individual candles or in a ring around the centre of the altar.

For each of the major arcana cards, I have listed candle colours, crystals and incenses and fragrance oils so you can enrich the energies of these physically two-dimensional but mythologically deep images.

The Fool

Candle colour: White

Crystal: Clear quartz

Incense and oils: Allspice, peppermint and sandalwood
For spells and rituals for new beginnings, optimism, unexpected opportunities and luck, for risky ventures, animals, babies and children, for travelling light and rediscovering the real essential you.

The Magician

Candle Colour: Yellow

Crystal: Carnelian

Incense and oils: Cinnamon, copal and dragon's blood
For spells and rituals for all matters of the arts, business, communication, healing, speculation and money-spinning, psychic development and protection against trickery and theft.

The High Priestess

Candle colour: Lilac

Crystal: Amethyst

Incense and oils: Bay, cedarwood and lavender

For spells and rituals concerning personal identity and spirituality, for secrets, for self-employment, for withdrawal from a situation of conflict, for people who live or work alone whether from choice or necessity and for matters concerning younger people especially women.

The Empress:

Candle Colour: Pink

Crystal: Jade

Incense and oils: Geranium, neroli and peach

For spells and rituals concerning domestic matters, fertility, motherhood, marriage, fidelity, family and middle-aged women; also all who care for others.

The Emperor

Candle colour: Deep blue

Crystal: Turquoise

Incense and oils: Frankincense, marjoram and kyphi

For spells and rituals for fulfilling ambitions, power, courage, success, prosperity, career, fatherhood and middle-aged men.

The Hierophant

Candle colour: Purple

Crystal: Lapis lazuli

Incense and oils: Juniper, sage and yarrow

For spells and rituals concerning learning, knowledge, health, wisdom, finding lost objects, breaking old restrictive patterns, for older people of both sexes and authority.

The Lovers

Candle colour: Green

Crystal: Rose quartz

Incense and oils: Rose, vervain and ylang-ylang

For spells and rituals for all relationships, especially love ones, for attracting love, for commitment in love, for choices in all matters and for sexual bliss and passion.

The Chariot

Candle colour: Scarlet

Crystal: Rutilated quartz or laboradite

Incense and oils: Benzoin, ginger and rosemary

For spells and rituals for travel, new ventures, house moves, resisting being pulled in different directions, self-confidence and independence.

Strength

Candle colour: Burgundy

Crystal: Malachite:

Incense and oils: Basil, carnation and cedar

For spells and rituals for increasing physical and mental energy, stamina and strength, for recovering from illness and improving chronic conditions, to resist bullying, for patience and to overcome obstacles.

The Hermit

Candle colour: Grey.

Crystal: Desert rose

Incense and oils: Eucalyptus, hyssop and thyme

For spells and rituals to prevent or overcome loneliness, for prophetic dreams, for starting again alone, for finding the way spiritually, for tuning into your inner wisdom, for personal integrity and discovering the truth about a matter.

The Wheel of Fortune

Candle colour: Orange

Crystal: Cat's eye or green aventurine

Incense and oils: Honeysuckle, fern and patchouli

For spells and rituals for prosperity and all money matters, good fortune and reversing a run of bad luck, for change of all kinds, for games of chance and for taking control of your destiny.

Justice

Candle colour: Dark Grey

Crystal: Banded agate.

Incense and oils: Gum arabic, lemon and marigold

For spells and rituals concerning negotiations, for decision-making, legal matters and any involving officialdom, for releasing anger about earlier injustices, for overcoming and resisting present injustice.

The Hanged Man

Candle colour: Dark green

Crystal: Bloodstone/heliotrope

Incense and oils: Cloves, fennel and tea tree

For spells and rituals for giving up compulsions and addictions, for beginning a new difficult but ultimately rewarding path, for ending destructive relationships, for initiation into deeper understanding and psychic awareness, for accepting the inevitable as a learning experience, for making a short-term sacrifice or loss for long term gain, for refusing to compromise.

Death

Candle colour: Dark brown or black

Crystal: Apache's tear (obsidian) or jet

Incense and oils: Cypress, myrrh and rosewood

For spells and rituals for endings that lead to beginnings, life transitions, moves of all kinds, leaving behind sorrow and regrets, laying old ghosts, divorce and separation rituals.

Temperance

Candle colour: Cream

Crystal: Blue lace agate

Incense and oils: Angelica, chamomile and lilac

For harmony and personal or domestic happiness, for healing, moderating feelings, words or actions, for peace making, for banishing excesses and obsessions, for inner harmony and for contacting your guardian angel or spirit guide.

The Devil

Candle colour: Inky blue, maroon or aubergine

Crystal: Red jasper

Incense and oils: Lime, saffron and pine

For spells and rituals for sudden or disruptive but necessary change, for releasing negative energies, integrating the shadow self into the personality, for psychic and physical protection against attacks and threats, for overcoming fears and free-floating anxiety, for binding magick.

The Tower

Candle colour: Dark yellow or natural beeswax

Crystal: Leopardskin jasper or snakeskin agate

Incense and oils: Sweet grass, vanilla and vetivert

For spells and rituals for removing restrictions and stagnation, for overcoming feelings of alienation, for sexual potency, for resolving property matters or structural problems, for protection at home, protection from natural hazards such as storms, for new directions and for recovery after any loss or reversal.

The Star

Candle colour: Pale yellow

Crystal: Citrine

Incense and oils: Magnolia, mimosa and violet

For spells and rituals for granting wishes and the fulfilment of dreams, for fame and stardom and all forms of recognition, the card of would-be writers, actors, entrepreneurs, musicians and dancers; also for moving abroad.

The Moon

Candle colour: Silver

Crystal: Moonstone

Incense and oils: Jasmine, lemongrass and valerian

For spells and rituals for love, for beauty, for healing, for women, for the cycles of life, for peaceful sleep, for any attracting rituals on the waxing moon and banishing rituals on the waning moon, for spiritual development and access to other dimensions.

The Sun

Candle colour: Gold

Crystal: Amber

Incense and oils: Chamomile, frankincense and orange

For spells and rituals for happiness, success, energy, lofty ambitions, major career boosts, larger and urgent sums of money, revealing hidden potential, travel to sunny places, renewal of health.

Judgement

Candle colour: Indigo

Crystal: Falcon's/hawk's eye (blue tiger's eye)

Incense and oils: Lemon verbena, lily and wintergreen

For spells and rituals for breaking free of guilt, renewal and rebirth, for forgiveness and mending of quarrels, for finding the right career, all weighty official and financial matters, breaking free of critical people and self-esteem.

The World

Candle colour: Multi-coloured

Crystal: Aquamarine

Incense and oils: Apple blossom, bergamot and heather

For spells and rituals for the expansion of horizons, business expansion, long-distance travel and house moves, relocation, promotion, freedom from the past, environmental and ecological issues, for self-confidence and a happy future.

The minor arcana or number cards

The suits

Pentacles or Discs: For spells and rituals for money, property, material security, home (so good for home moves), dealings with officialdom, stability, learning new things step by step, animals, business matters, gardening and the environment.

Cups or Chalices: Love and lovers, romance, marriage and partnerships, family, children, health and healing, psychic powers, pregnancy, celebrations, working with people professionally.

Wands, staves or rods: Career, independence, travel, creativity, sport, leisure, fun, the unexpected, change, inventions, risk-taking, self-employment.

Swords: Learning, logic, surgery and conventional medicine, science, technology, change under or after difficulty, swift and decisive action, justice.

The numbers

Aces: Spells for new beginnings, new energies, new opportunities in the area defined by the suit.

Twos: Spells for partnership issues, polarity magick, balancing magick, for a second career and for negotiations.

Threes: Spells for building up a business or relationship, for expansion and rebuilding, for increase, for marriage, conception and birth and for unity.

Fours: Spells for taking a risk, for overcoming fears and barriers to happiness, for financial consolidation, for resolving practical matters and for limiting the bad influences or negative behaviour of others.

Fives: Spells for resolving unstable situations, for all matters of communication, for moving on with life and for attracting unexpected or unlikely help or resources.

Sixes: Spells for love, for peace and reconciliation, for harmony and bringing families together, especially step relations fostering or adoption.

Sevens: Spells for all mystical and psychic matters, for holidays, leisure and sports, music and the arts.

Eights: Spells for learning new skills, changing career or turning interests into money spinners, for banishing what is no longer bringing happiness or old ways of living, for all kinds of moves, changes of location and lifestyle changes.

Nines: Spells for perfection, for self-confidence, independence and self reliance, for courage and for reviving projects or fulfilling dreams that have been put aside.

Tens: For spells for the successful completion of a dream, a project or life stage, lasting happiness, success or love, for fidelity. For restoring or renovating the home and for starting a venture or business with a marriage or love partner.

Court cards

Their characters will vary according to the suit. They can represent yourself, people in your life right now or whom you would like to come into your life, such as a new business partner or lover.

Pentacles or Discs: Patient, reliable, loyal, kind, practical, good with money, but can be dull and materialistic.

Cups or Chalices: Romantic, loving, gentle, dreamy, idealistic, and sympathetic, caring of others, but can be impractical and forgetful.

Wands, Staves or Rods: Exciting, fun-loving, creative, excellent communication skills, but can be impatient and fickle.

Swords: Clever, logical, witty, determined and committed, but can be dogmatic and sarcastic.

Pages: Children up to 15 and young women up to 30, sisters, female friends or cousins of any age or an older woman who is very immature; also a new skill or venture you are beginning or want to start, for either sex.

Knights: Young men up to 30, brothers and male friends or cousins of any age or men who act immaturely. There are many 40+ knights. They can also represent a period or action, fun or adventure you are planning or would like, for men and women.

Queens: Women of 35+, wives, mothers, aunts and grandmothers, also women in authority; they also reflect a caring nurturing period for men or women.

Kings: Men 35+, fathers, uncles and grandfathers, men in authority; they also signify a surge in ambition or success for a man or woman.

Further research

Choose between 10 and 20 universal symbols (depending on the time you have available) and use books and online resources to discover how they were used in different ages and cultures: for example, a heart, a butterfly, a bee or owl.

Note your findings in your symbol section in your Book of Shadows and add any personal divinatory or dream meanings. Note also how you have used/intend to use them in spells.

Update your list whenever you come across a new symbol.

Further information

Recommended reading

* Buchanan-Brown, John, *et al*, *The Penguin Dictionary of Symbols*, Penguin Books, 2004
* Cooper, J C, *An Illustrated Encyclopaedia of Traditional Symbols*, Thames and Hudson, 1979
* Eason, Cassandra, *Complete Guide to the Tarot*, Piatkus 2001/Crossing Press 2002
* Eason, Cassandra, *Tarot Talks to the Woman Within*, Foulsham/Quantum, 2003
* Tresside, Jack, *The Complete Dictionary of Symbols in Myth, Art and Literature*, Duncan Baird Publishers, 2004
* Wilkinson, Richard, H, *Symbol and Magic in Egyptian Art*, Thames and Hudson, 1994

Websites

* *Alternative Religions*
  Large site for information and graphics from a number of magickal traditions
  http://altreligion.about.com/library/glossary/symbols/bldefs/magicalsymbols.htm
* *Symbols.com*
  Huge online database
  www.symbols.com
* *Symbols.net*
  Another resource base for world symbols and images
  www.symbols.net

The Power of the Earth

The element Earth is significant in many ways in magick. It is the tangible plane on which magick begins and to which ultimately the released and amplified energy of the spell returns to take effect either as an inner change or an outer manifestation. It is the magick of hearth and home and folk magick. Its sacred substance salt is both protective and empowering and is used in folk and ceremonial magick alike. In the previous module clay, dough and beeswax, all Earth substances, were used to create symbols and after the spell were sometimes returned to the Earth.

Earth elementals as the most stable elemental force give spells and rituals form, the initial impetus to start the spell energies and fuel the other more aethereal, fluid and dynamic elemental aspects whether outdoors or around an indoor altar. Earth spirits, the personification of the living energies of plants, trees and minerals, are, even in urban magick, a source of instinctive wisdom and connection with the throbbing energies within the Earth (see also page 318).

Earth energies are manifest in nature as leys or energy lines, ancient stones, crystals, rock sculptures, underground waters and springs, the inexplicable lights that dance above the ground or the crop circles that create elaborate geometric signs that science struggles to explain. Because Earth energies are everywhere, even in high-rise buildings, they affect all spellcasting. The closer you get to the root earth or a place of earth power, the greater this positive charge becomes.

Finally, it is the domain of Mother Earth and the Earth Goddesses. Of all the creating Earth Goddesses, the most influential on modern generations has been Gaia, the Greek primal Earth Mother who has given her name to the 20th century and continuing ecological concept of a sentient or aware earth, the Gaia Hypothesis. Gaia was called by the Greeks the deep-breasted one, she from whom everything comes, and the first and the last. She was the daughter of Chaos or swirling primal darkness and emptiness. Emerging from this ocean of potential, Gaia, it is told, created every living thing, plants, animals, hills, mountains, waters and people.

In this module, we will move initially away from the altar to connect with and internalise the powers of the Earth, its places and creatures and learn more of its sacred substance salt. You may like to re read the magical associations of the Earth element on page 316 to remind yourself of its powers.

The elementals

Each of the four elements, Earth, Air, Fire and Water, is manifest through the essences or vital force of the four kinds of elementals, like an intense and speeded up form of the lifeforce. Elementals are considered the energy forces behind each act of creation and destruction in the continuing cycle of existence. They conduct and regulate the lifeforce through nature in an unbroken flow. Sudden surges or slowing of the flow of the power are experienced as natural disasters, such as earthquakes, forest fires, floods or drought, depending on which element is unbalanced.

Elementals seem adversely affected by factors such as global warming, pollution and deforestation and are struggling to keep the ice caps from melting. They energise the blueprint designs of the nature devas into the physical growth of flowers, trees or crystals. (The devas as Lords and Guardians of the four elemental directional Watchtowers in the magic circle are called the Old Ones.) As they open their gates elemental energies enter the circle to empower the ritual or spell and afterwards return with their Guardians to their own elemental realm (a good reason for closing your Watchtowers).

Elemental beings

Elementals don't exist permanently as separate entities from their element. However, they can appear as wavy flickering flame like figures, as swirling shimmers of water rising from a waterfall, as darting flashes of light in the air or as wispy mist rising over the land. People fleeing from forest fires have described how animated flames seem to curl like huge fingers to snatch at them.

When an elemental has finished its task, which could last anything from a few minutes to 1,000 years or more, they return to their own element in undifferentiated form. They can change size and appearance while they are animated, but remain as part of the same element. What is more, they cannot after the first creation brought the elements into being, be created or destroyed.

The elemental beings are therefore the bridge of power between the material and spiritual plane. This is why they come with a *Handle With Care* warning.

Elemental thought forms

In Hebrew and Mediaeval magick, elementals were summoned by magicians and shaped into a tulpa or thought form to carry out a purpose, after which they would be dismissed. I know some covens do create thought forms for very positive purposes, such as protecting the habitat of endangered species in distant places. However, I would caution individual witches and even covens unless you do have a huge amount of experience, as elemental energies are neutral and can easily change, even if they have been used for good.

I have come across examples of witches who recited all the correct ancient formulae, but could not return the elemental to its element and for a while suffered terrifying experiences, sometimes akin to vicious poltergeist activity. Some individual witches also try to keep an elemental spirit in a lidded bottle like a genie – and of course I respect their right to do so and hopefully their expertise. Animal familiars or power animals are much safer and I have written about these on page 688 as a more grounded form of Earth power. One of best-known familiars was the New Forest witch Sybil Leek's jackdaw, Mr. Hotfoot Jackson in the 1960s.

Personally I would advise working with pure elementals in settings where they already exist, caves or clearings in forests for Earth, mountain sides for Air, bonfires for Fire and rushing rivers for Water, so that you can connect with their power in situ rather than calling it into your altar place (unless you are using a circle and Guardians of the Watchtowers). They also have plenty of room to move around and you can leave the place with thanks and an appropriate offering, such as a crystal or flowers.

One way to keep elemental energies safely around your altar is to have a stone or pot of growing herbs in the north for the Earth elementals or a statue of Ganesh the Hindu elephant-headed God of Wisdom, a bird statue in the east or a pot of feathers in a jar for the air elementals, an amber crystal or a golden dragon in the south for the Fire elementals, and a silver fish or dolphin statue or a large sea shell in the west for the Water elementals. These will safely contain and filter any free-flying elemental energy.

Earth elementals

Earth elementals are manifest in both their positive and negative but sometimes necessary roles in nature. They give seeds the power to grow and the energy to flourish as mature trees. They continue to energise the growth/maturity/decay cycle through the scattering of new seeds until the eventual bark decays, the tree dies and is replaced with new green growth. In the case of a yew tree, this can take up to 2,000 years.

Earth elementals are also behind the movement of land masses, in erosion and the crumbing of stones to become earth and eventually sand and the ongoing growth of new minerals within the earth's crust. They are the forces that cause decay of bones, leaves and faeces in the earth, releasing necessary minerals that will cause new plants to grow to continue the food chain process. The London Natural History Museum has huge vivid displays that demonstrate this.

At their most powerful, Earth elementals are manifest in earth tremors, as earth lights, in crop circles, leaves on a tree shaken by the wind, rock falls, avalanches, snow and hail blizzards or within the centre of enclosed groves of trees. They are also concentrated in passages within caves, in railway and canal tunnels and in underground mines where they may be perceived as mine spirits; feel them at stone circles and near ley lines, especially on the festivals, where they can use the powerful and unstable forces of the parting dimensions to take temporary form. At such times they may be seen as dancing lights or figures round stone circles.

UFO sightings are very common over stone circles, such as Arbor Low in Derbyshire where more than 40 ley lines converge, at seasonal change points, especially on the Summer Solstice, the time of the union of sun (Fire) and Earth power. Some people attribute this extraterrestrial activity to the appearance of elementals as whirling metallic discs or at least that UFO sightings are made possible by the release of elemental power at times of intense natural force. Earth spirits have been reported dancing round Avebury Rings in Wiltshire on May Eve, which, like Halloween and Midsummer, is a major fairy festival.

Earth elemental energy may also be manifest in animal power: the bull, bear, buffalo/bison, elephant, mole, rabbit, squirrel, wolf, badger, snakes, spiders, moths and bees. I have written more of animals in magick in week 52.

Nature spirits

Many people throughout the ages have considered nature spirits to be objective beings and described them in remarkably consistent ways. Nature spirits live on a different level of vibration from humans, on the astral plane that is akin to the second orange level of your aura in terms of density. Because of this they do not have a solid physical body and so are invisible, except to children and those with clairvoyant sight.

Others believe their descriptions are the way the human mind sees and explains particular energy patterns in nature. Whichever is true, in outdoor magick or if you keep growing flowers and herbs near your altar, you will connect with these energies and they will bring vitality and lightness to rituals.

Earth energies

Earth spirits are among the most stable of the elemental nature spirits, but should not be underestimated, as they are very territorial. Some Earth spirits are thought to live in the home, on farms or in or outbuildings: for example, as the UK, sturdy, elf-like brownies or the Swedish Tomten or house elves. They can be helpful around the home and are believed to attract good fortune to the family, if they are respected, but can be otherwise mischievous or even malicious if angered. They may be mistaken for ghosts as they clatter around. Swedish families still leave them a dish of spiced porridge on Christmas Eve and in remote areas every Thursday night, the night the Tomten rest and play their fiddles.

The majority of nature spirits, however, do not live in houses but close to the earth, in forests or beneath the earth in mounds or hillocks. Their role is to protect the trees, the sacred sites, minerals, land and plants. They include forest dwellers, such as the Ancient Greek Dryads, female tree nymphs who are associated especially with willow, the oak and ash. There are also mine spirits, like the Tio of the tin mines of Bolivia in South America, where benign Earth spirits are under the care of our Lady of the Mineshaft, a name for the Virgin Mary whose worship replaced that of the old Earth Goddess.

Trooping earth spirits often come above ground to dance, especially after dark: for example, the dark or Earth elves of Western Europe, especially Germany, the Netherlands and Scandinavia. They are famed spinners, weavers and metal workers.

Some Earth spirits may be friendly and gentle to humans, guiding them if lost and conveying healing powers through encouraging the growth of healthy herbs, trees and flowers. But many are temperamentally more unpredictable or ambivalent towards humans. If we do see or hear them it is a real bonus and a reminder that life is much more than the material mundane world. Children, of course, can see gnomes or tree spirits quite easily, because they are totally open and Earth spirits are far more tolerant of them.

The origin of Earth spirits

The concept of different kinds of spirits dwelling in rocks, trees and water far predates Christianity or Judaism and still exists in lands like Japan. Here Earth spirits were not like our jolly modern garden gnomes, but mighty beings. Particular rocks and trees were venerated as the home of nature spirits with deity status. When the first wooden shrines were created, it was believed that by making them of sacred trees with the holiest tree and rock at the centre of the shrine, the power of the indwelling spirits could be transferred to the wooden shrine.

The same is true in India, where before formal shrines, rivers, springs, caves, trees and rocks were and still are considered by rural people to be the dwelling place of sacred Earth spirits. Enclosures and shrines marked areas in which these sacred earth spirits could be worshipped. The rock was the masculine symbol and the tree the female Earth spirit.

Earth spirits and earth energies

Earth spirits flourish around places where the Earth energies are most powerful, notably along ley or psychic energy lines beneath the earth. Legends of trolls, giants and Earth spirits are most common along these lines of unseen energy and it is likely Earth spirits can use this subterranean power source to charge themselves with vitality.

Other homes of trooping Earth spirits are ancient sacred sites, stone circles, monoliths or single standing stones, passage graves and ancient burial mounds and chambers, some dating back to 3500 BCE. These stones and their spirits are found from the Mediterranean to the Baltic and Russia, with the predominance along or close to the Western Atlantic coasts of Europe. The sites were created where energy lines met. Some, like the Korrs or Korreds, male Breton Earth spirits with huge heads and spiky hair, guard the ancient stones and stone circles from harm. Indeed, in Brittany it is believed the Korrs helped to create the original sacred sites and still frighten away those who would desecrate the stones. Earth spirits also frequent turf or stone labyrinths.

Elemental spirits and magick

Having said that elementals do not have a permanent form, gnomes, sylphs, salamanders or djinns and undines are usually described in magick as elemental beings, rather than nature spirits.

Elementals were first categorised by the Greek Neoplatonists around the 3rd century AD, though they were recognised much earlier as present in Earth, Air, Fire and Water. Mediaeval magicians and alchemists sought to manipulate their powers to gain mastery over nature. The alchemist magician Paracelsus in the 16th century gave names to the personified elemental forms: the gnomes of the Earth, who may also be manifest as rock sculptures, the sylphs of the Air, the salamanders or legendary Fire lizards, and the undines of the water.

Each of these four groups has an elemental king: for example, Geb, Ghob or Ghoab, the Earth elemental king who has domain over all other Earth spirits, such as dwarves or the dryads of the trees.

People have always felt a need to categorise and put beings into hierarchies. Had a Norse philosopher created the system instead of the Paracelsus (who, though German, used Mediterranean nature beings, rather than his native dwarf), the dwarf might easily have been the personified Earth elemental spirit.

In Norse cosmology, four of the strongest dwarves, Norðri, Suðri, Austri and Vestr, held the four corners of the heavens on their shoulders and gave their names to the four directions.

I do use gnomes and others as personified elemental forces when I need to work magically with a relatively stable elemental force. However, personally even then I keep the distinction of the gnome as the highest elemental nature spirit and regard them as a bridge between elementals and ordinary nature spirits. To me, gnomes and the like have feet in both worlds, rather than elemental in the sense of the rushing waterfall or earth lights hovering over a mountain. However, if you disagree, that makes no difference to the information I have given, only to how you use it.

Earth spirits

These are ruled by Geb, Gob, Ghob or Ghoab. He is described as a squat and shadowy gnome-like figure with crystal bright eyes that spends most of his time in jewel-filled caves on a gem-studded throne, or deep in the forests where his clothes blend with the trees. He oversees and cares for all the Earth spirits who work in mines, live below the ground or roam the forest places or fields.

Ghob is a gifted herbalist and cares for animals. His wrinkled face may be seen in rock sculptures or gnarled trees, and when he speaks his words can be soft as a woodland breeze or, if he is angered, shake the earth. His positive qualities, like those of the gnomes, are guardianship of the Earth, its treasures and natural wisdom and knowledge, but at worst he is materialistic, closed to new ideas and acquisitive.

His less benign subjects, the shape-shifting goblins or orcs, are as unfriendly to other fairies as to humans. They shun daylight, roam in bands and live in dark underground places or deep forests, forcing other creatures to work in their mines.

Gnomes

Gnomes have entered the folklore of many countries, especially Western Europe and even Scandinavia, once province of the dwarves. In physical terms, gnomes are the most solid of the elemental spirits and are said to live in caves and mines, guarding the treasures of the earth. Some inhabit deep forests and all live for up to 1,000 years.

Many are great metal workers and spend time in their underground forges, like the dwarves fashioning metals and digging for gems, though their main interest is in gold for coins and bars. They have wives and families and are all very strong.

Gnomes found in private and public gardens are slightly more sociable, though they are attached to the plants and wildlife and not the owners of the land. They vary in size from 30–90 cm (2–3 ft) and resemble garden gnome statues, though generally browner and more gnarled. Males usually have a peaked rather than a pointed red cap and wear blue or green with boots made from birch bark. Females may be seen in green and often have headscarves. The gnomes may or may not have white beards.

Garden and forest gnomes care for the earth, the roots of plants and for forest or garden wild animals and birds. They are said to be gifted herbalists, but generally only for the benefit of forest creatures. Gnomes are very similar to dwarves in appearance, but are slightly smaller and more graceful and can run fast for their size. Dwarves cannot come out in sunlight or will be turned to stone.

The trust of a gnome is a great gift and some witches keep model gnomes in their gardens in the hope of attracting the luck bringing and protective qualities of an actual gnome presence.

Six steps to absorbing elemental Earth strength for personal empowerment, healing and in ritual

1 Go to any old site as twilight is falling. Sit quietly for a while by the stones, connect with the Earth spirits and feel the throb of the earth beneath you. If you carry out rituals at any of these old sites, you need to raise very little power. It will flow upwards from the Earth and be vitalised by the nature spirits or the older, slower, huge, pillar-like brown guardians of the place, associated with the Landvaettir in Scandinavia. You will also experience pure elemental forces, especially if you stand on one of the spots where the energy lines converge (usually near the centre of a stone circle). On the Summer Solstice the Earth power might enable you to see the golden doorway in one of the stones (usually aligned with the Solstice sunrise or sunset) that will reveal other dimensions.

2 Walk barefoot on sand, soil or grass, press your hands against trees, trudge through snow or piles of leaves; sit on the earth or grass and allow the elemental strength to flow upwards through your feet and perineum. You can incorporate these sensations into spontaneous rituals and spells and find impromptu tools and natural circles in situ. Many less well known old sites are completely accessible for ritual and at certain times of the day and year are deserted.

3 When in a natural earth place, whether a park, a garden, the wilderness or an ancient site, hold your hands, palms flat a few centimetres above different flowers or herbs, or horizontally towards a tree trunk or a ancient stone. Relax and you will sense different kinds of energies that differ even among plants of the same species and among the stones. After doing this for a while you will start to feel very energised and harmonious. If you see any wilting flowers, shake your

fingers over them to pass on the energies and remove any choking bindweed close to them. This is excellent to do before a ritual to connect with the powers of the place. After the ritual, as well as grounding yourself, press downwards with your hands and feet. Any extra amplified powers you have generated in the ritual will be returned to the Earth and her essences as part of a mutual enrichment. You can also do this with growing plants in your indoor altar space.

4 Use holidays and weekends or days away and cheap travel to visit sites of antiquity, old caves and natural beauty or if you are working away in an unfamiliar city, find the local botanical gardens, urban wildlife garden or revived woodland, like the Sherwood Forest initiative around Nottingham in the East Midlands. You do not need to join expensive spiritual tours (unless you wish to). Armed with a guide book and a local trail marker you can discover old labyrinths and ruined abbeys with their medicinal herb gardens often intact that were, pre-1500, usually built on ley lines. Walk, touch and tune in. Take photographs and scribble down impressions for your Book of Shadows to inspire Earth magick and chants. Often a ritual will just happen at one of these places. Even on a compulsory guided tour you can usually find a dark or quiet corner or hold back from some history you can read up on later and leave a crystal with a blessing. These stored impressions, both in your mind and your Book of Shadows, will inspire you on dull grey days or cloudy nights indoors, when it is hard to visualise the power of the Earth.

5 Collect legends and information about local places and those you visit on holiday where there are stories or places associated with giants, trolls, fairies or witches, and also places where Earth lights or crop circles have been reported. Whether you believe that nature beings are an objective reality or an expression of the energies experienced in places of power by different people at different times, you can be sure there will be a huge surge of Earth power around the location. Take a pendulum and it may spiral and vibrate and amplify your clairvoyant impressions and visions. The actual experiences will open up your Earth energy channels that will increase your innate magical energies and act as a repository of stored power as you recall the experiences in your mind.

6 Work with the energies of animals, both pets and those in nature conservancies or who are wild in your garden or locality. In particular, study animals that live close to or under the earth in setts, burrows or caves. I have written extensively about animals in my *Natural Magick* book.

Soil and magick

In natural magick, clean soil can be an excellent substitute for salt as the Earth element in outdoor rituals for circle casting and for sprinkling around symbols especially those made of natural substances. As part of a spell or ritual, you can also plant seeds or seedlings in the cauldron or half fill it with earth. Afterwards, transfer the soil and plants carefully. Better still, use an old iron pot for the original ritual so they can grow in peace and perhaps be re-empowered in a subsequent spell if matters are slow moving.

Bury symbols of what you no longer need in your life in soil as part of the ritual. Set herbs or flowers on top of them to symbolise new hopes and new dreams.

Carry out private rituals to plant trees or bushy plants (in miniature pots if you do not have a garden) for memorable occasions, the birth of a child, your wedding, even your divorce or after a major commitment or breakdown in a relationship. The tree is a visible reminder that the old will be transformed into new growth or that what is good will continue to flourish. You can empower the soil first and bless the plants as part of the ritual.

Have your special wishing pot of earth or garden place that every time you get dispirited you push in a few seeds (any sort you like) and name them for a hope or plan. They may not all grow but some will and you can transplant those to bigger pots or a place in the garden. When you have wonderful flowering pot or flower or herb patches, you can see how far you have come.

When you want to bring reconciliation to your family, to protect your home or workplace or have some material need, light a candle and take a tray of soil or sand. Make miniature houses and towns out of earth, piling them up with your hands, as you did when you were a child.

Draw pathways between people and the places you represent. Draw protection round them or chant messages of peace or of new links that will bring what you need. Crystals such as moss agate or jade set in the outline of a house or workplace representation will encourage gradual growth and pressed into an outlined figure encourage a return to health. You can keep the earth pictures on your altar until the purpose is fulfilled and then smooth the soil for another occasion.

If you move house or leave home, take a small pot of earth with you as a connection, even if all the old times were not happy. Set it on your altar and hold it regularly to transfer the love and security.

The magick of salt

Salt is the most usual sacred substance used in spells and rituals to signify Earth and I have already described ways it can be used in circle casting either alone or mixed as sacred water.

Salt is found naturally as rock salt that is mined or extracted from salt marshes, and by dissolving seawater, the most usual magickal form. The name comes from Salus, Roman Goddess of health whom the Greeks called Hygeia.

Salt has always been regarded as precious because for early settlers around the globe it was the main preservative of food through the long winter months. Because salt is a universal symbol of health, happiness and prosperity, as you use it spiritually in your home and for your family as well as in ritual, good health and abundance as well as protection from all harm are naturally attracted. This may be because the spiritual connection with the salt and the energy emitted by empowered salt activates our own aura or spiritual energy field that acts as a protective filter or magnet on some level we do not fully understand from negativity (see page 625 for empowering salt).

Because salt was the one totally pure substance, it also assumed religious and spiritual significance throughout the ages as symbol both of purity and incorruptibility. Salt was used in many religions as Holy Water to ward off evil and increase physical strength. It is still used in the preparation of Christian Holy Water (see page 107 for preparing sacred water in magick).

Mediaeval alchemists regarded salt as one of the three major essences that made up life, with mercury (quicksilver) and sulphur, and it signified the human body.

Protective, health and abundance rituals using salt

* Draw the Alchemical symbol for salt (shown right) on the side of a white candle with a silver paper knife and leave the candle in the centre of your altar or the heart of your home where people gather. Do this on any evening during the waxing moon. Burn the candle right through to spread protection and abundance for the month ahead. Repeat monthly.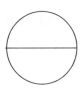

* Light a large plain white or beeswax candle for any urgent magical need, especially linked with healing or abundance, to change a run of bad luck or to overcome a huge obstacle, for yourself or anyone in need.

* Wait until the wax is melted around the flame, visualising your need coming to fruition. Recite the wish three times. Then sprinkle a few grains of salt into the flame so it sparkles, state your wish or need three times again, and blow out the candle, repeating the wish more three times.

* Continue each night as long as necessary or until the candle is burned through or will not light, on each occasion leaving the candle burning for a little longer. This is one of the most effective spells I know when there is a real crisis and so I felt I should share it. The flame can get fierce so be careful.

* On a Friday morning or whenever you have time on a Friday, sprinkle sacred salt water in the four corners of your altar room or anywhere you carry out psychic or divinatory work to keep the room purified. Say:

May only light and peace remain here.

* Tip any remaining water out of the front door. This can be carried out anywhere in your home where you feel negativity and especially over thresholds or round window frames.

* Starting on the night you first see the crescent moon, add three pinches of empowered sea salt to a small lidded ceramic pot, saying:

One for the Maiden for health, one for the Mother for abundance. Third for the Wise One for protection, Blessings be.

* Every evening do the same (use a small screw top jar if you are away from home and it is possible).

* On the night of the full moon, tip your pot of salt into flowing water (under an outside tap if possible), asking by the maiden, mother and wise one that it may bring abundance, health and protection into your daily life or that of a loved one.

* Afterwards send three blessings: one to someone who needs healing, one to someone who needs abundance and the third to someone who has wronged you.

* Wash the pot and when it is dry put the lid on with a single pinch of salt until the next crescent. Do three small kindnesses in the intervening period.

PRACTICAL ASSIGNMENT

Making the Earth element the basis for a whole spell

There will be times when you need to focus your altar and spell work on Earth energies alone, perhaps when you need a stable period in your life, to regularise finances or health, calm down emotions in a relationship, to settle yourself; whenever you need extra patience, perseverance or stamina to get you through a period of uncertainty or pressure or if your magical work seems to be remote from your everyday world and needs. There are many ways you can do this.

* Light green or brown candles at all the quadrants.

* Use dishes of dried herbs and flowers, Earth substances in each quadrant (each has its own elemental qualities): patchouli or heather in the north for Earth, lavender or fennel in the east for Air, chamomile or marigolds in the south for Fire and apple blossom or violets in the west for Water.

* Burn an incense mix or fragrance that is earth based (see page 136).

* Set four crystals, another Earth substance, at the four quarters, using stones that are linked with the respective quadrants: malachite, moss agate or rose quartz in the north, blue lace agate, amethyst or citrine in the east, carnelian, garnet or obsidian in the south, and a green calcite, jade or any fluorite in the west.

* Use a statue of the Goddess based on the Palaeolithic featureless Goddesses with breasts and swollen belly (you can often buy very cheap soapstone African ones or make your own) and either grain or a horn for the God.

* In the centre of the altar or your magick circle, have a dish of soil (use salt for the Earth element in the north).

* As you raise the power in the spell, rather than releasing it, direct the energy as you feel it rising to a climax into the Earth. Do this by scattering seeds on top of the dish of soil for an attracting ritual or burying dead leaves to banish sorrow.

* In either case allow your words to get softer and slower, ending with:

> *May the mother take all into her gentle arms and restore what should be renewed or reawakened in the fullness of time. So mote it be.*

* A group or coven could pass round the soil dish and scatter seeds with an empowerment or bury leaves with a blessing. Afterwards the soil and contents would be transferred to an outdoor patch. If outdoors, you could work round a patch of earth, perhaps instead of the fire if you were using the grid formation (see page 257).

Further information

Recommended reading

* Carmichael, et al, *Sacred Sites, Sacred Places*, Routledge, 1997
* Cunningham, Scott, *Earth Power*, Llewellyn, 1984
* Devereux, Paul, *Sacred Places, Ancient Origins of Holy and Mystical Sites*, Cassell Illustrated, 2000
* Palmer, Dawn Jessica, *Animal Wisdom*, Element, 2001
* Romani, Rosa, et al, *Green Spirituality, Green Magic*, 2004
* Simpson, Liz, *The Healing Energies of Earth*, Gaia Books, 2005
* Sigler, Michael D, *The Elementals*, Book Surge Publishing, 2005

Websites

* *Devas and Elementals*
  Good overviews, covering elementals, devas and spirit or energy orbs
  www.linsdomain.com/devas.htm
* *Order of the White Lion*
  Very comprehensive site on Elementals, Archangels and many other esoteric topics
  www.orderofthewhitelion.com/index
* *The Sacred Landscape – Cathrerine Yronwode*
  An excellent earth energies resource with many links
  www.luckymojo.com/sacredlinks.html
* *Sacred Sites*
  Another good starting point for on line sacred sites and earth energies resources
  www.sacredsites.com/index.html

THE POWER OF THE AIR

(*A*)ir is the least tangible element in magick. It is manifest in rituals through its effects, as incense smoke or fragrance and in nature by the sound of the wind in the trees or the sight of clouds moving across the skies. Yet it is an essential magickal force to lift the Earth component of the spell to higher spiritual levels. It initiates action on a symbolic level, carrying sound as the words of the spell are spoken and the athame, hand or wand stirs the air as it is moved.

Air magick is centred on movement, on initiating change, opening horizons, expanding possibility and triggering new beginnings in magick and in everyday life. Its sacred substance incense is set in the East of the altar.

Air elementals are the movers of energy, carrying seeds for germination, stripping dead leaves from trees and assisting birds on their migratory paths. Air spirits are usually winged, fairies, light elves, sprites who frequently assume the form of birds, the Spanish and Mexican Folletti who shape-shift into butterflies and travel on the wind, sometimes causing dust clouds.

Air is also the domain of birds, from the mighty eagle, symbol of the Great Spirit in Native North American lore to fabulous mythical creatures like Sielulintu, the golden Finnish Soul-Bird. On his behalf, small birds carried the souls of unborn children to their new families and return souls on death to the heavens.

Finally, it is the realm of the Angels and Archangels (of whom more later). In this module, I will explore some of the themes of Air spirits and energies and link them with your magickal work.

Air elementals

Air elementals are, like Air itself mainly seen through their effects, for even to the clairvoyant eye they are so fast moving only silver streaks of radiance remain in their trail. They carry spores and seeds, ensuring pollination and cross-fertilisation of plants and trees. At the other end of the cycle, they assist in natural decay by eroding mountain sides, uprooting trees, carrying on their breath the forest fire, rain and water surges that bring floods.

In the Chinese tradition they are known as the Dragon's Breath, as they transmit positive Ch'i or Qi, the invisible lifeforce, the flow of positive energy through everything, people, animals, nature and also homes and workplaces. The regulated gentle undulating flow of Ch'i promotes growth, health and vitality. But they also have their destructive side when they breathe too fast or too heavily. Bad Ch'i or Sha is fast and destructive and is believed to carry away good luck and prosperity and cause irritability and stress in those affected by it in their homes or workplaces.

At their most powerful, Air elementals are manifest as high winds, storms, sandstorms, dust clouds, whirlwinds, hurricanes, tornadoes, rainbows, comets and shooting stars. You can experience Air elementals if you are standing on the deck of a ship in a high wind or see their patterns in the clouds outside the cabin of an aircraft during turbulence, while walking on swing bridges, and in all high, open places, especially in unsettled weather.

Their force is also expressed through the power and flight of the eagle, hawk and birds of prey, in swooping flocks of birds, as butterflies, in carrions like the vulture that pick clean dead animals and birds. It permeates mythical creatures of flight, such as the Native North American thunderbird, the bringer of rain that spills from a lake on its back as it flies and whose flashing eyes create lightning and its vast eagle-like wings thunder. You can see the Elemental energy manifest in the constantly moving blue and silver auras around flying birds.

The Air dragons

Nowhere are the energies of the Air elementals better expressed than in the myths of the Oriental dragons. Air dragons are considered most fortunate and Dragon King temples were created so people could pray to the dragons for a good harvest, since the dragons controlled the rains and the seasons. They are associated with the Spring Equinox, the key festival for the Air elementals, when they are pictured bursting from the womb of the Earth, scattering the seeds of new growth upon the earth. As well as bringing rain, dragons could divert floodwaters away from towns. They would appear to herald a period of prosperity and fertilise the soil with their magickal semen.

However, when they fought, it caused thunderstorms, though the deep pools left by intense storms also gave growth to healing herbs such as the all-purpose red herb. If angered by mortals, the dragons would gather all the waters in a basket, thus creating drought. They might even cause an eclipse by swallowing the sun.

Elemental Air spirits and magick

Sylphs

Sylphs are the archetypal winged Air spirits that, like the Earth gnomes, are associated with the power of the elementals and so can be used in magick spells to generate Air energy. They reside on mountain tops, living for hundreds of years without seeming to age and can attain an immortal soul through good deeds.

They may assume human form for short periods of time and vary in size up to the size of a human. However, they are far more ethereal and slender than mortals, like all fey folk, and have huge iridescent wings. They are usually seen in the wind.

Sylphs are specifically described in the Ancient Greek and Roman tradition, but are found in many lands as winged air spirits or sprites. The classical sylphs are very slender and graceful, like transparent ballerinas, constantly moving as they float just above the ground or flying through the sky, creating wispy trails of light or mist. The Greek Muses who inspired poetry, dance and music were believed to be sylphs.

Their high soft voices may be heard in the wind, especially at seasonal change points such as Samhain. If you stand at a crossroads it is said you will hear all you need learn for the year ahead on the voices in the wind. Once believed to control the weather and as cloud spirits to direct the winds, sylphs have also been described from Classical times onwards as taking the form of large white graceful birds, like gigantic swallows.

The Butterfly Goddess of Minoan Crete whose images date from about 4000 BCE may have been an evolved nature being of the Air, because fabulous winged butterflies were one form the sylphs adopted.

Sylphs differ from angels in that they are much mistier and transparent and do not focus on human concerns or act as guardians. They also inhabit the second astral plane, whereas angels come from higher realms.

You'll find sylphs in wide-open spaces, in wilderness areas and in meadows, as well as higher ground. They will protect their own areas of land or a particular mountain or hill and may sometimes cause mists to shroud a place, even if all round or even higher land is clear. There are also wild sylphs that live in the wilderness and generally appear in bird or butterfly form, or just before a storm in high winds, leaving grey trails behind them.

If a high place of natural beauty is under threat, then sylph activity and sightings will increase. One example is the Sleeping Beauty, Sleeping Mother or Sleeping Goddess Mountain, on the island of Lewis in the Outer Hebrides, off the west coast of Scotland. The mountain appears like a sleeping Goddess when it is seen from a local stone circle. Every 18.6 years the moon appears to be born from this Goddess figure. A proposed wind farm would destroy the sacred site.

Sylphs' virtues are their vitality, their liberating power, their joy and their openness. However, they can be fickle and spiteful and encourage unnecessary risk taking by those who fall under their spell. They do not communicate directly with humans, but those who have seen them, usually very fleetingly, talk about being touched by a breeze that stirs the soul with happiness and a sense of freedom to try new avenues.

Sylphs are ruled by their queen Paralda, who resides on the highest mountain on earth or one of the mysterious sacred mountains of Chinese myth. She is silver with shimmering slivers of light emanating from her and is never still. Her touch can be soft, caressing and warm. But in an instant, she is sharp and suddenly icy as she blows away all our carefully laid out papers and plans in a sudden whirlwind, usually at a time we need to rethink or formulate. She is usually surrounded by silver birds and rainbow butterflies.

Other Air spirits

The spirits of the Air are not only those with wings, but also those who are light, aethereal and generally less fixed to the earth. However, they may live on or even within the ground, especially on hills, mountains, in windy places or where there are very open plains or meadow or grasslands. If you grow lavender or roses you may attract benign Air spirits to your garden. They will not stay long, but stir the air wonderfully.

In a previous module I wrote about the dark underground elves (see page 320). But the elves we think of most in fairytales and accounts by adults as well as children are described dancing in rings of toadstools. The light elves in Norse cosmology are the highest form of elves, characterised by their light blond or golden hair. Gandalf, immortalised by Tolkien as the Master wizard, was an elven king. From Tolkien, too, we learn of Galadriel, the lovely elven queen who like Ghoab rules over Earth spirits, but is herself a being of the air. Elves also appear throughout the folklore of Northern and Western Europe.

In Scandinavia, light elves, like their darker brothers, were the same size as humans, but slender and perfectly formed with delicate pointed features.

In Northern and Western Europe, elves tend to be smaller but like the Scandinavian elves are always beautiful young men and women, invariably with wings, who live in forest glades and flower meadows. They are creatures of the sun and of moonlight and are famed for their wondrous pipe and fiddle music, their singing and dancing and their skill with a bow.

However, were any human to come across the elves dancing and join (or even pause to watch) he or she would dance for what seemed like a whole night; but when morning came, many years would have passed. A special tune called the Elf King Song said to be the most wonderful tune in the world, but if mortal musicians played it, they would have to play until they dropped unless someone cut the fiddle strings.

Best known of all the Air spirits are the fairies of the Celtic lands. They live according to legend and recorded sightings, either in Fairy Courts or troops. The Sidhe or Sith were the name for Courtly fairies in Ireland, England and Scotland and also France (though the tradition was strongest in Ireland). They are described as beautiful opalescent or shining beings, often with shimmering wings. Although creatures of the Air, they live in subterranean fairy palaces of gold and crystal and are endowed with youth, beauty, joy, and great musical abilities. The Fairy Queen Oonagh has been described by the 19th century folklorist Lady Wilde, who collected accounts of fairy folk lore in Ireland, as having golden hair sweeping to the ground, dressed in silver gossamer glittering as if with diamonds, that were actually dew drops.

The Irish Daoine Sidhe were famed for their music and many aspiring musicians would sleep on a fairy mound in the hope of being transported to fairyland to be endowed with the gift of fairy music-making.

The smaller trooping fairies are much closer to the elves and in Celtic lands were the less noble groupings or tribes of fairy beings, associated with fairy rings and with green hillsides, fairy paths, woodland clearings and meadows.

Six steps to absorbing Air strength for personal empowerment, healing and in ritual

I   Collect feathers from different birds, either ones you find on the ground or go to a bird conservancy where you can buy more exotic kinds. Here you are using each feather as a means of connecting magickally with air and so it does not matter if you do not know its individual magickal significance. However, use light-coloured feathers for wishes or to attract what you need and darker ones for banishing what you no longer want or which is destructive.

Go to a high place such as a hilltop or to an open plain. Hold your feather close to your lips and whisper three times what or whom you wish to call into your life or to blow away what is redundant. Then release your feather into the wind. You can use a number of feathers, one after the other, a dark followed by a light, to replace what you are sending from your life with a call for new opportunities. Take a basket or pouch of feathers and continue until you have no more unnamed sorrows to lose or joys to seek.

2 Create a prayer stick, found in traditions from Tibet to Native North America, from a long, smooth, forked stick. Often they measure from the elbow to fingertip length, but for indoor altar work you can use a smaller one. Set one in the centre of your altar, embedded either in a dish of soil or tiny turquoise chippings.

Each day for the three days before the full moon, tie a feather, a sprig of leaves, a flower or a strip of paper on thread to the stick. Name a step to fulfil a personal goal or a step for someone else or as three daily steps to healing. You can write the steps as well as saying them aloud if you are using paper tags (luggage labels are ideal). Recite the first step on day 1, the first two steps on day 2 and all three on the day before the full moon.

On the day of the full moon wait until it appears in the sky (check the time of rising in a moon diary if it is cloudy.) Take the prayer stick and the tied feathers/wishes outdoors and set it in a mound of earth. Touch each attached item and rename the step. Then state the successful outcome you desire as a result of taking the steps in real life three times with confidence and end, *So mote it be*. Leave the tags to be blown away or decay as nature chooses.

For banishing sorrow or relieving a health problem, use dead leaves or dying flowers for each step. Leave the prayer stick indoors for the night of the full moon. Say the three steps aloud as you touch each leaf sprig (three for each sprig or flower) on the night of the full moon. State also the desired result.

Take the prayer stick outdoors on the next night, the first waning moon night when you see the moon in the sky. Put the stick in an exposed place, recite the steps and the successful conclusion and instead of, *So mote it be*, say:

Go in peace and in tranquillity. Blessings be.

3 Visit an open place, if possible on a windy day. Face the four directions in turn and call the four Ancient Greek and Roman Spirits of the four winds who are personifications of Air elemental energies. These are four brothers, sons of Eos or Aurora, the Goddess of the dawn and Aeolus or Aiolos, keeper of the winds.

Face north and call Boreas. Ask him to blow away anything that is restricting you, a seemingly immovable situation or destructive person in your life or unwelcome ties to the past. Name what you are losing and thank the Guardian of the North Wind.

Face east and call Apheliotes (Eurus in Latin). Ask him to bring the new beginning you need, any desired travel or new opportunities into your life. Name the change you seek and thank the Guardian of the East Wind.

Face south and call Notus. Ask him to bring the good fortune, the prosperity, health or success you need. Name what you seek and thank the Guardian of the South Wind.

Face west and call Zephyrus. Ask him to bring fertility, healing, peace, justice and reconciliation. Name what you seek and thank the Guardian of the West Wind.

Turn round nine times clockwise, reciting their names, then nine times anticlockwise and finally nine times clockwise. End as you face north again, saying:

May the power of the winds carry me to where I most wish to be.

The induced dizziness often gives a momentary out-of-body flying sensation in which you become the wind. Sit or lie down, steady yourself and enjoy the experience.

4 Find an Air place outdoors where you can tune into the sensations of the element. Explore any local hills or climb the steps to the top of a church or cathedral tower. If you are adventurous and fit, try windsurfing or hang-gliding and chant Air empowerments as you soar through the skies. If less adventurous, take advantage of cheap air fares and book a window seat from where in your imagination you can explore the lands high in the clouds.

5 Try Druidic cloud divination. Wait for a clear day when there are a number of white clouds, especially towards sunset when they are tinged with red, purple and pink. Go to a hilltop or plain with an unrestricted view. Ask a question and allow the clouds to form images, join together and part as an ongoing moving picture. Then sit quietly and let words and impressions flow through your mind that will expand the information from the images. Record them in your symbol section in your Book of Shadows.

When you need inspiration or encouragement, you may occasionally see an Angel formed of clouds at sunrise or sunset. Note what you were feeling just before the experience and what message the Angel seemed to bring.

6 Visit places locally and on holiday or during a weekend away that have fairy or elven names or associations. Usually they are a hilltop or glade and even if surrounded by houses have a sense of lightness and enchantment. In some lands you are falling over fairy and elf legends, the Isle of Man, Ireland, Wales, France especially Brittany with its enchanted Forest of Broceliande, Germany, the Netherlands, Denmark and Scandinavia. However, every part of the world has its indigenous mountain and Air spirits. Take a notebook and sketchpad and sit or lie in long grass and listen for whisperings.

The power of incense

Incense has been used in religious worship and formal magickal rituals in cultures as far apart as India, the Middle East and the pre European conquest of the Americas. It was used in religious ceremonies among the Assyrians and Ancient Babylonians, and on Egyptian monumental tablets kings are depicted with incense censers making offerings. God commanded Moses to build an altar of incense on which only the sweetest spices and gums were burned.

The daily renewal of these fragrant offerings was carried out by a special branch of the Levitical tribe. In the classical world also, incense was burned as offerings to the Gods when sacrifices were made. In Judaism, the Roman Catholic and well as Eastern Orthodox churches and in High Anglican churches, incense still forms an important part of ceremonies.

In mediaeval times the correct use of incense was central to ceremonial magick, each incense having a magickal and astrological meaning. Less fragrant scents were burned to drive and keep away demons in mediaeval demonology.

Incense as an offering

The traditional use of incense as a connection between the deities or higher forces of goodness and mortals is expressed in the following traditional and widely quoted incense or censing prayer that comes from the Ancient Egyptian Coffin Texts, number 269. These texts were intended to guide spirits after death safely through the Underworld. I saw it displayed next to a vast array of exotic incenses in Cairo and some of the most ornate gold censers I have ever seen outside a church and my Egyptologist guide translated it for me.

The fire is laid, the fire shines;
The incense is laid on the fire, the incense shines.
Your perfume comes to me, O Incense;
May my perfume come to you, O Incense.
Your perfume comes to me, you gods;
May my perfume come to you, you gods.
May I be with you, you gods;
May you be with me, you gods.
May I live with you, you gods;
May you live with me, you gods.
I love you, you gods;
May you love me, you gods.

In Ancient Egypt, incense burning was central to temple rituals of purification, in processions, at celebrations and at private rituals. Most precious of offerings, incense was burned to send prayers and praise to the deities by priests in the inner sanctum or naos of the god in the temple. However, it also had an important place in the lives of ordinary people or at homely household altars to honour the ancestors or ask the gods beloved by ordinary families Hathor, Isis, Bes or Tauret for blessings.

Lighting incense is still an almost instant way of separating ritual or contemplation from the everyday world.

Choosing incense for ritual

If you are unfamiliar with magick it may not always be clear that there are two kinds of incense. Combustible is the kind where you use the incense in stick, coil or cone form and light it directly. High quality incense in this form can be very pure and just as good as granular incense.

The second kind is non-combustible and can be any dried plant material, though it burns best with a proportion (a third plus of the total used) of a resinous incense, such as frankincense or myrrh. This you burn on a preheated charcoal disk or block in a censer or thurible, a heatproof container. You can mix a variety of petals, resins and herbs to create your own non-combustible incense to get the magickal meanings and fragrances you want or buy it ready mixed. Equally, you can burn several incense sticks in different fragrances and proportions: for example, two rose and one ginger incense stick to call for tender but passionate love.

Neither method is better than the other. It is a question of time and the kind and complexity of the ritual. There may be times when you want to dry the flowers, perhaps from a special bouquet or herbs from your garden and when dried pound and mix them with resin to make a personal incense mix. This takes about as long as it does for charcoal to heat and you this can be a part of the pre spell or ritual activity to make the transition from the everyday world along with crafting your symbol and/or rolling your beeswax candle. It can also be very companionable if you are working with others (more of this on page 569).

For instant spells or ones where you cannot have a lot of equipment, a variety of different fragrance sticks and cones will allow you to mix and match a precise spell purpose and you can even use incense as the symbol.

Incense in silent or passive ritual

In the module on fragrance magick I have written about making your own incense blends. Incense burning features in almost every module in ritual and for self-empowerment. Here I will focus on an important but little known technique that will enrich all your incense work when you are chanting aloud the purpose of the spell as you empower a symbol with incense power for the Air or use two incense sticks to raise the power using enchantment (see page 186).

Silent incense ritual is good for very personal, private magick and also for those needs or wishes that cannot easily be translated into a spell or ritual, sometimes because an issue is complex or we are so confused we just want to hand it to some higher force and say, *Please sort it out*. It is also a way of cultivating inner stillness that allows us to carry out magick by thought alone, the province of Air.

* Silent incense ritual uses incense without any other tools apart from a single white candle from which it is lit. You can work either in your altar place or anywhere indoors or out where it is quiet and you can be alone. If you have a partner with whom you are in total spiritual harmony, you could work together for the same purpose using two sets of incense. Work at sunrise or sunset according to the nature of the need.

* Copy the incense prayer above on to white paper with dark blue ink or learn it.

* Choose a single incense fragrance that reflects the purpose of the spell or if you prefer a blend (see below and page 551). Blends you buy may suggest a purpose in the name, but read the contents in advance so they are right for you.

* Prepare any incense you are making or mixing by stirring it slowly and rhythmically, but without chanting the purpose even in your mind.

* Alternatively, hold the sticks on cones in their burners for a minute or two, one in each hand and let the purpose flow into you effortlessly. If you cannot get the fragrance you need, frankincense, rose, lavender or sandalwood are good all-purpose substitute scents.

* Light the candle and then the incense, whether sticks, cones or loose powdered incense. If using sticks or cones, light two in separate holders from the candle and set them close together so that the smoke curls in a pattern. Do this in silence and do not consciously formulate the purpose, but allow the smoke to act as the wish or prayer.

- Preheat your charcoal for non-combustible incense.
- Read the incense prayer silently and then turn the paper over. If you have learned the prayer (which I prefer), say the words in your mind.
- Using your finger or one of the incense sticks, then write in smoke in the air:

> *So shall all be resolved in its own time and its own way. I lay my trust in the Goddess [or name the deities figure that for you offers protection and empowerment].*

- Wait for the prayer/message to be carried to the cosmos on the smoke as you sit facing the incense. Add more incense when necessary, if using incense on charcoal, until what you have mixed is gone or the charcoal no longer burns. Continue until the sticks are burned through.
- Allow words and images to float through your mind like clouds, but any conscious worries or forward planning that disturb you, push symbolically into the smoke with your hands, to be carried into the cosmos. For each concern that arises, think the words:

> *Blessed be.*

- When the ash is cool, scatter it on to earth.
- The ritual is closed as you either repeat the incense prayer in your mind or reread it. Blow out the candle, if it is still burning.

This apparently easy ritual is mentally and spiritually quite difficult so persevere and the results will increase both your spiritual harmony and over time your magickal control.

Ten incenses for silent ritual

I have listed where the incenses are resins and so are suitable for adding to mixtures or that burn well. You can burn non-resinous flowers and herbs, like lavender on rose petals, on charcoal to the same effect, though incense is strictly defined as containing resin (see page 551 for lists of magickal herbs, incense and flower meanings). Get the best quality sticks or cones you can afford.

Cedarwood: Cedarwood chips are an incense of the sun and have a warm woody smell. Good for purification of people, places and artefacts, for health concerns, for psychic, psychological and physical protection of self, home and possessions and for removing the unwanted influences or the control of others.

Cyphi or Kyphi: This contains resin and is best burned alone. This wonderful sweet and spicy Ancient Egyptian incense, used in the temple as part of the evening ceremony, is in fact a compound of up to 50 different ingredients (the average mix contains about 12). They include honey, wine, raisins, storax bark, saffron, sandalwood, frankincense, gum mastic, benzoin, cardamom seeds, galangal root, lemongrass and myrrh. You can still see representations of Kyphi recipes depicted on the walls of the temples at Edfu and Philae.

Really experienced witches with knowledge of the Ancient Egyptian world have their own secret recipe perfected over years. My friend Galatea recently made me some that I treasure and burn for special occasions. You can buy blends online or from good New Age stores. If you get the chance to visit Egypt or the Middle East on holiday you may find authentic Kyphi made by the same family for many generations.

If there is a late sunset this is a wonderful fragrance to use in silent ritual before sleep as it reduces distress and insomnia. At any time, it unravels complex problems and issues, cleanses old hurts and reassures you of a better tomorrow. It also reawakens dormant sexual desire.

Copal: This resin comes from the Mayan tradition, first said to be extracted from the original Tree of Life and it is still is used ceremonially in Central and South America. It has a soft, rich aroma and cleanses all emotional, mental and creative blocks. It also encourages contact with Angels or Spirit Guides and helps in overcoming the effects of quarrels and the removal of unwanted influences or addictions. Good for reassurance if you live in an unsafe area or alone and get nervous at night.

Dragon's blood: Another resin, this is a powerful spicy fragrance and some people do not like to burn it as single incense. Try it in incense sticks if you are uncertain as it is a wonderful empowerer and bringer of courage and confidence. Good for counteracting bullying or abuse and to encourage a surge forward towards dreams and desires whatever the obstacles. Excellent for men who are worried about their sexual or mental potency, and for men or women to attract or preserve passionate and enduring love; also for periods when one piece of bad luck follows another, to reverse the trend.

Frankincense: Frankincense resin, also linked with the sun and the power of Fire, is one of the original and most highly prized incenses. It will release the higher spiritual purpose of every experience, good and bad and also gives hope in despair, success in failure and protects against fears and threat, especially from powerful or official sources. It furthers any creative ventures and dreams and opens avenues to bring these into being; also for travel dreams and for leadership opportunities and for issues concerning fatherhood.

Lavender: A gentle Air fragrance, this not only soothes but also opens horizons and draws to us possibilities, support and resources. Excellent if you are exhausted or feel you cannot go on but cannot rest and to attract love, fertility, happiness and above all kindness and understanding even from normally unsympathetic or emotionally closed people. It also protects your home, your children, pets and older relations from harm and resolves worries concerning them.

Myrrh: Another ancient incense of the Water, myrrh resin is the alter ego of frankincense. It is gently healing incense for all sorrow or illness and is an incense of integrity and truth and promises that all shall be well. It also calls love forever, especially after reversal or past sorrow and restores what has been lost; good for matters concerning mothers and children.

Orris root: An incense of the moon, this is often used to preserve potpourri or stabilise other incense mixes. Its qualities are of preservation of love, home and resources, what matters most. With its delicate violet scent, it is uplifting when you fear loss or in uncertain times. Good also for allowing what must be secret to remain so, but also for protecting you from deception.

Patchouli: A leafy incense, patchouli is an incense of the Earth. Therefore it brings the blessings of the Earth, unexpected solutions to money worries that usually involve hard but productive work, stability and happiness at home and relief of worries over housing or property. It also offers protection against all harm and as a bonus enhances passion and sensual pleasures; also for environmental concerns and older people.

Rose petals: Fragrance of the Water element and of love, gentleness, happiness, abundance, fertility and healing, this is my favourite fragrance. If I am really sad, worried or hurt and cannot settle to anything, this is my spiritual sticking plaster and symbolises the essence of silent ritual. It restores trust in people and in life and will enhance your inner radiance and ability to attract love and all manner of abundance.

Sandalwood: Like frankincense and myrrh, sandalwood is a very ancient ceremonial incense and can be substituted for almost any other in ritual. Sandalwood offers inner harmony and peace and is good incense to start with if you find silent ritual difficult. It also helps the body and mind to heal themselves and to open your spiritual channels. It brings love and passion and the clarity, often in dreams, to find the missing steps to your path ahead or an unexpected solution.

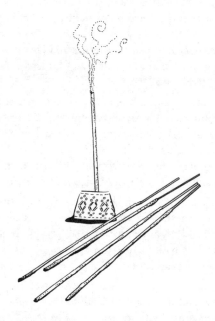

PRACTICAL ASSIGNMENT

Making the Air element the basis for a whole spell

✦ Use yellow or pearly grey candles at all four quarters.

✦ Burn incense sticks or cones at each of the four quarters of the circle or altar, using geranium or magnolia in the north, lemongrass or mint in the east, frankincense or dragon's blood in the south, and jasmine or vanilla in the west.

✦ Have feathers at all four quadrants, white in the north to signify the owl, grey or yellow in the east to signify the eagle, kestrel or falcon, red, golden brown or tawny in the south for the hawk, and black in the west for the raven.

✦ Make your circle with a smudge stick or incense and raise power in the same way by spiralling smudge as you move round the circle chanting.

✦ Hang wind chimes in your altar room and incorporate sound such as a singing bowl, pan pipe music or light, soft fast drumming into the spell.

✦ Open the four quarters by asking the help and protection of the four protective Archangels, Uriel in the north, Raphael, the Air Archangel in the east, Michael in the south, and Gabriel in the west (see page 576). Alternatively use the four winds as the Guardians of the Quadrants: Boreas in the north, Apheliotes (Eurus) in the east, Notus in the south, and Zephyrus in the west. Expect a very lively spell and be sure to close the Watchtowers at the end. Better still, also invite their father Eolus through the eastern gateway to stand in the centre of the circle and keep the winds under control.

✦ Hold a ritual outdoors on a windy day or on an open plain or hillside, tie long scarves round your wrists and neck and use your arms and feet to raise the power.

✦ Reread the list of Air attributes on page 137 and weave Air chants when you need a spell for a major new beginning, a change or for independence, travel, a specific career move or to succeed in an interview, examination or test.

Further research

Find out about some of the magickal creatures of the Air either online or in books. Examples include the Bird of Paradise, the Egyptian Phoenix (regarded as a Fire Bird), the Arabian Roc, and the Native North American Thunderbird, the enchanted Celtic swan maidens or the Scandinavian Valkyries, the winged horse Pegasus and Air dragons in the Oriental tradition.

Start a page for each in your Book of Shadows and as well as the myths weave your own chants and empowerments based on their unique qualities.

Work also with birds that have a rich mythology in different cultures, such as the raven, the crow, the hawk, the eagle, the crane, the stork, the nightingale, the swan and the owl.

Further information

Recommended reading

* Andrews, Ted, *Animal Speak*, Llewellyn, 1998
* Baxter, Ron, *Bestiaries and their Uses in the Middle Ages*, Sutton Publishing, 1998
* Bruce, Marie, *Magical Beasts*, Quantum, 2004
* Cunningham, Scott, *Complete Book of Incense, Oils and Brews*, Llewellyn, 2004
* Eason, Cassandra, *Complete Guide to Fairies and Magical Beings*, Piatkus 2002, Red Wheel/Weiser 2003
* Eason, Cassandra, *Smudging and Incense Burning*, Quantum/Foulsham 2001
* Froud, Brian, *Good Faeries, Bad Faeries*, Simon and Schuster, 1998
* Kavasch, E Barrie, and Baar, Karen, *American Indian Healing Arts*, Thorsons/Bantam US, 1999
* Kinsella, Thomas, *Incense and Incense Rituals, Healing Ceremonies for Spaces of Subtle Energy*, Lotus Books, 2004
* Llewelyn, Morgan, *The Elementals*, St Martins Press, 2003
* Neal, Carl E, *Incense Crafting and the Use of Magickal Scents*, Llewellyn 2003

Websites

* *The Feathers Site*
  www.geocities.com/felicitax/Magic.htm
  All about feathers and feather magick
* *Shamanic Visions*
  Comprehensive and well illustrated site on prayer trees and sticks
  www.shamanicvisions.com/sacredplaces_folder/prayertree.html
* *Incenses*
  Herbal incenses and information on making incense
  www.oller.net/incense-making.htm

THE POWER OF FIRE

F ire is the most volatile of the elements and provides the transformative energies necessary to translate intention into actuality in magick spells and rituals. It is the ignition of Fire power that generates the intensity and flash point to change the Earth component of the spell, lifted through the words and actions of Air into the release of power as the desired result. Furthermore, Fire is the creative spark that vitalises and energises the incense, the candle and the ritual fire.

Fire power has three aspects. The first is the intentionally lit ritual or bon (which means good) fire and the hearth fire at which it was believed the wise ancestors gathered to bless the home. Fire is manifest through lightning, meteorites and volcanoes and thirdly is the power of the sun. Indeed, it is believed by the Inuit and Sámi Reindeer people that the Aurora Borealis, the Northern Lights, are the fires of the beloved ancestors.

I have written about solar magick in week 39. There is also more on candle spells and rituals later, too, as they are probably the most common and central form of spellcasting.

Fire elementals are like their element, unpredictable and powerful, and their personifications include the salamander and the djinn. There is because of the fundamental instability of Fire a big overlap between fire nature spirits and elemental energies. Its earthly creatures are powerful and often ferocious, the lion, the tiger and the jaguar who in the Aztec world represented the sun God and the sun as it crossed the Underworld the Mictlan, at night and fought to be reborn each morning.

Energies are also manifest as the mythical fire dragon and the golden phoenix (symbol of transformation and rebirth, which burned itself on a funeral pyre every 500 years, only to rise again golden from the ashes). The latter you may have researched in the previous module. In this module we will explore the power of Fire in nature and in magick and examine ways you can use it to attract healing, transformation, fertility, power, joy, courage and confidence.

Fire in nature

For thousands of years, humans watched amazed as meteors blazed across the skies and meteorites fell to earth. These brought gifts, fire from the deities and rich deposits of iron or crystals such as olivine (peridot) or even occasionally diamonds embedded in the cooling rock.

Volcanoes, where fire from the earth's burning core erupts in flames, smoke and molten lava, were also associated with supernatural power. The Roman poet Virgil believed that the frequent eruptions from Mount Etna, in Sicily, were due to the giant Enceladus trying to free himself from the imprisonment beneath the mountain imposed by the gods.

If you carry a meteorite or volcanic lava they are both Fire elemental tokens and will offer powerful infusions of Fire power for courage, protection and to bring you good fortune (see more of this in the module on crystal power, page 530). In return, humans used fire as an offering to the deities and the spirits of the land.

Fire elementals

Fire elementals, like Fire itself, have dual roles providing light and heat to aid humankind, while at the same time being a force of death and destruction. They are certainly dramatic in their effects, such as sheets, forks or balls of lightning at the height of a storm. Lightning was believed to be the fury of the deities, as well as the earliest manifestation of fire. The forest fire can devastate whole areas of woodland in its path, killing animals, birds and humans. The elementals of Fire may also be experienced as volcanic activity, hot geysers and springs and in meteor showers.

But they also have many positive functions, including the power to filter non-harmful rays from the sun and transform the sun's light, essential for life, warmth and plant and animal growth. Through photosynthesis, they enable plants to produce from solar energy starches and sugars that we absorb through food.

They are attracted to and energise any source of kindled flame, including ritual festival blazes, with their ancient cleansing and fertilising properties. Elementals are also present in the hearth fire, traditionally the source of warmth at which the living and ancestors were once welcomed. Their energy ignites every candle lit to seek a blessing. In the modern world, they empower new forms of heating and cooking, as well as machine and vehicle fuels. But being the most ambivalent of the elementals they equally source global warming.

Ritual fires were and still sometimes are kindled by friction, because it was believed that wood contained burning fire. The West Coast Maidu American Indians tell that the earth began as a ball of fire that gradually cooled so that soil and trees grew on top. However, the roots of trees are still connected to this fiery centre and so fire may be created directly from wood (or the Fire elemental released, according to your perspective). Fire elementals would transform the offerings (or in earlier times the sacrifice) made on these ritual fires to ascend on the smoke and flames to the deities. For this reason, the ash of festival fires was scattered on the fields to convey the essence of the offerings and the fire power to make the fields fertile and to add necessary minerals to the earth (see ash magick on pages 348–9). In the same way, in the Hindu religion, the ashes of cremated loved ones from all over the world are still returned to the sacred river Ganges by relatives.

Elemental fire spirits and magick

Salamanders

Salamanders have been described as fire lizards or lizard people who originate from the Middle East in desert places. However, you can experience and work with their energies in any land. In shimmering heat, especially on sand, they resemble large golden upright lizards that come in and out of vision like a mirage. According to the power source (the sun is a great energiser), they can appear huge and occasionally manifest as beautiful, dancing females with lizard-like eyes and flaming hair. In Australian Aboriginal myth, the salamanders or Sleepy Lizard Women made their camp on what became Uluru (Ayers Rock), the red sacred hill that rose from the ashes after the camp of the Sleepy Lizard Women was burned.

Like the chameleon, salamanders are constantly changing colour and always moving like flame itself. Salamanders are creatures of the hottest part of the day and of high summer. Their natural home is in volcanoes or lakes of fire, but you can see them in large wood-burning bonfires and ritual fires; the larger the source of fire, the greater the perceived size of the salamander or indeed any other Fire spirit. At night, they can be manifest as sudden flares of light, big enough to light up the night sky for a moment or two, even though there is no lightning.

Unlike the other typical elemental spirits, such as the gnomes of the Earth element, salamanders, and indeed all Fire spirits, remain very close to the elemental power of Fire and are continually fuelled by the actual element. A Fire spirit will absorb the power of any fire it encounters and grow temporarily larger, more dynamic and more potent. But because they are made of balls of energy or light, Fire spirits tend to be far shorter lived than other elemental nature forms.

Like all Fire spirits, salamanders are readers of thought and mood. Therefore you should only carry out any Fire magick when you are calm and positive, and carry Water crystals such as fluorite or jade.

Salamanders will only work with you for a very short time and will remain in a particular fire source no longer than the fire lasts. However, you should limit any direct salamander contact to about five or ten minutes. Always leave them first and leave the fire burning safely or the sunny place you visualised them, so that they can return to their collective Fire source at the time of their choosing. Afterwards, splash yourself with cool water on your hairline, your brow, your throat and your wrist pulse points. Nothing bad would happen if you didn't, but you might feel irritable and jumpy for a while.

The good qualities that salamanders foster in humans are courage, willpower, and the determination and confidence to achieve anything or overcome the most fearsome opposition. Their faults are cruelty, aggressiveness and encouraging excesses of all kinds.

Their king is a flaming being called Djinn, a glorious fire-like creature with flashing ruby eyes, who is never still. He rules despotically all Fire spirits, sometimes with generosity and laughter, but at other times with the roar of a lion, snuffing them out of being on a whim. He lives in the heart of the sun or in other accounts in the hidden Emerald Mountains, and his fingers flash flames and lightning flares. He shimmers at the height of an electrical storm and may be seen striding in scarlet robes through the centre of a forest fire, occasionally rescuing a small animal or bird but as easily trampling one underfoot, for he is totally ruled by the moment.

Djinn dances through ritual fire, accepting the finest flowers and fruits as his own and sending out blazing embers or shooting flames to any who are not dancing, stamping or drumming to the movement of the flames. Djinn holds the sun at the heart of an eclipse, teasing the world that it may never return. But he tosses it back into the sky, because without its fire he too would cease to be.

Fire nature spirits

There are remarkably few Fire nature spirits, precisely because they are so unstable in form. In the Middle East, their land of origin, and especially in the Islamic tradition, jinns or djinns live on earth in a parallel universe and so are invisible, except to children and wise men or women. It was said they were created before mortals from smokeless fire and that their home is in the mystical mountains made of emeralds.

It is said that they travel with the speed of light. Jinns can take any form and it was considered to take the skill of a master magician to contain one in a lamp. However, the user of such a magick lamp had to be very careful what was asked for, as the genie would take the wish literally. Also, the number of wishes was limited, after which the genie was free and then could turn against the owner of the lamp, if the owner had been unwise with his or her wishes or unkind to the genie. In the Old Testament, King Solomon had a magick ring with which he summoned Jinns to help his armies win battles. Solomon was a master magician whose wisdom came from the secret book of the Angel Raziel.

Jinns are regarded as lower than Angels both because of their unpredictability and because they are creatures of Fire and so not immortal. I would advise even the most experienced witch against trying to persuade a Fire elemental to enter a bottle and be guardian of her home and, as with the salamander, to work outdoors, even when using an oil torch or lamp to which they are especially attracted.

Fire essences or fairies

I have learned a lot more about Fire essences over the past few months. Though they are called fairies, they are more like fire elves, winged and constantly moving, but much sharper than the normal fey being. They can give you a nasty burn if you are not careful when the hearth fire or candle starts sparking. They may be unpredictable, shoot out embers or tip over an unsecured candle at the height of excitement.

These essences are by far the most common and friendly of the unpredictable Fire spirits and may be seen in any open fire or hearth, around bonfires, in fires lit on beaches or lake sides and in the modern world round barbecues and chiminea or round flickering candles, especially beeswax. They like wood or fossil fuels such as barbecue coals. You may also see them on summer evenings after dark as fireflies. You will detect their presence by a sudden uprush of small flames or sparks or a candle flame that sparkles and dances even if there is no breeze, but they will not stay long.

If any choose to bless your ritual or spell then you will experience extra good fortune and abundance in your life, but I do not find they can be invoked or directly addressed; nor will they always be present in a candle or fire, though the less structured elemental force will be fuelling it.

Fire dragons

Dragons are the most powerful of the Fire creatures and may once have roamed the earth. Smaller Komodo dragons, which can grow to over 2 metres (6 ft) and still live in Indonesia, remind us of their strange beauty. The archetypal European and Scandinavian dragon is famed for being huge, six-limbed scaly, winged creature breathing fire that guarded the minerals and gems of the earth from the greedy.

Dragons symbolise the ability to overcome huge obstacles or odds through their stored Fire power that was released in the dragon's breath. Indeed, in the dragon-slaying legends, this power was absorbed into the hero, who thereafter became an even mightier warrior. The flames they breathed were pure Fire power and places where there was scorched earth where dragons landed after flight were regarded as sites of buried treasure, and in China and the Celtic world as the site of healing plants, especially for sexual potency.

In Scandinavia, dragons had place of honour on the prow of Viking ships as a symbol of power and courage and the ability to overcome tumultuous seas and enemies alike. In the historical Anglo-Saxon Chronicle, dated 793 CE, lights and flames in the sky were interpreted as fire-breathing dragons, who were warning of earthly disasters caused by human bad behaviour.

Calling dragons

Dragons are a wonderful focus for Fire magick since they take physical Fire spell power into the spiritual realms where now they exist and bounce it back, filled with energy to enrich our lives. Their power is represented in magick spells by tarragon, the dragon herb and dragon's blood incense.

Scatter circles of tarragon around a piece of gold jewellery or a gold-coloured item while burning dragon's blood and call on dragon power. In doing so, you can transfer the positive power of the dragon to the charm to bring you courage, abundance and fertility in the way you most need it. Also, add empowered tarragon (see page 570) to food or carry it in a protection/empowerment charm bag.

Any caves close to the shore on rocky hillsides are natural places to call on dragon power if you sit outside looking in and leave gold coins or small pieces of gold jewellery, such as an earring, as an offering in return for a wish, echoed into the cave. You can use a dragon figure on your altar as a focus for this golden energy, surrounded by small golden items, burning dragon's blood and small gold candles on the altar to connect with the energy.

Fire as an offering

As well as forming the means by which herbs, flowers and salt can be offered in ritual, the lighting of the Fire is in itself a sacred act. It returns to the gods their own gift of Fire as tribute and also by keeping a perpetual flame burning. In a number of cultures, women have traditionally been the guardians of constantly burning fires both in the home and as priestesses, tending the eternally burning flame of a state, city or country: for example, the Vestal Virgins of Rome.

The holy fire at the shrine of the 5th century Irish Saint Bridget in Kildare was dedicated originally to the Celtic Sun Goddess Brighid. It is believed to have burned unquenched for more than 1,000 years. It was tended first by 19 virgin priestesses of the Goddess called the Daughters of the Sacred Flame, and later by the nuns of the Abbey at Kildare.

When you have a day at home, you can keep a flame burning on your altar all day and replace it whenever it becomes low with an ongoing prayer or offering. For special occasions, use a longer burning candle (in a very safe holder or set somewhere it cannot catch fire) to signify a blessing for healing or for protection or abundance that need accumulated power.

Your Goddess candle lit first can act as your central flame for all other lights in a spell or ritual. You can also institute candle webs with friends and families everywhere using long burning candles. One of you can send a mail or message to ensure the next person lights their candle before the current flame burns low. This is a wonderful way of creating ongoing power for global issues such as peace, but also if you have a very sick friend or family member who needs a great deal of continuous strength.

Six steps to absorbing Fire strength for personal empowerment, healing and in ritual

I After dark, create a ring of fire for ritual. This fire can be as large and complex or as small and simple as you wish. If using small fires in metal containers or garden fire torches outdoors, make them sufficiently far apart so the fires will not close in and trap you in the centre. But you can equally use a ring of tea lights or candles indoors and sit in the centre. With small fires, pre-light them and cast a twig from a bundle into each fire as you say an empowerment over it.

You will use the fire source to initiate the power as the first fire or candle is lit and named for the ritual purpose. Then you will begin to raise the power as the second flame is lit from a taper or small fire torch from the first fire and also named. The third flame is lit from the second and so on clockwise until all are on fire. Each time you light a flame state the intention of the spell: for example:

I kindle this flame for the courage to be with the woman I love. Fire grow, fire glow. It shall be so by the power of the Fire.

When all the flames are lit move round the inside of the flames faster and faster repeating the empowerment. Leave a large space between the first and last flames so you and others can safely enter and leave the circle or if you prefer dance and chant round the outside after the flames are lit.

Release the power by calling out the final empowerment when you can chant or move no faster. Then sit quietly and let the flames die away.

If working with a group, each person can choose a small fire or candle and stand outside the circle behind it. The first person lights the first fire torch with a taper and says the empowerment and then carries the taper to the second person who is behind the fire on the left and goes to sit in the centre of the circle. This can continue round the circle with the words, Pass the magick on, as the light is passed from person to person. If the fires are pre-lit, each person has a twig and burns it in their fire, one after the other, again ending with the words, Pass the magick on, to herald the burning of the next twig.

You can either work repeating an empowerment for a collective or global need or each person makes their own fire affirmation and then everyone moves round in a circle, chanting:

Fire grow, for glow. It shall be so by the power of the Fire.

On the final release each can call their own personal Fire wish.

Candles or tea lights can be lit from a sitting circle if others are present, where each person reaches over to pass on the lighted taper and so the magick. The power can be raised by chanting as above and then for the final release the individual or collective wish is called at a prearranged signal by one person and every light extinguished at the same moment, to send the Fire into the sky. Fire circles are also very good for casting psychic defence around yourself or sending the power to the vulnerable.

2 For even more instant effect, whirl a large lighted incense stick really fast round yourself as you stand in total darkness, while calling faster and faster your need or desire. Then make a final spiral over your head bringing the fire downwards and vertically up again, as you release the power: wonderful at night if you need a burst of courage for the next day. Alternatively, in fire, against the night sky, write your personal magickal names and an affirmation of what you are and what you can achieve, with the swirling stick empowerments.

This is another excellent group or coven activity when one person lights their incense from a candle and says a prearranged group empowerment. For example:

May we be filled with the fire of love and healing.

Or:

May Sandra be freed from her overwhelming depression and know the fires of joy/life again.

He or she then takes the candle to the next person, returns to their place in the circle and begin to whirl their incense. When all the incense sticks are alight and moving, the group can chant faster and swirl faster. At the final call, each plunges their stick into an individual dish of sand or earth set in front of them and sits in the darkness, seeing in the after glow and the light of the single candle set in the centre of the circle, the fire carrying their wishes to the stars.

3 Fire offerings are an ancient tradition that is still central to Wicca and other religions. For example, in the Vedic tradition Homa or offerings are made to Agni, Lord of Fire to carry them to Vishnu, the Preserver God. Each kind of offering has its own significance: for example, aromatic substances indicate a blessing for health, milk the desired birth of a son, lotus seeds or lemon flowers prosperity and sesame seeds for both peace and acclaim.

Light a small fire or a large candle in a bucket or cauldron of sand and decide on your own symbolic offerings. You will need nine small ones, which in a candle could be nine petals or a fire nine flowers. You can use the herb or flower meanings beginning on page 551 or you could use common associations such as seeds for new life, dead leaves for taking away sorrow or what needs to be lost, orange or apple peel for fertility, seaweed for prosperity or the return of a lost love. In fact, you can name any symbol for a purpose or write on nine squares of paper what you wish to gain or lose as a single word or image. If for attracting, write the word larger on each piece of paper. If for banishing, begin with it large and reduce it. so by the last piece of paper it is barely visible. Cast the offerings one after the other into the fire or hold them in the candle until they catch light and drop them in the sand.

4 Fire and water as opposites come together in a fusion of power. There are a number of rituals where a fire is created on the shore as the tide is coming in and offerings are cast on it. The fire is below the shore line and so the sea washes over it. A variation is practised on seasonal festivals in a number of parts of the world, including Spain and Mexico. On the Summer Solstice, people go to the shore in great numbers and float candle boats into the sea to carry wishes and empowerments. This method is very effective for launching creative ventures or new enterprises that involve the fulfilment of dearly held desires.

Go to a lake, a deep pool or the sea and make nine small driftwood boats with flat pieces of wood you find on the shore. On each set a small beeswax candle or one made from organic materials that will not pollute the water. Light each candle in turn and float it gently on the water, naming your creative venture for each one and saying for each:

> May Fire carry [name] swiftly and powerfully to where it will find a welcome and expression. So mote it be.

When all nine are launched, send out nine proposals or offers of your services when you get home.

5 Find natural salamander and Djinn places, such as sand on a lake or sea shore in shimmering sun at noon or naturally sandy hillsides. On holidays, try to spend time in desert or sandy scrubland. If you cannot visit Egypt, a safe Middle Eastern country or Africa, there are deserts or rock and sand places in Spain, Greece and Turkey, and areas such as Arizona are natural salamander haunts. Anywhere lizards naturally live is a potential salamander site. If you cannot visit such places or live in a cold land, light a huge bonfire on a grassless area and set fire torches to attract salamanders to the light.

Half close your eyes and feel the warmth and excitement within you and know anything is possible. Project your wishes outwards aloud in a soft slow chant as you move your fingers slowly in spirals through the air and press your feet into the sand.

Study also Komodo dragons, iguana, chameleons, geckos and real salamanders in a conservation park and learn about their habitats. They have very different energies from snakes but were chosen as the magickal covering for the Fire elemental spirits. If you can manage close encounters you may get some very strange telepathic messages, often creative inspiration but remember they can be tricksters.

6 Ash magick is based in the incredible power with which fire transforms wood and other raw materials into energy and leaves a mineral rich residue, as long as the fuel is not polluted by chemicals. This mineral richness is the practical as well as magickal reason the ashes from festival fires were scattered on the fields to bring fertility.

Save ashes from your own festival fires in sealed containers to mix with soil when you need their particular energies: for example, the new beginnings of the Spring Equinox fires. Use a sprinkling of this empowered soil in charm bags or add it to earth in which new plants or crystals have been set, to symbolise new blessings coming from the old that has been buried. Festival ashes are also very protective against all harm and attract abundance if a few are placed in a sealed jar on the hearth or in the kitchen.

Burn different woods or pure herbal incenses: for example, hazel for justice, ash for healing or travel, and alder for security. Scatter a little on earth after the ritual to get the spell energies moving. Preserve the rest like the festival ashes in small, sealed jars and use as for festival ashes.

The power of candles

Candles offer an instant and safe form of Fire power in a confined space or indoors. Use as pure a candle as possible: for example, beeswax or pure wax rather than paraffin based. At its root, candle magick is simple and yet spiritually profound.

What follows are the basic steps to magickal candle burning. If you are an experienced witch, extend this into a prolonged private rite. Watch the candle flame for an hour or more and allow the magickal energies to pass to and fro between you and the candle, raising the power entirely within you without words or movements. Move the energies up a notch at a time in your mind until you are ready to extinguish the candle and catch the full force of the rite within yourself: heady stuff.

* The candle acts as the symbol for wishes or to attract or banish what you need. First purify it by setting it flat diagonally across the pentacle and touching the wick with the point of the athame or wand.

* Ask that the candle be made ready for the purpose for which it is intended (state the purpose) and that its released Fire may carry only what is pure, just and of worth. You can ask for the blessings of the Goddess, the lord and lady or any deity or Archangel connected with the purpose. I do not like the concept of exorcising candles, as described in some more formal Books of Shadows, because to me the word has negative connotations.

* The colour you choose and/or the astrological colour will be influenced by what the candle symbolises (see page 529).

* After purification, you could engrave the candle with any symbols or words you felt appropriate, using a special silver paper knife or engraving tool you keep for special candle magick work (though of course you can use anything, such as a metal nail). You could use an astrological glyph for a person (see page 451). Keeping special tools for special ceremonies does help to give you a good repository of spiritual energies and you can have a long wooden box for all your candles and related equipment.

* If you wish, you could then anoint the candle with a scented oil or pure olive oil to reinforce the purpose (see page 530 for more on this). However, this, like engraving, is an optional stage.

* Next you need to set the candle in the centre of the altar and light it either from the Goddess candle or if you prefer the God candle (lit from the Goddess

candle) or from a lighted taper, a slender wand-like candle used for this purpose.

* As you kindle the candle flame, quietly ask for the blessings of Fire to transform your purpose (state it again) into actuality. If the Fire elementals and spirits seem too unpredictable to trust, ask the blessing of one of the Archangels of Fire such as Uriel for melting away opposition and for protection, Samael or Azrael for cleansing and banishing or Michael of the Sun for attracting.

* The moon phase, day of the week etc may be significant, unless a need is urgent. For a really significant or major purpose, you could find when the moon is full in your time zone and locality (local papers are usually a good source for this) and light the candle at the precise minute the moon becomes full. For full effect, you would then extinguish it at the end of the minute.

* Generally, gaze into the flame and picture the fulfilment of your desire or petition. Extend this silent contemplation time for progressively longer periods as you become familiar with candle magick.

* If you wish, you can make a small offering into the melted wax round the flame, either a few herbs or salt.

* You need to decide in advance how long the candle will burn, whether all the way through to mark the ritual time, and if so whether or not you will keep vigil until it is burned. Alternatively, do you wish to extinguish it after speaking certain words aloud or in your mind and will relight it on subsequent days?

* If it was a banishing ritual, you could light a white candle of hope from a darker one, before extinguishing the dark one midway through the rite. You could light two smaller candles from the single larger one to mark a separation of two people, or conversely for unity start with two candles and light one single one from them both to signify coming together in love or reconciliation. In both cases, you can safely leave the separate candles burning to acknowledge the identity and free will of the people represented.

* A candle ritual can be one entirely of contemplation and quiet words or you can raise the power as with any spell with chanting or movement. To release power, cup your hands around the side of the candle, not touching it as you might burn yourself. With your fingers feel the releasing energy pushing into the candle and extinguish it with:

So mote it be.

When the power is released, you could close the rite softly with one of the old chants or runes, like:

I call on Earth to bind my spell, I ask for Air to speed it well,
Water make the magick flow and Fire to flame and let it grow.
One in four and four as one, the Five of Spirit, all is done.
Blessings be. The rite is ended.

* There is debate over whether you should snuff or pinch out candles that you do not wish to burn completely away. I believe the act of blowing out a candle is itself a magickal release of power and rather than holding the light in a snuffer,

you can send it forth to all who need it. What is more you are infusing the light with your own precious essence. The belief in not blowing out a candle dates from times when it was thought that the person would lose part of their soul when they sneezed or deliberately exhaled breath. But it is entirely your choice.

* You can buy candles with two or three wicks so that a new one can be lit each day in a three day ritual. Larger candles can have up to seven wicks. If you need a lot of power you can light all the wicks during a single ritual. Candles vary considerably in their burning times: the better quality ones may state the number of hours. In practice, if you use the same source of candles, you will be able to assess whether you need one that will have burned through by the end of an evening in a dusk ritual or it is an all night vigil candle: for example, on one of the Solstices.

* What should you do with the candle afterwards? If used for an attracting purpose and you have not engraved or anointed it, you can place it in its holder on the pentacle and touch its wick with the wand or athame once more. Say:

So is the candle freed from its purpose. Its work is done and I give thanks.

* You could then burn it around the home. For an anointed and engraved candle, relight it on the altar and leave it to burn through.

* For a banishing candle it is probably worth disposing of it in an environmentally friendly way.

PRACTICAL ASSIGNMENT

Making the Fire element the basis for a whole spell

* Use red, orange or gold candles at each of the four quarters of the altar.

* Dance, use rattles and or firm intense drumming as part of your spell or ritual to raise the Fire power.

* For a special ritual for power, protection or courage, create a Fire altar in the south of your altar room and face south. Add a dragon icon to symbolise the Goddess or a statue of Sekhmet, the lion-headed Fire Goddess of Ancient Egypt and Ra for the God. Put a dish of Fire crystals, such as amber, carnelian, desert rose or red jasper, in the north, frankincense or tarragon incense in the east, a red candle in the south and water in which amber or carnelian crystals have been soaked or better still burn a Fire fragrance oil, such as frankincense. Use a red altar cloth and red flowers. After the ritual, keep symbols of abundance on the altar, such as gold items of jewellery, gold-coloured flowers and coins, to draw abundance to your household in the way it is most needed.

* Alternatively, centre the spell or ritual round your fire dish or cauldron with a candle in sand. On a small altar, create a candle offering dish, a wide heatproof bowl with sand or soil in the middle piled as a mound to support a candle. Round the edges of the offering dish put a selection of Fire herbs (see page 140) or red, orange and gold-coloured flower petals as offerings.

- Use the lighting of the candle/fire and making the offerings to build up the power. If you want to include a lot of chanting, dancing and drumming, conduct a whole ritual based round the cauldron or Fire dish instead of the altar or a large metal bucket or pot with a candle in sand in the centre. You can burn wishes in the form of dried herbs or small branches on the fire. Alternatively, burn away what you no longer need as dead twigs or flowers.
- Use golden-coloured fruits, nuts and seeds in a Fire empowerment ritual. Either alone or in a group, light four golden candles at the four directions. In the centre of the altar set a gold-coloured dish (or one covered with gold foil or paper) piled high with the fruits etc.
- Name very fast all the positive attributes of Fire, both from the list on page 140 and all the things you associate with Fire at its most empowering. If in a group, let one person drum or clap to keep up the fast rhythm so the attributes are named by the unconscious mind. If alone, clap or drum softly.
- When no more words come, stop drumming eat a nut, seed or fruit for each Fire quality (you can use very small fruits like golden grapes or pre-cut slices of Satsuma). As you take each one, name the Fire power you are absorbing and how you will use it for yourself and then to help. In a group, take turns to eat and speak. When you/the group wish to add no more say:

By the power of the Fire I/we give thanks for these blessings.

Either collectively or alone, blow out all the candles at once, if possible.

Further research

There are numerous aspects of Fire traditions that can enrich your rituals. Choose one or more that fascinate you but about which you know little that you can weave into your rituals or add to your growing collection of symbols and myths in your Book of Shadows.

Explore some of the old myths about how Fire came to humans: for example, how in Maori legend, the inventor and trickster hero Maui stole fire for the people from the female Fire Guardian Maui-Tinihanga.

Alternatively explore the concept of the sacred flame among, for example, the Vestal Virgins of Rome, as well as other cultures where it was of ritual significance.

Investigate the magickal traditions of blacksmiths and metalworker that can be found from sub-Saharan Africa to Scandinavian dwarf lore.

Explore fire rituals in Shamanism.

Study the transformative role of Fire in alchemy where it signified sulphur, one of the three main elements.

Further information

Recommended reading

* Byock, Jesse, *Saga of the Volsungs, the Norse Epic of Sigurd the Dragon Slayer*, Penguin, 1999
* Eason, Cassandra, *Candle Power*, Blandford (Octopus Books), 1999, Sterling US, 2000
* Gamache, Henri, *The Master Book of Candle Burning, How to Burn Candles for Every Purpose*, Original Publications, 1998
* Ingersoll, Ernest, *Dragons and Dragon Lore*, Dover Publications, 2005
* Newcomb, Jason, *The New Hermetics, 21st Century Magick for Illumination and Power*, Red Wheel/Weiser, 2004
* Singer, Marian, *Dancing the Fire: The inside and outside of Neopagan festivals and gatherings*, Citadel, 2005
* Ward Helen *Working with Dragons*, Templar Publishing, 2004

Websites

* *Black Drago*
  Linked pages with a great deal of dragon information
  www.blackdrago.com/hist.htm
* *Dragon history*
  Good site on dragon lore
  www.dragon-history.com
* *Fire Ritual*
  Detailed essay on fire rituals
  www.net-info.nl/fire.htm
* *Fire Rituals*
  Illustrated with photographs, personal account of group fire rite
  www.hawkdancing.com/firerite.html
* *Hecate's Cauldron*
  Good general candle magick background
  www.hecatescauldron.org/Candle%20Magick.htm
* *Monstrous*
  Very detailed and informative dragon site
  http://dragons.monstrous.com/dragons_types_gallery_htm
* *Salagram*
  Comprehensive site describing Hindu candle and fire ceremonies with reference to other traditions
  www.salagram.net/CBR-page.htm

THE POWER OF WATER

All life came from the sea. Water is the first undifferentiated element in many creation myths from around the world and contains the potential for all life. In Genesis Chapter I, we are told:

2. The earth was without form, and void; and darkness was on the face of the deep. And the Spirit of God was moving over the face of the waters.

6. And God said, 'Let there be a firmament in the midst of the waters, and let it divide the waters from the waters.'

7. And God made the firmament, and divided the waters which were under the firmament from the waters which were above the firmament. And it was so.

8. And God called the firmament Heaven. And there was evening and there was morning, a second day.

Wells are considered in many cultures to come directly from the waters of the womb of the Earth Mother and so water from springs and wells has always been considered sacred and healing. Indeed, without water fertile land becomes desert and people, animals and plants cannot live.

Water is formless, shaped by its container, and in nature, too, whether by riverbanks, in a dam or by the shores of the land. But being an element, Water may become unpredictable and overflow or spill from the ritual bowl or cup and its waters rise above the riverbanks or tide line to flood the land. Every land has its flood story. After the terrible tragedy of the South East Asian tsunami on Boxing Day 2004, the Biblical account of Noah's Ark or the myths of Atlantis, submerged by Zeus with a huge tidal wave in a day and a night, no longer seem so unbelievable.

Spiritually water or wine is contained in formal magick in the sacred vessel of the chalice that symbolises the Holy Grail cup of Christ, the Celtic Cauldron of Dagda the Irish Good Father, or Cerridwen the Crone Goddess. In magick spells, Water is the flowing elemental force that connects the other elements, acting as the channel for the spell energies. Finally, it carries the transformed and released power of a spell to where it is most needed in the spellcaster's life. To do this, it connects with positive emotions generated by the spell that psychologically, as well as psychically, open up the horizons of possibility.

Water elementals like water spirits assume many forms because of the huge variations in the nature and character of water, from still deep ponds to fast flowing rivers, cascading waterfalls and tumultuous oceans. Water Spirits can be gentle, like the naiads, the nymphs of rivers, springs and the fountains who live in caves near or in water or under the surface of rivers and die if the water source dries up. But there are also the nereids of the Aegean, unpredictable and cruel as the sea, with their hypnotic voices calling through the mist. The nereids are said to drive mad any who perceive them under a full moon. Because they cannot have children themselves, legends tell how they kidnapped mortal infants and raised them in coral caves.

Water creatures likewise vary from healing intelligent dolphins and predatory sharks to fertile frogs and darting shoals of fish or fabulous coral, starfish and sea horses. In this module, we will explore some of the different kinds of Water energies and work with its healing and peace giving powers that can change almost instantly to a sudden spiritual weir or rapids to carry us on to another unexpected but exciting course.

Water elementals

Without the Water elementals there would be no life, for they are the creatures who give force to the rain pouring downwards and the hidden water courses, sacred wells and springs that rise through the earth. They offer pure water for drinking and healing and release it from the soil to nourish the plants and fill waterholes for the animals from the skies and the earth.

Water elementals direct water from the melting snows of mountain peaks, down ever widening rivers to the sea, and then cause water to evaporate and rise into the atmosphere in the never ending cycle. As the tides, Water elementals obey the moon and sun, but without warning they can encroach on the land as an unusually high tide or a rushing tidal bore turning a tranquil river into a cascading fury. They are not evil but neutral, and so their effects can be unpredictable, as with the other elementals.

Responsible for marine life of all kinds they are invoked in rituals by indigenous fishermen and hunters of sea mammals for a good catch and are offered the bones of slain creatures and the finest of the catch in age-old ceremonies. Sea pollution and over fishing by developed nations, as well as the unnecessary slaughter of young seals for their pelts, and keeping mammals such as dolphins and whales in unsuitable water parks, angers the Water elementals. It may be that their sporadic protection of fisher people and sailors is diminishing as a result.

Water elementals have been appeased with offerings for thousands of years and the principle of exchange for favours with humans is probably stronger with them than with any other elemental force except for the Earth spirits. If you cast offerings such as crystals, flowers, fruit or gold earrings into water and make petitions or wishes, good fortune and health will gradually flow into your life; from you likewise will flow away anything you no longer need in your daily world.

Like water itself, Water elementals will take on the form of any vessel in which water is temporarily or permanently stored.

Elemental water spirits

Undines are small, beautiful, water nymphs that dance upon the waves, shimmering with water rainbows. Sometimes they ride on the waves and appear as pearly foam. Because they are the most insubstantial of the Water spirits they are most usually perceived even by clairvoyants as distant rainbows on the waters, even on dark days. They also dance around rock pools at low tide or in salt marshes. In marshes, they may wear green glass beads.

Some Greek islanders claim kinship from the salt water undines. Though they are primarily spirits of the Aegean Sea, undines are found in different forms in other lands especially in warmer waters. They also inhabit freshwater sources such as marshlands, springs, streams and wells, but where possible stay close to the coast.

Smaller undines have wings, but unlike fairies that they resemble, they only live in plants and flowers close to water or near estuaries. Undines care for all the sea creatures and for water plants and coral.

The qualities they encourage in humans are harmony with the seasons, empathy with others and spontaneity. The faults they bring out are emotional manipulation, sentimentality and possessiveness.

Undines are ruled by the queen Nicksa, Nixsa or Neksa who rises from the sea, translucent, riding a giant seahorse or in a pearly or sea-green chariot pulled by pure white seahorses. She has long flowing hair, knotted with shells and a swirling cloak in all the colours of the sea, edged with pearls. She loves pearls above all other gems. Her voice may be soft and melodious, like the mermaids she also rules, or terrible as the stormy sea. She lives in deep coral caves far beneath the sea. Nicksa is attended by the oceanides, the beautiful sea nymph daughters of Oceanus, Titan Lord of the Sea.

Water spirits

Water spirits are generally polarised into either benign or hostile spirits and take quite definite forms according to the nature and movements of the water source they inhabit. Some of these nature essences are welcoming to humans, but others can be unpredictable or dangerous, reflecting the hazards of the actual deep or fast-flowing waters that they rule. One example of benign water sprites is the oreads, mountain spring dwellers that are believed to endow water with healing properties. For this reason, over many centuries floral offerings have been made to them at mountain or river shrines.

Malevolent spirits were believed to reside in deep dark pools or treacherous stretches of rivers. It was dangerous to bathe in these places, not only because of the malicious spirit, but also in practical terms because of hidden currents or sudden depth change.

Though some bad-tempered water spirits were given a generic name, like nacken in Sweden or nixes in Germany, others developed individual personalities and legends of their origin. The lorelei is now a term for any seductive water sprite near rocky or hazardous places on fast-flowing rivers in Western Europe. The original Lorelei was a beautiful young female water fairy that sat on the cliffs above the Rhine river and sang haunting songs. Her voice was irresistible, so luring sailors to their deaths on the rocks below, as they tried to climb to reach her and her voice moved ever further away towards lethal precipices.

Most famous of the sea spirits are the mer people, human from the waist up, the women with long golden hair and beautiful faces with fish or porpoise-like body in place of the legs. The men tend to be less attractive and can whip up storms if annoyed or jealous of sailors who are attracted to their women. Sailors have brought back tales of beautiful sea women with lovely voices, from all parts of the world and in all ages, telling how mer people have saved drowning sailors and guided ships away from rocks. Mermaids are seen most in shoals around islands that have magickal associations, such as Gotland in Sweden or Crete in Greece.

Six ways of using Water for healing, empowerment and in rituals

1 A sacred Water place can be set up anywhere in your home, in addition to your main altar. Its spreading energies will benefit family and visitors alike and ensure that abundance, peace and positive emotions flow freely through your home.

   Centre it around a small water feature or a tank of goldfish. In Feng Shui, goldfish are a symbol of prosperity and health and incredibly soothing. Enclose the space with green trailing plants, with tiny indoor lemon trees and Water crystals such as orbicular or ocean jasper, green jasper, pearls, green and purple fluorite, jade and aquamarine. You can add Water symbols, such as a lucky Chinese toad with a coin in its mouth, to encourage prosperity, shells and natural driftwood sculptures formed by the sea.

2 Wherever you live there will be legends of water spirits. Try to visit a variety of water places like still lakes with their beautiful lake women, such as the Welsh fair-haired Gwragedd Annwn. These fairy women, the same size as humans, live in underwater palaces in lakes close to the Black Mountains. On occasions, according to myth, they have taken human husbands, though they rarely stayed with them. Some local families still claim fey heritage. Lake women are famed for their healing powers and their kindness to the poor, mothers, children and pregnant women.

   Find out the stories and picture the spirits (you may even find artists' impressions in guide books or old local customs books). If there are no legends attached to the body of water that you can uncover, sit there at the place in the early morning and twilight and weave a story about one of the spirits you sense there.

   Scribble an image of the water people that come into your mind. Record your legend and maybe post it on a local website or in a local journal, emphasising it is a story. You may find other people contact you with similar experiences or someone recalls an actual legend that is frequently strikingly similar to the one that came to you from the collective well of wisdom. By such means over years the magick of a place is woven and enhanced by people's experiences and impressions.

3 Find a local Water place you can visit easily and frequently in different weathers and seasons. Tune into the changing moods of its Water sprites and try to focus on one individual sprite you sense is in tune with you.

   In your mind, ask their name and find a place close to the water where you can sit quietly. Each time you visit, take a small stone or shell from the shore line as a token and keep it with you between visits. Next time you go, cast it into the water or return it to the spot you found it.

At the same time, on each visit hide a small token of your own on or near the shore line: a very tiny crystal, a pearl from a broken necklace, a flower newly blooming in your garden, or tie a ribbon in natural fibre such as silk on an overhanging tree. Leave it with a blessing to the Water spirits. Whether they take it, leave it there or someone else finds it, then you are increasing the good energies of the place. You may find other people start to leave offerings and so you can over time create a water shrine.

4 Try to discover a holy well in your area. It may be in a churchyard, dedicated to a saint, and there may be an annual well-dressing ceremony with flowers or a celebration on the saint's special day. Explore the pre-Christian history and you may discover how the same water was once under the guardianship of a water nymph or minor water deity. The connection will be easy if you have a Bridewell (Brighid, the Celtic Triple Goddess), St Anne the grandmother of Christ wells (often formerly Ana or Danu the Irish Mother Goddess wells) and Lady wells dedicated to the Virgin Mary (the pre-Christian Mother Goddess, maybe as the Celtic/Roman Madrona or Matronae the three mothers).

If it is a sacred spring or well or water source that is pure, take a little water home with you after asking the Water guardian and/or the permission of the earthly guardian. You can use this for rubbing on your brow if you have a headache or feel stressed or for sprinkling round your home as a blessing.

5 Write a list of all the different kinds of water sources and list the kinds of blessings you feel each water source might offer: for example, still pools peace and reconciliation, the sea for power or the return of what is lost, fast-flowing rivers for moves of all kinds and travel. Then match each with the kind of offering most appropriate and decide whether it should be cast into the water, buried in the soil or sand near the water's edge or left below the tide line. These form embryo rituals and you can try out one or two contrasting ones when you next visit water.

6 Either in connection with the above or separately, create different Water chants and blessings to reflect the different energies, for the ebb tide, for waterfalls, for blocked streams, for waterholes where animals drink and even floods. These will greatly increase your capacity for spontaneous ritual and also help you to connect on a deep level with the Water element in spells and rituals.

Enhancing the power of Water in ritual

The Water element in magick is the least utilised element. We enrich Air with a variety of incenses to add significance. We can use salt, soil or herbs with different magickal meanings for the Earth element and appropriate candle colours for the Fire element. But Water can also be fused with different energies and there are numerous ways you can do this using crystals, cosmic energies like sunlight, fragrances, weather extremes such as storms and colours.

After making it you can empower your magickal water for its purpose by chanting over it and circling it with your wand or putting it in the chalice/ritual bowl for ritual. You would empower ritual water as for any sacred water at the beginning of a formal ritual by setting the water bowl on the pentacle, blessing it with the athame/wand and adding salt if you were using salt water for opening the circle. Having made your waters you can bottle, label and refrigerate them. You can buy a suitable bottle at pharmacies or from glassmakers. The glass should be clear for waters intended for energising, cleansing and empowering, dark for gentle healing or protective waters or can be the colour of the crystal used in making them. The waters will keep for several weeks.

As well as the Water element in spells and rituals, you can use your magickal waters in baths, for anointing or protecting your chakras, in house or altar room blessings and in making or adding to drinks. Blue lace agate water is excellent for defusing confrontational situations and softening critical words of sharp-tongued people. You can also put the waters in pet bowls or on plants to energise or heal them, sprinkle the water on wasteland to make it grow or pour it into polluted waters with a blessing.

Protective waters will form psychic and psychological boundaries when added to doorstep washes (with salt and pepper) or sprinkled round doors, thresholds, steps and window frames. You can also use them in spray bottles to cleanse or bless a room or your altar space.

Making empowered and protective waters

Add fragrance oils to water that will be empowered by the flower or herb oil you use: for example, basil for money spells and lilac or lily of the valley for happiness at home. (Use 10 drops of oil to 500ml/1 pt water.)

Infuse water with different crystalline energies by soaking crystals in them. For soft crystals, such as rose quartz for gentle love and healing, leave them overnight. For vibrant crystals like tiger's eye, which attracts abundance, you would soak them from dawn (when you wake) until noon or for at least six hours of daylight, whichever is longer. You will need a small round smooth crystal the size of a large coin in up to a mug of clear water. This could be tap water that has been allowed to run and bubble if relatively pure or a still mineral water (see page 532 for different magickal and healing meanings of crystals). The water will remain clear because it has absorbed the essence of the crystal rather than physical properties. Remove the crystal after empowering the water and allow it to dry naturally.

Infuse cosmic energies into your waters.

* Sun water can be made between sunrise and noon at the Summer Solstice or any bright sunny day for any eight hours, ending by 3 pm. You can set it in place overnight if necessary. Put the clear water in a large glass bowl in a place where the sun can shine on it. Cover with mesh to keep it unpolluted. You can leave the waters for longer until you get home. If you need sun water on a dull day, add two or three small sparkling citrine crystals to the water. Sun water is energising, health giving and good for success, confidence and prosperity spells.

* For moon water, leave a large bowl of clear water outside on the night of the full moon from dusk when it rises to when it sets at dawn. Put small white flowers round it and cover with fine mesh. If the night is cloudy, add three small moonstones to the water. Moon water is good for healing, love, travel and for protection.

* For star water place a large bowl of clear water under a starry sky on a clear night

and leave it until you wake. Star water is good for wish magick, for helping chronic conditions or illnesses and for achieving recognition or creative or artistic success.

Weather water

Rain water collected before it touches the ground i.e. in water butts or in bowls on low roofs, offers a traditional source of magick water. With the increase in acid rain there is need for caution. If in doubt do not drink it and add a drop or two of your favourite flower essence. It is excellent for garden and outdoor ceremonies, all growth magick using plants, whether for health or love, abundance magick, for positive change, for anti-drought rituals sprinkled on a bowl of sand or dried earth, and for reconciliation when tipped off a bridge into flowing water.

Storm and wind water can be made by putting clear water in a tall, lidded jug or glass cookware jar in a sheltered place outdoors well anchored with stones or secured in a hole for the duration of the storm or high winds. Use it in baths, drinks or anointing for courage, stamina when you are exhausted and cannot rest, for resisting bullying (good for teenagers and children, sprinkled round a school bag) and overcoming obstacles or to repel harm from your home. Add a few drops to a protective charm bottle you bury or hide outside your home to guard against burglars, vandals and damage to your property by storm or wind or as a doorstep wash if you live in a dangerous area.

Make snow water by leaving fallen powdery snow or ice from the freezer to melt (add a snow quartz to the latter as it melts), lighting a token candle near the bowl. Mix it clockwise and anticlockwise as it melts and name any reconciliation or melting of opposition you need. Tip the water on to earth rather than bottling it, or over growing plants to move things forward and melt stubborn people or hearts frozen with anger and indifference. Good in rituals to revive a love grown cold, melted just before the spell or ritual and used in the altar water bowl.

Colour infused waters are likewise traditional and you can leave your clear water in small appropriately coloured bottles. You can obtain coloured glass bottles (not plastic) from car boot sales, antique stores and from gift shops that sell Middle Eastern type perfume bottles with stoppers. Leave the water for a full 24-hour cycle. If you cannot obtain coloured bottles, stand clear ones on coloured Perspex for 24 hours or shine a coloured light bulb from a small lamp over the individual bottle for four hours. Leave the water in the bottle undisturbed for the rest of the 24-hour cycle.

Though the water in the bottle is still physically clear, it is infused with the magickal, empowering and healing colour energies. For example, orange is the colour of confidence and creativity and will heal problems with the reproductive system, aid fertility and help overcome addictions. You would use it as the water element in a spell, as well as to empower charms or to sprinkle around a manuscript you were going to send to a publisher or as a business proposal to an enterprise board (see page 512 for a full list of colours).

PRACTICAL ASSIGNMENT

Making the Water element the focus of a whole spell

* Set blue candles at each of the four quarters and a large conch sea shell or mother of pearl lined shell for the Goddess and a horn-shaped shell for the God.

* Put a glass or ceramic bowl half filled with water in the centre of the altar. For gentle healing, love or reconciliation rituals, release the power built up during the spell by moving your index fingers beneath the surface of the water and then anointing your top four chakras with water from your power index finger, to infuse your aura with the power of the spell. Alternatively, sprinkle some of the spell water round photographs of loved ones, pets or any place that is under threat to send peace and love. Tip some on plants that need reviving and use the rest in pets' water or to cleanse crystals and tools.

* Carry out an indoor sea energy ritual focused on shells (for love, abundance and fertility), seaweed for health and prosperity, pieces of driftwood for change, travel and house moves, sea crystals such as ocean jasper, blue and pink coral and aquamarine and play soft music of the sound of the sea or dolphins. Use heavily salted water, a turquoise candle and a sea incense such as kelp or a Water fragrance like lemon, poppy or eucalyptus.

* Sea magick will attract on the incoming tide, banish on the ebb and balance on the slack tides. Look up the tide times and turns (most powerful) of your nearest tidal water, even if the nearest shore is 100 or more miles away. If you are in the middle of a land mass, work with the moon phases, waxing being incoming, full moon tide turn and waning the ebb tide, as the moon rules the tides.

* End a spell for any Water purpose (see page 141), such as love, healing or reconciliation, with Water scrying to discover how the results of the spell will be manifest in your life. Sprinkle dried herbs such as rosemary, thyme or chives on the surface of a bowl of water kept on the altar during the rite.

* After release of power and before uncasting the circle, swirl the water with your receptive index finger to make moving images. Alternatively. drop wax from a coloured candle that is the same colour all the way through (otherwise the wax comes out white on the surface). Drip the wax on to the surface and you get both an initial moving image and a fixed one when the wax sets. Inks or dark-coloured oils are also effective.

* In a group, you can scry in a cauldron half filled with water or pass round the bowl to discover different interpretations of the image.

Further research

Continue exploring the myths surrounding the elements.

Research dolphins, whales, mermaids, undines, sea women such as the Jenny Green Teeth, a lovely Scottish water maiden who turned into a hideous hag and dragged young men she seduced to her watery home beneath deep pools and rivers; the Morgana sea women in Brittany said to be the spirits of drowned Druidesses, the Greek Circe or the Sirens, as well as Selkies or Scottish seal people, and fossegrim, the Norwegian waterfall fairies.

Weave chants and empowerments round their different energies to reflect different kinds of Water elemental powers and kinds of water from gentle streams to mighty oceans.

Further information

Recommended reading

* Conway, D J, *Magical Mermaids and Water Creatures: Invoke the Magick of the Waters*, New Page, 2005
* Dobbs, Horace, *Dolphin Healing, the Science and Magic of Dolphins*, Piatkus, 2000
* Fortune, Dion, *The Sea Priestess*, Red Wheel/Weiser, 2003
* Hawkins, Jaq D, *Spirits of the Water*, Capall Bann, 2000
* Muryn, Mary, *Water Magic*, Prentice Hall, 1995

Websites

* *Celtic Spirit*
  Sacred wells in the British Isles resource
  www.celticspirit.org/holywells.htm
* *Dolphin.Net*
  Good source of information on dolphin healing
  www.dolphinnet.org/directory/
* *Isodore of Seville*
  Everything about mermaids
  www.Isodore-of-seville.com/mermaids/
* *Share International Archives*
  Information about healing waters worldwide
  http://www.shareintl.org/archives/healing_water/i_healing_water.htm
* *Strange Magazine*
  Loch Ness monster and other lake creatures worldwide
  www.strangemag-com/nessie.home.html

THE MANY FACES OF THE GODDESS

The Goddess in her many aspects is central not only to witchcraft but also to any spiritual path. A woman can discover the higher energies of her own strengths as she walks though different ages and stages of her life, by identifying with Goddess persona that mirror those qualities. She can also draw down into herself the powers of the Goddess, as the moon (see page 236), the sun (see page 239), as a maiden, a mother, a wise woman, a Goddess of wisdom and justice (see page 244), a sensual love Goddess or indeed any appropriate Goddess energy to fill herself with power and light. Her earthly relationships with other women, mother, sisters, grandmothers, friends, women in authority and colleagues are likewise enhanced through the wise guidance of the Goddess who can help us to embrace the aspects of ourselves and others we may dislike or fear.

A man can work almost as easily with the Goddess as divine Alter ego, as gentle or passionate lover, a mother who offers tough love but will comfort him if he falls and with the fiercer aspects of the dark Goddess he may at first fear and push away. When he calls Goddess power into himself as opposed to channelling her into a magickal partner/the priestess, he can awaken his own anima energies in all its changing faces. Finally, he too can deepen earthly female relationships and free himself with kindness from any that are holding him back, such as an over-possessive mother or a critical or controlling partner.

The experienced witch can use this module and the next one as a resource for making new Goddess connections and also explore those Goddess forms such as the Three Sisters of Fate or the dark creative Kali energy that are less frequently bought into the circle. In this module we will work with the Goddess as the Mother of All, the Earth Goddess, the Goddesses of witchcraft and the Goddess in her transformative aspects.

The Mother of All, the pre-sexual pre-God stage

I have already written about the Goddess as the undifferentiated source of creation (see page 220). However, I would like to spend longer on this aspect, for whether you are a man or woman each magickal act is in a sense a recreation of the first generative spark. Some cultures of course and the major religions assign this creative role to the God form or rewrite the earlier more matriarchal friendly creation stories. The problem with that is that generally whereas the Goddess brings forth her mate and henceforth they relate as God and Goddess together, the male Godhead has more problems with the concept of an equal female power. One example of a Mother of All whose position has been altered over time is the supreme Hindu Mother Goddess Mahadevi. All the Hindu Goddesses may be regarded as aspects of Mahadevi though they have distinct personalities. In their earlier forms the Goddesses predate the Gods to whom they later became consorts.

Some older texts describe Mahadevi as creator of the universe who oversees the main cosmic functions, creation, preservation and destruction. The three supreme Gods of modern Hinduism, Brahma, the Creator, Vishnu the Preserver and Shiva the Destroyer assume these functions, it is said, by her will. According to one myth, Ammavaru, the Goddess who existed before the beginning of time, laid an egg that hatched into Brahma, Vishnu and Shiva.

Most fascinating magickally are the Celtic Mothers who may have evolved from Madron or Madrona, the Welsh Mother Goddess and mother of Mabon, who in some myths was stolen from her at three days old, but was rescued by Arthur/ Gwydion and restored to the world. A mother of the harvest, she is also linked with the washerwomen imagery of the Morrigu and so may also be a Fate/Rebirth Goddess. She gave her name to the Cornish healing well now known as St Madron's. Mabon is another name for the Autumn Equinox celebration (see page 80).

However, other more patriarchal writings attribute these cosmic functions as inherent to the male Gods. Nevertheless, they still acknowledge the Goddess in the consort Goddesses, some of whom are fierce and very independent, who transmit the Shakti, the female active divine energy that is necessary to empower the Gods through sacred sexual union.

But the best example of the Mother of All is the Ancient Greek Gaia.

The strength of Gaia

Gaia, the Greek primal Earth Mother, was called the daughter of Chaos or swirling primal darkness and emptiness. Emerging from this ocean of potential, Gaia created every living thing, plants, animals, hills, mountains, waters and people.

Gaia was depicted in Grecian art as a well-rounded mother figure, rising from the earth to which she remained connected. Her first creation was her consort Uranus, the starry heavens whom she split in birthing from herself, as a separate male element. She or her maiden form of Persephone (Kore) called Cura, created the first human from mud. Gaia insisted that since the man was created from her flesh, he should bear her name and be called her own. Zeus disagreed and so they divided ownership. Cura would possess the human in life. Zeus her grandson would claim the soul after death while Gaia would keep the body to be returned to the earth in burial.

Gaia was also the original source of prophecy at the Oracle at Delphi, since the priestesses derived their wisdom from deep within the earth.

The struggles of Gaia

In common with other creator Goddesses, Gaia struggled to give birth to her first children, the Titans and the Cyclopes. But Uranus hated the idea of sharing his power and he imprisoned them within Gaia's body, causing her untold agony.

Gaia pleaded for help and the Titan Cronos, Lord of Time also known as Saturn, the only child to be free, castrated his father as he lay with Gaia. So her children came forth and Cronos assumed sovereignty, later mating with his sister Rhea who became the younger Goddess of the earth. Some of the blood of Uranus fell on Gaia's womb and from the blood was spawned the avenging Furies and the Giants. The genitals of Uranus were cast into the sea and from the foam raised the beautiful Aphrodite, also called Urania, Goddess of Love. But Gaia was still the primal Earth Goddess. It was said that Gaia loved all her children the same, the beautiful and the hideous, cruel and benign.

Like the Chinese female Yin principle, Gaia is seen as the perfect mother who embraces all creation, without distinction, yet she could be cruel and allowed the castration of her husband because he stood in the way of the birth process. This usurpation of the old order by the new, instigated by the Earth Mother was an early motif in which the old God/king was replaced by force by the new younger God, often as the natural order of things, with the young stag in the herd killing the old. Priests of powerful goddesses such as the Anatolian Mother Goddess Cybele were often castrated or castrated themselves. Gaia is still a powerful female icon in the modern world.

Working with Gaia

Candle colour: Brown or green

Crystal: Moss or tree agate

Incense: Sweetgrass or patchouli

Add qualities you perceive in Gaia: See below.

For any creative issue or struggle or to establish your own identity and power; for tough love in mothering or marriage, for environmental and earth energy magick and for acceptance of what cannot be changed. A good icon for men struggling to free themselves of a father's influence or who have problems with authority.

The Goddess in witchcraft

You can use absolutely any Goddess form as your focus for spells and rituals and there may be a particular culture such as the Norse or Ancient Egyptian to which you are drawn. This may be one in which you have spiritual or soul ancestors that link with you through the collective well of wisdom. You may feel affinity through a past life and your Witch Guardian was probably a priestess in your chosen tradition (more of this in the practical assignment).

You can create special Charges for each of your favourite Goddesses. For example, Viviane Crowley has created a beautiful Charge for Aradia, Queen of the Witches as have the Farrars (see recommended reading, page 373). For each Goddess or Goddess combination I have listed some of the rituals you can carry out under their name as well as their candle, colour, crystal or incense. I have also written for each Add your own qualities. By this I mean list any additional strengths the Goddess suggests to you from meditating and reading. These will suggest other rituals or spells you can cast by invoking the particular Goddess energy.

I suggest you start a section in your Gods and Goddesses pages of your Book of Shadows for these and other Gods and Goddesses whose energies you would like to work with.

Aradia

Aradia is perhaps the most commonly invoked Goddess in Wicca, called the Queen of the Witches. The daughter of Diana we know most of her from Charles Leland's *Aradia, Gospel of the Witches* (1899), which I have referred to again in the recommended reading. If you can read the original, based on his information from the Italian Etruscan witches, you may be surprised at how radical Aradia's role is as champion of the slaves (it refers to ancient times) and the later church persecutions. The Italian witch tradition was said to be continuous from 500 BCE and has filtered into Wicca in a number of ceremonies devised by Gardner, as well as strongly influencing Dianic witchcraft.

Like many deities, Aradia has a fierce side and taught poisoning according to Leland. However, it is important to remember that the accounts handed down through history and myth of Aradia and other deities and their priestly castes are coloured by accounts of living through what were sometimes savage times. Such accounts need not in any way affect how you regard the silver daughter of Diana who was sent to earth to teach witchcraft in the most positive ways; it is a reminder that with all Goddesses and Gods their attributes can be affected not only by the myths but also the political and religious background of those who describe them. You also find in the Gospel of the Witches familiar words describing what Aradia's followers should do when she returned to the heavens:

> *When I shall have departed from this world,*
> *Whenever ye have need of anything,*
> *Once in the month, and when the moon is full,*
> *Ye shall assemble in some desert place,*
> *Or in a forest all together join*
> *To adore the potent spirit of your queen,*
> *My mother, great Diana...*
> *And ye shall all be freed from slavery.*

This echoes the part of the traditional Wiccan Charge of the Great Mother, which also talks of being naked in rites as a sign of being free of slavery. Viviane Crowley refers to Aradia in her Charge of Aradia as the daughter of the sea, wind, moon, dawn, sunset night and the mountains, embracing the idea of Diana her mother as the original creatrix Goddess. The Greek Kore/Persephone and Demeter are another famous witchcraft mother and daughter pairing (see page 382).

Working with Aradia

Goddess aspect: Maiden

Candle colour: White

Crystal: Moonstone or any stone with a hole in it

Incense: Poppy

Add your own qualities.

For any magickal spell (often paired with the Celtic Cernunnos Horned God), for courage and freedom, for mother/daughter or mother/child magick, for moon rituals, Earth rituals and for natural magick; also for enhanced magickal wisdom and knowledge.

Diana

If Aradia is Queen of the Witches, Diana is undoubtedly their main Goddess. According to Leland's account, Diana created the moon, stars, the rain and the sun. She divided herself into light and darkness and brought forth her brother/consort, Lucifer the Lightbearer, as the light of day and the sun. But he would not mate with her in heaven and so she had to come to earth. When he fell from heaven (in an amalgamation of the tale of the Biblical angelic war in heaven), Diana took the form of Lucifer's beloved cat to creep into his bed. They mated and Aradia was produced (read this fascinating alternative creation legend). Other versions say Aradia's father was Diana's twin brother Apollo.

To the Romans, Diana was the divine virgin (which meant she submitted to no man/God). She was the Goddess of the moon, of the earth and heavens, fertility and childbirth and Divine Huntress. Though she was originally the maiden/waxing aspect of the moon in time she became regarded as the moon in all its phases as Diana Triformis, the Triple Goddess (see below) and became one of the Romans' most important Goddesses.

She incorporated the worship of her Greek counterpart Artemis that continued especially at Ephesus, on the west coast of what is now Turkey, and no man could enter her temples. At Ephesus, her worship merged with that of the Virgin Mary, whose tomb was said to be located there with the establishment of the church of Our Lady of Ephesus in 431 CE. Diana of Ephesus is associated in this aspect with the Black Madonna (see below).

Working with Diana

Goddess aspect: Maiden/Mother

Candle colour: Silver

Crystal: Selenite or any holed stone

Incense: Jasmine or lemon

Add your own qualities.

For all magick. Use her powers in all phases of moon magick, for rituals when you seek to attain a goal (in her hunting aspect) and to protect animals, for strong female or male anima magick, for love and passion, for fertility and in assisting pregnant women to have a safe delivery; good for men who find strong independent women or female aggression of any kind hard to deal with.

Isis

Isis the Ancient Egyptian mother Goddess as Mistress of Enchantment is a central icon in modern Goddess worship, as well as witchcraft. She was so popular throughout the Roman Empire that at one time it was thought her worship would replace that of the Christian Virgin Mary with whom she is closely identified. She is idealised as the perfect wife and mother and one to whom ordinary people could relate, tell their sorrows and make offerings at her shrines.

Isis, who was once an earth dwelling deity, promised that everyone who followed her, not just kings and nobles, would have immortality. Her buckle amulet the tjet (see page 405) and images of her in her form of protective mother vulture were placed in the poorest of graves.

As devoted wife, Isis searched through the land and reassembled the dismembered body of Osiris, except for his phallus, which she magickally recreated, using chants and amulets. Then she breathed life into Osiris, so conceiving her son Horus, in a sense a virgin conception and birth, since she was the initiator and lifeforce.

As perfect mother, she suckled her infant in the papyrus swamps, hiding him from his evil uncle Set. Early Christians saw the Virgin Mary in terms of Isis and there is no doubt that Isis was the source of the numerous Black Madonna statues of mother and child found throughout Europe and the Mediterranean regions. Black Madonnas are a fascinating area to study.

Isis was known to the Egyptians as Au Set Lady of the Moon, Mother of the Crops. By Greek times, Isis had been elevated to Oldest of the Old, from whom all things arose, because since the Greek Sky Gods had usurped the earlier matriarchal focus there was a need for a personalised Gaia to whom women especially could relate. This also strengthened her unifying function among disparate peoples who needed to be welded together under a single political system.

Isis has been honoured in many forms: as Stella Maris, Goddess of the Sea, as Holy Virgin, Sacred Bride, Mother of Nature and perhaps most importantly in the Westernised ceremonial magickal system as Mistress of Enchantment. This esoteric image of Isis has formed the basis for recent art and literature and for her role as Lady of the Magickal Arts in the late 19th and 20th century Western magickal tradition, notably the Golden Dawn occult society. Dion Fortune distinguishes in accordance with the Western magickal tradition between Isis Veiled, the heavenly Isis, and Lady of the Moon and of the Mysteries and Isis Unveiled, the Goddess of Nature, mother of the Sun.

Like Demeter, Isis was the centre of mystery religions where the ritual dismemberment, death and resurrection of Osiris resulting in the birth of the divine child Horus were celebrated and the spiritual rebirth of initiates linked to the annual return of the grain. The second century writer Apuleius who was born in the Roman colony of Madura in Morocco and was initiated into the Mysteries of Isis, described her as an ethereal goddess of magick in his semi-autobiographical work The Golden Ass that was translated by Robert Graves from Latin. Apuleius wrote of the vision he saw in his initiation:

> . . . the apparition of a woman began to rise from the middle of the sea, with so lovely a face the gods themselves would have fallen down in adoration. Her long thick hair was crowned with an intricate chaplet in which was woven every kind of flower. Just above her brow shone a round disc like a mirror or like the bright face of the moon, which told me who she was. Her mantle was embroidered with glittering stars on the hem and everywhere else and in the middle beamed a full and fiery moon.

Working with Isis

Goddess aspect: Mother

Candle colour: Red

Crystal: Red jasper or bloodstone/heliotrope

Incense: Cyphi or any spice fragrance

Add your own qualities.

For all magick. For women's and gentle anima magick, for fertility, marriage and fidelity, mothering and protection, for moon magick on crescent and on the full moon, for restoring what has been lost, for sea magick, star and night magick (she was identified with Sirius, the star that heralded the annual flooding of the Nile) and for healing; good for men to work through the concept of wives and girlfriends as both mothers and lovers.

Hecate

When we talk of crone Goddesses in magick, we mainly think of Hecate, Goddess of the crossroads where three paths, past, present and future meet (or between the underworld, the earth and the heavens in classical terms), a remnant of her significance as a Triple Goddess. At crossroads, offerings were left to ask her blessings and to bring good fortune. She was protective especially to sailors and hunters in her ancient role as animal mother and of those falsely accused of wrongdoing and was patroness of midwives.

Hecate was one of the elder gods, a Titan, the daughter of Tartarus, the original Underworld and Nyx or Night the daughter of Chaos. She had then power over the heavens, earth and underworld, linking them in her person of Hecate Triformis. She was also Triple Goddess of the moon, carrying a torch through the skies, as she did in her role of underworld guardian and guide.

After the War of the Titans against Zeus, Hecate was the only Titan deity to retain her authority, but gradually this was eroded as the worship of Apollo the Sun God and Zeus took precedence over the Goddesses. She became associated more and more with the sad, dark abode of lost souls and wandering ghosts, guarded by her hell hound the three-headed Cerberus who stood at the gates of Hades. So, too, did she become uglier and more aged in her portrayal as she was absorbed into the myths of Rome from Greece.

Crossroads, once sources of prophetic power, became increasingly frightening, evil places where suicides and witches were buried. Hecate became identified with cemeteries and mills, the latter a relic of her former life-giving and regenerative role.

Hecate as the wise guide and initiator of women's mysteries may be found in the myths that describe her as Kore/Persephone's companion in the underworld. She did not rescue the Maiden Goddess and some ask why, if she was really kindly. But if we view the fall of Persephone into the underworld as her initiation from innocence and unawareness into experience through suffering, then Hecate could only stand there and comfort her while she learned the lessons that were necessary for her rebirth. This is one of Hecate's most important roles in our lives: not to make false promises, but to help us through the different stages of our lives.

Magickally, it is said Hecate will act as adviser and mediator for any woman's (or male anima) journey into their own psyche in which they confront fear and emerge stronger.

Working with Hecate

Goddess aspect: Crone

Candle colour: Black, dark blue

Crystal: Jet or obsidian

Incense: Myrrh or mugwort

Add your own qualities.

For protection, for making difficult decisions, for rituals to banish sorrow, fear or self-destruction, especially during the waning moon, for wisdom, taking away pain or illness, for night magick and winter magick, for safety while travelling, to induce prophetic powers; for overcoming fears of ageing and losing good looks; good for older men who find it hard to accept their wives growing older.

Kali, Goddess of transformation

The Bone Goddess is perhaps one of the oldest and most elusive goddess forms and has survived mainly in shamanic practices in Siberia and in folk myths, especially in Eastern Europe and Scandinavia. She is akin to such figures as the male Grim Reaper, but she is much more positive in that she not only calls people to death, but restores them to life in a new more perfect form.

Because shamans meet her when they undergo a ritual death and transformation as part of their initiation in her care, she is an image that can be helpful for anyone at major life changes whether physical, emotional or spiritual when a path or stage has become redundant or destructive. The dark time of the moon in astronomical calendars from new moon until you can see the crescent in the sky is the time associated with the Bone Goddess, the older sister or mother of the crone.

In Hinduism is the Dark Mother Kali and the Bone or Death Goddess, Chamunda. With their necklaces of skulls, they are perpetual reminders that death is as real as life, but is not the end, rather part of an ongoing cycle.

Some say Kali existed from the beginning of time as the Great Goddess herself and it was from her and by her that Vishnu, Brahma and Shiva was created. Vishnu calls her mother and grave. But in later accounts, Kali came into being when Shiva, whose body was covered by white ashes, taunted his gentle wife Parvati/Shakti for her dark skin. In fury, she carried out magickal rituals until her skin became golden inside. Parvati then shed her black outer skin like a snake. This being full of her anger formed the avenging destroying persona of Kali, half-naked with wild hair and protruding tongue, covered in blood that signified her power over life and death. Parvati is her alter ego with all anger gone.

Kali is beautiful yet terrifying at the same time and sometimes museums in the UK do not have statues of her, for they seem afraid of this untamed life essence. Dressed in a tiger skin symbolising fierceness and courage, around her neck are 50 human skulls, said to symbolise the 50 letters of the Sanskrit alphabet, indicating Kali is also an alter ego of Sarasvati, Goddess of Learning. Kali has three eyes so she can see into the past and future, as well as the present. Her third eye may also be regarded as the psychic eye associated with the Brow chakra or psychic energy point on the human body. On her girdle are human arms, but though in one hand she carries a severed head and the scythe of the reaper/severer of life in the other, her other two hands make gestures repelling fear and promising spiritual enlightenment, to those who worship her.

Kali is often pictured dancing on Shiva, whose body she trampled, destroyed and then danced on once more to restore him to life, transforming Shava (Sanskrit for corpse) to Shiva (the living one). Kali cannot exist without the male principle as a vessel for her energy and Shiva cannot activate his own power unless she kindles it. They are the lord and lady of the endless cosmic dance. Her ocean of blood with which she is surrounded, like the legendary menstrual blood of the Sumo-Babylonian Creator Goddess Tiamet that brought the world into being, is life-giving and maintaining, as well as destroying. This is the opposite of both the Oriental passive female Yin and active male Yang and the traditional westernised view of the initiating male and receptive female.

Kali strips away illusion and what is stagnant and redundant, like Cerridwen, the Welsh Crone Sow Goddess, both giver of life and devourer of her children, to whom she gives birth again and again. To her devotees, Kali brings mercy, bliss and the protection of the fierce mother, but because she is so powerful she can only be invoked by those with the purest of heart and intent.

Working with Kali

Don't work with Kali unless you are a very experienced witch as she is quite scary. Download her images, read about her and gradually allow her to show her kindly face. Then when you feel ready work with her first with the balancing energy of Parvati.

Goddess aspect: Bone

Candle colour: Dark red

Crystal: Ruby or garnet

Incense: Dragon's blood or nag champa

Add your own qualities.

For magick of transformation, for rituals when life cannot get any worse, for protection against fear, for working with aspects of mortality, for protecting the vulnerable and for men and women to heal bad relationships with older women, such as their mother.

PRACTICAL ASSIGNMENT

Who is my Goddess?

If you are an experienced witch you may already work with a particular Goddess. However, even if you are new to witchcraft you may already feel attracted towards a particular culture. For experienced witches you can use this activity to delve much deeper into your special Goddess and her priestess the Witch Guardian.

You will need for this walk into the past a clear quartz crystal sphere with inclusions or cracks. This to me is one of the most essential tools of witchcraft as well as divination and psychic development and you do not have to spend a fortune. Indeed you can pick one up for about £30, though if you can pay more the quality is better (that is not to say your insights will be better, just easier to connect with).

Ask for one as a present or save up to treat yourself. As witches we tend to be very generous towards others, but not so towards ourselves. Buy one from a mineral shop rather than a New Age store to keep prices down (unless you know the owner of a store who will keep an eye open for you when they visit the wholesaler).

* After dark in your altar place, light a horseshoe shape of small white or beeswax candles and in front of it set either your crystal ball or a bowl of water into which you have tipped a little back ink or used an infusion of mugwort, the traditional water darkener (see page 572 for making a mugwort infusion). Alternatively, a green teabag will make dark scrying water.

* Light myrrh, rose or sandalwood incense.

* Ask your Witch Guardian to guide you into the past that you may find your Goddess.

* Hold the crystal sphere so the light from the candles reflects within or ripples the dark water to create a doorway of light so that the lights of the candles reflect on the surface. Have no other light in the room.

* Wait and do not force. Before long, you will identify a pathway within the sphere that leads to a point or see a similar point in the water through the doorway. That is your entry point. When you feel ready, picture the point of light expanding into a shimmering rainbow curtain. Ripple the water again to see the curtain and breathe in very slowly and deeply. You may experience a kind of bump, like when a plane lands on the tarmac, and before you is the place of the Goddess.

* Each of us sees something different: a temple in sunlight, a mountain cave, a sunlit grove or steps leading upwards. Follow the path in your mind, being aware your Witch Guardian is with you, but may look different. If your Guardian is male he may resemble a priest, a wise man or a Druid.

* You may stand watching the world or you may find yourself there also. If you are patient you will hear chants, smell fragrances and see either a statue of your deity in an inner sanctum or a figure of light within the trees, and feel as though you have come home.

* You may be able to hold the experience for a while or it may fade quickly. *It* will leave *you*, not the other way as often happens in past recall, though you will sense

the presence of your Guardian and should thank him or her. If you are worried about entering the past, even in your mind, you can stand your own side of the rainbow curtain and ask your Guardian to lift it so you may see within.

* Put down the sphere or lift your eyes from the water and other impressions may come into your mind.

* When you are ready, light more candles, enough to record your experience. You might find you are writing in your Book of Shadows far more than you were aware of and feel prompted to write a praise poem or chant to the Goddess, even if you do not normally find written words easy.

* You can ask to return to learn more on another occasion or ask before beginning to be shown another form of the Goddess whose energies you need. But the first one will remain your special Goddess.

Further research

Find out more about your Goddess and her culture if you are unfamiliar with it. If you do know about her and she was no surprise, plan to visit a museum where you can see and perhaps handle some of the artefacts connected with her, so that the link with that world becomes deeper.

There may be a special place or collection devoted to her that you could visit on holiday.

Explore any literature in which she is mentioned or any poetry or old songs dedicated to her.

Further information

Recommended reading

* Baring, Anne, and Cashford, Jules, *The Myth of the Goddess*, Penguin, 1991
* Farrar, Janet and Stewart *A Witch's Bible*, Robert Hale, 2002
  You may already have looked at this it is very good for Goddess chants, rites and Charges.
* Hart, George, *Dictionary of Egyptian Gods and Goddesses*, Routledge and Kegan Paul, 1996
* Kinsley, David R, *Hindu Goddesses*, University of California Press, 1998
* Larrington, Carolyn, *The Feminist Companion to Mythology*, Pandora, 1992
* Leland, Charles G, Aradia, *Gospel of the Witches*, Phoenix Publishing, 1990

Websites

* *Aradia, Gospel of the Witches*
  Leland's book online
  http://www.sacred-texts.com/pag/aradia/index.htm
* *Charge of Aradia*
  A lot of other useful material as well
  http://users.erols.com/jesterbear/notes/crowley.html
* *Goddess World*
  Isis site listing almost 2,000 goddess names plus an article and litany names for Isis
  www.goddessworld.com/names.html

THE TRIPLE GODDESS

ne of the most significant forms of the Goddess in magick is the Triple Goddess, three varying aspects of the energies, distinct roles or life stages of the same Goddess power.

The Triple Goddess concept exists in a number of cultures and ages. She can be maiden, mother and wise woman crone or three sisters, whether the sisters of fate or three sisters who act as protectors and patronesses in three equally significant but differing roles. The three are one, just as the three phases of the moon are three aspects of the same moon. For this reason three Goddesses may be pictured facing three different ways but holding hands back to back.

The maiden, mother and wise woman

Each has her own colour used in magick and a number of covens do have their resident wise woman as well as the maiden and the mother/the high priestess. As a solitary witch you can incorporate all three aspects in your rituals. Use their magick separately for the different phases and add your own attributes to each.

Maiden Goddess

Candle and ritual colour: White

Crystal: Snow quartz or pink or white chalcedony

Incense: Lavender

Add your own qualities.

For new beginnings, creativity, love, trust, innovation, growth, health and vitality, optimism, children and young people, initiation of self or projects.

Mother Goddess

Candle and ritual colour: Red

Crystal: Red jasper or garnet

Incense: Rose or lily

Add your own qualities.

For fertility, commitment, fidelity, healing, nurturing, protectiveness of vulnerable, mothers and motherhood, for the home, for sexuality.

Crone

Candle and ritual colour: Dark blue or black

Crystal: Amethyst or sodalite

Incense: Myrrh or cypress

Add your own qualities.

For wisdom, taking away sorrow, illness and pain, for endings leading to beginnings, for reconciliation, in times of hardship, divination and prophecy, for finding what is lost, for keeping secrets, for older people and animals.

Maiden, mother and wise woman

Use the three energies, candle colours, etc together for magick of the rites of passage, for seasonal magick, for moon magick and for any rituals of change or transformation.

The Triple Isis

The Triple Isis is an example of how a single powerful Goddess can absorb the functions and qualities of other Goddesses especially as cultures merge their deities. The concept of the Triple Isis is Roman and Isis combined with two popular Graeco-Roman Goddesses to form Athena-Isis-Tyche. There are some good examples of Triple Isis statues in the British Museum dating from around the 2nd century CE. The three joined in one person the wisdom and feistiness of the Virgin Athena, the benevolence of Mother Isis and the luck bringing powers of Tyche, the Fate Goddess. Tyche is the equivalent of Fortuna who carried a horn of plenty and a steering oar because she was guardian of sailors.

Diana Triformis

Diana Triformis became a Triple Goddess in Rome as her power grew. As the lunar Diana, her name was associated with the waxing aspect of the trinity. The other two Goddesses joined with her as the Triple moon were Selene, the full moon (or sometimes Persephone), and Hecate, the waning.

Diana's image of the sacred antelope took precedence on Diana Triformis icons. Images of Diana Triformis (recalling her aspect as Goddess of childbirth) showing her sacred antelope, have been found on coins dating between 253 and 268 CE dropped as offerings into Romanised fertility wells: for example, on the Isle of Sheppey in Kent. Diana Triformis images were thought to have very powerful fertility powers and also acted as charms for success in hunting and battle. Her temples appeared throughout the Roman Empire for this reason.

The Triple Hecate

Hecate was once worshipped in all three phases of the moon and especially the Dark moon and this form of the Triple Hecate persisted in some parts of the Empire even after the rise of Diana Triformis.

Triple Hecate was depicted as a figure with three faces each facing a different direction, as three women holding hands back to back or on a statue with animal heads of a horse, dog and boar. To the Greeks the Triple Hecate Goddess was made up of Persephone, Demeter and Hecate. The Romans sometimes combined the Triple Hecate with Diana Triformis as Diana, Persephone and Hecate.

The Three Sisters

The Sisters of Fate

An ancient form of the Triple Goddess that persisted alongside the maiden, mother and crone, was the Sisters of Fate, who were sometimes pictured as crone Goddesses. They were spinners or weavers of the web of human destiny and even that of the deities and so were very powerful.

Sisters of Fate magick

For rituals for bringing good luck, changing your life path, for relationships especially tangled ones that need resolving, for spells involving different generations, for bringing people together and new members into the family, whether by remarriage or birth.

Candle colours: Three shades of purple

Crystals: Three rutilated quartz, smoky quartz or lapis lazuli (use the three different crystals if you wish)

Incenses: Sage, sandalwood or thyme

The Norns, the Norse Sisters of Fate

The guardians of the Well of Urd or Wyrd (Fate), sited beneath one of the roots of Yggdrasil, the World Tree of Viking and Germanic myth. At this well, the deities held their daily council. The three Norns, the Goddesses of destiny, nourished the World Tree with water from the spring. The three Sisters wove the web both of the world and the fate of individual beings, mortal and gods. They wove, not according to their own whims, but according to Orlog, the eternal law of the universe.

The first Norn, Urdhr, the oldest of the sisters, always looked backwards and talked of the past, which in Viking tradition influenced not only a person's own present and future, but also that of his or her descendants. The second Norn, Verdhandi, a young vibrant woman, looked straight ahead and talked of present deeds, which also influenced the future. Skuld, the third Norn, who tore up the web as the other two created it, was closely veiled and her head was turned in the opposite direction from Urdhr. She held a scroll that had not been unrolled, of what would pass, given the intricate connection of past and present interaction.

The Greek and Roman Sisters of Fate

In Ancient Greece the Fates were called the Moerae or Moirai, Clotho wove the thread of life, Lachesis measured it out and Atropos cut it off with her scissors of death.

The Roman Fates were very similar, called the Parcae, three very old women who spin the fate of mortal destiny. They were Nona, Decuma and Morta. Nona spun the thread of life, Decuma assigned it to a person and Morta cut it, ending that person's life.

The Furies or Erinyes, their alter ego, the three sisters of malign fate, Tisiphone, Megaera, and Alecto, were called *those who walk in darkness*. They were described by various myth weavers as dripping tears of blood, black and with hissing tresses of vipers. The original bringers of nightmares, they were formed from the spilled blood from the genitals of Uranus who was castrated by his son Cronos and so were born out of anger and destructiveness.

The Furies were not, however, indiscriminate in their destructiveness, driving criminals and wrongdoers to their death, usually by suicide, especially those who harmed their mothers who were under their special protection. They also pursued those who ill-treated the elderly and violated hospitality. It was said they made evil-doers long for their own death and acted as an external conscience in what were very brutal times.

What is more, in Athens was a temple to the Furies. Here rites were performed only by women and the Goddesses were depicted not as monsters but as huntresses, bearing torches with serpents wreathed around their heads. In this role they represented the crone aspect of Demeter.

The Creative Sisters, Mistresses of many Arts
Brighid, Brigid, Brigit, the Celtic Triple Goddess

Brighid is one of the most intriguing of the Triple Goddesses, associated with Ireland, Scotland, Wales, England and Gaul and was daughter or consort of the Dagda, the Irish Father God. The Romans linked her with their Minerva, Goddess of Wisdom.

In her triple aspect Brighid was patroness of poets, healers and smiths, Brig of poetry, Brig of healing and Brig of the forge.

Myths also suggest maiden, mother and crone aspects, but the elusive Brighid dances from category to category.

In maiden form, she is linked with lambing, cattle, milk and the maiden of spring who melted the winter snows. She replaced the rule of the Old Hag of Winter who in some legends was transformed into Brighid, as Brighid mated with the leader of the tribe. In this role she is the sovereign Goddess of the land, entering into a sacred bargain (in the guise of her priestess/a Druidess) with the ruler. He thereby promised to cherish the land and its people in return for her abundance.

In her creative maiden aspect, Brighid is linked to Robert Graves' ethereal White Goddess, inspiration of poets, musicians and writers. She created the first keening or mourning song when her son Ruadan was killed.

In her Mother aspect she was called Mary of the Gael, the Irish Mary, midwife and foster mother of Christ, baptising him with sacred milk, and so is a patroness of midwives. In her role as protectress of mothers and children, she distracted Herod's soldiers with a crown of candles so the Holy family could escape.

As a Water, healing and fertility Goddess, Brighid is associated with healing and fertility wells. On the Isle of Sheppey in Kent where I mentioned the well of Diana Triformis, about 10 years ago a team led by archaeologist Brian Slade excavated the Well of the Triple Goddess that had been later Christianised by the Anglo-Saxon Saint Sexburgha. Most significant was the discovery of a three-headed metal cast, depicting a heavily pregnant goddess squatting in the ancient position of giving birth, and similar broken beeswax images also found in the well of what is now called The Well of the Triple Goddess. This was linked the Brighid and also Sheelagh-na-gig, the crone-like birthing Goddess of the Celts.

It seems that women once broke these beeswax images into pieces and dropped them in the well as a private offering to the Goddess for fertility. Local evidence speaks of an indigenous ancient Goddess called Brid or Bridget, in Kent and her later cross pollination with Ireland's Brighid.

In her third aspect, Lady of the Forge, we connect Brighid with her Fire and solar aspects. Brighid was once a Sun Goddess, born according to legend at sunrise. As she entered the world, a shaft of fire blazed from her head linking earth with heaven. She is also associated with the household fire and the sanctity of the hearth as a place of welcome. The holy fire at the saint's shrine in Kildare, dedicated originally to the Goddess and then to Saint Bridget, who absorbed many of the Triple Goddess's qualities, is believed to have burned unquenched for more than 1,000 years.

Finally comes her connection with the ancient Serpent Goddesses, a form of the very wise mother Goddess, such as the Cretan Ariadne whose arms are shown wreathed with snakes and whose worship was linked with sacred bull worship (see page 387).

The Celtic Goddess Brighid was associated with the serpent especially in her crone or grandmother aspect. Christianity would have nothing to do with this aspect of female power. Indeed, in legend St Patrick stood on a hill in Ireland and drove all the serpents into the sea with his wooden staff and St Hilda in 657 CE did the same in Whitby in Northumberland. This may refer to drowning Druidesses, worshippers of Brighid, who would not convert. Nevertheless, in folk wisdom the connection continued. On St Bride's day (the Christianised Welsh form of Brighid in Wales), a prayer is said in folk custom to the serpent:

> Today is the Day of Bride,
> The serpent shall come from the hole,
> I will not molest the serpent,
> Nor will the serpent molest me.

Working with Brighid

Candles: Red, blue and white

Crystals: Carnelian, milky quartz and hematite, one of each

Incense: Hyacinth, chamomile or rosemary

Add your own qualities.

For melting the winter snows (especially around Oimelc Brigantia, 31 January-2 February), for healing, for all creative ventures, especially writing, for Water magick as patroness of sacred wells, for fertility, for transformation, for self employment and turning interest into money spinners (the smith aspect), for all matters of exchange especially concerning property or official matters (as patroness of the Celts and the Druids).

The Fierce Sisters of the Land and of Battle

Morrigu

The Irish Morrigu or raven Goddesses, Babh, Macha/Nass and Nemainn, are my favourite sisters and may have some connection with Brighid whose name is linked with Brigantia the warrior Goddess of the Northern England Brigantes tribes.

In later myth they were demonised as sexually insatiable, hideous, bloodthirsty crow or raven-like crones who could take the form of carrions as they swooped over the battlefield, carrying off the souls of the dead for healing and rebirth. We know that ravens pick off the flesh of corpses and this carrion aspect had magical significance in the matriarchal Celtic world, with the death mother being alter ego of the mother who birthed new life.

Tacitus gives us a clue as to her priestesses when he described the slaughter of many of the Druids, Druidesses and their children in 61 CE. He described the Druidesses screaming curses against the Romans, as raven-like. My own theory is that these mysterious raven women were perhaps a separate order of oracular Druidesses who wore black. They may have dedicated themselves to the Morrigu goddesses. Since the raven was a symbol of transformation and rebirth, the raven women may have been involved in sacred initiation rites.

The concept of the Morrigu may be much older than Celtic, dating back to Neolithic times when the Goddess was depicted with the head of a bird. Her priestesses were her flock and wore feathers on their robes and travelled astrally. Again this is a speculative link but one I am working on and so it is worth sharing.

Babh

She has become associated with the Bean Sidhe, the woman of the fairy who washes the souls of the dead before they enter the house of the mother. In Brittany she is known as La Lavandière. She also appears as a she-wolf in battle, a bear or a huge woman who placed a foot on either side of a wide, fast flowing river, indicating that either side could win the battle according to her choice. A sister of and prophetess of fate, it is believed she will herald the end of time when her otherworld cauldron overflows.

Macha/Nass

This is one of the most fascinating figures in Celtic myth and perhaps one whose persona changed most dramatically with the later telling of her story. She was dark mother of the fertile earth, ritually wedded to Lugh at Lughnassadh (associated also with Eriu) before sacrificing him for the land (see page 648). She was also described in early myth as a beautiful solar Goddess who encouraged creativity.

In her process of transformation from wise Goddess of the sacred land, death and rebirth to hideous crow came the account of how she married a rich, older widower called Crunnchua mac Angnoman and looked after his house. This may seem an unlikely willing choice for a powerful creatrix Goddess. She became pregnant. At the Assembly of Ulstermen, her husband boasted that his wife could outrun the king's horses. So although Macha was in labour, she was forced to run with the horses (she was also linked with Epona, the Celtic horse goddess). Macha won the race but at the finishing-post, she gave birth to twins and died, cursing the men of Ulster that for nine generations they would be helpless in the face of danger and in battle torn with agony, like a woman in labour.

This was perhaps the last action of pure power and because the king had failed to respect what had been set down as the sacred right of women to protection in childbirth, he and the other men were effectively deprived of their Goddess-given right to rule and the whole land suffered. This may also represent the destruction of the Druidesses.

Nemainn

Her name means frenzy and she was the wildest of the sisters She was called the confounder of armies and was the trickster unexpected aspect of the battle who could set armies fighting against allies, send down a storm or mists or appear out of the mist luring warriors on to marshy or unsafe land. Like the trickster Gods, such as the Norse Loki (see page 244), she was essential to preserve the chance aspect of fate and keep the cycle of creation and destruction flowing.

Candle colours: Indigo or dark grey

Crystals: Black tourmaline (schorl), amber and jet, one of each

Incense: Juniper, cedar or cypress

Add your own qualities.

For any situation where you are on trial or have to battle for what you need, to win through against all odds, for shape-shifting and astral projection powers, for bird magick and to reverse misfortune.

Triple Mother Goddesses

Different from the other triplicates but equally ancient are the triple mothers of fertility and abundance. They are found in Celtic lands, in Northern Europe and the Mediterranean, especially Northern Spain and Italy. These fertility mothers, who are also occasionally found in fours, were originally associated with the midwives of the new sun born on the Midwinter Solstice.

The Anglo-Saxons named Christmas Eve in Christian times and the Eve or the Solstice before that as the Night of the Mothers or Modraniht after the shadowy guardians of the hearth and home, the midwife Goddesses who protected women in childbirth and their infants.

The Madronae were Celtic Triple Goddess figures, each depicted nursing a baby or with symbols of fertility. Since the statues or stone reliefs we have of them date from the Roman people they are often a mixture of the Roman Matronae or Matres and the old Celtic Mothers. A typical stone relief triplicity dating from the 2nd century CE found in Lincoln, a Roman town, showed them seated, holding on their laps children, grain, fruit, symbols of fertility and good fortune.

They are usually shown wearing long robes with one breast exposed as if to feed a child. A 3rd century CE statue of four mother Goddesses found at the riverside at Blackfriars is now in the City of London Museum. It shows four females seated on a bench, holding bread, a basket of fruit, a suckling baby and one holding a dog. Three were obviously the three indigenous mother Goddesses, but the identity of the fourth is less clear. Could the woman with the dog, her hand resting on the shoulder of one Goddess, be Hecate, the reminder that birth and death were part of the same cycle?

Most fascinating magically are the Celtic mothers who may have evolved from Madrona, the Welsh Mother Goddess and mother of Mabon, who in some myths was stolen for her at three days old but rescued by Arthur/Gwydion and restored to the world. A mother of the harvest, she is also linked with the washerwomen imagery of the Morrigu and so may be also a fate/rebirth Goddess. She gave her name to the Cornish healing well now known as St Madron's. Mabon is another name for the Autumn Equinox celebration (see page 651).

Candle colours: Three natural beeswax candles or orange

Crystals: Amber, beryl, aragonite or carnelian

Incense: Orange, neroli or Sweetgrass

Add your own qualities.

For house and home, fertility, health, abundance and prosperity, for good luck, for protection and for all matters concerning mothers and children; a good icon for male witches working through mothering issues.

PRACTICAL ASSIGNMENT

The secret Goddess

Mystery religions originated in the Near East and the Mediterranean as ancient fertility cults linked with the willing death of the Corn God in the autumn and the resulting regrowth and resurrection in the spring.

Around the 6th century BCE, the mystery religions began to gain popularity as a focus for individuals in the Ancient Greek world, who no longer were satisfied with state religion and deities. These religions offered the concept of a caring mother Goddess and a saviour deity, her son, daughter or consort who died and was reborn annually, offering the hope of similar rebirth and eventual immortality for initiates in secret often subterranean ceremonies.

Most famed and probably most ancient were the Eleusinian rites associated with Demeter, the Greek Corn Goddess, whose death/rebirth cycle was with her daughter Persephone, called as the uninitiated maiden Kore (Greek for maiden). Other important fertility and initiation cults included the Ancient Egyptian Isis/Osiris resurrection cycles and the cult of Cybele, the Graeco-Roman Mother Goddess and her young consort Attis. Since I am focusing here on the Goddess, I will use the almost wholly Goddess-centred Eleusinian rites.

Eleusinian mysteries

The Eleusinian mysteries were held annually in honour of Demeter the Corn Mother and Persephone, her daughter the Corn Maiden. The Demeter mysteries may have started around the 13th century BCE in Mycenae. The festivals were built round the myth of how Persephone was abducted by Hades, brother of Zeus and taken to the underworld. The grieving Demeter searched for her daughter throughout the world and even in the underworld, and refused to allow the crops to germinate, thus bringing about winter and famine.

Eventually Hermes was sent by Zeus to the underworld to persuade Hades to restore Persephone to her mother. But because Hades had tricked Persephone into eating a single pomegranate seed, he was able to insist she returned to the underworld for three, (four or six, depending on the version) months of the year. As a result, Demeter grieved during the winter and no crops grow. Eleusis had welcomed Demeter as she sought her abducted daughter in the original myth and so had been given by her the gift of the first corn seeds and the right to administer her mysteries.

The rites were based in the city of Eleusis in Attica, not far from Athens and the site was used continuously until Christian monks destroyed it in the 4th century CE. The mysteries were held in March and September to coincide with the sowing and harvesting and every five years special ceremonies were held. In the spring ceremonial grain was thrown into the field and buried in the earth to bring forth new life. Images of the public ceremony depict Persephone as the sprouting corn. A virgin was chosen to represent the deflowering of Persephone and her sacrifice in a sacred sex ceremony. The first harvested corn was revered as Persephone herself reborn as the harvest or the divine child, union of Persephone and Hades and was placed in a basket. Bread baked from this corn was eaten in honour of Demeter.

Candidates were initiated during the September rites. Initiates were led through dark subterranean regions, symbolic of Persephone lost in the underworld, from which they were saved by the intervention of Demeter and so were themselves reborn as the Divine Infant. Accounts differ as to the parentage and name of the divine child. A sacred marriage between Zeus and Demeter was also re-enacted in some accounts of the mysteries.

Experiencing a personal new beginning

According to ancient texts, the rites of the mystery religions involve seeing secret things, hearing sacred things and tasting sacred things. It is quite possible to devise a private simple ritual of rebirth as part of your ongoing spiritual journey or in connection with the Spring and Autumn Equinox rites. However, you can also use it personally and magically after a setback in your life, an illness, a divorce or redundancy or simple a sense of loneliness and futility. You can carry out the stages one after another, perhaps once a week.

Seeing secret things

* Buy or create from clay or wire a symbol of what it is you want renewed: love, prosperity, good fortune or hope.
* Keep your symbol in a secret place and look at it when you are alone, as you hold it picturing all the good things resulting from your new beginning.

* Hold your symbol up to sunlight or moonlight to empower it. When not in use, wrap your symbol in white silk and keep it in a locked box or drawer.

Saying secret things

* These are simple empowerments or promises to yourself, encouragement, declarations that you are still yourself and that you will win through.
* Recite them as you hold your symbol. You may like to write them down and keep them in your box.

Tasting secret things

* The essential components of your ritual feast are bread and wine or dark red fruit juice as symbols of the earth and her bounty and the life blood that will flow within you and warm you again. As you eat and drink, visualise the strengths you need being absorbed and new life stirring.
* It may take many weeks or even months for the rebirth, but each time you fight back from adversity you become a little stronger.

Further research

Explore some of the other forms of the mystery religions and the theme of resurrection and rebirth in different cultures.

Further information

Recommended reading

* Crowley, Vivienne, *Wicca, The Old Religion on the New Age*, 1989, Aquarian/Thorsons
  A good source for Goddess work.
* Green, Miranda J, *Dictionary of Celtic Myth and Legend*, Thames and Hudson, 1992
* Husain, Sharukah, *The Goddess*, Duncan Baird, 1997

Websites

* *Dictionary*
  Online Goddesses and Gods dictionary, very comprehensive
  http://users.erols.com/jesterbear/notes/goddesses.html
* *Mary Jones*
  Thought-provoking Triple Goddess of the Celts article, but brings in other cultures; basis for personal research
  www.maryjones.us/jce/triplegoddess.html

MORE ABOUT THE GODS

The God is an important feature of witchcraft and of spirituality since he is the polarity of the Goddess energies and offers the necessary balance. A man can work with the different aspects of God energies and individual God forms to get in touch with the sparks of those energies and potential within himself. He can draw into himself the power of the God, as the traditional Horned One, but also the untamed power of the Green Man in the Wild Wood, the rebel. He can explore the responsibility as well as the power of the God King as protector of the land and the tribe and the sun at the height of power. The complex but relevant issues of the divine sacrifice who will die on behalf of the people and the land and the Underworld Lord of Winter unfold in myth and ritual. Finally, the male can ride upwards on the cosmic wheel once more as the newborn infant deity, dependent on his mother and helpless against the perils of the world, to experience the turbulent emotions of the jealous sibling having to fight for attention and survival with his alter ego twin.

His earthly relationships with other men, father, brothers, grandfathers, those who run with him in the social pack, men in authority who determine his career and those he must outrun and outfight to stay ahead, are likewise linked to the God energy. These interactions can be shaped through the wise guidance of the God who teaches the male witch to rely on self-knowledge and self-regulation, rather than constantly needing approval from others or wasting energy fighting against the shadows within.

A woman can and should work with the God as divine alter ego, as equal spiritual partner in love and in life, the inner father who fosters the balance between self-reliance and trust in others and the wild youth for whom there are no limits to possibility. When a witch calls God power into herself, she does not have to strap on a ceremonial sword and take the part of the God, nor divert God energies into her magickal partner/the priest. She can embrace them fully and without fear to awaken and communicate with her own animus in its myriad facets. Finally, she, too, can deepen earthly male relationships, and balance trust and self-reliance in relationships with the men in her life, in whatever capacity. Through God rites, she can gain or reinforce the confidence to stand by her own decisions and express her own strengths and independence without losing her essential capacity to care and be vulnerable and open.

The experienced witch can use this module as a resource for making new God connections and also to work with less structured God energies, such as the Green Man or the Goat Gods like Pan that they may experience less frequently in magick and life.

The God through the year

The cycle of the God in a number of cultures differs from that of the Goddess. She is ever present through the year, apart from a three-day sojourn in the Underworld at Samhain when she goes to be with the slain God and disorder rules in the world she has left.

We never see her as an infant or child, nor does she die. But the God spends up to a third of the year in the dual role of infant growing within the womb and Lord of Death while his alter ego, his twin rules on earth. Though we focus on the light twin/Sun God and Barley King in this module, the dark twin also experiences death and a time in the Underworld. We will examine the twin cycle of the God in the modules of the Wheel of the Year (see pages 636–660).

The Young God as the Horned One and the Green Man

The Young God is essentially the virile competitive God whose aim is to defeat all rivals (typified by the Dark God) and to mate with the Maiden Goddess to ensure the succession so that the new Sun King/Light Twin will be born on each Midwinter Solstice. His cycle lasts from the Midwinter Solstice to Beltane, when having impregnated the Goddess at the Spring Equinox he marries her in a woodland wedding and promises to defend her and the Greenwood (so beginning the transition to the God King).

He is symbolised by antlers, the stang (see page 121) or a single horn and by the erect phallus, and he begins his journey in the north of the circle, the place of the Horned God. So powerful is the energy of this God phase and so filled with the lifeforce that the Horned God assumes the main God form in Wicca and embraces all aspects and ages of the stag, bull or goat.

This is the oldest God form dating from Paleolithic times when the Hunter God or lord of the animals was entreated for a good hunt and also the animals were magickally called to the hunting grounds. This dual role as slayer and slain is expressed in the words of such chants as:

Cernunnos, Horned one – the Hunter and Hunted too, Horned God of the Earth.

In this older cycle as stag and the hunter of the stag, sacrifice came at the beginning of the hunting season (in Europe and Scandinavia around the Autumn Equinox). This explains why in some myth cycles the sacrificed grain god dies at the Autumn Equinox.

The Horned God was also probably the earliest tribal sacrifice icon of hunter-gatherer peoples, perhaps expressed in these very early societies by an actual fight between a powerful young male in the community, sometimes the leader's son, wearing antlers to represent the young stag challenging the old male for supremacy of the herd. This method of succession may have resulted in the death of the weaker party. This ensured that the leader was always physically strong and courageous. By Neolithic times, bulls were ritually sacrificed as offers for the fertility of the land as a symbol of the sacrifice God.

Witchcraft is made up of so many layers and different mythologies that the logical mind can get tangled up trying to create a single overall God/Goddess cycle. There isn't one, but on the spiritual/magickal level you can work with the various strands to create as in life itself a sometimes contradictory but rich treasure store of infinite possibility.

Working with the Horned God energies

Candle colour: Bright green or scarlet

Crystals: Malachite (amazonite for women), green jasper and leopard skin jasper

Incenses: Juniper, pine and sagebrush

For all magick as the God of witchcraft and king of witches, equivalent to Aradia/Diana as Huntress, for courage, change, energy, health, initiating enterprises, for freedom, abundance of resources, travel, breaking free of convention, for success in any physical or creative venture, for male potency, for passion, survival issues and for women for contacting their inner store of primal power, courage and desire for freedom and adventure.

Horned Gods and lords of the hunt

Horned deities appear as bulls, stags and goats in a number of cultures. The horn is a symbol of stored male virility, and the horned deity symbolises male power and sexual potency, but without the aggressiveness of the warrior image.

Cernunnos

Cernunnos is the antlered god, known throughout Celtic lands but under different names: Herne the Hunter, for example. He is father of winter, animals and the hunt, being invoked that the huntsmen might catch their prey. During the 1st century CE, the Romans assimilated some of the native deities of lands they conquered, and so the head of Cernunnos often appeared on monumental pillars that supported a Roman God. For example, a Roman pillar intended for a statue of Jupiter was discovered under the choir of the cathedral of Notre Dame during the 18th century and is now in the Museum of Cluny in Paris.

Among other native Gods, the carvings on the pillar depict the Horned God Cernunnos and the Celtic Thunder God Taranis emerging from a tree. In Celtic-Romano imagery, Cernunnos is often also shown with a ram-headed serpent and a stag, or he may be holding a bag of money.

The role of Cernunnos as lord of the forest was split with the coming of Christianity. In France, the divine huntsman became St Hubert, patron saint of hunters, having been, according to legend, converted to Christianity by a stag with a cross between his antlers. On 10 November, St Hubert's Day, huntsmen in red jackets play a fanfare on hunting horns outside Amiens Cathedral, before going in to celebrate the mass.

Freyr

The Norse Freyr or Frey was the Norse Hunting God who had a dual role as an Earth Agriculture God, possibly because Scandinavia and Germany still have a strong hunting tradition that existed alongside agriculture rather than supplanting it. He was the twin brother to Freyja, the Fertility and Love Goddess and some myths say the son rather than the consort of the Earth Goddess Nerthus. This suggests he may be a very ancient God, because originally Horned Gods were sons of the Earth Goddess. One of the Vanir Nature Gods, Freyr ruled over the weather and fertility and was frequently depicted certainly in earlier images with horns. The earliest images of Freyr date from the Bronze Age on rock carvings in Östergötland, Sweden. It would seem that his worship spread to Norway and Iceland.

His power animal was the golden boar called Gullenbursti whom he rode through the skies and who became a symbol at the Yule feast. Freyr's boar was also a symbol of the rising sun. In pre Christian times, the boar was sacrificed at Yule to Freyr so that he would bring abundance in the months ahead. It was also dedicated to Thor as lord of winter. In yet another aspect, as Freyr rode his boar through the skies around the Midwinter Solstice, the darkest and shortest days around 20/21 December, it was believed he brought light and the sun back into the world.

Freyr lived in Alfheim where he ruled over the light elves. It was said that at Ragnarok he would fight with an elk horn as his weapon. He was also invoked in Viking times for abundance, ships and sailors, oaths and bravery in battle. Ingvi Freyr was a later name for him and Ing was used by the Anglo-Saxons. According to the early mediaeval chronicler Adam of Bremen, an image of Ingvi Freyr was found in the pagan temple at Gamla Uppsala in Sweden and also in Germany.

The Bull Gods

The bull symbol is also ancient, dating back to early Neolithic images of the Earth Mother giving birth to a bull/Horned God figure who was her son/consort. In Catal Hayuk in Turkey, the largest Neolithic site in Europe that flourished between 7,000 and 500 BCE when it was abandoned, the Goddess is depicted giving birth to the bull as her child, surrounded by leopards. The God was signified by the bull on altars and in reliefs.

The bull birthing images were also painted in Neolithic vulva-shaped shrines that can still be seen in Malta and women gave birth in the shrines between huge bull horns for protection and safe delivery. The Goddess temples of the island of Malta in the Mediterranean are like no others in the world. The temple builders, perhaps descendants of the Stone Age farmers who arrived in Malta around 5000 BCE, created these mother temples from 2500 BCE onwards and then seem to have disappeared from history.

In the worship of the Anatolian Mother Goddess Cybele, a bull was ritually sacrificed on 24 March and his testicles offered to the Goddess to symbolise the castration and death of Attis her son/lover and his resurrection on 25 March, so that life might return to the world and the crops grow.

The Greek myth and Ariadne, the Goddess

The bull was also central to the Minoan Cretan cult and probably gave rise to the legends of the Minotaur as told by the conquering Greeks.

Because the Cretans ruled the seas, they demanded tribute each year from Athens of seven young men and seven maidens, who were sacrificed to the Minotaur/the bull worshipping cult. Theseus volunteered to go with those to be sacrificed in the hope of killing the monster and overthrowing the cult.

In the myth, the goddess Ariadne has become the gentle daughter of King Minos, rather than his Goddess, though there is archaeological evidence of her as a powerful Mother Goddess whose priestesses cared for sacred snakes, and she may have been the mother of the mythical bull. In Greek legend, the Minotaur, half man-half bull, was created when Poseidon enchanted Pasiphaë, Queen of Crete to mate with the snow-white bull Poseidon had sent to her husband King Minos. Minos had angered Poseidon by refusing to sacrifice the animal.

It was not until 1900 that British archaeologist Arthur Evans unearthed the huge palace at Knossos on Crete. In it was found evidence of a bull-worshipping cult and murals depicting the activities of the bull dancers trained in the fantastic art of bull dancing, a ritual form connected with bull ceremonies, culminating perhaps in the annual sacrifice of a bull to the Goddess. The complexity of the layout of the palace – actually a number of palace buildings that had been built on each other over the centuries – would have made possible the construction of a labyrinth beneath the palace, and Evans concluded that this labyrinth was probably connected with bull and Goddess worship, rather than imprisoning a monster. By no means has everyone agreed with Evans, but his theories have the intuitive quality that makes sense of history.

It is hypothesised that immediately before the annual sacrifice the Cretan high priest or king, wearing bull horns or a bull mask to resemble the Minotaur, ritually mated with the Goddess Ariadne in the form of her chief priestess or the queen. He entered the subterranean labyrinth, representing the womb of the Mother, where in the centre Ariadne waited. It was this yearly consummation of the sacred marriage that ensured the fertility of the land and the sea.

For the king, entering the labyrinth was to go into the tomb to symbolically face death and in mating to be ritually reborn, of the Mother – hence the female power. An actual bull died on the King's behalf (in pre-Minoan times the King may even have offered himself as sacrifice every seven years being replaced by a young strong man, a Theseus figure who killed him in combat, see page 393).

In the Mediterranean area, earth tremors were said to be the Bull God roaring beneath the ground.

Goat Gods

Most famous of the Goat gods is Pan, the ancient Greek herdsman's God of forests, flocks and fields. He is portrayed as half goat, with horns and goat legs and feet. Too wild to be allowed on Mount Olympus with the other deities, he roamed the groves of Arcadia, playing his magickal pipes and indulging his unbridled sexuality. In the secret magickal traditions of esoteric societies of the early 20th century, the invocation of Pan summoned his wildness back into a world grown complacent and spiritually arid.

In pre-Christian times, 14 February was not the day of St Valentine, but the time of lovers at the ancient Roman festival, Lupercalia, which was held on the spot where Romulus and Remus, founders of Rome, were said to have been suckled by the Wolf Goddess Lupa. The horned Fertility God, in the form of the Lycean Pan, or Lupercus as he was called in Rome, was central to the festival as he offered protection to the flocks from wolves. Because goats were sacrificed to Lupercus, the young men dressed up in goatskins and ran around the town, beating young maidens with goat thongs.

Puck, too, was a form of Pan in Celtic lands and passed into popular fairy lore as the mischievous figure we see in the works of Shakespeare and Kipling. But the older, pagan, Celtic connection remains in such phenomena as the Goat King in the annual Puck Fair held in Ireland at Kilorglin, County Kerry; and in the name of Puckaster Cove on the Isle of Wight, off southern England.

The Green Man

Like the Horned God, the Green Man, also known as the Hidden One and the Wild Herdsman, has his origins in pre-history. Some kind of tree image or man, perhaps formed from leafy branches, or a shaman dressed in greenery, may have had a place as a fertility icon in the rites of hunter-gatherer societies.

Just as the Horned God is lord of animals and the hunt, the Green Man is master of vegetation, the forest, trees, flowers and plants, fruits and vegetables. He is represented in western and eastern European May-time folk celebrations as a man covered with greenery. In Scandinavia where summer comes late, he is manifested in the more abstract form of the midsummer tree that is still created in Swedish local communities from freshly gathered greenery.

In some European traditions, the Green Man is ritually beheaded or cut down and then restored to the grieving May queen, to release, with his rebirth, the summer back into the world. From the first, the Green Man was a pagan resurrection symbol, representing the cycles of growth, decay, return to the earth and new growth for plants, humans and animals whose bodies after death contribute to the richness of the soil.

Wild nature

The Green Man is no tame icon. Indeed, it was his fierce expression that made him such a powerful protective image to Christians and pagans alike. His face etched in stone and wooden images in mediaeval cathedrals and churches is austere, a reminder of the darker power of nature to raise storms, whirlwinds and earthquakes.

Sometimes also known as Green George, he is associated with rain-making powers, both in southern and Eastern Europe, and features in Romany gypsy celebrations on St George's Day (23 April) or Easter Monday. A young willow or birch tree is cut down and dressed with flowers and ribbons. Accompanied by Green George (a combination of St George and the Green Man), the tree is taken to a river, and cast in as a substitute for Green George to appease the water spirits and ensure there will be enough rain to fertilise the crops.

Working with Green Man energies

Candle colours: Golden brown and any green

Crystals: Green and lemon chrysoprase or green aventurine (the luck-bringer)

Incense: Fennel, fern or rosemary

For rituals and spells to restore spontaneity, for escape from restrictions and outworn conventions, for following a unique path and valuing your individuality, for holidays and leisure, for good luck, for taking a chance, for unbridled passion and for earth energy magick, especially round ley lines or wild places.

Jack o' the Green

Jack o' the Green is the Green Man with the rest of his foliate body and he welcomes what was once the beginning of the Celtic summer. In 1583, he crossed the Atlantic, along with Morris dancers and a hobby horse (another symbol of fecundity in early summer folk celebrations). In England, Jack o' the Green still forms an integral part of the traditional Chimney Sweeps' May Festival weekend in Rochester, Kent. The person representing Jack, clad in a conical wicker framework covered with leaves, is ceremonially awakened at dawn on top of Bluebell Hill. He waits in the darkness for the call, sitting in the centre of a ring of 12 fires.

The legendary Robin Hood may also be a form of Jack o' the Green. Although he is identified in folklore as the dispossessed Robert Earl of Huntingdon, there are no records to confirm that Robin ever existed. Maid Marian, his lover, may have been a form of the pagan Maiden Goddess who annually renewed her marriage to the young Vegetation God in his most animated and human form, welcoming in the summer in a woodland wedding on a May morning. Robin is also linked with the Celtic horned Cernunnos or Herne.

The Trickster deities

Within the youthful vigour of the Horned God comes the Trickster aspect: sometimes forgotten, but which, if we are to embrace the shadow as well as the light aspects of the God, we need to explore in magick. What is more it helps us to understand the vital role of the Dark Twin who inherently is part of the Light Twin as his alter ego. This is the part of the horned god that Christians have focused on and demonised. He may be mischievous or malevolent, but his role is always to question the status quo and act as a catalyst for necessary change.

Working with the Trickster deities of change

As with Kali, wait until you are experienced and even then work with care. You don't need to be a practitioner of chaos magick, which is relatively modern, though I have suggested a book if this interests you.

With these deities you need to keep a counterbalancing God form for stability and work always in a positive mind. This is particularly important if you feel any bitterness or malicious feelings emerging, normal but often buried aspects of ourselves that can if transformed release power and creativity. Focus on the balancing God and keep the rituals quite short and structured.

Candle colour: Burnt orange or yellow

Crystals: Yellow jasper, meteorite or iron pyrites

Incense: Cinnamon, ginger or saffron

For change, for challenging the status quo, for laughter, for originality, for moving the immovable, for instinctual power, for breaking through stagnation and inertia, for spontaneity, for seeing through deceit, for removing what is destructive or redundant in your life, for facing your own negative aspects and acknowledging them rather than projecting them on to others and for accepting that in some situations you cannot win and so should move on.

Loki

Loki is the Norse trickster god of fire, magick and a great shape-changer. He is brother (either true or foster) and alter ego of the supreme sky god Odin – or his shadow side. Loki's malevolent deeds usually resulted not from his own evil actions but from tempting the deities to express their own hidden, weaker qualities, such as greed or vanity.

Loki belonged to a very old order of the Ettin giants. In some versions of the Creation myth, Loki, in his role as God of Fire, with Odin and Hoenir (the shining one), fought against the Frost Giants and eventually killed Ymir, the primal giant, from whose body they created the nine worlds and the stars, moon and sun. The world of the old Gods was condemned to end at the Battle of Ragnarok. When Ragnarok came, Loki led the legions of chaos against the Aesir, the old Gods, bringing in the more perfect new order. In this, neither Odin nor Loki had any part; nor did they survive the Battle of Ragnarok.

Set or Seth

In early myths, Set was brother of Horus the Elder (a mature version of and uncle to the young Sky God Horus) and Lord of Upper Egypt. Horus, the young falcon-headed Sky God is his alter ego. Set was originally defender of Ra, the Sun God's solar boat, against Apep, the chaos serpent, but he became demonised as the assassin of his other brother Osiris. Associated with the desert and the desert sandstorm, Set came to symbolise all that was arid, destructive and infertile. Why? Probably the myth was altered to take account of the changing political situation as Egypt moved into its dynastic eras around 3000 BCE.

As I said earlier (see page 366 in the chapter on Goddesses) it can be illuminating to look into the political situation behind the myths to see why deities were glorified or demonised. It may be that Set became demonised because he was the God of the losing side in the unification of Egypt around 3100 BCE. The mythological battle between good and evil, and specifically Horus and Set, may represent an actual struggle between the peoples who worshipped the two Gods during the pre-dynasty ages. By the Third Dynasty, the Horus kings were finally supreme and the vilification of Set became more intense; he became God of storms and whirlwinds and the red barren desert, murderer of Osiris and persecutor of the infant Horus, the original archetypal wicked uncle role. In his defence, his brother Osiris cheated on him and conceived Anubis, the jackal-headed God of rebirth with Nephthys, Set's wife.

As representative of the forces of chaos, Set had a vital role in the Ancient Egyptian world in ensuring that the forces of change could operate and for this reason, though defeated by Horus the younger, he was never killed. He was also associated with foreigners who were regarded as enemies by the Ancient Egyptians and with the pig, donkey, crocodile and male hippopotamus. He was shown with a human body and the head of the Set animal, a strange mixture of animals that includes a long tapering snout, large erect ears and bulging eyes.

The God King

The mature God King is found in numerous supreme God forms including the conquering Sky and Thunder Gods, as the All Father such as the Greek Zeus, the Norse Odin/Thor and as the supreme Father of Judaism and Christianity. This God form was associated often with the iron wielding conquering tribes who overcame the more mother-centred Neolithic farmers. The Sky God would marry the indigenous Earth Goddess (see Zeus and Hera and the Sacred Marriage on page 70) or as in Judaism/Christianity marginalise or sanitise her.

The Sky God is a very valid magickal form and I have suggested some Gods of this genre on page 237. He is also the Sun king whom I describe in the module on sun magick (see page 490). The focus here is on the God King as the Earth God, the stable father, farmer and protector of land and people. In this role he is symbolised by the magickal staff.

Earth Gods come from an older tradition than the warrior conquering Sky Gods and were largely surpassed by them, except in indigenous cultures where they still protect the earth and her food store. The Earth God was the idealised or archetype of the wise farmer and protector of the homestead and flocks whose life was regulated by the seasons. We see him also as a guardian king or leader who renews his vows of sacred marriage to the Earth Goddess at the beginning of the summer, promising to protect the land and people. When he breaks this vow, barrenness falls upon the land and he is alienated from his fellow humans, from animals and plants.

He rules from Beltane to Lughnassadh, the first grain harvest at the beginning of August. As caretaker of the Earth, symbolising potency in a peaceful creative form, the Earth God implanted the seed into the womb of the Mother. The emphasis on cultivating not conquering the land is a very positive image to carry forward into the modern war-torn world.

Working with the Earth God

Candle colour: Gold or orange

Crystals: Turquoise or orange jasper

Incense: Frankincense or copal

A wonderful stable power source for men and women, for rituals for employment, career, promotion, stability at home, mature relationships, steady growth in any area especially prosperity, for all fathering rituals and for positive contact with officialdom and authority, for creating firm foundations for a business, for attracting custom and resources and for protection.

Geb

Geb was the Ancient Egyptian Earth god. His consort Nut was the Sky Goddess, covered in stars, into whose womb Ra the Sun God returned each night. Like his sister/wife Nut, in the creation myths of Heliopolis and Hermopolis, he was the son of Shu, God of air, and Tefnut, Goddess of moisture. Geb was the father of Osiris, Isis, Nephthys and Set and Horus the elder. Therefore he brought seeded fertility as Isis, death and rebirth as Osiris, sterility and changes as Set the destroyer, as Nephthys, the Goddess of twilight, the protection in life and death and wisdom and justice as Horus the elder. He ensured the annual growth and ripening of the corn after the flood had receded.

Geb is shown as green with papyrus flowers growing from his body, reclining on one arm so that his body forms the undulating land. He usually has an erect phallus extending towards Nut to indicate his potency and connection with the fertilisation of land and the crops. Geb was in one major creation myth associated with laying the primordial egg, from which all life came. For this reason, some images depict him in human form with a goose on his headdress.

Freyr or Ingvi

Freyr is one of the most fascinating gods in any culture, because he spanned hunting and agriculture and remained equally beloved to hunters, farmers and indeed warriors. He is one of the few examples of the mature Horned God who combine hunting, voyaging and farming as did a number of Vikings. He adds the dimension of the explorer to the normally rooted Earth God persona (generally it is the Sun and Sky Gods who signify travel).

Some legends tell that Freyr was older than the Sky Gods, Father Odin and Thor, God of thunder, and that he once ruled the earth during a golden age of peace and prosperity. Freyr taught the people the arts of farming and animal husbandry. This dual role of Freyr may be echoed in the myth that he gave away his sword and his stallion to win Gerda, the beautiful giantess, which may be why he was to fight with an elk antler at the last battle. This legend may also offer us a clue to the sacred marriage in Scandinavia as he symbolically handed over his male power with his sword.

Freyr drove his wagon over the fields to sow the crops. This became part of a fertility rite, especially in Denmark and Sweden, and for hundreds of years in folk ritual his blessing and potency were sought at planting time to ensure the seeds will be fertile.

The Dark Lord

The third aspect of the God as the Sacrifice God, Lord of Death and Winter is not at all frightening, for he promises rebirth of the sun at the Midwinter Solstice and the new growth of crops in the spring.

In magick he is not the Grim Reaper (though that is a God form as are other similar Lords of Death, such as Ankou, the ancient Breton Death God, who take away human life at the appointed time). He himself willingly embraced death so that his people could live and he promised his protection in the Otherworld like the Egyptian jackal-headed Anubis (a Dark Lord form) to grant safe passage to light and rebirth like the sun.

In more savage ages, a defeated King would either kill himself or be sacrificed. Abdication was not always an option for the ageing ruler, though in Greek myth it is told that when Saturn or Cronos (Old Father Time) was deposed by Zeus he retired to Italy or some mythical island where he taught the people farming and ruled over a golden age of peace and plenty. However, Cronos was less merciful, killing his own father Uranus by castrating him.

The harvest sickle is the symbol of the Sacrifice and Death Gods and their reign is from Lughnassadh or the Autumn Equinox until the Midwinter Solstice. His alter ego is the Earth Mother who restores him to life.

Working with the Dark Lord

Candle colour: Indigo, black or maroon

Crystals: Desert rose, snowflake obsidian or laboradite

Incense: Cedar, cypress and parsley

For rituals of banishing what is old and outworn, for closing doors on the past, for waiting for the right time to act, for grieving for what has been lost, for rituals of transformation, for letting plans lie fallow, for trust and for making sacrifices in the short term for longer advantage, for idealism and altruism and for getting through all difficult transitions in life.

The Barley and Corn God Sacrifice

In return for the devotion of the people who worshipped him, the Earth God offered himself willingly for the fertility of the crops. Each year he would die with the cut harvest to be reborn from the womb of the mother first as the sun, and then he is fully renewed with the seeds in spring.

The Sacrifice God is found in a number of cultures from the 3rd Millennia BCE in Sumeria until Celtic times at the beginning of the 1st century CE. It was absorbed into Christianity as the Crucifixion/Resurrection.

Dumuzi

In ancient Sumeria, the Earth Father was called Dumuzi, a mortal shepherd who gained immortality and the role of lord of the crops and herds through his marriage to the Fertility Goddess Innana. The marriage brought fertility to the land, to both plants and animals.

However, eager to overcome death that took away so many things she loved and carried off her people, Innana descended to the Underworld to the realm of her sister Ereshkigal, Goddess of the Underworld, her alter ego, whom believed she could encounter and defeat death once and for all. Here she was forced to take off her clothes and fine jewels and she died and was hung from a stake. She was rescued through the efforts of Enkil, God of wisdom and sweet water, but was accompanied back to earth by demons that were to take a substitute back to the realms of death. When she came upon Dumuzi he was not in mourning for his love but had happily assumed the sole kingship in her stead. She became angry at his usurpation and allowed the demons of the Underworld to take Dumuzi away, whereupon barrenness fell on the earth.

She persuaded her sister Ereshkigal to allow Dumuzi's sister to replace him for half the year in the Underworld. Therefore when Dumuzi is in the Underworld the plants die. The sacred marriage takes place at the year's turn to herald the coming of spring and the renewal of plant and animal life with the return of Dumuzi to the world. This is one of the main sources from which the descent of the Goddess myth evolved (see page 654).

Osiris

For more than two millennia BCE Osiris was the most important of the Egyptian Earth Gods. He was appointed to rule the world by his father the Earth God Geb. Osiris taught the Egyptians agriculture and, as an early fertility and vegetation god, he was regarded as the embodiment of the corn. But his brother Set was jealous and tricked Osiris into getting into an ornamental trunk, which he closed and threw into the river. Later, Set dismembered the body.

After his body was mummified by his son Anubis, Osiris descended into the Underworld where he was reborn as the God who could grant to others immortality. Each night before dawn, he magickally joined with Ra and released him so that the sun might be reborn. Osiris likewise offered immortality and rebirth to mortals.

He came to represents the annual new growth of the corn, watered by the tears of Isis, the Nile flood, and so he ensured that the cycle of life, death and rebirth continued, as the corn was cut down but sprouted again. At the time of the harvest, the rebirth of Osiris as the ripened grain was celebrated and thanks given to Isis as Corn Mother who used her magick to give him life. As part of the rite, there was the ceremonial burial of grain in a small, flat, hollow, clay model of the Osirian mummy or Osiris himself. These were also placed in tombs.

Lugh

Lugh, the Irish God of the harvest and also the light (whose Welsh counterpart was Llew) had a festival at the beginning of August, called Lughnassadh. The celebration annually re-enacted his ritual marriage with Eriu, the Sovereign Goddess of the land. In the union, he transferred the remains of his solar strength to her so that the rest of the crops would ripen. He then offered himself as annual sacrifice to feed the people of the land. He was cut down as the last sheaf of grain; everyone hurled sickles at the same time, so no one would know who killed him. Lugh returned to the womb of the mother to be reborn as the new sun in midwinter. The legendary character John Barleycorn, cut down but reborn in the fermented ale, is a folk relic of Lugh (see more of this on page 648).

The Welsh version is even more dramatic. Blodeuwedd, the Flower Goddess, led Llew into his predestined death and a decay cycle by her infidelity with Goronwy the dark twin (see page 76 for this myth and the similar King Arthur/ Guinevere/Lancelot love triangle).

PRACTICAL ASSIGNMENT

Invoking the Wild God

If you read Dion Fortune's *The Goat Foot God*, there is a wonderful ending where Pan finally appears. We can invoke the Wild God, whether as horned stag, bull or goat or as the Green Man, as an antidote to modern living and to bring spontaneity and joy into magickal ritual.

* First you need to create your invocation chant. I have suggested an online version by Doreen Valiente, but there are others. Traditional Wiccan ones tend to call Cernunnos, but you can equally invoke Herne or Pan, write a Bull God chant, or incorporate Freyr riding through the skies on his golden boar into a Horned God chant of two or three names.

* Begin by describing your Horned God. You don't have to give him a name, but refer to him as the Horned One and create your own magnificent visualised God form. Alternatively, work with the Green Man or Jack o' the Green.

* Then bring in the setting, deep forest, a mountain side, an enchanted glade. You can picture an actual place you know where you sense Wild God energies or describe the most perfect setting imaginable.

* Finally, name the strengths you seek: courage, freedom, wildness, joy.

* Keep the chant short so you can memorise it. As you did in the chants module (see page 293), play around with the words until they have a rhythm. If in a group, you can work together, each adding a phrase or line.

* When you are happy with the chant, decide where and when you will call the God. Is it a sunrise or sunset ritual, after dark or a crisp autumn or winter's day in pale sunlight or mist? Do you want to try on May morning to waken the Green Man or the Autumn Equinox at dusk to call the stag? Do you want to go to an animal conservancy or deer park where you can wander through woodland and see the actual creatures? Is it a forest chant, best on a hillside, a special hilltop like Glastonbury Tor, near a chalk horse or giant figure etched into the earth or some natural rock sculpture, a sea shore or a garden?

* You may need to stay nearby overnight or for a weekend. You could make it an outing for the coven or group of friends, perhaps combined with a visit to a ritual at a sacred site or place of natural beauty. You may prefer to take yourself off alone to a place you have always wanted to visit, staying in a woodland chalet or caravan on a quiet, rural site if you don't want to camp.

* Will you drum to raise the power, clap or stamp as you chant or it is a chant for stillness, to be whispered softly into the breeze? You could work with a quiet chant in the garden or a local park, perhaps listening to Pan pipe music first through a headset.

* Begin chanting and increase the pace and intensity (unless it is a still, quiet call). Continue until you become part of the sound and can no longer consciously recall the words. Then when you feel you have reached a peak or that you are compelled to be silent, stop and wait.

* This is the hard part for you may have to wait an hour or more, maybe much less if you are lucky. Then who knows what you will see or hear? Pipes in the distance, the sound of hooves, the sight of a magnificent stag in the thicket or a strange green figure surrounded by luminosity in the distance. There may be mist or sudden sunshine and you may get the strongest vision in your mind and hear the returning call of the Wild One in your mind, on the wind or in a sudden animal call. Expect nothing and you will get something, even a strong inner bubble of joy that has you running and laughing or adding whole new verses to the chant: the answer from Cernunnos, Herne or Pan.

* The ordinary world will return, but for a time colours will seem brighter, bird song clearer and sharper. If you can, spend the day outdoors and as soon as possible try to visit a place where there are horned and hoofed creatures that you can move close to and experience the physical sensations.

* Try to weave the experiences into an expanded chant based on your insights of both the Wild God and the creatures that inspired the myths.

Further research

Choose a God theme that interests you and explore online and in books other mythological images and myths surrounding Wild, Earth and Sacrifice Gods. Locate different chants and poetry connected with them and copy the best into your Book of Shadows to use as the basis for your own rituals.

Further information

Recommended reading

* Dixon-Kennedy, Mike, *A Companion to Celtic Myths and Legends*, Sutton Publishing, 2004
* Fortune, Dion, *The Goat Foot God*, SIL Trading, 1990
* Green, Miranda, *Animals in Celtic Life and Myth*, Routledge, 1998
* Hine, Phil, *Condensed Chaos, An Introduction to Chaos Magic*, New Falcon Publications, 1995
* MacCulloch, J A, *The Religion of the Ancient Celts* (1911), R A Kessinger, 2003
* Neasham, Mary, *The Spirit of the Green Man*, Green Magic, 2003

Websites

* *At The Edge*
  Excellent photographs of Green men in churches
  www.indigogroup.co.uk/edge/green men.htm
* *The Goat Foot God*
  Dion Fortune inspired Pan site
  ww.geocities.com/wiccantwinpaths /godstuff/panstuff/pananddionfor tune.htm
* *Myth*ing Links*
  Excellent links sites to a wealth of Green Man information
  www.mythinglinks.org/ct~green men.html
* *Doreen Valiente Invocation to Horned God*
  www.sacredtexts.com/bos/ bos406.htm

AMULETS, TALISMANS AND CHARMS

(*A*)mulets, talismans and charms are symbols that store power or protection that can be released over a number of weeks or even months and years. They can serve as the symbol of a spell and gain their power as a result of the amplified and released spell energies. However, they may also be specifically crafted or bought ready made and filled with power to fulfil a specific purpose. In either case, they act as repositories of power, healing and protection when we cannot or would not want to carry out a ritual.

Wax or clay symbols are generally relatively short-lived materials and so are used for relatively short-lived talismans (see The Power of Symbols, page 303). However, some clay images of women with a baby or phallic symbols from altars of the Mother Goddess Hathor have survived from Ancient Egyptian times, as well as the more durable gold, crystal or faience amulets. This is because they were preserved in tombs or buried by the sands.

At this point, you might like to look back to page 99 on making tools for some basic magickal symbols that serve as charms. Look also at page 303, The Power of Symbols, and page 278 to remind yourself how to write names and wishes as talismanic shapes, using the square of Saturn. The following modules will teach you the runes, Egyptian hieroglyphs and the angelic scripts for marking talismans and charms, with the astrological and planetary glyphs on page 193. The most important Ancient Egyptian hieroglyphs are given in this module. The theme is continued later with spell bags, mojos and medicine bundles, Isis bags and crane bags.

Strictly speaking, an amulet is a protective symbol with natural protective qualities, usually made of a natural substance such as wax or crystal, sometimes crafted in the shape of a protective animal or bird or a body part, like a heart. It can be tuned magickally into a particular home or person and will last until the amulet crumbles or, in the case of herbs, loses its fragrance.

A charm is a small object over which magickal spells have been chanted or on which magick words are engraved or painted. It has no limits to its life as long as it remains intact and any visible markings do not fade. A charm increases in power as it is used. Generally it has a general ongoing attracting purpose, whether for love, money, health or good luck. It can be natural, such as a crystal, personally crafted by or for the recipient, or it can be manufactured.

A talisman is a charm made and/or empowered for a single specific purpose: for example, to attract success in a particular venture and not general success in unspecified areas of life. For this reason the talisman is more powerful than the charm. The time limit is generally imposed at the time of making and empowering. In practice, the terms amulet, charm and talisman are frequently regarded as interchangeable.

The Ancient Egyptians were the first to use amulets and charms in formal magick and so they have exerted great influence over modern usage. They empowered symbols, such as crystals or clay figures, with magickal words and substances, such as incense. Thus they could carry with them or invoke from the deities and ancestors power and protection that was regularly invoked from the cradle to grave and then into the afterlife. This concept is an extension of the word and image magick we have been working with.

Amulet power

E Wallis Budge (see further reading) defines an amulet:

as an object which is endowed with magickal powers, and which of its own accord uses these powers ceaselessly on behalf of the person who carries it, or causes it to be laid up in his house, or attaches it to some of his possessions, to protect him and his belongings from the attacks of evil spirits or from the Evil Eye.

Even though today we recognise that many misfortunes and ill health are not directly due to malign influences, the core definition is very valid.

There was a fundamental belief certainly in Ancient Egypt that a statue or any image of a deity or one of its animal representations could, if magickally charged and purified, be a receptacle for part of the soul or ka of the deity. Wearing or carrying a tiny statue or picture of a deity, animal or hieroglyph endowed the owner with some aspect, qualities or strengths of the divine power that was believed to dwell within the charged charm. The power would last as long as the amulet, if the wearer remained pure of intent and kept the amulet magickally cleansed.

Wax amulets are especially potent, because they have been created from the four ancient elements: Earth as the candle itself, Air as the smoke rises, Fire the flame, and Water the melting wax. The union is said to create a fifth element that is captured in the wax tablet.

The origin of amulets

The original protective amulets were animal parts or representations of animals made on tusks or bones. Marked talismanic images to attract good fortune were engraved on animal bones or tusks and were linked in early hunter societies with the success of hunting expeditions. For example, a human figure with the head of a lion, intended probably to endow the user with courage, was carved from mammoth ivory 32,000 years ago and was found at the Hohlenstein–Staddel Grave at Asselfingen in Germany. It was small enough to be carried and may have also been intended to give protection against wild beasts. It can be seen in the British Museum. Minerals and meteorites were also prized for their protective value.

Amulets made from specific parts of an animal were an attempt to transfer the animal's salient quality or strength to the possessor of the talisman. For example, a hawk's head or claw was sewn into children's clothes by the Inuit in North America to give the infants the clear vision and hunting ability of the hawk, and thus the power to survive in a society that still largely relies on hunting. In the Flinders Petrie Museum in London can be seen prehistoric Egyptian figures of animals in stone, ivory and clay, some intended to be worn: for example, a bone hair pin with an antelope on top and another with a bird on the pin head and a tiny ivory crocodile.

Some amulets were made in the shape of parts of the human body: for example, a phallus to bring fertility. Another popular charm was a miniature leg or foot to prevent mobility problems. In death, body part amulets were placed on the appropriate part of the mummy: for example, a crystal or faience foot charm on the foot of deceased so he or she might move swiftly in the afterlife. Colour was also significant for amulets and talismans and this is one way you can add significance to any talismans, amulets and charms you make or buy (see page 512).

Deity representations had both protective and empowering qualities. Beeswax images of the Celtic Triple Goddess were cast into sacred wells to call the fertility of the Goddess into the suppliant (see page 374).

Bees for abundance and good things and butterflies rebirth are symbols of the Mother Goddess from Neolithic times. Both remain excellent charm symbols. In Mediaeval Europe, holy relics were carried by pilgrims and sometimes the bones of saints or what were believed to be fragments of the true cross were believed to cure ills.

Special crystals had similar powers. One of the most famous healing stones was a diamond belonging to the biblical Abraham. It was reputed to cure instantly any sick person who looked on it. When Abraham died, it was reabsorbed by the sun. During the Middle Ages, healing gems were placed on the shrines of saints and accorded religious and magickal powers. One example is the sapphire on the shrine of St Erkinwald in Old St Paul's Cathedral in London. This was donated in 1391 by Richard Preston, a London grocer who made the offering so that people visiting the shrine might be cured of eye diseases.

Magickal amulets today

In the modern world amulets can protect people, homes, cars, possessions and places. Though the amulet does not need empowering, I always bless an amulet before use and ask that it may bring only good.

Unless worn as jewellery, amulets are often kept out of sight but unlike the mojo bag (see page 417) if they are found or touched by others it does not destroy their purpose. You might like to cleanse it with smudge or by sprinkling a hyssop infusion or three circles of salt round it. Keep it in a bag or a wooden box or bury the amulet in the garden or an indoor plant pot.

Magickal timings

Make or bless amulets on one of the three or four days after the full moon at dusk or just afterwards. Talismans and charms should be made/empowered on any of the three days before the full moon, again after dusk.

For a charm for change or major achievement, make it on the night of the full moon. However, I have found it is better made out of the direct light of the moon. Traditionally, the week before the Midsummer Solstice is said to be the best time of all for making protective amulets.

Old amulets are traditionally burned or buried on the eve of the Summer Solstice, but you can, of course, keep your amulets and charms for several years. If you don't want to replace your amulets annually, a better way is to wear or carry amulets and charms, the old and the new, from the Solstice eve, then, having empowered the new one at noon, remove the old one and keep it safe for special occasions, when you wear both.

Talismanic power

The actual word talisman comes from the Greek teleo, which means to achieve or bring into effect through the mind.

A visible talisman is an image or words engraved or marked on bone, stone, crystal metal, wood, paper wax or clay for a particular purpose. Synthetic materials are not so good. An invisible talisman is one empowered by reciting the words over the symbol (a spoken charm) or by writing the purpose in incense smoke over it. It portrays a symbol of what it is intended to attract into your life by sympathetic magick. For example, an engraved or painted acorn might be etched in a wax or clay tablet, so that your business will grow as the oak grows from the acorn (a sort of magickal shorthand).

You can make talismans for any positive purpose for yourself or other people. If you have a friend or family member who needs protection or a particular strength or healing, but you know they would not like to have it personally, you can keep a talisman (or amulet) with a photograph of them, as long as it is not an infringement of free will.

Charms

Charms are more general, open-ended power or protection and, like talismans, can be made of almost anything and either engraved or written visibly or invisibly empowered. Written charms often use a magickal alphabet or a shape, such as that formed by the Saturn square (see page 278) that can represent a message, such as protection or money, as well as a name.

By far the most numerous talismans in the Ancient Egyptian world were those representing a particular hieroglyph that would empower and protect both the living and the dead in their journey through the afterlife, when the charms were placed on the mummy: for example, the scarab on the heart. The symbols of power were engraved on crystals or gems or precious metal, such as gold, which symbolised the sun and immortality, or on symbols made of faience or glass. For ordinary people who could not read the meaning of the hieroglyph, the magick was doubly powerful.

Like runes, a hieroglyph releases the power of its meaning when written magickally. Somewhere between the 11th and 22nd Egyptian dynasties, 2040–1050 BCE, the written amulet became increasingly popular, whether a spell or an actual hieroglyph. Traditionally these word charms were written on papyrus.

You can draw your own hieroglyph charms on parchment or good quality white or dark paper with fine coloured ink pens, acrylic or glass paint and brushes or, if you are very skilled, with a special calligraphy quill. You can follow the amulet colours listed below or use your imagination. You can also draw the hieroglyph in incense smoke over the symbol, if you wish the purpose to remain secret.

You can create a hieroglyphic charm for a lover or family member and a newborn baby. You could write the name of the person in hieroglyphs (see page 451) and add one or two of the hieroglyphics of power listed below.

Wax hieroglyph charms were very popular in Ancient Egypt, because although they did not last as long as crystal or stone, they are excellent for a short-term talismanic need where power must be concentrated. This is still true in modern magick, because you melt the power or protection into the creation process and so it is truly absorbed. For example, there was an old spell in Ancient Egypt that involved melting wax while reciting the name of the desired person and saying:

As the wax melts, so may her heart be molten to me.

This has passed into westernised magick and afterwards the melted wax already empowered by the spell can be made into a heart-shaped charm on which entwined hearts or the hieroglyph of the heart is marked.

Colour is important for wax and crystal amulets, charms and talismans, and you can buy candles or beeswax sheets in a huge range of shades of the different colours.

Use the more vibrant shades for any fast-acting need or where power is needed to overcome obstacles or launch a venture.

Hieroglyphs of power

The Ba or spirit

For freedom, for starting a new life or venture, for spiritual power, for aiming high, for achieving dreams, for protection against criticism and those that unfairly block your path.

The Ba, a hawk with a human head, represented the spirit of the deceased that flew out of the mummified body and gave life to the spirit body that dwelled with the Blessed Dead. The hawk image linked it to Horus, the falcon-headed god.

The Ba amulet was traditionally made from gold, studded with gems, to indicate the immortality of its nature and in death was placed upon the breastbone of the mummy. You could use a sparkling yellow crystal such as citrine on which to draw the image.

The Boat

For travel, for holidays, bridging gaps between people, organisations or nations, for successful house moves and career changes, for moving into better times, for

protection on journeys of all kinds, for partnerships and where co-operation is necessary, for communication and writing skills.

The Sun God Ra crossed the sky each day in his solar boat. Ma'at, the Goddess of truth and natural law, rode in the sun boat, and even Ra was subject to her law and her allotting of the day and night, time and seasons. The Boat amulet usually took the form of model boats placed in the tomb, made of wood, on which the deceased could sail following the sun. But you can draw or paint one on a tiger's eye or a brown-banded agate.

Djed, Tet or backbone of Osiris

For physical and emotional strength and endurance, for protection against all harm and fears, for resistance to pressure or coercion, anti-bullying and all matters of justice and prevention of deceit or betrayal, for loyalty in permanent relationships and friendships.

The Djed represented the trunk of the plant that grew round the chest containing the murdered body of Osiris, that empowered with his strength, grew into a mighty tree. In a person's lifetime, the Djed amulet was used to protect the spine and to cure back injuries. On the mummy it would also ensure the deceased would rise up and stand tall and that Osiris would carry their spirit.

The Djed was traditionally made of gold or wood, but can be drawn on any deep blue stone, such as lapis lazuli or sodalite. You can also use the Osirian colour black, perhaps obsidian, jet or black jasper, or a green, malachite.

The Frog

For fertility, increased prosperity and better health, regeneration and renewed good fortune, for reviving past ventures and turning failures into success, for satisfying sexuality in a committed relationship.

The Frog is a Nile creature and as such is associated with abundance and fertility. The seemingly miraculous cycle of transformation from egg through tadpole to frog gave these creatures strong associations with resurrection. Heqet or Heket was the Frog Goddess, wife of the Potter God Khnum, who fashioned people from the Nile clay. She breathed life into the figures.

The amulet is good on a green stone such as jade, malachite, which was popular in Egypt, or an aquamarine, for water.

The Ladder

For career success, confidence, optimism, achievement in learning or tests of any kind, for psychic powers, for promotion, improvement in every area of life and good health.

The Ladder represented the means by which the deceased could gain access to the heavens. Osiris used a ladder created by Ra to ascend into the heavens and he and Thoth or Horus would help the deceased to climb the ladder. It was the forerunner of the pyramids.

Amulets or model ladders made of wood were placed in tombs right through the

Middle and Late Kingdoms, but you can draw or paint your ladder on any brown stone such as fossilised wood or brown jasper.

Menat

For abundance, prosperity, a return to health, unexpected blessings, gifts, fertility, creativity and sexual passion.

Menat is the symbol of nourishment, reproduction and fertility, of both humans and the land, represented by the annual flooding of the Nile. In myth, this was caused by the tears of Isis at the death of Osiris and the rich silt left when the water receded was her gift to the people. Anuket was the Goddess from whose womb the Nile waters flowed and she was bringer of abundance. She filled the grain houses and cared for the poor. It also represented the union of male and female and ensured fertility as well as nourishment in this and the afterlife.

This amulet was made in bronze or ceramic. You can draw it on any red crystal, such as carnelian or even reddish orange amber. It was carried ritually or worn as a pendant.

Nefer

For harmony, increased good fortune, beauty and radiance, joy, happy marriage and relationships, leisure and fun, for music, dance and the performing arts.

Nefer represents the ancient Egyptian oud, a lute type instrument with between nine and twelve strings. The amulet Nefer placed on the deceased promised eternal happiness. The perfect form and harmony of the instrument represented fulfilment and pleasure. Hathor with whom Isis is closely connected, was Goddess of music and dance, of joy and creativity and red is her colour.

The amulet was made of gold, carnelian or other red crystal or ceramic. You can use jasper, carnelian or reddish amber for your drawing of Nefer.

The Scarab

For new beginnings, restoration of what has been lost or stolen, for protection against all ills and harm and for fighting illness or depression, for transformation.

Sacred to Khepri, the God of the sun at dawn who was depicted as scarab-headed and was himself represented by the hieroglyph of the scarab, this amulet was a profound symbol of rebirth to the Egyptians. It was a beetle that laid its eggs in a small ball of dung to provide nourishment for the young. The Egyptians saw the beetle offspring emerging from the balls as a symbol of rebirth and transformation.

Khepri means he who rolls. Khepri was said to roll the ball of the sun across the sky, bringing each new day. In a mummy, the scarab, often imposed on a heart shape and given wings, was placed in the heart cavity.

Scarabs are found in a variety of colours and materials, including green marble, turquoise and blue faience. The green heart scarabs were inlaid with gold. But the most popular colour is sky blue and you can engrave your scarab on bright blue howlite or turquoise, or alternatively on rich green amazonite or malachite.

Shen

For permanence in all things, for fidelity, career and business security, for safety within the home and from external attack, for better days ahead, protection against sudden loss, for lasting happiness, health and long life.

Shen represents the orbit of the Sun around the Earth and so was a symbol of endless time. As an amulet placed upon the dead, it promised eternal life so long as the Sun endured. In funerary paintings on tomb walls, the protective sister goddesses Isis and Nephthys are pictured kneeling and resting their hands on Shen, which is sacred to Ra the Sun God. The amulet was painted in tombs and on coffins as well as on offering tablets. It was set close to the heart in the mummy.

As an amulet it was generally made of lapis lazuli, red jasper or carnelian, and you can draw it on any blue or red crystal.

Tjet or Buckle of Isis

The ultimate female power hieroglyph for all matters of female power, protection against abuse, strength and fertility, for protection of women, the restoration of lost love and for increasing magickal powers.

This amulet represents the Buckle of the Girdle of Isis, and is associated with the fertilising blood of Isis. There are numerous ancient chants that have passed from the funerary texts into popular folk tradition beginning:

The blood of Isis and the strength of Isis and the words of power of Isis

that can be woven into a protective chant to empower this amulet.

It was worn on the neck of the mummy to ensure maternal protection and rebirth in the afterlife, as Osiris was reborn through the magick of Isis. It also enabled the spirit to pass into the blessed realms and also to return to the body in the tomb when he or she wished.

The amulet is usually red whether carnelian, red jasper or red glass, though it can be crafted of gold. Sometimes there was a green crystal as part of the design.

The buckle of Isis is also important in knot magick (see page 661).

The Heart

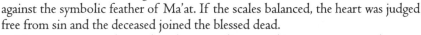

For determination, and willpower, discovering the truth about a hidden matter, for justice, for calming excess emotions, for being freed from unfair accusation or criticism, for employment and specially for getting the job you want, and for love.

The Heart was the source of good and evil intentions that to the Ancient Egyptians were quite as significant as thoughts. In the afterlife, each heart was weighed on scales in the halls of the dead against the symbolic feather of Ma'at. If the scales balanced, the heart was judged free from sin and the deceased joined the blessed dead.

You can use any red crystal, such as carnelian or red jasper, copper or silver.

The Vulture

For protection against all harm from whatever source, for freedom from illusion, for starting again under difficulty, for successful major life changes, for banishing what is destructive and for overcoming addictions; good for safe travel especially by air or long distance; for childbirth, mothers and children of any age.

The Vulture hieroglyph represents the protection and power of the Divine Mother Isis and was used as protection for the deceased with the ankh for life engraved on each talon. Isis demonstrated the power of maternal protection when she cared for Horus in the marshes, guarding him against his evil uncle who would have destroyed him. Her wings were also outstretched shielding Osiris and the Pharaohs.

Often made in gold, the vulture can be drawn on a yellow crystal such as citrine, or a clear crystal quartz or amethyst.

Wedja

For prosperity, self-employment, for all creative and artistic ventures, for inspiration, for fighting debt and overcoming job losses, for fame and recognition.

Wedja means fire and because fire was used by the Ancient Egyptians to forge metal and smelt gold, it represents prosperity. However, the hieroglyph was based on a bow drill that was turned in a shaped piece of wood (the lower part of the hieroglyph) to produce fire by friction, thereby generating vitality from itself rather than an external source of fuel.

It was often gold, but you can use any golden crystal such as tiger's eye or a rich red blood agate.

Spoken charms

These are generally spoken over the object to be empowered that may look like a perfectly ordinary object except that it has been empowered with the charm words and sometimes actions. It can empower a talisman for a single purpose or the more generally focused charm. It can be further re-empowered at any time you feel the power diminishing or after a personal reversal by saying the words over it.

Some objects may already be endowed with personal significance, a favourite piece of jewellery, such as alternately threaded jet and amber beads, and a silver pentagram pendant worn during ceremonies or a favourite ring. You can also use this method for empowering any engraved charm or talisman.

When writing spoken charms in advance, keep them simple and to two or four lines, rhyming, like this adaptation of the traditional healing rune or spoken charm I often use for healing crystals or herbs. It should be spoken softly throughout until you feel the charm is filled with the healing power:

Hear the rune I call to bind,
Body, flesh, soul and mind,
Balance, peace, alone remain
And [name sick person or animal] shall be whole again.

Another adaptation I use for healing and for peace and reconciliation charms or talismans comes from part of the Druidic prayer, as far as I know attributed to Ross Nichols, one of the fathers of modern Druidry. His book (see recommended reading) is an excellent source of Celtic chants and poems that you can adapt, as well as a good introduction to Wicca's sister religion. Though it does not rhyme, the words repeated as a soft regular mantra are excellent for any peace, protection or love charms or for ones you may bury in land to heal it or guard your home:

Grant, Goddess, thy protection; and in thy protection, strength;
and in thy strength, understanding; and in understanding, love;
and in love, the love of all Creation; and in the love of all Creation, the love of the Goddess and all
Goodness.
So may the circle be unbroken. Blessed be.

For creating an active or empowering charm use a fast punchier rhyme, spoken like a skipping chant faster and louder. For example:

By Maiden, Mother and Crone, I empower thee,
By Maiden, Mother and Crone, I bless thee,
By Maiden Mother and Crone, I purify thee
And by the Father/Horned One, I send thee free into the world.
So mote it be.

If working alone, hold your hands palms down a few centimetres above the charm, the power hand moving clockwise and the receptive hand anticlockwise, increasing the power and momentum of chant and movement until you release the power into the charm, by jabbing your index fingers into it with a final chant. For an unbreakable or solid charm, like a stone or silver ring, raise and release the power by tossing it rhythmically in your cupped hands as you chant.

In the case of a coven charm or one that the coven is empowering for someone, the group can pass it fast from hand to hand clockwise round a seated circle as all chant the charm words, raising the intensity to a height and with a final toss in the air (gently cupped if it is delicate) by the person who is leading the ritual, while everyone else jabs their index fingers towards it, infusing the power.

For a peace or healing charm, if working alone lower and slow the words to a whisper after raising the energy. Push the energies in very gently with your index fingers so you just touch the surface lightly while whispering the final chant.

In a group instead of tossing it you can draw the power gently into the symbol as everyone gently pushes the light towards it with their index fingers, by saying softly:

So may it be. Blessings be within the charm and enter those [name if you wish] upon whose
light it shines.

Metal charms

Metal charms and talismans, either engraved (see below) or invisibly empowered with a spoken spell or incense writing, are one of the most powerful charm materials and were also used for protective amulets. Charm bracelets with different charms, such as a boat for safe travel, a horseshoe for good luck, a key for a happy home and a heart for love, linked together on the chain, are not so fashionable. However empowered, they are ideal for integrating luck bringing and protection.

Metals have also been traditionally engraved with magickal purpose. Sometimes rings were etched inside with words of love. In Europe during the 16th and 17th centuries, posy rings (from the French poésie, meaning poetry) were engraved inside, so that the inscription was hidden from all but the wearer.

Because the ring is a perfect circle it symbolises love without end. The following was engraved on an old ring that is now displayed in the British Museum in London. It is made of gold and bears an image of clasped hands (a symbol of fidelity) on the outside. Inside the ring in a circle were images that substituted for words in the written love charm, clasped hands, followed by entwined hearts, followed by a knot, interspersed with the words:

Our hands [clasped hand image substitute] and hearts [heart image substituted] with one consent. Have tied this knot [knot image substituted] until death prevent.

Gold, metal of the sun, stands for success, wealth, ambition and lasting love. Silver, metal of the moon, is for secrets, magickal insights, moon power, new or young love and fertility, and the growth of health and abundance.

Copper, the metal of Venus, is for true and passionate love, health, healing, peace and family.

Iron, the metal of Mars, is common as a protective amulet: for example, a metal nail or stave or stake buried in the earth, or hammered into a door or furniture to protect your home and family against any kind of attack. It also appeared as nails in protective witch bottles (see page 426).

Tin, the metal of Jupiter, is for leadership, justice, power protection and abundance in all things.

Pewter, the metal of Saturn, is for security and stability, for protection of home and property. Lead, Saturn's other metal, was used for curse tablets in Roman tablets, but because it s toxic is not used in modern magick. Pewter incorporates the more positive aspects of banishing and binding charms.

Making charms from natural objects

Of course, natural items have power in themselves, like the acorn a symbol of the growth of lasting prosperity or success because it was the embryo oak tree (see page 414 for lucky roots and similar). Many Native American tribes believe in manitou, whereby if a person on finding a particular object has a psychic sensation, sometimes described as a sense of sudden excitement or awareness, the object thereby takes on great magickal and healing significance.

Anything can serve as a protective or empowering charm, from a rose worn or carried (its dried petals in a small bag if preferred) for an important love tryst, to the popular protective red natural fibre cord tied around the wrist as a bracelet that retains luck and protection until it breaks.

In Leland's *Aradia, Gospel of the Witches*, a pure white stone with a hole in the middle is described as the talisman of Diana and also it has become associated with Aradia. This book contains an invocation to empower it as a token of good fortune, but equally you can create your own chant.

The holey stone has an extensive folk tradition of healing and magickal power and if you can find a white one on a beach or lake side then it is a real luck bringer, worn on a cord round your neck or carried in the traditional red bag. Drilled ones do not count. Called the stones of Odin, as well as Diana/Aradia, they will send absent healing and give visions of other dimensions. They protect homes, workplaces, farms and farm buildings, warehouses and boats, if suspended on a red cord tied with three knots. Stones with three holes are especially powerful. They also guard children and animals and attract great good fortune in every way – and that's before empowering! If you can find a large one for a coven circle, your gatherings will be blessed.

A perfectly round red stone thrown in the air three times and caught each time while a spell is chanted is another luck bringer if the stone is then carried as a charm. Some of these stone empowering spells, like the round stone one in Leland's book, are not entirely positive. But you can create your own for good positive purpose (see the Witch's Rune on page 300 for a few ideas).

You can of course use any crystal, either as it is or with a symbol painted on or written over with incense smoke (see page 532 for the magickal meanings of different crystals). If you are very dextrous, paint on the crystal with glass or acrylic an image to make it a talisman or buy a small crystal or animal or bird.

In the *Gospel of the Witches* and also in the folk magick of Chile is described a lemon with pins stuck in it. In Chile, the lemon forms the body of a lucky pig. Coloured or silver pins were used in the Dianic version and in Chile the pig is sprinkled with salt and burned. The Dianic version has a less benign connotation of a lemon with 13 black pins stuck in it to hex someone, but I think we should blame the teller and not Diana. After the chanting, the lemon pig would be burned on the hearth fire or in a metal bucket half filled with sand, outside the front door if possible, to release the power of the charm – or burned by the recipient.

Pomanders made from an orange pierced with cloves and rolled in spices are another popular folk lore charm to bring happiness in the home, abundance, love and fidelity. The pomander is hung with red ribbons in the centre of the home so the air circulates.

If you do break your amulet or talisman you haven't lost the luck. Make a new one (any time in the month after dusk in an emergency) and wrap a small piece of the old one with it to transfer the luck. Bury the rest of the old one under a healthy plant or tree.

PRACTICAL ASSIGNMENT

Creating your wax personalised talisman or charm

Wax amulets are especially potent because they have been created from the four ancient elements: Earth, the candle itself; Air, as the smoke rises; Fire, the flame; and Water, the melting wax. The union is said to create a fifth element that is captured in the wax tablet.

* You are limited only by your imagination. You can create an animal shape by it cutting out of the wax for animal qualities or draw a circle and in it create a representation of a deity, an animal or what is the amulet is for, an image of baby or a lover in the circle of wax.

* You can alternatively use the hieroglyphic alphabet or the runic alphabet though this is used more often on stone or wood or angel letters (see pages 431 and 451) to write your name on the wax amulet. Alternatively, with the engraving tool you use to mark your candles, you could etch on it a word of power or the appropriate strength you need.

* You can create additional power and protection by endowing the amulet with a secret word of power or an adaptation of a deity name. For example:

    Diana/Artemis who with her silver arrows protects all women from harm.

* You never write this secret power down except in smoke and say it only in your mind. If the talisman or charm was for you, you could begin with, *I am* and your magick name/s spoken aloud, if you are alone.

Making a wax amulet or talisman

* The easiest method is to take a sheet of beeswax, preferably one coloured with natural dyes. Take a piece about twice or three times the diameter or length of the amulet/talisman. Thin ones break very easily.

* Melt it gently over a candle or for 'techno ease' use a hair dryer for a minute to soften the wax. Then you can press or mould the wax either flat or into any shape and cut round it or, better still, just press into shape.

* Put it on a tray or flat plate covered with greaseproof paper so it will not stick if you are going to engrave it. Use your own favourite symbol. Alternatively you can melt a beeswax candle.

* If you want a specific shape, such as a circle (potential), square (stability) or triangle (increase), drip the molten wax from the lit candle to create the shape you want. Use a metal tray or very strong greaseproof paper on the tray for easy removal (or use a wooden spatula).

* While the wax is still soft, engrave any talismanic symbols using your candle engraving tool, a small screwdriver, a paper knife, wooden skewer or a metal nail.

* When the wax is set if you melted the candle, ease it from the tray with a wooden spatula or very gently with a knife.

- Empower it with a spoken charm, by writing its purpose in incense or using the tool empowering methods in module 8 for a really important talisman or charm.
- Finally, wrap the amulet or talisman in fabric ready to place where you will keep it safely, or find a safe place to display it where it will not be touched except by you or the person for whom it is intended.

Further research

Continue with the symbol work you started in earlier modules.

Note any symbols that could be used either as amulets in a natural form or engraved to mark talismans.

Add your own associations to the conventional meanings in your Book of Shadows so that the symbols you use are personally meaningful to you.

Further information

Recommended reading

- Ball, Pamela, *Spells, Charms, Talismans and Amulets*, Castle, 2002
- Budge, E Wallis, *Amulets and Superstitions*, Dover Publications, 1978
- Germond, Philipe, *The Symbolic World of Egyptian Amulets*, 5 Continents Editions, 2005
- Kunz, George Frederick, *The Magic of Jewels and Charms*, Dover Publications, 1997
- Lippman, Deborah, and Colin, Paul, *How to make Amulets, Charms and Talismans*, Citadel Press, 1994
- Nichols, Ross, *The Book of Druidry*, Aquarian, 1990

Websites

- *Lucky Mojo*
  Huge online lucky charm resource base
  www.luckymojo.com/allluckyw.html
- *Virtual Egyptian Museum*
  A cyber-museum of antiquities
  www.virtual-egyptian-museum.org

Spell, charm and mojo bags

mpowered spell or charm bags or bundles of items are more complex and effective than a single charm. In them, you draw together different items with similar energies or combine different energies for a specific purpose: for example, to protect the home against natural disasters or human attack.

In Leland's *Gospel of the Witches*, a devotee invokes Aradia in a field at midnight carrying water, wine and salt and a talisman and a red small bag *which I ever hold in my hand*. These are used in a blessing rite to invoke the favour of Aradia.

A spell bag is defined as one made as part of a spell that is empowered by the spell. A charm bag is empowered less formally immediately after making. I have written about herbal spell bags, the most common form of bag, on page 413.

Though magick bags inevitably decayed over the millennia and we do not have the same archaeological evidence for them in early societies as we do for crystal amulets and charms, we can speculate their existence from the practices of remaining hunter-gatherer societies whose magick has been unchanged for thousands of years. They include the Sámi reindeer people in Lapland, the Inuit of North America and Canada, and the rainforest peoples of the Amazon and Africa. Other larger bags or bundles of items, like the Celtic Druid crane bag and the Native North American medicine bundle, belong to a specific individual and are an ongoing part of their spiritual life.

Likewise, some witches and covens have a private collection of magickal treasures that I call the Isis bag or pouch, named after the Mother of Enchantment. Others dedicate this to their own Mother deity. These bags reflect the traditions of the individual, a tribe or coven and contents may be added from sacred occasions: for example, a few perfect empowered seeds collected at the Spring Equinox or Ostara rites (see week 34).

Finally, the much-maligned witch bottle can be a real source of protection and positivity. It is from the 1500s that we have the first surviving examples of witch bottles as such, though protective charm bottles were used long before this. At this period they seem to have been created not only to repel witches but also to cause them harm and suffering. The modern witch bottle is much more benign and created by pagans and lovers of folklore, as well as witches, to protect the home, animals and family from harm and also to a lesser extent to transform any negativity it absorbs on your behalf into health and abundance.

Charm or spell bags

A charm or spell bag is a collection of items that may include herbs, roots, crystals, stones and feathers, coins, beads and tiny symbols made of metal, ceramics or formed from beeswax. It can be talismanic, created for a specific purpose with a specified time limit, or be created for an ongoing need, such as protection where it may be buried. Manufactured items can be used, but natural energies do seem to work best. The exception is if the item has some personal significance for you, like the stub of an airline ticket from a favourite holiday or a successful business trip to attract similar good things in future.

The bags are charmed or enchanted and will last if not buried either for a specified time or until any fragrance fades, when they are replaced for ongoing power or protection. You can make and empower bags for any positive purpose to attract good luck, love, health or prosperity to yourself or the recipient, to protect your home, car or property, or someone going on a journey, or as a gift for the birth or naming of a baby, a handfasting or a teenager leaving home. You can be really specific for a single focus bag, such as a love bag to attract a particular person, if it is right to be.

You can make spell bags, tied with nine knots for a binding purpose, to prevent someone being bullied or to stop burglars entering your home. Generally, however, witch bottles are more effective for binding work. Spell bags do not work for banishing as such (in my opinion).

The contents of a charm or spell bag

Spell or charm bags are made with three, five, seven or nine items of the kind and proportion you need for particular strengths or protection or to attract good fortune. A collective spell bag made by a coven or group for an individual or collective need can have 13 items or one for each member of a group (plus one to make the number odd). Make a spell bag on any of the three or four days before the full moon after dusk to attract good things; or on any of the three days after the full moon for protection; or on the night of the full moon (as for talismans made out of the light of the moon) for major purposes, change or urgent need and for conceiving a child.

Your dried spice or cooking herbs rack will be full of suitable contents. Ingredients need not be exotic. You can check pages 551–567 on herbs, to find the right magical ingredients. You can also improvise: for example, an old train ticket or plane ticket stub for travel, a small key for a new home, a ring for love and marriage. Look for small silver charms that come in all kinds of different shapes. You can improvise with softened beeswax or clay and craft tiny symbols and include if you wish a red thread knotted three times for protection. An iron nail will deter intruders to the home.

Sparkling or gleaming crystals like clear quartz crystal, citrine or golden tiger's eye, generally bring energy, focus and attract money; strongly coloured opaque crystals like red jasper, lapis lazuli or turquoise offer courage, power and success; soft transparent or pastel opaque ones such as rose quartz, amethyst or jade bring love or healing.

Darker crystals like smoke quartz or apache tear (obsidian you can see through) symbolise protection; gleaming dark ones like hematite or obsidian are fiercely defensive. Any banded or mottled stones like moss or brown agate or Dalmatian jasper (spotted, like the dog) carry security and stability and gentle growth. All agates are good for animals. They also protect property.

Lodestones (magnetic iron) are ideal for charm bags, either single or in pairs. Two that attract (one pointed and one round) will attract love or can be put in separate love bags like Adam and Eve roots, to be carried by a couple temporarily parted. A single pointed lodestone attracts money.

Roots are traditional in charm bags of all kinds: two Adam and Eve roots for love and fidelity; Archangel root (angelica/ masterwort) for protection of the home/healing; black snake root (black cohosh) for courage and passion; clover or trefoil (shamrock) for good luck; devil's shoestring for protection and employment; heather for wishes and lasting love; hawthorn berries for fertility and banishing harm; High John the Conqueror (poisonous) for money and success; lotus root for new opportunities and long life; Low John The Conqueror (galangal) for justice and success in all official matters; lucky hand root for employment, speculation and games of chance; and tonka beans (poisonous) for courage and good luck.

Natural items, such as nuts (fertility and prosperity), seeds in a knot of cloth to make them one item (for growth and gradual improvement in any area of life), small animal bones (for health, healing and good luck) and feathers (for travel, freedom and following dreams) can all be included. Different feathers have different meanings. You can find out from the myths and the behaviour of a bird its significance or just use a feather as a general focus. Lava or pumice (lava with holes) protects the home from natural disasters and intruders and attracts good luck.

If you wish, you can add a single drop of essential oil after making the bag (I don't count this as an item, though some practitioners do: it's your choice). You need only have a few all-purpose ones, such as patchouli for all financial matters or career, orange for fertility, marriage, happiness or abundance, pine for purification, prosperity, beginnings, anti-theft and psychic protection, or rose absolute for love, healing, good luck and protection of the family and home.

Making a charm or spell bag

Plan in advance the precise purpose of the bag and not only the components of the contents, but also the proportions you will need. If you regularly make spell bags, hoard small items to fill them, everything from packets of seeds to tiny silver or gold charms or earrings, hoop earrings being good for fertility and also prosperity. When you come back from abroad keep any coins, especially those with holes in the centre. Make sure that whatever you use is really dry to avoid your spell bag going mouldy. Aim for at least one fragrant item (two in a larger bag), then when the bag loses its fragrance you know it is time to replace even a more general bag.

If the bag is for you, add one item that is of personal significance to endow the bag and the purpose with your essence. Alternatively add something from your personal magick collection (see page 423 for making Isis bags), perhaps a shell, a stone you have found in a special place, a crystal, if you wish, or something small like a feather from your crane bag.

The bag

You can use either a circle of natural (if possible) cloth or leather, according to the size of charm bag you want. Most spell bags are pocket sized. For a household protection charm bag you could make one the size of a small evening bag. You can also use very tiny bags, the kind that hold a single crystal, for a root carried alone.

You can use silk, wool, velvet in different coloured fabrics according to the purpose of the bag: for example, blue for employment, career, justice, long-term and distance travel and house moves, leadership, and prosperity. See page 512 for a full list of colour meanings.

You can add further meaning by adding a different coloured cord for a secondary strength. However, if you prefer you can use a neutral colour bag for any purpose. Gather up and tie your cloth round the top when filled or make holes perforated round the edge for a drawstring. Otherwise, use a ready-made drawstring bag or fabric purse.

If you have the time and skill, you can embroider the ruling planetary glyph: for example, Venus for love (see page 215), the star sign of the individual for whom the bag is intended or a sigil made from the Square of Saturn that spells the purpose as a single word, such as money or love.

Assembling the bag

* Unless you are empowering the bag by making it the focus of a more general spell you will need a white or natural beeswax candle. You will also need two incense sticks, such as rose, lavender, myrrh or chamomile for a gentle purpose or ceremonial ones like frankincense, dragon's blood or sandalwood for more powerful urgent needs or protection. Have a separate holder for each incense to the left and right of the bag contents.

* Work after dark, outdoors if it is fine and add tea lights for extra illumination. Set out all your ingredients in advance separately in small dishes on a table or flat surface in the centre of the table or your altar. Spread out the cloth or open the bag you will use as the spell or charm bag.

* Begin by lighting the candle and then the two incense sticks from the candle while naming three times the purpose of the bag, who it is for and the timescale and say:

May it be so.

* Add each ingredient separately in the order that feels right, naming each one and its purpose. Add a single drop of essential oil with an empowerment to seal the bag energies (optional).

Empowering the bag

* You can use this method also for empowering talismans or charms (see previous module).

* Close or tie the bag with three six or nine knots (using a knot chant if appropriate – see week 50) and set it in the centre of the table or altar.

* Taking an incense stick in each hand, write with the one in your power hand the purpose of the spell bag, the name of the person and the timescale, if there is

one, plus a secret message of power. If the bag is for yourself, begin the incense empowerment with I am and your magick names.

❋ Then with the right hand incense stick moving clockwise and the other one anticlockwise a few centimetres over the bag, recite an empowerment or protection chant continuously. Be careful not to drop ash on the bag. An example chant for a talismanic one-purpose bag is:

Bring success and prosperity, if it is right to be; before the moon is past, so the spell I cast, will come to fruition.

❋ With spell bags even for protection and healing you need to build up the power to get them moving. When you can chant or move the sticks no faster, join the sticks for a second in the candle flame and say:

Flame and flare as I count three, one two three.

❋ Extinguish the candle by blowing it out on three. Return the incense to the holders, saying:

So power continue 'til the spell is done.

❋ Leave the incense to burn through.

❋ Alternatively, you can raise power with your wand in your power hand with the other hand keeping time anticlockwise or just your hands if you prefer, making the climax a dramatic sweep over the candle for flame and flare. Light the incense anyway.

❋ Up to four people can stand round the altar at the four directions and make a bag together or a coven can sit in a circle round the altar and each member add one of the 13 ingredients. If a larger number of people are present, for example, to make a bag for world peace or helping a famine area (the latter to be buried in an area of growing vegetation like a potato patch) each person can have a job, such as tying the bag with the required number of knots or leading a knot chant. You can tie a cord even around a drawstring bag.

❋ As each ingredient is added it is named aloud by the person adding it and the others present follow with:

So mote it be.

❋ The bag can be empowered by passing it round the coven or group clockwise as a simple empowering chant is made, maybe a variation of:

By the power of three, so we decree, nine by nine, the magick wind, within the seal, the power conceal, to work the charm, and none to harm, the purpose won, its work be done. Blessed be.

Keeping your bag

Once sealed your bag should not be opened. Unless the bag is a personalised or expensive one, I would be inclined to bury the bag along with items such as roots, nuts or bones after the allotted time span or when the bag loses its fragrance (three months is about maximum). You can scatter herbs, feathers or seeds to the wind. An outdoor protective charm bag tied to a tree or suspended high in a room may have a shorter life.

If the protection or purpose needs to be continued, take one item from the old bag for the new one. Whether ongoing or not, smudge any precious items you want to keep, such as silver charms, to free them of the bag charm.

If the bag is for someone else, give it to them as soon as possible after the spell. Name it for them if you cannot give it for whatever reason and keep it with a photograph of the person or animal wrapped in silk. There is no harm, because it is made for positive purpose.

It will not spoil the magic if the bag is seen, but it is better if you or the owner can keep it where it will not be touched. You could put it with your personal things in your bedroom, in a private drawer or locker at work or hidden in a high place in the home. Make very small charm bags to carry with you in a bag or pocket or keep in the glove compartment of a car or in luggage. Carry your bag at crucial times: for example, before an interview.

Mojo bags

In America, similar bags are called mojo. Originating in hoodoo, a form of folk magic still popular in the US today, the mojo like Hoodoo itself, draws upon an African tradition but has also incorporated Native North American and European magic. Though in recent years, hoodoo has adopted elaborate incenses, powders, oils and candles, much of its lore is based on an earlier tradition of very simple luck-bringing ingredients available even to the poorest people.

Mojo bags made and used by women living in the Memphis area are called nation sacks. The mojo bag has spread in popularity far beyond the practitioners of hoodoo and, like the Native American medicine or power bundle, is used by people interested in spiritual concepts who seek a traditional focus of power.

The term mojo probably comes either from a corruption of the European word magic or more likely the West African word mojuba, that means a prayer of praise. Mojo are small bags containing an odd number of symbols from 1 to 13. Symbols are drawn from objects manufactured as well as the natural world and are combined to attract or protect from particular energies.

They differ from the charm bag in that they are dressed with a liquid, either alcohol, an essential oil or special oils you can buy on line or from New Age stores, such as all-purpose Florida water or with mixed herbs and root oils with names like Love Come To Me. Traditionally the liquid is alcohol, such as barley wine for abundance and whisky or cognac for prosperity. The use of empowering but less aesthetically pleasing body fluids has fortunately died out and certainly is not advisable for indoor mojo. You can easily mix your own using cheaper fragrance oils with the properties you want: for example, cinnamon, rose and jasmine for lasting passionate love. Keep them in old fragrance oil bottles if you regularly make mojo.

Mojo must always be kept out of sight as if they are touched or seen by someone else they use the luck or protection.

Mojo colours and fabrics

Mojo bags are generally made of red flannel. However, more recently bags are also made in different colours suited to the wish and in natural fabrics or even leather, especially when used as more general charms.

* **Green** for success in any business venture and for gradual increase in fortune and money
* **Blue** for success or prosperity in enterprises or projects that you have already started; pale shades of blue signify peace and protection
* **Yellow** for speculation and attracting luck in uncertain times or necessarily risky enterprises
* **White** for anything new or for fast results, for health and for baby blessings
* **Red** for any absolutely any purpose, especially in the traditional red flannel, also for love and passion

The contents of a mojo bag

You can be as inventive as you like, but it is a good idea to use items that are of significance to you and are relatively easily obtained, so that the bag is in no way alien to your personal life context. Staying within commonsense folk magic roots carries inbuilt protection. At toy stores or antique markets, you can often find miniature loaves of bread for abundance or tiny dishes of fruit for health and fertility. Silver and gold charms are a good addition. Below I have listed some common mojo ingredients that you can combine.

* Lucky hand root, the root of the orchid most commonly used in mojo bags, traditionally placed in a bag to bring luck to gamblers. It will attract fortune to all forms of speculation or risk-taking, whether in a personal career gamble or a professional or personal decision involving uncertainty and needing luck. It is also helpful for finding a job, especially after a period of unemployment.

* Miniature playing cards, for example, the nine of hearts called the wish card that promises the fulfilment of hopes and dreams. The ten of diamonds is good in any mojo bag where fast results are needed. All diamonds are associated with prosperity, the house and home and officialdom. Hearts are for love, fertility, births and relationships, spades for speculation and risks, creative ventures, holidays and travel, and clubs are for learning, justice and medicine, tests, overcoming or avoiding disruption and new beginnings. A very tiny complete pack in a bag is good for doing deals of any kind, for turning your life or finances around and for contracts and property matters.

* A traditional silver dollar (you can buy this mail order) or other silver coin often combined with basil or dried kelp, wrapped in a green currency note, will bring money into your life and stop the outward flow. Chinese divinatory coins also bring unexpected wealth. Green currency notes (save them from holidays) are good in all money magick.

* High John the Conqueror root will attract new business if you are self employed and overcome slumps. It is good for the unemployed and for those returning to paid work after a career break or redundancy. Combine with a sugar lump or

twist of sugar in foil if you need to sell a creative idea or venture, like a book you have written, or face competition in an area of life.

* Gold, for example a gold ring, earring or collar stud or any small round gold object, will attract slow growing but lasting prosperity into your life, the restoration of health, happiness and confidence and lasting love. Gold chains symbolise successful partnerships and networking, new friends or the integration of new members to the family, as well as bringing reconciliation in family quarrels and avoiding rivalry.

* Broken chains and rings will remove and reverse bad luck. Add salt and rosemary to give extra power.

* A silver heart or two tiny worry dolls tied together with red cord knotted three times are good for love and three walnuts with three tiny fabric dolls ensure fertility.

* Tiny padlocks that are fastened represent safety in the home, to possessions and you personally as you travel as well as job security; unlocked padlocks or those with keys inserted, open the way to new opportunities.

* A small watch will help sustain effort for any long task or goal. It will also bring in work offers, especially for the self-employed. A watch works wonders for avoiding delays during commuting or holiday travel. Add High John the Conqueror root, salt and iron pyrites to a green bag if the odds are stacked against you financially or career wise.

* A broken watch will buy you time if there are bills you cannot pay until money comes in, or you are in danger of missing a deadline.

* Iron nails (if you can get ones from a horseshoe that is even better) defend house and property and also in a workbag protect against unfair tactics from rival firms or over-competitive colleagues.

* Salt has both protective and empowering functions and has for thousands of years been a symbol of incoming money, health and protection against negativity or accidents. A useful ingredient in any bag in a twist of silver foil.

* Pieces of out-of-date credit cards cut diagonally are a good symbol if you need to get loans or credit from a bank or other financial organisation.

* Angelica mixed with olive leaves will stop sniping and tension at home and work and is also good for preventing interruptions if you work from home. Hide a pale blue flannel bag with these and rosebuds and a blue lace agate for kind words if you have critical relatives or visitors.

* A St Christopher medallion in a mojo or worn on a chain guards you if you or family travel a lot. Place in a deep blue bag with coriander seeds, basil and sodalite crystals.

* Coriander or cumin seeds in a bag protect equipment, vehicles, premises and luggage.

Making and empowering the bag

* Create your mojo when you are alone in total silence after dark. Light a red candle and a single hyssop, lavender or rosemary incense stick.

* As you put in each item, name in your mind the purpose of the charm. Have at least one natural substance and one manufactured item for balance.

* If you have included any items that belonged to someone else in your mojo, purify them first with hyssop, lavender or rosemary infusion, 5 ml/1 tsp of dried herb to a cup of boiling water, left for five minutes. Strain the liquid, discard the herbs and sprinkle it over the artefact.

* Alternatively, waft a lighted hyssop, lavender or rosemary incense stick or smudge anti-clockwise over the object to remove the vibes of the previous owner. Some practitioners also make three circles of the above infusion round the bag or smudge over the bag before closing it for extra protection.

* Sprinkle a few drops of liquid on to the bag after filling to empower it, stating the purpose of the mojo in your mind, before closing (you need not count this towards the number of items unless you wish to).

* State in your mind for the final time the purpose for which it was created and then say in your mind as you close it:

    I made it; I empower it, I keep it. Mojo act for me and harm none. So do I decree.

* Even with a bag with a drawstring, secure the top with three red cords knotted together three times. You can seal this with a single drop of wax if you wish.

* Finally waft incense over it in three circles. Leave candle and incense to burn.

Keeping the mojo

Personal mojo are always carried, occasionally around the neck on a cord, but more usually round the hips or waist on a narrow fabric belt beneath outer clothes or concealed in a pocket, depending on the size of the bag. They are always kept out of sight. Those on work premises or for home protection are hidden near the door or in a locked drawer, again unseen.

Some mojo bags are only intended for short-term use: for example, a job interview. Others may have ongoing power. They will if necessary last for months unless they contain perishables. If created for an ongoing matter, for example, the continuing inflow of money or orders, replace the mojo when you feel the power waning.

Dispose of the old ones carefully by burying the contents, having thrown into water anything that will dissolve or naturally decay. Burn the bag.

PRACTICAL ASSIGNMENT

Plan a charm bag or mojo

* Look on pages 551–567 for details of herbs and roots, but try to be as ingenious as you can so that the items are relevant to the recipient, as well as the general purpose of the bag.

* Then make and empower the bag, adding for a special or urgent spell/mojo bag one unusual ingredient or item.

* Put this item in just before you close the bag, having spoken over it words of power, for a mojo spoken in your mind (allow for the addition in the overall number of items). This should be the one thing that makes it not just a love bag for Veronica, but Veronica's love bag, so that it could belong to no one else. This item should sum up the essence of the person and seem idiosyncratic and meaningful to no one except the maker of the bag. This is a sure-fire way of making the bag potent and keeping it fixed to its target.

Further research

Explore the world of the mojo bag online and/or use references from the previous module as well as this one to compile a list of charms suitable for adding to spell and mojo bags.

Further information

Recommended reading
* Bruce, Robert, *Practical Self Defense: Understanding and Surviving Unseen Influences*, Hampton Roads Publishing, 2003
* Frost, Gavin, and Frost, Yvonne, *The Witches' Magical Handbook*, Prentice Hall Press, 2000
* Paine, Sheila, *Amulets, A World of Sacred Powers, Charms and Magic Spells*, Thames and Hudson, 2004

Websites
* *Lucky Mojo*
  Probably the best mojo site on the internet
  www.luckymojo.com/mojo.html

NATIVE AMERICAN, ISIS, CELTIC SPELL AND CHARM BAGS AND WITCH BOTTLES

In this Module I will focus on the Native North American medicine bundle, the witch's Isis magick treasure collection, the Celtic Druid crane bag and the protective witch bottle. Each has qualities that can be applied to Wiccan practice, as well as enhancing our spiritual lives through contact with the natural world and ancient wisdom.

The medicine bag or bundle

From the Native North American tradition comes the medicine bundle, both the grandmother bundle/s of the nation and that of the individual. The collective bundle contains treasures handed down over generations, each with its own legend or chant and many with healing. Some contained only a few objects, while others could hold over 100, including charms, herbs, hooves and feathers. Contents were often dictated by dreams and visions and the official bundles would be opened before a special event or ritual as symbol of the releasing of the power. There were special bundles associated with major ceremonies: for example, the annual sun dance that has been revived in recent years.

The tribal medicine bundles were passed down by their guardians, usually the tribal chief or the medicine man or woman. Some of the older medicine bags contain objects that are more than 200 years old and even natural substances are perfectly preserved. The medicine men and women had special healing bundles, with contents that were passed down to successors to add to the apprentice's own items acquired during the long years of training.

An individual, much smaller bag like a pouch and worn round the waist was given to the adolescent boy or girl after their vision quest, when they spent time apart with nature to discover their power name. A totem item for the bag gathered on the quest would be brought back that symbolised this name. Again, it would be added to through the lifetime to mark personal milestones and became an ongoing source of power, healing and protection to the wearer. A person with the power name Running Horse might have a plaited charm made from the mane of a special horse they had ridden or loved as their special totem. Individual bags are still buried with owners or bequeathed to a chosen relative.

In some nations, a marriage medicine bag is given to a couple on their wedding day, including sweetgrass as a symbol of unity and a rattle to announce any pregnancies and births.

The Isis personal or coven witch bag

Some solitary witches and covens make collections of small treasured items, as well as their magickal set of ritual tools. This reflects their ongoing path. If you have not yet formalised your individual collection, you may like to do so as it forms a very potent repository of your magickal essence. Individual items can be carried in a small bag when you do not have time to make a charm bag. A coven or group Isis bag (or whichever Goddess you choose as its mentor) helps to define and focus the underlying collective spiritual energies.

Creating your own Isis or magickal bag or bundle

You will need a medium-sized satchel or drawstring bag to keep with you to collect items on visits to sacred sites, holidays and any empowered items from a seasonal ritual (see Celtic crane bags below). You can keep these items in a special box or drawer in your altar room. Some may be set on the altar for a time or relevant festival and then returned to the box after smudging.

Traditionally cedar leaves or sweet grass braids are kept with the artefacts and replaced regularly and you can add these plants to your coven or group Isis bundle. In your Book of Shadows, keep details about the treasures and how you acquired them. Some may get worn or start to crumble or represent an earlier stage in your development. You can return these to their own element with thanks: feathers and seeds to the air, ceramics, nuts and seeds (if you prefer) or beeswax to the earth.

You also need a personal bag for the most precious treasures, of the size that could be worn on a cord round your waist at ceremonies and private rituals or taken with you when you need power and protection in your daily life. The bag need not be large, just big enough to hold about 10 small items, and it can be whatever style you prefer, elaborately embroidered or plain. This will hold those items that are truly special: a beautiful crystal you were given or bought yourself, a perfect shell, a holed stone, a white crescent moon shaped stone you found after your first moon ritual, a crystal angel or silver fairy you bought at a wonderful festival when you did not have much money, a small piece of wood naturally formed into a face or animal, some dried orange blossom or roses from your wedding bouquet in a tiny bag, a lock of your child or a lover's hair or a silver locket you wore to your first dance, a small wooden or ceramic power animal that you saw crafted by indigenous artists.

A bead is a common addition to a personal magick bag in several cultures because of its protective shape (blue turquoise beads especially are traditionally associated with repelling the Evil Eye), and also because beads are associated with spiritual power in many religions: for example, Catholicism and Buddhism. In these traditions each represents a prayer or significant teaching and so if you handle your beads regularly, you will be able to tap into the magickal well of wisdom. Some people use a bead from a necklace they were given for a special birthday or one that commemorates a happy anniversary. Pearl, amber, jet and turquoise are the most suitable. Wrap any delicate items in individual pieces of cloth within the bag.

Items need no empowerment as you can take the bag along to esbats or put it in the moonlight on your private full moon ceremonies as a solitary. You can carry it at the Summer Solstice when you watch the dawn rise, when you marry, give birth and when you mourn. Smudge over your personal bag monthly to keep its energy field cleansed and pure. Set out the contents on your altar circling the Goddess candle before a special ritual.

You might like an even tinier bag so you can keep one or two items with you when you must travel light or to keep with you during a significant day. You can rotate the choice, putting your hand in the larger bag and asking to be guided to what will bring you the power, protection or healing you currently need. You can keep your larger personal Isis bag on your altar when it is not with you. Do not let other people use or handle your bag, because it is an expression of your inner self and so is precious.

As your spiritual life evolves and you acquire new beautiful treasures, you can replace ones you have outgrown by returning them to the larger box to be used on special occasions when you get out your full set of treasures, birthdays or anniversaries, as well as major magickal festivals.

A coven or group Isis bag

Every coven has it special tools, charms and artefacts. The collective Isis bag or bundle is an additional but I believe very valuable addition to group or coven work. It can be the size of a large, soft, fabric, ethnic shoulder bag. It could alternatively be a carved wooden box containing a roll of cloth with three horizontal cords to secure it.

The bag would contain those items that signify the heart or essence of your coven and any small treasures you set on your altar only on special occasions. There might be a beautiful crystal or fossil you have purchased with joint funds, a statue of your particular coven deity (or deities), items handed down or given to the coven by an older member, bags of empowered festival herbs (eight in all) that can be replaced in rotation as the new festival falls, a perfect or white, holed stone shell found on a group outing or holiday, or a statue of a tree spirit carved by a coven member or a clay Goddess they have made.

If you do not have a coven Isis collection, hold a meeting maybe after an esbat to see what you already possess that is not a tool but has some significance. Talk about the kind of artefacts you would like to represent your group or coven spiritually and magickally and aim initially to buy or make an item on each festival, to commemorate the birthday of the founding of the group and on the forming of a new offshoot coven (you could give the new daughter coven a treasure to start their collection).

These treasures can be set on the altar or an extra side table on special occasions, such as the handfasting of a member or the naming of a child. If a member dies, an item can be buried with them as grave goods or buried near the outdoor meeting place in their honour. The bag or box can be kept in the altar room and smudged along with the altar room. If the group or coven works outdoors or goes on a trip to a sacred site for a ritual, one of the items should be taken in a smaller bag to symbolise the heart of the coven.

The crane bag

In modern Druidry, the crane bag forms an essential piece of equipment for individual Druids and Druidesses. It was named after the bag created by Mannanann Mac Lir, Celtic Lord of the Sea and the Isle of Man from the skin of a sacred crane to carry the treasures of Ireland. One legend tells that the crane used was the maiden Aoife, who was enchanted by a jealous rival for the sea lord's love. Thereafter she lived as a bird in the house of the sea lord until her death 200 years later. However, some say she was the wife of Mannanann whom he punished because she gave the alphabet of knowledge to humanity. The original bags that might date back to Celtic times were made of crane skin or decorated with crane feathers.

A crane bag differs from the Isis bag in several respects, but the concepts can be adapted and combined, especially if you spend a lot of time outdoors or practise informal witchcraft. It contains only items found or made from nature and so is close to the medicine bag. A larger version (larger than the witch's satchel) is taken on journeys and outdoor rituals, both to collect treasures from the ritual site and to carry basic equipment such as a wand, a small bottle of water from a holy well and a tiny smudge stick in sage, cedar, rosemary or lavender for outdoor rituals. Also useful is a crystal pendulum that can be used for all kinds of work from decision-making to tracing ley or psychic energy lines beneath the earth, together with small purses for collecting herbs, leaves, flowers or berries without squashing them. You would also carry divinatory tools for outdoor work like runes or Celtic tree staves and a small bowl for scrying (see page 607).

You may find it useful to combine your private outdoor ritual tools with your collecting bag and you can often buy fabric bags with separate compartments (or go modern and use a large organiser bag). If you have a Crane bag you might collect leaves or berries from special trees (I have some fallen berries from the Glastonbury Thorn whose ancestor was planted by Joseph of Arimathea when he landed at Avalon – the old name for Glastonbury – bearing the Holy Grail). You might keep a stone from under a sacred waterfall, the first flower of spring in your garden.

Since many of the items are subject to decay they tend to be replaced regularly and buried, if possible where they were found or at a local place with similar energies. The exception is special crystals and stones.

Druids and Druidesses also have a small pouch that contains special more permanent treasures worn on the waist on a cord, perhaps a fossil you have made into an amulet, wooden divination tools like divinatory tree staves or runes in a small inner drawstring bag. Other common items include a dark and light stone each engraved with a seven-coil labyrinth. The design was etched on the stones and used respectively for moonlight and sunlight meditation.

If you have a nature-based crane bag, you can leave the more permanent contents of your crane bag open on their silk cloth to the full moon and from dawn to noon on the Longest Day of the year to absorb power.

Catalogue items with dates so that as you hold each in times of quiet contemplation, you can recall their original setting and the magick of the moment of collection.

Witch bottles

Defensive witch bottles filled with protective items date from before Roman times and continued to be made into the early 1900s There are fine examples of glass and stone witch bottles from different periods in the small and eccentric but fabulous Pitt Rivers Museum in Oxford, UK.

The witch bottle tradition was popularised in the 1500s when the witch persecutions made ordinary people terrified that witches might enter their homes through the chimney and doors and curse them. Counter-curse bottles were created to harm witches, as well as repel them. The corked stone bellarmine, bellamine or bellermine invented in the 1600s in Germany and also made in the Netherlands became the most popular kind of witch bottle. It was exported to the UK and Scandinavia, as well as parts of Eastern Europe.

Witch bottles are long lasting and self-recharging, as long as the seal remains undamaged by age or soil conditions where they are buried. Indeed, their power is said to last until they are found, which in some cases has been hundreds of years – and some are never discovered. A number were enclosed in walls or chimneybreasts rather than being buried. This makes it very important that the purpose is benign, not least for the sake of the energies of the earth in which it is buried.

A cross between an amulet and charm, witch bottles are very slow acting and need little empowering. You can make more active temporary ones for protection against specific threats or malice (see banishing magick on page 60).

Witch bottles do have transformative powers (especially if you use green or blue glass) to replace with positivity and healing, negative energies absorbed by the bottle. Nevertheless their role is primarily protective. They work by acting as a substitute for the maker or the person/group or place they are meant to protect, by deflecting unfocused negativity, creating an exclusion zone against deliberate ill intent and reflecting back any malice to the sender without in any way amplifying the ill intent (karma does that).

To make a basic witch bottle

* If possible obtain a stone bottle or flagon, the kind cider is sold in. The original bellarmine has a bearded face on the side. This was often mistaken for the Devil but in fact is a folk character whose origin has a number of conflicting versions. Otherwise use a dark thick green or brown glass. Some makers of real ale put their beer in such bottles, but you need one with a very wide neck. Have a look round glassmakers and car boot sales. Any small squat bottle or jar can be used and I have even seen them made from cookware storage jars. They are best with a screw top lid; otherwise find a suitable cork to fit. You will seal the bottle with wax.

* Make your witch bottle in bright sunlight to endow it with positive energies that are then sealed in the bottle, or after dusk by the light of a red candle if you need a lot of protection or have suffered a series of reversals or malice. The waning moon period is best and the stronger the protection needed the closer the day should follow the full moon.

* Before filling the bottle, even if it is new add a drop or two of pine or tea tree essential oil to hot water and wash the bottle well, rinsing with cold.

* Add a pinch of sea salt to the cleansed bottle and a pinch of pepper if you have

suffered a lot of spite or trouble. As you do so, ask the Wise Crone Goddess, protectress of witch bottles, that the bottle may be filled with light and transform what is not of good intent into blessings.

* Once bottles contained as well as sharp objects, urine, menstrual blood/semen knotted hairs etc. There are a number of these old recipes on the internet and I have suggested one or two good sites. I believe, however, that you can get the same effects from using herbs especially rosemary, and soured red wine, vinegar or sacred water darkened with mugwort. My reason is that urine was originally used in witch bottles to cause witches untold agony when they crossed water, and other bodily fluids similarly were added. (As a mother of five very earthy children there is little that makes me squeamish!)

* You can either half fill your bottle with the sharp objects and herbs and then add the liquid (practically easier) or you can half fill the bottle with the liquid and drop the objects in one by one while chanting protection (and top up the liquid if necessary).

* What sharp items should you use? Iron is the traditional protector and rusty nails can be bent into knots using small pliers, one by one as added. You can say for each:

Tangle the anger, bind the pain, tie up the malice, let no ill remain

or something similar. Iron is also very empowering.

* Razor blades are not so magickal and you can easily cut yourself.

* If you have a broken make up mirror (old powder compacts are good source) add the shards as this accords with the old, unfounded superstition that to break a mirror is bad luck. Therefore symbolically as you bury the bottle you are burying bad luck from present and future in the form of the broken mirror. But do not break a mirror deliberately. Mirrors reflect back any negativity and also are natural light-bringers.

* Thorns, symbol of the Norse Thunder God Thor's protection, balance the iron of Mars. Rose thorns give the added dimension of love and kindness and hawthorns are the traditional magickal protection of witches. Thorns are good for transforming negativity into positive energies.

* Rosemary is the best herb to add to your protective bottle for purification and also as a health-giving and abundance herb. If you can obtain the fresh sprigs (chopped for a smaller bottle), these are filled with the lifeforce, as well as protection. You could also use vervain or dill.

* For the liquid, you should use some darkened sacred water, sour wine or a deep red vinegar (yellow apple cider vinegar is also good for attracting positive energies).

* Cork your bottle firmly or screw the lid tightly. Seal with red sealing wax. (I got mine from Winchester Cathedral gift shop but it is obtainable in conventional stationers.) Otherwise, use a good quality red candle.

* Shake the bottle nine times, as you do so saying:

Keep away harm,
Keep away danger,
Keep from my door
False friend and stranger.
Drive away malice,
Drive away spite,
Guard my home/coven
By day and by night.

Where to keep witch bottles

If you made the bottle in sunlight wrap it in a natural fabric in a dark colour and bury it after dark. Keep the location secret unless you are burying a coven witch bottle. Traditionally buried under the doorstep or behind the hearth to seal psychic/actual entrances of harm, this is no longer so possible in modern times, unless you are doing major renovations. However, you can bury your bottle anywhere in a garden, best close to a tree.

You can make bottles just with herbs, crystals and darkened sacred water to bury deep in places under threat (wrap it in sacking so it will not break and hurt badgers or burrowing moles). I do not think you should bury personal bottles away from home, though some witches say that the protection will still work as effectively psychically as if within the boundaries.

You can bury a coven or group bottle into which each person has added a nail or mirror shard/thorn/herb and poured a little liquid, on land where you regularly meet for outdoor rituals. If you have a regular indoor meeting place, you can leave it to protect the place and create a new one.

Bury a full size bottle (about a litre) at least 30 cm/12 in underground or for a small one (a dark glass medicine bottle is ideal) in a deep plant pot of soil. If you really are cramped for space you could bury an essential oil bottle well washed with crystal chippings, dried supermarket rosemary and darkened sacred water. It is the bottle's purpose and not the physical size that determines its effectiveness.

If you cannot bury it, keep in a dark part of a basement or clear behind a pile of heavy objects that will not be moved. Conversely, you can store it as near to the front of the house as you can, perhaps in the front eaves of an attic. In an apartment you could erect a very high shelf near the entrance that can only be reached by a step ladder. But burying is always best.

PRACTICAL ASSIGNMENT

Making Druidic meditation stones

These are a good addition to your crane bag or Isis treasure bag.

* Find a medium-sized, flat-based black stone and a similarly sized white stone, about the size of a large coin. Pick your stones either on a shore, in woodland or near any sacred site.

* Alternatively, use a snow quartz (opaque white) or a black jet or onyx crystal.

* Draw a seven-coil labyrinth on each stone (or trace the one below). Use acrylic paint or permanent marker or etch the shape with an engraving tool or fine pointed awl or screwdriver, and then fill in the groove with paint or a permanent marker pen. Use silver or white on the black stone or crystal and black or gold on the white.

* You will need a light or white purse in a natural fabric for your white stone and a dark purse for the black one.

* Make your white stone in sunlight around noon and your black stone on the night of the full moon.

Using your Druidic stones for meditation

* Meditate on your black labyrinth stone in moonlight or by silver candlelight and your white stone in sunlight.

* Carry your white labyrinth stone as an amulet when you go to work, when you have a long or stressful journey (the white stone is good for soothing fears of flying), when you cannot rest and have a busy schedule or if you are anxious about an unfamiliar place or potentially unfriendly people.

* The black labyrinth stone will help you to rest after a stressful day, will protect you when travelling at night in a lonely place or alone on a crowded train, guarding you against psychological or psychic attack while you sleep and relieving pain that stops you sleeping.

Further information

Recommended reading

* Wallace, Black Elk, and Lyon, William, *Black Elk: the Sacred Ways of a Lakota*, Harper and Row, New York, 1990
* Moondance, *Wolf Spirit Medicine*, Sterling Books, 1995
* Telasco, Patricia, *Wishing Well: empowering your hopes and dreams*, Crossing Press, 1997

Websites

* *Unicorn Garden*
  Witch bottles and other interesting material
  www.unicorngarden.com/grimoire
* *Current Archaeology*
  Illustrated site with photographs and information about ancient witch bottle found at Reigate
  www.archaeology.co.uk/ca/ timeline/postmed/witch/ witch.htm

AN INTRODUCTION TO MAGICKAL ALPHABETS: THE RUNES

Magickal alphabets have an important role in writing magickal wishes or empowerments in spells, to burn as part of the spell or keep in a locked box for the required time frame of the spell. Single alphabet letters written in an ancient script act as a glyph or magickal sign on charms and talisman. This is because the runes and Egyptian hieroglyphs and to a lesser extent the Angel scripts release the actual power locked in the meaning when the glyphs are written. You can also write deity and Angel names or your own magickal names in one of the old scripts as part of an invocation. Magickal scripts are not part of everyday communication and because they are so old have accumulated power over generations of use. This stored antiquity can connect even a simple candle burning wish spell or letter written to an Archangel (see page 574) with the universal web of wisdom.

The power of the written word was considered immense in the ancient world and in Egypt spells were written on tomb walls and even the inside of coffins and on papyri to provide the necessary secret formulae to assist the deceased through the perils of the afterlife to reach the Celestial Nile in the Milky Way. The name of the deceased was carved on offerings tables outside the tombs so that people passing by, as well as the family, would know the name. By reciting it and making offerings they could keep alive the person's spirit or ka.

Inscribing an enemy's name on a pot and smashing the pot was a nasty way of destroying part of a person's soul and a pharaoh angry with a predecessor would wipe his name off statues. Of course, writing a name or spell is equally positive when used with good intent and by writing and reading magickal words they are animated. Even after the Christianisation of Scandinavia, runic inscriptions appeared on monuments to deceased nobles and royalty, recounting the deeds of the great Viking heroes to whom the person commemorated was likened in courage or achievements.

The magickal writing that I use in this module, the Norse runes, the Viking 24 symbol set, is in my opinion like the Ancient Egyptian hieroglyphs even more magickal than the traditional Angel alphabets we will work with later (see page

466). That is because runes like hieroglyphs are not alphabets as such and were used for primarily for inscriptions, on talismans and in magick rites.

Runes

Were you to learn only one magickal system, I would suggest the runes as the most straightforward, the most adaptable to modern magickal needs and also the most versatile both as the focus for spells and in creating talismans and charms. We know a lot more about its uses than the hieroglyphs, it is far more widely used than the ceremonial Angel scripts and much easier actually to write and make. You can draw one instantly on a stone you find in the forest, using a permanent red ink marker and have an immediate spell symbol, an amulet and if empowered a talisman or charm.

Runes were and still are a major divination system with the meanings of the symbols cast on the ground or selected from a bag, reveal answers and ways forward.

Using runes in magick

As well as using runes in writing names and wishes or etching or painting single ones on wood, self-hardening clay, stones, bones, metal, wax or crystal, it would be helpful for you to create a set of the 24 runes on stones, crystals etc, to keep ready for magick spells and create a second set for use in divination. Each set should be kept in a red drawstring bag, if possible of a natural fabric.

Runes even more than tarot are an excellent form of divination for witches, since they are made of the earth (as wood or stones) and can be cast on the earth. Therefore I will include in this module enough information to use the runes fully and continue the theme of scrying and divination more generally in the module on psychic development and scrying (page 607).

What is more, divination carried out immediately after the release of power in a spell or after the cakes and ale part of the ceremony (see page 633) does offer a means of seeing how you can apply the spell energies to the everyday world and discovering unexpected results that lead to further opportunity. In a private spell, a rune reading is a way of using the time waiting for a spell candle or incense to burn through in a positive way to make the transition between magick and your ordinary life.

When you have time, pick a rune in the morning by touch from the bag of magick rune symbols to enable you to read the prevailing energies of the day ahead. You can then carry it in a small red bag as your amulet charm of the day, empowering it with a purpose if you wish and returning the rune after smudging it clean to the larger rune bag at the end of the day.

Understanding the runes

Though an old form of magick, runes relate to the issues in the lives of modern witches that have concerned people throughout the ages, love, family, health, the home, travel, money and the fear of yet need for change.

Much of the modern interpretation of the runes is based on a series of Rune poems, the three main ones being the Anglo-Saxon or Old English Rune poem, the Old Norse or Viking Rune Poem and the Icelandic poem. Though they were written down by monks or Christian scholars, they are of great value and because of the similarity in systems we can gain knowledge from them all.

In addition we have the old legends such as the Prose and Poetic Edda (see recommended reading) to fill in the gaps and help us to understand the context of the runes. For example the Prose Edda was created by the Icelandic Christian historian and statesman Snorri Sturluson who lived between 1179–1241. He wanted to preserve the ancient tradition. But the set meanings are just the beginning and the more you use the runes, the less you will rely on conventional meanings and the more they will act as a stimulus for your own emerging clairvoyant powers that we last used in childhood but which never go away.

Runes and alphabetical correspondences

The most satisfactory way of writing in any magickal alphabet is to reduce any double letters coming together to a single letter, so happy becomes hapy, and unless there is a specific diphthong like Th that has a runic correspondence, use phonetic sounds so Ph becomes F or simplify so Sh is written as S and not S+H.

Keep spaces as they are in your native tongue. The conventional runic writings do not but it may be easier certainly at first. Keep to the left to right format. There are no capital letters or punctuation as such, so just separate words.

You can copy out the first two columns of the correspondences below the rune symbol and its Latin alphabet equivalent on a sheet of good quality white paper in red ink to keep in your altar room for reference. Once you are familiar with the meanings of the symbols, remembering them becomes easy.

Magickally it is better where there is a direct runic meaning correspondence to use the rune symbol rather than spelling out the attribute word. So for a money spell you could draw the symbol for Fehu (prosperity) rather than spelling out the word money in runic script.

When representing your magickal names in runes, consider just using the initials and then you have the further option of creating a joined or bind rune of the separate initials (see below). You could paint or engrave this glyph on magickal tools or write over them in incense smoke to empower them either when you first acquire or make them or for a special ritual. You could also write it in the air in incense smoke at the beginning of a spell after *I am* where others are present and you do not wish to use your secret names.

Letter	Rune	Rune name	Rune meaning
a/A	ᚠ	Ansuz	Communication inspiration, creativity, good luck, examination success, learning, fathering
b/B	ᛒ	Berkano	Regeneration, birth, fertility, new beginnings, peace at home, mothers, business ventures

c/C/k/K	Kenaz	Illumination, sexual passion, conception of child, protection of valuables
d/D	Dagaz	Hope, the end of a bad situation, transformation, regeneration, mastering new skills, increase in anything and fame and fortune
e/E	Ehwaz	Harmony, travel. partnerships, cooperative ventures, friendship, loyalty, fidelity, house or career moves
f/F	Fehu	Prosperity, abundance, property, a specific piece of good luck
g/G	Gebo	Gifts, marriage, love and family magick, partnerships and contracts
h/H	Hagalaz	Change to overcome stagnation or a redundant phase, protection of the home, defeating bad habits
i/I	Isa	Stillness, patience, binding, reconciliation, beginning negotiations
j/J (in traditional systems also Y)	Jera	Abundance, acquiring resources, fertility, rewards for input, talents or past efforts, the law
l/L	Laguz	Birth, initiation and rites of passage, increasing life force, awakening love and sexuality, courage for a new stage or uncertain venture
m/M	Mannaz	Health and healing, improved memory, balancing strengths and weaknesses, asking for help from whatever source
Ng/NG	Ingwaz	Fertility, potency, wealth, protection, anti-debt

n/N	†	Naudhiz	Urgent needs or desires, for self-reliance, breaking free, and manifesting inner power
o/O	◇	Othala	Home, property, family, security, relocation, animals
p/P	Ϛ	Pertho	Good luck, restoring what is lost, all risks and speculation, secrets
r/R	R	Raidho	Travel, journeys, action, legal matters
s/S/z/Z	ϟ	Sowilo	Success, leadership, power, ambitions, health and healing, wealth
t/T	↑	Tiwaz	Justice, wishes, fulfilling dreams, recovering from accidents, illness and reversals
u/U	∩	Uruz	Primal strength, courage, overcoming obstacles, health
v/V/w/W	P	Wunjo	Joy, pleasure, leisure, self-employment, holidays
x/X/th/Th	Þ	Thurisaz	Protection, strength, potency, challenges
Y	ʃ	Eihwaz	Endings leading to beginnings, banishing, balancing long-standing matters, protection
(not used in alphabet)	Y	Elhaz/Algiz	Higher self, turning bad luck into good.

The rune aetts

We have already met the aetts as the eight tides of the day. Here they refer to the division of the runes into three sets.

The first aett or set of eight runes is dedicated to Freyja the Goddess of love and beauty. You can ask her to bless her runes as you dedicate them or create one of them as a charm.

Fehu, cattle, wealth

Pronounced: Fayhoo

Strengths: Abundance, prosperity, the price that must be paid for happiness

Fehu is the rune of the cattle, which to the Vikings represented prosperity as tangible wealth that could if necessary be transported to a new land. The Norse Rune Poem warns that money causes strife among kinsmen, perhaps a reminder of the Wiccan rule that we should seek enough for our needs and a little more.

Good for all money, security and property magick, for reducing debt and as a good luck talisman for a single piece of luck.

Uruz, wild cattle, primal strength

Pronounced: Oo-rooz

Strengths: Courage, overcoming all obstacles, magickal power

Uruz represents the aurochs, huge, wild, very fierce oxen whose horns were worn on the Viking helmets, engraved with the Uruz rune to transfer by associative magick the strength of the creature to warriors. The Norse and Icelandic Rune poems talk of hardship for the herdsman and refinement by suffering using the images of iron and drizzle. Uruz is also associated with the original creative force.

Good for magick for business risks and speculation, for good health as well as against immoveable officialdom, for a surge of strength and courage.

Thurisaz, Thorn, hammer of Thor

Pronounced: Thoo-riz-saws (Th as in thorn)

Strengths: Protection, overcoming challenges and conflicts, potency, secret knowledge especially of magick

Thurisaz is the ultimate rune of defence of self, home, property and psychic or physical attack. It is associated with another harsh image, the thorn trees, although thorns can offer protection from intruders. In the Norse and Icelandic poems, it is associated with the Thurs, which means a giant in the Old Norse. It can also refer to Thor, God of thunder and courage who sought to protect Asgard, realm of the Gods from the Frost Giants. Thor's hammer also acted as a sacred symbol at marriages, births and funerals. The Anglo-Saxon rune poem relates how the thorn is cruel to anyone who lies on it and sharp to the grasp and so is protective.

Good for self-defence magick and sending back malevolence of all kinds.

Ansuz, the mouth, Odin, the God

Strengths: Inspiration, wisdom, idealism, creativity and communication

Pronounced: Onz-wars

Ansuz was a name for Odin, who was the God of poetry and communication. The Anglo-Saxon rune poem says that the mouth is the origin of every speech and the mainstay of wisdom. The Norse rune poem talks of estuary as the way of most journeys, conveying the concept that communication is essential for transforming inspiration into reality. What we say and how we say it can be crucial.

Good for magick for continuing or reviving good luck and for passing tests and examinations or career interviews, for all literary and artistic ventures.

Raidho, the wheel, the wagon, riding

Pronounced: Rye-though (Th as in Then)

Strengths: Action, travel, seizing opportunity and desired change

Raidho is the rune of the long and dangerous ride: the worst for horses, as the Norse poem says. The Norse poem also refers to the best sword being forged by Regin, the wise dwarf for the hero Sigurd, so prepare well and then be bold. Raidho was also the wheel on the wagon of the fertility God Frey or Ingvi (see the rune Ingwaz) and the sun wheel moving through the sky or the turning of the constellations. So movement could not be long resisted.

Good for magick for all forms of travel, journeys and success in legal matters.

Cenaz or Kenaz, torch

Pronounced: Ken-oars or Kayne-oars

Strengths: Inner wisdom, illumination, inner strength, the divine spark within creativity, conception of a child

Cenaz represents the cosmic fire from Muspellheim in the south that met with ice from Nifleheim in the north in the creation of the Norse world. The torch lit the great halls as well as more humble abodes and was made from pine dipped in resin. The burnishing, cleansing, purifying aspect of fire is emphasised in the Norse and Icelandic poems.

Good for magick for arts and crafts, for sexual passion and for protecting valuables of all kinds.

Gebo, the gift or giving

Pronounced: Gay-bow or gay-boo

Strengths: Generosity, all matters relating to exchanges, including contracts, marriage and partnerships

The Anglo-Saxon rune poem talks both of giving and receiving equally and that good fortune should be shared. The poem also talks of giving status to the outcast. In the society of the Nordic world, a person of property and recognition could confer status on an outcast by giving him land or animals.

Good for magick for all family matters, love and sex magick, commitment and for magickal knowledge.

Wunjo, joy

Pronounced: Woon-yoe (as in moon)

Strengths: Personal happiness and fulfilment, success on your own terms and recognition of worth by others

In the Anglo-Saxon poem, rune happiness is said to be experienced by one who has known sorrow and also who himself has power and blessedness: *Those who have experienced hardships value happiness in small ways.*

Good for magick for gaining favour from employers or those who can advance your cause, for living happy ever afters, for self-employment and businesses and to release the power of any spell over or within the named timescale.

The second aett is dedicated to Heimdall, the Watcher God and Guardian of the Rainbow Bridge that spanned the dimension between Asgard the realm of the gods and Midgard the world of mortals. He will sound the horn at the battle of Ragnarok. You can invoke him to bless the eight runes he rules over.

Hagalaz, hail

Pronounced: Har-gar-laws

Strengths: Embracing necessary change or disruption by natural events, positive transformation, future rewards

Hagalaz is the rune of the cosmic seed, for, according to legend, the world of the Viking Gods came into being when fire met ice and it melted. In the rune poems, the hail is called white grains, reminiscent of the harvest and though sharp to the touch quickly changes to water necessary for life and growth.

Good for magick for protecting your home and personal space, overcoming bad habits and for transforming any current disruption into a chance for a new better lifestyle.

Naudhiz, the need or ritual fire

Pronounced: Nowd-eez or Now-these

Strengths: Self-reliance, inner fire and inspiration, passion, unfulfilled desires and needs that should be expressed and achieved

Naudhiz, a Fire rune, is the spindle that generates the need fire by friction. This is the inner fire released from within the wood. Need fires were lit from early times all over Northern Europe on festivals such as Beltane and Halloween, and on the Solstices to give power to the sun. It is a rune of want and desire and because of this Naudhiz is associated with love magick. The Old Norse rune poem makes the link between fire and ice, the need fire being kindled to melt the frost.

Good for magick for attracting and keeping a lover, for urgent needs, powerful desires, a sudden surge of power and for breaking free.

Isa, ice

Pronounced: Ee-saw

Strengths: Waiting for the right moment, proceeding with care, patience, stopping the advance of a negative situation, necessary inaction

Isa is the rune of the fifth element in the Norse tradition. It is linked with the world ice from Nifleheim and the first being Ymir, the Frost Giant, who was formed by the continual action of heat and cold. The rune poems talk of the coldness and beauty of ice. The Norse poem sees it as a bridge between dimensions that needs to be negotiated with care by those who are perhaps blinded by the fear of going forward. But of course if we wait too long the ice melts and we cannot span the gap. Isa is also the icy glacier flowing imperceptibly from Nifleheim, indicating progress that seems slow but is occurring beneath the surface.

Good for magick for beginning any negotiations, reconciliation attempts and for gaining allies and taking the first steps.

Jera, the harvest

Pronounced: Yay-rar

Strengths: The results of earlier efforts realised, learning from old mistakes, abundance and the acquisition of resources

Jera, the good harvest or positive completion of endeavour was described in both the Norse and Icelandic poems as being of profit to all men. The Norse poem talks of the generosity of Freyr, the God of fertility of the land. The rune is a pagan version of the Biblical *As you sow, shall you reap.*

Good for magick for legal matters, set over the door at New Year to bring luck so long as the symbol lasts, for fertility rituals and fair rewards for outlay or effort.

Eihwaz, the yew tree

Pronounced: Eye-wars

Strengths: Natural endings, leading to new beginnings, banishment of what is redundant or destructive, what is of lasting worth, patience with slow moving matters.

Because the evergreen yew is the longest living tree, it was adopted by the northern peoples as a symbol of human longevity. It was also one of the trees burned as the sacred yule at the Midwinter Solstice and is called in the Norse rune poem, *the greenest wood in the winter, upheld by deep roots, a joy to the home.* For this reason, the rune is also in the Icelandic poem associated with the bow, often made from yew wood, as a symbol of new life from the old.

Good for magick for restoring the balance after disruption or change, for problem solving, for past life work and for banishing and protective magick.

Perthro, lot or gambling cup

Pronounced: Perth-row (as in row a boat)

Strengths: Discovering what is not yet known or revealed, allowing the essential self to emerge, taking a chance

In the tradition of the early northern peoples, gambling and divination were very close in function and decisions would be made from casting lots as whatever was cast would indicate, it was believed, the will of the gods. There is a mention of Perthro only in the Anglo-Saxon poem, which speaks of *play and laughter in the beer hall among bold men*.

Good for magick to keep secrets, to find and restore lost property, people and animals, for games of chance, gambling, speculation and foretelling the future.

Elhaz or Algiz, elk sedge, elk or eelgrass

Pronounced: Ail-hawz

Strengths: The higher self, spiritual nature, turning bad luck into good, seizing opportunities, taking the first difficult steps to happiness

Elk sedge is an old expression for a two-edged sword. The rune shape is taken as a splayed hand held out in defence or the horns of an elk, another translation, both of which can be used in attack or more usually as defence. The Anglo-Saxon rune poem, the only one to mention this rune, interprets the rune as eelgrass, found on marshes *that grimly wounds any man who tries to grasp it*. Once grasped eelgrass could be used for thatching, kindling for the fire and bedding for animals.

Good for magick for communication with ancestors, Angels and Spirit Guides, for psychic protection, for overcoming redundancy or unemployment, development of spiritual powers and past life work.

Sowilo, the sun

Pronounced: Sew-weel-oe

Strengths: Victory, success, wealth, potential, energy and expansion

Sowilo is a fire rune, the rune of the sun or the sun wheel, the sun moving through the year. It is seen in the Old Norse rune poem as light of the lands and refers to its holiness while the Icelandic poem talks of the sun as the *life-long destroyer of ice*. Other references describe how it causes the green crops to grow and that it is the hope and guide of seafarers. The sun is the most positive and potent symbol, especially in the world of the north where the sun was so precious. It can also be seen as lightning.

Good for self-confidence, health, healing, for leadership, career and knowledge.

The third aett belongs to Tiu or Tiw, the God of justice and of the guiding Pole Star. He will bless the eight runes under his protection.

Tiwaz, the Pole Star, a guiding star

Pronounced: Tee-wars

Strengths: Justice, nobility, self-sacrifice, following a dream, keeping faith, even in dark times

In the Norse and Icelandic poems, Tiu or Tiw is called the one-handed God, referring to the sacrifice he made of his most precious gift, his sword hand, to bind Fenris Wolf, as he was warned that the wolf would kill his father Odin. Tiwaz is identified as the Pole Star and also the God who symbolically presided over every assembly of justice and law. He was also God of war, because justice was sometimes settled by combat or even full-scale battle. It was believed that Odin and Tiu would allow the *just cause* to win.

Good for magick for recovery from illness, loss or accident or reversals, for public performances, fame and for competing against others.

Berkano, the birch tree, the Mother Goddess

Pronounced: Bear-kawn-oe

Strengths: New beginnings, rebirth, renewal, healing, fertility and mothering in all aspects

Berkano is another name for the old Nordic earth mother Nerthus whose blessings, like those of her husband Freyr/Ingvi, were associated with the sowing of crops in spring. The name also signifies the birch tree that *puts forth shoots without seeding*, according to the old rune verse. This says that we all contain within ourselves the power to regenerate our lives and to develop our unique gifts.

Good for magick for bringing happiness and peace to the home and family, for fertility and secrets, especially secret love, and for starting up business initiatives.

Ehwaz, the horse

Pronounced: Ay-wars

Strengths: Loyalty, fidelity, harmony between people or within oneself, moving house or changing career, travel

Ehwaz is associated with the horse, a sacred animal to the Vikings, especially the horse that carried its rider into battle. The rune, mentioned only in the Anglo-Saxon rune poem, emphasises the joy a horse brings to his rider and how it can make him feel like a prince.

Good for magick for calling aid in times of trouble, for swiftness in any venture and for friends and friendship.

Mannaz, man, humankind

Pronounced: man-norz

Strengths: Power of human intelligence, awareness of mortality, compassion and acceptance of the weaknesses and strengths of self and others

Man was seen in the ancient world of the north as a reflection of Odin in his three functions, as warrior, farmer and ruler/magician. Women were expressions of Frigg, wife, mother and wise counsellor. In Norse legend, the first man and woman were formed by Odin and his brothers Vili and Ve (after whom a sacred space is named), from an ash and an elm and called Aesc and Embla. At the destruction of the existing order at Ragnarok, their descendants Lif and Lifthrasir sheltered in the world tree and survived to repopulate the new world.

Good for magick for improving memory, for health and healing, for purification rites and prophetic dreams, asking for help, for balancing strengths and weaknesses where these are out of synch in a relationship or business venture.

Laguz, Water, the lake, the sea

Pronounced: law-gooz

Strengths: Initiation into life, emotions and awakening love and sexuality, following opportunities, intuition, travel, especially long-distance

Laguz is the rune of water or the sea and the ancient poems tell of the hazards of *churning water* and the *brine stallion* that does not heed its bridle. But the oak steeds, the name given to the Viking ships, did launch on huge seas and reached as far as America and Greece. So water is above all a symbol of courage and taking a chance on the unpredictable or unexpected.

For magick for birth and increase in energy and the lifeforce, for developing imaginative solutions and for all rites of passage magick.

Ingwaz, fertility, the Fertility God

Pronounced: Eeng-wars

Strengths: Protection, good luck and abundance in domestic life, male potency planting the seeds and then waiting for results

Ingwaz or Freyr drove his wagon over the fields after the winter to release the creative potential of the soil. The constellation called the Bear in Western Astrology was known as his Wagon in the Northern tradition. The old poems talk of Ingvi or Freyr riding his wagon eastwards or backwards as it is sometimes translated, in the opposite direction to the sun's daily journey. This referred to the sacrifice ritual that is seen in the festival of Lughnassadh/Lammas where the God died for the crops. He was traditionally the God of the hearth and his rune put into the walls or over doorways in houses and even churches as a protective device.

Good for magick for stopping resources draining away, for a satisfactory outcome to a matter, for fertility in all matters, to bind people together and to increase charisma.

Othala, the homestead

Pronounced: Oath-or-law

Strengths: Stability at home, in the family and family finances, protection of home, property and loved ones; the blessings of older people

In the Rune poems, Othala is said to be *beloved of every human* but this domestic contentment is linked with a good harvest, i.e. material comfort. Because Othala refers to land owned by generations rather than leased from a lord, it speaks of permanence and stability in family affairs. Though the Norse people were great wanderers, nevertheless, the homestead was important to them and establishing the new homestead, however temporary, in a new land was a priority.

Good for magick for inheritance, family loyalty, traditions and building or renovating the home, also for all practical concerns, for animals and any relocation or family additions for example through remarriage.

Dagaz, Day

Pronounced: Door-gawz

Strengths: Awakening, clear vision or awareness, light at the end of the tunnel, optimism of a better tomorrow

Dagaz refers to the moment of daybreak or dawn. The mid-point of the old northern day that began at sunset was the rising of the sun. The Anglo-Saxon rune poem, the only one to describe Dagaz, refers to it as *the Lord's messenger*. In Norse legends, Nott, the Goddess of night, gave birth to a radiant son, Daeg, who opened the gates of each new day.

Good for magick to increase status or position at work or in life, for increase in money and to bring recognition or fame; also for hope when all seems hopeless, transformation, to end a bad situation and for mastering new skills,

Bind runes

Bind runes consist of two or more runic shapes joined to form a single symbol when written, thereby amplifying the powers of the separate runes. These bind or joined runes appear in ancient inscriptions, carved on jewellery or objects. Practitioners can also weave their initials or two or more powers they feel typify their magickal self or potential as bind runes and use this as a signature glyph or magickal shorthand in spellcasting or for personal power and protection.

Bind runes are considered especially potent as talismans and charms when written, painted or drawn in red on a crystal, on a round wooden flat disk or stave, on a clay tablet, imprinted into wax and also when marked on the ground in the centre of the circle during a spell to create a powerful source of protection or strength.

* Make a bind rune the focus of an outdoor ritual of the energies you wish to attract or banish, drawn on the ground or with small branches arranged to make the shape.

* You could make the initials of someone you wished to bind from doing harm and wrap it safely for as long as stated by the spell, if you make the bind rune with kindness in your heart.

* Wear a bind rune round your neck, best of all on a natural holed stone, with your initials on for protection.

* Carry one painted on a wooden disc, crystal or pure white stone in a small red bag for luck or protection.

* Draw it on your computer or on paper at a meeting (like a doodle) at work in patterns to call the power or protection you need during a crisis or challenge.

* Draw a series of protective bind runes round your home in the earth or out of stones or small branches on grass and then smooth them or remove them so they are invisible, to repel negativity and attract good fortune and health.

* Bury a fertility bind rune to restore life to a neglected or abandoned place or outside your home if it is a sterile period.

* Place a fertility and potency bind rune beneath your mattress if you and your partner are trying to conceive a child.

- Make a large protective bind rune with bound garden bamboo canes fastened together with red twine in the three knots at each intersection. You can grow a climber like jasmine or honeysuckle up the canes to help the energies to grow.
- Draw one in the air before you sleep or go out or on holiday to protect your home and possessions.
- Draw a protective bind rune in incense smoke over luggage to stop it becoming lost or stolen.

If you no longer need a particular bind rune, don't throw it away as it has been a part of you. Keep it in a special drawer or in your altar room as you would any other memento as a reminder of what you have achieved. Alternatively, bury the bind rune and plant fragrant herbs on top. Some people believe that as the herbs bloom, so will their plans continue to evolve in ways not expected.

Above all, look for the hidden message in your bind rune as an extra rune shape that appears within the bind rune form as you combine two or more separate runes. The significance of a spontaneously formed inner rune might not become evident for some time (see below).

Making a protective bind rune

The most important form of bind rune is for protection. The Viking rune Thurisaz represents a thorn and the hammer or might of the Thunder God Thor or Thunor. When combined with Uruz, the rune of primal strength, the rune of the herds of wild cattle whose horns the Vikings wore in their helmets, the bind rune creates a symbol of might that will protect against any danger and shield from attacks of any kind. It also endows the wearer with the strength to survive and thrive in any environment and rise to any challenge.

There are of course other ways you could combine the same two runes as they can be at any angle to each other, upside down, horizontal or vertical, as long as the bind runes share at least one common line in drawing to join the power.

Creating extra runes in your bind rune construction, using the example of a fertility rune

Sometimes the runic shape created will create another rune within the bind rune that adds to the overall combined energies. This can happen spontaneously or you can play around with your chosen runic forms to create an extra inner power.

Let's experiment with a bind rune for fertility. This can be fertility for any purpose from a baby to getting your novel published or launching a hobby as a business. Ingwaz, the rune of the Earth God Freyr or Ingvi is the ultimate male potency and fertility symbol as well as a protector, anciently invoked to make the crops grow and to bring success to the hunt. Combine Ingwaz with Gebo, the rune of a couple joined in love and passion and another fertility rune:

If it is a child you are seeking you could add Berkano, the rune of the Mother Goddess and a representation of Nerthus, the Mother/consort of Ingvi/Freyr who was invoked for human and animal fertility as well as the land. You could also combine the three runes for a major creative or business venture or to bring life and passion back into a relationship:

Look into the above combination and you will see that the three runes have created a sideways Othala, the home or homestead. This adds a new dimension, a stable and happy home for a child or the firm foundations for a creative venture, especially a home-based one.

If you were reviving a relationship, the inner home rune would ensure the partners were happy as a permanent unit without interference from outsiders. It could even be used to guard against a destructive love rival who was trying to break up a home and family that maybe without interference could survive.

Suggested bind rune combinations

As you choose your rune combinations according to your magickal need, you can designate the different meanings individual runes have. Use the lists given on pages 433–435. For example, Gebo could signify a committed relationship, marriage or passion in a love or fidelity bind rune. It could also indicate a gift and so generosity and giving and taking in equal measure (or maybe needing to give time and effort for a while to stabilise a situation or to ask what is needed from the cosmos, whether health, abundance or protection).

Use as many runes as you wish and you may find two or three inner runes are formed spontaneously as you join your shapes.

For material success

Fehu, the prosperity rune; Sowilo, the sun and success; Gebo, the gift and generosity, casting your bread upon the waters; Wunjo, personal happiness; and Jera, for the harvest of past efforts in the sense of as you sow so shall you reap.

For better health

Mannaz, rune of replacing weakness with strength; Uruz, primal energy and the kicking on of the immune system; Berkano, for self-regeneration as the birch tree seeds itself; and Dagaz, light at the end of the tunnel, transformation and replacing exhaustion with energy.

For happiness or security at home
Othala, rune of the home; Berkano, the mother and loving relationships; Ehwaz, people living in harmony; and Ingwaz for protection of the home and abundance.

For love

Berkano, rune of permanent relationships (Freyr and Nerthus); Laguz, the positive flow of emotions; Gebo, another commitment rune; Naudhiz, the flames of love and mutual needs; and Cenaz for passion.

For strengthening your identity
Perthro, the essential real you and also good luck; Kenaz, your inner voice and the fire to aspire to what you want to be and do; Wunjo, for personal happiness, appreciated maybe after a downturn and focusing of what you want rather than pleasing others; and Thurisaz, the hammer of Thor to overcome any unfair criticism from others or self-doubt.

For long overdue change
Raidho, rune of the wheel, a rough but exciting ride; Eihwaz, the yew tree, closing old doors but taking what is good from the situation; Hagalaz, the hail and necessary disruption to get things moving; and Laguz, the water of the melted hail and the released seed within of the future. Perhaps also Tiwaz, the star, to guide you on your journey.

For reconciliation

Isa, melting the ice with care; Elhaz, the sharp marsh grass making the first difficult steps, towards a better state of affairs; Tiwaz, making compromises and being altruistic, rather than demanding justice; Sowilo, the sun, moving into happier times; and Ansuz, speaking wisely.

For travel
Raidho, the wheel, putting plans into action; Laguz, long-distance travel, Tiwaz, following the stars and dreams; and Sowilo, the sun wheel, following the sun.

Rune dedication

Whether for magick spells, as talismans or for divination, you need to dedicate your runes for use when you make them and again if charging a rune symbol for a specific purpose. If you are making a full set, you can dedicate the individual aetts and name as you light the candle their own special deity: for example, *These are for Freyja.*

❋ Light a red candle or small fire.

❋ Set your runes round it in a circle or a single rune for empowerment in front of it, on a white square cloth, on the ground or your harrow (see page 174).

❋ Using a hammer of Thor (you can often buy a small silver ornamental one or use an ordinary hammer very gently), bring it down three times in front of the candle and the rune/rune circle. After each bang, say:

> *I made/found this rune/these runes, I marked it/them in red, to seal with magick fire its power within.*
> *May the wise deities protect, empower and bless my work.*

❋ Put the hammer behind the candle horizontally. Face the candle flame and say:

> *I call on Freyja, the Radiant, on Heimdall the Protector and Tiw the Good God, burn with cosmic fire my rune/s the powers that I may shape it/them to my will with wisdom and for right purpose.*

❋ If dedicating after making, lift each rune in turn over the candle, chant its name three times and its purpose once. For example:

> *Fehu, Fehu, Fehu, named for prosperity, so mote it be.*

❋ Then pass it through the flame three times, saying for each:

> *Protect, empower and bring blessings by Freyja, Heimdall and wise Tiu.*

❋ Return the rune to its place round the candle and when you have empowered your rune/s leave the candle until it is burned through, still shining on them.

❋ If empowering a charm, you would name the rune's ruling deity as you lit the candle. Then recite the rune name nine times and its purpose three times as you held it above the candle. In addition, after the candle blessing you could write the rune name and purpose once in incense smoke (pine or cedar) over the rune. Alternatively, use an unempowered rune (apart from its initial empowerment when made) as the focus for the spell.

❋ Smudge the rune clean after its purpose is served and return it to your magick symbol set.

PRACTICAL ASSIGNMENT

Making your runes

* You will need 24 flat pebbles, crystals or clay tablets (the size of a large coin) all the same size and colour for your magick set and a further 24 for your divinatory set unless you decide to use the same set for both (up to you). One side will be marked and the other left blank, so each will need to have a reasonable surface on which to draw, with a marker pen or paint and a brush.

* Later you might like to craft special sets, painting crystals with special acrylic paint or etching the signs on wood or a stone using a screwdriver or awl and then painting red in the indentations. Some people varnish their runes but it is a matter of choice. If you are skilled in handicrafts, you could make metal ones.

* Alternatively buy a ready made set, smudge them clean and then dedicate/empower them as if you made them.

* You will need a bag of a natural red fabric in which to keep each set of runes and a small one for carrying a single rune as an amulet or charm.

* Traditionally runes are made just before sunset, the beginning of the Old Norse day, if possible outdoors. On each of your runes draw one of the symbols for each set.

* You can also make runes from twigs that need not be more than 10-12 cm/4-5 in long and just wide enough to etch the symbol on one side. You might like to use one of the traditional runic trees, the pine, the ash, the birch or the yew, but any dry, firm wood will do, Make sure all your twigs are the same size. Scrape away the bark at the top and etch on each. Or use an engraving tool or penknife to cut the symbol and paint it red or black.

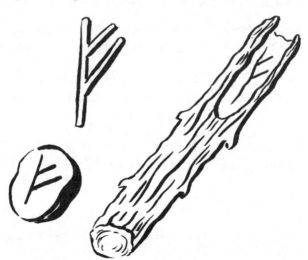

The runic symbol Fehu can be drawn or painted on stone or crystal or drawn, carved or burned on a twig or flat piece of wood.

Casting the runes

* Runes are traditionally cast at sunset or sunrise, outdoors when possible. But you can work at any time either at the end of a spell or when you need wisdom.

* In the evening light deep red and white candles and burn an incense such as pine or rosemary to increase psychic awareness.

* Formulate a question or allow your mind to go blank as you cast the runes.

* Kneel or sit and take three staves or rune discs from the bag, allowing you without looking inside the bag, to select the three that feel right.

* Holding the runes in your power hand, cast your runes on to the ground or on a cleared part of your altar.

* If the issue is complex or urgent, you can cast a second even a third time, three runes each time, allowing your hand to make the choice.

Interpreting the reading

Whether you have cast three, six or nine runes, the method is the same.

* First, note the positions of any runes in relation to others as they fell. If clustered they are connected. If one falls on top of another, the area indicated by the dominant rune is overriding or obscuring others.

* If they are scattered then there may be a number of unrelated issues or the questioner may, like the runes, feel fragmented.

* Next, look whether you have more marked or blank faces that will indicate whether the matter is one for action or a clear issue (the marked side uppermost) or whether hidden factors predominate (the blank). The blank side can also indicate that the time is not yet right to act.

* Then, in turn hold each rune in the order they were cast and allow any intuitive information to emerge. This may be as images, impressions or as words that come into your mind.

* Hold any blank-face runes and visualise a mist clearing so that the underlying factor can spontaneously form as images or impressions.

* Only then apply the meaning of the rune from the ideas given on pages 433–435 and see where it fits into the emerging picture.

* If reading for someone else, ask him or her to hold each rune immediately after you do, and then add their psychic impressions.

* Finally, put all the rune meanings together, either as a story or by drawing the symbols on paper and linking them with lines like a web. Allow your intuition to guide you.

* If you make a coven set for divination as well as magick, a question can be asked concerning the well being of a coven member, someone who is ill or a more global issue and the bag passed round the circle. One member can sit apart and close their eyes and as the bag goes round and round call Now three six or nine times. The person holding the bag pulls out a rune. The coven or group can all contribute to the meaning after the person holding it has spoken. This is an excellent way of resolving a dispute and families can also use the method with

the owner of the rune giving a brief explanation of some of the meanings of the runes selected as a guide before the others give intuitive messages.

Further research

Learn more about the world of the Vikings and their deities, so that you can understand the context of runic writing and spells.

Look online and in books for rune spells. The Thorsson books recommended below are especially full of ideas for making runic body shapes and chanting, as is the Jan Fries book.

Further information

Recommended reading

* Aswynn, Freya, *Northern Mysteries and Magick*, Llewellyn, 1998
* Blain, Jenny, *Nine Worlds of Seid Magic, Ecstasy and Neo Shamanism in North European Paganism*, Routledge, 2001
* Young, Jean, (translator) *Sturluson Snorri, The Edda of Snorri Sturluson*, Everyman, Phoenix, 2004
* Fries, Jan, *Helrunar*, Mandrake, 2002
* Larrington, Carolyne (translator), *The Poetic Edda*, World's Classics, Oxford Paperbacks, 1999
* Thorsson, Edred, *The Runecasters Handbook: The Well of Wyrd*, Red Wheel/Weiser, 1999
* Thorsson, Edred, *Futhark: Handbook of Rune Magic*, Red Wheel/Weiser, 1988
* Young, Jean (translator), *Sturluson Snorri, The Prose Edda*, University of California Press, 2002

Websites

* *Bewitching Ways*
  Good site with Wiccan emphasis
  www.bewitchingways.com/runes/ritual.htm
* *The Runic Journey*
  Rune spells and talismans
  www.tarahill.com/runes/runemagi.html
* *Irminsul Ættir*
  A truly comprehensive site of rune lore
  www.irminsul.org/ru/ru.html

MAGICKAL ALPHABETS: HIEROGLYPHS AND WITCHCRAFT

Many witches are intuitively drawn towards Ancient Egypt and feel a strong connection with its ceremonies and deities. A number have experienced clear past life connections and a sense of coming home when they visit Egypt, which they may have experienced though their lives in dreams and during meditation. Because Egypt does have such a strong influence on magick, a number of other witches connect instinctively through the common well of wisdom to this powerful tradition.

We have already worked with hieroglyphs of power (see page 402), but now we're going to explore lesser known hieroglyphs as a form of magickal writing. Like the runes, all hieroglyphs release inherent energies when written in a spell or empowerment. Hieroglyphs are a complex art and so I have limited this module to an overview and basic methodology that will enable you to write magickally in hieroglyphs.

Hieroglyphics

Hieroglyphics is a Greek word meaning holy writing. Indeed, the Egyptians believed that the system had been developed by the God Thoth to preserve the words of Ra and to write down his own magickal secrets. In fact, the ancient Egyptian phrase for writing means God's words, emphasising the association between script and the power of the Gods.

Hieroglyphs contained not only meaning but were themselves repositories of the power they represented. For example, the ankh is the symbol of the union of Isis and her husband Osiris and people would leave small bronze representations of the ankh at temples to ask for favour, in this case for a fruitful marriage.

The Ancient Egyptians were so impressed with the power of writing that they feared that words could literally jump off the page at them. The British Museum holds a funerary papyrus in which the name of Ra's serpent enemy is written in red ink. The final hieroglyph that makes up the name is struck through with knives to stop it harming the deceased.

The transcriber of the words of Gods and scribe par excellence was Thoth whom some myths say was present at creation and spoke the words of power that brought the world into being (an alternative to the Heka myth with Thoth in his role as the oldest of the deities). Thoth is pictured as a man with an ibis head or as a baboon (baboons are very active at dawn and because of this the Ancient Egyptians believed they were paying homage to Ra and were therefore sacred creatures). In either form, Thoth is often portrayed with a palette, a water jar, a reed pen and papyrus to take down the words of Ra or to record his own magickal formulae.

Working with hieroglyphs

Hieroglyphs began as simple pictures, which linguists call ideograms. For example, this simple picture of a mouth represented a mouth:

and this picture of water represented water:

But the scribes soon discovered that, although you can say a lot with simple pictures, they are limited if you want to express more complex ideas. For example, for spelling out a Pharaoh's name on his statues or the name of a foreign threat in curse magick, the Egyptians needed a more complex alphabet. They moved towards this goal by taking some of the more common ideograms and giving them character values. For example, their word for mouth was something like the symbol for the Sun God Ra (we can't be sure because the Ancient Egyptians did not record vowel sounds, so our knowledge of Egyptian vowels are based on guesswork). Therefore the mouth and Ra were linked and the mouth symbol was empowered and took on magickal as well as practical meaning. The scribes then decided that the ⬭ ideogram would have the value of its first letter, so in the hieroglyphic alphabet, this figure stands for R.

The 〰〰 water ideogram was given the value of N, linked sometimes with Nut and the Celestial Nile in the Milky Way where the blessed dead farmed the Field of Reeds. So putting these hieroglyphs together formed the Egyptian word Ren, which means the name that was part of the soul. The Ren or name part of the soul had to be read and spoken after the person had died so that the whole spirit remained intact after death.

Hieroglyphs and the English alphabet

Hieroglyphs were often assigned values for single consonants as the table below shows. Some of the letters do not have equivalent sounds in English so this table is an approximation.

* Copy it out on a piece of high-quality paper and next to each hieroglyph note the magickal meaning summarised in the list below.

* Use black or blue on white. Alternatively keep coloured pens or paint and a fine brush in the six traditional Egyptian colours: green, black, blue, red, white (on black or grey paper) and yellow, so you can create colour hieroglyphs.

I have given the Egyptian meanings of each colour later (see page 000) as this can add to the magick, as many hieroglyphs you see on painted tomb wall inscriptions are coloured.

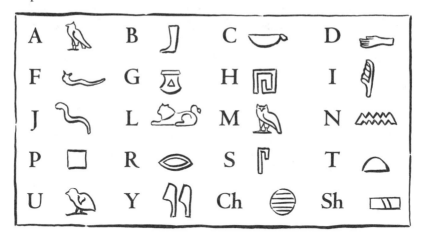

Using the letters magickally

Because hieroglyphs were considered magickal and each letter has an associated object or animal, you will find that as you write the letter correspondence to create a name or word of power, the subsidiary meanings of the letters are released as a bonus, even when you just use them alphabetically to write your name or a spell word. You can also use the individual letters in a different way as charms as an expression of the power of the meaning (rather than as a letter value) and release the power of the built-in meaning instead of using them as an alphabet (an extension to the charm hieroglyphs you learned earlier in the course). Alternatively if you find the concepts of the letters having independent meanings confusing or unnecessary, just do a pure translation of your name/s and power words.

Read the meanings below once and then forget them. Since each meaning is positive whether or not you are aware of it as you use the letter value, positive energy will be released automatically as a by product to give you strength and harmony in your spell and life. These are the associations with the letters I have developed over time and the deities whose strengths add background magick to the letters. However, other researchers and writers assign different significance, so as you read more and, most importantly, work with the letters yourself, you may come up with a better system of magickal associations that work for you.

While most of the alphabet letters below are not as individually potent as the pure charm hieroglyphs (see page 402), the more you use the alphabet hieroglyphs in magickal writing and/or as charms, the more easily you release the inherent powers of each and build up a personal store of power in the individual letters. Those hieroglyphs linked with your magickal name/s and initials will take on special significance and in time as you write them will generate an instant release of confidence, energy and protection.

Hieroglyph magick is written not spoken, as no one knows for sure how the people of 5,000 years ago pronounced the hieroglyphs. Nevertheless, some scholars working with modern Middle Eastern languages have hypothesised how the hieroglyphs might have been said. If you visit Egypt, hire a private local Egyptologist guide through the hotel (for not much more than the cost of a package day coach tour). He or she will teach you the pronunciation of the deity names and other words, as well as offering a crash course in hieroglyph inscriptions. I have mentioned deities in this section that I have not described before in the course and so have added details so you can picture them.

There are other single consonant hieroglyphs, but I have left them out because they are for sound values that we do not have in English. You will notice that there are two extra characters in the chart at the end: for the Sh sound as in Sharon or Charlotte and Ch for Charles or Cherry. These hieroglyphs do not have great magickal significance, but may be useful in writing a word. However, if you are writing your initials you could use C for Ch (hard as in Charles) and S for Sh or Ch (as in Charlotte). Use the English sounds to guide you. The other peculiarity is that there are no vowels apart from an optional A and I (but over the years a symbol for U has been added and now is used in magickal writing).

A, the vulture
A true power amulet representing the protective power of Isis the divine mother, in death as well as life. Therefore it is a symbol of protection from any powerful external force.

Deity: Isis

Magickal significance: Protection

B, the leg
Associated with swiftness of purpose, running to reach a goal or away from danger.

Deity: Anukis, the Goddess of the lower Nile, pictured in the form of a desert gazelle, embodying peace, swiftness and grace, also represented as a woman with a high feather headdress.

Magickal Significance: Travel

C or K, the basket or offerings dish
Sustenance, nourishment or a gift according to what you conceive as the contents of the basket. An alternative hieroglyph not pictured for S and K, the stair, signifies ambition or the desire for elevation in the worldly sense. Can also be used for Ch (hard).

Deity: Amenti, a Goddess represented with the head of a sheep, a human head and the crown of Lower Egypt or with papyrus flowers on her headdress, lived near a tree at the edge of the western desert. She welcomed the newly deceased at the gates of the afterworld with fresh bread and water to sustain them.

Magickal significance: Abundance, especially in times of need

D, the hand

A related hieroglyph for two fingers represents Horus or Thoth, in some versions helping Osiris to climb up the ladder to the heavens. By association the hand is an instrument of help.

Deity: Thoth, God of wisdom, and Horus, the falcon-headed Sky God

Magickal significance: Unexpected help to achieve a goal

F, also V, the viper

Swift, sharp defensive action, for the viper only stings humans if under attack, bringing to an end what has outlived its purpose.

Deity: Buto, cobra Goddess; symbol of Lower Egypt whose sacred place was the prehistoric town of Buto. She is sometimes depicted as a cobra on the crown of the pharaoh, fixing the enemies of the Pharaoh with her fiery eyes and then spitting poison into their faces. She also administers the death sting to the pharaoh when his time on earth is ended, and did so for Cleopatra.

Magickal defence: Defence especially against those who act spitefully or try to steal ideas, property or lure away loved ones

G, the stand

Lifting or supporting someone in time of need so they can see the way ahead, linked with bringing healing. A related hieroglyph to this, the Pillow of Gold, has the sacred power meaning of uplifting the spirit of the mummy so it can see the way over the horizon.

Deity: Anubis, the black jackal God was the God who both healed the living and prepared the body of the deceased so that it might be preserved. In his jackal-headed form, he was son of Nephthys and Osiris and the alter ego of Horus. He embalmed and mummified his dead father and performed this role for all the deceased so that they might survive, like his father, in the afterworld. Anubis also acted as guide and protector. He is also pictured as a black crouching dog/jackal, placed to guard tombs or sacred shrines. In this role, Anubis was called the guarder of secrets.

Magickal significance: Hope and overcoming difficulties

H, the courtyard or quarter of a city

Signifies the strength of hearth and home and their welcoming sanctuary.

Deity: Hathor, the Mother Goddess, in her role as a Domestic Goddess, was worshipped on family altars, as well as in her great temples such as Memphis and Dendara. Women would make offerings for a good husband or leave fertility images in order to conceive a child. As well as her image as a cow, Hathor was portrayed as a beautiful woman, wearing a crown of cow horns with the sun disc between them.

Magickal significance: Domestic happiness, a home

I and also Y, single and double papyrus reeds respectively

The reeds were used to make papyrus for recording wisdom and so signify knowledge and learning; also the fate that is marked out that sets marker points ahead.

Deity: Seshat writes in the books of fate and as a Fate Goddess attended the coronation of kings and major festivals. Seshat also marks out the dimensions and directions for a new temple and for all sacred buildings. Also mistress of writing and all books, she wears a seven-pointed star above which is a bow or sickle shape and a panther skin over her robe.

Magickal significance: Learning, good memory

J, the serpent

A serpent rod was used to open the mouth of the mummy to free the soul, so by association here the serpent is a symbol of freedom from restrictions and from the past; also defence against malice.

Deity: Buto, also known as Uajdet (see viper above), was regarded as the Snake Goddess and a serpent's head amulet was placed on dead bodies to prevent snakebite in the afterlife and to guard against malice.

Magickal significance: Freedom

L, the lion

For Ancient Egyptian magick, as in the modern world, the lion was associated with courage and nobility. Plutarch reports that the lion was worshipped by the Egyptians who decorated their doorways with open lion mouths as guardians to represent the rising of the Nile because the river began to rise when the sun was in Leo.

Deity: Sekhmet the Lion Goddess was Goddess of both war and healing and doctors practised in her name. Known also as a lady of magick, especially magickal healing and protection, she is frequently pictured with the head of a lioness with the sun disc on her head. She can take the form of a lioness. In her more usual lioness-headed form she carries an ankh or sistrum.

Magickal significance: Courage, leadership

M, the owl

Traditionally associated with wisdom and the moon, the owl is also a bird of warning. It signifies both listening to your own inner warnings and prompting and the wisdom of the moon and secrets of the night.

Deity: Isis in her hidden lunar aspect or Khonsu, the Moon God, the alter ego of Horus. His name means to cross, because he crossed the heavens every night in his lunar boat. Khonsu is depicted in human form with a crescent moon supporting the full moon disc. He was invoked for driving away malevolent spirits.

Magickal significance: Intuitive wisdom, secrets

N, water

Associated with the life-giving fertility of the Nile and with all aspects of growth, health and abundance.

Deity: Nut, the creating sky mother, the mother of Ra into whose watery womb he passed each night to be reborn through her thighs at dawn. She was associated with the Celestial Nile along which Ra sailed the sun boat by day. There are many representations of her body covered with stars and this image was painted on tomb lids in the hope she would grant rebirth, as Ra was reborn.

Magickal significance: Birth and rebirth

P, the stool

Offered a respite, a resting place, a seat of contemplation and was also a domestic symbol of the home and of children.

Deity: Tauret, Taweret or Thoueris, as benign and protective Goddess, was shown as a pregnant hippopotamus with huge breasts and sometimes the tail and back of a crocodile. She was mainly a Household Goddess, protective of the home, the family, pregnant women and those in childbirth and babies and children. She was frequently depicted holding knives to drive away danger from those she protected.

Magickal significance: Family and children

Q, the hill

The primal mound that rose from the waters on the morning of the first creation and so is associated with creativity, with firm foundations or a higher or different viewpoint.

Deity: Atum, the creator who according to the first creation myth rose out of the swirling waters of chaos. Because there was nowhere to stand, he created the first mound. He is depicted in human form wearing the double-headed crown of Egypt. Atum's creatures are the snake, the bull and the lion and the desert lizard.

Magickal significance: Creation, generation of wealth

R, the mouth

Opening the mouth was vital after death so that the deceased person might utter the words of power that would enable him or her entry to the next world. The mouth could therefore represent the power to communicate clearly and to be reborn.

Deity: Ra or Re, the Sun God. The cosmic egg in some creation myths contained Ra, the Sun God and his birth set time in motion. He was identified as the sun at its full power and is depicted by the symbol of the sun and also in his solar boat. He became associated with rebirth as the sun is reborn each morning.

Magickal significance: Renewal and new beginnings

S, a bolt of cloth

First letter in the word seneb, meaning health and was often used on its own as magickal shorthand in inscriptions for the whole word seneb. Seneb has come to represent the whole concept of health and wellbeing. In the tombs of pharaohs and nobles, the three signs ankh, wedja and seneb were written after his name, endowing eternal life, prosperity and health in the next world. Can be used as soft C as in Celia and Sh.

Deity: Imhotep or Imouthes. Once the scribe of King Djoser, Imhotep created the step pyramid for his master. He was also skilled in medicine and healing and performed a number of healing miracles. After his death he was made a God and continued to be a source of healing for those who came to his temple near Memphis to receive healing in dreams. In time he became known as the son of Ptah and Nut, and was pictured as a youth wearing a skullcap and carrying a scroll.

Magickal significance: Health and healing

T, the loaf

This was regarded in all ancient societies as the staff of life and so the possession of basic needs. Therefore it is a symbol of the Wiccan Enough for our needs and a little more and of deciding priorities.

Deity: Satis, Lady of the Nile waterfalls, was pictured pouring water into the dry earth to revive it. She is shown as a beautiful woman with the white crown of Upper Egypt and two gazelle horns. She appears frequently with her mother/sister Anukis and like Anukis was invoked to fill the grain store.

Magickal significance: The granting of needs rather than wishes

W, the chick

Symbol of young life and opportunity for growth and potential, this signifies enthusiasm and new beginnings; also, striving for perfection.

Deity: Nefertum. The young God of the lotus flower from which he is pictured emerging on the first sunrise. He is lord of the lotus, of all perfumes and oils. His name is linked with the hieroglyph Nefer, the Ancient Egyptian oud, the musical instrument that symbolises harmony. He represents perfection. Nefertum is depicted either as a beautiful head rising from a lotus flower, a child with a side lock sucking his thumb, sitting inside the lotus or as a youth with a lotus headdress.

Magickal significance: Beauty of the natural, innocent kind

Writing in hieroglyphs

Although some books offer approximations of vowel sounds, the truth is that the scribes did not bother with vowels, using what is the equivalent of our speedwriting (although we have A and I hieroglyphs). To add to the confusion, the scribes did not put spaces between words and put the hieroglyphs in combinations that looked attractive to them. It's no wonder that the secret of reading this script was lost for 2,000 years!

If you get no further with the study of hieroglyphics, you can use the above chart to write your name or a phonetic equivalent. While in Cairo I bought my daughter Miranda a charm pendant as a souvenir and I was able to have her name put on it in hieroglyphics. This came out as Mrnd as they did not use the I or A. If you wish, you can choose to do the same and work just with consonants (although the A is a strong hieroglyph of protection).

Mrnd is:

I have deliberately written the name vertically because that is how it appears on Miranda's long pendant and, conveniently, hieroglyphs can be stacked in this fashion. The rule in this example is that you read from top to bottom.

More confusion

Hieroglyphics can be read from left to right or right to left. One theory to explain this is that right-handed scribes using a reed pen found it easier to write as we do, dragging the pen across the paper from left to right. But right-handed masons, using a hammer and chisel to carve inscriptions on stone walls, found it more convenient to work from right to left. So how can you tell which way to read? The answer is look for faces, see which way they are looking and read towards them. Take my name Cassandra, for example, which can be written:

I have deliberately included the A sounds here to show the bird faces for clarity. They face left, so begin reading from the left towards the faces. This is as the name might be written if I were mentioned by a scribe in a papyrus. I have also combined N and D in the Egyptian version so I have just the water (ND) instead of water (N) followed by a hand (D) followed by the mouth (R). This is because the ND sound tends to get combined when the English version of my name is pronounced. I have also left in the double S, but could have reduced it to a single (your choice).

But this second version is equally valid and has the water (N) and hand (D) followed by the mouth R separate:

This time read towards the faces from right to left, as if my name was on a stone monument where people would leave fabulous offerings (I can dream). Read towards the faces. Also note another change here. The N (water) glyph has been put on top of the d glyph. Scribes would often stack small hieroglyphs in this way for neatness. When you come across a pile like this you read from top to bottom and then carry on with the horizontal words.

Try the art

In fact it is all quite logical and easy once you are in the swing. To the Ancient Egyptians, the simple act of writing their names in hieroglyphics was an empowering event. So now try transcribing your ordinary and magickal names and the names of friends and family into hieroglyphs using the chart. Don't worry about vowels (except for A and I if you wish). As I have said, my name could be written as Cssndr or Cassandra or Casandra or Csndra or Cssnra or a number of permutations. Which is right? Any or all of them.

* First work out the English shorthand phonetic version you are using.

* Left to right (for matters of short-term or urgent needs and right to left for longer term or slower acting wishes or events (not a hard and fast rule):

Here I am as Cssnr (with the ND combined), left to right. So, for instance, Mark could become Mrk or stay Mark.

* Think phonetically. The C in the chart is a hard C and can be used to write Kate or Karen. For Celia, use the S symbol. For Victor or Valerie, there's no V so use an F. For X, use C and S together.

* Experiment with writing from left to right, right to left or vertically top to bottom (if you want to make an impression or get to the top).

* Continue stacking the hieroglyphs until you find a shape that is pleasing and feels magickal, just as the ancient scribes did. Usually names were enclosed in a frame, which is called a cartouche.

Cassanra above, left to right

This gives us another clue to reading; read towards the line at the end of the cartouche.

They could also be vertical, thus:

The owl, mouth, water and hand above are Miranda as MRND top to bottom, reading to the line marked at the bottom of the cartouche. Easy!

Magick names and spells

Once you can write your magickal name/s in hieroglyphs and create a formation that is right, use it on magickal charms (use elongated stones or crystals if you have a long name or stack the letters. Write your magickal name/s on a small parchment or high-quality white vellum and tie it with red ribbon to keep on your altar or, if small enough, in a gold tube on a pendant. This is a good way of saying I exist, I matter, so don't mess with me! Or I will succeed, I will find love: whatever is your current magickal affirmation. Or use just your magickal initial/s on a crystal, a stone, on wax or a clay tablet carried in a small green bag as a personal empowerment or for protection.

If hieroglyphs seem complicated you can use just the first letter of a word for a full-scale magickal wish, as long as you know what it signifies: for example, L (the lion) for love, and of course courage and success in love. You can also make love tokens by enclosing yours and a lover's name or initials in the same cartouche or making a pattern with your initials in hieroglyphs, even one written over the other for unity and commitment/consummation.

Write your hieroglyph initial in incense smoke or the spell word initial (L and the lion for love) over a symbol such as a bag of herbs or a crystal or anything used as the focus for a spell. Do this near the beginning of the spell. This will fill it with power or protect the person it is intended for, according to the nature of the spell. Alternatively say I am and write your magickal initial/s in smoke or with your finger at the beginning of the spell over the symbol.

You could write a spell wish or names of people in hieroglyphs on paper as the focus of spell and burn it as part of the spell, a usual way of releasing hieroglyph energies. Alternatively when you are really clever with the art, use the meaning of the letter in your writing as a lucky charm. For example, L is lion and so courage and nobility, good for leadership and not just L for love.

Each letter can be linked with its deity in a spell and you could invoke the relevant deities whose letters you have used as part of a charm empowerment or in the spell. For example, L for love is LV, the empowering Sekhmet, the Lioness Goddess and Buto, the protective Snake Goddess.

More hieroglyph wisdom

Another type of hieroglyph is the determinative, which is a 'silent letter' that helps to tell us what the word means. Imagine that you were writing to a friend using a vowel-less alphabet and wanted to tell him that you had gone down to the beach to buy a ht. How would he know whether you had bought a hat or a beach hut? One way to let him know would be to add the determinative. So if you wrote:

the picture of the hat would make certain there was no mistake; while,

with the picture of the house would tell him you'd bought a hut.
However, if you wrote:

then the picture of the sun would indicate that the letters HT stood for hot or heat.

Two common determinatives are these:

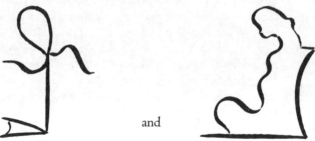

and

They stand for man and woman respectively and were often added to the end of a name to indicate the sex. These symbols are good in a fertility spell written after baby or BBY (the leg twice or singly followed by the double papyrus reed followed by the male or female symbol according to whether you want a male or female child if you have a preference As a bonus, since B, the leg, is swiftness and Y is knowledge you should conceive a clever baby soon.

So, feel free to create your own image when writing a spell message at the end of the hieroglyph (the end is where you finish reading) to expand on the hieroglyph message.

The colours of magick

The colours used in Ancient Egypt have survived thousands of years, mainly because they were created from mineral compounds. They can still be seen on statues from tombs and from paintings on tomb walls. I have written about colour generally in a later module, but these are the specific colours used in Ancient Egyptian magick. Some magickal practitioners who feel connected with Ancient Egypt use these colour correspondences rather than the more general ones given on page 512.

Use a particular colour when writing your name or initials in hieroglyphs that seems to typify for you the magickal quality you possess or strive to possess. You can also write whole words in either one colour or a mixture according to the magickal name: for example, using green linked with the rebirth Osiris in a love spell (The L lion and the V viper letters for LV) to rekindle a lost love.

Choose an appropriately coloured crystal or wax and on it etch or paint either a hieroglyph of power (see page 454) as a charm. Or use the crystal/wax tablet you have formed as a symbol of a particular power in a spell with a magickal initial drawn on it or written over it in incense smoke: for example, green malachite for strength, fertility and growth in your life perhaps after a setback, or to make that love grow or regrow, using red paint for the passion of Hathor, the Fertility Goddess.

Visit a good quality art shop or stationers that has calligraphy equipment or look online and you will find an array of inks, paints and fine brushes.

Black (khem or kem)

This had none of the gloomy or evil connotations of black in the modern world. Indeed its name, km, is linked with kmt or kemet, means the Black land and was one of the names for Egypt, referring to the rich silt deposited by the Nile flood. Therefore black was primarily a colour of fertility and rebirth. Life came from the dark primordial waters.

It also was the colour of the Underworld and specifically of Osiris, the Underworld God who caused the constant cycle of regeneration and was instrumental in giving the blessed dead rebirth. Osiris was also shown as green.

Anubis, the God who was responsible for embalming the body, was depicted either as a black jackal or dog or a black jackal-headed figure with gold limbs. Most famous are the ka or soul statues in pure black and gold of the ka of Tutankhamun guarding the entrance to his tomb. Once the statue stood in front of the naos, the gold shrines that enclosed his coffins.

Blue (khesbedj or irtiu)

Blue is a very powerful colour, used to represent the sky, especially the starry heavens and the body of Nut the Sky Goddess, as well as the waters of the Nile. Beautiful papyri paintings plus those on coffin lids depict a rich lapis lazuli blue (the pigment was made from the crystal) studded with golden stars to signify the body of Nut.

The Benu, the heron or phoenix that was the first creature to perch on the mound that rose from the primeval waters, is also blue. Blue is the colour of Thoth, the God of wisdom and writing, in the form of a blue baboon. The hair of the deities was made from blue lapis lazuli.

So blue can be used for wisdom and also for power of the sky and flowing waters, but also powerful protection.

Green (wadj)

This was primarily associated with and often made from the green crystal malachite, itself of the copper family (see page 540). Green symbolised life and growth and the green strip of land growing on either side of the Nile that even today is ploughed by bullocks and tilled by hand using implements that date back thousands of years. Green is especially associated with the green papyrus stem and leaves, itself the hieroglyph or sign for green, a plant used in making papyrus for writing. Uajdet, the Serpent Goddess was protectress of Lower Egypt whose symbol was the papyrus and she, too, was sometimes also called the green one.

Osiris was depicted with a green face and skin to represent the regrowth of the crops and his power over vegetation. For this reason, deceased people were likewise depicted on coffins and on tomb walls with a green skin to signify their rebirth.

Green was popular for amulets, especially the healing and life giving ones. The colour turquoise, associated with Hathor and the rising sun, also signified rebirth.

The blessed field of reeds in the afterlife was sometimes described as the malachite fields and Horus's wings were green.

Red (desher)

Red is a mixture of power and danger. This was the colour associated with the desert on either side of the black fertile land, Deshret, the Red Land.

Red ink was used in writing to indicate someone who was an enemy. In its negative aspect, it was associated with Set, God of evil and chaos, and of storms, though he was necessary for the universe as part of the balance. However, red was not only a colour of danger, but it also signified victory and was creative and life-giving in its forms of fire and of blood, especially the menstrual blood of Isis, whose amulet tjet, her girdle, was often in red jasper or carnelian. Red is also the colour of Hathor for fertility and especially passionate love and deep feelings in a long-term relationship.

Like gold, red is a solar colour, associated with the rising and setting sun and so the Sun Gods, especially Ra.

White (shesep and hedj)

This was perhaps the earliest colour to be used, and in such a hot country was an important colour since it reflected the light. Therefore from prehistoric times it was associated with purity, sanctity and, of course, ritual and so was the natural colour for priestly and kingly robes. Even the soles of priestly sandals were white.

The name of Memphis, a sacred city for thousands of years, translates as the city of white walls because a white wall originally enclosed it. The statues still shimmer white in the sunlight. White alabaster or calcite was used both in temple construction and for objects used in ritual, while the Great Pyramids at Giza were once coated with white limestone to radiate the sun and form a symbol of the Sun God and life.

Silver, a rare metal and the substance of the bones of the Gods, was also called khdj and a symbol of lunar light. Silver and gold together symbolised the moon and sun.

Isis in her moon aspect and Khonsu the Moon God often wear white.

Yellow (kenit and khenet)

This was another solar colour and a symbol of all that was permanent and could not be destroyed. Gold was Ra's colour and the flesh of the Gods. It was also the colour of pharaohs after death, since it was believed they had become deities, hence gold funerary masks and coffins. But any and all of the deities were created in gold to indicate their power and divinity and the solar Lion Goddess Sekhmet could be golden yellow, as fierce protectress and healer.

The development of magickal writing

Complex spells were often written in Hieratic, the cursive form of writing, examples of which were first discovered in the 6th dynasty town in Elephantine in the ruins, but may be much older. As magick became more popular, spells were written in demotic script used by educated but more ordinary people. This began around the 25th dynasty about 900 BCE.

PRACTICAL ASSIGNMENT

Working with hieroglyphs

Work with the hieroglyphs of the initials of your magickal name/s so that you can form it/them in your mind or visualise or draw on paper when you need instant power or protection.

Also, spend time designing the right formation for you of your ordinary/magickal names as an icon of power within a cartouche.

Further research

Find a museum with Egyptian exhibits or make plans to visit one in the near future. Many city museums have a good Egyptian collection; follow their attached labels and try to read the inscriptions and the significance of their creation. You will, of course, find discrepancies from my very basic guide, but you can use this as a spur if you are interested to get to grips with the intricacies of this exotic form of magickal writing.

Further information

Recommended reading:
* Ashcroft–Nowicki, Dolores, *The Ritual Magick workbook: A Practical Course of Self-Initiation*, Red Wheel/Weiser, 1998
* Collier, Mark, *How to read Egyptian Hieroglyphs: A step-by-step guide to teach yourself Hieroglyphs*, British Museum Press, 1998
* Kamrin, Janice, *Ancient Egypt Hieroglyphs*, Henry W Abrams Inc, 2004
* Robinson, Andrew, *The Story of Writing: Alphabets, Hieroglyphs and Pictograms*, Thames and Hudson 2000

Websites
* *Hieroglyphs*
  Two good references for understanding hieroglyphs
  http://hometown.aol.com/egyptnew/hiero.html
  and
  http://members.aol.com/egyptnew/glyph.html
* *Isodore of Seville*
  Good resource and links site
  www.isodore-of-seville.com/hieroglyphs/middle/

MAGICKAL ALPHABETS OF THE ALCHEMISTS AND ANGELS

Magickal alchemical alphabets date from mediaeval alchemy and ceremonial magick traditions and reached their height of popularity around the 16th and 17th centuries. They were an ideal way of concealing magickal formulae and passing wisdom between magicians (especially useful during times of persecution). Most are a variation of the Hebrew and Greek alphabets and so in some of the alphabets the individual letters have magickal and spiritual significance of their own. They have continued in popularity among ceremonial magicians to the present day because of their complexity and relative obscurity.

Some are called Angelic alphabets (such as the Enochian and Celestial) because knowledge of them was attributed to the Angels who, it is said, dictated them to such magicians as Edward Kelly in 1583, the medium of Dr John Dee. Dee was astrologer to Queen Elizabeth. There are slight variations between Dee's and Kelley's interpretations. Angel alphabets are often but not exclusively used for Angel magick but you can equally use any magickal script in Angel/Archangel invocations. Dee's Enochian alphabet and Angel-based ceremonial magick were influential upon the Order of the Golden Dawn and upon Aleister Crowley.

There are a number of magickal scripts still in existence from the formal ceremonial traditions. Most popular among witches and one of the two I have chosen is the Theban script often called the witches' alphabet, because it has straightforward correspondences with the English/Latin alphabet we use. It could be argued that the increasing popularity of the internet and the free fonts that are available as downloads have made these once secret systems so freely available they have lost their point. However, they are so far removed from everyday writing and have acquired magickal significance because of their usage over centuries. What is more, if you are to be fully proficient you would need to study them for a long time.

There are variations between alphabets even with the same name as individual occultists copying from old manuscripts added their own letter forms. One is no more right than the other and you may also make variations if you learn a system well. Some of you may already use a magickal script regularly in spells and in making charms and talismans and so this may be a good chance to learn a second or third alphabet.

Magickal alphabets

The 16th century occultist Heinrich Cornelius Agrippa is credited with the creation or certainly transmission of four of the most popular magickal alphabets. Three, the Malachim, Angelic or Celestial and the Passage Du Fleuve (Crossing the River), are strongly influenced by the Hebrew and Greek alphabets and have a number of similarities. The Malachim is the most straightforward and popular of these scripts and it is ideal for Angel as well as more general work magick.

A fourth alphabet, the Theban, transmitted by Agrippa like the other three in *The Three Books of Occult Philosophy* is the most popular in witchcraft and the easiest to learn. Agrippa dates it from the 13th century or before, created or used by a mysterious mage Honorius. It would have been used in Europe originally to transcribe Latin words, the main language of ceremonial magicians and alchemists, into a secret form. It does not have Hebrew or Greek correspondences.

I would suggest you choose one of the two magickal alphabets I have given and, if possible, download the free fonts from the internet. Put the size up to 36 points so you can see the letter formation clearly and print out the alphabet. Then you can copy it (blue or green ink on cream or white paper) to keep near your altar. Practise writing your magickal initials/names, angel or deity names and basic single word spell wishes until you are confident about writing in it.

Get to know this alphabet before learning another, if you wish. You will find free fronts for all the major magickal scripts on the internet so if you know the Theban well already you can substitute another.

Theban or witches' alphabet

* Write left to right and the same letters for capitals and lower case. You can leave spaces between words.
* Etch single letters for the initials, names or as a shorthand for a magickal wish on candles.
* Anything you would write down in magick can be made more powerful by transcribing into Theban script.
* Use the initials of your magickal/names for creating a personal charm or talisman.
* Write a single word, a longer spell wish or whole sentences on paper to burn as the focus of a spell.
* Record secret information in your Book of Shadows in Theban.
* Write love letters in Theban and keep in an envelope with fresh flowers on your altar for seven days and then burn it. Send the same letter in ordinary writing to the intended, if appropriate.
* Use the script for writing deity names as a written chant or charm.
* Etch the script on stones to cast into the sea or rivers to call abundance or specific wishes or to bury under a tree for banishment.
* Use in positive binding spells and wrap Theban words written on paper in soft cloth or freeze them in ice in a freezer rather than making an image. You can tie the paper with three knots.

- If you work within a coven or magickal group you can send e-mails or letters to other coven members (to transmit healing or magickal formulae) in Theban. Check the spelling carefully to avoid misunderstandings if writing by hand, as some of the letters are quite similar.

- Write the name of those to be healed in Theban script in your healing book.

- When you are proficient, use Theban script to write wishes and empowerments in incense smoke over symbols in spells or over crystals to act as charms or talismans.

- Mirror everyday correspondence on the magickal plane by writing an ordinary e-mail or written correspondence and then transcribing it in Theban script. Print out the Theban version and keep it on your altar, empowering it with salt, incense, candle flame and water for the four elements or leaving the light of an appropriately coloured candle to shine over it until the candle is burned through. This will greatly strengthen the effect of the ordinary mail.

- You can do the same using a Theban computer font, as well as an ordinary font, for prewriting a copy of any ceremonies or special chants. Print out the Theban copy on high-quality paper the night before the ceremony or a major event in your daily life and sleep with it beneath your pillow. You will find you can remember the words of the ordinary English version so much more easily the next day. We should not despise high-tech methods to add to our magick and make the preparations easier.

- You can also write by hand or print Theban written charms to be filled with the power of the full moon and the Summer Solstice dawn sunrise.

ꡝ	A	ꡟ	I/J	ꡏ	R
ꡢ	B	ꡑ	K	ꡛ	S
ꡏꡒ	C	ꡒ	L	ꡞ	T
ꡏ	D	ꡘ	M	ꡤ	U
ꡔ	E	ꡠ	N	ꡬ	W
꡺	F	ꡏꡨ	O	ꡟꡯ	X
ꡟ	G	ꡏꡪ	P	ꡫ	Y
ꡟ	H	ꡞ	Q	ꡏꡦ	Z

The Malachim Script

The second alphabet we will use is the Malachim script that is based on Hebrew and Greek and was very popular in the 17th century, though it was created much earlier. The Hebrew equivalents and their meanings do give the individual letters extra power and meaning and therefore single Malachim letters make powerful charms (see below). This script is also commonly used for writing Angel and Archangel names and invocations, instead of the Celestial alphabet, but you can use the Theban letters if you prefer.

There are a number of minor variations of Malachim, but this is a common version. If the font you download is slightly different, information that you should download alongside the font should give the same Hebrew letter correspondences, so you can draw in your font letter correspondence on this page for reference.

In Malachim, there is no difference for capitals and lower case except for capital S, which is Shen and lower case s Samech or Samekh, capital T Theth and lower case t Tau. If you download a font on your computer this will happen automatically according to whether you enter a lower or upper case S or T. You will notice some letters are the same in the chart below, F, U, V (Vau), W and E and O (Ayn) and I, J and Y (Yod) where there are not direct equivalents.

Though Hebrew is written right to left, fortunately our mystic ancestors used this script left to right. These are not the actual Hebrew letters but since they have taken Hebrew names we can legitimately make the connection. These Hebrew correspondences will also be of help if you use the Passage du Fleuve or Celestial (Angelic) alphabets.

Using the Malachim script in magick

❋ Use it for any of the purposes I have listed for the Theban.

❋ Etch it on candles you burn in Angel/Archangel rituals and for etching the Angel initial on the candle in the rituals (see page 528).

❋ Write petitions to Angels and Archangels in Malachim script.

❋ Create charms for people or magickal wishes as you did with the Theban, using initials or whole words. Alternatively, you can use the Hebrew meaning and write the single letter to call the magickal powers I have listed for each letter.

❋ Because Malachim script is based on Hebrew, it is powerfully defensive and can be used in all forms of protective magick and for positive banishing magick.

Malachim	Latin equivalent	Hebrew equivalent	Meaning
	A	Aleph	Aleph means ox or bull and in many traditional creation myths the Divine Cow is seen as source of life. The bull was also used as a symbol for God and represents creative and undifferentiated force, the pure lifeforce and spark of life that permeates all animate and inanimate forms; magickally, brings power and energy.

Malachim	Latin equivalent	Hebrew equivalent	Meaning
	B	Beth	Beth means house and so is the vessel of life, the bodily house of the spirit and so can be used for the home and also the body as the sacred home of the spirit; magickally, use for all magick connected with the home and for health.
	C	Cheth	Cheth is a fence or enclosure that talks about bringing spiritual powers into everyday life and also safety from all harm; there is also the suggestion of agriculture, the need to plant seeds that will grow in the future; magickally, use for protective and also for all growth magick.
	D	Daleth	Daleth, the door and the coming of abundance, new life and light; the concept of opening a doorway into fertility, creativity and opportunities once not available; magickally, use for opening closed doors and increasing business.
	E	Ayn	Ayn or Ayin, the eye, the physical eye and so things being revealed, but also the clairvoyant inner eye and also the ability to see the long term goal rather than the immediate gain.
	F	Vau	Vau is the nail, a symbol of connection between the spirit and the body, the magickal and the everyday, higher sources of power and our own inner wisdom; magickally, use to channel spiritual wisdom and Angelic sources.
	G	Gimel	Gimel means camel, a means of crossing vast tracts of barren land, a symbol of reconciliation, communication and spanning dimensions; magickally, use for travel, relocation and overcoming a barren or unprofitable time.
	H	He	He is a window that is also related to the universal lifeforce and so represents illumination, inspiration and hope; magickally use for understanding what is complex or hidden, and for making a major breakthrough.

Malachim	Latin equivalent	Hebrew equivalent	Meaning
౭	I	Yod	Yod, the smallest letter in the Hebrew alphabet, the hand that extends to other seekers and so a symbol of support in need, love, friendship and unity; use in love and joining magick, also for unexpected help.
౭	J	Yod	See I.
౨	K	Kaph	Kaph is a cupped hand, but can also represent an open hand or palm that reflects the processes of alternately giving and taking, winning and losing, as the wheel of life turns; magickally, a good symbol for calling good fortune and prosperity.
౮	L	Lamed	Lamed, the Ox-Goad that drives animals along but that can only be used with kindness; a symbol of wise justice and also a spur to noble action and challenge; use magickally for justice, official matters and for moving forward when tired or dispirited.
H	M	Mem	Mem, the waters or seas, and so a symbol of unconscious wisdom, of initiation and also of emotions, ebbs and flows in life; magickally, use for love, for attracting and banishing magick.
Ɏ	N	Nun	Nun, the fish who swims in the waters, and so a symbol of easy transition and passage to whatever is desired; also means to sprout or generate and so the concept is one of transformation, of new from old, joy out of sorrow and above all new beginnings; use for wealth, health and all growth magick.
▢	O	Ayn	See E.

Malachim	Latin equivalent	Hebrew equivalent	Meaning
	P	Peh	Peh is the mouth, from which comes both the breath of life and words; indeed sometimes a lightning flash is seen coming from the mouth of a sage; magickally, refers to any form of creative communication from writing to prophecy the growth of knowledge and inspiration.
	Q	Quph	Quph is the back of the head, seat of the brain, associated with the unconscious world and sleep, spiritual experiences begin in and through the imagination; intuition and dreams are its themes; magickally, use for the granting of wishes and increased imagination.
	R	Resh	Resh is the head or face and there is a link with the sun who is the brilliant face of the solar system, so conscious thought emanating in the head, fuelled by visionary inspiration offers a path of discovery and potential fulfilment; magickally, a symbol of power, potential, courage and leadership.
	S upper case	Shin	Shin is the tooth, biting through what is worth consuming to feed the body and spitting out what is not of use; the lines on the true Hebrew letter offer the magickal significance that is linked with the spirit descending in tongues of Fire; magickally, use for attracting resources and banishing the redundant.
	S lower case	Samekh or Samech	Samekh, a rough stone set up on end, new beliefs and theories are tested as it were against a touchstone and previous apparent certainties modified when illumination is shed upon them; magickally, a symbol of truth, integrity and what is of worth.
	T upper case	Theth	The celestial serpent who, like the alchemical ourobos snake, swallows his own tail and therefore signifies life without end, perpetually restoring and nourishing itself; magickally, a symbol of permanence and self-reliance.

Malachim	Latin equivalent	Hebrew equivalent	Meaning
	T lower case	Tau	Tau is a seal or witness, expressed in the Tau cross formed liked a capital T that is the point where Earth and Heaven meet; there are many complex associations with this symbol, but the meaning is both boundlessness and completion; magickally, it means perfection, completing a task and an awareness that anything is only a stage.
	U	Vau	See F.
	V	Vau	See F.
	W	Vau	See F.
	X	Tzaddi	Tzaddi is the fish-hook, the means of probing the unconscious waters of the psyche and drawing out what is of substance, the hook also lifts the seeker out of the material world towards the light of true fulfilment; magickally, it is a means both of moving upwards in any area including career and specially the fulfilment of dreams of fame and recognition.
	Y	Yod	See I.
	Z	Zain	Zain means sword, the sword that can cut through false attachments and illusion and is a symbol of rebirth and integration of our shadow side and potentials; magickally, a defensive symbol.

PRACTICAL ASSIGNMENT

Work with the magickal alphabets

Spend time learning one of the alphabets above or another chosen one so that you can start to work with it in spells, charms and rituals.

Further research

Using the references below, research another alphabet that interests you. If you are interested in the Hebrew associations, any books about the Kabbalah/Qabalah will give you insight into the Hebrew mystical world.

Further information

Recommended reading

* Agrippa, Heinrich Cornelius, Von Nettesheim *et al*, Turner, Robert (translator), *The Fourth Book of Occult Philosophy*, Nicolas-Hays, 2005
* Fortune, Dion, *The Mystical Qabalah*, Red Wheel/Weiser, 2000
* Parfitt, Will, *The Living Qabalah*, Element, 1988
* MacLean, Adam, *A Treatise on Angel Magic*, Magnum Opus Hermetic Sourceworks, Red Wheel/Weiser, 2006
* Pennick Nigel *Magical Alphabets, Secrets and Signs of Ancient Scripts including Runes, Greek, Hebrew and Alchemical*, Red Wheel/Weiser, 1997
* Skinner, Stephen, Rankine, David, *Dr John Dee's Enochian Tables*, Golden Hoard Press, 2004

Websites

* *Omniglot*
  Good site with links to free Celestial alphabets font download sites; good for Malachim and Theban alphabet correspondences and general information
  www.omniglot.com/writing
* *Free downloads for Angelic/celestial fonts, also for similar Enochian alphabet*
  www.steliart.com/angelology_celestial_alphabet.html
* *Coven of Cythrawl*
  Excellent site plus free download of Theban fonts
  www.coven-of-cythrawl.com/Theban_script.htm
* *Free font Malachim*
  www.geocities.com/SoHo/Lofts/2763/witchy/alphabets.html

THE MOON

The moon is central to witchcraft, for the full moon is the focus of a witch's monthly esbat whether she is a solitary practitioner or coven member. Throughout the month, the moon provides a source of power that reflects magickally and personally the life rhythms of the witch. Images on a vase from Ancient Greece dating from the 2nd century BCE show a priest and priestess drawing down the moon into her body. He holds a sword, she what appears to be a wand in her hand.

The full moons have been important in a number of cultures including China where the Chinese New Year is marked by the first full moon in February. The Native North Americans and the Celts marked the passage of time by the full moons of the year, each of which heralded a natural change in the migratory cycles of animals and birds, weather conditions and the growth of crops.

I have already written about the moon phases and details of moon deities from around the world can be found on page 234. In this module we will focus on drawing down the moon ceremonies, on incorporating the different names and energies of the full moons throughout the year into our magick and personal lives and using the moon as it passes through the different astrological signs each month for different kinds of spellcasting.

Drawing down the moon

This is probably the single most important ceremony in magick. The full moon is the time when the Moon Goddess and lunar energies are not only at their most powerful but also most accessible. Traditionally, the full moon is drawn down into the High Priestess by the High Priest in a formal ceremony where in an altered state of consciousness she and all present are able to merge with Goddess energies and be empowered by them. A usual form for channelling the Goddess is the Charge of the Goddess, of which I wrote on page 239. The High Priestess (or whoever speaks the words) may feel a sense of not being possessed but blessed and filled with Goddess light and wisdom.

I will focus on two ways of drawing down the moon in which solitary witches or covens work directly with the full moon in the sky. Full moon energy can be channelled by any practitioner, beginner or experienced or indeed any moon lover standing beneath the moon who wishes to be empowered and blessed. I believe that drawing down the moon connects with and ignites the divine spark within us all, and whatever your religion is a positive natural as well as supernatural experience. There is not a great tradition of drawing down Moon God power, but there is no reason why men and women cannot try what is a subtly different approach, or men call on the Moon Goddess to enter them, a very profound and spiritual experience.

To many witches, the full moon night is sacred to Diana and indeed Leland, before Gardner, wrote of Aradia, telling her followers to meet once in the month: *when the moon is full to adore the spirit of your Queen, my mother Great Diana*. Other witches call on Aradia, Diana's silver daughter on this night or my own favourite Greek Moon Mother Selene, after whom the moon crystal selenite is named.

Why the full moon?

Since in the old world the new day began at dusk, at the major festivals moonlight was important both for providing light and ritually signifying the presence and blessings of the Moon Mother. A full moon on a festival, which would rise around dusk, was regarded as especially mystical and fortunate. The extreme midwinter full moonrise, occurring every 18 years 7 months, marked a complete ritual cycle and on this day the rebirth of light was especially potent, because it was mingled with the tides of change signified by the full moon.

The full moon was chosen for the monthly esbat or coven meeting for the practical reason that in the times before electricity not only witches but ordinary village people could meet and dance after work was done. Dancing in the moonlight, they would stir the earth energies for success of the crops and the health of the animals on which the community depended. The moon as symbol of fertility further strengthened the rites. Often the seasonal celebrations would be moved to a period when the moon would be bright.

A basic but powerful drawing down the moon ceremony for solitary practitioners or magickal gatherings

If you do not belong to a tradition that has a set ritual for drawing down the moon or would like to experiment with different methods, all you need for the following ritual is the moon, water in a cauldron or a clear glass bowl and some silver bells on a small hoop or string (optional). Alternatively, you could use a small round pond or a rock pool as your water source. You can carry out this rite in any place where the moon shines down upon you, preferably outdoors, even if the moon goes behind clouds.

* The bowl or cauldron should be in front of you as you face the moon or in the centre of a group of people or a coven.

* Hold any bells in your receptive hand.

* Stand in full moonlight looking up at the moon. For the first time try when the moon is shining brightly. When you are more experienced, you can visualise the brilliant moon rays even if it is very cloudy.

* If more than one person is present stand in a circle with enough space between you to spin round separately.

* Raise your arms wide and high, palms uppermost and slightly curved (some people hold them flat). Stand with your legs apart so you make a pentagram with your body with your head as the apex.

* Call the Moon Mothers into your life and your heart with a chant. I work with Isis, the Celtic Rhiannon, Selene and Diana.
* You can with a group devise a simple repetitive group chant in advance that you can chant to call and dance down the moon. The private chant I use and adapt from time to time is:

> Draw down the moon, draw down the power, Moon Mothers, I call at this hour.
> Draw down the moon, draw down the light, Diana, Rhiannon, mothers of night;
> Isis, Selene, come to me be with me, mothers tonight, Be with me, lady, be with me soon,
> that we may be one, lady of moon.

* Dance round the water chanting and spiralling moonwise (anticlockwise) and if you have bells use those as you move.
* Then when you are spinning fast, stop and turn round on the spot in small moon wise circles, still chanting. This works whether you are alone or with others.
* Circle your arms as you move in front of you, over and round your body, chanting faster and moving faster in your tiny circle until you become dizzy. Let the movements and words flow and don't worry if they change as you become more enchanted.
* With a final call:

> Come to me, be with me, Mothers of Moon

sink to the ground, look up and the physical moon will come rushing towards you. This is a purely physiological effect but is the most effective psychic method I know for bringing together the experience on all levels.

* You may spontaneously speak or sing aloud or hear words channelled from the Moon Mother or see images of light and moonbeams circling round you.
* If you wish, you can now use the absorbed rush of power and inspiration to direct a wish skywards or send healing by pointing with both hands fingers outstretched in the direction from which fulfilment will come or towards which healing will be sent. Or point your fingers towards your Heart chakra or any of the chakra points to fill yourself with power. Your fingertips may sparkle either in actuality or within your mind.
* When you are ready, direct your outstretched fingers towards the water and send the final light into it. Gaze into your bowl of water into which the moon is shining and images will enter your mind. If it is a cloudy night, light tiny silver candles round the bowl,
* If working with others, each of you should draw close to the water in a tight circle kneeling or sitting or pass the bowl round the group and each person can speak a few words or describe images.
* Unless the weather is bad remain in the moonlight, singing, dreaming and scrying in your bowl of moonlit water Over the months of working with the full moon you may receive a great deal of personal insight through moon scrying and begin to retrieve information from the collective well of wisdom or even recall past worlds and other moons.

* Don't forget to make your moon water (see page 359) for baths, drinks, for healing and as the water element in magickal spells with a strong moon focus.

A more complex ceremony

Again you can work alone or with others. I will describe a solitary ritual, but you can as easily adapt it for others, choosing one person to act as the Goddess focus, assisted by everyone present who will then absorb the channelled power.

* First, you need a moon altar. If outdoors away from your usual garden altar, set a large, white, flat stone, preferably round, to act as a moon altar. Some practitioners keep a large, round stone in the garden for full moon ceremonies.

* Light four silver candles in the four quadrants on it plus a conch shell for the Goddess if you wish and a spiral shell for the God. Outdoors you can use small glass enclosed night-lights that will not blow out in the wind.

* In the centre, set a bowl of either seawater or water in which you have mixed three pinches of sea salt moonwise with a small silver knife.

* You can edge the bowl with shells, moonstones or small white flowers and light jasmine, lemon, lemon balm, myrrh or poppy incense (see page 202 for a list of moon fragrances).

* If you wish you can anoint the candles with moon oil before lighting after casting the circle. You can use a few drops of jasmine, lemon, lemon verbena, vervain, sandalwood or myrrh essential or fragrance oil mixed with a little sweet almond or olive oil (see page 530 for anointing candles). Lemon, lemon verbena and vervain are sacred to Diana and Aradia.

* Alternatively, work with the cauldron as the centre on the ground instead of a stone and set the candles etc round it. An old-fashioned goldfish bowl is also ideal for scrying and drawing down the moon.

* Cast a circle in the usual way and raise your athame or willow (moon) wand to the moon at a 60-degree angle.

* If in a group, one of you should stand in the centre facing the moon to signify the manifest Moon Goddess and to act as the main channel for moon power. The group should arrange themselves in a horseshoe formation so they can see the moon and the person taking the part of the Goddess.

* You or everyone present as they raise the athame or wand to the moon should say:

> By seed and root, by stem and bud, by leaf and flower and fruit, I call you Mother Moon,
> Lady Luna, to enter this blade with blessings.

Luna was the Roman name for the Full Moon Goddess.

* Next, if working alone touch the centre of your forehead with the blade and directing it towards your feet say:

> Blessed be the feet that walk within your paths of light.

* Next, direct the blade towards your knees and say:

Blessed be the knees that kneel upon the silver earth in praise.

* Kneel still holding the athame or wand.
* Next, direct the athame towards your womb (or, for a male witch, the genitals) and say:

Blessed be the womb/the source of procreation that ever renews and generates new life.

* Next, direct the athame towards the heart, saying:

Blessed be the heart of love, of beauty and of strength.

* Finally, touch your lips very gently with the blade, saying:

Blessed be the lips that speak the words of mystery and of truth divine.

* If in a group, you can form a circle round the person acting as the Goddess and direct your blades towards her as you all speak the words together, kneeling at the appropriate point and afterwards moving back to the horseshoe. She remains silent, standing with her athame pointing directly upwards to the moon.
* If working alone, stand and raise the athame again toward the moon and say:

By seed and root, by stem and bud, by leaf and flower and fruit, by Life and Love, do I call you gracious Goddess to fill me with your blessings and your wisdom.

* If in a group direct your blades towards the figure in the centre and speak the chant together, adapting the words. Again the Goddess figure remains silent with her athame raised towards the moon.
* If alone, now lower your blade and, facing the moon, make the pentagram position legs and arms apart and arms raised. Begin an invocation, whether you speak as Aradia, Diana, Isis, your favourite Moon Goddess or the Great Mother (using the Charges on page 223). Make it simple enough to say by heart. My favourite, amalgamated from a variety of sources for my solitary rites, is:

I am the moon upon the deep waters, I am the moon upon the shining waters, I am the moon upon the flowing waters. I am the moon among the stars, child of the moon I hear you call and so I come to you. Safe you are once more within my watery womb, safe within my loving arms, beloved child. I your Goddess, the stars, the moon, the watery deep, your mother, I am you, you are me, we are one, we are the moon.

* If you are in a group, the Goddess designate speaks while the others sway softly. Then whether alone or as the Goddess in a group, continue to chant the words softly and begin to sway also rhythmically until there is a shift of consciousness inside and you feel lighter, filled with moonbeams, warm and no longer separate from others and the cosmos (even if working alone).
* As a group you will be aware of the magick working and the central figure being filled with light and the light radiating into every person present.

* When the glow becomes almost unbearable, if alone raise the athame and touch the surface of the water with it saying (or the central figure of the group says softly):

I am the moon and I still am myself. And so I speak with blessings and humility by the light of the moon and through the light of the moon and with the light of the moon.

* If in a group, all should point their athames towards the Goddess designate as she touches the water.

* Now, sit or if in a group the Goddess figure should softly say, Down, and all sit. Put the blade on the ground and, looking into the water, speak from the heart. In the group each person looks into the water or passes the bowl round and speaks spontaneously.

* Then when no more is to be, either boil the water on a small camping stove in a heatproof pan to return it to the cosmos or tip it away in an environmentally friendly way, perhaps into a deep pot of earth as salt water can damage grass or growing plants. While the water is boiling away, watch the moon and perhaps create quiet spontaneous chants.

* When you are ready, uncast your circle, blow out the candles and walk beneath the moon, dreaming or if with others talking softly of matters of the heart.

Working with the full moons through the year

Hunter-gatherers and later farmers recorded the lunar cycle as marks on rock, bone or wood to create the earliest calendars. In contemporary indigenous traditions such as the Native American, the names of the different full moons still echo the qualities of each season.

These Native American moon names show a remarkable similarity to the Celtic calendar. For example, the April/May moon in the Celtic world was called Glamonios, which means growing green shoots and is Frog or Blossom Moon in some Native North American calendars, reflecting the mating of the frogs after their winter hibernation and the return of the blossom on the trees.

Calendars were originally created with direct reference to what was happening in the natural world. In early lunar calendars, it was reflected that certain events such as the migration or return of certain birds or the arrival of the herds occurred regularly after a set number of full moons. So the concept of the moon months evolved, tied into the land and its creatures upon whom humans depended. Therefore from any point by counting forward it could be calculated how many moon months would elapse before, for example, spring returned.

Blue moons, where more than one full moon occurs in the same month, have always been regarded as especially potent.

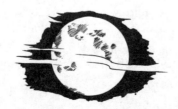

The Celtic lunar calendar

The Roman historian Pliny reported that the Druids calculated their months and years by lunar time. For the Celts, specific moons heralded not just times of bird migration or crop growth but also when the roads were sufficiently dry for travelling to markets, fairs or to seek justice, so that people could make plans to travel two or three moons ahead.

The archaeological source of our knowledge of Celtic lunar calculations is the Coligny calendar, which consists of surviving fragments of a huge bronze plate measuring, when it was intact, 152 cm/5ft by 107 cm/3 ft 6 in. The calendar, named after the location where it was discovered in Eastern France in 1897, was engraved in Gaulish, but with Roman letters and numbers. It has 12 cyclical moon months and it seems from the 62 consecutive months recorded that an additional two months were included (one every two-and-a-half to three years, consisting of 30 days each). This extra magickal biyearly month was called Ciallos, the month of no time.

If you follow this time cycle on a 19-year solar time basis (i.e. 235 lunar months), it is accurate to within half a day, the time it took to train as a Druid and not far off the time between Midwinter-full moon cycle, 18 years plus six full moon cycles (see page 330).

This Coligny calendar ran from full moon to full moon. Another theory suggests that the Romanised Gauls replaced in its creation an earlier Celtic calendar that was 13 lunar months long.

Working with the moon months

If you have access to the internet, there are many excellent online lunar calendars/calculators for the Coligny and some lunar almanacs also include the Coligny and Native North American months. After two-and-a-half years, you can choose to name a full moon Ciallos in the cycle when there is a period of unseasonable weather or great natural upheavals, since it is associated with transitions either in nature or in lifestyle. Keep this spare month for every two-and-a-half to three years to catch up or use if a moon name does not feel right for what is going on. There is no substitute for looking in the sky and matching moon to name.

Most importantly, go back to the practices of the people who made their notches and related the moon in the sky to what was happening in the natural world and to the crops. Over the next year, you can create moon names for each of the moons to reflect the events in your world urban or rural. For me, for example, the full moon in January represents Reckoning Moon when my very chaotic tax accounts are due. Also after Christmas it really is a time for assessing what works and does not work financially, career-wise and emotionally to plan the coming year's diary. To the Celts the January moon was Angantios, Staying At Home Moon and to the Native Americans Gnawing on Bones Moon, reflecting the difficulty of hunting when the weather was so bad.

* In a diary, mark full moons to make your calendar and start day 1 and lunar month 1 as the nearest full moon to when you begin this module. Of course, it does not matter how many full moons there are in the calendar year because once

you have named your 12 listed full moons you start again.

* Keep notes of how each full moon makes you feel. Over a period of two or three lunar years you will discover definite energy patterns emerging, so that you can plan your year and anticipate natural change points to take advantage of the energies of the moons.

* Try to fix full moon celebrations to reflect their different qualities, using different crystals, incenses and symbols related to your own region You can empower a related charm, whether a crystal, bag of herbs or a symbol, that you an carry until the next full moon.

* If you live in the southern hemisphere, you could move the moon names forward six moons or change them completely.

* As in Native North America, where the large number of moon names reflects very different climates, you can adapt the moon names according to what is going on around you: for example, Hurricane Season or Monsoon Moon (see the practical assignment on page 488).

* You can either use the moon name for the calendar month it falls in, carrying over a second blue moon right at the end of one month to the next month, or go from full moon to full moon. I think the second works best magickally.

* I have briefly listed the moons and the kind of magick you can perform either on the full moon itself or the two days on either side. These are a synthesis of lunar names I have gathered and used over the years. You can find other Native North American names in the websites I have listed at the end of the module.

Coligny name	Native North American name	Full moon date	Ritual
Samnios Seed Fall	Hunter's or Trading Moon	Oct/Nov	Making an end to what is not fruitful, drawing up realistic plans for the coming year, seeking rewards for past efforts made, storing resources such as money.
Dumannios, the Coming of Deep Darkness	First Snows or Frost on the Grass Moon	Nov/Dec	Bringing light into the darkness, seeking inner as well as outer illumination and inspiration, for trust in a better tomorrow, candle rituals for rebirth and new beginnings.
Riuros, the Time of the Long Coldness	When Wolves Huddle Close Moon	Dec/Jan	Material security, the home and family, rituals for older people and welcoming people back into your life, rituals for absent or estranged family.

Coligny name	Native North American name	Full moon date	Ritual
Angantios, Staying Home	Gnawing On Bones Moon	Jan/Feb	Acceptance of life as it is, seeking joy in what one has, not fretting for what one has not, conserving strength, health and resources.
Ogronios, the Time of Shining Ice	When The Geese First Lay Moon	Feb/Mar	The stirring of new hope and trust, releasing potential that has been frozen, conception and planning new initiatives.
Cutios, the Time of the Winds	Purification or Eagle Moon	Mar/April	Change, clearing away the stagnation and inertia, banishing bad habits and negative influences.
Glamonios, Growing Green Shoots	Frog or Blossom Moon	April/May	New horizons and opportunities, employment, fertility, love, speculation and creative ventures.
Simiuisonnos, Right Time or the Time of Dancing	Flowering or Full Leaf Moon	May/June	Joy, permanent relationships, maximising opportunities, potency and fertility.
Equos, the Time of the Horse	Strawberry Moon When The Buffalo Are Calling	June/July	Travel, moves of all kinds, house or career, expansion.
Elembiuos, Claim Time	Ripe Corn Moon or When The Young Geese Take Wing	July/Aug	Justice, promotion, recognition and financial gain, resolving official matters.
Edrinios, the Time of Arbitration	Harvest Moon or Dark Butterfly Moon	Aug/Sept	Reaping what has been sown, abundance, assessing life and resources with a view to shedding what cannot be used.
Cantios/ Song Moon	Nut Moon, When The Birds Fly South Moon	Sept/Oct	Final burst of energy for tasks undone, salvaging relationships and missed opportunities.

The zodiac and moon spells

The moon travels around the Earth every $29^1/_2$ days. In its orbit, it passes through each of the sun or zodiac signs each month, for about two-and-a-half days. Each period is potent for particular kinds of spells. Of course, the emphasis will vary according to whether the moon is waxing, waning or full, and you could get more than one of these phases within your two-and-a-half day period. The full moon gives a burst of power to the waxing qualities, but can also be used for change and to launch a waning venture.

For this reason, I have divided each sun sign phase into two. Some practitioners only cast one zodiac-related spell a month, working with the sun phase the full moon falls in during that month. Others cast a single zodiac spell related to the sun sign of the current crescent moon. However, I believe that the moon and sun sign energies combined are helpful if you have specific issues within a month and can wait to cast your moon spell at the right time. As it enters the new sign or right in the middle is most potent. Almost every daily newspaper astrology column will give you this information or you can get it on line or from an almanac.

I have listed which candle colours, incenses and crystals belong to each sun sign. Each sun sign also has healing power for specific areas of the body that is amplified by the moon's presence. The waxing moon in a sign increases energy and self-healing and the waning aspect takes away pain and illness. You can add this information to the magickal timings section of your Book of Shadows.

Moon in Aries

Waxing
For courage, independence, self-reliance, self-employment, action, health, assertiveness, launching major ventures or life changes, energy and passion.

Waning
For anti–bullying and aggressiveness, to reduce hyperactivity.

Use for healing the face, head or brain.

Candle colour: Red

Incense: Ginger or Cinnamon

Crystal: Red jasper

Moon in Taurus

Waxing
For spells for fertility, love, radiance, money, material security and to acquire beautiful things.

Waning
For losing weight, for overcoming possessiveness and emotional blackmail, anti-debt and to protect possessions.

Use for healing the throat, neck or ears.

Candle colour: Pink

Incense: Apple blossom or rose

Crystal: Rose quartz

Moon in Gemini

Waxing

For speculation and games of chance, for passing examinations and tests, for healing using surgery or medical intervention, for communication, travel and moves of all kinds. Also for good luck.

Waning

For protection against deceit, gossip and spite and to reverse bad luck.

Use for healing the shoulders, arms, hands, or lungs.

Candle colour: Yellow

Incense: Lavender or lemongrass

Crystal: Citrine

Moon in Cancer

Waxing

For spells for happiness at home, for family, children and fidelity, also for keeping secrets and for all moon spells.

Waning

For protection of the home, family and against accidents or hostile neighbours.

Use for healing the chest or stomach.

Candle colour: Silver

Incense: Myrrh or poppy

Crystal: Moonstone

Moon in Leo

Waxing

For spells for success, power, leadership, fame, prosperity, career and abundance, potency, childbirth and for nobility of purpose.

Waning

For reducing the negative effects of critical people, for overcoming problems with bosses and financial shortages and losses.

Use for healing the upper back, spine and heart.

Candle colour: Gold

Incense: Frankincense or orange

Crystal: Amber

Moon in Virgo

Waxing

For health and healing, for animals, for striving for perfection, for any detailed matters, for employment, for skill with hands, for gardening and the environment and for keeping to diets.

Waning

For banishing illness and any form of addiction or compulsion, for helping clumsy children or adults, for overcoming unemployment, for personal safety.

Use for healing intestines or nervous system.

Candle colour: Green

Incense: Fennel or patchouli

Crystal: Jade

Moon in Libra

Waxing

For spells for marriage and partnerships, for peace and harmony, for justice, the successful outcome of court cases, for charisma and for compromise.

Waning

Use to prevent lack of commitment, infidelity, laziness and inertia and in anti-war and conflict spells.

Use for healing ailments of the lower back or kidneys.

Candle colour: Blue

Incense: Peach or vanilla

Crystal: Blue lace agate

Moon in Scorpio

Waxing

For transformation, wish magick, sex magick, to increase psychic powers and for any strongly felt desires or needs, for recovering what has been lost or stolen.

Waning

For protection against psychic attack, anyone seeking revenge, against vandalism, jealousy and criminals.

Use for healing the reproductive organs.

Candle colour: Indigo or Burgundy

Incense: Sandalwood or mimosa

Crystal: Opal

Moon in Sagittarius

Waxing

For travel, adventures, house moves, horses, publishing and creative ventures, for happiness and optimism, for good ideas, for sports and for finding lost pets.

Waning

Protection on journeys and against getting lost, for preventing pets straying or being stolen, for slowing or reversing money losses.

Use for healing the liver, thighs or hips.

Candle colour: Orange

Incense: Hibiscus or sage

Crystal: Turquoise

Moon in Capricorn

Waxing

For commitment in love and business, for financial security, for all official matters, for wise caution, for steady promotion and career success, for stable business ventures, for perseverance and overcoming obstacles though persistent effort.

Waning

For overcoming depression and self-doubt and for releasing money that is tied up or disputed.

Use for healing the knees, bones, teeth, or skin.

Candle colour: Brown

Incense: Magnolia, vetivert

Crystal: Garnet

Moon in Aquarius

Waxing

For spells for original ventures, for the success of inventions, for any intellectual matters, for humanitarian issues, for friendships and for developing unique gifts and talents, for alternative medicine.

Waning

For overcoming intolerance, bad habits, prejudice and inequality and for banishing loneliness and isolation.

Use for healing the calves, ankles and blood and personality disorders.

Candle colour: Purple

Incense: Benzoin, rosemary

Crystal: Amethyst

Moon in Pisces

Waxing

For spells for new love or love after loss, for music and the performing arts, for balancing two commitments or having two careers, for adaptability, for merging two families and for telepathic powers.

Waning

For overcoming rivalries and people pulling you in different directions, for reconciling quarrels and custody or divorce disputes and for overcoming excesses or imbalances of any kind.

Use for healing the feet or lymph glands.

Candle colour: White

Incense: Lemon or sweetgrass

Crystal: Clear quartz or clear fluorite

PRACTICAL ASSIGNMENT

Creating a full moon year

※ Create your own full moon year, using the Celtic or Native North American moon year as a guide. You can get other ideas online.

※ You can link the moons with both your own regional climate patterns and your magickal and daily world. You may need three or four words to sum up your picture of the individual moon energies. For example, the Celtic Moon Ogronios, the Time of Shining Ice, contains the image of the sun starting to melt the ice. In the Native North American world it is sometimes called When The Geese First Lay Moon or in other traditions Little Bud Moon. In the relatively mild Isle of Wight off the south coast of England, I call it my Looking For The Greenery Moon. When I see this moon I am looking for the first spring flowers and feel the stirrings to get on the road again after spending the winter huddled by the radiator writing. It is the time when I am out enjoying any moments of early sunshine and feel that I am ready to try new things, even though I said Never again just before Christmas. This full moon, the one usually before the Spring Equinox moon I celebrate by buying lots of hyacinth bulbs to decorate the altar and bluebell fragrance candles from the local garden centre that is opening for the first time after the winter. Knowing this moon is coming is my year turning and it is the time when my beloved caravan site opens for the season, even though the weather might may be freezing and muddy.

※ If you live mainly in town, you can follow the monthly lunar energies by watching the changing leaves in the city squares and escaping to the countryside and coast at weekends.

※ The importance is not the calculations and the set names but writing your personal lunar calendar, living by it and celebrating the coming of the moons ritually. If your moon times are out of the step with the solar clock, have a double date system in your diary. Still keep business appointments and remember birthdays by the modern solar date, but know that these occasions also occur on the third day of the Migrating Geese Moon, or whatever you call the moon in the sky.

Further information

Recommended reading

* Cashford, Jules, *The Moon: Myth and Image*, Cassell Illustrated, 2003
* Eason, Cassandra, *Night Magic*, Piatkus, 2003 and Kensington/ Citadel 2004
* Galenom, Yasmine, *Embracing the Moon, A Witch's Guide to Rituals, Spellwork and Shadow Work*, Llewellyn, 1998
* Grimassi, R, *Italian Witchcraft: The Old Religion of Southern Europe*, Llewellyn, 2000 Publications, Minnesota, USA
* Guiley, Rosemary Ellen, *Moonscapes: A Celebration of Lunar Astronomy, Magic, Legend and Lore*, Cynthia Parzych Publishing Inc, 1991
* Lucy, Janet, Allison, Terri, *Moon Mother, Moon Daughter: Rituals and Myths that celebrate a Woman's Coming of Age*, Fair Winds Press, 2003
* Paungger, Johanna, Peppe Thomas, *Moon Time: The Art of Harmony with Nature and Lunar Cycles*, Rider, 2004
* Wood, Gail, *Rituals of the Dark Moon*, Llewellyn 2004

Websites

* *Powersource*
  Excellent site about Native North American moons, customs at the times of the moons etc
  www.powersource.com/cocine/ cermony/moons.htm
* *Pib Burns*
  Extensive myths site, including a large lunar section
  www.pibburns.com/mythtopi.htm
* *Roman Britain*
  Comprehensive site on Celtic full moon Coligny calendar
  www.roman-britain.org/coligny.htm
* *Sacred Texts*
  Gardner's Book of Shadows, Drawing down the Moon ceremony
  www.sacred-texts.com/ pag/gbos/gbos01.htm

THE SUN

(⋆A⋆)s a Druidess and a witch I value the sun and moon equally. Witchcraft is sometimes said to be religion of the moon and Druidry the religion of the sun with its public rituals performed in the eye of the sun. Druid ceremonies are held mainly during daylight, though some begin or end in the dark: for example, on the Solstices.

As well as drawing down the moon/Goddess into the priestess, witches draw down the sun/God power into the priest, especially at seasonal solar change points such as the Equinoxes or Solstices. For witches, the Sun is also a potent force, just as the moon is part of Druidry. Many witches celebrate whether with a minute or two's contemplation and blessing or occasionally ceremonies at the four sacred day markers, dawn, noon, sunset or dusk and midnight, time of the dark or visualised sun as it shines on the other side of the world. Finally, witches spontaneously derive power and healing from the essential solar life force called in Druidry awen, the inspiration of pure gold.

Best of all we don't have to wait for the once a month full moon, for the sun is there every single day we need power and inspiration. So sun power can be drawn (though often it is not) whenever needed and the experience can be totally spiritual and empowering in a witch's private life as well as ceremonially.

Because this is a less familiar topic maybe even to more experienced witches, I have extended it to a double module.

Drawing down the power of the Sun Goddess or God

Solitary male practitioners may find drawing down the Sun God a direct route to connecting with their own divine core. The moon/sun, anima/animus division is one traditional to alchemy with King Sol and Queen Luna joining to produce the divine child, the philosopher's stone and, it is said, the key to immortality. However, female witches can claim some advantage. Because there is such a strong tradition of Sun Goddesses (see page 239 and the recommended reading for a list of some of the best known), a female practitioner can likewise readily draw down the sun to illuminate her animus side. Men can, of course, draw down the Moon Goddess as I suggested in the previous module, but the tradition of Moon Gods is by no means as strong as that of the solar Goddesses.

Solar Goddesses tend to be very hands on in creation. According to myth, the Celtic solar Goddesses Sulis, Aine and Grainne did not ride though the skies but actually walked the fields and hilltops in their summer finery, not only indicating the time of harvest but also helping to cheer a tired worker or soothe a crying baby.

Then in the celebrations of harvest home leading the processions, they bound their spirit into the grain maiden created from the last sheaf.

You can draw down the sun power as God or Goddess regardless of your own gender, most easily at noon on the Summer Solstice or on a Sunday, the day of the sun, again at noon on a brilliantly sunny day. But as you become more experienced you can also draw down the sun at dawn or during a vivid sunset. These three daytime sun ceremonies are called drawing down the visible sun. The dark sun at midnight I have described in the next module, as this is more complex.

Drawing down the visible sun

The Ancient Egyptians believed that by speaking words to the sun we became the sun spiritually and in power terms. This concept reached a height during the relatively short period when the sun called the Aten was worshipped as the only deity during the 14th century BCE. The Aten was depicted not through statues but also as an image of the solar disc with rays emanating from it that ended as ankhs, the key like symbol of immortality.

The Aten's patron on earth was King Akhenaton (the glory of the Aten) who changed his name from the family name Amenhotep IV (Amun or Amen is at peace). He ruled for a relatively short time from 1352-1336 BCE, yet his actions gained him the name of the Heretic King and his name was removed from many of his monuments after his death, so it was believed destroying his immortal soul.

What he said was that without the sun there is no life and that we all receive our own inner radiance from the undifferentiated source. He also left the legacy of a wonderful Great Hymn to the Aten, traditionally recited each morning facing the sunrise. You can create your own chant of praise; I have given my version of this on page 495.

Creating the call to the sun

For male or female, solitary practitioner or coven member who shares in a more formal maybe God-focused drawing down the sun rite, creating your own private call to the sun helps you connect more easily with its life-giving radiance when you participate in a more formal shared ritual. A number of witches, men as well as women and not just beginners, have said that they feel far less personally connected with the drawing down the sun/God ceremony. By adding this preliminary private step even in coven work, the sun becomes as real and as loving as the moon.

Wherever you draw down your personal sun, in an Ancient Egyptian temple, your local park, the garden or on the beach in brilliant sunshine or as the sun rises blood red over a snowy landscape, you need a solar chant of power to harmonise your inner self with the solar rhythms.

You might wish to create an all-purpose praise poem in your Book of Shadows to recite when you call the sun on special occasions and perhaps when working in a group to weave into collective calls. For inspiration, there are many sites about the Great Hymn to the Aten on the internet, as well as in almost any general book on Ancient Egypt.

Also draw together lines to say aloud or in your mind on Solstices and Equinoxes as you celebrate in more general rituals the rise and fall of sun power, knowing it will rise again and with the differing radiance intensity, to add to more general celebrations. Most importantly to me, create single or dual lines of empowerment to be spoken anywhere you find yourself at dawn, noon, sunset and midnight (see below for channelling the sun at midnight), when you need inspiration, courage, hope or the reassurance the sun will rise again and tomorrow really is another day.

Or you can speak spontaneously when you are out and about; look up and there is the sun shimmering over office blocks, breaking through the mist or ascending at great speed over a vast plain.

Chants you create may vary according to the solar deity focus you relate most easily to or, if you prefer, in your mind create a golden figure, God or Goddess that you can just call Sun Father or Mother. Some women work better with a Sun God and some men with a Sun Goddess. Incorporate into the chant what you love about the sun, based on your own life experiences and memories of precious sunny days. Weave in sun images, animals, birds that you associate with the sun and herbs and flowers that seem appropriate. I have suggested some on page 213. State also why you need and value the sun in your life and all the positive attributes it has for growth, warmth and fertility.

You can create a collective coven chant, perhaps during a picnic on a lovely sunny day to be used when you don't feel you want to use a more traditional God ceremony. However, you could adapt the Hymn to the Sun you create as part of the more formal Sun God call (generally the Charge of the God, see page 230). The God representative would speak on behalf of the coven, framed against the sun.

Beginning your sun ceremony

Choose the time of day that is best for your ceremony, brilliant high noon for full power, the optimism of the new day dawning or the healing of sunset. Clear conditions are best, though of course you cannot look directly at the sun at any time. In time you may be able to visualise the orb. Although Sunday is the special day of the sun, you can choose any day that feels right.

Decide on the kind of sun energy you want to focus on for this particular ceremony, a loving Sun Mother to bring joy, abundance and a sense of well being, an aesthetic Sun God for spiritual and mental clarity and focused creativity or a warrior to empower you and give you the courage of purpose. Alternatively, use your personal solar deity focus or the sun itself as your icon of light, life and health-bringing powers. Remember to give thanks for life or to send the sun as light beams perhaps through a crystal sphere to those who need it spiritually or actually.

Find your sun place where at particular times of year the sun casts radiating beams or dancing rays. You may have to wait for just the right conditions for your first personal and private sun encounter or make it part of a holiday abroad, using a spectacular Mediterranean or tropical sunrise or West Coast sunset. It may help to hold a clear crystal sphere or rainbow quartz as you speak (any with fractures inside will reflect rainbows).

The sun rite

In fact, you need no materials except for yourself, the sun and some water. But you may prefer to set the outdoor altar or a rock with sun symbols for the ceremony, whether alone or with others. For winter rituals, wrap up warm. Clear winter sunlight bursting through clouds or shimmering on ice has a special radiance.

* If you want to, in the centre of your rock or altar place a brass or gold-coloured dish (use gold foil if necessary) filled with gold jewellery, golden crystals, gold coloured coins, golden flowers and fruit to be empowered by the sun. A group can each contribute items that have significance for them.

* Next to it place a glass bowl of sparkling mineral water. Afterwards the water will be charged with the power of the sun chant and you can use it in baths or to splash on pulse points.

* Place your athame at your feet so the blade faces the sun.

* If alone raise your arms high and wide, palms uppermost, and set your feet quite widely apart, to make a sun pentagram with your body.

* Speak the words of your empowerment aloud unless there are too many people around. Wait until you feel the light beginning to enter you.

* Move your arms so they are extended horizontally either side of your body, with your palms still uppermost to absorb the light. At this point breathe in the golden light through your nose, slowly and gently, exhaling darkness through your mouth. As you continue breathing, visualise the light spreading to every part of your body from your toes right to the tips of your fingers and the crown of your head. Allow the light to extend now beyond your body, forming a shield of golden rays all around you and above you so that you are enclosed in a shimmering sun sphere.

* Gradually move your arms and hands so they cross about waist height and repeat in succession in the rhythm right for you raising, extending and enfolding yourself with light as if you were splashing the light over yourself.

* Cease deliberately breathing in gold when you feel that you are completely filled with the radiance. Stand with your palms still uppermost close together in front of your body with elbows bent.

* Say slowly and with confidence three times:

I am filled with the light of the sun. I am pure light.

* Raise your athame to the sun and allow the energies to flow between your body, the blade and the golden sun sphere both surrounding you and in the sky.

* Kneel or reach down and touch the water with the athame, saying:

Shaft of light, enter the waters of the Earth that life may grow and flow ever from Sun to Earth and Earth to Sky so long as the Sun shines and the Waters of the Earth do flow.

* Set the athame horizontally between you and the bowl. Splash a few drops of the newly made sun water on your hairline, brow, throat and wrist pulse points, saying:

Lord/Lady Sun enter my spirit, enrich my mind, transform my words and warm my heart.
Blessings be.

✳ Listen and you may hear a message from the Sun Mother or Father.

✳ If you face opposition or spite, shake your fingers and see golden sparks emanate from your fingertips like miniature sun rays. Extend your arms in a circle over your head so you create a psychic protective force field of sparks all around you that will gently repel any malice.

✳ Make a sign, perhaps touching the place between and just above your eyes that is regarded as the third psychic eye, the Brow chakra, a spiritual energy point. Or you may prefer to touch your heart or make a circle in the palm of your hand. As you do so, say:

When I touch my brow/heart, I will invoke the power of the Sun within me wherever I may be, no matter how dark the hour of day or night. So mote it be.

✳ Look upwards and picture the Sun Mother or Father or a whirling spinning solar disc and gradually allow the radiance and the God/Goddess to fade, knowing you can recall the sun into your life any time you are in need, just by making your psychic sign.

✳ Spend the rest of the day or at least part of it in the sunshine and the next day do something amazingly brave or dynamic to make the most of your new power.

The coven and the sun

In a coven, you would need the water bowl and the dish of golden objects to be empowered on the central outdoor altar or the ground. The chosen Sun God/Goddess figure would stand in the centre of the circle facing the sun with the bowl and gold dish between him or her and the sun. That person then speaks the words of the solar deity either the Charge of the God (see page 230) or the Hymn to the Sun or a mixture of both, holding the athame towards the sun.

As he or she speaks, the other members in the circle focus their athame blades towards the sun. As the sun deity's words fade, they direct the light caught in the blades directly towards the solar plexus of the sun persona. Then the sun deity persona would wheel round sunwise (clockwise) nine times on the spot, pointing the blade towards the coven members in turn, filling them with the channelled divine light. There would be a chant as the sun figure turns based on the theme of:

Draw down the sun, draw down the power,

chanted by all faster and faster.

The power is released with a final call as everyone's athames are finally raised to the sun for a final time and then directed inwards to the individual's solar plexus, seat of the personal sun. The group and the sun figure do this at the same time.

Afterwards all except the sun figure direct any residual sun power via the athames into the central bowl of fruit/flowers etc that can be shared. The sun figure then touches the surface of the water bowl with the athame and says:

Be blessed by the divine wisdom light and healing of the sun.

Each person can anoint themselves on the Brow chakra, beginning with the deity figure by passing the water bowl round the circle, saying, Blessings be. If you prefer, the sun figure can after anointing themselves anoint everyone else.

Cassandra's Hymn to the Sun

This is my sun chant based on a mixture of my own version of the Hymn to the Egyptian Aten and my own favourite sun deities. You can set yours in any culture or place, describing your personal river Nile and sun deity, keeping the sun on the water theme. If you are an urban witch you can use any inland waterway.

As a Midlands Witch I have a great affection for the restored Gas Street Canal Basin in the centre of Birmingham. Once, when I was really scared about a forthcoming television appearance, I directed my Hymn to the Sun at sunset looking out of a plate glass hotel window on a traffic island from which I could see the canal, calling on my water witch family ancestors.

Once you have created your Sun Hymn or Charge you should learn it by heart. It's best not to read it, but if you prefer you can read it in your chosen sun setting and build up to a climax with the last line. But it doesn't matter at all if you forget lines and improvise others. That is how I improve mine every time I describe it.

Shen that I incorporate in my chant chorus is the Ancient Egyptian hieroglyph for the orbit of the sun round the earth and shows the sun rising over the horizon. It means permanence so long as the sun shines.

Because the Aten Hymn to the Sun was spoken at dawn, I have written the chant from that perspective, although I incorporate noon. In practice, you can use it at dawn, noon or sunset, maybe adding a line or two about the sun setting if it is a sunset call. You could emphasise that the sun never sleeps but shines on the other side of the world and will rise again for us in the morning.

Greetings to you, great sun, as you break the bonds of the night. The birds rise in the light; young animals stir and leap with joy while their mothers turn their faces to the warmth after the chill of the night.

The serpents of my fears, the scorpions of old sorrows and the leonine demons of doubt that trouble the dark hours, flee as your golden shafts of radiance rise as Ra sails his sun boat across the sky.

Saule of the Baltic lands dressed and crowned with gold, walks amongst the ripening fields of corn. Sol of the north chases her brother the moon around the skies and laughingly outpaces him, never looking behind at the encroaching wolf-like darkness. For she loves and lives this day and the next and the next and fears not Ragnarok, the final battle.

I am a daughter of the light, child of Sekhmet, fierce sun lioness of Egypt who protects those she loves. I rise with golden Apollo and hear his song echoed by the daughters of the winds. The sky is radiant, first purple, scarlet, then golden.

Mother, Father Sun, I sing in my heart bathed in light and I consign my fears to bright sunbeams. I am the sun and walk in hope to be reborn each morning in faith like you and to live on not only in my life but in my descendants and my deeds so long as the sun itself endures.

Shen, Shen, Shen, be golden and glorious eternally and make me glorious at this hour.

Repeat the last line over and over faster and faster and louder and end with a final *Be glorious* or substitute the name of your favourite sun deity for Shen.

The four sacred ceremonies of the sun in Ancient Egypt

Because Ancient Egypt was such a sunny land, the four solar times were inbuilt into daily temple ritual. Of course in the modern world we do not have time on a daily basis to celebrate the passage of the sun formally, but occasionally to celebrate the passing of the day ritually does connect you very powerfully with the solar rhythms. You can also visualise the rites as you greet the sun, however briefly, during the day and night during periods when you are busy.

You might like to look back now at the pages on the Ancient Egyptian altar, although you can carry out the ceremonies using a standard Wiccan altar or even an unadorned table (see page 171). You could also adapt the rituals below to give them a purely Wiccan emphasis to celebrate the four change points.

Traditionally, the most important ceremony of the day was at sunrise, then at noon and at sunset. Sunrise was a special healing time and sunset good for empowering charms and protective amulets. Noon brought power, confidence and energy, pure solar lifeforce. The hour before sunset was considered especially good for divination. Midnight was considered by the Ancient Egyptians the time for protective magic and the banishing of sorrow and problems and for encouraging prophetic dreams.

When you have a whole day or two free, carry out all four purification ceremonies, at dawn, noon, dusk and midnight. If you have a sistrum or a bell, you can ring it at the beginning of each ceremony and again to close the ceremony.

The ceremonies are based on the indoor altar but are very beautiful outdoors, since you can focus on the actual sun in the sky or the lightest point on the horizon for the first three and look towards the southern hemisphere for midnight.

Dawn

This ceremony is especially dedicated to Horus, the falcon-headed Sky God or indeed any Sky God.

* Work facing the east or the direction of the actual sunrise as it is only true east on the Spring and Autumn Equinoxes (21 March and 21 September in the northern hemisphere and the other way round in the south). Do this even if you cannot see the sunrise directly.

* Carry out the basic altar purification with water. I have varied it slightly here to take account of working with the actual sun, but use the earlier version if you prefer. Take the bowl of water on the altar and scatter a few drops of water at each of the four corners of the altar, beginning in the south-west corner and proceeding clockwise. At each corner, say:

> *With the waters of the celestial Nile [or your favourite water source],*
> *I purify this altar and this ritual.*

* Facing east again, next hold your dish of water between your hands and raise it over the centre of the altar and say four times, one for each of the main directions:

I purify this water by the sacred lotus, the setting sun, the wise papyrus and dawning of the new day. May only goodness and light enter herein.

* Now walk to the south and sprinkle a drop of water in each of the four cardinal directions on the altar in turn, south, west, north and east, saying:

So does the sun rise each day and life is renewed.

* On a roll of white paper write in black ink the names of any people you know who are ill or animals or places that need healing. You can ask for healing for yourself of worries as well as actual illnesses. Read them aloud one by one and say:

Horus, hawk of dawn, may he/she be healed and restored as the day is renewed.

* Roll and secure the paper with a white ribbon and leave it all day on the altar.

Noon

This is the special time of Ra, the Sun God (or a focal Sun God).

* Purify the altar with water, even if you did so at dawn.
* Fill large glass bowl with water and set it in the centre of the altar so it fills with light. If it is a dull day, supplement with gold candles. Surround the bowl with a circle of white flowers. Use silk or paper if you cannot get real ones.
* Light frankincense, orange or rosemary incense sticks, fragrances of the sun, one at each of the four cardinal directions of the altar. Set them in tall holders (bottles will do).
* Walk to the south and take the southernmost incense stick (use a broad firm based one that can be easily carried) and walking clockwise around the altar nine times (the sacred number three by three), saying:

Lord Ra, blazing fire of the noonday sky, fill me likewise with power and light and bless my altar and my life.

* Walk back to the south and splash the sun filled water on your face and make three declarations of power or confidence concerning your life. These can be for yourself or others. For example:

By the power of the high sun, I will overcome prejudice at work and gain promotion. By the power of the high sun, I will prevent by legal means my local wildlife marsh from being drained for a landfill site. By the power of the high sun, I will stop overloading my body with caffeine.

* Take your wand (Egyptian or Wiccan) in your power hand and as you speak, raise it and bring it in front of you, flicking it from left to right in a slashing movement, Egyptian style, saying after each empowerment:

So I speak and so it shall be done.

* Tip the rest of the sun water in clear glass bottles for use in your bath and to revive plants.

Dusk

This is my favourite ceremony and can be adapted any time after coming home from work, ideally as the rays of sunset filter on to the altar. This is the time of Hathor, Goddess of women and the home (or any Sun Goddess). Face west or the direction of sunset as you work.

* This time, purify the altar just with rose perfume, the scent of Hathor. This is her special time so it is very potent for sunset work. Sprinkle the four directions at the edges of the altar clockwise, with single drops of rose cologne or water in a small bowl. You can add a few drops of rose essential oil to water in a bottle and shake well to make a simple rose essence water.

* Begin anointing the altar from the west, saying:

> With your fragrance, Lady Hathor, I welcome the light of evening and with it let flow away all sorrow and regrets for what was not fulfilled, keeping joy in what was achieved.

* Now set your mirror, the special tool of Hathor, in the centre of the altar. If you cannot see the sunset, light orange and red candles, the colour of Hathor. You may wish to incorporate mirror divination at the end of your dusk ceremony, looking into the mirror with sunset or candles reflected into the glass and ask questions, allowing the answers to flow as images in your mind or the glass.

* But first breathe in the light of sunset or the candle light slowly and gently through your nose and then equally slowly and gently blow the light after each in breath in a gentle invisible ever radiating circle of swirling red, purple, pink and orange light reflected in the mirror, enclosing yourself and protecting your altar and your home and family. Once you get into the rhythm, on the out breath sigh the words:

> Bless and protect all, Lady of the West.

* Use also your gentle breathing to remove pain or sorrow from yourself and others, by continuing the gentle breathing, adding to the out breath:

> Bless, protect and heal.

* Then sit quietly allowing the visualised Hathor sunset to swirl around you, taking away all unresolved conflicts and tensions.

* When it is dark, extinguish any candles, saying:

> Rest within the womb of your mother, weary sun, to be reborn in the morning.
> May I do likewise.

Midnight

You can carry out this ceremony late in the evening if you do not wish to stay awake until midnight. If it is a clear night, draw back the curtains so that you can see the stars. If not, visualise a ceiling covered with stars. This is the time dedicated to Nut, the Sky Goddess whose body was arched over the earth and covered with stars and within whose body the Sun God and his solar boat travelled the night to emerge at dawn. You can obtain many beautiful pictures of her arched over the earth. Alternatively, use a Mother Goddess you love.

* Light your oil lamp or a large white or beeswax candle. Purify the altar with incense. Use jasmine or mimosa, scents of the night or sandalwood, another traditional night fragrance.

* Face north, the direction of midnight and the northern constellations that so fascinated the Ancient Egyptians.

* Light a single incense stick or add incense to a preheated censer and walk round the altar sunwise to the north holding it. Now begin a circuit north to east and back to the north, making a clockwise smoke circle round the outside of the altar, enclosing yourself also saying:

Wise Nut, Mother you absorb all into gentle sleep. Bring sleep to me also and all who also lie awake in pain or in anxiety or have no place to rest their head.

* Gaze into the bubbling oil of your lamp and see pictures.

* If you are working by candlelight, drop coloured essential oils or dark fragrance oils on the surface of a small bowl of water and let images form spontaneously that will answer questions you did not even know you were asking. Even if you do not wish to carry out a divination, minutes spent gazing into the candle or lamplight and inhaling slowly and gently a night fragrance (see page 170) from your incense stick, can mark the easy transition between day and night and the conscious and unconscious world.

* It is a good time for past world visions, perhaps holding a statue or ancient Egyptian symbol. Even those of us who do not have a direct link with the Ancient Egyptian world can in the stillness of the night tune into other lives for illumination on present situations and future possibilities. At this time you may talk to your Witch Guardian or perhaps a wise Egyptian spiritual ancestor who makes him or herself known at the midnight ceremony.

* If you have no time even to purify your special area, spend just a minute or two in your Egyptian sanctuary perhaps when rising or coming home to mark the dawn and dusk solar tides and drawing strength. At such times, anoint yourself with a drop of perfume on your forehead, brow, throat and wrists saying softly for each:

Bring to me and to this sacred place the power of the old land, the fertility of Kemet [the rich dark silt of the Nile], the warmth of the sun and the life of the waters.

PRACTICAL ASSIGNMENT

Your personal sun chant

Create and learn a sun chant using and adapting the suggestions in this module.

Further research

Work with the myths of the Sun Gods and Goddesses in different cultures to discover your personal icons.

Further information

Recommended reading

* Kerenyl, Karl, Stein M (translator) *Goddesses of the Sun and Moon*, Spring Publications, 2003
* McCrickard, Janet, *Eclipse of the Sun: Investigation into Sun and Moon Myths*, Gothic Image Publications, 1990

Websites

* *Tour Egypt*
  Full text of Hymn to Aten
  www.touregyptnet/hymntoaten.htm
* *David Rankine*
  Charge of the God by David Rankine
  http://www.avalonia.co.uk/horned%20god/index.htm

THE dARK SUN

Once you incorporate the sun more fully into witchcraft, you discover that it has subtle mysterious energies, just like the moon. In this module, we will work with the sun at midnight and eclipses, with the Celtic Druid Awen, the inspirational lifeforce of the sun associated with prophecy and all forms of creativity and with the mystical solar doorway of light at ancient sites that leads to other dimensions.

Solar eclipse magick

Once you are comfortable drawing down the visible sun, you can progress to working with the sun at midnight and when there is an eclipse in your region.

Partial eclipses of the sun occur when the sun is partially obscured by the moon's outer shadow and annular eclipses of the sun when the moon is on the far side of its orbit from the earth and its inner shadow is not large enough to cover the sun. In this case, there is a ring of bright sunlight round the moon. In the even rarer total eclipse, only the sun's outer edges are visible. Eclipses are well worth travelling to see for their magickal powers. However, you can also work with webcam images and also pictures on websites such as the NASA site listed at the end of the module. This explains more fully the reasons for different types of solar eclipse and when and where you can see future ones.

When a solar eclipse of any kind occurs, at least twice a year, it is magickally a time of great change. Wherever the eclipse is occurring, you can use the time to bury symbols of the old and plant seeds of the new on top. The energies always bring rapid results and can move stagnant or seemingly insurmountable obstacles to progress. If you do experience an eclipse in your region, empower eclipse water for banishing the old and bringing in the new by leaving water outdoors from before the sun is obscured until just afterwards.

Mythologically, eclipses have been described in China as a dragon eating the sun and arrows were fired against him. In Africa, a snake was blamed for eating the sun. In Tahiti, more benignly the sun and moon were seen as making love and unlike in many lands where it was feared, the eclipse here was a favourable sign. Those who could predict eclipses in earlier times wielded great power because they would promise to restore the sun in return for rich rewards.

Studying eclipse images online or in astronomy books, especially of the total eclipse where there is only a faint ring of light round the dark moon sphere, is a good way of seeing physically what you need to visualise psychically for drawing down the dark sun at midnight. If you do witness a partial or annular eclipse, you might just have time to use it as the focus to draw down the dark sun and as the sun emerges, feel the sun power reawakening in you like a rebirth.

Drawing down the sun at midnight

* Stand or sit in total darkness and picture the sun shining on the other side of the world as if you were seeing it through a sun-shaped hole opening in the blackness.
* As a focus to represent the eclipsed sun, you can use a single white candle indoors in a totally blacked-out room or outdoors on a moonless and starless night away from any streetlights.
* Create yourself a special sun at midnight chant, calling on the dark sun to fill you with inner fire and light and to shine brilliant against the blackness. It is a wonderful symbol for renewed hope and for restored health in times when you may doubt or despair.
* Light the candle and face the darkness beyond the candle, as if you were looking at a dark screen. There are two techniques that are equally effective.

The point of light

* Look into the external darkness and focus on the exact place the sun will occupy and picture there a single dot of light.
* Concentrate on that spot, visualising the blazing ball of fire building up from the spot of light.
* Now transfer your gaze to the candle flame and see that, too, as a blazing sphere of light.
* Return to the visualised sun in the sky and ever more rapidly transfer your gaze between the actual and ever-growing and pulsating perceived light source.
* When you can feel power and light throbbing within you, act as a channel between the candle and sun at midnight.
* Raise your hands high over the flame, then thrust your outstretched fingers towards the perceived sun and you may sense fire shooting from your fingers towards the visualised sun.
* Repeat until you can mentally see that the sun image in the sky flares and momentarily fills the whole sky. If you wish, you can hold your athame in your power hand and a small silver paper knife in the other.
* As the sun fades (for you will only hold it a short while), you may still see the golden glow temporarily in the sky.
* As you practise, you will find that it takes less time to transfer the light source and the sun will remain longer in the midnight sky and gradually make the sky seem light as day as opposed to the glowing sphere set against blackness. But that may take months or even years as it is a real test of psychic control.
* As you become skilled you can make the candlelight source even smaller, until you are working in total darkness. In time, too, you may experience travel to other dimensions.
* If you do this as a coven or group, standing facing the darkness in a horseshoe with a huge white candle in the centre, you may light up the whole sky.
* Keep a chant going to maintain the rhythm and use the intensified speed and intensity to hurl the final light into the sky. You would point towards the

candle with your athame in each person's power hand to absorb the light rather than holding hands above it. You then transmit the light to the visualised sun with all the athames with a prearranged call:

Fire find your source and bring back the sun.

✳ As a group you work with your power hand only.

The dark sphere

Call the sun and picture a dark sphere ahead of you in the sky, just lighter than the dark sky.

✳ Stand with your hands by your side. This time breathe in darkness and imagine pure light leaving your body and strengthening the visualised sun.
✳ As you continue, as with an eclipse, see the solar rays beginning to shoot from behind the dark sphere and gradually spreading to cover the sphere, which becomes lighter and lighter.
✳ Now raise your arms and direct your hands, fingers outstretched and palms down towards the sun disc. Visualise sparks of fire emanating from your fingertips. Chant:

I am pure light, I am radiance. I am the dark sun no more. The sun at midnight is as brilliant as noon. Light surround and enfold me. Darkness is no more.

✳ This is quite tiring and you might only hold the vision for half a minute.
✳ If you wish, light an incense stick in a sun fragrance, such as frankincense or chamomile, and let any pain, sorrow or fear rise to the skies on the smoke.
✳ Occasionally carry out this ceremony just before dawn, so the natural light will follow soon after your vision. This is especially evocative over the sea.
✳ In time, the sun at midnight will transmit messages for you. If you are not too tired, light a candle and drip white wax on the surface of water in a dark glass bowl. Whether or not you formulated a question, the moving wax will tell you the action needed in your life and the cooled wax shape indicate the most likely outcome of action.

Awen, the sound of the sun

I learned the following techniques during my training as a Druidess and increasingly the sister religions Wicca and Druidry are moving closer together. Phillip Carr Gomm, Chief of the Order of Bards, Ovates and Druids, has worked a great deal in this area and I can recommend any of his books. If as witches we can take wisdom from different sources we can make our Craft rich and we can equally enrich the traditions of other forms of nature spirituality as well as everyday life with or magickal knowledge.

If you attend or watch a public Druidic ceremony, you will hear those assembled and maybe be asked to join in calling nine Awens. Rather like the Buddhist mantra AUM, this is the Druidic name for the life and inspirational force of creation behind the universe that is transmitted through the sun's rays. Some Druid/esses identify this as the sound that called forth creation.

The sound is something like AAH-oo-en, or AAH-oo-Wen, as three equally weighted syllables as a monotone. But, in practice, when you have a lot of people calling Awen in the dusk or early dawn light or you are standing within a long barrow or passage grave alone chanting, the sounds merge. Then Awen becomes more like the sound of the sea, of wind rippling through plains of corn or the cries of the birds going home at night, especially if it is called on a rising note.

La Hogue Bie Passage Grave in Jersey and West Kennet Long Barrow in Wiltshire are my favourite solitary spots for calling Awen in an enclosed ancient space and hearing the sound echo right over the walls and roof and bounce back into my Throat chakra. The sound really rolls round the walls.

If you are standing looking over the sea (mid afternoon seems best), you might also witness the sun forming the three rays as pictured below in the Awen symbol. Whenever I call the three or nine Awen looking at the three-pronged symbol made by the sun in the sky, I always see three ravens that land close by. It freaks my son, although I haven't told him about the Morrigu, the three Celtic raven sisters.

Practise calling Awens, three, six or nine in monotones, continuing in sets of three to raise power. Then, using ascending or descending scales, sing your Awens in a cave, a tunnel, in dense woodland, in a valley of rocks or an old quarry. Let the echoes swell your voice in an old burial chamber or as the rays of sun fall upon water. Best of all stand on a cliff overlooking the sea or an open plain near water where Sea/Water, Sky and Earth meet, the three natural realms of the Celts. The sun makes up the fourth element, Fire, and is the generative power.

Awen, the symbol of the sun

Awen is the symbol of the three rays of the sun reaching through the sky to the earth or sea and transmitting the vibrant life force and inspiration.

There are two different explanations for its form. One says that at the time of the midsummer sunrise, the sun casts three spreading rays of light, the Awen, which open the gates of Annwyn, the doorway to the Celtic Otherworld. The other view is that they represent the points at which the sun rises on the Equinoxes and Solstices: that is, due east at the time of the equinoxes, as represented by the central bar of the Awen. At the time of the Summer and Winter Solstices, the sun rises in the east-north-east and the east-south-east respectively. These would form the bars on either side.

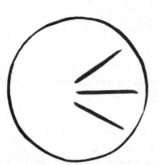

An Awen turned to face the east shows the direction of the winter and summer solstice sunrises

The rays are sometimes positioned within the centre of a triple circle to represent the three Celtic realms of Earth, Sea and Sky (see page 147)

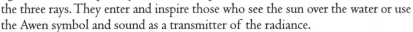

Working with Awen, the inspiration of the Sun

The triple sun rays shed pure liquid gold light. This liquid light is sometimes portrayed as three drops distilled from the three rays. They enter and inspire those who see the sun over the water or use the Awen symbol and sound as a transmitter of the radiance.

In Celtic lore, they were the inspirer of bards and of prophecy and are also associated with the cauldron of rebirth of the Solar Crone Goddess Cerridwen. Like Druids and Druidesses, witches can use the Awen symbol in ritual or meditation to absorb the inspiration and solar lifeforce. In the Celtic world, the focus is on Sun Goddesses, rather than Gods.

* Draw your Awen with or without the three drops in sand, earth or soil or create one out of seeds, small nuts or twigs. Surround the rays with a circle to focus and concentrate the power. Make it large enough to walk and sit inside Alternatively, as I have done at my home, create a permanent one out of small stones or shells in your garden and surround it with an enclosing circle of pure white stones. You can also use white glass nuggets.

* Work in sunlight when you can so the circle is filled with light and the pebbles or nuggets gleam.

* If working outdoors, stand or sit within the Awen so you are facing the sun with your feet or perineum (the Root chakra) directly over the point where the three sunbeams converge.

* In your power hand, hold a sparkling yellow citrine or clear crystal quartz. On the ground between you and the sun, set a bowl half-filled with either sparkling mineral water or water from a bubbling tap.

* At dawn visualise a beautiful Sun or Fire Goddess haloed around the sun as you look towards it. The Triple Goddess Brighid, brilliant and vibrant as fire, in her maiden form was said to hang her gold and scarlet cloak on the sun wheel that radiated golden rays (see page 377).

* At noon, picture a Sun Mother: for example, Grainne who in very ancient Irish legend gave birth to her sun daughter Aine at the Midwinter Solstice in the passage grave at Newgrange, as the Midwinter sunrise illuminated the inner chamber.

* Alternatively, at sunset visualise the Crone Cerridwen in the colours of the descending sun directly ahead of you, stirring a cauldron of pure gold whose essence radiates as a rich rivulet of liquid gold around the Awen circle.

* Feel also the golden soil of the Earth Mothers warming you beneath, heated by the molten volcanic forces, the sun beneath the surface of the world.

* Breathe in the golden light of the sun through your nose, slowly and gently, exhaling darkness until you create a steady continuous rhythm and are no longer aware of your breathing but only the inflow of light from all around you, above and beneath and around into every pore.

* As you continue breathing, visualise the light flowing upwards, from your toes right to the tips of your fingers, downwards through the crown of your head, inwards like a rushing waterfall of light, in which up is down, in is out and you are the cascading light. This is sometimes called making a light body.

* Now begin your call of Awen, at first low and slowly and then higher and with greater intensity, but maintaining a comfortable pitch so you do not tip over psychically, but remain still and golden within the heart of the billowing waterfall of gold light.

* Continue chanting until you can see light radiating from within you and you feel connected with the source of power and inspiration flowing from the sun.

* Hold the moment when you feel totally at one with solar power and then allow the Awens to fade slowly and become slower until they are no more than a whisper. Finally, sit still and silent.

* Dip the index finger of your power hand into the water three times and lick each of the three water drops. For each drop, name a creative gift or project you would like to develop or launch. This symbolises the three drops of pure inspiration that splashed from the Cauldron of Cerridwen on to the fingers of the boy Gwion, foster son of Cerridwen. He licked his fingers to cool the pain of the burning brew. After a shape-shifting cycle to escape Cerridwen's anger for the brew was not for him, he was swallowed in the form of a grain of wheat by Cerridwen (shades of the Persephone/Demeter cycle). Gwion was reborn from her womb as the bard/magician Taliesin nine months later. After nine days in the darkness of the Petre Ifan Cromlech burial chamber in Wales, Celtic Druids and Druidesses were initiated and restored to the light with three drops of liquid from a magickal sun brew.

* Take now your citrine and either draw over it with your index finger of the power hand or paint in gold the Awen symbol to act as a talisman.

* Tip away the rest of the water outside the Awen towards the sun.

* Allow the radiance within you to fade slowly, knowing it is always with you although unseen, for you are now a daughter or son of the light.

* Thank the Sun Goddess and wise Cerridwen who has watched over you while you work and she may reward you with a few words of inspiration or a creative surge that can be manifest in your life.

* If your Awen is only a temporary one, erase it; if permanent, bury a small offering close to the sign, such as a crystal or a few herbs.

* Launch your creative project as soon as possible.

PRACTICAL ASSIGNMENT

Special sun ritual

Each one of my big magick books has a secret I have learned that I would like to share with you. This time it is opening the doorway of light on the Summer Solstice or in brilliant sunlight.

This is a very special sun ritual that is not specifically Wiccan or Druid based, but is totally magickal and life-changing as you look momentarily through a doorway of pure light. Mystics experienced such moments of unity with the cosmos and total bliss after perhaps 30 years of contemplation and Abraham Maslow the American psychologist described them as a peak experience. The poet TS Eliot talked about them as being, *sudden in a shaft of sunlight.* I wonder if he had seen one of these golden doorways.

You may experience this golden doorway just once or many times, and you may see it as I did totally unexpectedly, but in either wood or stone and always in bright sunlight. It generally appears either at a change time in the year, around one of the eight festivals or at one of the three daily solar change points: dawn, noon or sunset.

I once saw the doorway of light on a deserted summer evening in the side of the ruined tower on Glastonbury Tor and again in the magickal Breton Forest at Broceliande near the Tomb of Merlin where it is said Vivien, Lady of the Lake, has imprisoned Merlin in nine magick rings. Another time incongruously was when the sun rise bounced off an urban disused metal gasworks.

In addition, there are places and times you can look for the sun doorway. However, because this is such an unusual and mystical experience it may occur in the most unlikely place and time rather than in the predicted places below at the expected time. Golden doorways have most frequently been reported:

* On the Summer Solstice (around 21 June) most frequently in one of the central stones in a stone circle and even more often the stone aligned to the Summer Solstice sunrise or set. There are many stone circles on moorlands: for example, in Cornwall, Wales, Ireland, Scotland, the Lake District, in Derbyshire and throughout Brittany, with totally free access, usually built where a number of ley lines cross in the middle and a dome of water rises from the earth to meet them. The ancient stone power is charged by the sun and especially the Summer Solstice. Luckily the energy lasts all day so if people are celebrating the Solstice at the circle you can wait until they have gone. Walk round with your hands outstretched, palms uppermost close to but not touching the stones and you will feel the right stone.

* At single standing stones on May Day morning right up until noon, or an hour or so before sunset on May Eve.

* Between two matching oak trees as the sunlight colours the leaves, beautifully and poignantly in the sudden final brilliance just before sunset, on the Spring Equinox around 21 March, on May Day, the Summer Solstice and also, if you get a bright sunny 31 October, Samhain afternoon.

* In the side of a single hawthorn tree on a plain or hilltop around the Spring Equinox, May Eve and Day and the Summer Solstice, especially in the morning; also when blackthorn blossoms in winter.

* In the trunk of a twisted elder tree any time in the month of May.

* In apple trees laden with golden apples (not green or red) any time around the Autumn Equinox (around 21 September).

* The sun will strike the stone or a tree and a golden keyhole shape will appear like a huge golden butterfly. The light will extend over the whole stone momentarily as an archway or spread between the trees like a gate opening and you will suddenly see deep inside the gold. Do not touch the tree or stone but sit or stand close (not in the space between the trees) and don't blink if you can help it because the doorway of pure gold will open only for a few seconds though it seems much longer.

* What will you see? Some people have described the scene as resembling the golden Celtic Otherworld with crystal palaces, golden apple trees, rainbow birds and clear fountains; others like a Garden of Eden. However, the majority of people recall sensations of warmth, light, total peace, reconciliation and healing, like coming home sometimes for the first time or like childhood Christmases and fairytales, all combined. The experience will feel as though it lasted for hours and may reveal glimpses of the past or occasionally future words or star realms. Whatever you see will be better than could be anticipated and is immensely reassuring that there is far more than this life. *The heart of magick* was how a witch friend described her golden doorway, like spiralling gold and diamond lights, flowers of every colour but richer than earthly ones. Others have described angelic beings, fairies, clan animals, unicorns and one Druidess saw the golden phoenix newly risen.

* Then the doorway is gone – and usually you stumble or skin your knuckle on a stone, and the sun goes in, a reminder that real life is here to stay.

* Your golden doorway doesn't make your problems disappear or turn you into Mary Poppins. Indeed, you may realise that you need to change your life because suddenly you are aware of your own potential and having experienced a moment of pure joy do not want to settle for second best in any part of your life. Above all, you saw into the heart of the sun and you didn't burn up. You don't have all the answers on a postcard, but magick makes sense; and you won't ever be so scared of what scares you most again.

Further research

Find out about eclipses and also locate stone circles and standing stones you might visit.

Further information

Recommended reading

* Gurtnman, Ariel, Johnson, Kenneth, *Mythic Astrology, Archetypal Powers in the Horoscope*, Llewellyn, 1995
* Willis, Roy, *The Complete Guide to World Mysticism*, Piatkus, 1999

Websites

* *Williams College Solar Eclipse Expeditions*
  Beautiful eclipse images
  www.williams.edu/astronomey/eclipse/
* *NASA Eclipse*
  Information on eclipses, photographs, dates of future eclipses and where you can see them, a very comprehensive site
  http://sunearth.gsfc.nasa.gov/eclipse/eclipse.html
* *Coven of Dynion Mwyn*
  Very good Druid site
  www.tylwythteg.com/tylwyth.html
* *Alchemy Works*
  Sun and Fire correspondences, a lot of sun herb information
  www.alchemy-works.com/planets_sun.html

COLOURS IN MAGICK

In the module on spellcasting (see page 177) I described the colours of the aura and chakras that form your personal rainbow energy field. That energy field links with the universal rainbow energy field, itself containing the collective auras of people, animals, places, crystals, plants and even what we would regard as inanimate objects, such as houses and artefacts. The aura of houses and objects, especially old ones, is made up of the feelings and experiences of those who have lived in them or used them. Then there are the higher vibrational coloured rays of Angels, the colours, too, of nature, essences, ancestors and Spirit Guides. This is the colour pool from which we draw in magick and our private spiritual work.

Candles are one of the most important ways of animating and releasing colour magickally, but also have their own innate powers beyond that of their colour. When they are lit, candles generate the Fire element and transform the wax of the candle (Earth) into smoke (Air) and melting wax (Water) and so are powerful transmitters of colour energies. Crystals, another dynamic transmitter of colour, also rely very heavily on colour symbolism to define their strengths, though these are enhanced or modified by their composition: for example, agates are stones of balance, jaspers of strength and quartz brings changes. There is more on the use of colour specifically through candles and crystals in week 42, as well as an examination of their other essential properties.

Colour

Each individual witch carries within her the most powerful source of colour generated through her chakras or psychic energy centres and filtered via the aura. During spellcasting she draws colours from the universal energy field that are intensified through the spell process to enhance and strengthen her aura (see page 178).

In magick, colour is a key factor in determining the nature and intensity of the energies that are introduced into a spell though appropriately coloured candles, crystals, herbs, flowers and other artefacts on the altar. The colours are empowered and released by the spell to send, for example, rich green rays to a person we wish to attract or someone unknown who would make us happy. On a personal level, colour is an instant and very accessible way of absorbing energy to enhance or modify the witch's inner rainbow.

Colour is a magickal code and like a computer zip file has many levels of meaning, being associated with specific elemental and astrological as well as natural qualities. For example, red is the elemental colouring of Fire and also the colour of the fierce planet Mars and the astrological sign Aries, as well as related strengths such as courage, assertiveness, passion and action, and the association with lifeblood. The physiological and psychological effects of red to stimulate strong feelings and a desire to act on those feelings are fairly universal and red therefore has similar meanings in many cultures and ages, as does calming cooling blue and green for growth.

How colour magick works

The three primary colours from which all other colours can be mixed, red, blue and yellow, hold the seeds of colour energy, as does pure white, the synthesis of all the rainbow colours. The ancient Egyptians believed that red, yellow and blue corresponded to the body, soul and spirit respectively.

All colours vibrate at different frequencies and affect us physically, as well as psychologically as healing and energising white light, dynamic and warming red, cooling and calming blue, growth-inducing green and soothing pink. Let's use the example of red, the most dynamic colour. Its colour energies can be released in a variety of forms magickally and personally, by burning a red candle, using a red crystal to make colour infused waters (see page 531) or by setting on the altar and empowering red symbols such as a red wax or velvet heart for passion. Natural foci, for example, red flowers or red apples release Prana, Ch'i or the lifeforce in a pure form, which can also be absorbed by breathing in the colour.

In a spell for overcoming seemingly insurmountable obstacles or for strong protection against harm, you could put red candles in all four quadrants of your circle to create a defensive red force field. What is more, the amplified red is absorbed quite spontaneously into your aura during the spell, so that in the days after the spell you radiate the necessary determination to act decisively and attract dynamic opportunities to you. The red of the spell strengthens your own red Root energy drawn via your feet and perineum from the Earth as you dance or stamp your feet during the spell or blow out the red candles.

Colour symbolism

The divergent cultural stream through the ages enhances basic colour meanings as the myths and practices flow into the general magickal tradition. For example, black, though associated with death and endings, carries within it the message of rebirth and renewal, of new growing from the old and creation from destruction. This has partly come from the Ancient Egyptian colour system where black was linked to the rich black silt around the Nile after the flood receded and so a symbol of rebirth and fertility.

However, where elemental associations are concerned and to some extent astrological colours, there can be variations that may be explained by the qualities of the element emphasised by the particular magickal tradition. I see the Air, the element of dawn and spring, as the clear citrine yellow of the messenger God Mercury and the early morning and a number of traditions use this association. However, Vivienne Crowley links Air with blue, perhaps the blue sky and that, of course, is equally valid. The vital thing is to establish in your mind and in your Book of Shadows your own colour correspondences that work for you or your coven and keep to that reference system.

Colour meanings in magick

You can weave magickal spells to activate the strengths inherent in the colours, using the deity names, the ruling planet (see page 213), the Archangel, the crystals and the elements. Some of the associations are linked with days of the week (see below) and if you follow those you can add linked fragrances to your colour meanings. Gradually, magickal associations come together to form an intertwining web of power, so each spell or ritual becomes infused with layer upon layer of symbolic significance.

You can also use coloured candles, crystals, flowers or infused waters for healing. The following are the most popular associations for the colours. White has two entries because you have the dazzling white brilliance of bright sunlight and the softer white glow of moonlight. Each shade has different properties.

White, bright

White is the colour of pure lifeforce, representing great potential and boundless energy and links the earth with the cosmos.

Use bright white in spells for fulfilling potential, for increased energy, optimism and enthusiasm, the free-flowing lifeforce, originality, new beginnings and for innovations of all kinds. It is potent also for bringing or restoring prosperity when fortunes are low, for breaking a run of bad luck, and for all matters concerning fathers; also good health, vitality, spiritual development and contact with one's higher self and Angels, Spirit Guides and divinity; for purity and cleansing rites. White can be used as a substitute for any other colour magickally.

Planetary ruler: ☉ the Sun

Day of the week: Sunday

Deities: Dagaz, the Norse God of the dawn who rode his chariot, drawn by a white steed, Skjin-faxi (shining mane). Brilliant beams of light radiated from its mane in all directions, scattering the night. Also, Sopdet or Sophis, the Ancient Egyptian Star Goddess of Sirius, the brightest star in the sky, whose rising heralded the Nile flood. She was depicted with a star on her head. Also, Grainne, the Celtic Crone Sun Goddess who woke the fertility of the earth every spring after the long winter and in whose honour hilltop fires were lit and processions led at Midsummer and the harvest.

Archangel: Michael, Archangel of the sun

Element: Air

Gems and crystals: Aragonite, diamond, clear fluorite, clear crystal quartz, Herkimer diamond, opal aura, rainbow quartz, white sapphire, white topaz, zircon

Sun sign: ♌ Leo, the Lion (23 July-23 August)

Aura meaning: A clear white aura reveals that the possessor is very healthy, well-balanced and spiritually evolved. This spirituality is part of their everyday philosophy and does not stop them succeeding in whatever they try. They tend to be at the centre of any social gathering.

Chakra: Crown

Healing: Whole body healing, for general health and healing, integration of mind, body and soul; also the brain, neurological disorders and auto immune system problems. White light is a natural pain reliever.

Antidote: Green or brown

White, soft or cloudy

Soft white is the colour of nurturing, of maternal milk and also of the moon, and so moderates the initiating dynamic power of bright white with a gentler pace and a slower unfolding of potential.

Use soft or cloudy white in spells for protection against negativity, for pregnancy, mothers and for babies and small children, for restoring hope, for success in writing and poetry, for gradual new beginnings after loss, for intuitive awareness, for the granting of wishes and fulfilment of dreams, for recovering from illness, depression or exhaustion, for discovering secrets (see also grey) and for calling someone from afar.

Planetary ruler: ☽ The moon

Day of the week: Monday

Deities: The White Goddess of the Celtic people, who inspired writers and poets. Also, Selene, Greek Goddess especially associated with the full moon, sometimes forming a triplicity with Diana and Hecate. She rises from the sea in her chariot drawn by white horses at night. Also, Berkano, the beautiful Silver Birch Tree Goddess whose ancient worship is still recalled in folk custom in lands as far north as Russia at the old Whitsun, when the birch maiden is made from a young birch tree and adorned with flowers.

Archangel: Gabriel, Archangel of the moon

Element: Water

Gems and crystals: Calcite, howlite, milky quartz, milky opal, moonstone, pearl, selenite, snow quartz

Sun sign: ♓ Pisces, the Fish (19 February-20 March)

Aura meaning: A cloudy white aura will tell you that the person is gentle and very nurturing, a natural counsellor and also a dreamer rather than a doer, a listener rather than a speaker.

Chakra: Sacral or Crown

Healing: Hormonal disorders, breast or womb problems, postnatal depression, problems with lactation, all matters concerning pregnancy, childbirth and mothers and babies.

Antidote: Yellow for an infusion of logic

Red

Red is the colour of movement, courage, change and strength, representing action and determination.

Use red in spells for action, courage, assertiveness, power, determination, stamina and strength, sexual passion, potency, sensual pleasures and the consummation of love; for the impetus for positive change and for taking the initiative. It also represents competitiveness, standing out against injustice and protecting the vulnerable and loved ones under threat; for survival and for overcoming seemingly impossible odds.

Planetary ruler: ♂ Mars

Day of the week: Tuesday

Deities: Mars, the Roman War God, who as God of both agriculture and war, represented the ideal Roman as farmer, protector and wise ruler and then as conqueror. Also, Bellona, the Roman Goddess of war, the female counterpart of Mars whose chariot she drove into battle. Also, Sekhmet, the Ancient Egyptian lion-headed Goddess of fire who sent out her obsidian arrows against her enemies but used them protectively to defend the sick and vulnerable.

Archangel: Samael, Archangel of cleansing fire

Element: Fire

Gems and crystals: Blood agate, fire opal, bloodstone/heliotrope, garnet, jasper, red tiger's eye, ruby

Sun sign: ♈ Aries, the Ram (21 March-20 April)

Aura meaning: Not an easy personality to live with, but one to whom life is constantly a challenge, the word no is absent from the vocabulary; at its most noble red indicates a crusader for justice; can indicate great passion.

Chakra: Root

Healing: Stimulates the entire system, building up energy stores, good for raising blood pressure and improving circulation, promoting cellular growth and activity; used in healing blood ailments, especially anaemia; linked to reproduction and fertility, the feet, hands, skeleton, uterus, penis, vagina; helps with impotence. Red should not be used with people with high blood pressure or extreme anxiety states, although it helps lift depression.

Antidote: Blue

Orange

Orange is the colour of confidence, joy, creativity, fertility and abundance, inventiveness and independence.

Use orange in spells for self-esteem and confidence, strengthening identity and establishing personal boundaries between self and others and for independence; for balance and negotiations, for happiness and wellbeing, for the media, for music, physical and mental fertility, for creativity and all creative and artistic ventures, and for abundance of all kinds.

Planetary ruler: ☉ Sun

Day of the week: Sunday

Deities: Apollo, the God of light and most glorious of the gods who inspired musicians and artists. Also, Ana or Danu, ancient Mother Goddess of Ireland and the old Gods. She was the original owner of the cauldron of rebirth called Annwyn that was filled with pearls and guarded by nine maidens. Also, Heket or Heqet, the Ancient Egyptian frog–headed Goddess who assisted in childbirth and breathed life into the clay figures created by her husband Khnum, the Potter God.

Archangel: Metatron, Archangel of light and the heavenly scribe

Element: Fire

Gems and crystals: Amber, aragonite, beryl, calcite, carnelian, calcite, celestine, jasper, mookaite, sunstone

Sun sign: ♐ Sagittarius, the Archer (23 November-21 December)

Aura meaning: A natural negotiator, emotionally secure, without any prejudices or preconceptions about people and invariably self-confident, creative and sunny in temperament, unless personal space is invaded.

Chakra: Solar plexus

Healing: Ovaries, large and small intestines, spleen, gallbladder and bile, circulation, used to increase the pulse rate, stimulates maternal milk, helps dissolve kidney and gall-stones. Orange rays are good for kidney weakness and inflammation, menstrual and muscle cramps and allergies, arthritis and rheumatism, also sinus problems. Orange is also used to strengthen the immune system. An antidepressant, but should not be used for long periods of time or with people with high stress levels; substitute a shade of peach for gentler energies.

Antidote: Indigo

Yellow

Yellow is the colour of a logical mind, of focus, financial acumen, especially in speculation and technological expertise.

Use yellow in spells for logic, focus, improving memory and concentration, for learning, for passing examinations and tests, for mastering new technology, for clear communication; good also for job changes and overcoming money problems; for all- money-making ventures and speculation, for persuasion, adaptability and versatility, for short-distance or short duration breaks, for recovery through conventional methods of healing, especially surgery. It is also potent for repelling envy, malice and spite and to protect against those who would deceive.

Planetary ruler: ☿ Mercury

Day of the week: Wednesday

Deities: Mercury, the Roman winged messenger and healer God (known as Hermes to the Greeks) and was the son of Jupiter. Carrying a healing rod entwined with two serpents that could induce sleep, he travelled between the heavens, Earth and Underworld. Also, Aesculapius, the healer son of Apollo and the mortal Corona, who became a God after Zeus killed him with a thunderbolt for raising the dead. The first shrine dedicated to Aesculapius was built in Athens in the 5th century BC by Sophocles. Also, Iduna, the Viking Goddess of eternal youthfulness, health and long life who possessed a store of golden apples that endowed immortality to all she favoured.

Archangel: Raphael, Archangel of healing and travellers

Element: Air

Gems and crystals: Calcite (yellow and honey) chrysoberyl, lemon chrysoprase, citrine, jasper, rutilated quartz, topaz

Sun sign: ♊ Gemini, the Heavenly Twins (22 May-21 June)

Aura meaning: Yellow indicates a clear thinker, quick to learn, able to concentrate for long periods, very adaptable and a natural communicator of ideas rather than emotions (leave that to green). Yellow people are natural healers, especially through conventional medicine.

Chakra: Solar plexus

Healing: Area around the solar plexus, stomach, and liver; provides energy for the lymphatic system, promoting a healthy metabolism and is used to balance blood sugar, relieve indigestion and liver ailments and constipation. Believed to stimulate the nervous system and improve memory and concentration, yellow relieves nervous exhaustion. Yellow may also be beneficial with the treatment of arthritis and rheumatism, eczema and skin problems.

Antidote: Violet

Green

Green is the colour of the heart, of giving and receiving love on many levels, of beauty and of growth in every aspect of life.

Use green in spells for love, fidelity and commitment, to bring beauty into your life, for the acquisition of beautiful possessions; for harmony, for horticulture and the environment; also for healing people through natural methods such as herbs and crystals and for healing the planet, especially the land and forests. Because of its association with growth, green can be used for the gradual increase of all energies, especially health, wealth and resources, as well as the ultimate bringer of good luck.

Planetary ruler: ♀ Venus

Day of the week: Friday

Deities: Aphrodite, the Cretan and Greek Goddess of love and beauty, born of the foam, associated with the sea, as well as with passionate love. Also, Innana, a Sumerian Goddess, queen of heaven, Goddess of beauty, abundance, fertility and passion, famed for her loveliness and her lapis lazuli necklaces formed from the stars. She was the first Goddess of the morning and evening star, a legacy that has passed via Innana and Astarte to Aphrodite and Venus. Also, Venus, as the Goddess of love, fertility and beauty is the Roman form of Aphrodite. By her liaison with Mercury gives birth to the young God of love, Cupid.

Archangel: Anael, Archangel of love

Element: Earth and Water

Gems and crystals: Amazonite, aventurine, chrysoprase, emerald, fluorite, jade, malachite, moss agate, tourmaline

Sun sign: ♍ Virgo, the Maiden (24 August-22 September)

Aura meaning: Indicates sympathetic connection with other people and with the world, a person who is in harmony with themselves, as well as others; a natural healer with crystals and good at gradually increasing prosperity and opportunity through gentle but persistent effort.

Chakra: Heart

Healing: Heart, lungs, respiratory system, ulcers, infections and viruses, especially influenza, bronchitis, fevers and colds; green, like blue, lowers and stabilises blood pressure and acts as a general boost and calmer for the emotional and physical system; counters panic attacks, addictions and food-related illnesses. It is good for tired nerves and can help with heart conditions. Green is a good healing colour because it stimulates tissue and cell growth and general body regeneration. Emerald green is usually the colour applied in healing.

Antidote: Neutral: generally needs no antidote, though orange can be used

Turquoise

Turquoise, a mixture of green and blue, is the perfect synthesis of emotion and wisdom.

Use turquoise in spells for power, leadership, earthly success, connection with ancient wisdom, for travel, to discover truth and to overcome attempts to hold power over you or intimidate you.

Planetary ruler: Sirius B

Day of the Week: Thursday

Deities: Tiu, the Norse God of the Pole Star called the spirit warrior, God of justice and of altruistic action, because he sacrificed his greatest strength, his sword arm, to save the other deities. Also, Hathor, the Ancient Egyptian Mother Goddess whose magick mirror revealed others as they could become. Also, Sarasvati, Hindu Goddess of medicine, healing and divine knowledge, for her river was said to flow from the heavens to earth. In later Hinduism, she became Goddess of music, poetry, speech and learning and the wife or daughter of Brahma, the Creator God.

Archangel: Metatron, the teacher

Element: Air

Gems and crystals: Chrysocolla, bornite or peacock ore, cobalt and titanium ore, turquoise

Sun sign: ♐ Sagittarius, the Archer (23 November-21 December)

Aura meaning: In whatever situation it occurs, you know the possessor is very wise and can assume a number of responsibilities simultaneously, giving equal weight to all. A leader and in public or personal life inspires and gives great love. They are, however, not personally ambitious or success orientated, but believe in what they do. If you believe in reincarnation, it is said turquoise people are old souls who have lived before.

Chakra: Throat

Healing: The immune system, the throat, upper back, asthma, respiratory problems and swellings of all kinds. It influences the thyroid gland and is used to control inflammation, to calm nerves and to heal skin complaints, such as eczema.

Antidote: None needed

Blue

Blue is the colour of idealism, of acquired or traditional knowledge, of learning from experience whatever the age of the person and of wise leadership qualities.

Use blue for matters of justice, for career and employment, especially promotion, for acquiring traditional knowledge, for leadership opportunities, for authority and power used wisely, for long distance or long term travel and house moves; for marriage and partnerships of all kinds, for expansion of business and financial improvement based on past efforts, for idealism, for drawing down healing powers from higher sources and to heal air pollution and the seas.

Planetary ruler: ♃ Jupiter

Day of the week: Thursday

Deities: Dazhbog, the Sun and Father God who is called Grandfather of Russia. He travels in a chariot across the sky, bringing with the morning light, justice and abundance. The seven planets act as judges for him. Odin, the Norse Father God, known as the All-Father, God of inspiration, wisdom and poetry as well as war. Also, Ma'at, the Ancient Egyptian Goddess of truth against whose feathered headdress the hearts of the deceased were weighed to test their worthiness.

Archangel: Sachiel, Archangel of abundance and the harvest

Element: Air

Gems and crystals: Aqua aura, angelite, blue chalcedony, blue lace agate, blue quartz, celestite/celestine, cobalt aura, kyanite, iolite, lapis lazuli, sapphire, topaz, turquoise

Sun sign: ♎ Libra, the Scales (23 September-23 October)

Aura meaning: This subject has natural authority and a keen sense of justice and will probably be a gifted orator; also as soft celestial blue, the colour surrounding natural healers who channel healing from Angels or Spirit Guides.

Chakra: Throat

Healing: Thyroid gland, throat, the left side of the brain and the nervous system. A natural antiseptic, blue relieves fevers, cures sore throats, inflammation of the skin and mouth, helpful for teething in infants, for childhood rashes, cuts, bruises and burns; effective for all pain relief, blue decreases hormonal activity, lowers blood pressure and pulse rate. All shades of blue, such violet and indigo, relieve migraines and headaches.

Antidote: Red

Purple

Purple is the colour of the spirit, of imagination, dreams, psychic powers and intuitive insights and the seeker after truth.

Use purple for spiritual knowledge and increasing psychic powers, for finding answers through dreams, for any form of teaching or counselling work, for banishing what lies in the past but is still troublesome; for diminishing pain, for contacting friends and family members with whom you have lost touch or who live far away; for spells concerning older people and for protection physically, mentally, emotionally and psychically.

Planetary ruler: ♃ Jupiter

Day of the week: Thursday

Deities: Osiris, Father and Underworld God of the Ancient Egyptians, who promised all, not just pharaohs and nobles, immortality if their hearts were pure. Also, Saga, Norse Goddess of wisdom and prophecy who released the gift of storytelling to the world and encouraged the people to transmit their wisdom in verse. Also, Athena or Athene, Greek Goddess of wisdom, born from the head of her father, the Goddess of wise counsel, both in peace and war, of intelligence, reason, negotiation and all forms of the arts and literature.

Archangel: Raziel, Archangel of mysteries

Element: Air

Gems and crystals: Amethyst, ametrine, charoite, fluorite, lepidolite, sodalite, super seven, sugilite, titanium aura

Sun sign: ♒ Aquarius, the Water Carrier (21 January-18 February)

Aura meaning: A gentle, mysterious soul who is in tune with others and with the world on a deep intangible level and who is a natural clairvoyant and healer, drawing healing powers through prayer and from divinity. Indigo children have been defined as very spiritual children, adult before their time, having trouble accepting the world as it is.

Chakra: Brow or Third Eye

Healing: Headaches and migraines, problems with scalp and hair also helpful for sinusitis and all mucous problems, sciatica rheumatism, arthritis and in easing childbirth, for healing all addictions and neuroses and also problems with nerve endings and connections.

Antidote: Orange

Pink

Pink is the colour of the peacemaker and wise counsellor, the mender of hearts and healer of emotional sorrows.

Use pink for reconciliation and the mending of quarrels or coldness, for happy family relationships, for friendship, gentleness and kindness, for very gentle binding magick; for all matters concerning children and teenagers, for girls entering puberty and women entering the menopause, for young or new love and the growth of love and trust after betrayal or a setback; good also for healing psychological trauma and abuse especially left from childhood and to bring quiet sleep.

Planetary ruler: ♀ Venus

Day of the week: Friday

Deities: Frigg or Frigga, the Norse Mother Goddess and patroness of women, who had the gift of prophecy and knew what even Odin her husband could not see, but would never reveal her secrets. Also, Parvati, the benign and gentle Hindu Mother Goddess, consort of the God Shiva, Madrones, the three Mother Goddesses of the Celts and Romans who protected children and mothers and ensured enough food for the people.

Archangel: Zadkiel (also Archangel of Thursday in his abundance role), Archangel of gentleness and integrity

Element: Earth

Gems and crystals: Coral, kunzite, mangano or pink calcite, morganite, pink chalcedony, rose quartz, tourmaline

Sun sign: ♉ Taurus, the Bull (21 April-21 May)

Aura meaning: Gentle, nurturing, kind, patient and tolerant of others, an aura seen around mothers, especially new ones, no matter how difficult the birth.

Chakra: Heart

Healing: Glands, eyes, head, migraines, ear problems, psychosomatic and stress induced illnesses. All family ills and those connected with babies and children.

Antidote: Dark blue

Brown

Brown is the colour of stability, security, reliability and practicality.

Use brown in spells for all practical matters, security, the gradual accumulation of money, for self-employment and learning new skills, especially in later years; for the home, property, institutions such as banking, for animals and for conservation of old places and traditions. Brown is good also for absorbing pain and panic, for finding what is lost or stolen and for increasing strength after an illness or in later years.

Planetary ruler: ♄ Saturn

Day of the week: Saturday

Deities: Ingwaz, the ancient Norse Fertility God who brought new life to the land each spring and then retreated to allow his efforts to come to fruition. Also, Tellus Mater, the Roman Mother Earth in whose name oaths were sworn. Also, Mata Syra Zjemlja, Mokosh or Matka, the Slavic Earth Mother whose name means Moist Mother Earth. She is the Goddess of fertility, birth and midwives. A Fate Goddess, she spins the web of life and ordains when the individual threads shall be cut.

Archangel: Cassiel, Archangel of compassion and wise silence

Element: Earth

Gems and crystals: Banded agate, brown zircon, desert rose, fossils, fossilised or petrified wood, leopardskin jasper, rutilated quartz, and all the sand-coloured and brown mottled jaspers, smoky quartz, tiger's eye

Sun sign: ♑ Capricorn, the Goat (22 December-20 January)

Aura meaning: Loyal and a realist with an ability to build on the most unpromising beginnings and to persevere through difficulties; good with money but very cautious with purse and with heart; they are patient with animals and older people.

Chakra: Root

Healing: For feet and legs, the bowels, the large intestine, for older people and animals, for healing chronic conditions; for restoring nature and for slowing any growths; good against panic attacks and nightmares or free floating anxiety and also hyperactivity.

Antidote: Green

Grey

Grey is the colour of compromise, adaptability and the ability to merge into the background.

Use grey in spells for casting invisibility around yourself to create a low profile in times of danger or unwelcome confrontation, for neutralising unfriendly energies and feelings, for compromise, for peacemaking, keeping secrets and to repel psychic attack.

Planetary ruler: $\female$ Mercury (sometimes called Hidden Mercury)

Day of the week: Wednesday

Deities: Isis veiled, the hidden mysterious aspect of the Ancient Egyptian Goddess Isis. Also, Tiwaz, the Spirit Warrior of the Norse Gods who symbolised the Pole Star, Persephone or Kore, the Greek Maiden Goddess who was abducted by Hades, God of the Underworld, and became Queen of the Underworld for the winter months, returning to the world as the light-bringer in spring.

Archangel: Sandalaphon in his role of Archangel of carers and what is yet to be revealed

Element: Air

Gems and crystals: Apache tear (obsidian), banded agate, laboradite, lodestone, meteorite, smoky quartz

Sun sign: $\mathbb{I}$ Gemini, the Heavenly Twins (22 May–21 June)

Aura meaning: A keeper of secrets, but also good at making things happening behind the scenes and always willing to find a compromise; occasionally has a double life.

Chakra: Root

Healing: Good for healing any kind of lesion, wound or burn and for reconnecting tissues and nerves; anti panic and will help addictions and obsessions as well as phobias; relieves chronic pain and illnesses especially of muscles.

Antidote: Clear white

Gold

Gold is the colour of perfection, of striving after high achievement, visions and global rather than personal vision.

Use gold in spells for attaining perfection, fulfilling a great dream or ambition, for all sun magick, for an urgent or large infusion of money and resources; for a long and happy life, for a major leap forward, for discovering your unique potential, for recognition and fame, to recover after a huge setback, for contacting Angels and for healing when the prognosis is not good or a patient is not responding to conventional treatment.

Planetary ruler: $\odot$ the sun

Day of the week: Sunday

Deities: Aine, another Celtic Sun Goddess, sister of Grainne, Goddess of the sun and moon, Goddess of cattle and corn and the harvest. Svarozhich, the Slavic Fire God who gave power to the winter sun and lit fires at the harvest to dry the gathered crops before they were ground into grain. Ra or Re, the Ancient Egyptian Sun God who was portrayed as the sun at its full power and depicted by the symbol of the sun and also in his solar boat.

Archangel: Uriel, Archangel of transformation and alchemy

Element: Fire

Gems and crystals: Gold, boji stones, clear quartz crystal, diamond, cuprite (copper nugget), polished iron pyrites, tiger's eye, topaz

Sun sign: ♌ Leo, the Lion (23 July-23 August)

Aura meaning: A sign of the visionary, the perfectionist and noble spirit, one who is destined for great things and for fame and will make a real difference to the world; also marks one who will become wealthy, but will use that wealth for the good of others.

Chakra: Crown

Healing: Nervous system, spine, skin, addictions, obsessions and compulsions. It is the most powerful healing colour of all, associated with long life, minor miracles and long periods of remission.

Antidote: None needed

Silver

Silver is the colour of the moon and the Moon Goddesses, of mysticism, magick and clairvoyance.

Use silver in spells for establishing natural cycles for fertility, for all moon, star and night magick, for increased financial good fortune, for bringing the unexpected into your life, for discovering the truth about a matter, for increased intuition and for women's magick of all kinds.

Planetary ruler: ☽ The moon

Day of the week: Monday

Deities: Arianrhod, Welsh Goddess of the full moon, time and destiny, who turned the Wheel of the Stars. Her mystical fountain of wine, offered eternal health and youth for those who chose to spend their immortality in the afterlife. Also, Britomaris, the Cretan Moon Goddess, who was adopted by the Greek invaders as protectress of all who sailed the seas. She was also a prophetess and is linked with Ariadne, the Fate and Fertility Goddess of the Minoans. Also, Khonsu or Knensu, the Ancient Egyptian Moon God, whose name means to cross, because he crossed the heavens every night in his lunar boat. He is depicted in human form with a crescent moon supporting the full moon disc.

Archangel: Ofaniel, the Archangel who rules the individual days of the moon cycle and their Angels

Element: Water

Gems and crystals: Moonstone, rainbow moonstone, selenite, silver, hematite, rainbow obsidian, pearl, white opal

Sun sign: ♋ Cancer, the Crab (22 June-22 July)

Aura meaning: A person who is very spiritual and fey, who can pass easily between other dimensions, tiny silver flashes or stars are signs of the teacher; also often appears around the time a woman is about to conceive a child; it remains throughout pregnancy and after childbirth; can be a sign of newly awakened sexuality.

Chakra: Sacral

Healing: Silver is a natural cleanser and will draw illness or pain out of the body; for relieving nightmares and insomnia and for easing the passing of a loved one.

Antidote: Needs none

Black

Black is a ceremonial colour and is a strong symbol of transformation and rebirth as well as psychic protection.

Use black in spells for endings, for banishing sorrow, guilt, destructive influences and for acceptance of what cannot be changed, for working within limitations and restrictions, for mourning, for rebirth and for reducing chronic pain; also for blocking a negative or harmful force.

Planetary ruler: ♄ Saturn

Day of the week: Saturday

Deities: Saturn, the Roman form of Cronos, God of time, Jupiter's father who was deposed by his son. Saturn was sent to Italy, where he taught the farmers agriculture and engineering and established a golden age of peace and plenty. Also, Badbh, the Irish Morrigu Crow, Raven or Vulture Goddess who also assumed the form of wolf or a bear. Vulture Goddesses picked clean the bones of the deceased so they might be reborn. Also, Chamunda, the eight-armed Hindu Goddess, who wears a necklace of skulls, but promises to those who can look her in the face, rebirth in a new more perfect form, and to her devotees protection and relief from suffering.

Archangel: Raguel, Archangel of ice and snow, who protects against their ill effects

Element: Water

Gems and crystals: Black opal, black pearl, black coral, tourmaline (schorl) jet, obsidian, onyx, snowflake obsidian, tektite

Sun sign: ♑ Capricorn, the Goat (22 December-20 January)

Aura meaning: This tends to appear in small patches as knots, jagged places or dark spots and indicate stress or blockages However, you may see an overall black aura where depression or trauma have obscured the natural colours.

Chakra: Root

Healing: Only used in healing after invasive treatments, such as x-rays or chemotherapy, or strong medicines, to absorb and so reduce toxicity.

Antidote: Clear white

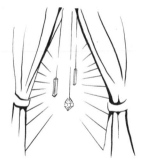

Colours in magick

Think of your spells and rituals as paintings.

* What colour mix do you want and in what proportions? For a spell for justice you need blue, but you may also want to add orange to give you the confidence to argue your cause and red for determination if you are tackling a bully or an organisation with a lot of power and maybe not many scruples.

* Which is the predominant colour you need and what shades? A soft green for encouraging a new love to blossom or a vibrant green to obtain your heart's desire or to bring commitment? What about the symbol? Do you want a silver heart for spiritual love, a red felt passionate heart or a soft pink velvet one to melt the heart of someone who is estranged?

* Do you want to use your usual altar cloth or the one of the season or would it help to have a cloth of the colour of the spell purpose to give the spell a firm foundation, a golden brown for a prosperity spell? Or if you are aiming high or need an urgent fast infusion of money, you could add a gold cloth or at least one with gold stars or suns on it.

* Keep an eye on the off-cuts basket in your local fabrics store so you can make a whole range of coloured cloths or coloured runners to set on the indoor altar.

* Have a range of different coloured purses or drawstring bags in natural fabrics to hold symbols empowered with colour for different purposes, for herbs, for different coloured crystals and for spell bags (see page 413).

* Keep crystals in different shades in all the colours I listed above (see also page 532 on crystal meanings for specific coloured crystal meanings). For example, a vibrant carnelian will launch a creative venture and a soft orange calcite warm frozen, stiff limbs or relieve gall bladder pain.

* Have a selection of candles in different sizes, colours and shades, including the astrological colours listed in the next module so that you can use them to represent people. If you make your own beeswax candles there is a huge range of naturally dyed beeswax sheets on sale online and they are also excellent for making symbols (see page 303).

* Buy coloured, self-hardening clay or make different dough mixes with flour, sunflower oil and water with added natural colourings. Use these to craft talismans and charms and engrave the colour's ruling planetary glyph on it (see page 213).

* Use coloured dried flower petals or herbs instead of salt for the Earth element.

* Empower the elemental Water in the west with a crystal of the colour of the qualities you need. Leave the crystal overnight in the water the night before the spell and take it out just before you carry out the spell.

* Have fresh flowers in the colour or colours whose strengths you are invoking in the spell near the centre of your altar. They will continue to filter the energies into your life in the days after the spell.

* Before beginning a spell for a particular purpose, eat foods or drink juices in the relevant colours to absorb the strengths.

* Alternatively, breathe in visualised coloured light from the flowers or any source of colour in the setting you are casting the spell: for example, a green forest. Very softly inhale each in breath. Pause momentarily and then gently push the out breath through your mouth as a sigh so that the light is spread around the altar and will infuse the symbol and tools. Pause momentarily again and take another slow in breath, establishing a slow regular rhythm until the altar feels infused with the colours.

* Use different colours of fruits, vegetables or unprocessed foods (lightly cooked where necessary) as your focus in personal spells. Once it is empowered you can eat the food after the spell to absorb the charged colour.

* Carry out spells entirely with one colour for candles, crystals, flowers etc. Stage-manage a spell so that the whole scene is bathed, for example, in silver moonlight or you have golden brown earth, blue or grey sky, a green tree and maybe some growing flowers to add the colour mix you need.

PRACTICAL ASSIGNMENT

Working with colour

Begin your own colour section in your Book of Shadows and list natural places that are good sources of colour at different times of the year: for example, when your local bluebell wood is usually in bloom.

Further research

Explore different colour systems not only in Wicca but also other traditions such as the Native North American world where different nations assign different colours to the directions. Try to work out what it was about their life and world that gave rise to the associations.

Further information

Recommended reading

* Buckland, Ray, *Practical Color Magic*, Llewellyn, 1996
* Klotsche, Charles, *Color Medicine: The Secrets of Color/Vibrational Healing*, Light Technology Publications, 1993
* Sun, Howard and Dorothy, *Colour Your Life*, Piatkus, 1999

Websites

* *Real Magick*
  Good healing colour article with links to other useful articles
  http://realmagick.com/articles/79/1979.html

CANDLES, CRYSTALS AND COLOUR

In the previous module I introduced the framework of colour. Here colour is related to its main channels of power, candles and crystals. However, I will also expand the theme of candles and crystals to work with their other properties in magick. There is also more about candles in the module on Fire (see page 349), and crystals have formed a central focus for making amulets and talismans as the single most effective and probably ancient form of charm.

The magick of candles

Burned with empowerments, the candle is transformed into a magickal substance, a vibrant pool of wax that can be crafted into an amulet, charm or talisman when engraved. Fragrances both in scented candles and oils added to the candle in anointing further enhance the magickal properties of the candles (see pages 551–567 for the magickal qualities of different fragrances).

Engraving a candle with astrological glyphs, words, names or symbols of power in one of the magickal alphabets, such as runes, endows the candle with the etched-in power that is then released during burning. Rune symbol candles in red or natural beeswax are among the most potent engraved candles, since rune energies become even more dynamic when burned. Candles are often used in spells to represent people, using their astrological colour. You can also burn a candle to signify the wish or desire, again using the appropriate colour.

There are various ways of creating your candle focus:

❋ Use the colour meaning of the candle: for example, in a love spell you would have one pink and one green candle and move them closer together each day over the three days before the full moon. Light each from the other. Blow the candles out at the end of the spell on the first three nights, sending the love to the lover known or unknown (the person who would make me happy). On the fourth night on the full moon, light the candles on a metal tray so they touch and as they melt the wax mingles (ready for a love talisman to be created).

❋ For banishing you would use a dark and a light candle. In the dark one burn dark wool, naming what you no longer want in your life. Then light the white candle from the dark to symbolise a new beginning and blow out and dispose of the dark candle.

* For marriage or a deep commitment, light one white or unity candle from two separate smaller candles to signify the coming together of the two of you in love. Maybe let the single candles continue burning as well, so you don't lose your separate identities. You could also have candles for any existing children, so they could add the light of their candles to the flame of the unity candle.

* If ending a relationship, light two smaller dark blue candles from a purple or indigo joint one. If you have children together or business interests, you could leave the joint one burning to symbolise co-operation or the family unit that survives. Even in a bitter or unwilling parting, doing this alone two or three times can help you to mark the separation symbolically and so gradually accept the inevitable.

* On a cumulative spell you could use the same colour candle: for example, a series of small white candles for improved health or energy. Light one candle on the first night, make an empowerment and blow the candle out, sending the healing light to wherever needed. On the second night, relight the original candle plus a second white candle from the first and so on for as long as you need, up to nine nights. You would say the empowerment once for every candle alight. On the final night, all nine candles would be left to burn through.

Astrological candle magick

If you know a person's birth date you can light an astrological colour to signify them and if you wish a second colour for the spell wish meaning. It is most effective to do this on the first night of the crescent moon, either alone or, better still, with friends or your coven. Each person present would take their astrological candle colour, anoint it with oil and engrave on it the sun sign glyph (see below). They would then choose a second candle colour, according to their most pressing need for the month ahead.

All present sit in a circle next to their candles and surround the two candles with jewellery, coins, fruits, flowers, any symbol to signify abundance. In the middle of the circle is a huge silver candle embedded in a cauldron or deep pot of sand. The coven maiden or the youngest person present lights this to indicate the beginning of the ceremony and a blessing should be spoken by the oldest person present or the coven wise woman.

Each person draws their sun sign glyph and writes a wish but no name on a strip of the appropriately coloured paper for the wish. When ready, the wish is placed in a pot near the cauldron. All the candles are lit: the astrological candles in turn from the central candle and the individual wish candles from the individual lighted astrological candles at the same time by a prearranged signal. This is a very action-led ritual, but if you wish you can include a collective soft crescent moon chant.

Then in turn each person takes a wish from the central pot, reads it aloud (it will probably not be your own) and singes it in the candle flame, dropping the wish to burn out in a large tray or pot of sand or soil in the centre. (You can drop it in the cauldron to burn, but I have found this can be a bit of a fire hazard.) When this is done, each person recites their wish in their mind nine times and makes a promise about what they will give in return to others (all silently).

Then on a prearranged signal, the candles are blown out except for the central one, which is left burning for the rest of the evening. Generally this is an informal ceremony with an opening and closing blessing, rather than circle casting.

You can of course do this all alone and light candles for people you care for and burn wishes for each of them in your central flame. It really still is very magickal and of course you can make all wishes and promises aloud.

Astrological candle colours

♈ Aries, the Ram (21 March–20 April)
Red
Keyword: Action

♉ **Taurus, the Bull (21 April–21 May)**
Pink
Keyword: Beauty

♊ **Gemini, the Heavenly Twins (22 May–21 June)**
Yellow
Keyword: Communication

♋ **Cancer, the Crab (22 June–22 July)**
Silver
Keyword: Sensitivity

♌ **Leo, the Lion (23 July–23 August)**
Gold
Keyword: Leadership

♍ **Virgo, the Maiden (24 August–22 September)**
Green
Keyword: Perfection.

♎ **Libra, the Scales (23 September–23 October)**
Blue
Keyword: Harmony

♏ **Scorpio, the Scorpion (24 October–22 November)**
Indigo or burgundy
Keyword: Intensity

♐ **Sagittarius, the Archer (23 November—21 December)**
Orange or turquoise
Keyword: Expansiveness

♑ **Capricorn, the Goat (22 December–20 January)**
Brown
Keyword: Wise caution

≈≈ **Aquarius, the Water Carrier (21 January–18 February)**
Purple
Keyword: Idealism

)(**Pisces, the Fish (19 February–20 March)**
Soft white
Keyword: Intuition

Anointing candles

Anointing candles is a good way of infusing a candle with power as you rub the oil into the wax and focus on the purpose and/or the person it represents. Anointed candles are more flammable so anoint them unlit and use a large metal tray underneath them when burning. You can use a fragrance anointing oil or pure virgin olive oil. You can buy anointing oil from candle and New Age stores or add one or two drops of a perfumed essential oil to a quarter of an egg cup of pure olive oil. If engraving a candle, do it before anointing.

Each fragrance has a magickal meaning (see pages 551–567). You can make candle infusion oils in different fragrances and keep them ready for different spells. These are very magickal because the oil is steeped with the fragrance for several days and not just added before the anointing. So too does making your own anointing oil endow it with your personal essence and positive feelings.

* Pour a small quantity of the oil into the eggcup and if not ready made, add the essential oil drop by drop. With any oil gently swirl it nine times clockwise, nine times anticlockwise and nine times clockwise again, picturing light and power pouring into the oil.

* Rub the oil with the index finger of your power hand, anointing down the body of the candle from the top but not around the wick area. As you do so, speak aloud a soft chant that sums up the spell or candle purpose. You need use only a small quantity of oil, as the action is symbolic.

* Stop just below halfway and then rub from the bottom of the candle upwards with the index finger of your receptive hand, again chanting. Work to just above half way, so that the rubbed in oil overlaps in the middle.

* Light the candle.

Crystal magick

With crystal wisdom, trusting your own feelings is the key to rediscovering ancient crystal knowledge that as witches we can access relatively effortlessly from our predecessors. If you are new to crystal work and want to choose a crystal as a spell focus, begin with the known, the colour, until you gain confidence.

Hold it in your cupped hands to activate your sensitive palm chakras and psychic powers. You will feel the inner powers and purpose of an individual crystal. Visually, a vibrant crystal will radiate fast energy, a soft transparent or pastel crystal gentle transformative or soothing energies, and a muted solid crystal will absorb pain or sorrow and provide slow but sure stability.

Next try with your eyes closed holding one after the other, two crystals of similar size and shape and the same colour but a different shade and composition. Work with, for example, a gleaming golden brown Tiger's eye and a muted brown banded agate. Visually, you would know the tiger's eye was more active, but there is a lot more information to be gained from your crystal once you move beyond the physical senses.

You would naturally choose a gleaming golden brown tiger's eye rather than a softer brown banded agate for calling abundance into your life when you urgently need it, because it not only looks but also feels golden and vibrant. You are linking with its aura that is actively and instantly releasing energies to call good things into your life. In contrast, your banded agate feels as well as looks stable, slower but more lasting in its effects and so would stop that instant infusion of abundance from flowing equally fast out of your life.

There are times when the difference isn't so obvious: for example, between a red jasper strengthening and a balancing red agate, unless you are a crystal expert, but you can feel the difference.

Go into a shop that sells a wide range of crystals and hold different ones, at first with your eyes open so the colour and shade will give some guide. Then close your eyes, feeling through your psychometric powers what energies each crystal releases that could be amplified through spellcasting.

When you get home check below and from the internet the magickal and healing meanings of the crystals you touched. You may have seen images in your mind as you held them (clairvoyance), heard words (clairaudience) or felt impressions (clairsentience). Even if you are relatively new to crystal work, you might be surprised how accurate you were.

Using crystals in spellcasting
Start a personal collection of crystals you use for magick and healing work, photograph them for your Book of Shadows and keep notes of how you use them and with what effect. Get to know a few familiar ones really well, rather than buying too many. I have listed some suggestions below. Find out all you can about your chosen crystals, not only from books and also online but working with them and seeing what you find from actually holding them and using them.

Try making different crystal waters by soaking individual crystals in a glass or small still mineral water bottle. Add these waters to baths, drink them and use them as the Water element in different spells: for example, jade water in a love rite. Keep detailed notes of your impressions. You can also use four elemental crystals for an instant altar anywhere or even on your desk at work (see page 135 for a list of elemental crystals). Try aventurine or rose quartz for north and Earth, citrine or amethyst for east and Air, clear quartz crystal or amber for Fire, and any fluorite or aquamarine for west and Water.

Create empowered crystal talismans and charms to carry with you, to keep at home or work, in your car and to add to charm bags (see below). You can also magickally programme a crystal before using it for a healing spell by using its own candle colour and oils/incenses and adding an empowerment.

You can charge stones to be sent to someone who is sick or to be set beneath a pet bed. Keep crystals with photographs of places or people far away who need healing. Similarly, bury a charged crystal in spoiled land, cast into polluted waters, bury on hilltops or hang single crystals in a charm bag from trees to heal the air. If you are at work, you can carry out the crystal spell entirely in your mind. Name and visualise the central symbol or use another crystal related to the need.

Pointed crystals can be used outwards to repel harm or the power directed in all directions to draw back what you need: for example, a new job, a lover or money. Point them inwards to absorb strength, protection or healing. Gentler crystal points, like amethyst, also send healing powers to improve the atmosphere and darker ones like smoke quartz will help to lower your psychological profile and filter negativity. On a desk at work or pointed outwards on window ledges at home, dark crystals will keep you safe from all forms of harm.

A clear quartz point, the good fairy wish crystal, will give a rush of energy that purifies and brings light and can be pointed in the direction of what or who it is you seek to enter your life. Use a smoke quartz point to circle as you talk on the phone to someone potentially confrontational or touch one in your pocket as you wait for a late-night taxi, outwards to repel unwelcome intrusion into your space.

Cleanse crystals you use as talismans or charms with incense or smudge when they have been working hard or monthly, by passing a pendulum over them nine times anticlockwise. Plunge the pendulum into clear water, shake it and then pass it nine times round the crystal to re-empower. You can charge any tired crystal, amulet or talisman by passing a pendulum nine times round it clockwise. You can also keep crystals near a large piece of polished amethyst for 24 hours or bury them in soil and then wash under running water to cleanse and re-empower. Noon sunlight, full moonlight, starlight and ancient stones will also recharge magickal crystals. Dawn to noon on the Solstice morning is best of all.

Crystal meanings

I have listed for each the associated oils, candle colours etc so you can empower the chosen crystal for any particular purpose in a spell and then carry or wear it as a talisman or charm or as part of a charm bag. Use an incense stick in the relevant fragrance to write over it the purpose for which you are empowering the crystal.

The empowerment can be used as part of the original spell or recited nine times while holding the crystal to programme the crystal for its purpose. If not casting a whole spell, you could even use the candle and incense as part of the empowerment.

Every time you hold the crystal in your daily life, recite the empowerment nine times (silently, if necessary) to activate its power or protection.

I have also listed crystal magickal healing powers.

Amazonite
Composition: Feldspar

Colours: Blue green or turquoise, to darker greens with white lines, opaque

Zodiac sign: ♒ Aquarius, the Water Carrier (21 January–18 February)

Element: Earth

Candle colour: Turquoise

Herbs, incenses and oils: Basil, bergamot, fennel, mint, patchouli

Magickal: Protects against others taking advantage of you, whether in the home or at work; attracts customers and new orders to a business. Use amazonite in all money spells, to bring good luck and when gambling or speculating.

Healing: Amazonite is a general health-bringer, but especially helps female breast problems, the throat and the thyroid gland in efficient functioning.

Empowerment/affirmation: I have the right to expect fair treatment and consideration from others.

Amber

Composition: Organic gem made from fossilised resin from coniferous trees that existed about 30 million years ago

Colours: Translucent, yellow or golden orange, sometimes brown, often containing fossilised insects or tiny plants

Zodiac sign: ♌ Leo, the Lion (23 July–23 August)

Planet: Sun

Element: Fire

Candle colour: Gold

Herbs, incenses and oils: Frankincense, bay, marigolds, saffron, St John's Wort

Magickal: Protects against physical harm, mental hostility and psychic attack. Use it in love magick to call a twin soul; also in all goddess rituals. For fertility, wrap a rounded amber and pointed jet crystal in a red cloth bag, tied with three red knots and place beneath the mattress during lovemaking.

Healing: Amber improves short-term memory, soothes sore throats and inner ear balance problems and relieves depression and anxiety.

Empowerment/affirmation: I am filled with the radiance of the sun.

Amethyst

Composition: Quartz with very large crystals

Colours: From pale lilac and lavender to deep purple, translucent, semi-transparent and transparent, also purple and white

Zodiac sign: ♒ Aquarius, the Water Carrier (21 January–18 February)

Planet: Jupiter

Element: Air

Candle colour: Dark blue/purple

Herbs, incenses and oils: Patchouli, lavender, chamomile, rose, sweetgrass

Magickal: Removes negative earth energies that may make a house feel cold or unfriendly; good placed on a computer table to avoid excessive strain on eyes and mind; effective in any healing spell. Place under a pillow to drive away nightmares and psychic attack. Use in spells to reduce the power of addictions of any kind.

Healing: Often called the all-healer because it heals people, animals and plants and even recharges other crystals with its healing powers; especially effective against migraines and headaches, gall bladder and stomach disorders.

Empowerment/affirmation: I am in control of my body and like myself as I am.

Angelite

Composition: Sulphate/anhydrite, opaque and veined with wings, but smooth when polished; celestite that has been compressed for millions of years

Colours: Pale or mid to celestial blue, lilac or violet, also white or grey

Zodiac sign: ≈≈ Aquarius, the Water Carrier (21 January–18 February)

Planet: Uranus

Element: Air

Candle colour: Pale blue

Herbs, oils and incenses: Chamomile, cedarwood, lemon verbena, rosewood and vanilla

Magickal: Protects against angry people at work or home and calms them; also defensive against prejudice or intolerance of your way of life. Use it in all Angel and Archangel spells and for calling absent family members or friends who have lost contact, who are estranged or cold towards you.

Healing: The crystal regulates fluid imbalances and aids a gentle weight loss programme; soothing for sunburn. It works for whole-body healing, especially when combined with sound or sound wave therapies.

Empowerment/Affirmation: I turn anger into love.

Aquamarine

Composition: Beryl

Colours: Clear light blue or blue green, the colour of a calm sea; occasionally a watery green

Zodiac sign: ⊂ Pisces, the Fish (19 February–20 March)

Planet: Neptune

Element: Water

Candle colour: Turquoise

Herbs, oils and incenses: Eucalyptus, kelp (seaweed), myrrh, tea tree, vanilla

Magickal: Ensures safety when you travel, especially overseas or on a boat; for justice spells to resolve legal matters favourably and usually amicably. Use in all sea rituals. Cast a tiny aquamarine enclosed in a shell tied with twine on to the seventh wave for a really important wish or to call a loved one home or into your heart.

Healing: Aquamarine relieves sore throats, tooth and gum problems, fluid retention, bladder and kidney disorders, colds and upper respiratory difficulties. Add an empowered one to a fish tank for healthy marine life.

Empowerment/affirmation: I open my heart with love and forgiveness.

Aventurine

Composition: Oxide, quartz, containing mica that can sometimes give aventurine a metallic, iridescent glint

Colours: Light to darker green, often a soft mid green, opaque; also red, peach and blue

Zodiac sign: ♊ Gemini, the Heavenly Twins (22 May–21 June)

Planet: Mercury

Element: Earth

Candle colour: Mint green or silver

Herbs, oils and incenses: Bay, oakmoss, parsley, patchouli, sagebrush

Magickal: Protects against money losses, accidents and psychic intrusion; known as the gambler's stone, the luckiest of all stones in games of chance and competitions, often placed in charm bags for good fortune and money.

Healing: A crystal for relieving eye problems, panic attacks and irregular heart rhythms; a fertility stone. Also eases genito-urinary problems.

Empowerment/affirmation: I attract good fortune into my life.

Banded agate

Composition: Oxide, cryptocrystalline quartz, chalcedony

Colours: Vast number with curved bands of colour, browns and fawns of all shades are very common; some take their names from the place a particular variety was discovered: for example, banded pink Botswana agate

Zodiac sign: ♎ Libra, the Scales (23 September–23 October)

Planet: Mercury

Element: Air/Earth

Candle colour: Dark yellow or fawn

Herbs, oils and incenses: Anise, ferns, lemongrass, sweetgrass, sagebrush

Magickal: Protects against excesses of any kind; also to prevent you absorbing the sorrows and negativity of others into your energy field. Good for stability to take examinations or tests and interviews without panic; also for steady financial increase or good investments for the future.

Healing: Good especially for skin troubles and stomach upsets, colon, liver, spleen and kidney imbalances. Keep a banded agate near to the site of the problem.

Empowerment/affirmation: I walk through life at my own pace and to my chosen destination.

Blue lace agate

Composition: Agate:

Colours: Usually pale powdery blue, sometimes brighter periwinkle blue with white lace threads through, opaque

Zodiac sign: ♒ Aquarius, the Water Carrier (21 January–18 February)

Planet: Neptune

Element: Water/Air

Candle colour: Pale blue

Herbs, oils and incenses: Fern, star anise, vervain, vetivert, yarrow

Magickal: The stone of the peacemaker; make blue lace agate water for kind words and avoiding confrontations at family gatherings; use also to protect against and calm irritability. Use in spells when you need to communicate something important at home or work; also for sea or air rituals and to cleanse pollution.

Healing: Relieves sore throats and aching or swollen glands in the neck; also eases skin irritations and panic attacks, especially before speaking in public. For throat problems, soak a crystal in water for eight hours and drink or gargle with the water.

Empowerment/affirmation: I speak the truth that is in my heart, but with gentleness.

Blue calcite

Composition: Calcium carbonate, either polished smooth or as water ice

Colours: From pale to mid-blue, sometimes with white veins; semi-transparent to translucent

Zodiac sign: ♋ Cancer, the Crab (22 June–22 July)

Planet: The Moon

Element: Water

Candle colour: Silver

Herbs, oils and incenses: Ambergris (artificial for environmental reasons), jasmine, mimosa, violet, yarrow

Magickal: Deters crime, if placed on inner window ledges and near doors or valuable equipment. Use it in rituals to connect with water spirits and as offerings to water deities; heals quarrels and discourages factions or cliques. Also use to give you creative dreams to provide solutions to dilemmas while you sleep.

Healing: Relieves neuralgia, sore throats, hormonal headaches, the menopause, temperatures, burns and scalds and sunburn. Blue calcite increases the speed of wound healing.

Empowerment/affirmation: I put aside divisions and dissent.

Carnelian/cornelian

Composition: Chalcedony

Colours: Translucent orange to red, also occasionally yellow or brown

Zodiac sign: ♌ Leo, the Lion (23 July–23 August)

Planet: Sun

Candle colour: Orange

Element: Fire

Herbs, incenses and oils: Copal, frankincense, juniper, orange and rue

Magickal: Protective against fire, storm and malevolence of all kinds, also acts as a shield from attempted psychic intrusion into your thoughts; guards against accident especially related to building or DIY and kitchen mishaps. Good for all love and sex rites, especially in rekindling increase passion that has faded in an otherwise loving relationship. Place a carnelian under each corner of the mattress. For spells and in charm bags for courage, self-confidence, creativity and independence. Fire magick is more effective if you circle a red candle with carnelians.

Healing: Increases physical energy. A stone both of fertility and male potency, carnelian can relieve PMS and menopausal symptoms and overcome sexual anxieties that prevent orgasm. Relieves addictions of all kinds, especially problems centring on food that may be linked with low self-esteem.

Empowerment/affirmation: I am as courageous as a lion/lioness.

Chrysoprase

Composition: Chalcedony (quartz) with nickel

Colours: Apple green, opaque, can vary through lighter greens, also lemon

Zodiac sign: ♉ Taurus, the Bull (21 April–21 May)

Planet: Venus

Element: Earth

Candle colour: Mint or apple green

Herbs, oils and incenses: Apple blossom, lemon balm, rose, vervain, vetivert

Magickal: In mediaeval times, chrysoprase was engraved with the image of a bull to give strength and protection to the wearer. Protects against stagnation. Use in rituals to bring fresh energies into your life and home by opening all the windows and doors at home and afterwards place a chrysoprase near the front and back or patio doors. This and other chrysoprase spells will attract abundance, love, health, happiness and enthusiasm. At work, chrysoprase is excellent for beginning a new job, a new venture or project.

Healing: Good for ears, eyes, stomach ulcers, liver problems and skin perforations or infected areas; a powerful detoxifier, especially of pollutants in the atmosphere or caused by necessary but prolonged medication.

Empowerment/affirmation: I open myself to love and to opportunity.

Citrine

Composition: Quartz

Colours: Yellow from pale to golden yellow, honey or dark orange; always sparkling

Zodiac sign: ♊ Gemini, the Heavenly Twins (22 May–21 June)

Planet: Mercury

Element: Air

Candle colour: Lemon yellow

Herbs, oils and incenses: Almond, bergamot, lemon verbena, lily of the valley, papyrus

Magickal: Citrine will drive away fear and danger, and protect against negative people, atmospheres and unfriendly ghosts. It also helps us to feel less alone when we are far from home. Excellent for rituals of prosperity, you can charge a citrine with energies of abundance by burning a yellow candle next to your citrine at dawn. Blow out the candle and send the wish to the lightening sky, then keep the crystal in your purse; also for spells for new beginnings, travel and optimism.

Healing: Aids efficient functioning of pancreas, liver, spleen, gall bladder and digestive system, relieves back pain, skin problems and allergies. Effective also for depressive illnesses or phobias.

Empowerment/affirmation: I attract abundance into my life.

Clear crystal quartz

Composition: Silicon dioxide, crystalline

Colours: Clear, glassy, sparkles in the sun (other quartzes are listed separately)

Zodiac sign: ♌ Leo, the Lion (23 July–23 August)

Planet: Sun

Element: Air/Fire

Candle colour: Gold

Herbs, oils and incenses: Bay, frankincense, orange, rosemary, St John's Wort

Magickal: Clear crystal quartz will absorb any negativity and transform it into rays of healing and positive feelings. It will also act as a channel for angelic powers and spirit guides. Use for any empowering or energising purpose.

Healing: If you only had one crystal for healing it would have to be clear quartz. Quartz crystals will absorb energy from sunlight, the life force in flowers, trees and all plants and will draw down light from angels, from the God or Goddess and from the cosmos. They will store this energy that becomes concentrated, to be released in healing. Crystal quartz brings pure vitality when tiny quartz crystals are added to bath water or clear crystal quartz left in water from first light to midday is drunk or splashed on pulse points.

Empowerment/affirmation: Each day is a new beginning.

Hematite

Composition: Iron oxide, a very heavy stone

Colours: brilliant silvery black, steel grey metallic, also dark red or reddish brown, with a red streak

Zodiac sign: ♈ Aries, the Ram (21 March–20 April)

Planet: Mars

Element: Fire

Herbs, incenses and oils: Dragon's blood, ginger, juniper, parsley, saffron

Magickal: Known sometimes as the lawyer's stone, hematite will help with all legal wrangles or matters of injustice and is especially good for neighbourhood or boundary disputes. Bury hematite at the corners of your land or in pots at the four corners of your house to keep out all forms of malice, to guard against fire and reflect negativity back to the sender. Hematite is good to counter fears of flying and to prevent jetlag.

Healing: Hematite will draw out pain, illness and improve muscle weakness; good for all blood disorders, in the formation of healthy red blood cells and to stop excessive bleeding, whether from a wound or during menstruation or childbirth.

Empowerment/affirmation: I draw my own boundaries.

Jade

Composition: Jadeite and nephrite/silicates

Colours: Transparent to opaque, from a pale through to dark green

Zodiac sign: ♓ Pisces, the Fish (19 February–20 March)

Planet: Venus/Neptune

Element: Water

Candle colour: All shades of green

Herbs, incenses and oils: Chamomile, lavender, mugwort, rose, patchouli

Magickal: Jade is especially protective for babies, children and women, especially when pregnant or as new mothers and young lovers; good for gentle love and fidelity spells; for health and healing and for animal welfare.

Healing: Jade is used in modern times, as formerly, for kidney and bladder problems and for hip and arm socket disorders; effective against fluid retention, blood sugar imbalances, and lung and eye problems and preserves youthfulness of body and mind; especially good for healing pregnant women, mothers and babies, children and small animals.

Empowerment/affirmation: Life and health flow within me.

Jet

Composition: Organic; fossilised wood that has been turned into a dense form of coal and, like amber, of great antiquity

Colours: Black or occasionally very dark brown, opaque but glassy

Zodiac sign: ♑ Capricorn, the Goat (22 December–20 January)

Planet: Saturn

Element: Earth

Candle colour: Very dark purple or black

Herbs, incenses and oils: cedar, cypress, ivy, hyssop, myrrh

Magickal: In home and business, jet will help to stabilise finances and to take practical steps to overcome debt problems; eases grief of all kinds; good for property matters. Place one at home or work facing the outer door to keep negative people and vibes at bay. Though a Mother Goddess stone, jet often represents the God energies in witchcraft. Use it in spells for the safe return of loved ones and for leaving the past behind; also for psychic invisibility.

Healing: Jet eases toothache, neuralgia, migraines, stomach pains caused by irritations of the colon or bowel and colds. Traditionally used to relieve labour pains and prevent nightmares. Use a piece to allow a very sick or old animal to let go of life gently.

Empowerment/affirmation: My ancestors live within me and fill me with their wisdom.

Lapis lazuli

Composition: Silicate of sodium calcium and aluminium, with some sulphur

Colours: Opaque, rich medium to royal blue, violet blue and azure, even greenish blue, sometimes mixed blues, with flecks of iron pyrites (fool's gold); the gold looks like stars

Zodiac sign: ♎ Libra, the Scales (23 September–23 October)

Planet: Jupiter

Element: Air

Candle colour: Royal blue

Herbs, oils and incenses: Black cohosh, lemon, sandalwood, sweetgrass, thyme

Magickal: Protects against the fears and dangers of the night; against betrayal and psychic and emotional vampires. Use for star and night magick, for promotion, house moves, for leadership opportunities, for female power rituals (it is the stone of the Egyptian Sky Mother Nut) and to unite the family.

Healing: Lapis lazuli eases headaches, migraines, eye strain, problems with the lymph glands and the ears and nasal passages and reduces pain and inflammation; good for children with any form of autism or Asperger's Syndrome.

Empowerment/affirmation: I speak the truth without hesitation and without fear or to seek favour.

Malachite

Composition: Copper carbonate

Colours: Emerald to grass green with black or occasionally pale green stripes, bands, swirls or marbling, opaque

Zodiac sign: ♒ Aquarius, the Water Carrier (21 January–18 February)

Planet: Uranus

Element: Earth

Candle colour: Emerald green

Herbs, oils and incenses: Cedar, fennel, parsley, pine, sage

Magickal: The best crystal for cleansing and protecting workspaces against all the pollution and toxicity of noise, from over bright fluorescent lighting and harmful rays emitted by electrical equipment. Place near a computer or phone to filter out negative communication and potentially harmful energies. Keep near white goods at home in the kitchen and by televisions and home PCs; also for protection if travelling by air or on congested motorways; and for increased business success.

Healing: Malachite is one of the best antidotes for the adverse effects of the modern technological modern world; specifically it eases toothache, gum infections, sinus blockages and headaches and aids heart, stomach, liver and lungs to function more effectively.

Empowerment/affirmation: I will not absorb the negativity of others or my own self-doubt.

Moonstone

Composition: Feldspar

Colours: Translucent white, cream, peach, pink, grey and less commonly blue, all with an iridescent shimmer

Zodiac sign: ♋ Cancer, the Crab (22 June–22 July)

Planet: Moon

Element: Water

Candle Colour: Silver

Herbs, incenses and oils: Jasmine, lemon, mimosa, myrrh, poppy

Magickal: Moonstones protect travellers, especially those who travel at night and on or over the sea. Frequent travellers should keep one in the glove box of a car for safe night driving and as protection against road rage; also potent against psychic attack and all supernatural malevolence. Use in moon magick and for wish magick and fertility spells. Leave on the bedroom window ledge from the crescent to full moon in an egg shell; prick it with a silver pin on the night of the full moon to signify conception and cover the eggshell and crystal until the next crescent moon. Repeat if necessary.

Healing: Moonstone is especially healing for all illnesses in women, though it helps with hormonal and thyroid problems with both sexes. For women it eases troubles with fluid retention, PMT, menstruation, pregnancy, childbirth, the menopause and fertility problems. Emotionally, a moonstone helps to lessen mood swings, insomnia, nightmares, and hormonal and stress-related headaches.

Empowerment/affirmation: Wishes can come true if I believe they will.

Moss agate

Composition: Oxide, chalcedony (quartz), smoother and more translucent than tree agate

Colours: Colourless with profusion of deep green tendrils inside of hornblende that may make it appear green, also pale blue or a deeper green with pale blue or white inclusions, translucent to opaque

Zodiac sign: ♍ Virgo, the Maiden (24 August–22 September)

Planet: Earth

Element: Earth

Candle colour: Moss or olive green

Magickal: Called the gardener's crystal, moss agate soothes panics and fears of the unknown; it brings gradual increase in any attracting spells; whether for money, love, health, promotion or happiness; a good offering for nature spirits and essences especially earth based ones; also for animal and plant spells.

Healing: Empowered and worn next to the skin or added to a bath, moss agate stimulates healthy cell and tissue growth; carry if you have a cold.

Empowerment/affirmation: I draw strength and harmony from the natural world.

Obsidian

Composition: Volcanic glass/magma, formed when lava hardens so fast no crystalline structures are created; the kind that is called Apache tear is sufficiently transparent you can see light through; most obsidian is opaque though shining in the polished form we usually buy it: the more opaque obsidian is, the more concentrated its powers

Colours: Black, dark smoky grey as Apache tears, mahogany brown (see also snowflake obsidian)

Zodiac sign: ♏ Scorpio, the Scorpion (24 October–22 November)

Planet: Pluto/Saturn

Element: Fire/Earth

Candle colour: Burgundy

Herbs, oils and incenses: Basil, mint, parsley, pine, sandalwood

Magickal: Very protective both from negative people and from psychic or psychological attack; a traveller's stone, especially by night. Use seven opaque obsidian arrows pointed outwards and recite what you need to return or come into your life; good for employment spells and also to drive away those who would wish you harm. Use Apache tears in smudging rituals and to carry with you on spiritual journeys to ancient sites etc; Apache tear is an amulet against sorrow, especially if you have experienced a lot.

Healing: Obsidian is an effective pain reliever that improves circulation and artery health, also bowel problems; use to recover from shock whether after an accident, an operation or physical or mental trauma or domestic violence. Apache tear eases depression; also relieves pain and blockage in the lower parts of the body, especially the lower spine and feet.

Empowerment/affirmation: I will not squander energy on useless regrets but focus on what can be achieved (black obsidian); tomorrow really is another day (apache tear).

Purple Fluorite

Composition: Halide/fluorspar

Colours: Purple, lavender, blue (as Blue John from Derbyshire, UK); fluorite is found in green, colourless, its purest form red and orange, transparent or semi-transparent and usually very gentle in its shades

Zodiac sign: ♓ Pisces, the Fish (19 February–20 March)

Planet: Neptune

Element: Water

Candle colour: Lilac

Herbs, oils and incenses: Apple blossom, chamomile, clary sage, rosewood, sweet pea

Magickal: Reduces hyperactivity and over concern with work; will bring peace into the home and workplace and calm pets; use in study spells and whenever you will be questioned whether legally or in a job interview or presentation to stay calm and focused; good for Angel, Spirit Guide and Archangel Work and any water-inspired rituals.

Healing: Relieves stress headaches, earache, throat and tonsil infections; builds up resistance, especially against colds, flu and childhood illnesses that can make adults ill if caught in later years.

Empowerment/affirmation: I need not fear; my Guides and Angels watch over me.

Red jasper

Composition: Chalcedony quartz

Colours: From a brick red through orange to a brownish red hue, red includes poppy jasper and brecciated or mottled jasper; some poppy jaspers have a bull's eye pattern in grey, brown or yellow (other jaspers are listed separately)

Zodiac sign: ♈ Aries, the Ram (21 March–20 April)

Planet: Mars

Element: Fire

Candle colour: Red and burgundy

Herbs, incenses and oils: Cedar wood, dragon's blood, fennel, ginger and mint

Magickal: The stone of the warrior, red jasper offers defence against physical threats and from psychic attack; protects against accidents and bad luck and will return any negative energies to the sender. Use in spells to increase passion; for success, overcoming obstacles, for courage and confidence; also for any Fire rituals.

Healing: Red and orange jaspers help with menstrual and menopausal difficulties, aid circulation and relieve anaemia or toxicity in the blood. Useful as a fertility crystal, after a prolonged period of artificial contraception or if you are undergoing treatment for conception.

Empowerment/affirmation: I reach out to and welcome life's experiences with courage.

Rose quartz

Composition: Quartz

Colours: Transparent or sometimes translucent pink, from pale to bright; the paler shades are transparent

Zodiac sign: ♉ Taurus, the Bull (21 April–21 May)

Planet: Venus

Element: Earth

Candle colour: Pink

Herbs, incenses and oils: Apple blossom, feverfew, geranium, lilac, mugwort, strawberry, vervain, ylang-ylang

Magickal: Drives away nightmares and deters bullying, helps to heal and prevent abuse of any kind. Use in rituals to attract gentle love and romance or to call a lover when the crystal is empowered by the crescent moon, for family harmony, for reconciliation and to reduce addictive behaviour, especially food disorders associated with a poor self-image; also for fertility magick.

Healing: One of the best healing crystals; rose quartz will ease pain or tension and heal cuts, bruises, and emotional wounds, such as grief, stress, fear, or anger and past abuse that overshadows the present. Rose quartz can ease a young girl through problems with menstruation.

Empowerment/affirmation: I will be as kind to myself as I am to others.

Rutilated quartz

Composition: Quartz with golden rutiles inside that are sometimes called the hair of Venus

Colours: Clear to occasionally smoky quartz with golden yellow to brownish red needles inside that can form patterns and stars within the crystal

Zodiac sign: ♌ Leo, the Lion (23 July–23 August)

Planet: The sun

Element: Earth/Fire

Candle colour: Gold

Herbs, incenses and oils: Basil, frankincense, garlic, neroli, nutmeg, orange

Magickal: Protects all who live or work in or near town centres; counters prejudice in the workplace. Use for spells of prosperity and developing latent creativity and hidden talents; also to bring out new talents later in life and for any spells concerning people from their fifties upwards to find fulfilment and new opportunities.

Healing: Rutilated quartz relieves bronchitis and asthma and will slow conditions made worse by time or ageing, for regenerating brain cells and for improving the condition of blood vessels and veins; said to bring healthy and shining hair if the head is brushed with rutilated quartz regularly.

Empowerment/affirmation: I can see beyond the superficial to the deeper meaning.

Smoky quartz

Composition: Quartz (also called cairngorm)

Colours: translucent, tinted smoky brown or dark grey by natural radiation

Zodiac sign: ♑ Capricorn, the Goat (22 December–20 January)

Planet: Saturn

Element: Earth

Candle colour: Indigo

Herbs incense and oils: Carnation, mimosa, ivy, mullein, patchouli

Magickal: Protects the home and work premises. It guards vehicles from theft, mechanical breakdown and the driver against road rage. Use it for channelling the wisdom of earth spirits at old sites; also in spells when things seem bad to find the way forward; hold it up to sunlight or candlelight and call better times.

Healing: Smoky quartz melts knots, pain and tension in limbs and muscles, cleanses the adrenal glands, kidneys (good for dissolving kidney stones) and the pancreas; also relieves anxiety, psychological sexual dysfunction and insomnia.

Empowerment/affirmation: There is always light beyond the darkness.

Snowflake obsidian

Composition: Volcanic glass/magma in which a few grey feldspar inclusions appear as the obsidian begins to crystallise

Colours: Black with white spots or small white flower shapes, opaque

Zodiac sign: ♑ Capricorn, the Goat (22 December–20 January)

Planet: Saturn

Element: Earth

Candle colour: White

Herbs, oils and incenses: Hyacinths, lemongrass, lemon verbena, sweet tobacco and yarrow

Magickal: Protects against guilt at having personal negative emotions and allows you to express these creatively and instigate positive change; good in animal healing spells especially for horses. Add to a charm bag to mix protection with luck bringing; helps you to discover the truth about a person or situation; also for closing doors on the past.

Healing: Snowflake obsidian improves circulation and the efficient processing of fat within the body, lowering cholesterol and encouraging cells and skin to grow healthily; removes pain and replaces it with warming energy.

Empowerment/affirmation: I walk towards my future with confidence.

Sodalite

Composition: Lattice silicate

Colours: Deep blue with white flecks of calcite that can sometimes be quite large; the whiter the stone, the more active its properties; occasionally indigo

Zodiac sign: ♋ Cancer, the Crab (22 June–22 July)

Planet: Moon

Element: Air

Candle colour: Indigo

Herbs, incenses and oils: Hyssop, lavender, mugwort, rosewood and violet

Magickal: Overcomes fears of flying and protects all travellers; good for justice spells or house moves that involve relocation, or after a loss; also for any matters and rituals concerning older women/wise women. Amethyst has similar properties for older women's magick.

Healing: Soothes, calms physical or emotional overheating and so is good for menopausal hot flushes and menopausal symptoms generally; calms a racing pulse, heart or blood pressure in both sexes and in people of any age. Sodalite also balances blood sugar levels and relieves inflammation, pain from burns, and problems with ears, throat, sinuses, mouth and thyroid, pituitary and lymph glands or mouth.

Empowerment/affirmation: The best years are yet to come and I welcome their wisdom.

Tiger's eye

Composition: Oxide, quartz, brown and gold striped; chatoyant, reflecting light in a wavy band so the crystal gleams translucently

Colours: Honey or golden brown bands

Zodiac sign: ♌ Leo, the Lion (23 July–23 August)

Planet: The sun

Element: Earth/Fire

Candle colour: Gold

Herbs, oils and incenses: Bay, blessed thistle, Neroli, spearmint, sunflower

Magickal: Traditionally protective against the evil eye or in the modern world against verbal or psychic attack or emotional blackmail by someone in a position of power; a stone of courage, it attracts prosperity in spells or charm bags and encourages a positive response to and by officialdom. Keep a tiger's eye in a money pot to which you add a coin every day. Keep the pot in a warm place to bring a steady inflow of resources into your life.

Healing: A stabilising stone that slows an overloaded or stressed mind and body and offers strength to an exhausted system; reduces cravings for the wrong kind of food and food binges, cigarettes or alcohol; eases stomach and gall bladder problems, ulcers, sprains and strains and bruises.

Empowerment/affirmation: My efforts will bring results if I persist.

Tree agate

Composition: Oxide, quartz, coarse and knobbly, even when polished

Colours: White with green, tree-like inclusions or veins (see also moss agate which is very similar in mineralogical terms but looks and feels different), opaque

Zodiac sign: ♊ Gemini, the Heavenly Twins (22 May–21 June)

Planet: Mercury/Earth

Element: Earth/Air

Candle colour: White

Herbs, oils and incenses: Apple, cedar, cherry blossom, peach, pine

Magickal: Protective for air and car travel and for preserving family links; use in spells for increasing influence through networking and the gradual expansion of business; for all family spells and for tree magick of all kinds

Healing: Tree agate relieves small bone, vein and capillary problems and calms people who worry about their health.

Empowerment/affirmation: I make connection with others who share my path.

Turquoise

Composition: Phosphate of aluminium with copper and traces of iron

Colours: Opaque, light blue/blue-green

Zodiac sign: ♐ Sagittarius, the Archer (23 November–21 December)

Element: Air/Fire

Candle colour: Bright blue

Herbs, incenses and oils: Carnation, honeysuckle, lemon, lemongrass, mistletoe, sandalwood

Magickal: Protects animals and birds from being stolen or straying; stops horses and people from stumbling; keep travellers safe; guards against financial, professional or personal misfortune and malpractice by others; use for all spells for power, leadership, earthly success, connection with ancient wisdom, for travel, to discover truth and to overcome any organisation or individual who holds power over you and is seeking to silence or intimidate you.

Healing: Turquoise relieves migraines, sore throats, rheumatism, arthritis and bone disorders as well as inner ear, eye problems, lung and chest infections, asthma and other allergies. It also eases cramps and stomach acidity and gives the body resistance to fight viruses and infections.

Empowerment/affirmation: I do not fear power in myself or others.

Yellow jasper

Composition: Chalcedony quartz

Colours: Single coloured yellow, often mustard or burnished colour through to sandy beige, brown, also mottled; opaque

Zodiac sign: ♑ Capricorn, the Goat (22 December–20 January):

Planet: Saturn

Element: Earth

Candle colour: Sandy yellow

Herbs, oils and incenses: Chamomile, fennel, hops, melissa (lemon balm), patchouli

Magickal: Protects against spiteful neighbours and work colleagues. Place near your workspace to stop others gossiping in your absence; good for all earth magick and as an offering to earth spirits and guardians; use also in spells for any home or property matters, to learn or improve practical skills and to rebuild after a setback.

Healing: Relieves problems and pain from the digestive system, especially liver, gall bladder, gall stones and large intestine; also nausea, fat intolerance and chronic indigestion.

Empowerment/affirmation: I absorb the power of the earth and so am safe and cherished.

Birth crystals

Empower your own birth crystal on your birthday and at significant periods during your life. The more you wear and carry it the more powerful it will become and you can leave it in the centre of your altar while casting any personal spell to absorb the energies.

There are a number of different stones given in different traditions to correspond with the zodiac signs. The discrepancies come because over thousands of years and in different cultures the month stones as they were then called varied both according to those most available in different parts of the world and because of spiritual and religious associations. Zodiac birthstones as such were not introduced until the early 18th century. The list I give combines several of the traditions where there is agreement, as well as more modern associations made by jewellers' associations.

Because you may not wish to mark your precious zodiac crystal you can empower it by drawing over it your zodiacal glyph nine times in incense smoke.

♈ **Aries, the Ram** (21 March–20 April): Clear crystal quartz, diamond

♉ **Taurus, the Bull** (21 April–21 May): Rose quartz, emerald

♊ **Gemini, the Heavenly Twins** (22 May–21 June): Citrine, white sapphire

♋ **Cancer, the Crab** (22 June–22 July): Moonstone, pearl

♌ **Leo, the Lion** (23 July–23 August): Carnelian, golden topaz

♍ **Virgo, the Maiden** (24 August–22 September): Jade, blue sapphire

♎ **Libra, the Scales** (23 September–23 October): Lapis lazuli, opal

♏ **Scorpio, the Scorpion** (24 October–22 November): Obsidian, black pearl

♐ **Sagittarius, the Archer** (23 November–21 December): Turquoise, blue zircon

♑ **Capricorn, the Goat** (22 December–20 January): Garnet, ruby

♒ **Aquarius, the Water Carrier** (21 January–18 February): Amethyst, clear spinel

♓ **Pisces, the Fish** (19 February–20 March): Heliotrope, golden beryl

PRACTICAL ASSIGNMENT

Empowering crystals

Plan your own crescent moon or indeed full moon candle magick wish ceremony. By the light of the candles, empower your birth crystal and one to represent the purpose of the ceremony.

Further research

Visit or plan to visit a mineralogy store or the geological section of a museum to find out more about how crystals look when embedded in rocks and about their history and traditions.

Explore also the world of fossils, which are a good way of accessing past lives or connecting with other dimensions.

Further information

Recommended reading

* Bruce, Marie, *Candleburning Rituals*, Foulsham, 2001
* Bourgault, Luc, *The American Indian Secrets of Crystal Healing*, Foulsham/Quantum, 1977
* Cunningham, Scott, *Encyclopaedia of Crystal, Gem and Metal Magic*, Llewellyn, St Paul, Minnesota, 1991
* Eason, Cassandra, *Candle Power*, Blandford/Octopus/Sterling, 1998
* Eason, Cassandra, *Fragrance Magick*, Quantum/Foulsham, 2002
* Eason, Cassandra, *The Illustrated Directory of Healing Crystals*, Collins and Brown, 2004
* Larkin, Chris, *The Book of Candlemaking: Creating Scent, Beauty and Light*, Sterling, 1998

Websites

* *Lucky Mojo*
  Though about Hoodoo traditions, there is a lot of high-quality general information about candle magick
  www.luckymojo.com/candlemagic.html
* *Candles*
  Extensive site on candle-making
  www.joellessacredgrove.com/candles.html
* *Crystals*
  Extensive site on crystal healing and uses
  www.astrologyzine.com/crystal-3.shtml
* *Different aspects of crystal lore.*
  www.crystallinks.com/crystals.html

Herb and Fragrance
Magick

It would be hard to imagine magick without fragrances, flowers, herbs and evocative incenses. In The Power of the Air (see page 328), I wrote about using incense in silent ritual. Here I will further explore making and empowering your own incenses if you wish or combining ready-made incenses or incense sticks to release the appropriate magickal energies to fine-tune your spell or ritual. I have also written about creating herbal and floral spell bags for power, protection and healing and how to use magickal herbal infusions.

Because this is a course in witchcraft, I do not propose to offer you specific incense recipes, but rather to provide the necessary information so that you can create your own mixes, based on your magickal needs. For experienced witches, there is the chance to develop an extensive resource of recipes by combining planetary and elemental associations with the magickal meanings and the all essential pleasing fragrance.

I know it is very easy for me to use tried and tested incense and herb bag mixes (my daughter Miranda is the family incense-maker). However, I recommend that you experiment with different proportions and fragrances to craft spell bags and incenses for their precise and often unique needs.

I have listed the magickal meanings of the most common herbs, spices, tree bark, leaves and flowers. Any of these can be used whole in magick as a focus or symbol for a spell: for example, a pot of basil empowered with a green candle in whose soil coins are buried. Basil is a herb of prosperity and in its living form signifies growth. I have marked with an asterisk(*) those herbs and flowers that are especially good in incense and generally have a pleasant fragrance.

Herbs and their meanings

Herb	Magickal meaning	Planet	Element	Botanical name
Acacia, gum resin, also known as gum arabic from a very similar tree, acacia vera*	Secret love, optimism, making friends	Sun	Air	*Acacia Senegal*
Adam and Eve roots Sold in pairs, one long and pointed, the other round	Love, marriage proposals and fidelity; good in charm bags	Venus	Earth	*Orchis*
Agrimony	Protection, peaceful sleep, returns negativity to sender	Jupiter	Air	*Agrimonia eupatoria*
Allspice*	Money, luck, healing, passion, fertility	Mars	Fire	*Pimenta officinalis*
Alder	Prosperity, security, stability, house moves	Venus	Water/Fire	*Alnus glutinosa*
Almond/ almond blossom*	Abundance, prosperity, fertility and love without limits	Mercury	Air	*Prunus dulcis*
Anemone	Calling a lost love back, keeping secrets, secret love	Mars	Fire	*Anemone pulsatilla*
Angelica* *See also* archangel root	Banishes hostility from others, protection especially for children and against attacks on the home, healing, brings energy, health and long life	Sun	Fire	*Angelica archangelica*
Anise*	Reduces fears of attack and anxiety about ageing and infirmity	Jupiter	Air	*Pimpinella anisum*
Apple/ apple blossom*	Fertility, good fortune, abundance, health, love and long life, the birth of boys	Venus	Water	*Pyrus*
Ash	Expansion of horizons, travel especially by sea, courage, healing, strength, prosperity, creating poetry or any inspired writing	Sun	Fire	*Fraxinus excelsior*
Archangel root Root of angelica/ masterwort	Protection of the home, healing, contact with guardian angels, luck in speculation and money matters where there is a risk; good in charm bags	Sun	Fire	*Angelica archangelica*
Balm of Gilead	Love when carried as love amulet, brings visions of other dimensions and spirits, protection, healing	Venus	Water	*Commiphora opobalsamum*

Herb	Magickal meaning	Planet	Element	Botanical name
Bamboo	Protection, especially of household boundaries and against the negative thoughts of others; good luck, especially in money matters	Moon	Water	*Bambusa vulgaris*
Basil*	Love, protection against intruders, accidents and attack, brings courage, wealth, fidelity, fertility, astral travel, conquers fear of flying in the real world, good against road rage, attracts money, brings good luck to new homes or for home moves	Mars	Fire	*Ocimum basilicum*
Bay leaf*	Protection, psychic powers, healing, purification, strength and endurance, marriage, fertility, fidelity, prosperity, preservation of family and home	Sun	Fire	*Laurus nobilis*
Benzoin* Resin	Purifies negativity and bad atmospheres, attracts riches and business success, personal power, confidence and a sense of wellbeing; good for promotion or career rituals, power and self-confidence	Sun	Air/Fire	*Styrax benzoin*
Bergamot*	Successful property deals, reduces addictions, fears and the hold of destructive relationships, brings new love, brings opportunities in the area you most need them, good for all forms of communication, increases radiance, charisma and persuasiveness; encourages returns on investment and attracts fast money	Mercury	Air	*Menthe citrate*
Birch	Cleansing, health, new beginnings, protection of young children and animals	Venus	Water/Earth	*Betula alba*
Bistort Also called snakeweed or dragon's wort	Fertility, also deters malice in others and increases natural intuitive and divinatory powers, good for overcoming spiritual or psychic blockages, repels malicious communication	Saturn	Earth	*Polygonum bistorta*

Herb	Magickal meaning	Planet	Element	Botanical name
Bladderwrack Also kelp/seaweed	Protection against accidents or illness, especially at sea, sea rituals, wind rituals, brings action after stagnation, attracts money to the home; wishes	Moon	Water	*Fucus visiculosus*
Blessed or holy thistle	Spirituality, protection against psychic attack and all dangers, guards women and babies	Mars	Fire	*Centaurea benedicta*
Bluebell*	Constancy and faithfulness; brings understanding in relationships; also good luck and truth	Venus	Water/Earth	*Campanula rotundifolia*
Caraway seed	Protection of property against theft or damage, passion, health, improving mental powers; good in charm bags	Mercury	Air	*Carum carvi*
Carnation*	Red: passion, calling absent love; pink: acceptance into group; white: maternal love, love in later years, truth; yellow: anti-spite, protects against unfair criticism	Mars	Fire	*Dianthus caryophyllus*
Catnip* Also called catmint	Cat magick, love, beauty, happiness in home, fertility	Venus	Water	*Nepeta cataria*
Cedar*	Healing, purification, money, the home; protecting tools and special artefacts, good luck, fidelity in love, mature relationships	Jupiter	Air/Fire	*Cedrus libani*
Celery seed	Potency, money, protection, bringing travel; good in charm bags	Moon/ Mercury	Water	*Apium graveolens*
Chamomile*	For affection, gentle love, increases self-love especially after abuse, restores confidence after bad luck, fertility; good for all spells for children, babies and families, for family happiness, mending quarrels, for protection against anger and malice, for attracting money and winning it or prizes, for lessening obsessions and addictions and healing sorrow or abuse, also attracts money	Sun	Water	*Anthemis nobilis/ romanis*
Cherry* Also cherry blossom	New love, fertility, increasing psychic powers	Venus	Water	*Prunus avium*

Herb	Magickal meaning	Planet	Element	Botanical name
Cinnamon*	Success, healing, powers, psychic powers, money, passionate love	Sun/ Mars	Fire	Cinnamomum zelanicum
Clove	Protection, banishing negativity, love, money, healing	Jupiter	Fire	Syzygium aromaticum
Clover	Protection, money, love, fidelity, banishing negativity, success, good luck, employment, two leaves for love, three for protection and four for good luck in every way; carry in a charm bag	Mercury	Air	Trifolium
Cohosh Also known as snake or squaw root	Black (male): love, courage, protection, potency; blue (female): restoring natural cycles and harmony to stressed modern lives especially for older women, fertility, also anti-spite	Moon	Fire/Water	Cimicifuga
Coltsfoot*	Love, visions, peace and tranquillity, protects horses	Venus	Water	Tussilago farfara
Columbine*	Courage, love, the lion's herb, retrieves lost love; crushed seeds good in love mix	Venus	Water	Aquilegia canadensis
Comfrey	Safety during travel, to protect travellers and their luggage; money (use root), health	Saturn	Earth/ Water	Symphytum officinale
Copal* Resin	Protection, purification, especially good for cleansing crystals; use in incense for special occasions, for spiritual purposes and for all times when you, your property or home need protection, also for overcoming bad atmospheres and quarrels and the removal of unwanted influences or addictions	Sun	Fire	Bursera odorata
Coriander	Love, health, healing, passion, ensures clarity of thought and creativity brings optimism; seeds protect property	Mars	Fire	Coriandrum sativum
Chrysanthemum*	Brown: animals and animal healing; red: passion, marriage and motherhood; yellow: ending relationships; white: truth and love forever	Jupiter	Air/Fire	Chrysanthemum

Herb	Magickal meaning	Planet	Element	Botanical name
Cumin	Protection, especially of homes, property and cars (seeds), fidelity, returning malice to sender	Mercury	Air	*Cuminum cyminum*
Cyphi/kyphi* Contains resin	Reduces distress, purification, evening temple incense, healing, problem solving, reduces hurt, reawakens sexual desire	Sun	Fire	Mixture includes honey, wine, raisins, storax bark, saffron, sandalwood, frankincense, gum mastic, benzoin, cardamom seeds, galangal root, lemongrass and myrrh
Cypress*	Long life, healing and comfort in sorrow, reduces the pain of loss and injustice, good for gentle banishing and binding spells, for moving forwards after a period of stagnation, for blessing rituals and for all forms of protection, use for restoring what has been lost or stolen and for connecting with people from the past	Saturn/ Mars	Earth	*Cupressius sempervirens*
Daffodil	Forgiveness, finding and keeping one true love, also fertility and good luck	Mercury	Air/Water	*Narcissus*
Devil's shoestring	Protection, gambling, good luck, power, employment; root good in charm bags	Mercury	Air	*Viburnum alnifolium*
Dill*	Keeping home, loved ones and land safe from enemies and those who have envy in their hearts, also for money (use seeds in money spells), passion, luck	Mercury	Air/Earth	*Anethum graveolens*
Dragon's blood* Resin	Love magick, protection, dispels negativity increases male potency, courage, confidence, leadership	Mars	Fire	*Daemonorops draco*
Elder*	Increases clairvoyance, good for overcoming negativity, for all nature spirit magick, healing, good for older women	Venus	Water	*Sambucus canadensis*

Herb	Magickal meaning	Planet	Element	Botanical name
Eucalyptus*	Overcoming obstacles and misunderstandings, cleanses and banishes all negativity and anger and offers physical, psychological and psychic protection, moves long-standing problems towards resolution (so good for court cases and official matters or neighbour-hood disputes), good for passing tests and examinations, for health and for healing spells, also for job opportunities and travel	Moon	Water	*Eucalyptus*
Fennel*	Important herb for all forms of travel, holidays, relocation and journeys of all kinds, courage, house moves, protection, healing (especially protects animals and small children), brings together people or situations that are pulling in opposite directions, also strength, perseverance to win through whatever the obstacles, diminishes jealousy and possessiveness, disarms hidden enemies	Mercury	Air/Fire	*Foeniculum vulgare*
Fenugreek	Associated with increased prosperity over a period of time, in not only resources but also health and strength, healing; use seeds in money spells	Mercury	Air	*Trigonella foenum-graecum*
Fern*	Rain making, protection, luck, riches, finding hidden treasure, restoring youthfulness, health	Mercury	Air	*Pteridium aquilinum*
Feverfew	Reduces addictions, bad habits, the hold of destructive people, guards travellers and all who must go to unfamiliar or hostile environments, prevents accidents	Venus	Water	*Chrysanthemum parthenium*

Herb	Magickal meaning	Planet	Element	Botanical name
Frankincense* Resin	Ambition, authority, expansion of business interests, travel and confidence, also for creative ventures, leadership, promotion, employment, prosperity, and contact with other dimensions; an all-purpose fragrance for ritual magick and for healing	Sun	Fire	*Boswellia carterii*
Galangal Also called Low John the Conqueror root	Justice, success in all official matters, also for examination, increases passion, good fortune, also family happiness; good in charm bags and as a substitute for High John the Conqueror	Mars	Fire	*Alpina officinalis*
Galbanum* Resin	Called the mother resin, loved by the Ancient Egyptians and good for healing, for bringing calm, acceptance, good for mothers and all mothering issues, stability and the home	Saturn/ Moon	Earth	*Ferula galbaniflua*
Gardenia*	Healing, to attract love, for peace and nature spirit magick	Moon	Water	*Gardenia*
Garlic	Health, psychic protection, especially against unfriendly spirits, calling the wise ancestors, passion, bringing security from thieves, attracting money, domestic protection	Mars	Fire	*Allium sativum*
Geranium*	Happiness, friendship, the growth of love, gentle love, bringing or restoring harmony to the home or workplace, and healing coldness and indifference, diminishes self-doubt, fear of failure or inadequacy, guilt trips and over-critical people, as well as deterring intruders, brings fertility and good health, use also to attract good news and welcome visitors	Venus	Earth	*Pelargonium*

Herb	Magickal meaning	Planet	Element	Botanical name
Ginger*	Exploration, energy and health, brings or renews passion to love, good for all money-making enterprises, especially speculative and to reverse the outflow of finances, for travel, new ventures and enterprises, for originality and innovation when a new, bold approach is needed, for adding speed to any need in a hurry; use root as substitute for galangal	Mars	Fire	*Zingiber officinale*
Hawthorn berries	Fertility, banishing harm, fertility, marriage and general happiness, attracts good luck, protection of property against bad weather, especially storms, courage; use in charm bags	Mars	Fire	*Crataegus oxacantha*
Hazel	Wisdom, justice and the success of all official matters, good luck, fertility, knowledge and inspiration, psychic powers; use nuts in charm bags	Sun	Air	*Corylus*
Heather*	Pink: good luck; purple: faithfulness forever, also money and gambling; white: granting of wishes, especially if found growing wild	Sun	Earth	*Calluna*
Hibiscus*	Gentleness, family love and happiness, healing, love and passion later in life	Saturn	Earth	*Hibiscus*
High John the Conqueror root	Money, success, protection against psychic attack or ill wishers and depression (poisonous, so handle with care); good in charm bags	Mars	Fire	*Ipomoea*
Honeysuckle*	Commitment in love, babies, growth of wealth and career opportunity, good luck, psychic powers	Jupiter	Earth	*Lonicera caprifolium*
Hops	Healing, peaceful sleep, money, transformation, recovery from loss or debt, good in sleep pillows and charm bags	Mars	Fire	*Humulus lupulus*
Hyacinth*	Regaining lost love, overcoming opposition to love, new beginnings	Venus	Water	*Hyacinthus orientalis*

Herb	Magickal meaning	Planet	Element	Botanical name
Hyssop	The ultimate cleansing and purification, especially as infusion, removing negative influences from property, precious artefacts, places and people	Jupiter	Air/Earth	*Hyssopus officinalis*
Iris*	Clear communication, receiving long-awaited news, reconciliation, love after loss	Mercury	Air	*Iris*
Ivy	Marriage, fidelity, committed relationships, overcoming possessiveness or emotional blackmail, restoring lost love or after betrayal	Saturn	Earth	*Hedera*
Jasmine*	Attracts love and increases passion, for secret love, making dreams come true, discovering the identity of a secret admirer, enhances male potency and female fertility, also for peace and for enhanced psychic powers, deflects potential hostility and unwanted influences and emotional vampires or those who drain finances, increases self-love, personal radiance and melts emotional blockages and fears; use for all night and moon rituals	Moon	Water	*Jasminum officinale*
Job's tears seed	Protects against any sorrow, lessens pain or sickness, also guards against personal and household accidents; three seeds for good luck, seven to grant wishes	Saturn	Earth	*Coix lachryma*
Juniper berry*	Banishing negativity, increases male potency, new beginnings, money, luck, to purify homes and to protect against accidents, thieves and all forms of illness, justice	Sun	Fire	*Juniperus communis*
Knotweed	To encourage loyalty in lovers or friends, for keeping promises, health; for all binding spells	Moon/ Saturn	Earth	*Polygonum aviculare*

Herb	Magickal meaning	Planet	Element	Botanical name
Lavender*	An all-purpose herb and flower for protection, especially of children quiet sleep, long life and health, purification, happiness and peace, gentleness in love, friendship, mending quarrels, money and luck, banishing guilt, anti-abuse of all kinds, attracts new love and romance, encourages kindness and gentleness in love and lasting faithful love; also for family happiness, for animal spells, deterring bullies, for attracting friendship and romance, for slowly improving finances; use in all healing and health spells	Mercury	Air	*Lavendula officinale*
Lemon*	For night magick, for purification, new beginnings and overcoming obstacles, removing addictions and destructive ties from the past, also for good luck and prosperity, travel and house moves, for energy	Moon	Water	*Citrus limon*
Lemon balm* Also called melissa	Increases abundance and all good things in your life, reverses bad luck and grants wishes, draws love and promises long life	Moon	Water	*Melissa*
Lemongrass*	Repels spite, gives protection against spite, thieves and bad neighbours, increases passion, for moves of all kinds, removes what is redundant in your life, also to banish sad memories and past failures that hold back present and future achievements, blows away stagnation, attracts unexpected money or resources	Mercury	Air	*Cymbopogan citratus*
Lemon verbena*	Purification, maintains love and friendship, increases family happiness	Saturn	Air	*Lippia citriodora*

Herb	Magickal meaning	Planet	Element	Botanical name
Lilac*	Domestic happiness, brings you the home you want, encourages and blesses permanent relationships, drives away unfriendly ghosts and all malevolence from the home	Venus	Water	*Syringa vulgaris*
Lily*	Encourages spiritual powers, brings and keeps happy marriage and permanent relationships, for all mothers and mothering spells, to break possessive love, good for solving mysteries and crimes, anti-ghosts; also for purification rites	Venus	Water	*Lillium*
Lily of the valley*	Return of happiness, pregnancy, gentle or first love, improves memory and focus (poisonous, so use with care), fairy magick	Mercury	Air	*Convallaria magalis*
Linden blossom*	Justice, co-operation with others, partnerships of all kinds, dealing with officialdom	Mercury	Air	*Tilia europaea*
Lucky hand root	Employment, luck, protection, money, safe travel, gambling; good in charm bags	Venus	Water	*Orchis*
Magnolia*	Beauty, sensuality, love of nature, nobility and idealism, for fidelity and lasting love	Venus	Earth	*Magnolia grandifolia*
Marigold*	Protection, prophetic dreams, legal matters, increases psychic powers, growing love, marriage, money	Sun	Fire	*Calendula officinalis*
Marjoram, Sweet*	Protection, happiness, health, drives away loneliness, alienation and fears of separation or abandonment, good for increasing family loyalty, resolving divided loyalties, encourages compromise; also for increasing commitment in love, increases money flow, good for all joint ventures	Mercury	Air/Earth	*Origanum marjorana*
Meadowsweet*	Lasting love, happiness, reconciliation, diminishes rivalry, increases peace within the self, between family members or more globally	Jupiter	Air	*Spiraea filipendula*

Herb	Magickal meaning	Planet	Element	Botanical name
Milk thistle	Health and healing, fertility, pregnancy, mothers and children, healing, care of animals	Mars	Fire	*Carduus marianus*
Mimosa*	Riches, increasing beauty, older love or love after loss, overcoming grief, sustains love in bad times, also for connection with absent lovers and for grieving for loved ones who have died or left us forever, also for keeping secrets and secret trysts	Saturn	Earth	*Acacia dealbata*
Mint*	Money, love, increasing sexual desire, healing, banishing malevolence, travel, protection especially while travelling against road rage and accident	Mars/ Mercury	Air	*Mentha*
Moonwort	Money, love, magickal associated with phases of the moon, harmony and healing	Moon	Water	*Botrychium*
Mugwort*	Strength, psychic powers, prophetic dreams, healing, astral projection, drives away danger, increases fertility, protective on journeys of all kinds, especially from predators human and otherwise	Saturn	Earth	*Artemesia vulgaris*
Myrrh* Resin	Protection, banishing negativity, healing, spirituality; use to begin again after difficulty or loss, excellent for post-redundancy and retirement spells, for all who would or already work in alternative therapies, good for spells against prejudice and war, for all blessings, especially homes; an important ritual magick fragrance	Moon	Water	*Commiphora myrhha*
Nettle*	The ultimate herb of protection of the home and family, banishing negativity, for healing, for passion; good in protective mixes and bags	Mars	Fire	*Urtica divica*

Herb	Magickal meaning	Planet	Element	Botanical name
Olive	Peace, mending of quarrels, forgiveness especially of our own mistakes, abundance, healing, and fertility	Sun	Fire	Olea europaea
Orange*	Marriage, fertility, abundance, health, passion, luck and money, good for developing creative talents, personal fulfilment and for success	Sun	Fire	Citrus sinesis
Orris root	Love, protection, divination, positive change, prosperity; preserving what is of worth; good as a fixative	Venus	Water	Iris florentina
Parsley	Passion, physical, emotional and psychic protection, anti-bullying, divination, purification, good luck, abundance, takes away bad luck	Mercury	Air	Petroslinum sativum
Passion flower*	Finding a twin soul, love forever, the reuniting of lovers	Mars	Water/Fire	Passiflora incarnata
Patchouli*	Fragrance of the Earth and Earth energies, attracts money and money-making opportunities, good for healing the environment, brings stability to business ventures and property matters; use for spells for sacred or committed sexual relationships and for physical strength	Saturn	Earth	Pogostemon patchouly
Pennyroyal	Strength, protection, peace, banishes debt and the outflow of money	Mars	Fire	Mentha pulegium
Peppermint*	Purification, energy, love, healing, increases psychic powers, cleansing and stirring of fresh energies, for protection, especially during travel, in banishing spells and in attracting good fortune, brings money, increases passion and also improves mental acuity; use to see through con artists and illusion	Mercury	Air/Fire	Mentha piperita

Herb	Magickal meaning	Planet	Element	Botanical name
Pine* Pinon pine is resinous	Healing, fertility, returns hostility to sender, drives away all harm, good also to resist emotional blackmail and psychic attack, purifies just about everything and everybody, especially homes, good against tricksters and liars, use to discover the truth about a matter associated with birth, baby blessings and new beginnings, inspiration and illumination, so good for increasing fame and getting creative projects off the ground, also for courage and prosperity	Mars	Air/Earth	*Pinus*
Poppy*	Peace, pleasure, increasing imaginative and creative gifts, quiet sleep, remembering ancestors	Moon	Water	*Papaver*
Rattlesnake root	Protection, money, good fortune for gambling, competitions or speculation	Saturn	Earth	*Polygala senega*
Rose*	An all-purpose herb and flower, the ultimate love herb for all love, fidelity and relationship spells, money, healing, especially babies, children, animals, older people and all who have been abused, brings good luck, psychic protection, travel, fertility, family joy, to increase personal desirability; pink: first love, attracting love at any age, also healing; red: love forever, commitment in love and fidelity, also health; white: secret love and all secrets; wild or dog: identifying a secret admirer, holiday or long-distance romances; yellow: repelling jealousy, an older lover or love in later years	Venus	Water	*Rosa*

Herb	Magickal meaning	Planet	Element	Botanical name
Rosemary*	Bringing lovers together, increasing passion, increasing mental powers, improving memory and concentration, for tests and examinations, for learning anything new, for justice, and career success, banishing negativity, also for purification, healing, quiet sleep, preserves youthfulness, encourages money to flow into your life; a substitute for heather to bring good luck	Sun/ Mercury	Fire	Rosemarinus officinalis
Rue*	Healing, protects against illnesses of all kinds and speeds recovery from surgery or wounds, increases mental powers, brings love enchantment; banishes regrets, guilt or anger; used especially in infusions for purification	Sun/ Mars	Fire	Ruta graveolens
Sage*	Long life, good health, wisdom, protection, grants wishes, improves memory, justice, prosperity, leadership, anti-bullying, career success, healing, examinations and tests, house moves and renovation, acquiring knowledge or learning new skills	Jupiter	Air	Salvia officinalis
Sagebrush*	Purification, banishing negativity, leadership, success, prosperity, health and healing; use as smudge or herbal smoke stick	Venus/ Jupiter	Earth	Artemesia
Sandalwood*	Protection, healing, spirituality, contact with Guardian Angels, passion, wealth, also enhances sexual magnetism and commitment in love, helps to deflect anger, unfair criticism and spiteful words, to enhance self-esteem and a positive body image; an all-purpose fragrance for any formal magick	Moon/ Jupiter	Water/ Air	Santalum album
Sweetgrass*	Protection, wisdom, purification, all women's and Earth magick; use as a smudge or herbal smoke braid	Saturn	Earth	Hierochloe odorata

Herb	Magickal meaning	Planet	Element	Botanical name
Tansy	Health, long life, conception and pregnancy, invisibility against potential danger; associated with spring	Venus	Water	*Tanacetum vulgare*
Scullcap/skullcap	Money, employment, business partnerships and investment, attracting gifts and resources, love, fidelity, peace	Saturn	Water/Earth	*Scutellaria galericulata*
Solomon's seal*	Protection, banishes all negativity and hostility, wisdom, leadership, success, power	Saturn	Earth/Water	*Polygonatum officinale*
Tarragon*	Associated with dragons and serpent Goddesses, courage, new beginnings, shedding the redundant, career, prosperity, regeneration in any and every aspect of living, helps the user to focus on new targets	Mercury	Air/Fire	
Thyme*	Health, healing, prophetic dreams, overcomes misfortune and brings luck, career opportunities, increases psychic powers, improves memory, good for purification and cleansing places and objects, courage, long-term prosperity, connection with Earth power, drives away fear and danger, anti-bullying, good for tests and examinations	Mars/Venus	Water	*Thymus vulgaris*
Valerian*	Love and love divination, quiet sleep, purification, protection against outer hostility, inner fears and despair, reconciliation, reuniting those parted by anger or circumstance	Mercury/Venus	Water	*Valeriana officinalis*
Vanilla*	Love, passion, increases mental powers, fidelity, marriage vows and renewal of vows, money, wellbeing, health and harmony, preserving youthfulness	Venus	Water	*Vanilla aromatica*

Herb	Magickal meaning	Planet	Element	Botanical name
Vervain*	Love, transforms enemies into friends, purification, peace, money, prophecy, preserves youthfulness, peaceful sleep, healing, protects the home, attracting the blessings of nature spirits and wights who guard the land on which even urban homes are built	Venus	Earth	*Verbena officinalis*
Vetivert*	Love, money, anti-theft, protects against all negativity, starting businesses, for wish magick and to attract good luck or to break a run of bad fortune; good in gambling and speculation, in finding new or self-employment, also for all practical ventures, crafts and hands-on skills	Saturn	Earth	*Vetiveria zizanioides*
Violet*	Restoring trust, fulfilling modest ambitions; keeping secrets and secret love; use in charm bags or infusions with sugar for love	Venus	Water	*Viola odorata*
Wintergreen	Protection, healing, good luck, deflects hostility, reduces debts and misfortune	Moon	Water	*Gaultheria procumbens*

Working with fragrance

Be a collector of fragrant materials so that you truly have your witch's kitchen. Dried herbs, spices and flower petals keep for many months and if you have a selection of jars at home you can add to your collection as you shop, visit markets, go on holiday or call at garden centres. Of course, you can also dry your own herbs and flowers. Head for the bazaars in Middle and Far Eastern countries as you will obtain resins for a fraction of the price you would pay from a store.

* It is easy to dry your own flowers and herbs from the garden by hanging them upside down in a warm, dry place where the air circulates until they are crumbly but still fragrant.

* Cooking herbs and spices from glass kitchen jars — the kind you buy in a supermarket — can be mixed with a resin for almost instant incense.

* Scour the internet for suppliers of more unusual herbs and resins as you may get a better deal on slightly larger quantities. Try first with one or two purchases so you can gauge the quality and reliability of service.

* Start a wish list in your Book of Shadows or on your computer of fragrances you would like to acquire and tick them off as you acquire them with date purchased.

As you do with any other ingredients in your kitchen, keep a note when stocks are running low of staples such as dried lavender or rose petals, that can be used for almost any mix, as well as one or two basic all-purpose resins, such as frankincense or myrrh.

✹ It is always helpful to have jars of ready-made incense as well as a variety of incense sticks and jars of dried herbs ready for spell bags in a hurry.

✹ Even if you are skilled in incense making, build up a large collection of high-quality incense sticks in a variety of fragrances. The really cheap ones burn too quickly and the fragrance is not so authentic.

✹ Incense sticks are ideal for raising the energy in spells, one in each hand, for writing magickal messages, names or talismanic glyphs over symbols or crystals and herb bags.

✹ Incense sticks form an instant Air element when you do not have the time or space to use loose, non-combustible incense (see page 336 for the difference between this and combustible incense). They are also perfect for background protective or empowering energies for divination, other spiritual work and around your home.

Incense wisdom

✹ Have a long spaghetti jar filled with individual incense sticks in a wide variety of fragrances and keep it topped up. When doing a spell if you feel something is missing or you really cannot decide the best incense to use in a ritual, turn the jar round nine times clockwise and open it. With your eyes closed, pick as many incense sticks as feel right. This always works, once you trust your inner wisdom and Witch Guardian to guide your hand.

✹ With incense sticks, as with loose incense, rely on the purpose of the spell to suggest the right proportions/number of sticks of each fragrance: for example, how much gentleness (lavender) to passion (ginger) to long-lasting love (bay) in a love mix.

✹ Single fragrances (with or as a resin for a loose mix) are effective and can provide one concentrated energy.

✹ If you are new to witchcraft, working with individual incenses will give you the chance to get to know your fragrances and their effects individually.

✹ Note in your Book of Shadows not only the magickal meaning of any incense you used, but also your own impressions and maybe visions as you use it. Then combine two fragrances, and so on. This is where using individual sticks can help you to attune and see what works for you.

✹ You can move two or three different fragrance incense sticks close, so the fragrances mix in the combined smoke. You can also combine fragrances by adding different loose incenses one after the other to burning charcoal.

✹ Even if you're an experienced witch, you might find that working with a single incense fragrance for a while is a way of refreshing the magickal palate and reminding you of what is special for you.

Magickal herbs, spices, tree and flower meanings

In the table on pages 551–567, I have given the planetary and elemental connections of fragrant materials, so that you can use these broader categories when you need a surge of energy or protection: for example, herbs of Venus to bring love, or two or three Fire herbs for creativity. I have included tree bark and leaves as herbs and given the botanical name of the source plant.

I have also indicated which substance are resins, because if you are making your own incense you will need at least a third of resin so that your mixture will burn well on charcoal discs in your censer or burning dish.

I have suggested fragrances that I personally like, but you should experiment and adapt accordingly: for example, some people hate vervain or say sage gives them a headache. Most herbs and flowers are very good tempered and mix well and you rarely make a truly foul brew. Lavender, hibiscus, jasmine, mimosa, rose petals, lemon balm and lemon verbena, bay leaves, most of the fruit blossoms, mint, sage, rosemary, thyme and chamomile are very fragrant. Banishing/cleaning incenses are generally more pungent.

Herbs can have a different elemental correspondence from that of their planet so that though the Sun is a planet of Fire, it may rule a herb that has for example strong Air qualities, like gum arabic. You could make a Jupiter incense mix for success or justice or a Water mix to get whatever you are casting the spell for flowing into your life.

You can orientate a whole spell to a planet or element. In, for example, a Fire-based spell where you were casting a spell for creativity to get a book accepted by a publisher, you could burn frankincense resin with dried orange blossom, marigold and rosemary, plus other fire ingredients for the Air, use dried rosemary herb instead of salt for Earth and a rue infusion, sacred to Aradia and Diana, for the Water element. You could even anoint your candle with a fire oil or burn one in a Fire fragrance, such as frankincense.

If you meet an unfamiliar herb or flower and cannot find its associated planet ask yourself what it feels like, smells like and if it is similar to any other herbs or flowers.

Making, empowering and using magickal incenses

Making your own incense does enable you to empower it as you work, but you can empower ready-made granular or powdered incense to burn on charcoal or your incense sticks before use.

If making your own incense use a mortar and pestle, a large one so you can mix the herbs and flowers more easily. There really is no substitute for this tool and they are widely obtainable in cookware stores, as well as online. The secret of a good incense is that it is a very fine powder.

Spend a little time devising what you want to put into your mix. Aim to have at least two fragrant substances in a mix.

You can have a charcoal disc ready burning and experiment with small quantities of a basic mix before adding extra ingredients.

Because you need to pound and grind herbs and flowers for your incense mix, you can empower the incense as you mix. I have found that it takes about as long for a charcoal disc to heat as it does for you to mix incense and so you can combine the two activities at the beginning of a spell. Concentrating on the magickal intention for which the incense will be used, create a mixing chant just two or three phrases over and over that name the ingredients and the purpose for which they are being mixed. You can do this even when empowering a single resin.

* First, pound any leaves and petals in the mortar. Chop roots beforehand very finely and crumble bark and large dried petals. Mix them all against the sides until you have a fine or grainy powder.

* Next, add the resin beads or granules. Pound and mix these well into the powder, as the smoother the incense the better it will burn.

* Mid-way through, add a drop or two of essential/fragrance oil, if you want to, but use it sparingly so that the moisture is quickly absorbed by the mix.

* Mix the incense faster and faster for any dynamic purpose, such as calling love or prosperity, increasing the speed and intensity of the chant until with a final pound and call, you release the power into the mix.

* For a healing, peace or reconciliation mix, for example, lavender, lilac, rose and myrrh, endow softer energies by chanting faster and mixing faster until you can feel the powder filled with energy. Then chant and mix slower and quieter, ending with a final, smooth, slow downward movement of the pestle, pushing the power into the herbs as your words fade into silence.

You can mix up batches of incense and store it in sealed jars for future rituals. Do a mini empowerment by mixing it in a small dish to link it to the specific purpose of the spell as you set the altar.

You can make up basic core mixes for love (rosemary, lavender, rose and myrrh) or prosperity (basil, frankincense, mint and sage) and then add individual ingredients for specific spells. Keep notes of your different mixes and rough proportions in your Book of Shadows so that you have a database for future mixes.

If you are using ready-made, loose, powdered incenses, mix them with a mortar and pestle and chant before use as if they were homemade (though of course you need not be so vigorous or prolonged in the mixing).

You can also empower your incense sticks or cones by placing them in the container in which you are going to burn them. Chant over the container as you turn it nine times clockwise or pass your wand clockwise nine times or your hands the right one clockwise and the left one anticlockwise. Recite the purpose and the named fragrances nine times.

Herbal and spell charm bags

Herbs and flower spell charm bags without any other added items can be empowered during a spell, either with the ingredients added one at a time to a bowl as the spell focus in the centre of the altar or added to the bag before the spell. In the former case, you would fill the bag after the release of power but before closing the quarters or closing the circle. Herb bags alone, rather than ones where you include metal or wax items, are very good for matters of the heart and healing or where you need very gentle energies or increase or banishment.

Alternatively, as with charm bags, you can make the creation a mini ritual in itself (see page 413 for full details of making and empowering charm bags).

Generally herb spell bags do not contain resin or oil. When adding the ingredients one at a time to the central bowl or the bag, you can list them as part of the spell/empowerment. For example:

Rosemary for passion that he will desire me, rose petals that we may live as one and loving bay that we will be together forever in trust and in fidelity.

You can either choose a number of herbs and flowers in advance to put in small dishes to fill the bag or put the jars of dried herbs and flowers on the table or altar where you are making the bag and take from them as you need. As with incense, you can make your herbal spell bag based on magickal meanings or devise elemental or planetary bags.

As you become more confident in your innate magickal wisdom or for special bags, for example, a charm bag for a friend's wedding or to help a loved one through a crisis, you can trust your psychic powers to choose the best ingredients:

* Hold a clear crystal pendulum over either the different jars or at least 10 different herbs and petals in very small dishes. Ask the pendulum to indicate which are the right ingredients for this bag (specify the need aloud).

* Though as a rule you add three, five, seven or nine ingredients, go with the pendulum. It will vibrate, feel heavy and pull down over the right ingredients if you hold it a few centimetres above each jar/dish and you will feel instinctively which are right.

* If you are creating a pre-planned mix but want to personalise it, afterwards hold your pendulum over the different jars in turn and ask it to indicate an extra secret ingredient that will activate the spell bag contents. You may be surprised at the choice, but it always works.

You can also put an individual magickal root or a number of berries in a very small drawstring bag of the appropriate colour: for example, the tear-like seeds called Job's tears are protection against any sorrow and are said to absorb pain or sickness. Three in a bag also brings good luck and seven will grant wishes made when the bag is sealed. Or Low John the Conqueror root is carried either in a blue bag or in a pocket to a court case, tribunal or enquiry for a speedy and satisfactory resolution.

Herb bags are said to be active until the fragrance fades, in which case they should be replaced or can be charged for a particular event or period. When they are inactive or no longer needed, the herbs should be scattered in the air if used for attracting purposes and buried if the bag was created for banishing or binding purposes. You would then empower a new bag if necessary. If not expensive or of personal significance, I would advise throwing the old spell bag away.

Infusions

Magickal infusions or herbal liquids can be used many ways in magick:

* For cleansing: for example, hyssop infusion for purifying artefacts, especially ones that you have bought or for cleansing the area around your altar space especially outdoors. Asperge the whole area with hyssop infusion and twigs tied together (hazel, oak or ash if possible).

* As a substitute for the Water element whether in a spell or ritual and to cast a circle to add particular strengths to the spell or ritual (you can match the incense and infusion magickal, planetary or elemental meanings).

* For protecting an area, such as a lemon or lemongrass infusion on doorsteps (in a floor wash), sprinkled round household boundaries, in front of garages or round possessions or cars, and a vervain infusion to banish harmful ghosts.

* Pour a money-drawing infusion such as basil or sage down external drains and internal water outlets to prevent money or resources draining out of your life and to call money back.

* Use planetary infusions as offerings at special ceremonies: for example, moonwort or jasmine for full moon ceremonies, rose infused water for Venus and love on a Friday or violet water for secret love on the same day. Pour them into the earth, round growing plants or into running water with an invocation (much better for grass and plants).

* Add a small quantity to a bath to draw into you the strengths you need or, for example, with a rose petal infusion, to radiate charisma and beauty into and from your aura.

* As empowered teas to absorb magickal qualities such as mint to attract money and success and chamomile for gentle love, fertility in any way or happiness. Check in a herbal book that the herb is safe to drink and in what dose and if you are pregnant always consult a pharmacist before taking any herb internally.

How to make an infusion or decoction

* To make an infusion, soak the herbs or herbal tea bag in water that has just been brought to the boil. Use 5 ml/1 tsp dried herbs or 15 ml/1 tbsp fresh herbs to an average tea cup.

* Pour the water on to the herbs, stir nine times clockwise to attract and anticlockwise to repel, naming quietly but firmly nine times your purpose.

* Cover and leave for five to ten minutes and drain off the herbs and discard. (Alternatively, you can put the herbs in a small muslin bag in the cup and then you do not need to strain.)

* Stir the strained liquid again either nine times clockwise or anticlockwise according to the purpose and add:

So mote it be.

* For a decoction to extract healing and magickal agents from roots and barks, you need to stir the mix constantly as you boil it and you can add power by chanting as you do this. You do not need to empower or stir after you have strained it, as

you have added the power in the making. Again, work clockwise to attract and anticlockwise to banish or bind.

* The roots etc should be powdered, crushed in a pestle or finely chopped and 30 g/1 oz added to 500 ml/1 pint of cold water. Some decoctions are better if left to stand overnight before brewing.

* The mixture should then be simmered until the water is reduced by half.

* Strain before using and squeeze the herb to get out all the liquid and discard the herbs as with an infusion.

* When possible, make your infusions a few hours at the most before you need them though they will keep if refrigerated.

PRACTICAL ASSIGNMENT

Personalised fragrances

What herbal/floral mix signifies you, the strengths and qualities you value most in yourself and those you aspire to? Plan and if possible create your personal incense.

Further research

Discover what you can about 10 herbs or flowers that I have not listed and try using some of them in ritual or in incense making.

Further information

Recommended reading

* Culpepper, Nicholas, *Complete Herbal*, Bloomsbury Books, 1992
* Cunningham, Scott, *Encyclopaedia of Magical Herbs*, Llewellyn, 1997
* Cunningham, Scott, *Complete Book of Incense, Oils and Brews*, Llewellyn, 1997
* Rodway, Marie, *A Wiccan Herbal*, Foulsham/Quantum, 1997
* Vickery, Roy, *A Dictionary of Plant Lore*, Oxford University Press, 1995

Websites

* *How to make herbal infusions, decoctions and teas*
  Excellent site for infusions and other herbal remedies you can adapt for magick
  www.herbalremediesinfo.com/ infusions.html
* *Scents of Earth*
  How to make incense, including without saltpetre
  www.scents-of-earth.com/ makeyourownna.html
* *A Modern Herbal*
  Good incense plus link to traditional Herbal A-Z index
  www.botanical.com/botanical/ article/incense.htm

Angel And Archangel
Magick

It can be hard to understand how Angels fit into witchcraft since they are traditionally associated with more formal Judaic, Christian and Islamic religions. Here they are regarded as intermediaries between God and mortals. However, through the Jewish mystical system the Kabbalah and later in mediaeval angelology, they have maintained magickal associations with the powers of the four elements, with the four directions and seasons, the four winds, the seven older planets and the 12 zodiacal constellations. The Angels of the Kabbalah come from an ancient Jewish tradition, dating from times when old Israel incorporated the earlier pagan Gods worshipped by the tribes and transformed them into Angels serving the One True God.

Because witchcraft is a very spiritual religion, it is quite possible not only to ask for the protection of your Guardian Angel during magick, but also to work with the traditional Archangels as a focus for rituals. There are also specific Angels of the zodiac and month who can be invoked in modern magick.

Archangel rituals and working with Archangel hours are no different from deity rituals in essence. However, they are focused more round making an invocation to the Archangel using their special crystals, rather than an increase and release of power as in spells (see page 222 on praying to the Goddess). Archangel magick can also involve writing a letter to the Archangel or asking for a blessing.

For solitary and coven witches alike, in private work the Archangels offer a very deep connection to the spiritual heart of witchcraft as a religion and so are well worth incorporating into spiritual work. You may choose a particular Angel or Archangel focus for your year and a day dedication or ask the four core Archangels Michael, Gabriel, Raphael and Uriel to guard the four Watchtowers on this special occasion.

Archangels

Magick has its own Archangel. The Archangel Raziel, whose name means secret of God, is the giver of magickal secrets and divine mysteries. Raziel is credited with writing the esoteric Book of the Angel Raziel that contained all earthly and heavenly knowledge. He gave it to Adam as consolation for losing Eden, but other Angels became jealous and threw it into the sea.

God ordered Rahab, Angel of the deep caverns of the sea, to restore the book to

Adam. Thereafter the book passed to Enoch, then to Noah and finally to King Solomon who derived from it his magickal powers and wisdom. However, it is said that only Raziel can reveal its deepest secrets to Angels and mortals whom he favours and who are sufficiently pure of heart.

It is to the 5th century philosopher Dionysius that we owe the formalisation of the nine ranks of Angels that still form the core of more formal angelology (see Further research, page 592). The Judaic Angels became divided into Seraphim, Kerubim (Cherubim), Thrones, Dominations, Powers, Virtues, Principalities, Archangels and Angels.

Like the deities, Archangels represent specific archetypal or idealised qualities and so are invoked for these strengths and gifts. There are many Archangels whose names are given in different forms of religious writings and so the names of the seven main Archangels vary according to the tradition in which they appear. If you want to know more of these, the books at the end of this module will offer you information on the different traditions.

In spite of their elevated roles in the seven heavens, Archangels are concerned with our spiritual welfare and in assisting us to aspire beyond purely private concerns. However, they will also help with our practical difficulties and if you need a lot of power or sudden urgent aid, try the relevant Archangel. In some ways, Archangels are easier than Guardian Angels to visualise, because there are a number of descriptions drawn from different sources to guide us. These create a picture of the individual Archangel, not only the physical appearance, but also specific roles governed by them and associated crystals, candle colours etc. If you visit art galleries, you will see them portrayed in great works of art and a number of the images can be downloaded for non-commercial purposes from the internet.

Working with the Archangels

Keep a page in your Angel journal for each Archangel and note down any information you come across whether on the internet, in churches or cathedrals, art galleries, or during your own rituals or moments of quiet contemplation. Over time, you might draw up your own concept of the Archangels that may be entirely different from traditional lore. If it works for you, then trust your own insights. Archangels like Angels are made of pure energy and light and so it is we who give them their earthly form according to how we perceive them.

Each of the seven traditional Archangels is linked with one of the ancient planets: for example, Sachiel with Jupiter. Their correspondences are very similar. Archangel-focused magick does differ from its associated planetary magick in that you can, of course, ask them for help in personal areas. However, at the same time Archangels have global foci and are frequently invoked for peace in a war-torn land or to assist with famine.

When you can carry out globally focused rites, under the threefold law you spontaneously call similar blessings in your personal life. For example, you might ask Michael, Archangel of the sun, to bring abundance to a land where there is great poverty and in doing so Michael will bring what you need in the weeks ahead in the way that is right. This might be an opportunity to earn some extra money or a new friendship that would lead to a pooling of mutual resources and strengths or an exchange of help. Archangels are very good at helping us to help ourselves.

You can also naturally ask for help for someone you know who is sick or in trouble, whether a person or animal, or for the resolution of a local issue that affects your community and for protection of loved ones. Witches I know with relations in any of the forces ask Samael to keep them safe and bring them home at the end of their duty. However, you can ask for what you need materially as long as you make a specific *and in return I will...* Although all magick operates on the Cosmic Exchange principle, this is a major feature of Archangel magick and you should repay in the area ruled by your chosen Archangel: for example, joining a local tree-planting day if you have asked Anael the Archangel of Friday and the planet Venus to bring you love.

The four core Archangels

We have most information about the four Archangels who are central to angelology and Angel magick. I have spoken about them in other modules including psychic protection (see page 281), but I will give an expanded version here so that you can see where they fit into the pattern of the days of the week and the planetary hours. In fact, Uriel does not feature in the days of the week or the planetary hours, but Samael, Archangel of cleansing Fire appears instead. Like Samael, Uriel is linked with Tuesday and Mars, though standing in the north and earth you could as easily associate him with Saturn. There is another Archangel of Tuesday, Camael, Archangel of courage who is pictured either as a crouching leopard or as a warrior in red and green armour riding a leopard. The differences occur because of the overlap of systems. In practice, Uriel remains one of the four elemental/directional Archangels, but Samael or Camael appears in the days of the week and Samael always in the planetary hours.

Uriel, Raphael, Michael and Gabriel will guard your four quarters whether of your magickal circle, your protective square or your home. They share the magickal correspondences of their elements and planets, but I will give them again so you can carry out rituals without referring back. However, you might like now to remind yourself of the four Archangel protective invocations on page 289.

Uriel

Uriel, whose name means fire of God, is the Archangel of Transformation. Uriel is a regent or guardian of the sun and the sharpest sighted Archangel in heaven. He is the Archangel who brought alchemy to humankind, the sacred art of transmuting base metal into gold to refine spiritual as well as actual gold, believed to be the way humans can find the way back to paradise. He guards the gates of the Garden of Eden with his fiery sword until we are wise enough to return. He warned Noah of the flood (Raphael showed Noah how to build the Ark).

Uriel is a pure pillar of fire and brings warmth to the winter and melts the snows with his flaming sword. Picture Uriel with an open hand holding a flaming torch and in the other a sword of fire, dressed in rich burnished gold and ruby red with a bright flame-like halo like a bonfire blazing in the darkness.

Uriel is patron of all who undertake creative work, those who relieve disasters, bailiffs, students and teachers, chemists, industrialists, goldsmiths, safety executives, blacksmiths, electrical and gas workers and fire personnel.

Direction: North

Season: Winter

Time of day: Midnight

Day: Tuesday

Element: Earth (magickally)

Planet: Mars

Colour: Ruby red

Incenses: Basil, copal, sandalwood, ginger

Crystals: Hematite, obsidian, rutilated quartz, tiger's eye

Metal: Burnished gold, brass

Personally, invoke Uriel for courage and for protection against bullies and danger of all kinds, especially in the home and against fire and electrical faults, for older people, for animals, for the fulfilment of a long-term spiritual or personal path, for quelling anger in others and transforming our own powerful emotions such as fury, jealousy, resentment and spite into impetus for positive change and for focusing ourselves single-mindedly on a task.

Globally, call on Uriel to protect against the effects of extremes of cold, to melt rigid attitudes and indifference of authority and corporations towards the plight of others, to protect against nuclear accidents and dangers and the unwise use of the world's fuel resources and those who are short of resources such as fuel and shelter and to make the world a safer place.

Raphael

Raphael, whose name means God has healed, is the Archangel of medicine and also of all forms of healing and science. He healed the earth and gave Noah a medical book after the flood receded and also healed the blind Tobit in the Holy Scriptures. Raphael gave King Solomon a magickal ring to help him in building his great temple. He is also Archangel of the four winds and the traveller's Archangel, especially of the young and vulnerable who are far from home.

Picture him carrying a golden vial of medicine, with a traveller's staff, food, often a fish, in his wallet to nourish travellers, dressed in the colours of early morning sunlight, with a beautiful green, healing ray emanating from his halo.

Raphael is patron of the blind, of joyful meetings and celebrations, of nurses, of physicians, of shopkeepers, bus drivers, technicians, scientists, healthcare workers, travellers, all who work in technology, especially software production, tour operators, the self-employed, youth workers, taxi drivers, chiropractors and packers.

Direction: East

Season: Spring

Time of day: Dawn

Day: Wednesday

Element: Air

Planet: Mercury

Colour: Lemon yellow or misty grey, but often also perceived as green

Incenses: Lavender, lily of the valley, pine, thyme

Crystals: Citrine, yellow and orange calcite, yellow jasper, golden beryl, lemon chrysoprase

Metal: Aluminium, mercury

Personally, invoke Raphael for healing and health, for business ventures, technological expertise, for scientific breakthroughs, travel and relocation, young people, successful buying and selling, for protection against road or travel accidents, especially by air, road rage and in hazardous situations, and for ingenuity and adaptability, for learning languages and for clear, wise communication.

Globally, call upon Raphael for resolving neighbourhood matters, for peace and tolerance between people of different religions, backgrounds and ethnic origin, for communication and co-operation between nations, for a free and wise media everywhere and the dissemination of unbiased information, and also against technological and chemical pollution, especially during travel and the adverse effects of modern living.

Michael

Michael, whose name means who is like to God, is the supreme Archangel, Archangel of the sun. He oversees the natural world, the weather and the growth of crops. He is the leader of all the great warrior Angels who fight against evil and he is often shown trampling the Devil underfoot. Michael appeared to Moses as the fire in the burning bush, and rescued Daniel from the lions' den.

Michael is pictured with golden wings in red and gold armour with sword, shield, a green date branch and carrying the scales of justice or a white banner with a red cross. He is the ideal young golden-haired warrior and is one of the chief dragon-slaying Angels. In Muslim lore, Michael's wings are said to be the colour of green emeralds.

Michael is the patron of grocers, sailors, administrators, car repairers and garage mechanics, railway workers, police, mechanical engineers, lorry drivers, construction engineers and builders and metalworkers.

Direction: South

Season: Summer

Time of day: Noon

Day: Sunday

Element: Fire

Planet: Sun

Colour: Gold

Incenses: Chamomile, frankincense, marigold, rosemary, sunflower, sage

Crystals: Amber, clear quartz crystal, Herkimer diamond, opal or Angel aura, golden topaz

Metal: Gold

Personally, invoke Michael for abundance and prosperity where there has been a lack of it, for developing leadership qualities and opportunities, for striving for perfection for what the alchemists call spiritual gold, for all creative ventures, for original ideas and new beginnings, for energy, joy, health, for property matters, for middle age, men and fathering issues, for spiritual awareness of divinity, Angels and Spirit Guides and self-confidence.

Globally, Michael will aid the revival of barren land despoiled by industrialisation or war, for overcoming drought, for cleansing air pollution, for bringing enlightenment in the face of prejudice and intolerance, for overcoming corruption that harms the vulnerable and for wise and responsible world leadership; to slow down global warming, the resolution of territory disputes peacefully and wisely and for international aid work both ongoing and after disasters.

Gabriel

Gabriel is Archangel of the moon and with Michael he is the highest of the Archangels. His name means God has shown himself mightily. Archangel Gabriel carries God's messages and reveals the answers to the questions we carry deep in our hearts. He was herald to Elizabeth, telling her that though long past childbearing years she would give birth to John the Baptist. He also took the news to Mary that she would have a son Jesus. Gabriel chooses the souls of children to be born and teaches them in the nine months their spirits move between the mother and the heavens. When the child is born, Gabriel presses his finger on its lips so that the child will keep the secrets of the heavens, so creating the cleft below the nose.

Picture him in silver or clothed in the blue of the night sky with a mantle of stars and a crescent moon for his halo, with a golden horn, a white lily; alternatively with a lantern in his right hand and with a mirror made of jasper in his left.

He is patron of the household, of communications and postal workers, of all in the hotel or hospitality trade, of market researchers, dieticians, conference planners, secretaries, desktop publishers, family practitioner doctors, women's aid workers and translators.

Direction: West

Season: Autumn

Time of day: Sunset

Day: Monday

Element: Water

Planet: Moon

Colour: Silver

Incenses: Eucalyptus, jasmine, lily, myrrh, lilac, rose

Crystals: Aquamarine, aqua aura, moonstone, milky quartz, opal, pearls, selenite

Metal: Silver

Personally, invoke Gabriel for protection, for safe travel especially across water, for matters concerning families, women, infants and children, mothering, pregnancy and fertility, for diminishing self-destructive tendencies, for peace in the home and at work, for healing, psychic development and divination, especially scrying in water, and keeping secrets, for boats and sailors.

Globally, call upon Gabriel for clean water projects, to protect water creatures and cleanse polluted seas, lakes and rivers, for wise fishing of the seas and rivers, for protection for fishermen and sailors and against floods and tidal waves, inclement weather and extreme seasonal effects.

Other Archangels associated with days of the week and the main planets

With the four Archangels above, the following make up the seven traditionally used in spirituality and ritual in connection with the traditional planets and the days (also the hours, see page 199). Though I refer to the Archangels as he, they are androgynous and some people see Anael and Gabriel, as having a more female focus. There is some overlap with the roles of the four overseeing core Archangels and so you have some choice over whom you invoke.

Sunday: Michael

Monday: Gabriel

Tuesday: Samael (also Uriel and Camael)

Wednesday: Raphael

Thursday: Sachiel

Friday: Anael/Hanael

Saturday: Cassiel

Samael/Sammael

Samael is Archangel of severity and personal integrity. He is the Archangel of cleansing fire and of overcoming all obstacles in the way of truth. One of the seven regents of the world and said to be served by two million Angels, he is also called the dark Angel who in the guise of the serpent tempted Eve. In this role, that may seem hard to understand at first, he was a true tester of faith and someone who introduced the concept of free will, rather than blind obedience into the Garden of Eden. He may not be an easy Angel to work with and one you might like to leave until later in your explorations. He challenges the status quo and demands that we examine our motives and make our own choices, rather than go along with the way things have always been or the majority view. Samael insists on integrity and honesty of purpose, so we may have to do a fair amount of mental cleansing and also take care of our bodies.

Visualise him in midnight blue and red, with blue and red flames in his halo and midnight blue wings, sweeping through the skies, waking the slumbering Angels and scattering slumbering mortals on earth, with a huge, dark gold sword.

He is patron of all military personnel and all security forces, aid workers and peace campaigners, of wise politicians and officials at every level, historians, crossword and quiz writers, school and college examiners and inspectors, driving test instructors and examiners, and fitness trainers.

Day of the week: Tuesday

Element: Fire

Planet: Mars

Colour: Red/indigo

Incenses: Allspice, cinnamon, dragon's blood, ferns, fig

Crystals: Blood or red agate, garnet, ruby, iron pyrites, titanium aura

Metal: Iron and steel

Personally, invoke Samael for all matters where truth is of the essence, for independence, courage, making your own decisions and if necessary standing alone for an unpopular cause you believe is right, to resist bullies and to protect the home, car, furniture and personal possessions against thieves, vandalism and damage by fire, storm or flood; also to overcome addictions and destructive habits or the power of bad influences on ourselves and loved ones.

Globally, call upon him to overcome dictators, those who are cruel to others whether human or animals, against unfair imprisonment and bad prisons, to stop wars, guard against terrorism and relieve the suffering of those in war zones or former war zones; also for oppressed minorities and endangered species.

Sachiel

Sachiel, whose name means the covering of God, is called the divine benefactor and the Archangel of charity. He is one of the mighty Cherubim and orders the four elements Earth, Air, Fire and Water and is likewise one of the seven Archangels who stand in the presence of God. He has also become associated with good harvests, taking over this role from the pre-Christian Grain Gods.

Picture him in robes of deep blue and purple, carrying sheaves of corn and baskets of food with a rich purple and golden halo and blue and purple wings.

He is patron of charity workers, insurance and bank workers, lawyers, bosses, solicitors and judges, also of agricultural workers, town planners, farmers and supermarket workers.

Day of the week: Thursday

Element: Air

Planet: Jupiter

Colour: Deep blue and purple

Incenses: Fennel, honeysuckle, lotus, sage, sagebrush

Crystals: Cobalt aura, blue topaz, angelite, lapis lazuli, sodalite

Metal: Tin

Personally, invoke Sachiel for justice, for increasing abundance and prosperity and also for increasing knowledge and learning, for loyal and mutually enriching partnerships both personally and in business, for finding the right life path and career and advancement; for idealism and altruism and, like Michael, for leadership and authority with responsibility, for travel and house moves, rehabilitation after crime or restoration after financial loss, redundancy, breakdown or illness.

Globally, call upon Sachiel for good harvests, for relieving lands where there is famine or disease, for international and national justice, for the fairer distribution of resources and to restore run down areas or cities where employment has been lost, for honourable and efficient administrators of law and justice, for reducing the world debt wisely and for alleviating world poverty.

Anael/Hanael/Hamiel

Anael, whose name means glory or grace of God, guards the gates of the west wind. He was one of the seven Angels present at creation and rules over all kingdoms, kings, queens and more recently over presidents and prime ministers. Anael took Enoch to the heavenly realms and he is another Archangel of the moon, as well as Archangel of love, of healing remedies and crystal healing. Anael is the Archangel most invoked for gradual growth, whether love, health or money.

Picture Anael, like Gabriel, with a more female focus, surrounded by rose and green light, with silver wings and delicate features with his hands full of flowers, especially roses.

Anael is patron of alternative healers, gardeners and horticulturists, all partnerships, carpenters, day care centre and preschool workers, textile workers, mineralogists, counsellors, night workers, call centre staff, pharmacists, dancers, glaziers, florists and social workers.

Day of the week: Friday

Element: Water

Planet: Venus

Colour: Rose pink, light green

Incenses: Hibiscus, apple blossom, cherry, rose, strawberry, valerian

Crystals: Green jasper, rose quartz, pink calcite, green fluorite, chrysoprase

Metal: Copper

Personally, invoke Anael for beauty, radiance and charisma, love, marriage, the arts, music, the environment, for matters concerning children, pets and animals, for all matters of reconciliation, the joining together of families in remarriage, as well as in marriage and having children, for fidelity, friendship, for the gradual growth of all things, including health and love, for gardens and herb skills, and to develop a spiritual career in the psychic arts or alternative medicine.

Globally, call Anael for reforestation, for protection of the ozone layer, the preservation of mineral resources and for protecting animals in the wild, for local wildlife, encouraging wildlife preserves and breeding programmes, for kindness to animals and birds, bringing nature into cities and for peace in our times, especially between traditionally rival nations or groups within those nations.

Cassiel

Cassiel is called the Archangel of tears and solitude who weeps for the sorrows of the world and also helps to heal them. Some have linked him to the primal darkness before creation. He is Archangel of the mind and of memory and of the expansion of traditions, ancient wisdom and spiritual knowledge and of great thinkers, also the Archangel of balance who unifies all things, darkness and light, sorrow and joy, night and day. Cassiel is the Archangel ruling over games of chance and good luck.

Picture him as bearded, riding a dragon (Cassiel loves dragons and dragon power), wearing dark robes with indigo flames sparking from his halo.

Cassiel is a patron of estate agents and mortgage brokers, university professors, investors, stock brokers, architects, inventors, geniuses and of gamblers, also those who work with old people and the disabled.

Day of the week: Saturday

Element: Earth

Planet: Saturn

Colour: Indigo/black

Incenses: Cypress, patchouli, mimosa, violet

Crystals: Black onyx, brown jasper, jet, snowflake obsidian, black tourmaline, green aventurine

Metal: Lead, pewter

Personally, invoke Cassiel for patience, for help with all slow-moving matters and for practical or financial worries that can distract you from the path of spirituality, for matters concerning older people, your living arrangements and any house renovations, for healing or alleviating chronic illnesses and overwhelming sorrow or grief, for inheritance, debt worries or problems with officialdom, also for the restoration of good luck.

Globally, call upon Cassiel for the conservation and restoration of ancient sites and beautiful buildings, for preserving traditional values and wisdom, for the restoration of the knowledge and homelands of indigenous peoples, for compassionate farming methods and for the preservation of manufacturing industries and the preservation and creation of farming resources at home and also in underdeveloped countries.

Archangel rites

You may decide to carry out a monthly Archangel ritual on his day or when there is a need. You may relate to one of the Archangels or perhaps one seems appropriate as a coven guardian. However, mainly Archangel rituals tend to be personal. Try working with the different Archangels, those eight listed above and others you may encounter in the course of your reading or online explorations.

* Choose the Archangel whose wisdom you seek.

* In the evening or early morning, both good Archangel times, light the appropriate candle colour and incense (or a fragrance oil if you prefer).

* Hold one of the Archangel crystals or a clear crystal sphere between your hands.

* Welcome the angelic presence and do not always make a petition or request. Instead occasionally use the ritual to reflect on the qualities of the Archangel and how they are or could be manifest in your life to help others or the planet.

* You can also create in advance a series of different Archangel blessings that you recite from your Book of Shadows. These summarise the strengths of the particular Archangel and list how these qualities bless yourself/others/globally (see the practical assignment, page 591).

* If you wish, on the weekday of the Archangel you could copy out the blessing on a scroll of paper during the ritual, tie it with the ribbon colour of the Archangel and keep it on your altar for six more days.

* On the eighth day, the next day of the Archangel, re-read the blessing as part of the ritual and afterwards put it away until next time. You would not need to rewrite it unless you wished.

- Some people rotate the Archangel blessings over a seven-week cycle (Uriel and Samael alternate to keep the seven).

- End the ritual by asking aloud for healing for those in need from the particular Archangel and blow out the Archangel candle to send the light where needed.

- Alternatively, begin your ritual by asking aloud as you light the candle for the blessing you seek addressing the Archangel as *Wise Sachiel or Gentle Anael*, and if it is something you seek for yourself adding what you are willing to offer in return. Speak aloud softly, as though to a wise father or mother.

- Leave the timescale of the answer to the Archangel: *When it is right to be* or *Even in the manner and time of your choosing*. Trust is a major component in Angel magick.

- In addition to speaking aloud, you can write a letter to your chosen Archangel, using cream paper and green ink. You may like to use the Theban or Malachim alphabet or if you prefer an Angel script such as the Enochian or Celestial you have downloaded from the Internet.

- Write your name, the person, animal or place the blessing is for and that of the Archangel in the magickal script, or if you prefer use your normal handwriting for the whole letter. How little or how much you use the scripts is your choice. The letter writing can be a central part of the rite and you can light additional candles to give you sufficient illumination to write by.

- Write freely and if you are writing a personal concern, then perhaps you can incorporate a more global aspect. For example, you might if writing about your need for abundance to Sachiel, mentioning that you know that your current need is not on the same scale as a family in another part of the world who has no food but right now this is a pressing problem for you. Say how you can help by participating in an event to help hungry children abroad that is being organised at work (maybe you had thought you would not bother).

- Alternatively, you could focus a letter to Samael concerning a peaceful resolution to, for example, the aftermath of the war in Iraq and say that you too are experiencing family disruption and would welcome an end to conflict in your home in the manner and timescale most appropriate, as this is making an elderly relative ill with worry.

- When you have finished writing, seal the letter with wax in an unmarked envelope and set it beneath the crystal.

- Blow into the candle flame three times and ask for healing for any who need it, regardless of which Archangel you are invoking and send peace to someone who has hurt or offended you.

- Blow out the candle but leave the incense to burn and end by naming the Archangel three times, saying:

  So am I blessed and healed by your presence and your wisdom. I thank you and I end this rite with blessings and in joy. Blessed be.

- Leave the letter beneath the crystal overnight or through the day until sunset if you began at or near dawn.

* Sometimes, too, if you keep paper and pen ready you may be moved to write words from the Archangel as response or hear a still deep voice like music in your head. However, often the answers will follow in your daily world.

* Expect little and you may be very pleased with the swift positive response in your life. Keep the letters tied with green or white ribbon in a box. You can store them in a special place when the box is full. You can substitute clear quartz and amethysts for any Archangel crystals and frankincense or sandalwood for any Archangel incense. Pure white or beeswax candles can be used for any Archangel.

Your birth Guardian Angels and their zodiacal correspondences

Each sun sign period has its own Guardian Angel who can be used personally as your special Angel to empower your rituals any time of the year. You can also invoke the appropriate zodiac Angel and use his candles, incense etc when you are empowering a zodiacal charm or when you are carrying out, for example, a moon in Aries spell (see below).

In addition a zodiacal Angel will, if invoked in the chant, empower spells during his zodiacal period or whenever you would call on a particular zodiacal strength in a spell or ritual. For example, if you were carrying out a spell using two zodiacal glyphs engraved on candles for two people in a love spell, you could call on their ruling zodiacal Angels.

Each of the angels also rules over a month and again you can use them to strengthen your spells that are themed around the strengths of the individual month (see the list of magickal timings on page 197). You can also use them as spell guardians and bring in their names, candle colours etc for any spells you carry out during the month they rule. Each day also has its own Angel. Each individual Angel also has qualities you can invoke in magick or meditation during your birth month or period or any time you need his qualities that are intrinsic to your personality strengthened.

I have given only a brief description of the angels as so much less is known, so you can see them in your own way.

♈ Aries, the Ram (21 March–20 April)

Ruling Angel: Machidiel (or Malahidael), the Innovator, Angel of March. He rises with the spring and brings love, new beginnings and new hopes as the new growth appears in plants and wildlife. Picture him with sparkling golden red halo and wings

Keyword: Optimism

Message: Believe in yourself and be confident for all shall be well

Colour: Red

Crystals: Carnelian, diamond or Herkimer diamond.

Incenses: Cedar or dragon's blood

Planet: Mars

Element: Fire

♉ Taurus, the Bull (21 April–21 May)

Ruling Angel: Asmodel, the creator of what is of worth, Angel of April. A high Cherubim angel, Asmodel is an Angel of beauty and beautiful places and artefacts, and encourages all to create beauty whether artistically in our homes and in the way we live our lives. Picture him or her surrounded by soft pink rays.

Keyword: Creativity

Message: Beauty, grace and harmony will surround your work and home life

Colour: Pink

Crystals: Rose quartz, emerald

Incenses: Rose, apple blossom

Planet: Venus

Element: Earth

♊ Gemini, the Heavenly Twins (22 May–21 June)

Ruling Angel: Ambriel or Ambiel the messenger is from the angelic order of Thrones where he is described as a Prince. He is Angel of May and he brings change and challenge, causing us to question our current direction and to seek new knowledge or skills we need to fulfil our destiny.

Keyword: Learning

Message: Be open to new ideas and you will make many friends on life's journey

Colours: Pale yellow, grey

Crystals: Citrine, sapphire

Incenses: Lavender, lemongrass

Planet: Mercury

Element: Air

♋ Cancer, the Crab (22 June–22 July)

Ruling Angel: Muriel the Healer, whose name means myrrh, is the Angel of June. Muriel is also one of the leading Dominion Angels, but nevertheless is concerned with nurturing the weak, protection of the home and healing those who are sick, in pain or distressed. Said to possess a magickal carpet on which sleepers travel to astral realms. Picture Muriel surrounded in silver moonbeams. Sometimes Muriel is given strong female energies.

Keyword: Gentleness

Message: I will bring you beautiful dreams and keep safe your home and family day and night

Colour: Silver

Crystals: Moonstone, pearl

Incenses: Lemon balm, jasmine

Planet: Moon

Element: Water

♌ Leo, the Lion (23 July–23 August)

Ruling Angel: Verchiel, sometimes called Zerachiel, the joy-bringer is the Angel of July. Another Dominions ruler, Verchiel is an Angel of the south, of the sun at its height and full power. Picture him in shimmering gold with a halo of sunbeams.

Keyword: Pleasure

Message: Enjoy today and do not fret about yesterday or tomorrow

Colour: Gold

Crystals: Clear crystal quartz, golden topaz

Incenses: Frankincense, orange

Planet: Sun

Element: Fire

♍ Virgo, the Maiden (24 August–22 September)

Ruling Angel: Hamaliel, the perfectionist, is the Angel of August and is a leading Angel in the order of Virtues. Not the easiest of Angels, Hamaliel, an energetic and practical Angel, expects us to put our affairs in order, to sort urgent paperwork and to clear up any backlogs of essential tasks. This is based on the traditional need to get in the early ripe grain harvest using the long sunny days so we are ready for the winter. Picture Hamaliel surrounded by misty forest green.

Keyword: Perseverance

Message: Together we can bring order to chaos and sort out any muddle or uncertainty

Colour: Green

Crystals: Jade, opal

Incenses: Patchouli, thyme

Planet: Mercury

Element: Earth

♎ Libra, the Scales (23 September–23 October)

Ruling Angel: Zuriel, the teacher and Angel of justice, is the Angel of September and a high Angel in the order of Principalities. He is mainly known as the Angel who prevents humans doing impulsive stupid things or overreacting. Zuriel encourages calm, reasoned thought and compromise. Picture Zuriel with shimmering, pale blue wings and halo.

Keyword: Idealism

Message: I will protect you against unfair treatment and you will get your reward for what you do now that seems not appreciated

Colour: Light blue

Crystals: Lapis lazuli, blue topaz

Incenses: Lemon verbena, vanilla

Planet: Venus

Element: Air

♏ Scorpio, the Scorpion (24 October–22 November)

Ruling Angel: Bariel or Baruel, the wise one and Angel of small daily miracles, is the Angel of October. He is a member of both the Virtues and the Archangels. He knows about the past and frees us from repeating the same mistakes, so we can learn from our personal and family history. Picture Bariel in the colours of sunset.

Keyword: Understanding

Message: Miracles do happen and unexpected help will come to you to resolve a long-standing worry

Colour: Burgundy

Crystals: Aquamarine, aqua aura

Incenses: Pine, mint

Planet: Pluto

Element: Water

♐ Sagittarius, the Archer (23 November–21 December)

Ruling Angel: Adnachiel or Advachiel, the voyager, is the Angel of November He is ruler of the Choir of Angels. He assists in any mental discovery, whether taking courses, examinations or learning a new hobby, as well as actual voyages, both holidays and relocation or house moves. He guards us as we travel on journeys long and short. Picture him with yellow robes and a globe of the world in his hand.

Keyword: Curiosity

Message: Follow me to the world that is waiting just over the horizon

Colour: Bright yellow

Crystals: Ruby, turquoise

Incenses: Sage, sandalwood

Planet: Jupiter

Element: Fire

♑ Capricorn, the Goat (22 December–20 January)

Ruling Angel: Anael or Hanael, the protector, is the Angel of December. He is chief of the choir of Principalities and Virtues. We met him in his role of Archangel of Friday, marriage, children and reconciliation, but here he advocates rest and withdrawing from the frantic outer world to an inner stillness. He helps us to wait and to plan so that we will recognise the right moment to move forward in our lives. Anael sometimes has a strong female focus. Picture him (or her) as an Angel of roses with pink and green rays all round.

Keyword: Caution

Message: We are all worthy of love and I will bring and keep love in your life forever

Colour: Indigo, brown

Crystals: Garnet, tiger's eye, titanium aura

Incenses: Hyacinth, myrrh, cedar

Planet: Saturn

Element: Earth

≈≈ Aquarius, the Water Carrier (21 January–18 February)

Ruling Angel: Cambiel, the watcher, is the Angel of January and Archangel of the night who nevertheless has an awareness of all the possibilities in the days ahead. He encourages us towards independence from the need for the approval of others and to develop original ideas and enjoy our uniqueness. Picture Cambiel still and silent with a halo of stars and midnight blue robes.

Keyword: Inventiveness

Message: Being alone is not the same as being lonely so treasure solitary moments

Colours: Dark blue

Crystals: Amethyst, blue lace agate, any zircon

Incenses: Lemon, rosemary

Planet: Uranus

Element: Air

ⓧ Pisces, the Fish (19 February–20 March)

Ruling Angel: Barakiel or Barchiel, the bringer of fortune, whose name means lightning of God, is the Angel of February. He is an Archangel and one of the ruling Seraphim. He is traditionally invoked by those needing good luck and says that what we regret most are the things we never tried. He promises that the love and trust we freely offer others will be returned three times from many sources. Barakiel is also the Angel of hail and the storm, so picture him in dark robes and with dark wings that momentarily blaze as lightning flashes shoot from his halo.

Keyword: Opportunity

Message: Follow your dreams even if others laugh at them for you can make them come true

Colour: White, mauve

Crystals: Coral, fluorite

Incenses: Honeysuckle, sweetgrass, lotus

Planet: Neptune

Element: Water

Archangel hours

Each hour of the day and night has its own Archangel. These hours, as well as the relevant day of the week, offer you the concentrated energies of the ruling Archangel for rituals or for contemplation or prayer. Use the Archangel hours in exactly the same way magickally as you do the planetary hours (see page 192).

Archangel hours have a wider focus than planetary energies, concentrating more on the needs of others and more global and spiritual concerns. However, you can also incorporate them into your life both in magickal ritual and in your everyday world to answer personal needs, especially spiritually focused ones and in spells for others you know. You can work with the associated fragrances, either as incense, oils or smudge. You can also focus on their specific crystal and, holding it, connect with their powers.

Archangels are also remarkably useful in your daily life. If you have an important phone call to make or a decision to make during the day at home or work, you could use the hour of the Archangel who would best further your cause. You might choose them rather than the planetary hour if the matter was of deep significance to you or involved moral choices. Equally, at night you could choose the appropriate hour to focus on particular powers you need for the coming day or perhaps to ease pain or worry that will otherwise keep you awake.

You can calculate Archangel hours in precisely the same way you did for the planets and may like to reread this now. The Archangel rules the first hour after dawn of his own day so Michael will always rule Hour I after sunrise on a Sunday, as does the Sun, Michael's planet.

Sunrise to sunset

Hour	Sunday	Monday	Tuesday	Wednesday	Thursday	Friday	Saturday
I	Michael	Gabriel	Samael	Raphael	Sachiel	Anael	Cassiel
2	Anael	Cassiel	Michael	Gabriel	Samael	Raphael	Sachiel
3	Raphael	Sachiel	Anael	Cassiel	Michael	Gabriel	Samael
4	Gabriel	Samael	Raphael	Sachiel	Anael	Cassiel	Michael
5	Cassiel	Michael	Gabriel	Samael	Raphael	Sachiel	Anael
6	Sachiel	Anael	Cassiel	Michael	Gabriel	Samael	Raphael
7	Samael	Raphael	Sachiel	Anael	Cassiel	Michael	Gabriel
8	Michael	Gabriel	Samael	Raphael	Sachiel	Anael	Cassiel
9	Anael	Cassiel	Michael	Gabriel	Samael	Raphael	Sachiel
10	Raphael	Sachiel	Anael	Cassiel	Michael	Gabriel	Samael
11	Gabriel	Samael	Raphael	Sachiel	Anael	Cassiel	Michael
12	Cassiel	Michael	Gabriel	Samael	Raphael	Sachiel	Anael

Sunset to sunrise

Hour	Sunday	Monday	Tuesday	Wednesday	Thursday	Friday	Saturday
I	Sachiel	Anael	Cassiel	Michael	Gabriel	Samael	Raphael
2	Samael	Raphael	Sachiel	Anael	Cassiel	Michael	Gabriel
3	Michael	Gabriel	Samael	Raphael	Sachiel	Anael	Cassiel
4	Anael	Cassiel	Michael	Gabriel	Samael	Raphael	Sachiel
5	Raphael	Sachiel	Anael	Cassiel	Michael	Gabriel	Samael
6	Gabriel	Samael	Raphael	Sachiel	Anael	Cassiel	Michael
7	Cassiel	Michael	Gabriel	Samael	Raphael	Sachiel	Anael
8	Sachiel	Anael	Cassiel	Michael	Gabriel	Samael	Raphael
9	Samael	Raphael	Sachiel	Anael	Cassiel	Michael	Gabriel
10	Michael	Gabriel	Samael	Raphael	Sachiel	Anael	Cassiel
11	Anael	Cassiel	Michael	Gabriel	Samael	Raphael	Sachiel
12	Raphael	Sachiel	Anael	Cassiel	Michael	Gabriel	Samael

Using magickal hours for Archangel rituals

When you are using angelic hours and days in a ritual, you can mix and match your needs by using more than one Archangel energy on the same day or in the same ritual. For helping a woman who is having a difficult pregnancy you would carry out the ritual on Monday, Gabriel's day, in the first hour after dawn and again on Raphael's hour, the second after sunset. Alternatively, you could use Gabriel's hours for both but empower Raphael's crystal citrine to send to the woman afterwards.

If you invoked just one Archangel you would carry out a prayer or simple rite on his day at his sunrise or sunset period or both on that day and night. You could repeat the ritual weekly on his day on the special hours for extra energy and to keep up the flow of power through your life. You can carry out your rituals indoors or outdoors if it is a fine day.

PRACTICAL ASSIGNMENT

Angel blessings

Angel blessings are a good way of getting to understand on a deep level the different Archangel powers and how they enrich your life, that of loved ones and the world generally. They follow the same purpose as the Charge of the Goddess but are more personalised and focus on a single Archangel. You need one for each Archangel and can also write them for other Archangels you encounter in your reading or online. You can write them as part of a ritual or at a special time using the candle colour and incense of the chosen Archangel. Record them in your Book of Shadows.

As well as the ways I suggested, you can read aloud the blessing at the beginning or end of a ritual or, indeed, recite it as an empowerment whenever you need to call on the strength of the Angel but cannot carry out a ritual. It need only be short and as you work more with individual Archangels you may rewrite it.

You can also give blessings to friends or loved ones on occasions such as a wedding (Anael) or a new job (Sachiel), or use the zodiac Angels to create birthday blessings. For a birthday send the Angel crystal, flowers in the zodiac angel's colour or a special candle as a birthday gift with the blessing written on a scroll tied with ribbon in the Angel or Archangel colour.

Further research

There are nine Choirs of hierarchies of Angels. Divided into threes, I have given you a basic outline below of the role of each as I have mentioned them in the zodiacal Angels. Use the Internet and books to find out more about the nine Choirs and why they were divided in this way.

The Highest Order or Choir of Angels

The Seraphim

They have been described as concerned with the harmony or vibrations of the universe and regulate its movements.

They have six wings and four faces so they can see in all directions and carry flaming swords. They have been called the Angels of pure love, light and fire and ensure that divine love is transmitted through the different levels so that eventually it reaches human, animals and plants.

Their light is so brilliant that apart from divinity only the supreme Archangel Michael can look upon them, and they stand guarding the veil that divides pure divinity from creation.

Below them are:

The Cherubim or Kerubim

They have been portrayed as the guardians of the fixed stars, the constellations and all the galaxies and as the warrior Angels. They keep the heavenly records about the lives of humans and are the Angels who transmit light and knowledge right through the universe to humans.

They have been described as dazzlingly radiant blue Angels, sometimes with four faces and wings; also as winged sphinxes or lions with four beautiful faces, many all-seeing eyes and wings, and they are linked to the four winds.

Below them are:

The Thrones

These Angels are the bringers of justice and oversee the planets (these also have individual Archangels, of course).

Thrones are concerned with overcoming human cruelty and oppression and they send healing energies towards persecuted nations or groups, who are unable to live, learn, work or worship freely.

They are called the charioteers or sometimes the chariots of divinity and have been described as brilliant spinning wheels of light with many eyes, so act as an energy source for spreading goodness and justice though the world.

The Second Order or Choir of Angels

The Dominions

Dominions are said to be the oldest of the Angels in terms of creation and are the leader Angels, carrying orbs and sceptres. They have been called priests/princes and form the control centre for the other ranks of Angels higher and lower. Dominions ensure things happen. They are also concerned with how spiritual principles operate through earthly authority and so have a hard job, since people, especially world leaders, won't always listen.

The Dominions perform major miracles.

The Virtues

The Virtues are gentler and associated with love, working miracles on earth, bringing patience, quiet strength and the practical application of world peace through the efforts of organisations and individuals.

They are responsible for the natural world and with bringing blessings and abundance to the material world. They rule the weather and the elemental energies of Earth, Air, Fire and Water, and regulate rain and sunshine for growth and also carry out the instructions of the Dominions.

We don't know much about their appearance except that they are often surrounded by mists or the colours of sunset and have starry crowns.

The Powers

Moving ever closer to the earthly realms, the Powers are the cosmic police force who not only deter wrongdoing, often with a timely warning, but also assist souls who are lost both in life and after death, by sending angelic help.

These are the Angels of birth and death who ensure our guardians are with us as we enter and leave the world and help those with any severe illness or disabilities to reach their potential (and support those who care for them).

You often see pictures of Angels of death and birth in green, gold or red robes and these are the Angels depicted in the brilliantly jewel colours of hosts of Angels in mediaeval paintings. They can also be warrior Angels resplendent in gold and red armour and shining swords.

The Third Order or Choir of Angels

The Principalities

They are concerned with the organisation of large collections of people in practical settings people have created to live or work in. They especially oversee the fair distribution of resources (another uphill task), discrimination issues and all teaching and learning situations, colleges, schools, universities; also alternative spirituality. They are also called the ministering Angels, a term sometimes applied to the Archangels and Guardian Angels, as well.

They look like ordinary Angels, but tend to be taller, more brilliant and with shimmering wings and haloes.

The Archangels

The Archangels are the most fascinating of all Angels and are multi-level.

On one hand, individual Archangels, such as Michael, work with the highest levels of Angels and often have elevated roles within the seven heavens. They also rule individual planets, seasons, directions, days of the week and hours of the day. They tend to be identified by individual robes and symbols. Archangels are the supreme messengers in many religions and ages.

The Angels

These are our very own Guardian Angels, but also Angels of healing and nature that live close to humans and can be easily contacted. They protect us and guide us throughout our lives. We see them in our own way, but always surrounded by light.

Further information

Recommended reading

* Davidson, Gustav, *A Dictionary of Angels*, Simon and Schuster, 1994
* Eason, Cassandra, *Touched by Angels*, Quantum/Foulsham, 2005
* Newcomb, Jacky, *A Treasury of Angels*, Element/Thorsons, 2004
* Parisen, Maria, *Angels and Mortals, the Co Creative Power*, Quest Books, 1994

Websites

* *Paranormality*
  Extensive site and links about paranormal, supernatural and unusual phenomena
  www.paranormality.com/archangel.shtml
* *Angelic Website*
  Excellent A-Z of Angels
  www.DanielKudra.com
* *Catholic Encyclopedia*
  Large range of pages on Angels and Archangels and Kabbalistic information
  www.newadvent.org/cathen
* *Crystalinks*
  Information on the nine choirs of Angels
  www.crystalinks.com/angels/html

MAGICK AND PSYCHIC DEVELOPMENT

In the modern world, magick has become separated from awareness of the psychic senses and divination, though they are three strands and expressions of the same power. As I have said before, the more skilled you become at magick the more your psychic powers spontaneously develop in everyday decision-making as well as in the ability to know instinctively the right herbs, crystals and moon times for a spell. So, too, practising witches find themselves becoming automatically more expert in divination, in receiving psychic messages and interpreting omens both from the natural world, such as the sound of the wind in leaves, and using different tools, whether tarot cards, runes or a magickal mirror.

However, the more you work on developing your psychic senses, the more effective your spellcasting and rituals become, and the more tuned in you are to the powers of the deities and to the essences of the natural world. What is more, at the end of every ritual or more formal spell after the release or direction of power, the excess magickal energy can be used to enhance private or collective divination to give meaningful and profound insights.

Scrying, perceiving images in a reflective surface, is the most common form of divination practised by witches, most frequently by using the reflective surface of water in a bowl, cauldron or natural water source illuminated by sun, moon or candle light. You can also work with tarot cards, runes, a pendulum or, my own favourite form of scrying, the crystal ball. Some witches use a dark mirror illuminated by candles or the metallic or clear glass Hathor mirror sacred to the Ancient Egyptian Goddess of women and joy. There is more about mirrors on page 615.

In the first part of this double module we will focus on psychic powers and how they can enhance magick.

Mind powers

In the module, What is magick? (see page 50), I described how psychic powers were intrinsic to the processes of magick. Magick is empowered and enriched by our innate psychic abilities, such as using psychokinesis or mind power to move wishes into actuality. When you call upon the elements at the four quarters or empower symbols or cast circles with their magickal substances, you can not only imagine the elemental power of the crashing sea, but also see it clairvoyantly as though you were by it, hearing its crashing waves clairaudiently as if you were on the sea shore and smell and taste the salt clairsentiently. This ability brings the elemental power to life and so our bowl of salt water or chalice of pure water imbibes the spell with sea or waterfall power though our psychic connections.

Psychokinesis

The term psychokinesis is derived from the Greek words *psyche* meaning breath, life or soul, and *kinein* meaning to move. Psychokinesis, the power of the mind to affect matter, is popularly associated with spoon-bending feats and with poltergeist activity, whereby a stressed person, especially a teenage girl, unconsciously causes plates or sometimes heavy objects to fly through the air. However, such occurrences are rare and psychokinesis is most usually and less dramatically manifest every time we select a tarot card from a face down shuffled pack to answer a question, or a pendulum gives a yes/no response or guides us to a place of positive earth energies for the centre of an outdoor circle. Our unconscious mind influences the selection of the card or movement of the pendulum in the way that gives the most appropriate symbol or answer, using the instrument of our hand.

In magick, the psychokinetic power of the mind draws to you mentally what you most want in attracting magick, holds inactive a harmful influence in binding magick, or sends or keeps away what you do not want in banishing magick. The spell or ritual structure and the symbol into which these psychokinetic powers are poured are amplified as you use the same mind power to absorb energy into the circle, symbol and yourself from the natural world, the earth and the skies and the elemental substances. In a coven, the collective energies use the same psychic channels and, whether in a solitary or group rite, the release of power externalises the increased and magickally charged psychokinetic energy to bring about the desired result in the daily world.

Psychokinesis also transmits the amplified spell energy into your aura so you attract to you opportunities – or send out a psychic barrier of defence against what you have banished in the spell. Through psychokinesis, too, we can connect to the well of the wisdom of all times and places and so can recall ancient wisdom and practices without knowing precisely how or from where the knowledge comes. Invariably, when you check it is accurate.

So, psychokinesis is probably the most important power in witchcraft and one you need to keep finely tuned by practising it in daily situations.

Developing psychokinesis

My favourite psychometric practice and that of a number of other witches is finding a parking space in a hurry. You should not use this when you don't need to, for example, if you just want to go into town window shopping, as psychokinesis works best where there is a real need. But if you have an urgent appointment or are running late collecting young children who will worry and there is a good reason why you did not allow extra time, visualise your car parking into a place as close to your destination as possible.

✻ Begin calling in your mind and visualising the vacant space about five minutes before you need it. This also acts as a way of reducing wasteful free floating panic.

✻ Make the experience as multi-sensation filled as possible. Though you may visualise a particular spot you know, you can add *or wherever will best serve this urgent purpose* (in case another witch has got to your spot first).

✻ Picture the leaves on the tree if there is one next to the chosen space or any distinguishing features and if it is spring smell the blossom on the tree. Hear in your mind the sound of the engine revving as you reverse in, the touch of your arm on the fabric of the car seat as you turn to check if it is clear, as well as the relief and satisfaction and finally yourself locking the car as you leave.

✻ Create an empowerment chant to recite as you make the picture clearer and clearer in your mind using clairvoyance (psychic seeing) as if you were turning the focus dial on a camera or binoculars.

✻ Since the psychokinetic process is two-way, you need to tune into your internal radar a minute or two before you turn towards your chosen spot and you may feel instinctively you should drive instead into another unfamiliar street. Say:

Show me where the right space is for [specify need] if so it is right to be.

✻ Trust your radar which may feel like a buzzing sensation in your ears and you may discover it has led you to a new even more convenient parking area that has just opened up or that normal restrictions have been lifted on a street on this particular afternoon, maybe because of road works elsewhere.

Remote viewing, a form of clairvoyance where you tune into somewhere beyond the physical eye range, is another name for this ability. If you are already an expert remote parker, set yourself harder tasks to draw to you something hard to find that you need: for example, a replacement for a broken cup in an unusual design from a well-loved family crockery set that is no longer made, a part for your favourite ancient coffee maker (I once found a new filter in a Spanish market).

With an ongoing need like a piece of crockery, recite the need every morning and visualise finding it. In your vision, you might even be able to locate a particular shop in a back street of a town you occasionally visit or a new stall at a weekly car boot sale you regularly attend.

If you are running late for work, ask for the means to get you there fast. It may be your usual hourly bus is running late or a colleague who has taken a diversion because of road works or dropping off a family member somewhere unusual, will pass your bus stop and see you. You may be prompted to walk down a particular street or to walk to the next bus stop – and there is your lift to work waiting.

When you are really competent, anticipate the tarot cards that you or someone you are reading for will pick out when answering a particular question. I use three packs of identical tarot cards to lengthen the odds of it being by chance.

Note your successes and devise ongoing exercises to attract what is needed and where it may be found.

Telepathy

The lift to work I mentioned probably brings in another power, mind to mind communication or telepathy. Telepathy is another central power in spellcasting and works in connecting with the mind of people or animals to send magickal strength, protection or healing via the spell or to draw a lover back to you. It is close to psychokinesis in many ways. The word telepathy comes from the Greek tele (distant) and pathe (occurrence or feeling).

This was the way the ancient hunters linked into the location of the herds, as well as calling them to the nearest hunting grounds. The telepathic powers were amplified through ritual and cave paintings portraying the successful hunt.

There are countless spontaneous examples of this mind-to-mind communication that can span oceans instantaneously. It usually occurs between close relatives and friends at a time when one of them is experiencing strong emotions, whether love or distress, and occurs very strongly between mother and child of any age. The telepathic communication may be seen in the mind as images, heard as words, sometimes a warning. It may be experienced as feelings of love, fear or a desire to find the person who has appeared suddenly in their mind that causes him or her to change their normal pattern of behaviour in response to the telepathic message. Sometimes the telepathic channels are spontaneously used to send psychokinetic energy as strength or protection to a loved one who is in danger.

Let's look at the old folk magick candle spell:

> 'Tis not these pins I seek to burn, but a lover's heart to turn.
> May he neither sleep nor rest till he has granted my request.

The candle representing the lover is lit and pins inserted in the wick. Now while pure psychokinesis might work and draw the lover to your door willingly or otherwise as the wick representing his/her heart is pierced, that is a bit dubious under the Wiccan Rede. Telepathy, on the other hand, will make the lover think of the abandoned or neglected partner and draw him to contact the spellcaster by the time the candle has burned past the pins and they have fallen out. But he or she will do so willingly as a result of feeling the telepathic love vibes amplified by the spell, a subtle but vital difference magickally.

My version of the candle and pins spell is based on telepathic connection:

> 'Tis not these pins I wish to burn
> But a willing heart to turn.
> As I softly speak your name,
> I call you love through candle flame.

Love spells, protective spells, healing spells and banishing or binding spells involve the connection between the mind of the spellcaster or the collective thoughts of a coven and the subject of the spell. Some love spells call a lover as yet unknown. The unknown lover may feel a surge of love coming their way and the message, Find me, and may even dream of the spellcaster sending out the love vibes to find the right target. The recipient may not even consciously be aware of the love call, but their movements often change as they are unconsciously guided to the place where the positive encounter will occur seemingly by chance. The spellcaster, too, may as a result of the spell be guided to the event at a particular time.

Usually there is a built-in protection in the recipient on a deep unconscious level that only if the call of love is the right one/at the right time will he or she respond. The spell energies or chant, in the case of the candle spell, increase the innate telepathic powers. Telepathy also enables us to align our minds with different deity qualities, whether we draw these into ourselves and speak as though we were the deity or calling upon the protection and power from beyond us: for example, the Archangels to guard the four quarters of a circle.

Developing your telepathic powers

It is quite easy to practise strengthening telepathic links with loved ones, coven members and friends, although ironically with the increased use of mobile phones the art is declining even in the witchcraft community. At most pagan festivals, mobile phones are jangling away even in spite of signs asking for them to be switched off.

* Begin a section in your Book of Shadows for spontaneous telepathic experiences and note incidents for several weeks or months, seeing if there is a pattern both with certain people and times when you are especially receptive. Note what you were doing and your mood before and after the experience.

* If you have young children or can borrow friends and relations' offspring, ask them a question silently or ask them to fetch something for you without speaking, and note if and under what circumstances they respond.

* If you have a pet, ask a friend to pet-sit for you and change your normal time of coming home after work or from an outing. Animals invariably sit by the door or on an outside wall five minutes before you return. At a pre-arranged time, when someone can monitor the animal while you are away from home, start to talk in your mind to your pet and mentally stroke it, asking the sitter to note any unusual reaction.

* With a co-operative partner, spouse, parent, coven member or best friend, focus on the person at a time of day when you do not normally have contact. Do not warn them in advance of your intention. Mentally send a message of love or ask for a piece of information and ask him or her to phone or e-mail you as soon as possible. If this does not work first time, don't give up. It may be the other person was preoccupied. Repeat the question and mentally turn up the volume of your thoughts.

* When you are together and quiet mentally ask a question or ask the person to make you a drink, again at an unusual time and if you do not get a response, persist at five minute intervals, turning up the psychic volume of your inner voice.

* If you want a person to get in touch, you may find that using the photograph of a person or holding one of their possessions (psychometry making an appearance: see below) will open telepathic channels.

* Play drawing games within the coven where one person leaves the group, draws an object, turns the drawing over so it cannot be seen, returns to the group, visualises the drawing and the others try and draw it.

Psychometry

Psychometry, the art of psychic touch, is linked to both psychokinesis and clairsentience or psychic sensing that I will describe later (see page 607). This psychic touch operates through the sensitive chakras in the palms of the hands and fingertips and feet that respectively link with the Heart and Root chakras (see page 179 for a reminder of these).

One aspect of psychometry involves the ability to detect information about people, places and events, past or present, by holding an artefact, connected with that person or place (and so is a key power in divination). It also acts as a transmitter of our personal psychic energies. These energies pass through psychic touch into the spell symbol and any artefacts we use, for example, the bowl of salt or the athame in an ongoing, two-way process of mutual empowerment and enrichment. What is more, psychometric energies activate contact with the energy fields of tools, magickal substances and the spell symbol, just as electricity can leap between two poles.

What we are doing is transmitting the essential energies from the aura or energy field: for example, of the salt as we sprinkle it around a symbol, from the Air as we raise the athame, from Fire as we move the symbol close to the flame of the candle, and so on. This energy is amplified by our own inner powers as we draw upwards energy from the Earth as we stamp or walk round the circle.

Think of yourself as receiver, transmitter and power transformation house of the different spell energies and, if you are working with others, through the touch their hands in a circle or spiral dance and the energies from their athames etc. Natural sources of energy, such as flowers, herbs and crystals, have strong psychometric energies that can be released as you touch them, breathe in the light or chant over them and so permeate the spell space with their powers. No wonder we can so easily produce a cone of rainbow stars through the psychometric interchange within a magick circle.

Developing psychometric powers

Magickally, the best way to develop your psychometric power is by tuning into artefacts or buildings that are very old and so have a lot of stored information. As a bonus, psychometry with such objects and places may trigger off your own past life recall.

Make hand contact with a very old wall, at a castle or ruined abbey, cupping both hands round any artefacts you are allowed to hold, resting against old chimney breasts where people sat and talked over the centuries. Haunted buildings hold a lot of concentrated energy from former residents and you may connect with the actual spirit or more usually the impression or imprint they have left on the aura of the place.

Sit in pews or the choir stalls in old churches or cathedrals, in reconstructed rooms in industrial museums whose furniture and artefacts are typical of the period if not the exact ones from the original building. Run your hands along the wood, press your feet against old tiled or wooden floors and sink into a deep sofa or press your spine against the leather of a stagecoach seat to make a connection.

Go to museums where there is a hands-on policy and handle pottery from different periods. One of the best museums I have visited is the Museum de Cluny on the Left Bank of Paris, built on the site of an ancient abbey and Roman baths where you can touch stone columns from Celtic times, Roman statues and mediaeval Black Madonnas, though more delicate artefacts are behind glass.

In each case close your eyes and, if possible, touching or cradling the artefact in both hands, begin to breathe very gently and slowly in and out through your nose, feeling your own boundaries melting and those of the artefact or building expanding so that you merge temporarily and enter the aura of the place or artefact. Information may be channelled as impressions, emotions, and physical sensations or through sounds and images. Then slowly push away from the source and as you concentrate again on slow gentle breathing, become aware of your own boundaries re-establishing.

As you become more experienced you may not even need to make physical connection but using the leaping electricity principle merge the aura round your fingers with that of an artefact as you extend your palms facing outwards towards them and your fingers curved slightly inwards. Once you are sensitised, you can imprint your psychometric impressions on places as well as artefacts, so some day people will see you there.

Visit places of beauty or personal significance. Press hard with your feet downwards and then if possible sit so your perineum is on the ground and your hands touching the grass or rocks. Look at the view or building intently and focus on every detail, every sound and every fragrance. Deliberately induce a mood of peace or happiness and now with your hands push the air all round you. You are imprinting your power and presence in aether of the place. Then practise pressing with your fingers into crystals and symbols in personal spells, imprinting them with your positive feelings and strong desires that will be manifest through the spell.

If working with others or as a coven exercise, you can play games where everyone puts a flower they have deliberately imprinted with their energies into a central container. In turn each flower is passed round and people comment on the feelings and information they receive as they hold the flower. Use different flowers so they can be identified by their owners. The owner focuses on their own flower when it is passed to them and comments as if she was unfamiliar with it. It may reveal deep buried feelings she did not know she still had, as well as future potentials.

Clairvoyance

Clairvoyance or clear-seeing is sometimes called second sight and like intuition is believed by some researchers to reside in the Third Eye, seat of the Brow chakra, the psychic energy centre most associated with all forms of spiritual and psychic functioning.

Clairvoyance that you used when finding a parking place is central to spellcasting. It enables you to go beyond just visualising the elemental guardians and focal deities, the elemental places, the coloured cone of light that is raised and released, but to empower them with life through your psychic vision so powerfully that they are manifest and others may see them. This is the power that enables you to see into the past and the future possibilities, the paths you could choose to walk In a group, you can sit around a central fire or huge candle in darkness and create a joint vision, perhaps of past world, a mystical temple or a world across the universe.

Often in magick we are drawn to people from our soul family with whom we may have shared past lives. Even if you do not sense this, you can within the coven focus on the same vision of a past or an alternative dimension world perhaps across the galaxy, reached via the flame in the centre of the circle.

An experienced witch can help the others by raising the power into her Third Eye/Brow chakra but even relative beginners will be able to tap into this collective glimpse of a world that can be accessed around the flickering flame where dimensions are very thin. However, the best way to develop your clairvoyance is by practising divination either for yourself or others (see page 603).

Clairaudience

Clairaudience is primarily the ability to hear words or sounds that are not part of the material world, which may be wisdom channelled from wise guides, nature essences or Angels. When we channel the Goddess/God, the Sun God and the Moon Goddesses through our Charges, we are speaking clairaudiently the words of the Goddess/God transmitted through our vocal cords (almost a form of mediumship). This is one of the most potent ways of evoking or calling from within us and kindling our own inner Goddess/God divine spark, as we at the same time invoke or call down the God/Goddess power from above.

Every time we say *I am*... and use our magickal names or that of a deity we are tuning into, the generative power of sound that is central to clairaudience and all we can say is the words were given to us. The prophecy we may display after calling down the Moon Goddess is transmitted into our minds and others may comment that our voice changes. Many witch healers are aware that the healing voice they use as opposed to their daily tones is certainly inspired from a higher source as well as from within. The wisdom we receive from divination after any spell or ritual comes as much in words as images and may sometimes be phrases or verses from sacred works or great poetry drawn from a timeless source.

Experienced witches say that on occasions as they carry out a spell rehearsed in advance suddenly the words are not the planned ones, not even theirs and only afterwards do they realise they had dropped the paper on which the preconceived ceremony was written – and yet spoke for half an hour without hesitation.

Many of the lovely words created by great witches such as Doreen Valiente are truly clairaudient whether we read or memorise them. Even if we work alone, just as we can hear our chants and spell words echoed by the elemental guardians, the nature essences, our Witch Guardian, our wise ancestors and the deities or Angels we invite into the circle, so, too, we can use the psychic sounds of ritual to transmit our spell purpose into higher realms.

The physical sounds of spellcasting or ceremony, whether chanting, drumming or dancing in a repetitive magickal way, create an altered state of consciousness in the spellcaster that is akin to the Shamanic trance. As the sound intensifies as the power is raised, so it moves beyond the physical and creates the vibrations to convey the spell intent to higher levels. Here it is transformed and returned to fulfil its purpose. The final call of power breaks the psychic sound barrier.

Developing your psychic ear and voice

Because the modern world is so noisy and discordant, clairaudience is a power that is under utilised even in witchcraft. The following sounds can be used to expand psychic awareness and you can work alone or make it a coven exercise, perhaps on a day out.

* Gregorian chants. These are still used in monasteries but have entered the wider spiritual field as a conscious-raising tool. Gregorian chants are a single-line melody, known also as plainchant or plainsong. However, choral music, preferably heard in a high-vaulted cathedral, works as well.

* Bird song, if possible in natural surroundings, both in the day and as they swirl round before nesting for the night. The call of seagulls can be especially evocative.

* Water from a river running over stones, especially a fast-flowing water course or a waterfall.

* The sea in all its moods.

* Wind rustling through leaves in a forest or grove.

* Children playing.

* The calls of animals and birds in the countryside or at an animal conservation park. Camp in or near a forest at night to hear the night calls.

* The sound of a storm or heavy rain on a roof.

* Markets with street vendors and fairgrounds. The latter should not be the modern kind with loud music, but with the old steam organs and carousels that are enjoying a revival.

* Church or temple bells.

* Ship and tug hooters at a port and vendors selling fish on the beach.

Find your source of sound and sitting in a comfortable place where you will not be disturbed, close your eyes and focus on that particular sound. Allow others to gradually fade as though you were tuning in a radio to a specific frequency. The sounds may trigger images, fragrances, tastes, impressions or whole scenes of other times and places when birds sang, bells called people to church for a wedding or a Sunday service.

You will find that the scenes you experience during these psychic exercises do have particular significance for you and will recur both in the everyday world, often in unexpected contexts, as core symbols in dreams, scrying and as you explore other dimensions. Keep a note of experiences in your Book of Shadows.

Divination with the voices of the natural world

Other societies, for example, the Native North American and Australian Aboriginal peoples, have long known that the natural world has many voices, carrying wisdom on the wind, the flowing rivers and in the call of the birds and animals. Indeed, wise animals and birds, often identified as the clan or species father or mother, will impart wisdom and sometimes healing powers at times when individuals withdraw into solitude for a period.

* Begin by standing in a circle of trees when it is windy, whether in your garden, a park or a forest and allow your mind to become attuned to the rhythm of the rustle, followed by a lull.

* When you are ready, ask a question in your mind or recall an area of your life in which there is uncertainty.

* Listen to the leaves and the wind as they intermingle as though a person was speaking to you. The message is sometimes in verse or in a single phrase, followed by a lull.

* Scribble down any words, images or impressions that came into your mind.

* Do not ask any more questions, but if you sit quietly you may gain other words or impressions.

* In the evening sit quietly by candlelight and as you transfer the material to your journal recreate in your mind the actual sounds and insight will come.

* You can also work with fast-flowing water over pebbles. If necessary you can create your own source using a hose and a bucket of pebbles. Church bells especially when playing different parts of a tune, a choir singing in Latin or another language you do not know, can also channel wisdom. In this case, do not ask a specific question and, if possible, record the music or work from a CD so you listen first and then can write down any impressions afterwards. Bird song, too, holds many messages and the dawn chorus or the last calls at night are very evocative.

Clairsentience

Clairsentience, psychic sensing or instinctive awareness is, like its sister intuition, a power that many people already possess, although again they may not trust it. It is our psychic antennae or radar that is finely tuned into both our own and the universal energy field and so may be our wisest guide both personally and in magick. You may go into an unfamiliar house or ancient site and know instantly something bad happened there and if you carry out research you will usually discover you were right.

In the everyday world, this knowing, based on what you feel, whether jaggedness, as someone smiling but potentially malicious collides with your aura, or a sense of harmony and trust, even with a perfect stranger, can guide you through a social or business minefield and bring you safely to the other side. In witchcraft this sense, so difficult to describe, is very valuable, enabling you to take many shortcuts by tuning into prevailing energies or being able to know instinctively whether a site is right for a ritual, whether you should leave candles burning at the end of the ritual, whether someone is sending negativity towards you or the coven or if it is just free-floating anxiety, whether to ask a friend or coven member if they need help or just to wait quietly by until asked. Even without a pendulum or your herb book, you suddenly know that on this occasion thyme would work better for the ceremony, even though rose petals are the suggested fragrance.

Clairsentience is the fine-tuning of all the other senses and can call upon them all. It is the perfect antidote to the modern tendency to do everything, even witchcraft, by the book (and I say that as an author). What feels right is the key and often an instinctively led spell or ritual will tune into the prevailing energies of the time and place, the current energies of the spellcaster/s and maybe the unvoiced real need of the person for who the spell is being cast or who needs healing.

As we rush round making sure the tools are in the right place, the moon is where it should be in a zodiac sign and we know all the elemental chants and the coven Maiden has her crown of 13 primroses, stop and ask yourself: *Does this feel right?* If so, go with it or if not discard the lot or the part that feels wrong and trust your psychic radar. A clairsentient witch instinctively knows the right words for the occasion and the right actions and setting. This creates a quiet confidence and serenity that enables solitary practitioners and coven members to practise the kind of witchcraft that is right and unique to them.

Working with fragrances

Of all the aspects of psychic sensing, fragrance seems to offer the easiest route to developing clairsentient powers. Certain fragrances, usually those that open psychic pathways, possess a long tradition in different ages and cultures. They offer almost instant access to the collective folk memory in which they have strong roots. The result is that your psychic channels become sensitised to picking up information by this route, even in other contexts. Even if you are experienced psychically, you may find this method helpful. As a by-product, these fragrances usually trigger strong past life recall and also seem to help you to effortlessly blend beautiful incenses. You can work alone or in a group.

* Buy a variety of herbs, fruits or flowers from the following list or visit a garden where they may be growing. If they do not grow in your region, substitute fragrant or strong smelling ones that are indigenous to the region. Alternatively, burn them as fragrant candles, incenses or in separate small oil burners. Initially, choose three or four from the following and if your sensory palate gets overloaded sniff a single coffee bean in between fragrances:

Basil	Lemon verbena
Bay leaves	Lilac
Eau de cologne mint	Mimosa
Eucalyptus	Orange
Honeysuckle	Peppermint
Jasmine	Pine
Lavender	Rose
Lemon	Sage
Lemongrass	Thyme

- Hold or sniff each separately, closing your eyes and concentrating not so much on what you see and hear, but what you feel, peace, joy or sudden knowledge about a place or time where the fragrance had significance.

- Work next with other strong smells, spices such as cinnamon, garlic, ginger, baking bread, old-fashioned soap and furniture polish, oil, tar, wood smoke. Some of these you may find in natural settings and you may also discover that the lesser but valuable taste buds evoke feelings and sensations.

- Visit the ocean or a salt lake or marsh, close your eyes and taste the tang of the sea and note the strong emotions and sometimes scenes it evokes.

- As a group, pass the fragrances round and together build up a series of impressions and visions that will enhance all your fragrance work as well as tuning you into practical magick for any occasion.

PRACTICAL ASSIGNMENT

Developing psychic powers

Develop one form of psychic awareness that interests you and of which you know little.

Further research

Find out more about research into psychic powers and whether any of these studies might enhance the practice of witchcraft.

Further information

Recommended reading

- Eason, Cassandra, *A Complete Guide to Psychic Development*, Piatkus 2002, Crossing Press US, 2003
- Eason, Cassandra, *Psychic Party Games*, Piatkus, 2005
  A wide range of psychic games for festivals and covens.
- Lonegren, Sig, *Spiritual Dowsing*, Gothic Images, 1986
- Radin, Dean, *The Conscious Universe, the Scientific Truth of Psychic Phenomena*, New York, Harper Collins, 1997
- Sheldrake, Rupert, *Dogs that Know When Their Owners Are Coming Home and Other Unexplained Powers of Animals: An Investigation*, Crown Publishing, 1999

Websites

- *The Mystica*
  Good psychokinesis background and research
  www.themystica.com/mystica/articles/p/psychokinesis_pk.html
- *New Age Directory*
  Information on extra-sensory perception (ESP), including telepathy, downloadable tests and material for activities
  www.newagedirectory.com/esp/esp.htm

PSYCHIC DEVELOPMENT AND SCRYING

Divination means consulting the wise divus or diva, God or Goddess or divine energy source. This source can be the divus or diva within the witch, the wise evolved inner spirit or the divine spark that connects us with the universal well of wisdom and future potential.

However you can also invoke and draw wisdom through divination from the Goddess/God, your Witch Guardian, from wise ancestors spiritual and actual and from your Guardian Angel or after a ritual with your chosen Archangel. The inner and outer sources of divinity powers unite in the process of exploring through divination the potentials for the future that is imprinted on the aether. This is not fortune-telling, but exploring what is possible given the present life path influences conscious knowledge. However, it goes deeper to bring into consciousness those potentials and opportunities not yet accessible to the conscious mind, because it moves beyond measured clock time. Clock or measured time is an artificial though necessary form of dividing life into meaningful segments and co-ordinating with the timeframes of others, but time measurement has taken many forms throughout the ages and different cultures. A person talking on the telephone from the UK to Los Angeles is thinking of going home from work as the person in LA is arriving early at the office to start their day and the conversation takes place outside those timeframes in terms of personal connections.

Though many witches are expert tarot or rune readers, scrying, seeking wisdom using a reflective surface as a medium, has traditionally been the divinatory art most favoured by witches. Scrying which comes from the Old English for to descry or perceive dimly, can take many forms. At its most natural and simple, this is gazing into a lake or pool of water by full moonlight and rippling the surface with the branch of a moon tree like the willow. Scrying in cauldrons after a full moon ceremony follows this tradition. Scrying, especially using water, is almost universal. At its most elaborate, the crystal ball and the magick mirror have brought more organised systems of interpreting wisdom, but at root they follow the same techniques.

Scrying and magick

The insights of divination, whether by scrying or using a more conventional method, such as tarot or runes, emerge in the form of symbols or sometimes words or images in your mind. There may be a particular focal deity you relate to and call upon to bless your divinatory work. For the Vikings it was Freyja, who taught magick to the Gods, Mother Frigg, who saw all things from her chair in the stars, or Saga, the Goddess of wisdom. Isis is another popular deity from the Ancient Egyptian world or Hathor, mother of the magickal mirror.

If you work after spellcasting, your scrying will reveal how the spell purpose will develop and what you need to do to ensure its success. This can be very helpful after healing magick. You can then devise and cast future spells to hasten the opportunities revealed and to guide any people who appeared in the scrying bowl to find you by increasing the connection magickally. You may also learn more of your present, future and past worlds as you scry and can ask specific questions within this spiritually charged time and space.

You can bid farewell to the elemental guardians before you begin scrying, but leave the circle cast so you can sit within the still charged circle. Uncast the circle in a serene slow way at the end of your scrying. Alternatively, close the quarters afterwards if you are scrying after a major festival or for guidance on an important issue to draw on their wisdom. You can scry not only at the end of a ritual but any time you need answers or to clear away the pressures and irrelevancies of daily life.

* Prepare yourself by creating a magickal space and time, lighting one of the divinatory incenses, sage, thyme, rosemary, mugwort, frankincense, myrrh, sandalwood or rose and a candle.

* Cast a circle round yourself for private divination or make a blessing at the beginning and end.

* Pass your hands nine times over the bowl or cauldron filled with water or over the crystal ball or mirror. Ask that you may be protected and guided in the ways of truth, light and wisdom. You can call on a special deity or angel to help. Do this whether scrying alone or to answer the questions of another person.

For group work you can jointly answer a coven-related question or advise individual members on decisions by passing round the seated coven a scrying bowl, crystal sphere or a mini cauldron or gathering round a large central cauldron. If this is not part of a ritual or at the end of a spell, each person can light a candle in turn round the circle and ask that the work be blessed. Afterwards they would be extinguished in reverse order of lighting, with each person speaking a few words as part of a collective closing blessing. Each person names out loud an image they see. Speed is of the essence to keep the momentum going and to prevent the conscious mind intruding or reminding you that the process is illogical.

In a group you need one person to act as a scribe to record the images and afterwards read them out one by one so everyone can contribute to the meaning after the original perceiver has expanded on what she saw, heard and felt about the image. This is an excellent way of resolving sensitive coven issues and also of helping less experienced members of a group to channel, for example, Goddess wisdom after drawing down the Goddess.

If working alone you can work with an image at a time and so build up the answer step by step. A good time to scry is after your Year and a Day ceremony to discover your future path and tasks, especially if you use the water or a crystal sphere that was part of the ceremony.

Scrying into a crystal ball

This is the easiest form of scrying since the crystal sphere provides a tangible focus for the clairvoyant eye. Every witch should have a crystal ball as it can be used in so many ways: as a focus in abundance spells, charged for psychic protection, used in light ceremonies for amplifying and transforming sun, moon and candle light into healing rays to fill you with power or to be directed towards a person, animal or place as absent healing. It will radiate ongoing health, protection and abundance throughout your altar place that will permeate your entire home and transform negativity to light and will constantly renew its own energies. You can also connect with your spiritual guardians within a crystal sphere as its centre vibrates at a sufficiently high level for them to be perceived by the physical eye.

* Choose a sphere (clear crystal quartz is the best) with inclusions or cracks inside the ball that form rainbows and patterns. These are often the cheaper kind but are perfect for scrying.

* If you have the chance, buy your crystal ball personally from a crystal store where there is a large selection, rather than by mail order. You can obtain a good sized crystal for about £35 and you can get stunningly beautiful ones for under £100. Normally I am not in favour of buying expensive magick items, but with the crystal ball I would sooner find the right one and make economies elsewhere.

* Look inside a number of spheres and one will reveal images immediately and feel right when you hold it.

* A crystal ball will become uniquely yours the more the use it, though if you belong to a coven you may decide to have a large crystal sphere as one of your coven treasures.

Beginning crystal sphere scrying

* Spend time by sun, moon and candle light at the end of personal spells or whenever you have time to sit quietly with candles and incense or in bright natural light, identifying images in the cracks and patterns of the sphere. Gradually your inner or clairvoyant eye will take over from the physical eye without you realising it, because clairvoyance is in essence an extension of physical seeing.

* Hold the ball to the light in your cupped hands so that you are also making psychometric (psychic touch) connections.

* Note in your Book of Shadows symbol section what the different images you perceive suggest, in terms of what you feel about the image (clairsentience) words that come into your mind (clairaudience) and as you hold the ball what you see as well as the basic image (clairvoyance). Some scryers see the image as though it were alive or set in a context or wider scene that provides more information and an image may change.

* If there is a bird, what kind of bird? A nesting bird, a bird in flight coming to land or waiting, a huge winged eagle, a vulture or a song bird? Is the bird free or in a cage? Is the cage door open? Is the bird happy, afraid, at peace, defending its territory, focused on its prey?

Developing the art

* Now for the next stage. Does the bird relate to the way you are feeling or is it someone else and does it have a message for you?

* When you are identifying images easily one after the other and interpreting them, start to ask questions and use the images and related information to answer the questions. You can read the ball for others as well as yourself, but always ask them to hold the ball and tell you what they see.

* Sometimes you may be aware when you look into the ball at the start of a session of the presence of a particular deity, Angel or guardian and you may catch an image of them in the ball as you hold it upwards to the light. They, too, may have come with a message, so listen and do not be in a hurry to move on to the next stage.

* Even if the answer seems cryptic or the image unrelated to your current situation, you can be sure that within the next day or two you will hear something on the radio or television, see a book you are drawn to or that is open at a particular page or meet someone you did not expect to encounter and the answer will become clear.

* If you feel blocked devising a ritual or in understanding some information that is either badly explained or has a missing link, look into the crystal ball and write down all the images you see. Then let your pen carry on writing as you hold it loosely in your power hand and relax. You will discover that the missing link is provided in the words.

* Occasionally you will see golden light sparkles, rays or pure rainbow images in your crystal ball, even when there is no obvious light source. These rainbow images always hold personal insights for you, often at a time when you are dispirited or feel that though you know a lot the spontaneity and joy of early exploration into magick is temporarily missing.

* Note which colours of the rainbow appear (it may be two or three) as these may be telling you the colours you need in your life right now or for healing.

Cleanse your ball after use by leaving it in sun, moon or starlight for an hour or sprinkling clear water over and around it with a blessing. You can initially cleanse and charge it in the same way or by using a method on page 608.

Scrying with water

Water scrying is a natural part of witchcraft but can sometimes seem daunting and the water empty of images. The first method for scrying is one I have taught that seems to overcome psychic blocks almost instantly and even for experienced water scryers stimulates clairvoyant powers that result in richer conventional water scrying than with other less focused methods.

Sea witches use a similar technique with shells and sea water in a large domed bowl (like an old-fashioned goldfish bowl) and the swishing sound of the shells also triggers clairaudience. Try shell scrying next time you are by the sea.

Herb scrying

Herbs moving on the surface of water create physical images that can be interpreted by your psychic senses in the same way images in the crystal sphere take on life. For herb scrying you will need a clear glass bowl so that you can see the herbs from outside as well as in as you hold it.

For individual scrying, you can either use a cereal bowl size or a larger fruit bowl. A fruit bowl or an old-fashioned goldfish bowl is ideal for a group or coven. You can also use a cauldron as long as there is plenty of light whether natural or candlelight to shine on the surface of the water.

You will also need jars of dried culinary herbs in any one of the four traditional divinatory fragrances. These are parsley, sage, rosemary and thyme and they give clear images, as do dried chopped chives, tarragon and basil. If you wish, you can choose dried chopped herbs according to their magickal meanings to represent the subject under scrutiny. If you want to use more than one herb, pre-mix them in a small dish.

* Half-fill the bowl or cauldron with clear water.
* The secret of successful herb scrying is adding a few herbs at a time and either swirling the bowl clockwise three times or stirring the water with the index finger of your power hand.
* Either allow images to form or ask a question or pinpoint an area of concern.
* Almost immediately some herbs will form a single predominant image or picture on the surface. Some people see a whole scene and interpret that. Swirl the water round until you get the first clear image that is larger and clearer than the rest. This first image defines the true issue or question, which may be very different from the one you thought you were asking.
* If you aren't getting anywhere, close your eyes, open them, blink and say out loud what the image is. You have only a few seconds before the rational mind interferes.
* Swirl the water or bowl again for your second image. This will tell you what is the best action or alternatively if inaction is better.
* Now swirl a third time and read as many images as you can identify. These images will tell you the likely outcome of any action or inaction and may form a story or time line from where you are now.
* Spend time analysing the images, most of all what they made you feel as you did

with the images in the crystal ball. Record your insights in your symbol section in your Book of Shadows.

A group can ask a pre-planned question aloud for a coven issue or individuals can take turns to ask for collective input to a personal question. One or two people add the herbs. The bowl is passed from person to person and each person identifies an image as with the crystal ball. Later, the group should work with these images to extract as much information as possible. You can also use a cauldron and gather round it and call out images as they appear.

Oil and water scrying

The Ancient Egyptians, Greeks and Romans would use the bubbling oil in a lamp to answer questions. You can often buy these oil lamps in museum shops or in some modern garden centres and with care they are an excellent form of divination. Another method used by Ancient Egyptians was to float drops of cold oil on the surface of a ceramic bowl of cold water. You can occasionally still see the method in tourist bazaars on stalls where scented oils are for sale. Because the oil is constantly moving, this is a very effective and easy method. I prefer this to hot oil as you can create a series of images very slowly and it is very good for showing the way ahead or untangling dilemmas. Oil scrying is better for individuals rather than group scrying.

Use dark coloured oil that contrasts with the water, in a clear glass or pale ceramic bowl. The cheap fragrance oils you buy for oil burners are ideal. Very dark virgin olive oils are also traditional and give strong physical images. I have also experimented with a smoked glass bowl and used a yellow olive oil on the surface of the shadowy water. This method seems to work best in the hour before sunset, a traditional scrying time.

* Sit facing the sunset if it is visible from the scrying place. Remain silent.

* When you are ready, drip the oil drop by drop either through an eyedropper or using a fragrance or essential oil bottle, allowing it to swirl and form images. If you are sparing with the oil and pause between drops to allow the oil to swirl, you will build up a series of images, each evolving from the first.

* As the shadows deepen, light a pure white or beeswax candle at the back of the bowl to cast light on the oil. Allow the shadows to form part of the imaging process.

* Afterwards you may find it easier to draw the images randomly on a page in your Book of Shadows and then to study the page by candlelight, allowing your deep mind to make the connections. The images will together give insight into an aspect of your life, leading you gently into the future so that you can make wise choices.

Water and ink scrying

Ink scrying remained popular in the Middle East right through the Middle Ages. One version involved tipping ink into the palm of the hand and reading the formations created by the lines and grooves. However, that is a very messy method.

Like oil and water scrying, ink scrying also works well for individual witches rather than a coven activity, as images can quickly blur. If you buy black, blue or red ink cartridges, the kind you use in pens, in a plastic tube, you can use them much as you did the oils. This scrying method is good for specific issues or choices concerning family and your immediate circle.

* Fill a glass bowl with water. Work at sunset and sit facing the sunset, if possible, where light shines on the bowl.

* Prick the narrow end of the ink cartridge. Alternatively use waterproof ink in red, blue or black or two colours one after the other, and a thin brush or ink nib pen for each colour.

* Drop by drop, put the ink very gently on the surface and as it swirls name images. You should get three or four images before the water clouds.

* If you wish, you can then light candles around the black water and gaze into that for further clarification.

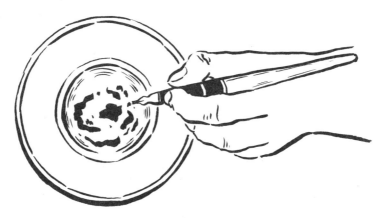

Wax and water

This method is popular at festivals and can be carried out in the cauldron or a bowl using festival candles as a group as well as a personal activity.

* Use a bowl of clear water in a glass bowl or the cauldron. At the back of it set a horseshoe of four candles in strong colours: for example, bright red, blue, orange and green. Buy the kind where the colour penetrates right through the candle for best effect. If using white candles, darken the water with mugwort or any other dark coloured herbal infusion or a little black ink beforehand.

* Light the candles, one from the other, left to right as you face them. As you do so, name the main question at each candle.

* Focus on the candlelit water for a moment without trying to discern any images. Let your mind to go blank and merge your consciousness with the water.

* Then taking the first candle in your receptive hand and the second in your power one shake a few drops from each simultaneously on the surface of the water. Then rapidly take the third and fourth candles and add them to the water. You will need to be very fast in order to read an image before the wax sets.

* At first you may find it easier to read two separate images as you add the two sets of wax. These refer to the aspects of the current situation that are changing or new and unexpected opportunities that are opening.

* When the wax sets, you will obtain a second more permanent image from the joined four colours or maybe separate images, referring to what will pass several months ahead if change is made or opportunity seized.

* You can add fresh wax at any time as the first is hardening to create an interim image of potentially fruitful avenues. Some people interpret a whole scene in the hardened wax.

In a group, you can have different people gathered around the cauldron or a large bowl and choose one person for each colour. You could use up to seven or eight different candle colours in a large cauldron, each person dropping the wax quickly, one after the other without an interval (as many as you like). All present can interpret the images as they form and harden. You may get a number of different but related images and insights.

Using water and sun, moon or candlelight

Scrying in lakes with either moon or sunlight shining on the water and trees overhanging it to create patterns is probably the oldest form of scrying. Water and light scrying is good for both solitary practitioners and as a coven activity and is still the most popular form of scrying among modern witches. It can be carried out either in a small pool, a large cauldron or a large flat clear bowl.

It is especially potent on the night of the full moon after the moon has been drawn down, but can also be carried out in bright sunlight after the drawing down of the sun. Other good times include after a handfasting or baby naming, on Samhain Eve, Beltaine Eve, the night before the Summer Solstice after sun down and at noon on the Solstice day (using sunlight on the water instead of candles), as well as on the Midwinter Solstice sun return, perhaps supplemented by candlelight.

* Darken the water either with mugwort or black ink and place a horseshoe of pure white or natural beeswax candles behind the bowl so the light shines on the water. This also works well with bright full moonlight.

* If you work outdoors or near an open window or on a sheltered balcony or patio, the breeze will create patterns on the water.

* When scrying with a bowl and candles indoors stir the water first clockwise then anticlockwise, then clockwise again. If using the full moon as your light source, stir anticlockwise, then clockwise, then anticlockwise again.

* Use a clear quartz crystal wand or a smoothed twig from one of the magickal trees such as elder, rowan or willow to stir the still water each time before reading a new image in the water. Some practitioners do this even outdoors in a breeze for psychometric connection.

* If you find it difficult to discern images, look through half-closed eyes and concentrate on the patterns of light, considering first what feelings or ideas they evoke and then imagining a golden wand of light tracing images on the surface of the water. Continue until you can get no more images.
* Generally insights come at the moment the image is perceived.

Mirror scrying

There are two kinds of mirror scrying practised in modern witchcraft, one using the traditional witches' dark mirror and the second through clear glass, though this is usually carried out around sunset or in semi-darkness rather than bright sunlight.

The earliest mirrors were made of highly polished metal or crystal. The origin of magickal mirror scrying is attributed to the Ancient Egyptians and especially to the Goddess Hathor the Ancient Egyptian Goddess of joy, love, fertility, marriage music and dance and protector of women. Hathor mirrors were originally made of polished silver or bronze with an image of Hathor on the handle, and you can adapt a highly polished silver plated tray if you wish to try scrying with metal.

In an equally old tradition, mirrors, especially bronze ones, were consulted in Ancient China, perhaps as early as 4,000 BCE to determine what would come to pass. They were believed to reflect the universe. The Greeks used bronze mirrors to see into the future and in Ancient Rome practitioners called specularii were highly regarded as soothsayers. According to myth, Vulcan, God of fire and metalworkers and husband of Venus, fashioned a mirror that showed past, present and future. The mirror was given to Penelope, wife of the hero Ulysses. Merlin, King Arthur's magician, used his magickal mirror to warn the king about plots and potential invasions by enemy forces.

The Aztecs and Mayans scried the future by watching the sun at eclipses through black obsidian mirrors. Black glass or crystal mirrors, called witches' mirrors, were popular in mediaeval times, and now are treasured by a number of witches, though they tend not to be used more generally in divination. Mirrors are also excellent for past life work.

Mirror scrying tends to be a private art, though a coven can one at a time look into a dark mirror, speak what comes to them and then pass on the mirror.

Hathor mirror magick/clear mirror scrying

According to myth, Hathor was allowed to see through the sacred eye of her father/consort Ra the Sun God or in other legends the moon eye of the Sky God Horus. In this way, she had knowledge of everything on the earth, in the sea and in the heavens and the thoughts as well as the deeds of humankind.

Hathor also carried a shield that could reflect back all things in their true light. From this shield she fashioned the first magick mirror. One side was endowed with the power of Horus/Ra's eye so that the seeker could see everything, no matter how distant in miles or how far into the future. The other side showed the gazer in his or her true light and only a brave or pure person could look without flinching.

The methods I describe for Hathor mirror magick apply to scrying with a clear or shiny metal mirror, but the basic information about the significance of the sizes of images etc holds true for scrying with dark mirrors if you use them for divination. You may find a Hathor metal mirror in a museum shop. There are a number of online museum shops and it is well worth seeking one out for pride of place in your temple.

But you can use any round mirror and some practitioners of Hathor magick prefer to use a swivel mirror on a stand. You can also work with a single-sided conventional mirror with a handle. Years ago, dressing table sets with embossed handled mirrors were very common and these can still be picked up cheaply from car boot sales and are absolutely perfect.

Clear mirror scrying is potent for bringing to the surface issues concerning personal identity and potential areas of development. As it was in Ancient Egypt, mirror divination is effective for discovering the identity of a future partner, and for answering questions about love, fidelity, marriage and permanent love relationships, fertility, family concerns, for discovering the location of an item or animal that is lost or the truth about a matter that is hidden from you.

Beginning mirror divination

In the past I have found any mirror divination hard but the following method I have recently discovered does seem to work well. The mistake I made was to expect to see an image as clear as a normal reflection. In fact in this most elusive of psychic arts, even with sunset scrying, when the reds, pinks and purple light floods the mirror, images appear quite faintly, sometimes as a light shimmer, at other times forming in a shadow, maybe an outline, or a grey formation, coming together in a shape and as quickly dissolving like wisps of mist, always fleeting. On other occasions, the image can move in and out of vision, like the ripples clearing from water after a stone has been thrown.

What you are left with afterwards is a strong impression in your mind, often more powerful than images seen more tangibly in other forms of scrying. You might think you saw nothing except that you are left with this image that released from the reflective mirror becomes very clear and vivid in your mind. So persevere, as it is a wonderful route into other dimensions-and suddenly it will work.

* Work during the hour before sunset so you catch the sunset colours in the glass unless the mirror scrying follows a spell or ritual. In that case, leave the mirror in the south-east of the altar during the spell.

* You may at first find it easier for any mirror scrying to work in semi-darkness, even with a clear mirror, unless you are working with the sunset rays in the glass.

* Light three red candles, Hathor's colour, so that the light catches the mirror reflections. In more modern magick, orange and pink have also become her colours.

* Light rose incense, Hathor's fragrance, on either side of the mirror so the smoke can be seen rising in the mirror reflection.

* Tilt the mirror angle so that you do not see your own face reflected, unless you are seeking to discover yourself in your true light (see the method below if you want to try this).

* Ask a question of Hathor and wait for the images to form in the mirror in the reflected light and shadow. These images will be made of the light shimmers and shadows and may even just be outlines, forming and dissolving.

* If you experience difficulty, close your eyes, open them, blink and look at the mirror, naming whatever image you perceive or sense you perceive. Once you have an image either look away or close your eyes again, open and blink. Continue until you have evoked five or six consecutive images.

* If you can get a round or oval shiny silver, copper or pewter tray, hold that to catch the sunset light or candles and scry with that. Then flip the metal mirror over, close your eyes and say:

Show me myself as I could be in my true light.

* Open your eyes and you will get an instant image of your reflection in the metal as you could become. I promise you will be pleased.

* You can also stand reflected in a clear mirror close your eyes, open them rapidly blink and ask to see yourself as you could be.

Interpreting the mirror images

You can interpret mirror images as you do any others evoked during scrying. From early mirror work evolved a series of rules for mirror scrying that have survived into modern magick. However, you may prefer not to use them if they conflict with your more spontaneous interpretations.

* An image moving away says that an event or person is either moving away from the scryer's world or that a past issue or relationship may still be exerting undue influence on the scryer. You will sense which is true.

* Images appearing on the left of the mirror suggest actual physical occurrences that have or may influence the everyday world in the near future.

* Images appearing in the centre or to the right tend to be symbolic.

* Pictures near the top of the mirror are important and need prompt attention.

* Those in the corners or at the bottom are less prominent or urgent.

* The relative size of the images can indicate their importance.

* The closer they are to you the more they are significant and indicate action or opportunity by you.

* Images that change into another reflect the next stage is coming fast in your life.

* A scene rather than an image occasionally signifies either a past world or that a number or people or factors will be influencing your immediate future.

* An image, however fleeting, that fills the mirror signifies your essential life and future and says that you, not others, need to be centre stage in your priorities.

Dark or witches' mirrors

These are gateways into other worlds and what you see may appear like a grainy black and white still photograph or like an old-fashioned black and white silent film in which the images flicker intensely.

Your dark mirror should be made of darkened smoky glass and not, as you often see, a black tile-like substance. I used to work with the shiny opaque kind, but the dark glass ones that look almost opaque until candlelight shines in them are by far the best. The finest example of a dark witch mirror I have seen was in the Museum of Witchcraft at Boscastle that has a wooden frame carved in the face of a witch. You can scry in a darkened mirror as you would in a clear one.

However, this is not their traditional usage. According to Cecil Williamson, the original collector of many of the items now in the Boscastle museum, dark mirrors could form a home for one's familiar spirit (see page 34). A figure could often be seen reflected in the darkened glass as you looked into it, standing behind you. You could talk to the shadowy person reflected there, who would help, teach and advise you but you must never turn round.

If this sounds a little spooky for you, try the following:

❋ Hang your dark mirror on a wall in your altar room away from windows or doors that might illuminate it. Some witches swathe it in dark silk when not in use, just as some wrap their smaller clear scrying mirrors in white silk.

❋ Set a tall table in front of it so that you can position a pair of tall white candles to shine into the glass as you look into it, making a doorway of faint light.

❋ Unlike clear mirrors, you stand or sit so you can see your own reflection unless you prefer not to. By seeing yourself you are setting your spiritual inner self within the mirror and so other dimensions.

❋ You can if you wish make a pathway of candles so they reflect within the mirror into the darkness and this is a wonderful pathway to past worlds or other dimensions, especially after spellcasting.

❋ Unless you are still working within a circle, cast a protective circle of light round yourself and the glass by projecting and visualising the complete circle as you stand facing the mirror.

❋ Light protective incense such as rose, myrrh or lavender so the reflection of the smoke swirls in the glass.

❋ If you wish, hold a protective crystal whether your Guardian stone if small, or smoke quartz, rutilated quartz or amethyst.

❋ Close your eyes and ask that you may see, or, if this would worry you, sense the kindly presence of your Witch Guardian, a wise ancestor or teacher or your Guardian Angel.

❋ Open your eyes slowly and you may see in the mirror or feel the gentle loving shadowy presence form behind you and be filled with love and peace. Ask if they have a message or teaching for you and the words will flow into your mind.

❋ When you are ready, thank the Guardian and say:

Go in peace and in blessings until we meet again.

❋ Close your eyes and when you open them do not look into the glass but blow out the candles one by one and sit enjoying the fragrance.

❋ In the unlikely event you ever you feel afraid while using a dark mirror or find it hard to break the connection even with your loving guardian, say:

Blessings be.

Blow out the candles fast one after the other and then say:

Go in peace. I remain myself and separate. So mote it be.

Smudge yourself in the incense smoke.

You will not have called anything bad, nor can your spirit get trapped in the glass. That is the stuff of bad B movies. However, occasionally there are times when earthly matters naturally cloud our mind and we can project our fears into the glass in ways that may frighten us.

Dark mirrors are not for everyone and you are no better or worse a witch for not using one. I don't use one right now as I have a lot of earthly clutter and stress, and so I talk to my guardian in the clear crystal ball.

PRACTICAL ASSIGNMENT

Scrying ceremony

Devise a separate ceremony for scrying on special occasions, including circle casting, a special blessing, choosing divinatory and protective incenses, crystals etc. If possible, find a natural setting for your scrying.

Record the ceremony in your Book of Shadows.

Further research

Research into old methods of scrying in different cultures and see what can be extracted from those practices to enhance your own scrying work.

Further information

Recommended reading

* Andrews, Ted, *Crystal Balls and Crystal Bowls: tools for Ancient Scrying and Modern Seership*, Llewellyn, 1995
* Crowley, Aleister, et al, *A Symbolic Representation of the Universe: developed by Doctor John Dee through the scrying of Edward Kelly*, Holmes Publishing Group plc, 2001
* Eason, Cassandra, *Scrying the Secrets of the Future*, New Page US, 2007 Includes mirrors.

Websites

* *The Paranormal*
  Extensive links including scrying from a Wiccan perspective and how to make dark mirrors
  http://paranormal.about.com/od/scrying
* *Museum of Witchcraft, Boscastle*
  Fabulous museum and an excellent website
  www.museumofwitchcraft.com

RITUALS AND CEREMONIES

This module draws together many strands of earlier work. Before beginning, refresh your memory about formal rituals by rereading the modules on the basic tools of magick (page 99) and the altar (page 157), as well as the four elements (page 134) and magickal timings (pages 192 and 202).

For seasonal festivals, rites of passage, such as baby naming ceremonies and handfasting, as well as the monthly esbat on the full moon, a more formal ritual brings sanctity and marks the occasion as significant in the life of the participants. In modern society, whole months can flash by unnoticed and unmarked. Particularly if you are a solitary practitioner, magick may have to be squeezed in with a dozen other pressing demands on time and energy.

Suddenly it is full moon and you have to fit in a hurried ceremony and maybe rearrange your schedule to have that brief precious time (I know from my own life). Even in a coven, ritual can become a chore if people are travelling long distances after working late, or have to work round family needs at the weekend. It can be with a sinking feeling you realise you promised to organise the Spring Equinox for over 20 families and the event is two days away...

Some more formal spells can also incorporate more formal ritual aspects: for example, for healing or in response to an ecological disaster or national or international tragedy. The difference between ritual magick and natural folk magick is, I believe, one of degree, like the difference between organising a formal dinner party and a spontaneous picnic.

There are many traditions of formal magick and it is an area where you need to experiment and, if experienced, make sure your practices are still right for you and not just inherited. In this way, every occasion is sacred but still pleasurable. Ritual or formal magick works as well for the solitary practitioner as the coven member. Indeed, the solitary practitioner has a great deal of personal flexibility both in planning and adapting the ceremony on the day and a lack of pressure to ensure all flows smoothly.

The following suggested structure can be used as a basis for planning any special event, including your seasonal celebrations, an esbat, to empower special symbols in a formal spell and, of course, your approaching Year and a Day ceremony. There will be some overlap with earlier material and variations on it so that the structure can be seen as a whole.

The ritual year

Because the majority of witches are not just witches, but also employers, employees, parents, lovers, spouses, grandparents, best friends, and members of committees, societies and sports clubs, forward planning is essential for your ritual year. Use any of the witchcraft almanacs (see page 219) or diaries to plan the year ahead, noting the full moons and the seasonal festivals as well as milestone birthdays, anniversaries etc, and global events such as World Earth Day around 22 April that you would like to mark with a more formal ritual.

Be realistic about what is possible without causing yourself stress, but prioritise your magickal times as you would any other commitment. You may have to perform a short, private, full moon rite after a Great Aunt's 80th birthday party because magick and your Great Aunt will never mix. But try to mark as sacrosanct those times that are important to your spiritual and ceremonial life. Perhaps you could even try to plan a weekend away to a special place for one or two of them, so you can enjoy a ritual with friends, your coven or alone with the nature essences.

If you are a solitary practitioner or relatively new to group or coven work, note any major witchcraft festivals, open circles, large pagan moots or Druid gatherings in your area or that you could travel to, so you can see how other people organise and carry out formal rituals. Often there is a website address you can contact in advance to find out details and what if any offerings you should take along.

Equally, once you are confident, you and a group of friends or your coven could plan some open events. Sites such as Avebury Stones are awash with groups on the Equinoxes and you may need to plan your festival on the weekend before or at an earlier/later time than normal (you can check with the site custodians). However, there are plenty of quiet woodlands and smaller sites where you can work freely.

Gatherings such as the huge Stonehenge Summer Solstice dawn are an excellent way of getting to know people and to participate in different ceremonies, formal and informal. One Autumn Equinox at Avebury my daughter Miranda and I joined three ceremonies at Avebury (one by accident) and still made it up Glastonbury Tor for our own private ceremony at sundown.

Above all remember that if family members get sick or there is a crisis at work and if you have to miss a festival, that does not make you a bad witch but a good person, who puts human need first – and that makes you a very good witch indeed. You can always carry out a substitute, short, private empowerment anywhere.

1 Planning

If you're working as a solitary, some of the aspects I describe below will not apply, but you may want to invite friends and family to share in seasonal celebrations or a family/personal milestone. The practical aspects may not seem relevant to witchcraft, but advanced planning means that you can relax, whether celebrating alone or with others. You can focus on the magickal energies and not where you put the matches.

✸ What is the purpose of the ceremony or ritual and who/how many will attend?

* Is the date and timing of the ceremony dictated by the occasion: for example, a Beltane Eve ceremony or a weekend close to the festival when you have time and people can meet?

* Alternatively, is there flexibility so that you can use the right moon phase (and also maybe which star sign it is), day of the week or planetary/Archangel hour of the day/night on which to begin? If it is a full moon esbat, you can craft the ritual around what else is going on magickally and astrologically and the kind of moon it is (see page 482) and so its specific energies: for example, an autumnal hunters' moon will be very different in focus and surrounding energies from an early Spring When The Geese Lay Moon.

* Where will the rite be held? This will affect the kind of circle casting and the nature of the rite, if there is room to dance/drum and if the area is private. When working alone you will want privacy, but in an unfamiliar and maybe remote place you need to think about security issues. Rural campsites, forestry huts or caravans on sites with few facilities usually have areas where you can be undisturbed.

* Are there any restrictions/extra facilities: for example, a road close by or people passing as at Avebury stones or a fire dish in situ (with permission) at the Rollright stone circle near Banbury in Oxfordshire?

* If you are working at your indoor or outdoor altar, how will you decorate it and the room/garden?

* How will you position anyone else taking part? Four of you, one for each element round the altar, you and a lover facing one another across the Goddess/God altar candles, or, a full coven? Even as a solitary, you may organise friends or family who at a seasonal rite or milestone such as handfasting or baby naming may be unfamiliar with the beliefs behind the ceremony or the nature of the rites. Even at a formal ceremony, it is very easy to involve non-pagans in a relaxed way so that they can participate fully and often afterwards want to know more.

* If working alone, how can you place the artefacts, especially a larger one like a cauldron or fire dish, so you can move easily between stages of the rite?

* If after dark, how will you illuminate the site and can you incorporate this as part of the ritual: for example, by using large directional candles, outdoor torches or a ring of tea lights indoors? In your garden, could you position fairy lights to light the altar area or paper or metal lanterns containing tea lights? You can hang a larger lantern from your staff embedded in the ground.

* Who will be playing a major part (easier in a coven)? If you are organising an open circle or organising a ritual at a festival or pagan moot or camp, then newcomers need a little extra input as, with a little explanation, even someone new to magick can take a full part.

* If you have a regular group you can share the responsibilities and e-mail necessary information and even words to be used.

* Are you going to write the ceremony and chants? Should you keep everything short and repetitive and encourage improvisation? If working with newcomers,

you can adapt familiar chants with easy refrains or sing them in advance before the ceremony begins and also explain anything unfamiliar.

* Will the centre of the rite be a dramatic representation of a Goddess/God myth from your favourite culture or a seasonal myth? Are there parts to be learned or will people read (think about lighting)?

* You don't have to be part of a group to act out the great myths, but can write the story as a poem or a praise dialogue to be spoken by you as part of your private ceremony. Drama is one of the most powerful ways we can connect with deity energies in our formal rites. You could adapt the Demeter/Persephone myth (see page 134), the Descent of the Goddess (see page 394) who strips off all her finery and goes into the Underworld to ask Death why he takes away all she loves, especially the Slain God. Some act this out at Samhain and call it the first Resurrection. He explains to her that death is inevitable but that through her love there can be rebirth and so her Lord/Death and the slain God return as one resurrected with great celebration. If it is Samhain, he tells her he will be reborn as her son if she trusts that the sun will not die at Midwinter.

* Another myth that can be acted out alone as well as with others is the progression of the Maiden-Mother-Crone and how each learns to give way to the other and not fear the change, especially during the three dark days when the Maiden lies in darkness in the arms of the Wise Grandmother/Midwife before she walks into the light. There are masses of such ceremonies online and in books, but best of all are the ones you write yourself.

* It is often easier not to have long speeches that can get lost on the wind. Instead have plenty of action, group chants and even drumming to keep everyone warm, involved and moving.

* If you are working alone, you can just have a brief order of ceremony and maybe some key words so that you immerse yourself fully in the rite.

* What tools will you need, what incenses, candles etc. and what will serve as an altar if you are not working at home? Even details such as how you will transport things to the site if it is across a field or in the middle of a wood can be planned by an advance visit unless you are familiar with the site or have help.

* Can you cope with adverse weather or winds (a mini gas blowtorch about the size of a cigarette lighter is a useful tool)?

* If alone you can work as easily in as outdoors. If a lot of people are coming, is there an alternative venue or somewhere to warm up afterwards?

* If someone can't come, can you easily substitute someone else?

* Finally, remember: you might have to change everything at the last minute when you find you have large number of people in a very small space. If you hit problems adapt if possible (people never notice) and if it all goes wrong start to sing or chant to get the energy flowing again and give yourself five minutes to get back on track.

Preparing the area

* First use an ordinary directional compass to ascertain the four directions or calculate approximations from known places.
* Then cleanse the area by asperging or sprinkling with a small bundle of twigs dipped in water and/or sweeping (see page 167).
* Indoors you can smudge the room with a herbal smoke stick in sagebrush or cedar or a cedar or pine incense stick in alternate clockwise and anticlockwise circles (see page 162). Both indoors and out add a chant, such as:

> *May only goodness and light remain here and this area be dedicated for the greatest good and highest purpose.*

* See page 222 for personal preparations and ritual purification.
* Set up your altar using as many or as few of the tools as you require. Even in formal magick few may be better than more. Plan how you will use the tools and magickal substances in the specific ceremony.
* You can anoint or carry out a mini dedication, if you wish (see page 161). Otherwise just pass your hands over the altar, the power hand clockwise and the receiving hand anticlockwise at the same time, palms down. Say:

> *Blessings be on this altar and this work.*

* Pre-light anything that needs to warm up, like charcoal, and have substitute candles etc in case any won't light or go out quickly. I tend to light a second charcoal disk or block about five minutes after the first so that I don't run out of incense fuel at the crucial point.

2 Mark the beginning of the ritual or ceremony formally

* Ring the bell at each of the quarters of your visualised or actual circle, starting in the north where the bell is (or use a Tibetan singing bowl, Tibetan bells or a drum).
* Alternatively, make an opening blessing, calling on the protection you will be using, the four Archangels at the quarters, God/Goddess of light or specific deities. State again that you are working for greatest good.
* Then light the Goddess and God candles left to right, lighting the right God candle from the Goddess.
* Do the blessing and lighting the candles facing the altar looking north. Raise your arms high and wide as you speak the blessing.
* You can practise a blessing in advance or just let the words come. Try something simple, like:

> *Bless this ritual/spell, Mother and Father, keep harm outside and peace within.*
> *Bless me as I come in joy/bless all who gather here this day.*

* If others are present and have not yet come into a circle face them as you make the blessing.

* Now light the elemental south candle. If you are using one of the directional candles to serve as the elemental candle as well (that is, part of the salt, incense and water set) you light it later.

* Light any incense or incense sticks from the Goddess candle (burn the charcoal early if you are using loose powdered incense).

* To bless the salt, set the salt dish on the pentacle and touch it with the blade of the athame, saying:

Blessed be this salt and sanctified in the name of the Goddess.

* Repeat the process and blessing for the water bowl.

3 Casting the circle

These are two very simple ways of organising circle casting at a ritual. There are other variations for spellcasting that you can use also in rituals on page 185.

Circle casting really is very simple, but because there are such a huge variety of ways of circle casting I have tried to cover as many as possible. Once you choose your method it soon becomes second nature. There are no absolutes and if you are experienced and yet circle casting doesn't flow, spend time working out what you want to do and how.

* Alone, cast your initial physical/visualised circle in the earth sealed afterwards with the triple circle of salt/water incense and fire. Or you can use the triple circle by itself both to form and seal the sacred circle. It does not matter if you are preparing the salt/water at the altar without a physical circle as you have made the blessing and lit the candles to sanctify the rite.

* If a group rite, after the blessing you can lead any guests into the ritual area, all joining hands and spiralling until you make a physical circle joined by hands left palm up right palm down. Their hands form the physical circle, which you can if you wish then reinforce by drawing one to enclose them physically in the earth or in visualised light round them or just seal with the triple circle of salt/water, incense and fire after consecrating the salt/water.

* After sealing, you could have a chant about how the circle remains as our hearts hold the power and can then signal the dropping of hands.

* Alternatively you can ask any present to enter after an initial physical circle is cast by you either marked in the earth or drawn at waist height in light with the wand or athame as you walk round the boundaries of your projected circle. Explain in advance what you are doing if newcomers are present, so they aren't standing awkwardly round wondering what to do. After the circle is cast, they enter through the gateway (see page 252) and stand around the perimeter of the circle.

* If you are using a sacred salt and water mix to make one of the triple sealing circles, prepare this ritually at the altar directly after the physical or light circle casting, using the athame and pentacle (see page 107). You can ask someone present to help you. Salt and water are the Goddess elements blessed by the athame, the God tool.

* After you have consecrated the salt/water, you can cast the triple sealing circle of first salt water, then incense, then the candle or if you prefer salt, incense and

finally water droplets. You cast this behind the group as they face inwards.

* You can use three different people walking either one after the other round the outside of the circle carrying the salt water, the incense and the flame, to cast or seal the circle in procession so the three triple circles are created almost simultaneously, one on top of the other. Or you can choose three people to make the circles one at a time, each walking round once in turn.

* Create simple elemental casting chants according to the substances you are using and the nature of the ritual.

* Finally, close the gateway after the triple sealing circle is cast and enter the circle for the last time. Then walk round the inside of the circle, sprinkling each person present as they face you with a few drops water/salt water (see page 625), saying:

Blessings be or *You are welcome.*

* You can sprinkle yourself with the sacred water if working alone, facing north.

4 Opening the quarters

At each of the Four Watchtowers waits the elemental guardian whom you can invite into the circle to stand at the four watchtowers or quarters and to release and amplify the four elemental powers you are calling. They also act as spiritual protectors during the ritual. In earlier times they may have faced outwards to watch for physical dangers coming from the four quarters. You can use the Archangels Uriel in the north, Raphael in the east, Michael in the south and Gabriel in the west.

One of the most common ways of greeting the four guardians is to make the appropriate invoking elemental pentagram at its own quarter after you have called the guardian. Alternatively, you can use the Earth invoking pentagram we have already met at all four quarters. Four different people can do this.

But first let me introduce for new witches the four elemental pentagrams that in no time will become second nature.

You use the invoking pentagram to open its own element at the quarters and the banishing to close. These are generally drawn from chest height with outstretched and bent arm at about a 60-degree angle to the body facing outwards to the watchtower. They can be drawn the size of a large dinner plate or a small round shield according to your choice. Draw them with your athame, your wand, the index finger of your power hand or in the darkness with a huge incense stick so you make your pentagrams of Fire. Imagine you are drawing them on a closed door.

* To invoke an element (open a watchtower), draw the pentagram starting from the point opposite its elemental point on the pentagram (see diagram below to remind you of the elemental points).

* To banish an element (close the watchtower), draw the pentagram starting from its elemental point on the pentagram.

* Invoke towards and banish away from the element you're working with.

* Pentagrams are either visualised in their own colours, green for Earth, yellow for Air, red for Fire and blue for Water or as being a brilliant electric blue.

These diagrams are to remind you of the elemental positions, so you know where to start drawing:

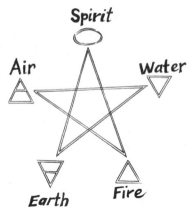

The pentagram and the elements

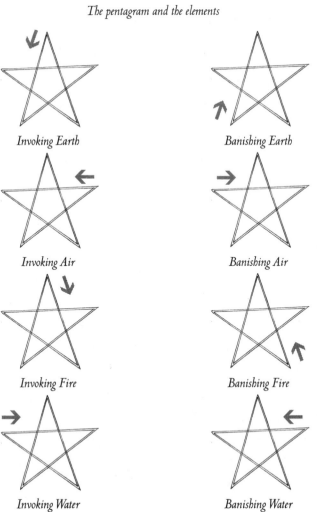

Invoking Earth	*Banishing Earth*
Invoking Air	*Banishing Air*
Invoking Fire	*Banishing Fire*
Invoking Water	*Banishing Water*

Greeting the guardians

* Light any candles at the elemental quarter as you face outwards from the circle.

* Raise both arms in greeting (palms flat and uppermost) and make a greeting. Outdoors or in a larger indoor circle you can physically visit the four quarters in turn. On a smaller altar, face the direction as you greet it. Welcome each guardian in turn and ask for their appropriate power and protection. In some traditions the words used are:

Hail and welcome.

* You then make the invoking elemental pentagram. Everyone present faces that direction, raises their arms, echoes the *Hail and welcome* or the greeting that is used. If they wish, they can then draw the appropriate pentagram.

* I have noticed that some practitioners make the pentagram before the greeting, after or instead of candle lighting (like knocking on the psychic entrance before calling). Again, it is your choice.

* Greet the guardians in your own way. I sometimes first name the guardian with:

Welcome to this circle and this rite in light and in purity.

* Make a refrain in the greeting that anyone else present can easily repeat. You can make the elemental call as elaborate or as simple as you wish.

* You can also drum open the four quarters, which is very evocative if you are working alone, slowly and regularly in the north, lightly and very fast in the east, with slow drum rolls in the south, and gentle flowing beats in the west. You can combine the four rhythms to raise the power. A Shamanic rattle works as well, too.

5 Inviting in the wise ones

You can invite chosen ancestors (spiritual and actual) into the circle, your Spirit Guides and Guardian Angels and those of any present to give their protection and blessing.

* Face west and either blow a horn, call with your voice, make nine short drum beats, ring the bell three times or strike the ground with your staff to invite them in. Remember: you are respectfully requesting their spiritual presence, not summoning them, and their presence is a bonus and privilege.

* If outdoors, swing round in a complete clockwise circle from the north with arms open wide, palms outermost and vertical, asking any benign fey beings and nature spirits if they wish to attend into the circle.

* Finally, face south, open your arms wide again and ask if any deities (you can name them) would bless your circle and ritual.

* Whether you are working alone or with others, this can be followed by a unifying chant such as:

We are the old people, we are the new people, we are the same people wiser than before

then in the next verse, *stronger than before*, then *younger than before* and as many variations as you can create (see page 302 for sources of these popular chants). Or you can adapt the Isis Astarte chant to welcome whoever you have invited in, be they nature spirits, ancestors or deities.

6 Defining ceremonially the purpose of the ritual

This is the place where you state the specific purpose of the rite and begin the ceremony proper. If working alone, you would begin with *I am* and state your magickal names. Then:

I come here to this place at this hour to...

If you were carrying out a seasonal celebration, this is the point where you would set your seasonal offerings on the altar. If others are present, each person would bring a symbol of the season/the ritual purpose such as Earth Day in to the centre as an offering. In a more general rite, you could have a deep bowl or cauldron bowl to collect symbols of something each person wished to discard from their life, perhaps a dying flower. By its side would be a second bowl or cauldron to which they would add some seeds, an acorn or nut for the new beginnings they wished to bring into their life to replace the old. As the organiser, you need to have spare offerings such as flower petals, tiny crystals or small fruits for those who have not brought anything along. However, this rite works as well for a solitary practitioner and you can bury the symbol of the old in soil in which you plant the seeds as part of the release of power stage (see below).

At a handfasting or baby blessing, each guest would offer a small crystal or flower as a gift.

You may have a central stone and perhaps a guardian of the festival or ceremony to accept the offerings and sit in the centre to receive on behalf of everyone the purpose of the gift as each person names it (or may prefer to do so silently). The mother would do this at a handfasting or a baby naming. The offerings are now blessed on the offerings dish with the four elemental substances, salt, incense, candle and water, and then the four sacred tools in turn, first the pentacle, then the tip of the athame, then the tip of the wand, and finally the chalice would be circled over them with appropriate elemental blessings.

Alternatively, if you were not using ritual tools you could in turn pass the offerings dish round the circle and ask anyone present to endow it first with an Earth strength or quality, then round a second time for the Air, the third time for the Fire and the fourth time for the Water. This can be a good point at an esbat for everyone to bring a tiny gift for another coven member or a few coins for a charity the coven is supporting. Alone you would offer either a symbol or a suitable small gift to be sent to someone in need or donated to a charity or a dish of fruit to be shared with your family and friends the next day.

If you were going to carry out instead or as well the calling down of the Goddess, God, moon or sun, you would bless the person acting as the divine figure or call forward all who, for example, were going to re-enact the story of the Descent of the Goddess to encounter death and acknowledge his sway and, in the versions I like, accept rebirth from her. Then you would either anoint them and bless them with the ritual tools (see page 99) or use the ritual substances and tools as part of their empowerment on your behalf.

Alone you would bless yourself with the substances and tools or anoint yourself (see page 478 for the *By root and bud and flower* chant and the *Blessed be my feet* prelude chant) before beginning the chant.

This would be the point in a handfasting where the couple would state their intention and the priestess/priest joining them ask if they came willingly, who came as their Goddess sisters and brothers and would anoint them. In a baby rite, the Goddess parents would be called forward.

7 The body of the ritual

This may involve raising of power to charge the offerings with the energies of the season. Alternatively the speaking of the Charge of the Goddess/God would begin or the acting out of the drama of the seasons/Goddess/God cycle and may be prolonged or short. There may be a praise chant of the season/circle dance and prayer for the occasion, if the Goddess/God Charge is not made. The couple would make their vows and the Goddess parents promise to care for the child.

Alternatively, after or instead of the Goddess/God Charge or drama it can be the beginning of the symbolic Great Rite, the Cakes and Ale ceremony where the body of the God is offered as the grain in the cakes and blessed and the athame raised to bless the wine or the blood of the Slain God. I have described this at the end, so not to slow down the sequence now. If there is a raising of power to be released, the Cakes and Ale blessing would follow the release of power or the Goddess prophecies prompted by speaking the Charge.

If very clever, you can weave the Cakes and Ale blessing into the end of the drama, especially if the God and Goddess come together.

8 Releasing the power: the resolution

* The power is set free from the offerings/symbol or pushed back into them gently as the chant subsides into silence, especially if it is a festival or formal spell for healing and peace of healing.

* If you had two bowls for what was to be lost and gained, you would now bury the symbols of the old in a large pot of soil, adding the seeds on behalf of everyone with a blessing.

* If you are following the Cakes and Ale ceremony now, the athame blade and chalice, God and Goddess, are united in the symbolic Great Rite. If a couple were alone, they could follow with the actual Great Rite, having made offerings of cake and wine to the Goddess Mother Earth.

* Alternatively, after the Charge of the Goddess/God or drawing down the moon or sun, the figure assuming the divine power on behalf of others would speak spontaneous prophetic words.

* In a drama cycle, all is resolved: for example, in the Descent of the Goddess myth the Goddess returns bringing with her the resurrected God (in my version) unless at Samhain. In the Midwinter rite, the Sun King is born.

* In handfasting, the couple tie the knot and leap over the broomstick or run through a flower arch, tossing the bouquet.

* The child would be named and his or her special candles lit and the first one left to burn. The others are blown out to be relit at later times in his or her life.

* The cakes would now be blessed if not already and then the athame blade plunged into the chalice. Offerings of cake and wine, ale, mead or fruit juice are made to the Earth Mother. You would eat and drink if you are working alone, asking for a blessing and making one for each mouthful. In a group, the cakes and chalice of wine are passed round with blessings or taken round and given with the refrain Blessings be from giver and recipient.

9 Returning the energies

Don't be in too much of a hurry to close the quarters as this is a very special time whether for scrying, sending healing blessings, singing or drumming softly or making wishes for the future into a candle flame or by dropping them as herbs or flower petals into the cauldron. Each person can speak Goddess-inspired wisdom after the Charge or help create what happened after the resolution of the myth. Alone, this is a good time for inspired writing in your Book of Shadows.

If offerings were not made earlier this would be a good time for each person to put a flower or crystal into a basket that is passed round while speaking a blessing, or to quietly pass the symbol round and make low soft promises of practical ways you all personally will help to bring the spell to fruition. In a handfasting, the crystals collected earlier would be given to the couple, filled with wishes. At a naming ceremony, a tree can be planted for the infant.

10 Closing the quarters

* First face south. If you invited deity energies, open your arms wide as you did when calling them and thank them, saying:

Hail and farewell until we meet again

or whatever words you choose to use and ask that they may continue to bless you and your work.

* Face west and bid any ancestors farewell by banging the staff or ringing the bell precisely as you did to call them and give thanks, saying finally

Hail and farewell until we meet again [or your chosen words].

Ask that they will continue to guide you with their wisdom.

* Straight afterwards go to the western perimeter of the circle and close the elemental gateway of Water. Raise your arms high and wide and palms flat and uppermost and bid:

Hail and farewell to the guardians of the west.

Thank them for their protection and strength and asking that they will bring peace into the world, saying:

'Til we meet again.

* Again everyone present faces west and echoes *Hail and farewell* or the response to the words used. Make the banishing Water pentagram if you wish, either before or after the farewell.

* Then slowly in turn close the south, then the east and finally the north gateways, again bidding:

Hail and farewell 'til we meet again

and asking the guardian of the south for continuing joy, of the east for continuing opportunities and of the north for continuing protection.

* You can either make the appropriate elemental pentagram at each quarter or use banishing Earth at them all (or none at all). Extinguish any directional candles as you go.

Some people close the gateways in the same direction they opened them, from north clockwise and you can do this straight after bidding the ancestors farewell by moving clockwise to the north. Again, extinguish direction candles.

11 Uncasting the circle

The earlier farewell and extinguishing the directional candles is considered by some witches adequate uncasting. You may also conclude as follows:

* Finish with a chorus or three of:

May the circle that is cast forever be unbroken, may the love of the Goddess, be forever in our hearts. Merry meet and Merry part and Merry meet again.

* Now if you prefer uncast just one circle (any triple circles have all merged by now, see page 250).

* Face north, but if others are still in the circle turn round slowly anticlockwise as you make the blessing. Again, others close clockwise.

* If you cast your sealing triple circles round a circle of people, lead them out in a spiral with an uncasting chant, such as:

We leave this place willingly, we joyfully uncast the circle that we made. Within us the enchantment, inside us dwells the sanctity, the circle lives forever, safe in our heart. Merry meet and merry part and merry meet again.

* Then alone or with others make your closing blessing, maybe an echo of the opening one, or:

May the circle that is be open but remain unbroken in my/our heart/s and life/lives. Blessings be.

* All the nature essences will now depart peacefully.

12 Afterwards

Whether alone or with others, it is important to avoid an anticlimax. This is the point where you would share out any empowered offerings of the feast. It is good to take away one another's offerings. You would give the crystals or herbs to the mother of the child or the couple, and generally there is a small exchange of gifts, such as a packet of wildflower seeds for all present to take home. If you did bring small coven gifts, such as a tiny bag of herbs or incense or a single crystal in a pouch, get everyone to close their eyes and in turn take a gift from the Goddess.

You need to decide in advance what you will do with any symbol you empowered, if you carried out a formal spell as part of or as the rite.

If in a group, often musical offerings or poems are spoken and a bring-and-share meal enjoyed. If alone, you should have prepared something specially good to eat and drink afterwards, and sit outdoors or listen to music by the fire. Leave the altar candles burning until you leave the site and then extinguish them in either order, sending the light to whoever needs it, not forgetting yourself.

The Cakes and Ale/Chalice and Blade

If you work as a solitary practitioner you may not use this as part of your ceremonies but it is very beautiful and a way of uniting the Goddess/God power within you. It will also make any ritual significant and sacred. Leland in Aradia described making and blessing ritual crescent moon-shaped cakes in honour of Diana, made of honey, salt, meal and wine to be consecrated and eaten at ceremonies.

* All you need is a small cake or biscuit made with honey for each person plus one as an offering, and a chalice filled with wine, fruit juice or a special water, such as a full moon water you made on the night of the full moon (see page 359).

* Set the cakes towards the north of the altar on a dish or plate marked with a pentacle if you wish and the chalice or goblet in the west.

* Raise the cakes skywards in front of the altar as you stand in the south of it, facing north.

* Then lower them to solar plexus level in front of you and make an invoking Earth pentagram or a cross over the cakes with your power hand as you hold them in the other. Rest the plate on the altar if there are a lot of cakes, saying:

> *May the abundance of the Mother and the bountifulness of the Father bless and nourish,*
> *sustain and protect me/you all my/your days.*
> *Blessed be.*

* You can choose a man to hold the dish and a woman to bless them (or either sex can do this) as they speak. The person blessing them says the words. Put the plate in the centre of the altar.

* Now take the chalice/goblet in your receptive hand and your athame in your power hand and gently lower the tip of the knife so it almost touches the surface of the wine or juice. This represents the joining of Goddess (in the chalice) and God energies in the knife. Say:

As male to female, God to Goddess so in this wine/juice is joined in power and love, strength and compassion, striving and acceptance.
Blessed be.

* Return it to the centre of the altar to the right of the cakes.

* If more than one person is present one can bless the cakes and two people bless the wine. They are usually the same people who blessed the cakes, but you may prefer to share the duties. Often the athame is held by the female and the cup by a male for the crossing of energies, but two women or men can carry out the ceremony.

* Then you should take the cakes, scatter a few crumbs from one of the cakes on the ground or into an offerings dish indoors. and say:

I return this gift to the Earth Mother in gratitude for blessings received. Blessings be to your Mother and to me/all here gathered.

* After the ceremony, feed the rest of this cake to the birds.

* At this point if there are two people involved, they can offer each other a cake and then pass them round any one else present. Each person can say Blessings be or add a blessing before eating. Some people kiss the person to whom they are giving the cakes/wine on each cheek.

* You should then return the plate to the altar and take the wine, dropping a little on the ground and thanking Mother Earth again for her blessings. Pour this offering into a dish if indoors and you can put the crumbs and liquid outside after the ceremony.

* Now drink or offer it to the other person who blessed the chalice. He or she will take a sip and offer it to you to or the other person who carried out the blessing, saying:

Blessings be.

* Then, if others are present, pass the cup round so each can take a sip, saying Blessings be and perhaps add a blessing before passing it on.

PRACTICAL ASSIGNMENT

Creating a ritual

❋ Work towards creating an actual ritual, whether for yourself or to involve others. If possible incorporate a mini drama. Feel free to devise your own myths about the God and Goddess and record them in your Book of Shadows or publish them on the internet to inspire others.

❋ Practise the movements and order bit by bit and reread until you are confident.

❋ Then shut the book and go for it. It does not matter at all if you miss out stages as you are the magick.

Further research

Using online Books of Shadows and the books I have mentioned in earlier modules such as the Farrar's Witch's Bible, to study the construction of different ceremonies, partly to reassure yourself there is no single right way, but more importantly to draw ideas that you can adapt for your own work.

Further information

Recommended reading

❋ West, Kate, *The Real Witch's Handbook*, Harper Collins, 2001

Websites

❋ *Ceisiwr Serith*
Excellent site about the descent of the Goddess myth, though I don't agree that Wicca is poor in myths
www.ceisiwrserith.com/wicca/legendofthedescent.htm
Also refer back to:
www.pagan-library.com
www.sacred-texts.com/bos/index.htm

FESTIVALS:
OIMELC TO LITHA

I have already devoted three modules to the all-essential Wheel of the Year since it is in essence the Witch's calendar. In this and the next module I aim to give you some background to the festivals and their associated herbs, crystals and artefacts. In this way and using your creativity, you can weave your own festivals whether as a solitary witch, with friends and family as many solitaries like myself do, or in a magickal group or coven.

If you live in the southern hemisphere then as I suggested in earlier modules you can move the festivals round six months. But in other lands you can adapt the festivals to fit with what is going on outdoors in terms of tree and flower growth, as well as climate. For each and every festival you should where possible include natural plants and herbs at their particular stage of growth from your own region.

If you think of the Wheel of the Year like a Ferris wheel, it operates in terms of the downward ebb and the upward flow and these are natural mirrors of our own yearly energies. So, too, with the God/Goddess myths there are times when the animus rules, when we must trust the anima or the two powers within us are in perfect balance. Instinctively, you will feel the changing energies for about a week before each festival and can ride its power for a week or two afterwards. The restlessness that even domesticated animals display at natural and seasonal change points can be expressed in the excitement of the festival and launch the next surge in your life. The energies of the different festivals will carry you forward on an upsurging festival, allow you to consolidate or plan on a balancing one and prepare you to shed excess baggage and leave what is completed with satisfaction as the wheel goes down. You know as you greet winter that spring is not far ahead.

For every festival you celebrate, in your Book of Shadows write the ongoing story of your personal wheel as it turns each year: what is happening right now and how you feel about it, what you hope to be doing by the time the next festival comes in six weeks' time and your plans and dreams for when the wheel reaches this point again in 12 months' time. I find these mini targets more inspiring and attainable than the once and for all New Year resolution.

The first four festivals

In this module we will work with the festivals of Oimelc at the beginning of February, Ostara, the Spring Equinox in mid-March, Beltaine at the beginning of May, and Litha, the Summer Solstice in mid-June. However, you can step on the wheel at any point and can turn to the second module if the approaching festival is in that section. Refer back to modules 5, 6 and 7 for the introductory information on the Wheel of the Year and to 17 and 18, 28, 29 and 30 for the respective paths of the Goddess and God through the year.

I have given myths from the Celtic, Christian, Northern and Mediterranean traditions so you can create your own dramatic performance for the ceremony in your coven or with friends and family. If you are working alone, you can tell or ritually act out the part of the myth that seems to resonate most with you. The re-enactment or retelling of myths is one of the most potent ways we have of connecting with the deeper truths behind a festival and as you adapt or rewrite them with the resolution you feel is right you are adding to the mythology of the future. Record these myths in your Book of Shadows or publish them on the internet or write your own mythology book. Covens, too, should keep records of how a drama altered in the enactment and how someone improvising when they forgot their lines in fact created just the right feeling and a new perspective.

Imbolc or Oimelc

31 January–2 February, a cross-quarter day

Focus: New ideas, for the promise that winter will end, for planning the future and for putting out the first shoots of new love and the growth or regrowth of trust; for taking the first steps to launch any projects that start in a small way; for rituals to regenerate any areas devastated by neglect or pollution in your life or more globally; for melting rigid attitudes that may have led to conflicts between families and work colleagues or the isolation and alienation of disadvantaged groups through prejudice; rituals for newborn infants, babies and young animals.

Element: Fire/Earth

Direction: North-east

Cycle of the year: The Maiden Goddess displaces the old hag of winter; the God as the helpless infant is protected and nurtured by the mother's milk; also the Young/Horned God who mates with the hag transformed into the maiden. This is the maiden's awakening into womanhood as spring melts the winter, but conception does not take place and so a theme of the festival is awakening. The dark brother still holds sway but the young God of light is growing in power.

Nature of festival: Light/candles

Energies: Rising

Symbols: Milk, honey, seeds, early budding flowers and greenery

Animal: Serpent, black cat

Tree: Willow: with her willow wand, the Goddess melts the snows of winter

Incenses, flowers and herbs: Angelica, basil, benzoin, celandine, crocus, heather, myrrh, snowdrops, violets

Candle colours: Pale pink, green, blue, white

Crystals: Dark gemstones such as the garnet and bloodstone/heliotrope, also amethyst, rose quartz, moonstone

Celtic tradition

At dusk on 31 January in the pagan calendar, candles and sacred bonfires were lit to attract the sun and there was a procession clockwise around the frozen fields with blazing torches, led it was said in pre-Christian times, by the Maiden Goddess herself or a huge grain maiden pulled on a cart made from the last sheaf cut from the previous harvest. This was believed to contain the spirit of the grain mother Brighid who brought back life to the land on this night. A festival of healing of the land as well as people and animals was held. Eight candles were placed in a circle in water and lit so that the light rose from the water of the Goddess, the unity of Fire and Water.

Right through mediaeval times, a girl representing Brighid arrived at the door of the main house or farmstead of a village on 31 January eve with cows and a cauldron, symbols of plenty, where her straw bride bed would be created close to the fire, adorned with ribbons and blessed with honey and milk by the women of the household. This referred to the deflowering and awakening of the Maiden Goddess. The local men would enter the circle of firelight and ask for help with their craft or agriculture and make a wish on the bride bed of the maiden chosen to represent the young Goddess.

Bridget crosses, none of whose three or four arms are parallel, were woven from straw or wheat to hang around the house for protection. They are still a feature in Irish homes today.

Norse and Anglo-Saxon associations

The Anglo-Saxon Offering of Cakes ceremony to the deities asked for a thaw that the first ploughing might take place early. In Scandinavia, Disting, the festival of the family ancestors, was associated with future prosperity, because it was a time the cattle and resources remaining after the winter's forced inactivity were counted. In Iceland, Thorrablót was dedicated to Thor as god of winter. He was asked to drive back the Jotuns, the Frost Giants, so that spring would come.

Christian associations

On Candlemas Day, 2 February, all the church candles that would be used for the coming liturgical year were blessed at high mass. Blessed candles were also distributed to the congregation. Each person was given a blessed candle that acted as protector of the home against storms, fire and flood and protected cattle and crops against evil. Traditionally, a lighted candle was placed at each window of houses on 31 January (dating from Celtic times) or on Candlemas Eve, 1 February, and left to burn through.

On the following day, the feast of St Blaise, the newly sanctified church candles were used by priests to bless the throats of parishioners, so that they would be free from all respiratory illness in the coming months.

In the Christian calendar the anniversary of the Purification of the Virgin Mary occurred 40 days after the birth of Jesus, the occasion also when he was taken to the Temple on 2 February and was hailed as the light of the world. Candlemas was also the day for predicting the weather for the coming weeks and the arrival of spring weather. The US Groundhog Day, 2 February, follows this tradition.

Mediterranean associations

In Ancient Rome, at the rites of Juno Februa, animals were brought out of their winter hibernation, candles were lit in homes to drive away evil spirits and blazing torches cast into the river Tiber.

In Rome, 15 February, the love and fertility festival that gave rise to modern Valentine's Day customs, Lupercalia, was dedicated to Lupa, the Goddess she-wolf who suckled Romulus and Remus, the twins who founded Rome. Love and sex rites by young unmarried girls and men were performed in the Grotto of the She-Wolf to bring fertility to animals, land and people.

Ritual activity

* Place a ring of eight candles for the Wheel of the Year in the centre of your home or magick circle.

* Set a dish in the middle of the candles, filled with ice and a jug with fresh milk. Each person present should light a candle clockwise, then stir the ice clockwise with a wooden spoon and name a personal or global situation where feelings or indifference needs to melt.

* If more than eight people are present, place extra candles in an outer ring round the eight candles. If fewer or you are working alone, light each candle and stir eight times each time, but you can make the same wish as many times as you need.

* While the ice is melting sing, chant or softly drum. When it has melted, tip it on the ground or if indoors on a plant.

* Afterwards drink the milk and eat seed bread and honey, foods of the feast.

Alban Eiler, Ostara or the Spring Equinox

Around 20 March–22 March, a quarter day

Focus: Fertility and positive life changes, new beginnings and opportunities, for new flowering love, for initiating creative ventures, travel, house moves, clearing what is no longer needed in your life; anything to do with conception and pregnancy, children and young people, mothers, for healing, spring-cleaning and casting out what is no longer of worth, welcoming the winds of change; rituals to cleanse the seas and air of pollution, for new peace-making initiatives of all kinds, also to encourage attitude changes towards international, national and local issues.

Direction: East

Cycle of the year: The Maiden Goddess opens the doors of spring and mates with the young, virile, triumphal Horned and Wild Woodland God to conceive the child of light who will be born on the Midwinter Solstice the following December. The light and dark brothers fight and the light twin kills his brother, so henceforward the days will be longer than the night. The dark twin descends to the Underworld or the womb of the mother, like the seeds planted in the earth, to await rebirth.

Nature of festival: Rebirth/eggs

Energies: Balanced

Symbols: Eggs, especially painted ones, feathers, spring flowers or leaves, a sprouting pot of seeds, pottery rabbits and birds, feathers and anything made of dough or clay

Animal: Hare

Tree: Birch

Incenses, flowers and herbs: Celandine, cinquefoil, crocus, daffodil, honeysuckle, hyacinth, lemon, primroses, sage, tansy, thyme, violets (the latter also for Oimelc)

Candle colours: Yellow and green

Crystals: Sparkling yellow crystals, such as citrine, golden beryl, rutilated quartz, chrysoprase, aventurine

Celtic tradition

Alban Eiler means in Gaelic the light of the earth that returns after the winter from the Otherworld and also rises from the earth to cause the growth of plants. Bonfires were lit and the corn dolly from the previous year was burned or the effigy of a straw sacrifice man symbolising the awakening of the sacrificed Grain God. As at Beltaine, the Nyd fire was kindled using an oaken spindle from nine different kinds of sacred wood. The ashes were scattered on the fields when sowing for fertility.

The sun (in Christian times Angels) was seen to dance in rivers in the Spring Equinox to celebrate the resurrection of light and this water was considered to bring healing and fertility. Dough cakes marked with the cross of the Earth Mother were eaten to absorb the fertility of the year. These survive as hot cross buns.

Norse and Anglo-Saxon associations

Ostara is the Viking Goddess of the moon and spring, the maiden aspect of Frigg, the Mother Goddess, after whom the festival is named. Her white magickal hare led to the tradition in some lands of chocolate Easter rabbits and it was the hare that brought eggs for the children or hid them for them to find. Rabbits were also a symbol of fertility as they began to reproduce. Painted fresh eggs, again a sign of spring when the hens began to lay in natural light, are another ancient fertility symbol and were placed on the shrines of Ostara.

Christian associations

In the early Christian tradition, candles were extinguished on Easter Eve. The paschal candle was lit from the Nyd fire, which was kindled outside churches using an oaken spindle from nine different kinds of wood. Sometimes the effigy of a Judas Man was burned. Charred sticks were taken from the fire and placed on newly kindled home fires or kept through the year as protection against thunderstorms.

St Cyril of Jerusalem described the profusion of light on Easter Eve as being as bright as day, and Constantine the Great made the Easter Eve celebrations even more dazzling by placing lights not only in basilicas, but also in streets and squares. Homes were also illuminated with candles in every window to welcome the resurrection.

Eggs were painted and dedicated to the Virgin Mary in Germany, Eastern and Western Europe, parts of the Mediterranean, Russia and in Mexico and South America. In Poland, it is said that Mary painted eggs in bright colours to delight her infant and so Polish mothers continue the custom.

Mediterranean associations

The Phrygian Goddess Mother Cybele, much beloved in Greece and Rome, brought her sacrificed God consort/son Attis back to life on the Spring Equinox.

The Eleusinian Mysteries celebrated the restoration of Persephone the grain maiden to her grieving mother Demeter. In the spring rites at Eleusis, grain was thrown into the field and buried in the earth to bring forth new life. Images of the public ceremony depict Persephone as the sprouting corn. A virgin was chosen to represent the deflowering of Persephone and her sacrifice in a sacred sex ceremony (see page 382).

Ritual activity

* Sweep your home, the ritual square and/or a specially constructed circle in the earth (from flowers or drawn with a branch or the staff in the earth). Scatter dried lavender heads or any fragrant, lavender-based potpourri in the circle or square area.

* Then using a bristle or besom broom, or long twigs tied together in a bundle, one for each person, preferably from a pine or thorn tree, sweep the sacred area sweeping outwards in anticlockwise circles.

* Chant as you work:

> *Dust to dust away you must. Health and luck and joy to bring, be gone winter, welcome spring.*

* When all the lavender is gone, sprinkle clockwise with small bowls of water, left out before the ritual from dawn (again one for each person) towards the centre of the circle as you dance or spiral clockwise.

* As you do so chant:

> *Enter new light and life, welcome Maiden of the spring, welcome health, luck, love, joy and new beginnings.*

* Chant and sprinkle faster and faster, finally leaping over your broom that you have set horizontally on the ground close to the altar and call:

> *Enter, maiden; welcome spring.*

Beltane or Beltaine

30 April–2 May, the second most important cross-quarter day of the year and the beginning of the Celtic summer

Focus: Fertility whether for conceiving a child or improvement in career, business or financial matters, for increasing commitment in love, for passion and the consummation of love, for creative inspiration, improving health and increasing energy, for optimism and self-confidence; for abundance in every way and for generosity; for people in their 20s and 30s; for giving up bad habits and for rituals to send strength for freedom of speech, action and beliefs everywhere.

Direction: South-east

Cycle of the year: The marriage of the Goddess as May Queen, the flower maiden to the God in his woodland form as the Green Man; the last appearance of the Maiden Goddess. The mating is the wild form of the sacred marriage solemnised at the Summer Solstice when the God will become the God King.

Energies: Rising

Symbols: Fresh greenery and blossom, especially hawthorn (indoors only on 1 May), also ribbons, staffs or staves decorated with flowers and ribbons

Nature of Festival: Fire/flowers

Animal: Cow

Tree: Hawthorn

Incenses, flowers and herbs: Almond, angelica, ash, cowslip, frankincense, hawthorn, lilac, bluebells, marigolds and roses for love; also any flower or light floral fragrance

Candle colours: Dark green, scarlet, silver

Crystals: Clear crystal quartz, red ox-eye, Herkimer diamond, golden tiger's eye, amber, topaz

Celtic tradition

The beginning of the Celtic summer when the cattle that survived the winter in barns were driven between twin fires for cleansing. The major theme of this festival was the interlinked fertility of the fields, the animals and the people.

Sundown on May Eve heralded the signal for Druids to kindle the great twin Bel-fires from nine different kinds of sacred wood, willow, hazel, alder, birch, ash, yew, elm, rowan and oak, by turning an oaken spindle in an oaken socket, on top of the nearest beacon hill: for example, on Tara Hill, County Meath, in Ireland, former home of the Tuatha de Danaan, the Hero Gods of old Ireland. As time went on every village would have its twin Beltaine fires, which were attributed with both fertility and healing powers. They were lit in the name of the Gallic Sun God Belinus or the even earlier Gallic Solar and Fire Goddess called Belissima by the Romans. Winter was finally dead as at midnight on May Eve, Cailleach Bhuer, the old hag of winter, cast her staff under a holly bush and turned to stone until six months later on Halloween.

The God bridegroom, in his form as the Green Man, Jack o' Green or Robin Hood, led the procession to his woodland wedding, made up of Morris dancers, like him dressed in foliage, bearing horns or darkened with soot. The wild God crowns his bride with flowers and promises one day to crown her with gold.

Young men and girls made love in the woods and fields on May Eve to bring fertility to the land as well as themselves. They gathered flowers and May blossoms from the magickal hawthorn tree to decorate houses and to make into May baskets that were left as gifts on doorsteps. This custom certainly lasted well into Victorian times and is recalled in Rudyard Kipling's poem 'Oak, Ash and Thorn' that begins:

> Do not tell the priest our plight,
> For he would think it a sin,
> For we have been in the woods all night,
> Bringing summer in.

Tales of the wicker man come from this time or the possible ancient Beltaine human sacrifice that was selected if he chose the charred portion of the Beltaine cake that was divided into 13 pieces and placed in a bag.

From Celtic times, sacred wells have been considered potent on 1 May for both healing and fertility. Traditionally, the ritual should be finished by sunrise, but any May morning energies will work as well. This continued when the wells were Christianised.

A time of great fairy activity, especially around standing stones and stone circles as the fairies moved to their summer quarters.

Norse and Anglo-Saxon associations

From 22 April–1 May was the nine-night festival named Walpurgis in Germany, the Netherlands and Scandinavia, after the Goddess of this festival, Walpurgis or Walpurga. She was Christianised as St Walpurga. The nine nights represented Odin's nine nights hanging on the World Tree Yggdrasil to acquire wisdom and his resurrection. The fires were lit at midnight as light returns to the world. On Walpurgisnacht, 30 April, the wild hunt through the sky for souls led by Odin ended and the dead and nature spirits roamed freely for the last time after the long winter as light prevailed.

In Iceland and parts of Scandinavia on May Day there was the Sigrblot or victory blessing celebration to ask for success in future trading and raiding parties, once the weather was fine enough for the men to travel.

Christian associations

Six weeks after Easter comes the Christian Whitsun when the Holy Spirit descended to earth in tongues of flame. Sophia, Goddess of Wisdom who in early creation stories was present at the beginning of the world, was associated by the 2nd century Gnostic sects with the Holy Spirit, both of whom had the white dove as their symbol.

Mediterranean associations

The Goddess is manifested as the May Queen, Maia, the Greek Goddess of spring who gives her name to the month.

Flowers that typify the festival are named after the Roman Goddess of flowers whose festival, Floralia, lasted from 26 April until 3 May. She was called Khloris in the Ancient Greek tradition and was the wife of Zephyros, God of the west wind.

The flowers came from her mouth and were scattered by the wind. Young people would collect baskets of flowers and children make tiny floral images on 1 May.

Ritual activity

* On May Eve or the night of 1 May, either alone or with a group, make a small fire and burn as many different kinds of wood as you can easily obtain. Alternatively, use one or more tree types local to your area.

* Ask questions. Look in the flames for images to predict the months ahead. If others are present, you can all work to see and interpret each person's questions as you stand around the fire.

* When the fire is burned through, one person should scatter some of the ashes to the winds, everyone present calling out at the same time their personal wishes for the future creativity or fertility in any way.

* If you are working alone and do not wish to make a fire, use a large green candle and three large incense sticks or loose incense in one or more the fragrances of the festival and scatter those ashes in your garden, making wishes as you go.

* Leave the candle to burn through and look for images in the area around the flame.

Alban Heruin, Litha, Midsummer or Summer Solstice

Around 20–22 June, a major quarter day

Focus: Power, joy and courage, male potency, success, marriage, fertility of all kinds, especially for older women, for people approaching middle age; happiness, strength, energy, self-confidence, identity, health, wealth and career; also for maximising opportunities, seizing chances and enjoying the present. This power can be harnessed for tackling seemingly insoluble problems, bringing light and life and hope; also for tackling major global problems such as global warming, famine, disease and preventing cruelty to people under oppressive regimes and intensive farming methods where livestock suffer.

Direction: South

Cycle of the year: The Goddess gives birth to the dark twin and so becomes the Mother Goddess. In turn, the God is now the God King and they enter into a formal sacred marriage in which he promises to lay down his life for the Goddess, the land and her people. Ritually, this is the first ceremony involving the Great Rite. The God reaches his height of power and God and Goddess are equal at the coronation. But by the end of the day he knows that he will grow weaker.

Nature of festival: Sun/gold

Energies: The high turning point as full power begins to wane from this day

Symbols: Brightly coloured flowers, oak boughs, golden fern pollen that is said to reveal buried treasure wherever it falls, scarlet, orange and yellow ribbons, gold coloured coins and any gold jewellery that can be empowered at the festival, any golden fruit or vegetables

Animal: Bear

Tree: Oak

Incenses, flowers and herbs: Chamomile, dill, elder, fennel, lavender, frankincense, orange, marigolds, rosemary, sage and sagebrush, St John's Wort, lemon verbena, vervain, any golden, red or orange flowers

Candle colours: Red, orange, gold

Crystals: Amber, carnelian or red jasper, sun stone; also sparkling crystal quartz spheres

Celtic tradition

Litha means light and Alban Heruin the light of the shore as the sun floods over the land ripening the crops. But it is bittersweet for the Sun God and Goddess who want the day to last forever. Because she loved him, bonfires were lit and sun wheels made of flaming cart wheels were rolled down the hillsides to prolong the light on this longest of days. The Goddess, or her representative, cast her bouquet of summer flowers on a hilltop fire to add her power to the sun. The cauldron was the symbol of the Goddess giving forth her bounty on the Solstice and may be filled with small golden coloured fruits and crystals as coven gifts.

The Celtic solar and lunar Goddess Aine was seen at the Summer Solstice Eve festival on her sacred hill by maidens who looked through a gold ring at the moon. The height of the festival has always been first light falling on Solstice morn, like a shaft of gold across standing stones and stone circles, linking the dimensions.

Stonehenge is oriented to mark the sunrise and moonrise at the Summer and Winter Solstices, built long before the time of the Celts. Druidic ceremonies based, it is believed, on Celtic ones are held at dawn and noon on the Summer Solstice at sacred circles such as Stonehenge and some groups and individuals still keep vigil from sunset on the previous evening. At sunset of the Summer Solstice at Stonehenge, another significant ritual point, the heel (sun) stone outside the circles, casts a shadow on the altar stone, thus marking the beginning of the dying of the year.

Norse and Anglo-Saxon associations

Overseas trading, raiding and fishing reached its height at this time. As the longest day of the year transferred to the Midsummer celebrations of modern Scandinavia, the ancient Midsummer tree, linked to the Green Man, formed the centre of dancing and music.

In the ancient Germanic tradition, mountain and cliff top fires were lit on the eve of the Solstice and later on St John's Eve, 23 June, to give power to the sun.

The Norse god of light Baldur was slain by his blind brother Hodur. In the traditional version of the legend, the young Sun God was doomed to remain in the Underworld until the last battle, Ragnarok. But a more positive version tells that Hel, the guardian of the Underworld, was so moved by the tears of his mother that she allowed the Goddess of spring, Ostara, to restore him each year to the world at Yule for half of the year.

Christian associations

The Christian festival of Midsummer is very close to St John's Day on 24 June. John's own mother was long beyond childbearing years and thus regarded as a virgin birth. In the early Christian Celtic tradition, John was linked with the dark brother of the solar deity who would in a variation of the Celtic myth cycle after the Longest Day rule the waning year.

The ancient, possibly pre-Celtic myth of the Oak King who ruled from Midwinter to Midsummer and the Holly King who ruled from Midsummer to Midwinter became linked to the Christian tradition and oak fires were burned at Midsummer right until Victorian times. Married women who wanted to get pregnant would walk naked in a garden at midnight and pick the golden herb of midsummer, St John's Wort, on the Eve of St John. Young girls would not eat anything all day and they would pick the same herb to put under their pillow to dream of their true love.

Mediterranean associations

In the Basque region of Northern Spain, the sun is still revered in folk custom as Grandmother Sun. Her worship has been transferred to the Virgin Mary who is associated with mother Mari, the Storm Goddess in whose wise bosom Grandmother Sun sleeps at night. On Midsummer Eve sun vigils were held until recently to see the Sun Goddess touch the mountain tops and dance at dawn. The watchers would then bathe in streams in the magickal Midsummer waters that are still believed to have healing and empowering properties.

Juno, the Roman Mother Goddess, was patron of marriage and of childbirth and she protected women from birth to the grave. June, her month, is considered to be the most fortunate for marriages.

Ritual activity

This works as well whether you are celebrating the festival alone or with others and is based on an old Scandinavian folk custom.

* At dawn, set a basket of seven different species of flowers where they will catch the first light of the Summer Solstice. Make sure there are enough flowers for each person to have several.

* At noon, each person should weave the seven kinds of flowers on to a small circle of wire, using threads in red, yellow, green and blue to attach them.

* As you weave, silently name for each flower over and over again in your mind or whisper your dearest secret wish for fulfilment in the next 12 months whether for lasting love, a child, the success of a creative venture, happiness, travel, success, health or spiritual wisdom.

* When finished, the circlet should be hung on a shady tree and you should circle the tree nine times clockwise, nine times anticlockwise, nine times clockwise again, clapping a rhythm until the world spins, chanting:

With seven flowers sweet I call my secret dream. Come to me as I dance the Midsummer Tree, come to me in my sleep, come to me in my waking, that when I next dance the Midsummer tree, I shall know the joy of the seven flowers sweet.

* If you are working alone you can adapt the chant to fit your desire: for example, if for lasting love:

. . . that when next I dance the Midsummer tree, it shall be my wedding day.

* At sundown, take your wreath from the tree and hang it over your bed. Go straight to bed when it is dark. Picture yourself walking as you drift into sleep along a pathway of flowers into mist that slowly clears to reveal how and when you will attain your desire. This may continue in your dreams.
* Leave the wreath on the wall of your bedroom until it fades and then release the petals to the wind or use the flowers in incense.

PRACTICAL ASSIGNMENT

Creating a myth cycle

Choose at least one of the four festivals and create a myth or drama that you can weave in your Book of Shadows to begin to create your own Wheel of the Year myth cycle.

Further research

Choose a festival and research similar dates in other cultures such as India, China or Native North America.

Further information

Recommended reading
* Gilchrist, Cherry, *A Calendar of Festivals; Celebrations around the World*, Barefoot Books, 2005
* Luenn, Nancy, *Celebrations of Light, A Year of Holidays around the World*, Simon and Schuster Inc, 1998

Websites
* *Living Myths*
  Myths of the Celtic year and good links to Ancient Greek Native American and the myths of other cultures
  www.livingmyths.com/Celticyear.htm
* *Branwen's Cauldron of Light*
  Norse traditions and lots of good links including the Norse/ Germanic pantheons and a great deal of information about witchcraft traditions, including the Italian Stregheria
  www.branwenscauldron.com/ resources/Astaru.html

Festivals: Lughnassadh to Yule

In this module are the other four festivals of the ritual year. As you read, weave into these and the previous festivals events in your life that have mirrored their energies. If there are any loose ends, mark in your calendar ahead how you might use the appropriate festival, perhaps by celebrating it in a special place or by incorporation of personal symbols to resolve these issues. In this way you can achieve spiritual closure or move on from a stage that seems each year or at least regularly in your life to prove problematic. Acknowledge and also celebrate ritually your personal harvests and achievements and plan your next year's sowing.

In this module I will write of Lughnassadh, the first grain harvest at the beginning of August, the Autumn Equinox, the second harvest in mid-September, Samhain at the beginning of November and the traditional beginning of the ritual year, and finally the Midwinter Solstice in mid-December and the rebirth of light. Use any altar formation you wish, Wiccan, Norse, Ancient Egyptian or your own unique arrangement that is right for you.

Lughnassadh/Lammas

31 July–2 August, a cross-quarter day

Focus: Justice, human rights, freedom from abuse of any kind; for partnerships, personal and legal or business, for signing contracts or property matters; promotion and career advancement and the regularising of personal finances; for journeys to see friends and family or on business and the renewal of promises and fidelity; also willing sacrifice for the greater good, natural justice and karma, trusting the cosmos to provide by giving without seeking immediate return; for people in their 40s and 50s.

Globally, the festival energies are good for rituals for fighting through legal redress for injustice for oppressed people or creatures, especially making sure that workers in Third World countries are not exploited financially; for teaching new skills so that people in poor lands and deprived areas may have a chance to create their own prosperity, for all acts of unpublicised charity.

Direction: South-west

Cycle of the year: The God renews or in some myths makes for the first time the sacred marriage with the Goddess in the Celtic form of Eriu/Nass, the Irish Earth

Goddess. In this he promises to defend and die for the land, a ceremony undertaken by King/Leader and priestess of the Goddess, another Great Rite ceremony. In one of the magickal transformations from Maiden/Mother/Crone, Eriu was pictured as a hag who was made lovely by the golden light of the sun. The Sun/Grain God transfers his remaining light and warmth to the Goddess for the continuing growth of the crops. He willingly sacrifices himself for the growth of the rest of the crops and his spirit enters the grain. He assumes the role of Sacrifice God/dark lord and descends to the Underworld, back into her womb, to be reborn on the Midwinter celebration as the infant Sun King. The final battle of the light and dark twin cannot take place until the Autumn Equinox six weeks later and so the myths divide again. In some myths, the twins fight and the light twin is mortally wounded and takes six weeks to die.

Nature of festival: Transformation, bread

Energies: Waning

Symbols: Any straw object such as a corn dolly, a corn knot or a straw hat or a horse or goat (symbol of the Norse Thor) tied with red ribbon, harvest flowers such as poppies or cornflowers, container of mixed cereals, dried grasses, and stones with natural holes; bread and dough

Animal: Stag

Tree: Alder

Incense, flowers and herbs: Cedarwood, cinnamon, fenugreek, ginger and heather, myrtle, poppies, sunflowers, any dark yellow, deep blue or brown-gold flowers

Candle colours: Golden brown, dark yellow

Crystals: Fossilised wood, dark yellow and any brown jasper, banded agates, titanium aura, fossils

Celtic tradition

Because of the dry roads it was a time for travelling Druidesses and Druids (and Viking courts) to arbitrate in disputes; also the time for making and renewing vows and contracts when temporary marriages were made for a year and a day by the couple joining hands through a large holed stone called in Scandinavian tradition an Odin stone.

In the old harvesting rites, that continued right through mediaeval times, everyone hurled sickles at the last grain in the field at same time so no one would know who killed the God.

Bread was made from this sheaf to be offered to the Earth Mother. From this also was fashioned a Grain Mother decorated with the scarlet ribbons of Cerridwen, the Celtic Mother Goddess or in Scandinavia the red ribbons of Frigg, the Mother Goddess. The Grain dolly would be hung over the hearth of the main homestead to bring health, abundance and protection to the whole settlement throughout winter. Smaller grain knots and dolls were made from other grain that was cut on this day. These were hung in barns and smaller homes through the long winter and returned to the fields as ashes on the Spring Equinox the following year.

On Lughnassadh, hilltop processions and fires were held on the tops of hills associated with the Mother Goddess, such as the Irish Aine and Grainne. Hilltop ceremonies were also dedicated in England to Sulis, the Celtic Sun and Water Goddess, Romanised as Sulis Minerva. She was particularly worshipped on the man-made Neolithic Silbury Hill near Avebury in Wiltshire that was built in 2600 BCE. Here on the full or harvest moon nearest to Lughnassadh, when the sun set as the moon rose, the light would be reflected in the moat then surrounding Silbury Hill. It was said that milk was pouring from the Great Mother's breast into the water and it was time for harvesting to begin. Lughnassadh fires still burn in parts of the world where there is Celtic ancestry.

Norse and Anglo-Saxon associations

Lithasblot, the first harvest, was a celebration among farmers to give thanks to the Earth Mother for the riches of the first ripened grain. Bread in the shape of the sun wheel was made and gifts of food and money offered to the poor in order that the deities would bless the farmers. Fairs and horse fighting were traditional. Freyr was patron of horses and the first harvest and so invoked for success.

The August crayfish or herring celebrations may date back to older festivals of the harvest of the lakes and seas as offerings of the finest of the catch and gold were made to the sea deities. Courts were held, disputes were heard and judgements given.

Christian associations

In the Christian tradition, the festival was called Loaf mass or Lammas and a loaf baked from the first harvested sheaf was offered on the altar. On 15 August, at the feast of the Assumption of the Virgin Mary into heaven, a bannock was made from bread and milk to be broken by the father and given to the family.

Mediterranean associations

In the classical world, the festival of bread was dedicated to Corn Goddesses such as Demeter in the Greek tradition, the Roman Ceres and Juno the Roman Mother Goddess.

Ritual activity

* Either alone or in your group or coven, each person takes an ear of grain or a long grass with seeds. For a group you can have a sheaf of grain in the centre of the circle. Burn a few grains on a central fire, in the cauldron or in a huge orange candle, embedded in sand.

* Name a matter where you need justice or feel resentful about not getting what was rightfully yours. Say:

   By the Father and the Mother, Justice shall be done in due course and what owed paid. This I know and this will sustain me.

   You can, if you prefer, work on behalf of a friend or family member or to address a more global injustice.

* Cast the rest of the grains on to the ground to be blown away or lie fallow until the spring, saying:

   I forgive and let go of anger or burning resentment for any wrongs that have been done or deeds that should have been done that were neglected.

* Now hold the stem into the candle or fire until it breaks and say:

  Now I am free of the burden that has so long held me back.

* Each person can carry out the burning when they feel ready and speak in their minds if it is private.

* If any of these issues concern family or love estrangement, contact the person or people shortly afterwards to make one last attempt to resolve matters and if not give up for now, knowing you have done your best.

Alban Elued, Mabon, Autumn Equinox

Around 21–23 September, a quarter-day

Focus: The completion of tasks, the fruition of long-term goals, for mending quarrels and forgiving yourself for past mistakes, for receiving money owed asked for on the earlier festival, for assessing gain and loss, for family relationships and friendships; for material security for the months ahead, for abundance in all aspects of your life, for issues of job security or the need to consolidate finances; all matters concerning the retirement and older people; for healing.

Globally, rituals concentrate on positive steps to ensure enough food, shelter and resources for vulnerable communities and individuals, relief of flood and famine, protection of endangered water creatures, dolphins, whales and fish whose death involves great suffering; also for peace, especially where initiatives have already been set in motion.

Direction: West

Cycle of the year: Ancient tales tell of the death of the old Horned God at the hands of his successor or by offering himself to the huntsmen at the beginning of the hunting season. The God's dark lord of death and winter is in the Underworld, the womb of the Mother awaiting rebirth. While the Goddess mourns for her love she must prepare for the harvest over which she presides. But she is tired herself and getting heavier with the light child. The dark twin challenges and kills the light brother who returns to the Earth/the womb, becoming one with the dark lord and the two legends temporarily merge again. The dark twin ritually mates with the Goddess to ensure his successor.

In a strange variation of the light/dark myths, Blodeuwedd, wife of Llew, the Welsh God of light, is instrumental in bringing about the death of Llew at the hands of Goronwy, the dark twin and the dark magician. Llew becomes an eagle whose physical deterioration progresses as pigs, icons of Cerridwen, mother of regeneration, ate the rotting flesh as it fell to the ground. Llew will not be released from the form of the eagle until his rebirth at the Midwinter Solstice. This treachery myth reflects the need for the new dark twin to be born at the Summer Solstice so the wheel continues to turn and is a reminder that even the deities are subject to the turning wheel and must play their part.

Nature of festival: Reconciliation, fruit and nuts

Energies: Balanced

Symbols: Copper-coloured, yellow or orange leaves, willow boughs, harvest fruits such as apples, berries, nuts, copper or bronze coins, pottery geese

Animal: Salmon

Tree: Apple

Incenses, flowers and herbs: Ferns, geranium, myrrh, pine, sandalwood, Solomon's seal, Michaelmas daisies and all small-petal purple and blue flowers

Candle colours: Blue for the autumn rain, green for the Earth Mother

Crystals: Blue lace agate, chalcedony, aqua aura, rose quartz, all calcites

Celtic tradition

Alban Elued means light on the water in Gaelic, and the sun is moving away over the water to shine on the Isles of the Blest, the Celtic Otherworld leaving the world with encroaching darkness. The gathering of the second or green harvest of fruit, nuts and vegetables and the final grain harvest marked the storing of resources for the winter and barter for goods not available or scarce. Feasts of abundance and the offering of the finest of the harvest to the deities were a practical as well as magickal gesture, part of the bargain between humans and deities. Rotten fruit and vegetables were fed to animals where possible or left to form compost to enrich the soil.

In traditional celebrations, a priestess would carry a wheat sheaf, fruit and vegetables and distribute them to the people. A priest representing the slain God given the name of John Barleycorn, would offer ale, made from the fermented barley cut down at Lughnassadh. The harvest feast served as a magickal rite as the food was eaten and the barley wine of the slain god drunk that there would be enough food to last the winter. This may be the origins of the Cakes and Ale ceremony, so it is a good time to include it in your festivity using the harvest bread and barley wine as offerings.

Some Druidesses and Druids still climb to the top of a hill at sunset on the Autumn Equinox day to say farewell to the Horned God, lord of animals, as he departs for the lands of winter.

Mabon, after whom the festival is called, is another name for the divine son of Modron, the great mother, also called the liberator and another form of Llew. He was captured and taken into the Underworld when he was three nights old and restored after three months with the help of wise animals (later versions say Arthur) on the Spring Equinox. This was in time to defeat the dark brother, Goronwy.

In other myths his mother was Arianrhod and he was brought up by a magician/shepherd and returned to his mother in disguise as a bard to claim his name, sometimes at this festival, more often at the Spring Equinox.

Norse and Anglo-Saxon associations

The second harvest recognised that winter was not far away. The finest of the crop and fruits and the first meat of the hunting season that began at this time were offered in sacred feasts, to be shared with the deities in a request for a gentle winter and enough food to last. The Anglo-Saxons called this holy month.

The Autumn Equinox in many lands in the northern hemisphere still signals the beginning of the hunting season. In Scandinavia, huntsmen leave the entrails of animals on rocks in the forest, a relic of the ancient offering of the first animals.

Christian associations

In Christian times God rather than the Goddess was thanked for the harvest. The finest of the fruits and vegetables and bread baked from the grain would be set on the altar as an offering and afterwards distributed to the needy.

Michaelmas, the day of St Michael, the Archangel of the sun was celebrated on 29 September with a feast centred on geese. Since St Michael was patron saint of high places and replaced the pagan sun deities, he was an apt symbol for the last days of the summer sun. Goose fairs were held and workers in the fields often paid with slaughtered geese.

Mediterranean associations

In Ancient Greece, the rites of the greater Eleusinian mysteries took place at this time in honour of Kore/Persephone and her mother Demeter. The harvested grain representing the divine child, union of Persephone and Hades or in earlier Mother Goddess worship Persephone, herself reborn as the harvest, was placed in a basket and bread baked from this corn was eaten in honour of Demeter.

Candidates were initiated during the September rites. A sacred marriage between Zeus and Demeter was also re-enacted.

Ritual activity

* Whether working alone or in a coven or group, have a deep dish filled with autumn leaves and another dish of mixed nuts and berries.

* First, pass round the circle the dish of leaves. Each person takes one, whispers what is being left behind that did not work out and gently blows away the leaf saying:

Go in peace.

* Next, pass the dish of nuts and berries round the circle. Each person takes and eats one, then says what they wish to take forward with them from the harvest of personal achievement in the months that have passed.

* Then one person carries the remaining leaves to the west outside the sacred space and scatters them to the winds. A second person follows with the remaining berries and nuts and leaves them on the ground, in the west, the direction of autumn, for the birds and animals.

* If working alone, select and blow away as many leaves as you wish, each leaf followed by eating a berry or nut, naming as many losses or gains as you choose, both personal and global.

* Scatter any remaining leaves and drop the remaining berries or nuts on the ground, saying:

What is lost and what is gained are now set free in equal measure. Blessings be on all.

Samhain, 31 October–2 November

The major cross-quarter day of the year and the beginning of the Celtic winter and New Year

Focus: Remembering the family ancestors, for looking both backwards to the past and into the future, for protection, psychic and physical; for overcoming fears, especially of ageing and mortality, for retired people and those in their 70s and 80s; for marking the natural transition between one stage of life and the next and for laying old ghosts, psychological as well as psychic.

Globally, this is a time for rituals to aid charities and initiatives to help families and the elderly, the sick and terminally ill; also for the preservation of ancient sacred sites and the cultural heritage of the world, including the wisdom of indigenous peoples.

Direction: North-west

Cycle of the year: The Goddess descends into the Underworld to visit her lost love, the Sun King and the world is in mourning. This is sometimes linked to the Descent of the Goddess ceremony. Meanwhile, in her absence timelessness rules good and bad spirits and fairies roam free, and the ancestors come to visit families. The dark brother rejoices at his supremacy and usurps the throne in the absence of the Goddess.

The Cailleach, the Crone Goddess of the Celtic World, moves to the fore at this festival. She is the winter sun that shines from All Hallows to Beltane Eve and Grainne or Dia Greine, the Celtic Crone Sun Goddess rules the rest of the year. They are mother and daughter in a revolving cycle. The Crone comes from under her stone and picks a new holly staff, symbol of the Holly King who has six more weeks to hold sway.

Nature of festival: Past worlds, nature spirits, fey energies

Energies: Waning

Symbols: Apples, pumpkins, nuts and autumn leaves mingled with evergreens as a promise that life continues, salt, scary masks, fantastic costumes, lanterns

Animal: Raven

Tree: Silver fir

Incenses, flowers and herbs: Cypress, dittany, ferns, garlic, nutmeg, sage, thyme, pine, large white flowers, rose petals, rose fragrances, spices

Candle colour: Orange, purple

Crystals: Lapis lazuli, sodalite, dark amethysts, smoky quartz, jet, obsidian (apache tear)

Celtic tradition

Samhain means summer's end and the acceptance that the nights get longer and the weather colder. It was the time when the herds were brought down from the hills and family members returned to the homestead for the winter. The animals that were to be kept during the winter were driven though twin fires in a dark mirror of Beltaine so that they might be cleansed of disease and parasites. Others were slaughtered with reverence and salted to be preserved for food. At this time of no time, the family spirits returned shivering to seek warmth at the family hearth.

In legend, Jack o' Lantern, who had three times rejected the advances of Macha of the Morrigu in her guise as Death Goddess to come with her, is condemned to wander forever throughout the darkness that is neither life nor death, with only a single lantern to guide him.

In pre-Christian times, the fires of Ireland were extinguished at sunset on Samhain. A fire was kindled by the Arch Druid/Druidess on the hill of Tlachtga in Ireland and every great family carried home torches to rekindle their hearth fires, which thereafter were kept burning. There are many Irish Halloween tales of fairy enchantment and battles between good and evil on Halloween night when the Fomorii, a misshapen violent people, the evil gods of Irish myth, came forth to wreak harm, enslave whole tribes and take their riches for themselves. They sometimes appeared with only a single hand foot or eye. However, the Tuatha De Danaan, the tribe of the Goddess Dana, using the magick of Halloween, defeated the Fomorii at the second battle of Magh Tuireadh and became the leaders of Ireland.

On Halloween in Ireland, people still watch out for the Fairy Rade (Ride), led by Finvarra, the king of the dead, and his fairy queen Oonagh. Mortals who cross their path on Halloween night are in danger of being captured by them. Often Finvarra's hosts of fairy folk attend a fair with revelry and dancing and all kinds of wonderful goods displayed. But should a mortal sample any of the fare or attempt to buy any of the magickal items with the fairy gold he has found scattered in a fairy ring on Halloween, he or she will be enchanted forever.

Norse and Anglo-Saxon associations

The Old Norse festival like others worldwide honoured the ancestors. It also focused on thanking the God Freyr for the harvest stored and the animals killed in the hunt and from the farms for the winter. The celebration made tribute to the land wights, asking their protection on the homestead and the animals in the cold months ahead. The similar festival of Winternights may have been celebrated a little earlier in some regions around the old start of winter in mid-October, when travel and trade finally ended. Divination began for the year ahead, and sitting on a burial mound all night at this time was believed to bring prophetic powers.

Odin's wild hunt took to the skies and the slain warriors rode with him. The Viking tradition has its dark Odin (Uller God of the snow and ice) who ruled in the winter when Odin went riding with his ghostly entourage.

Christian associations

St Patrick in Ireland challenged the Druids with his own fires that it is said burned brighter than theirs.

In many lands from France to Scandinavia the Christianised Halloween is called All Hallows Eve and the following two days All Saints and All Souls days (or a day close by) are occasions when the family dead are remembered with flowers and photographs in the cemeteries.

In Mexico and parts of Spain, too, people still celebrate Halloween in its traditional sense. El Dia del Muerte (the day of the dead) is All Souls' Day in the Catholic calendar. The feast is spread over two days. On 1 November departed children are remembered and on 2 November the ghosts of adults are honoured.

In Mexico, people in towns, cities and villages make a path with bright yellow flowers from the cemetery to their house to guide the dead to their homes to visit them. The houses are full of ornaments, pictures of the dead, the things they personally used, the foods they liked, flowers and incense.

Mediterranean associations

In Greek myth, Persephone is abducted by Hades and the world thrown into winter and barrenness as Demeter her mother the Goddess of Grain searches for her. Hecate guides Demeter through the Underworld with her torch, but cannot find her. Rome has its parallel myth of Proserpina, Ceres her mother and Pluto, God of the Underworld.

Ritual activity

* Place a clove of garlic on a north or north-west-facing window of a room in which you are sitting or on the north-west side of your outdoor altar or ritual circle. If others are present set nine garlic cloves to the north-west side of the protective area. Say:

May only good enter here.

* Light a purple candle, one for each person present.

* Focus on a deceased relative whom you believe guides you; alternatively, on a distant or spiritual ancestor to whose culture you are attracted. This might be a Spirit Guide.

* Gaze into the candle flame and hold a small amethyst, smoky quartz or apache tear to the candlelight. In the crystal or flame or your mind's vision, you may see your beloved great-grandmother smiling and hear her wise, comforting words or sense her presence. Alternatively, you may see, hear or feel a gentle breeze and be given a picture of a past world.

* If alone speak words of love aloud to your chosen ancestor. If others are present, each person in turn makes a blessing aloud to the departed ancestor or Guide and recalls someone beloved who may have recently died.

* When you are ready to end the experience, thank whoever you connected with, saying (at a prearranged signal if working in a group):

Go in peace and blessings on your own paths of wisdom.

* Blow out the candle and in the darkness you may see as though etched in light a possible pathway ahead if you choose to take it.

* Finally, walk around the room, altar or enclosed area clockwise (one after the other in a group) in the darkness, saying nine times:

May all be blessed and protected. The rite of the ancestors is ended.

Alban Arthuran, Yule or Midwinter Solstice

Around 20–22 December, a major quarter day

Focus: For the rebirth of light and hope, for domestic happiness and security, family togetherness, anything to do with the home and property and for financial security; for long term money plans, for patience and for accepting what cannot be changed; for very old people, for carers, for welcoming home travellers or estranged people and for restoring enthusiasm and health in those who are worn down by illness or lack of hope.

Globally, this is a time for rituals of renewed faith in the face of despair and cynicism. for work to provide homes and shelter for people, birds and animals, more efficient and humane welfare services; the regeneration of famine or war-torn lands; improving conditions in all institutions.

Direction: North

Cycle of the year: The Horned God/the young Sun God/the light twin is born on the Midwinter Solstice, which is the time for the incarnation of divinity in the sacred stories of many religions, including Christianity and Mithraism.

Nature of festival: Rekindling extinguished flames, light in the darkness

Energies: Turning point as the energies begin to rise again

Symbols: Evergreen boughs especially pine or fir, small logs of wood, especially oak, pine and ash, holly and ivy, gold coins and jewellery, silver and gold ribbons and baubles, tiny wrapped presents to be opened on the Solstice after the coven meeting or at Christmas.

Animal: Bull

Tree: Holly

Incenses, flowers and herbs: Bay, cedar, feverfew, frankincense and myrrh mixed, holly, juniper, pine, rosemary, sage and all spices, poinsettias, scarlet and white flowers and rosemary

Candle colours: White, scarlet, gold, purple for what is being left behind

Crystals: Amazonite, malachite, garnet, snow quartz, snowflake obsidian, opal aura

Celtic tradition

Alban Arthuran means in Gaelic the light of Arthur and refers to the rebirth of Arthur as the divine child, the Mabon (in some myths he rescued the Mabon, see Autumn Equinox for tangled tale of this elusive child). After the Midwinter Solstice when the physical and psychic crisis point of the overwhelming darkness had passed, people held feasts as a magickal gesture to attract abundance. They hung lights from evergreen branches to encourage the trees and vegetation to sprout green again and to give power to the sun.

In rituals in many different lands on Midwinter night, all lights are extinguished at dusk and the Crone Goddess or the person representing her invites those present to walk into the darkness with her, an act of pure surrender and faith that light will return. In some myths it is the three mothers, the Celtic Madrones or the Romanised Matronae who are the midwives of the Sun King.

In passage graves throughout the world, such as the pre-Celtic Newgrange in

Ireland, people waited for the first shaft of light on the Solstice morning to illuminate the inner shrine.

Norse and Anglo-Saxon associations

Because of the long nights and bad weather, people gathered in homesteads for 12 nights or even longer to feast and ask that the deities would bring abundance. On the night of the Solstice, Freyr was said to ride over the world on his boar that shone with light restoring light into the world. Later this role was transferred to Baldur. Huge wooden wheels were set alight and rolled from the tops of hills or mountains, into water where possible. The boar, crowned with laurel and rosemary in honour of Thor, lord of the winter, formed the feast. The father of the family put his hand on the boar's head, called the Boar of Atonement and swore he would be faithful to family and fulfil clan obligations.

The Anglo-Saxons named first 21 December and then in Christian times 25 December as the Day of the Infant. Christmas Eve or Solstice Eve was called the Night of the Mothers or Modraniht after the shadowy guardians of the hearth and home, the midwife Goddesses who protected all women in childbirth and their newborn infants.

Christian associations

In 320 CE, the Christian Church placed the date of the birth of Christ as 25 December to overwrite the pagan births of earlier Sun Gods at the Midwinter Solstice. In Ireland today a candle is left burning in a window on Christmas Eve to guide the Virgin Mary on her way.

The most famous Midwife Goddess of Christmas was St Bridget. According to myth, immediately after Christ was born, she placed three drops of water on the newborn infant's head, in accordance with Celtic birth custom, thus thoroughly confusing those who try to keep a consistency of dates. However, it is probably a Christianised legend from old Ireland.

Mediterranean associations

Mithras, the Persian Sun God, whose cult spread throughout the Roman Empire, was born in a cave at Midwinter, predating the birth of Jesus. Some legends record he emerged from a rock (Mother Earth). Attis, consort of Cybele, was also born on this day.

In ancient Southern Europe, the Mid-Winter Solstice was called Brumalia, the return of the unconquerable sun.

The Egyptian Mother Goddess Isis gave birth to Horus, the young Sky God on this night, secretly in a cave and, as with the infant Jesus, Horus had to be hidden, because the reigning King, his uncle Set, like Herod, would have killed him.

Ritual activity

* Stand in the centre of a candle light circle. If alone, light small white candles or tea lights one by one round the circle. If in a group, each person can light their own candle or tea light with a blessing and sit behind it facing the centre of the circle. In the centre, light a single dark purple candle (even for a group).

* If others are present, choose one to be the Crone and ask if those present will walk into the darkness in trust that light will return. If working alone, hear your

Witch Guardian speak the words or say them on her behalf. Say softly: I will walk into the darkness with you, Wise Grandmother and Midwife, in trust that light will return.

* Extinguish all other candles so all that is visible is the flame of the dark central candle After a few minutes of silent reflection, light a white candle from the dark and say:

> *The Sun is reborn and light returns to the world. Blessings be.*

In a group the Crone/midwife would say this.

* Look into the white candle flame, and say:

> *The dark times are ended and light returns.*

* Blow out the dark candle and from the light candle, if alone begin to relight the circle of small candles or tea lights by carrying the central candle round the circle. Light each with a blessing for Christmas for someone in the family or who is absent.

* If others are present they can bring their candle or tea light to the main central candle and as it lights, name someone to whom they wish to send love who is away for Christmas or who is sick or estranged. Alternatively, the Crone can light the small candles by walking round the circle.

* You can create a full drama of the Sun King being reborn from this ceremony, whether you are alone or in a coven.

PRACTICAL ASSIGNMENT

Making progress

Continue to work on your festival dramas or poems and chants.

Further research

Explore either Halloween rites around the world or other Sun King birth myths from different lands.

Further information

Recommended reading

* Crowley, Vivianne, *Celtic Wisdom: Seasonal Festivals and Rituals*, Sterling, 1998
* Hewitson, Jennifer, Illustrator, *The Witches' Datebook*, Llewellyn, 2007

Websites

* *Bartleby Online Bookstore*
  Links to extracts from Frazer's Golden Bough
  www.bartleby.com
* *A Druid Fellowship*
  Irish Druidic site with information on the Norse Wheel of the Year and also a series of good articles on the Neopagan world of myth
  www.adf.org/articles/cosmology/norsewy.html

USING KNOT MAGICK

In this module, I would like to draw the strands together in the form of a perennial witchcraft favourite, knot magick. This stores and then releases concentrated magickal energy.

Knot magick is a deceptively simple yet powerful magickal technique. A single cord shaped through knot tying and empowerment is in itself a spell, used for attracting, protecting, banishing, binding or healing energies. It is the most portable kind of magick and can either be crafted at home, within a magick circle, as a coven activity or anywhere you find yourself such as a hotel room or workplace: even on a deserted station platform at night where you can touch the knotted cord and say the chants in your mind.

Many witches routinely carry a small knotted cord wrapped in silk or in a silk purse in their bag, briefcase or pocket for energy and protection while travelling or to give energy or protection during the day. You can craft in advance any number of empowered knot cords in different colours for different purposes for they have no time limit on their use until the cord frays.

Your pre-created knot cord provides an instant spell or talisman when you are in a hurry and you may also have a number of protective knot cords around your home, workplace or even in your car. To the uninitiated they look like a decoration. Mine are always so amateur-looking I say my children made them at playschool, but they are nevertheless very powerful indeed and I rarely travel without one. For example, a knotted yellow and brown cord in the glove box or hanging inside the car guards against road rage and road hazards while commuting, and a dark blue one reduces fear of flying if untied during take-off and landing.

Magickal knots

Magickal knot tying has been practised for thousands of years. We know that the Ancient Babylonians used knot tying to cure headaches and that the Ancient Egyptians made seven magickal knots tied in red cord in honour of the seven daughters of Hathor, especially in love magick. According to the Ancient Egyptian Leyden magickal papyrus, seven knots were especially powerful. Seven knots were used to fasten charms and amulets around the ankle and neck.

One of the knot's main functions was to act as a magickal barrier, as protection against harm and illness. One spell in the Leyden magickal papyrus tells of a strip of linen on which 12 deities were drawn and then the strip was tied into 12 knots, the final creating a circle, and it was worn as a necklet. According to the ritual, the linen was blessed with beer, bread and incense, dedicated to the gods.

In Ancient Egypt three deities were specifically associated with knots. The first of these, Anubis, because of his association with binding the mummy, rules knots for preservation and protection. His knots are black (or you can use dark blue or purple) and he rules binding, protective and banishing knot magick (see below).

Second is Isis, with her famous knotted girdle, the tjet that was a hieroglyph (see page 405), associated with menstrual and life blood. She rules knots for increasing energy, prosperity, female power and fertility. She is a good patroness of any attracting or wishes knot magick. Her knots tend to be red cord or thin red or natural linen.

The third deity is actually seven sisters. The seven daughters of Hathor, the sisters of fate, were represented by seven separate ribbons or cords of red and these were used both for love knots, for good luck and to drive away or bind those who would do harm, especially against young children and women. The seven Hathors were named in spells as Lady of the House of Jubilation, Lady of the Stormy Sky, Lady from the Land of Silence, Lady of the Black Earth, Lady with Hair of Fire, Lady of the Sacred Land and Lady whose name flourishes through Power.

Knot ladders

Some witches make ladders of knots, which may not look like ladders at all unless woven into an intricate pattern, but are most usually knotted triple cords in which feathers, beads, shells or stones are tied into the knots. Traditionally there were 40 beads knotted into a witches' ladder, which I have also seen joined as a circle and that can act as a kind of rosary in reciting empowerments A 40-knot empowerment is a fairly permanent powerhouse and can be given to witches by other witches for birthdays, anniversaries, initiation ceremonies, perhaps with some of the witch's hair (with permission) bound in. You could also make a coven or private one for major healing or peace.

Many modern witches' ladders have only nine feathers or beads attached and may be hung in the home, near the altar, placed on the altar or even worn as bracelet or neck adornment during ritual. It can be a real act of kindness to make a witches' ladder, tying into it good wishes or even a wish cord for another solitary practitioner you meet.

Long ago, witches' ladders had a nasty reputation for tying up people's hairs in a death wish spell, but today they are most often used in healing. I have suggested resources for information on witches' ladders (see page 673), but also look on the internet yourself for photographs of other people's witches' ladders and commercially made ones to inspire you. If you make a beautiful one, then photograph it to inspire others on the internet or send the image to me and I will display it on my website for you to keep the tradition alive.

Making knot cords

Though 9 ft or 9 in (the 3 × 3) is traditionally recommended (maybe as modern Euro-witches we should use 9 m or 9 cm cords), you can use any suitable multiple of three for the length of your knotted cord.

Choose either undyed wool, cotton, thin ribbon or any natural fibre or a colour that signifies the purpose of the ritual (see page 512 for colour meanings). A cord made of triple strands is considered most magickal or if the thread is very thin you could braid six or nine strands together to make a single cord. Braiding your own single cords is easy if you tie one end to a ring attached to a chair or work with a friend or another coven member helping one another to make cords ready for knot tying. You can chant as you make them to endow the cords with light and sanctity and picture light and peace entering them.

As well as your personal cord that you wear in ritual or use during your altar work, it is a good idea to have a wooden box of spare cords in different colours, secured at one end so they do not become unravelled and wrapped in silk within the box. A coven or magickal group may have its store of coloured cords, including longer ones (9–12 ft) so each person can hold a cord in their power hand or one in each hand, each looped and knotted loosely in the centre over a secure stake or staff in the ground or round a tree.

The coven can dance and spin round to make cord webs for healing and harmony, using all seven rainbow colours in different shades. This web weaving takes a bit of practice at first, a bit like maypole dancing, but is an effective way of raising power and releasing it. Alone you can knot one end of the cord round a tree (again, you need a 9 or 12 ft cord) and wind yourself in and out and spiral round. What you lose in making a communal web you gain in being filled with the power of the tree and the nature essences that will spiral with you as light beams.

If you have long hair, you can knot nine hairs from your hairbrush or cut from your head if you wish for a protective knot cord, or use a pet's hairs in the same way to guard them from harm. Some witches keep a lock of their child's hair from his or her first haircut, knotted or mingled knotted hairs from a lover and yourself on your wedding day for lasting love. These personal knot charms are very precious and should never be undone, but kept in a special place wrapped in silk.

You can make family unity hair knots (ask lovers and family members if you may keep their hair). You can also make life chains by adding a strand of hair to a personal hair knot charm on each of your birthdays. This is traditionally buried with the witch.

If you use strips of linen or a single long thin linen strip for knot tying Ancient Egyptian style, you can write along it the names of three, seven (as in the Isis, Astarte chant) or nine empowering or protective deities from any culture. Alternatively, mark their initials in either hieroglyphs, Malachim or Theban script at regular intervals along the strip in fabric marker pen at regular intervals and tie knots over them. In a seven-knot chant, you could also draw the seven planetary glyphs or Archangel initials in magickal scripts. You would weave these names into the knot chant (see Hathor chant below).

For any knot spell, you can use three, seven or nine separate cords or ribbons end to end and, if keeping the chant, tie the final joining knot of cord 1–7 to make a circle. Alternatively, tie a knot in the untied end of cord 7 and leave the ends loose. For special occasions or coven knot spells use long thin scarves in rainbow colours.

Using knots as a focus for different magickal powers

❋ A series of three, seven or nine knots can be tied for attracting magick. Each knot is empowered in the tying to act as a storage cell for energies that can be released, one knot every day or occasionally together, one after the other, for a huge release of power at a crucial time.

❋ If the knots were important or long lasting, you could tie one a day, repeating the cumulative chant on successive days up to the relevant knot number and on the last day of tying reciting the whole chant.

❋ The knots can represent a multiple sequence of the qualities needed in gaining a particular strength, a number of steps to fruition or the same wish recited for each knot if it is a vital or ongoing issue.

❋ Use a red knot cord to tie two images together face to face for love and commitment. Create two tiny poppets, featureless fabric dolls filled with herbs and a tiny rose quartz for a heart, and bind them together with a three-knot cord chant, stating:

> *We are joined willingly, lovingly and faithfully. May it be so throughout eternity.*

❋ Tie lovers' garments together with the old words as you fasten with three knots:

> *Three times the lovers' knots secure, firm be the knots, long the love endure.*

❋ Use a knot cord for binding magick, to tie a wax, clay, dough or fabric image with a cord secured with three, six, seven or nine knots to prevent the named person represented by the image doing harm.

❋ Alternatively, freeze a knotted cord in the coldest part of your freezer in a container to hold things stable and bound, perhaps to keep a pressing debt problem under control or a chronic illness from getting worse. Protective knot spells would come under this category, which you would hang near an entrance to your home or behind an office door with feathers tied in the knots to bind the power of any who entered from doing harm. After three months or when the cord has served its purpose, set the feathers free into the air, having first deprogrammed the knots by saying:

> *The cord has served its purpose. I now release all energy as healing into the sky to be transformed to light and healing. Blessings be.*

❋ Finally, knots are good in banishing rituals. Tie three knots in a cord to signify what you wish to banish from your life or a destructive hold over you whether a person, a situation or a bad habit. Burn the knots one after the other in a candle flame (set on a metal tray or have a container of earth or sand nearby to drop the burning cord into). Three knots is usually sufficient in banishing magick (see page 668 for a more detailed spell).

❋ Alternatively, you can bury rather than burn the still knotted cord in earth to bury an illness or a run of bad luck. As the knot cord decays, so will the bad influence, bad luck or sickness diminish; good for ongoing slow problems that you can only put right step by step over months rather than weeks.

- For healing, you could secure an empowered three, seven or nine-knot cord to a tree near a sacred water source, having dipped the knotted cord in the healing water after empowering. This is very traditional and often a ribbon rather than cord is used in the colour related to the illness or sorrow (see page 512 for healing colours).

- Healing spells can be either attracting knot spells or banishing, according to the nature of the illness. In practice, it might be better to use balancing magick and combine the powers. Work with a double knot cord to represent the polarities sickness/health, exhaustion/energy, depression, sorrow/joy, and pain/harmony.

- You would make and empower two knotted cords with the same number of knots: for example, a dark blue one to banish pain or an illness and alongside it would set an empowered red knotted cord. You would create the banishing knot cord first, then the attracting, and keep them side by side, undoing a banishing knot followed by an attracting knot each day. However, instead you could tie together the two separate coloured cords in seven or nine knots for healing and then undo the dual-purpose knot, the one colour to take away the illness and the other to restore health.

- You can use balancing knot magick for any positive purpose: for reducing debt and increasing prosperity, for ending loneliness and attracting love. There are no end of polarities you can join together in your knots. You can create a binding knot cord if you are being overwhelmed by something or someone, the first cord to hold the situation steady and then the second knotted cord to build up your resources or energy to be released each day. This is very empowering if you just want to stop the world while you get back on track.

- You can tie 13 cords together as a coven exercise or one with each member of your family or magick group naming for each knot something that binds you together in love (good for reconciling differences). If your family has quarrels or some members distance themselves, tie a cord on behalf of each one of them and yourself in love and keep your unity circle with photographs of the people and a pot of growing roses.

- Some covens have a special knot staff that they pass round so that each member can tie a knot on the attached cord.

Storing and releasing magick in knots

Whereas when we store magick in an empowered charm or crystal it is released very slowly, even in gentle knot charms the act of tying the knot accompanied by a chant imbues the knot with fast concentrated power. The act of undoing, cutting or burning the knot is equally intense and swift acting. Knots are released in the order they were tied for attracting magick and for banishing magick in reverse order.

Ex-Scout and Guide witches are at a distinct advantage. But in essence it doesn't matter what your level of proficiency is (I have handfasted couples with a granny knot and they are still happily and willingly bound). Knots on knot cords need to be fairly easily undone, but it is the significance that you endow them with that matters at the end of the day.

Knot tying order

You don't need to stick rigidly to the number or order of knots given here, as sometimes a matter will need a lot of power and then you would use nine regardless. Six knots are not used so much except for tying charm, spell or mojo bags, but there is no good reason why not.

Three knots for love and fidelity, also for energy and banishing magick

1–3–2

Or

2–3–1

Seven knots for love, marriage, family, pets or healing, but also for protection, binding and banishing as Hathor knots

6–2–4–1–5–3–7

Or

6–4–2–1–3–5–7

Nine knots for work, happiness, healing, health success and power and any important or urgent matters

8–4–2–5–1–6–3–7–9

Or

8–6–4–2–1–3–5–7–9

Nine knots for money, property, travel and all practical matters

1–6–4–8–3–7–5–9–2

Nine knots for any wish magick, for protection or for binding and banishing

1–6–4–8–3–9–5–7–2

Whatever order you use, note it down so you can undo them in the correct order. The spell would still work if your forgot the order, but it just makes the power that little bit stronger to keep to the sequence. You ordain the purpose and programme in the knots' purpose and if you wish target them by the chant as you tie and untie.

Knot chants

There are almost as many knot chants as there are witches, the majority based on variations of:

By the knot of one, the spell's begun.

Nine is most common and Doreen Valiente was one of the earliest people to record the nine-knot chant. Seven is also the basis for traditional knot chants and is often linked to deities, including the seven Hathors in the Ancient Egyptian tradition or crafted round the days of the week, the planets or Archangels. Three-knot chants as well as focusing on love can be linked to any magickal triplicates, like the three phases of the moon, when you would tie the three knots on the crescent and then untie on the full, the middle of the wane and the crescent again. Deity energies frequently empower the chant. You could link the knots to Maiden, Mother and Crone energies or to Horned God, God King and Dark Lord knot rites. For each knot, name the deity quality it represents who will assist in the fulfilment of a need or as a banishment of harm.

Rightly, witches are taught to focus on knot tying chants, but we also need to make untying them a ritual, however short, even a line or two of empowerment. This is especially true if you cut or burn knots. Just as you programme your knot in the tying, so you need to direct its energies in the untying in words, renaming the person, purpose and which number knot you are undoing. For example:

By the knot of three, my love for James is free. Fly swift, knot power to my love that he may feel its power and come to me/call me/return to me.

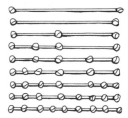

Releasing power in balancing magick

Nowhere is the releasing chant more important than in balancing magick. If using two separate cords, perhaps to attract health and banish illness or even to bind, say, the effects of an addiction while banishing its cravings, you always endow with a chant the banishing cord first and then follow with a separate attracting chant for the second cord. Then for the releasing of the banishing energy, you would include such words as:

Go from me, leave me. . .

followed by:

Come to me. Stay with me/soothe. . .

You could use the same knot tying order for both if you wished for ease of tying and untying. However, if you had made a dual cord where two colours were tied together, you would make a combined chant in the creation. For example:

Knot one to ease Sue's pain and fill with energy again,
Knot two that sleepless nights may end and in sweet dreams her life may mend,

and so on. You would repeat the relevant knot chant three times as you untied the knot.

A three-knot chant for energy

Best made when it is windy outdoors or near an open window, any time during the waxing to the full moon; the more powerful the energies become the closer to the moon the cord is tied. Use a single white cord.

✺ Tie the first knot at the right-hand end of the cord, as you do so, saying:

May the four winds enter this knot and hold the power within.

* Blow over the knot three times.
* Tie a second knot at the other end of the cord and a third one in the middle, as you do so, repeating the words. Each time blow over the knot as you tie it.
* Then blow three more times over the knotted cord, once over each knot in the order you tied them, more forcefully than before, and say:

> *Knot of three,*
> *Till you are free*
> *Hold tight your power*
> *Until the hour*
> *I call thee.*

* Keep the cord safe where a breeze can blow over it. When you need a sudden increase in energy, untie one of the knots, and say:

> *One knot of three,*
> *The power's in me.*
> *Energy*
> *Thus do I free*
> *So mote it be.*

* Re-hang the cord until needed again.
* Untie the other two knots as necessary, modifying the chant to *two knots of three* and finally *three knots of three*. When you have used all three knots of energy, bury or burn the cord.

A three-knot banishing spell

This is one of the most effective banishing spells I know, especially for breaking a destructive, abusive relationship, for banishing guilt or regrets, addiction or anything that holds you back. Though it should be a waning moon spell, sometimes we can't wait. All you need is three dark coloured cords (9 in each is long enough) and a dark purple candle. Put a big metal tray under the candle or a separate container of soil or sand for the burning cords.

* Light the candle and tie cord 2 to cord 1 with the words:

> *This is the knot that binds me to... I seek to be free of it.*

* Now tie cord 3 to cord 2 and repeat the words.
* Join one end of cord 3 to the free end of cord 1 with a knot and say:

> *So am I locked in the cycle of... Yet I shall be free.*

* Hold the knot joining the ends of 3 and 1 in the candle flame so they begin to burn and say:

> *I cut the cord between [name the person or situation] and me. So mote it be.*

* As the cord breaks, say:

> *The cycle is broken between. . .*

* Put out the burning cord in the sand or on the tray so the whole cord does not burn, unless that is what you wish. You can get rid of it all once and for all.

* Two knots remain. You have the option of continuing or waiting until another day. If you do not wish to continue, blow out the candle and send the light to the destructive person or bad habit.

* When you are ready, pick up the cord and hold it taut by its ends over the cord joining 2 and 3. Hold it in the flame until it begins to burn. Say:

    I cut the cord between [name the person or situation] and me. So mote it be.

* When the cord breaks drop it on the tray or in the sand and put it out, unless you want it all to burn.

* Again either blow out the candle and send light or burn the final knot. Use the same words and hold the final knot in the flame until it breaks. When the final knot is burned, either leave the cord to burn through or when it is cool throw it away after the ritual. End by saying:

    I am free. Blessings be on all.

* Leave the candle to burn out. You may need to repeat the spell with another cord if the situation is long-standing or very painful.

A seven-knot Hathor love knot ritual

This is a full ritual to show how knot tying can be central to quite a formal spell or rite. You will need seven red ribbons or cords, each 9 in long. Although you can use the separate Hathor names for each knot (see page 110), let's use the basic Hathor name for simplicity. Hathor herself was the Goddess to whom women especially prayed to and left offerings for a husband and faithful love. The spell can be used by men or women. Similar spells are still used in Egyptian popular folk magick. However, you can use Hathor knot magick for any purpose, such as fertility, health or abundance by adapting the basic chant and for banishing or binding, as the daughters of Hathor were fiercely protective.

* Light a red Hathor candle just before sunset, her special time. Purify the altar with perfume, incense and water (see page 161). You can carry out a less formal spell by a normal circle casting and candle lighting. Set seven separate red ribbons or thin cords for the daughters of Hathor on the altar in front of the candle.

* Light your incense, on this occasion a stick, using frankincense or sandalwood for any knot work if possible. However, rose is a good substitute for love magick.

* Have also two offering bowls, one for crumbs of bread and the other traditionally for beer, wine or dark fruit juice. Beer in Ancient Egypt was very nourishing, rather than alcoholic.

* Speak as you tie your seven cords together:
  Knot 1: *That he/she may come to me, Hathor guide the way.*
  Knot 2: *That he/she may see and like me as I am, Hathor guide the way.*
  Knot 3: *That he/she may be kind and gentle in word and action, Hathor guide the way.*

Knot 4: *May he/she grow to love me more each day, Hathor guide the way.*

Knot 5: *May he/she be faithful and never give me cause to doubt, Hathor guide the way.*

Knot 6: *May our love grow deeper with the years, Hathor guide the way.*

Knot 7: *May there be always unity through bad times as well as good so long as the water flows and the sun shines, Hathor guide the way.*

* Do not join the ends together, but tie a knot in the end of the seventh cord to seal in the power.

* Anoint both ends of the joined ribbons, first the knot joining 1–2, then the single knot at the end of ribbon 7 with a single drop of rose essence or water and then from left to right the remaining five knots, saying for each:

   Fragrance of Hathor, perfume of love, bring and preserve love within these knots.

* With your incense, reproduce the knots from left to right over the ribbons in smoke, repeating the knot chant.

* Leave the incense to burn and the knotted love cord on your altar.

* Begin on the next dawn or when you wake and it is light. Untie the knot to the far left (1–2), reciting only its chant and leave the loose ribbon/s on the altar next to the rest of the cord. Continue until you have all seven ribbons free on the seventh day.

* Leave all the ribbons on the altar until all are free and bury them beneath a living tree, traditionally fruit bearing.

* Wait a week and if your love has not come, repeat the spell. Then if it still does not work, wait a month and repeat as the energies are building. Make sure you do go out as usual, perhaps finding new interests, but do not actively seek love for example, in a singles bar. Egyptian magick tends to be slow but powerful.

This is also a good spell for regaining lost love or if you want it, to make a faithless partner turn to you in love. You can also adapt it for any purpose: for example, for protection, each knot listing a fear or aspects of specific hostility and saying for each knot:

   Hathor protect me today.

Again, untie one knot each day, but for banishing or binding bury the seven ribbons beneath a bush that is dying or in unplanted earth.

Three nine-knot spells

These are some of my favourites and show the way you can adapt your knot magick for any purpose.

A knot wish spell

Traditionally a sunshine spell between noon and 3pm. Sundays are good, as is the Summer Solstice at noon.

* Name your wish aloud.

* Place the nine pieces of cord or, for a special wish, different coloured scarves on a table and slowly tie a knot in each until they are all secured together in a circle.

As you work, say with increasing intensity:

> *By the knot of one, the wish be spun.*
> *By the knot of two, wish, come true.*
> *By the knot of three, the power's in me.*
> *By the knot of four, I make it more.*
> *By the knot of five, wish, be alive.*
> *By the knot of six, the spell is mixed.*
> *By the knot of seven, my cause is leaven.*
> *By the knot of eight, I make my fate.*
> *By the knot of nine, the wish is mine.*

* Toss your knotted scarves or cords into the air and catch them and then spiral around, waving them and chanting nine times:

> *My power renewed,*
> *The dream is true,*
> *The wish is free.*
> *So mote it be!*

* Gradually slow down and reduce your chant to a whisper, until you are still and silent.
* Sit and make a nine-day plan for materialising your wish. Each morning untie one of your knots as you repeat the whole chant.

A second knot wish spell

This spell is much slower than the last, but no less powerful. Take your time holding the cord taut as you tie the knots and formulating your wish. For this use a single longer red cord.

* Tie nine knots in the cord
* Keep on repeating the rhyme for each particular knot until that knot is tied. As you work, speak the chant more and more loudly and intensely, but not faster:

> *Knot one renew*
> *My power knot two.*
> *In courage be,*
> *I tie knot three.*
> *The power is more, I make knot four.*
> *And so I strive within knot five.*
> *With fate not fixed, I tie knot six.*
> *My strength is leaven, I tie knot seven.*
> *I master fate, and so knot eight.*
> *The wish is mine within knot nine.*

* Pull the cord taut and say with confidence:

> *The wish is mine*
> *Within knot nine.*
> *The power is free.*

So I decree
And it mote be.

✹ Either hang the knots on your wall as a talisman or undo one each day.

A third knot wish spell

This knot spell is useful if you need immediate fulfilment of the wish. Again, you need a single red cord or a thin red scarf long enough to tie nine knots in.

✹ Take up the scarf or cord and tie nine knots in it, but this time very loosely, one knot on top of the other. As you do so, speaking the chant from the spell above or one you create.

✹ When you have finished tying the knots, you can if you like untie them rapidly, one after the other, as you call out the final power chant from either the spell above or the previous spell nine times. Otherwise, keep the knotted scarf or cord as a talisman.

A nine-knot chant for success at work

This is an example of how you can use the nine-knot format for any purpose. Use a triple green cord long enough to hang in your workplace, best behind a door or if self-employed behind the door of your workroom or near your work bench, desk or station. Make it at night, preferably at midnight, during the waxing to the full moon. Light a green candle and work only by that light.

✹ Pass each end of the cord in turn through the flame very fast, so it does not catch light, and say:

So enter power. Flow constantly, gradually and easily, towards prosperity.

✹ Working slowly, tie nine knots in the cord, as you tie each one, reciting the appropriate line from the chant below. Knot the cord in what feels a natural order or from the suggestions above:

With the knot of one, success begun,
With the knot of two, much work to do,
With the knot of three, increase be,
With the knot of four, open every door,
With the knot of five, let business thrive,
With the knot of six, contracts are fixed,
With the knot of seven, new work is given,
By knot of eight, my future's great,
By knot of nine, all can be mine.

✹ Hang the knot cord behind the door and only undo a knot if things at work are stagnant. If you undo a knot, repeat the whole spell as you retie a new ninth knot so that all nine knots are restored.

✹ Replace every three months or if you sense the energies are waning.

✹ Smudge over it weekly with sagebrush or cedar.

PRACTICAL ASSIGNMENT

Create your own knot ritual

Create a knot ritual to attract, one to bind and one to banish.

Further research

Using online resources and books experiment with different kinds of knots and decide if you can create an all-purpose knot for knot spells and tying spell bags or if some kinds are better than others.

Alternatively, explore the witches' ladder.

Further information

Recommended reading

* Budworth, Geoffrey, *Complete Guide to Knots and Knot Tying*, Lorenz Books, 1999
* Judkins, Steve, *Knot Know How*, Fernhurst Books, 2003
* West, Kate, *The Real Witches' Handbook*, Thorsons, 2001

Websites

* *Lucky Mojo*
  Good section on magickal knot spells and other useful advice on magick
  www.luckymojo.com/spells/practicaltips.html
* *Angelfire*
  Excellent site on knot magick for different purposes
  www.angelfire.com/fl3/wicca1132/knots.html
* *Earth Witchery*
  Good site for witches' ladder info
  www.earthwitchery.com/witchesladder.html
* *Good article on making Witches' ladder*
  www.geocities.com/Area51/Chamber/7227/ladder.html

MAKING YOUR OWN TOOLS

Some witches are naturally talented at making their own tools and artefacts, whether fabulously embroidered or silk screen-painted altar cloths and robes, glass painting to create a beautiful chalice from an old wine glass, intricately carved wands and even their own athame. Other witches are gifted at writing chants, organising ceremonies or getting bus-loads of people from A to Z and producing tea for 60 on a wind-whipped hillside. Others are skilled in healing, setting up an interactive Book of Shadows on the internet or learning complex chants and lists of magickal correspondences. All these gifts are equally valuable.

The witchcraft community is about exchange and whether you are a solitary witch or part of coven there are ample opportunities for pooling resources. If you find natural crafts difficult, as I do, there are many good sources of hand-crafted tools, robes and artefacts of all kinds. You will find them at reasonable prices on the internet and at witchcraft festivals, at country fairs and at pagan gatherings. You are giving a craftsperson a chance to earn a living from their gifts and a small company will often produce a unique athame, chalice or pentacle to your specifications if you are able to wait a few weeks (or even months) for it.

Equally, if you can make Goddess statues, Green Men, drums, candles, incense or wands, then get yourself a stall at fairs and festivals or sell via the internet. The smaller pagan gatherings hire stalls at very reasonable rates and you can work your way up to the bigger festivals if you choose. Many online traders are one-person organisations and use PayPal for their credit facilities. There is nothing wrong with using the talents the Goddess gave you to make money and then you can offer your products at cheaper rates to people who are genuinely impoverished and give everyone pleasure with your creations.

If you are naturally good at making things, run workshops at festivals and local fairs to pass on your skills. One of the considerations as you approach your Year and a Day initiation is what you can give to others and pass on of your unique life view and talents to other witches. Put a how-to article on the internet or through one of the forums. I would be delighted to host any on my site that do not have a home.

Learning the skills

Most of us want to make our own wand, even if we buy a beautiful crystal or carved one for special ceremonies. What is more, we can all engrave tools with glyphs using a pyrography tool, like an electrically heated pen, on wands or wooden handles of athames. Some witches design their own monogram to put on all their tools. There are many woodcraft courses available at local colleges, and you can make entire altar sets out of wood. There are also metalwork classes if you are interested in making an athame. This is a much more specialised art and can be quite dangerous, unless you know what you are doing.

The following tools are relatively easy and very satisfying to create. These are just suggestions and if you have a better way of making a wand or pentacle, then please let me know and I will credit you in future books. I have written in more detail about beeswax candle and incense making in my natural magick book and some of the basic information in this module comes from that book, but I have learned new ideas even since writing that book and have incorporated them here.

Making a wand

I have described making two kinds of wand, the first the wand used in Wicca and Druidry, and the second the Ancient Egyptian wand. The Egyptian wand is very protective and often displayed on a bedroom or altar wall at home when not being used for magick.

Wands in witchcraft and Druidry

Element: Fire

Direction: South

Energies: God

Qualities: Inspiration, intuition, passion (in every way)

See page 104 for the traditions of the wand, which is one of the four sacred treasures and also its uses in magick.

Choosing the wood

Wands can be straight, slightly curved and tapering to a point or twisted like corkscrews (you occasionally find one of these twisted pieces of wood and they need hardly any empowerment and no adornment to make them into wands).

You need a piece of wood about a thumb wide at the base. Look for a relatively straight branch tapering to about the width of your forefinger at the pointed end and about 30–45 cm/12–18 in long. Some traditions insist a wand should be 21 in long, but if you find a piece that is right but shorter go with that. I personally find 21 in too long except for outdoor rituals.

Other practitioners recommend cutting the wood so it is the same length as from the middle of where your inner upper and lower arm join to the tip of your middle finger on the same hand (usually the power arm). Best of all is to find a fallen tree length that does not need cutting.

Driftwood

This is surprisingly effective since it is already smooth, the bark has been worn away and as long as it is still firm it contains the power of the sea. Driftwood may come from hundreds or thousands of miles away, In the UK, for example, wood is washed up that has come from Africa and South America and so brings with it the history and culture of its origin and the sun that has dried it.

Tree branches

Fallen fresh branches may be on the ground if there has been pollarding, tree felling or a high wind. Don't use wood that is green as wand wood should always be relatively dry, even when taken from a growing tree. Damp or green wood can shrink and crack.

You can cut a small branch from a growing tree, but you must ask the permission of the dryad of the tree (as well as its earthly owners, where necessary). If you feel a cold breeze or sense resistance, try another tree or wait until another day. If you wish, use a pendulum and ask it to lead you by its positive (usually clockwise) swing to the right tree for your wand.

Traditionally, wands are cut on the day of the full moon, if possible when the moon and sun are both in the sky just before sunset, but you may choose a day that has personal significance. Another popular wand-cutting time is on a Wednesday, the day of Mercury/the Archangel Raphael during the first hour after dawn, the hour of Mercury and Raphael.

It is up to you how elaborate or simple the cutting ceremony and whether you want to cast a circle round the tree. Use a small hacksaw, as this is easier and kinder to the tree than breaking off a branch. Cut lightly diagonally to give you a firm end to hold. You may need a stepladder unless you are a regular tree climber. The wood should be dry with leaves growing on it.

If you want to be really formal use a boline, a ritual white-handled knife. Bert, a local environmentalist who made me a special wand and has taught me a great deal of natural lore, says you should cut the required length of branch at five 45-degree angles, giving the remaining branch a five-sided point for regrowth (other wand experts have confirmed this). Remember to thank the tree and leave an offering, such as a crystal, closing the circle if you cast one. Crumble a few biscuits near the roots for wildlife.

Even better, some green witches say, is wood from a dead tree or from branches that have been on the ground in dry weather and dried out. You should be able to see the grain, the finish of the wood, and it will not shrink. It is also if completely dry ready for use and so you can make your wand in situ. If it has been lying a while, check it is not starting to rot inside. Some environmentalists believe that cutting a living tree is like cutting off a finger, whereas a dead tree branch is a gift Mother Nature has made available freely in its next stage of evolution.

Magickal wood for wands

Wands can be made of almost any wood (not elder – see below – unless you find it on the ground, as it is a magickal tree that you should not cut or burn). The following meanings also hold true for staffs (or staves, the correct plural, I believe). You can create or buy wands in different woods as well and maybe a crystal one for healing and special ceremonies (see page 532 for crystal meanings).

Alder is the wood of stability and so brings magickal desires and energies into the here and now.

Apple wood is very fertile and will help to spread abundance and creativity; also used traditionally for casting circles and in love magick.

Ash is the world tree that formed the axis between earth and heaven. It is also a healing tree and the tree of travel and travellers and so is good for portable altars; good for your special wand and for healing magick; also for drawing down the sun and God rituals.

Cedar is the wand of truth, integrity and purity, and so demands high standards of the user. It is also very good for cleansing other artefacts and tools; good for binding and banishing magick.

Elder but only if you find a fallen branch, is associated with fairy and nature spirit magick (see page 319) and is good for any visualisation work and also for work with fairies and nature essences.

Hazel is the traditional tree of wisdom, knowledge and justice and so grounds magick in a secure foundation. It is linked with the magick of the sun, like the ash. The wand should be cut from a tree that has not yet borne fruit; another choice for a ceremonial wand and also for balancing magick.

Oak is a tree of great strength and wisdom and will help you to develop your inner understanding of the deeper significance behind even simple rituals; also for those who wish to progress further in magick and are prepared to accept the extra responsibilities; another really special wood but some will only work with fallen branches. Popular with Druids and Druidesses.

Pine brings courage and inspiration to your work; a good wand for mothers and wise women and in divinatory work.

Rowan is both magickal and protective, if you work mainly in an area where there are security problems or extremes of weather or you are new to magick.

Willow, the moon tree is wonderful for moon magick, drawing down the moon, for Goddess work, for women and younger witches, and will develop your divinatory/prophetic powers; for the magick of the mysteries and mysticism.

Making the wand

You should remove any leaves and twigs as soon as you cut or find your wand wood. In more formal practice, the wand is left for a year and a day in a dry safe airy place. But this may not be practical for a first wand. If you find a really fine piece of wood, you could preserve it for a year and a day to make a second wand (perhaps for your second Year and a Day ceremony in 53 weeks' time).

Unless totally dry from a dead tree, wood should be left about a week in a warm place where air can circulate. An airing cupboard is ideal. This means you still have time to make a wand for your first Year and a Day ceremony, or if you wish you could carry out your ceremony in a place where you know there are dry fallen branches and cut it and use it totally unadorned in your ceremony.

Each wand will retain some of the essence of the tree spirit, even driftwood or dead wood where the actual spirit may have moved on. I am always very wary of buying a wand or staff whose maker declares it to contain a tree spirit per se (and usually charges you a great deal extra for the resident).

- Strip off the bark if you wish. Some people leave at least some of it on and, especially with twisted wooden wands, this looks beautiful.
- Sand or rub it smooth or at least smooth enough so you can hold the wand comfortably without getting splinters. Leaving some nodes adds character.

* I believe that unadorned polished wands are the most magickal. However, you can if you wish bind the handle with cord, add cords, runes etched on small holey stones tied with a cord, crystals or charms.

* You can optionally inscribe one side of the wand with natural magickal symbols from a natural alphabet like runes (see page 431) or your magickal name, the one you use or would use with other witches in runic (see also pages 451 and 466 for other symbols).

* Carve either with a heated pyrography tool or a very fine awl, the finest blade of a pocket knife or a red hot screwdriver in a camping gas cooker flame or an ordinary gas cooker flame (be careful). Bolines can be used, but often are not fine enough unless you have one with a slender blade.

* For an unadorned wand, after polishing write your power names and magickal wishes in incense stick smoke. Alternatively, draw runic symbols in the air over it with smoke to represent the different energies you want to endow your wand with. You can repeat this monthly or whenever your wand seems to lack power. You can also do this over adorned wands to keep the energies active. Ritual magick symbols are, I think, rather heavy for wooden wands.

* Sometimes the wood will already be marked with a distinctive spiral or eye and you can accentuate this with a thin brush and a subtle brown wood paint. Buy sealing oils for the wood from a DIY store to preserve your wand and give it a subtle sheen. Try to use a natural based ones such as linseed oil and varnish after engraving.

* You can give your wand a crystal point if you wish, traditionally a narrow pointed smoky or clear quartz crystal. You need to make a narrow split in the top of the wand with a pocket knife so the crystal will slide in and remain firm (have a couple of spare identical crystals in case one falls out. You can use natural glue if you wish for a snugger fit.

* Once the varnish is dry the wand is ready for dedication (see page 112). This could be the time you endow it with incense smoke symbols to make it your own.

* At the same time, make a simple, small, unadorned and unpolished twig wand (9 in) for when you travel to sites and cannot carry much in the way of equipment.

Caring for your wand

Whether or not you treat your wand with preservative or varnish or buy one that has been treated, polish it before and after use each time with a soft cloth kept especially for the purpose. Once a week use furniture polish, the old-fashioned lavender or beeswax kind in a tin. This cleanses the wand psychically and increases its power.

You can make or buy a long pouch in leather or a natural fabric to keep the wand in. One sold to hold a larger alto recorder musical instrument or flute may be ideal.

If you haven't used the wand during the week, spend a few minutes holding your wand and picturing light beams and sparks flowing in and out. Leave it out under the full moon for three hours or the noon day sun for an hour (even if the moon or sun is not visible because of adverse weather) once a month.

Ancient Egyptian Wand

Element: Air

Direction: East

Energies: God

Qualities: Seeking, sending out, restoring order, protection

See page 123 for the background to these wands.

Egyptologists refer to this type of wand as apotropaic, which means they were protective against evil.

Balsa boomerang wand

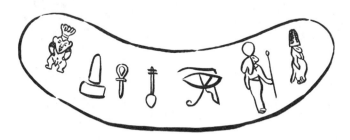

Image 1, reading from left to right is Bes the divine dwarf who protected women in childbirth and the home with his dual knives; image 2, the hieroglyph Wedja, which means prosperity; image 3, the Ankh of immortality; the next is Nefer, the hieroglyph for harmony; then the protective eye of Horus, then Hathor, Goddess of women, the home and fertility; and finally the hippopotamus and fertility Goddess Tauret, guardian of the home and women in childbirth.

* Use a strip of balsa wood 30 cm/12 in long by 7. 5 cm/3 in. You can make it larger or smaller as required and cut it into the classic boomerang shape.

* Decide on the symbols you want on your wand and copy them from pages 123–131 (if you do not like the design on this page) on to tracing paper. Alternatively, trace them from downloaded images of Egyptian deities from the internet. Lay the tracing paper on the wand and, pressing hard, draw over the tracings. As balsa wood is soft, you will leave an indentation that you can draw over with a paint pen or paints and brush. Or just draw them directly, if you prefer.

* You could write a hieroglyph spell or your magickal name in hieroglyphs and a cartouche on the back, but do not press so heavily that the design goes through to the other side.

* If you are skilled in wood carving you can use ordinary light coloured wood to carve your boomerang shape and decorate that.

* If balsa feels too lightweight try Milliput, modelling putty, used for restoring porcelain, ceramics and other antiques. There are similar brands in different parts of the world. You can get it from DIY stores or direct from the Milliput company (see further information at the end of this module). The Milliput I used comprised two tubes containing putty and a hardener that have to be mixed

together to produce a clay-like substance that within eight hours will set as hard as stone. It does need to be mixed thoroughly, so wear gloves during the process.

❋ The putty is pliable enough to be formed into the boomerang shape. Then you can draw your Gods, Goddesses and symbols of power on the wand using a blunt stylus. When the putty has set, you can paint it.

The Milliput 'ivory' wand

My DIY efforts always look home-made, but personally crafted artefacts are very magickal, because they are imbued with the essential self.

Making or buying a staff

Primary element: Air

Direction: North or east

Energies: God

Qualities: Protection, stability, the power of the earth guardians

See page 120 for its many uses in ritual.

The staff is a tool of natural rather than ceremonial magick and also of Druidry. It is nevertheless an important tool in outdoor rituals, not least acting as guardian in the north or east just outside the circle. Often in the twilight you may see a shadowy guardian resting against your staff and you feel suddenly safe and know your ritual is blessed by the Land Spirits or Wights.

Staffs are widely available ready-made in country stores, gift shops at woodlands, animal and bird sanctuaries and at all kinds of rural fairs and gatherings. The staff may have an animal or bird head and is often elaborately carved and polished. You can choose one with your personal power animal. Fortunately, the art of woodcarving is returning and a local craftsperson may make one to order.

Traditionally, staffs are made of yew, ash or hazel, but it is your choice and you can refer to the list of woods above. If making your own staff or indeed ordering one, make sure it is heart height or the same height as you are. Some practitioners prefer shoulder height, tall enough for support but manageable. It is carried in the power hand. Staffs are used vertically in magick.

You can make your own staff from a tall branch so the staff is about a broomstick width, tapering slightly at the end. Hold it upright so that you can see if it feels right. The end you hold is usually cleft on a homemade staff, so you can hang a lantern or your crane bag or small antlers to make a stang (see page 121) from it when it is set upright in the earth or grass. You need sturdy tools to cut and smooth a staff. You may prefer to use a fallen dry branch that only needs the leaves and twigs taken off.

* Dry wood as for a wand. Rub the bark until it is quite smooth and varnish with clear wood varnish.

* If you want to adorn it before varnishing, engrave runes on it. You can write your magickal name in runic or the word Protect in runes or use the symbols Thurisaz or Ingwaz the runes of protection (see page 446). Alternatively, engrave a staff with symbols that are personal to you or perhaps an image of your power creature. You can have staffs of different woods.

* When not in use, stand it upright behind the house or bedroom door at night. I keep mine by the fireplace of my living room in the day when I am not using it or some practitioners prefer to put their staff just inside the altar room door rested diagonally as a symbolic barrier.

* Smudge over your staff monthly with sagebrush or cedar, unless it has been outdoors a lot as that is a natural cleanser.

Making a pentacle

Element: Earth

Direction: North

Energies: Goddess

Qualities: Sensations, stability, nourishment

See page 101 for more on the magickal qualities of the pentagram.

A pentagram is a pentacle enclosed is a circle. As an emblem, it is found naturally inside apples and watermelons and represents the four natural elements combining to make the fifth element Aether, Akasha or Spirit on the uppermost point.

Ways of using the pentacle in ritual:

* Your pentacle can stand in the north of the altar as a totally flat circular plate formed of the pentagram design or with the design of the encircled pentagram in the centre of the plate or dish.

* A dish with a pentacle on can stand in the centre of the altar for holding the symbol of the ritual. You can pass the focus of this pentacle through the four elements on the altar for amplified power or round a circle of assembled participants for each to empower with a wish or blessing.

* You can also on an indoor altar use small flat pentacles dishes at each quarter to contain the elemental crystal and herbs and use chalices etc engraved with it.

* The pentacle is used at the beginning of a ritual to bless the salt and water and then for making sacred water to cast the circle and bless any participants, by resting the water and salt bowl on it to empower them with the athame or ritual knife.

* Like the wand, the pentacle can empower any other tool, including the wand, and is itself empowered by the wand (see page 112 for empowerments and cleansing of tools).

* You can also use a free-standing upright pentacle set in the north of the altar during a ceremony as the Earth element ritual tool to ground the spell, balance the energies and keep out all but benign energies.
* You can also make talismans with pentacles etched on, invoking for power and banishing for protection.
* You can also wear a silver pentacle on a chain round your neck, perhaps with your magick name in a magickal alphabet on the back, as a sign you are a practitioner of the craft. This is good for solitary practitioners to join spiritually with the wide witchcraft community.

How to choose a pentacle

Pentacles are everywhere in New Age stores, online and at every pagan festival. Therefore it is easy to purchase pentacle plates, dishes and altar ware, jewellery and an upright, free-standing pentacle. Dishes are usually ceramic or wood and free-standing pentacles made of brass, silver, copper, bronze or wood or any metal that can be engraved.

To make the pentacle your own and in case it was made by someone who designed the pentacle stamp with little knowledge of pentagram drawing, light a ceremonial incense stick in frankincense, Dragon's blood, myrrh or sandalwood. Over each pentacle item, light a red candle and make first the banishing pentagram (see below) to cleanse and protect and then an invoking one to empower and make it yours. Add chants if you wish and use either your wand, athame or index finger of your power hand. Leave the candle and incense to burn through with the item in front of the candle.

To make your own clay pentacle

Making relatively fragile pentacles that you can replace when they begin to crumble is an ancient art. Wax pentacles were used by witches in the times of persecution so if hostile visitors came they could be thrown on the fire and the evidence destroyed. To me, these fragile home made pentacles in wax and clay are therefore a tribute to the witch ancestors. All pentacles are traditionally made on or around the night of the full moon.

* Roll out a circle of soft clay, the size you need for your pentacle using a wooden rolling pin. Unless you have access to a kiln, use self-hardening clay. Roll into a thick circle and smooth the edges with a slight lip all round. You can make different sizes for different purposes.
* Draw a pentagram on a circle of thin paper or tracing paper cut to precisely the same size as your clay, Make an invoking pentagram and then with your power index finger go over the lines in the other direction to make a protective banishing one and then again over the same lines in the other direction again for an invoking one.
* Make sure the five points touch the edges of the paper circle. Practise drawing pentagrams and use a ruler if necessary to get the lines straight. You can enlarge or shrink the images in this chapter as a template if you prefer.
* If you used tracing paper, place it over the clay and press down with a broad-tipped pencil on the outline. Redraw over the outline so it presses through and

appears on the clay. If you used thicker paper, place the pentagram drawing directly on top of the clay circle and use a sharp pencil, toothpick or thin-bladed paper knife.

* Follow the design on the paper so your implement pierces the paper and creates a dot pentagram on the clay below.

* Remove the paper and join up the dots on the clay with a modelling tool or pencil and make into a smooth or slightly raised line. Do this following the lines in an invoking direction as you create the physical pentagram. Then trace over the finished pentagram on the clay with your index finger in the banishing and then the invoking direction again.

* Put on greaseproof paper or wooden board, loosen with a palette knife or spatula and leave it to harden.

* Empower with the wand or by another method (see page 112). Alternatively, enchant the original circle of clay as I suggest for making a wax pentacle below.

Wax pentacles

These are even more flimsy but my favourites and will hold their power until the wax crumbles. They are firm enough to act as a dish for symbols or as a talisman to guard you or tools if you make the wax quite thick.

The easiest way is to soften a large natural beeswax sheet of the kind you use for making rolling candles. You can buy this in different thicknesses or pre-soften the wax with a hairdryer or over a candle and mould it in your hands. Alternatively use a very large, squat, beeswax pillar candle and stand it on a large, flat, metal holder. Secure the candle by lighting it and dripping on the holder. Holders with spikes are ideal as you can fill in the wax hole while still warm after the candle has melted and they tend to give an even circle of wax.

* Enchant the candle by moving your hands on either side of the burning flame (without getting too close) as though your hands were snakes dancing in unison. As you do so, in your own words, endow the candle with whatever you seek the pentacle to do, to give security to spells to act as a protection etc.

* Build the chant to a crescendo and then release the power by making an arch over the candle with your hands, crossing your hands and bringing them earthwards either side of the candle.

* Leave the candle to burn through and when the wax is still molten mark a circle in the wax with a fine tipped screwdriver, thin-bladed paper knife or the special art engraving tool you keep for engraving candles.

* Within the circle, make the pentagram so it touches the edges, again an invoking Earth pentagram, then draw over it very lightly with the tool in the banishing direction and then the invoking again over precisely the same lines you first drew in the wax.

- Finally just before the wax hardens, redefine the outline circle with your knife so the pentacle separates from the remaining wax. Ease with a spatula on to greaseproof paper on a tray and leave until hard.
- Bury the old pentacle when it crumbles but add a little of the old clay or wax when making a new one.

Making a sistrum

Element: Air

Direction: North-west

Energies: Goddess

Qualities: Joy, fertility, female authority

The sistrum is a metal rattle that is used to begin and end ceremonies and to enhance power through sound. It was often seen in Egyptian art in the hand of the Goddesses Isis, Hathor or Bastet, the cat-headed Goddess of women and children. You can use it instead of a bell or for meditative/shamanic rituals.

- Buy a thin sheet of tin in a craft shop and three long, thin, copper rods.
- You will also need tin snips like pliers that slash through it like dress-making scissors, so that you can cut the tin.
- Begin by cutting a piece of tin 30 cm (12 in) by 7.5 cm (3 in). Use heavy gloves during the cutting because the edges of tin are sharp. For the same reason it is worth turning over the edges of the metal with a pair of pliers.

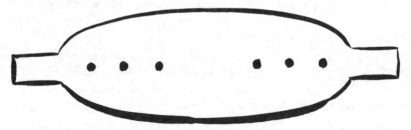

Sistrum template

- The two ends of the metal for the sistrum need to be tapered at the ends so that they can be fixed to a handle. These fixing tabs on the tin will need to be less than the width of the wood.
- Punch six holes, three at each end, with an awl or even a screwdriver: tin is very easily worked. They will need to be equidistant, so that when you bend the tin to the cow-horn shape and insert the copper rods, they run straight across.
- Fold the tin to the cow horn shape.
- Cut the rods to the required length with the tin snips and insert them through the sets of holes, bending them to stop them from falling out.
- You can use an old wooden handle and force the ends of the metal in or use a rounded stick and tack the ends to the top with tin tacks. I used a small piece of broken branch from the local forest.

✳ If you wish, you can make small discs of tin with holes punched in to thread on the copper rods to sit in the middle of the sistrum. I omitted the extra rattles, as some Egyptians did; the rods make a surprising amount of noise on their own.

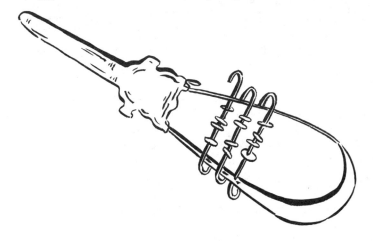

Your finished sistrum

PRACTICAL ASSIGNMENT

Developing your gifts

Decide on your own special gifts to witchcraft in any field and think of ways you can develop them.

Further research

Explore websites, craft fairs, witchcraft festivals etc to study the adornments and magickal glyphs that are used by crafts persons on magickal tools.

If you were having one magickal glyph on all your tools to mark them as uniquely yours, what would it be?

Further information

Recommended reading

* Buckland, Raymond, *Complete Book of Witchcraft*, Llewellyn, 1997
  Best on making your own athame
* Harris, Eleanor and Philip, *Crafting and the Use of Ritual Tools*, Llewellyn, 2002
  Includes Athames, wands and staffs
* McArthur Margie, *Witchcraft for Families*, Phoenix, 1994
  For Wiccan crafts and foods etc
* Polson, Willow, *Witch Crafts, 101 projects for creative pagans*, Polson Willow, Citadel/Kensington, 2002
  Includes sewing crafts such as making spell bags, also making pentacles etc; fun and informative

Websites

* *Witchway*
  Good site for making your own broomstick
  www.witchway.net/hallows/besom.html
* *Earthwitchery*
  Another comprehensive site that includes information on broomstick-making
  www.earthwitchery.com/besom.html
* *Making altar tools*
  Links to articles on crafting tools including besom
  http://paganwiccan.about.com/od/diytools/
* *Milliput company*
  Website that tells you all about this modelling material
  www.milliput.co.uk
* *Willowroot*
  Especially good on consecrating wands
  http://realmagicwands.com
* *College Wicca*
  Good for decorating wands
  www.collegewicca.com/Bosfiles/wand.html
* *Wands*
  Very comprehensive site with instructions including different woods to use
  www.sacred-pathways.com/Wands.html
* *Athame*
  Equipment for making your own athame
  www.witchcraftshop.co.uk/index.php?cat=0136

PREPARING FOR YOUR YEAR AND A DAY CEREMONY

(*A*)lmost a year has passed since the course began. For a number of you it may be longer as you may have had commitments, holidays, crises and opportunities in the daily world that have meant you have needed to take longer to study the material. Alternatively, you may have decided to spend longer on areas that interest you or conversely, if experienced, you may have studied only those parts that you felt might be of value and so finished early. Certainly there will be many books yet to read and avenues to explore, as the modules are meant to be an impetus for ongoing work.

You may be unsure whether you want to go ahead and make a dedication to yourself and the Goddess at this stage, in which case wait and practise the Craft for a while until you feel ready to make a commitment. Some people never want to make any formal declaration and yet still practise witchcraft. Essentially, this is a hard dedication and initiation to make because you are not making it to a coven, with ongoing support and a set ceremony, though you may have followed the course with others and be ready to create a joint ceremony with them on this special day. You are making promises to yourself, as well as to the Goddess/God, or however you picture the divine source of goodness and light and those can be hardest of all to keep.

This marks the completion of the first stage in a lifetime's journey. In your ceremony, you are not saying that you know a great deal about witchcraft (though you do), but that you accept the principles of this highly moral craft and that you accept also the responsibilities of taking on the role of wise man or woman to those you meet in daily life as well as the witchcraft community.

You may live in an area where you cannot talk about your beliefs and practices. Nevertheless by your example, the way you live and relate to others and your reverence for nature, as a wise man or woman you can make a real difference. Your healing and psychic powers will evolve the more you practise magick and dedicate your gifts to the service of others. Once you walk through the doorway into committed witchcraft you become a different person in the very best way. In the months ahead you will increasingly express your magickal gifts in a variety of ways, through spells and rituals, through writing, teaching and by practical work as a caretaker of the earth and all her creatures.

You may find other magick and psychic courses, be they day, residential or online, or craft your own through books, workshops and online resources. I hope to publish the second and third years of the course before too long.

If you are a Solitary practitioner you may decide to find a coven or at least a regular pagan moot, or if a coven member you may suddenly realise you want to work alone for a while or accelerate your learning so you can run your own coven one day. As a result of studying witchcraft, you may be prompted to go all out for a career in the psychic or healing fields or decide that you need first to make your mark in earthly terms as a priority, or, as most witches do, follow the dual pathway of the true hedge witch who walks between the dimensions with a foot in both worlds. There are many choices and sometimes a dedication and initiation can clarify for you your future intentions, if not the precise path.

There are only two more topics I wish to introduce: that of the witch's familiar and the difference between dedication and initiation, before moving on to the ceremony construction.

The witch's familiar

You by now know your Witch Guardian well and she may stay with you throughout your path. However, you may find over the months ahead or even during the ceremony that another spiritual persona draws close to assist you in future with particular tasks such as healing or to take you to the next level of awareness. But your first magickal teacher will never leave you. You also have your special Spirit Guides, your wise ancestors, spiritual and actual, and your angelic protectors and these, like your Witch Guardian will be with you in your special ceremony.

Traditionally witches also have an animal familiar, which may be a pet, a cat, bird, dog, a horse or even a small animal like a hamster that is connected with you on a very deep level and daily gives you power, energy and healing. I currently have two black cats (I always end up with black cats, however hard I try otherwise) that sit either side of me during rituals and spook the neighbours by doing so.

In times past it was believed that these familiars, which might include mice or frogs, contained a magickal spirit, and in the times of persecution these were identified, erroneously, as demons. Witches were often unfairly accused of shape-shifting into animal form to do harm to neighbours who might see a toad on their doorstep at a time of family illness or when a cow stopped giving milk. Animals were regularly burned or hanged alongside their owners during the witchcraft persecutions and it was often claimed a hideous black demon was seen leaving the creature who was in reality a much loved pet and protector of the person accused of witchcraft.

To many modern witches, their familiar is a particular pet that after its death seems to reincarnate into subsequent pets that just turn up as strays. You will know this one for it is your soul mate. But for other witches the familiar may be a wild animal or bird that turns up and sits close whenever you are performing an outdoor ritual or are just in urgent need of reassurance you are on the right path. Mine is the blackbird.

You may dream of this creature and see it in unlikely places. Invariably you end up (again, usually by synchronicity or meaningful coincidence) with a ceramic, painting or photograph of the creature and its icon becomes a magickal focus for its creature energies. If your familiar animal or bird has not come, you can be sure it soon will, maybe a species you loved in childhood.

For some people, however, the attraction is to a more exotic creature, such as a wolf that you might see occasionally in a sanctuary but that is a recurring theme in your life. You may collect wolf music and wolf images. This is a true spirit familiar, akin to the Native North America power totem, and you may already have its image on your altar or painted on your staff and incorporate it into magickal chants.

The following exercise is a very good way of connecting with your familiar pet, favourite wild animal or power creature. If it is an actual animal or bird you encounter daily, you can repay their magickal and spiritual energy by the loving care you give them and by offering them healing or strength when they are tired. I leave out food for my garden blackbird and when I forget he comes close to the house and eats the cat food instead while they watch, amazed.

Walking on the wild side

It is easiest to start with your pet or by going to a place where you know you can see a representative of the wild bird or animal who appears at ritual and other significant times. Otherwise you can use the power icon or photograph that typifies a more exotic and less frequently seen power animal or bird.

* First create and then use a magickal animal chant to make the connection that will henceforward call the power of your animal before a ritual, even if he or she is not physically there.

* Once you have established the chant, whenever you use it you may hear in your mind or externally the beating of wings, feel the soft brush of fur against you or become aware of the fast breathing as a more exotic creature stalks through the forest You may be linked to your exotic creature through some deep ancestral past or a past life.

* Look through half-closed eyes towards the creature or icon, not too close if the creature is wild and might run or fly away if disturbed.

* Tune into the creature's breathing pattern whether physically heard or imagined, slow and deep or tiny panting breaths. Match the creature's breathing either aloud or in your mind.

* Picture you and the creature moving closer step by step as the visualised breathing gets louder and your own breath gets correspondingly louder and assumes the animal breath pattern. Listen to online nature clips or videos if you are uncertain of the rhythm.

* A pet may move close enough for you to stroke them rhythmically as you breathe in time with them, but they must take the initiative. The wild creature may also approach but you should remain motionless.

* As you continue to breathe animal style, imagine your skin touching its fur or feathers and the strengths of your creature flowing into your own body. This tactile contact may actually be happening with your pet but you pet will seem different, magickally charged, and its aura will glow.

* Keep breathing and moving closer in your mind until your skin and their feathers seem to merge and you share one physical form.

* You are now within the creature's psychic space so that you can see through their eyes and hear through their ears, breathe as their rhythm. If visualised, the creature may be at rest or moving fast, either hunting or hiding or you may suddenly perceive your pet running in a forest or if a bird soaring high or perched in a tree.

* Feel the ground beneath you or the air round you and the throb of the energies from your familiar making your heartbeat and your mind pulsate (even if your body is sitting in your living room still stroking the physical cat).

* When you feel filled with the animal strength, thank your host and allow the boundaries to begin to re-emerge as your animal very gently recedes.

* Mentally move away, re-creating the separate boundaries between you and the creature once more and gently withdraw your own essence back into your body by gentler in breaths and longer, slower out breaths as you assume your own breathing pattern.

* Continue to practise connecting with your power animal until you can step almost instantly within your animal's power and protection when you need it, just by picturing them and making their chant. You may find a conservation park where you can study your exotic creature at close quarters.

* You might like to give your power animal a name so you can call softly in your mind or sing their chant when you need assistance or for the creature to empower a ritual. You can give your pet a secret magickal name for ritual work.

Dedication and initiation

Once it was said only a witch could make another witch and I respect those who believe that. But increasingly solitary witches wish to mark ceremonially their own spiritual commitment to the Craft and acknowledge the positive spiritual change that working with witchcraft brings within the practitioner. The Year and a Day ceremony I am suggesting involves both initiation and dedication.

Initiation is a rite of passage, a spiritual rebirth involving leaving part of the old self and life behind and moving on to a new higher level of awareness. In a sense, any ceremony is the outward marking and acknowledgement of the inner changes that have been occurring during the study and practice of witchcraft.

Dedication is the conscious commitment to the Craft and can be made at any time during study or practice, but I believe is especially appropriate after a Year and a Day, because then so much more is understood of the implications and the degree and nature of commitment to magick as a way of life.

So dedication and initiation go hand in hand, and even if you are an initiated coven member you may wish to solemnise your private contract with the Goddess.

PRACTICAL ASSIGNMENT

Preparing your ceremony

Even if you do not feel ready for your ceremony, this is a good point to prepare its form and to consider what aspects are for you significant. You can keep these notes in your Book of Shadows and look back at them during further study and magickal work. You may revise them from time to time.

A Year and a Day ceremony

Work through these questions and then plan the ceremony. Because you are at the end of the course I will no longer say, *Call the ancestors from the west* etc' but do check back to the ritual structure of module 47 and other relevant modules listing herb associations and so on and the extensive material you have acquired in your Book of Shadows in your planning. If in doubt, trust your intuition and your pendulum as what is right for you. This really is all about you.

Aims and achievements

* What has/will a commitment to witchcraft involve giving up in my personal life and are these sacrifices worthwhile for me?

* Have I developed a Wiccan Rede of my own that accords with my deeply held spiritual values and is workable in my daily life as well as magick?

* How have I developed spiritually, emotionally and in terms of knowledge and wisdom over the last year? In what ways have been the greatest achievements?

* What disappointments, failures, practical, spiritual and emotional problems, as well as lack of support or opposition from others, have I encountered during the course that are related to my studies or have made study difficult? Are these insurmountable or have I become more resourceful and better at merging the different aspects of my life?

* Who has been helpful to me and how can I maximise the level of support so that the road ahead is easier?

* How do I see my road ahead during the next 12 months magickally and personally? What are my aims and how can I realistically achieve these?

* Am I ready to take on the role of wise man or woman, even at this level of training? How do I see this role in relation to others within the witchcraft community, friends, family and colleagues?

* What are my special gifts that I can bring to witchcraft and how can I develop these, use them for the good of others and, if appropriate, make it financially more viable for me to devote more time to spiritual work? Is there one area of expertise I could develop over the next 12 months?

* Do I want to initiate other life changes as a result of my magickal work: for example, to study or practise healing or divination, change my place of residence, career or relationships? Or should I continue on my present life path and incorporate witchcraft into it more and more? Or do I need to go more slowly?

* What blessings do I seek from the cosmos and the Goddess and what can I offer in return?

* Do I feel ready to offer teaching to others, whether of specific gifts, to disseminate my own knowledge and insights in writing articles, on line or practically?

* Could I organise festival celebrations or events for friends and family, offer a workshop or talk to a local non pagan group?

* Should I seek more or less formal contact with other witches and pagan organisations or do I need more time in private work and study?

The ceremony
The practicalities

* Where do I want to hold my ceremony: at my indoor or outdoor altar, in a place of natural beauty or sanctity, a harrow on the mountain side or within a grove of trees?

* When should I hold my ceremony? After a year and a day from beginning the course or after another month, two months or an unspecified time when I feel ready? Should I link it to a particular phase of the moon: the crescent to mark a rebirth, the full moon to walk into my dedicated, initiated period with joy and power? Or do I want an end of waning or dark of moon ceremony to mark the ending of my old world and pure trust that I will be reborn as the moon is as a wise man or woman? Do I want to link it to a moon entering a particular star sign that is my own star sign? Is there a forthcoming Wheel of the Year festival, the first of a month or a particular day of the week whose planetary or Archangel energies mirror my own path to witchcraft?

* Will it be a day or night ceremony or begin at dawn and continue with ceremonies at noon, sunset and maybe midnight, Egyptian style? What planetary or Archangel hour is most appropriate to begin and are there any actual astronomical events or alignments that would enhance the occasion?

* Is there a particular star or constellation visible that has magickal meaning for me? Should I begin when both the sun and moon are in the sky at the same time (check your astrological diary or an online almanac)?

* Do I want to begin precisely as one monthly zodiacal period ends and another begins and span the changeover period in my ceremony to mark the passage into a new magickal state?

* Am I inviting friends and family, coven members or my magickal group to attend? Or is it better as a totally private occasion, attended by my Witch Guardian, spiritual or historical ancestors, my animal familiar, Spirit Guides and Angels and the nature essences?

* What should I wear or do I want to be sky clad? If outdoors or in a public place, would this be safe or wise alone? Do I want two robes, one to wear for the first part of the ceremony to signify my old life, in which case could it be an old one? Then would I want a new white one to put on after initiation? If not, what colour is right? If I am immersing myself in water as part of the initiation, do I need something to wear, such as a white swimsuit or shift if in a public place?

* Is there any new special magickal jewellery, such as jet and amber beads or silver pentagram earrings, that I could like to dedicate during the ceremony to replace some older non-magickal jewellery I could wear for the first part (essential if working sky clad)?

* What about cords: maybe a waist cord to burn to signify the end of the old and a new one ready on the altar to be tied round the waist to signify the new magickal self?

* How can I signify walking into the darkness of the unknown, putting a scarf round the eyes or a sleep mask in daylight or extinguishing candles at night?

* Is the day or evening after the ceremony going to be part of a general period of magickal activity or celebration and do I want to spend the time before in quiet contemplation?

* If I am planning an outdoor ceremony or to go to a particular place and the weather turns bad in spite of forecasts, or for some reason I can't get there, do I want to have an alternative venue or would I sooner wait until the factors are right? What am I prepared to compromise on and what is sacrosanct?

Preparing for the ceremony

* What kind of an altar do I wish to use or do I want to work in an entirely natural place and find a rock or tree stump?

* What tools do I plan on using, a full formal altar, an informal setting using key artefacts (what is key to me?) or do I want to go to my beautiful place and find a twig wand on the ground and use for offerings the flowers and leaves I know I will be growing?

* Which incenses, herbs, flowers, candle colours and crystals are truly mine? Do I want to make a Year and a Day charm bag or empower a crystal to carry the power forward in the days and weeks ahead?

* What kind of offerings will I make: symbolic ones like salt or petals in a candle flame or crystals to bury at the site, and herbs or even a small tree to put on top to symbolise the burial of the old and growth of the new?

* Should I write the ceremony in advance or should I just create the order of the ceremony and let the words come inspired by the occasion? Or is it all between me and the Goddess and I will speak and move as the moment takes me?

* Who is my focal deity for the ceremony? Or do I want to work with God and Goddess energies and in what aspects? How will I address them: Lord and Lady, by specific deity names and, if so, which? How will I represent them: with candles, crystals, statues, a shell and a horn? Or should I craft representations out of clay or wax before or during the ceremony?

* When I begin *I am. . .*, what magickal names will I use? Do I want to leave one of my old magickal names I have outgrown, perhaps saying it for the last time and burning it in a candle flame on the altar?

* What accompaniments do I need: chants (do I need to write or learn any?), drums, a sistrum, a bell?

* What do I state I am leaving behind and what embracing? What blessings do I

ask for and what will I promise? How will I define my new role: *I am a priestess, witch, wise woman or man*? Don't be afraid to take on the mantle of what will be a lifetime's journey because if you assume the responsibility seriously and with humility you will be helped to do good.

* If others are present, how do I see their role in the ceremony? As celebrants joining in simple chants, as sponsors if experienced in magick who will help me make my promises and lead me into the unknown in darkness? If working as a group, shall we all make our dedications one after the other with the others assisting the individual, or make silent private dedications and come together for the opening, closing and at key parts of the ritual? Could we make an actual doorway out of a flower arch to walk through into the new life?

* Will there be circle casting and will I move within it to signify the new life or work for the whole ritual within it? Is a circle formation too restrictive? If not, how will I draw protection at a time when I am vulnerable spiritually: with a large magickal grid formation (see page 257) or by visualising light extending all round? Could I work in front of a particular standing stone, sacred well, lake or tree and ask for protection from the Guardians of the place to stand around it? Or should I work within a natural circle of trees encircled by the nature essences and make a protective blessing at the beginning and end?

The ceremony

It is very important that each witch crafts her own ceremony. Once you have written it or outlined the stages you can draw up a list of everything you will need. The following are the stages that I consider important but you can add others or reshape according to your priorities. You can adapt these for a more spontaneous format.

If a group rite initiating several people, you can ask one another question's, such as: *What is your name? Why are you here*'. You can also receive one another's offerings, anoint and help one another to walk through the doorway into the new life. This will take a little more planning in advance.

Purification and protection

* Asperge and cleanse the area and personal purification, whether a ritual bath and/or anointing the chakras.

* Put on a clean but old robe (or sky clad wearing old jewellery) to signify the old and work barefoot, if possible.

* Purify and charge the altar and tools.

* Light candles, set on the altar new jewellery and the robe to be worn after the initiation. Organise the crystals, herbs etc to be empowered for a charm bag that will carry on the energies after the ceremony; also, put any offerings in place.

* Cast and bless circles.

Beginning the rite

* At the Altar. Statement: *I am* and (new) magick name. Any old name would be spoken and written for the last time then burned in the Goddess candle.

* Greeting the focal deity/deities.

* Opening the quarters.
* Welcoming the Witch Guardian ancestors, nature essences, Angels, etc. You can assume the Witch Guardian will be by the guardian stone or near the north of the altar inside the circle waiting. But it is respectful to invite her in and thank her for her care on the year's road that you have travelled together. You may become aware of a shadowy new guardian who will help you through the doorway into your new life.
* Opening prayer or chant followed by your declaration:

I seek to dedicate . . . and I seek initiation from . . .

* Name focal deities, wise ancestors Witch Guardian, spiritual witchcraft community worldwide past and present and whoever you choose to guide your path. If you sense a new guardian with you add:

Guardians blessed but as yet unknown.

Dedication

* Make offerings, for example, salt into the Goddess flame or flower petals burned in the flame, or bury a crystal in a pot of earth or the soil near the altar if possible, giving thanks for blessings received and asking for blessings on this rite, *from all the wise ones here present.*
* Then state, *I offer. . .* and make promises you feel able to keep, responsibilities you will take on.
* State your new title, witch/wise woman or man/priestess or priest of the lord and lady, Goddess and God or name deities to whom you relate. Ask for the help of your chosen force or if you prefer call yourself a priest/priestess of the light. Then ask of these deities for the specific blessings and strengths you seek.
* Empower yourself and chosen symbols, new jewellery and/or robe with the elements and ritual tools in a way that seems meaningful. Make a dedicatory chant or prayer.

The initiation proper

* Take the cord tied round your waist and burn it in the Goddess candle, saying you are cutting ties with what holds you back from the light, also shedding weaknesses, doubts and fears about your path (name them).
* Acknowledge the need to walk through the doorway of the dimensions into the darkness of the unknown and accept rebirth Ask if you may be admitted and call on the wise Crone to hold your hand.
* There may be two trees you could stand between.
* Remove your old robe and any jewellery if working clothed or the old jewellery, in a public place keeping on a simple shift.
* Bury the jewellery with the crystal and lay the robe on the ground and walk across it.
* Either extinguish all candles except a tiny light, if dark, or in the day cover your

eyes with a loose scarf or sleep mask and state that you walk into the darkness in trust and perfect love etc.

- Stand motionless if you eyes are covered (for safety reasons unless others are present to guide you).

- Stand in silence. Where you travel will depend on you, but you need not be afraid because your Witch Guardian and maybe your new Guardian will hold your hands. Let yourself float and fly or lie safe within the arms of the Earth Mother and leave your sorrows, fears and any illness in the dark.

- When you are ready (with others they will do this for you), remove the mask or scarf or light the candles and you will be flooded with light and love and joy.

- If possible, immerse yourself now either using a tub of water, a pool, lake or the sea or just wade out a way and splash.

- Anoint your chakras if more appropriate, using perfume or a few drops of rose or lavender essential oil dissolved in almond or pure olive oil, adapting the *Blessed be my feet* chant on page 478.

- Put on your new white initiation robe and any empowered jewellery from the altar.

- Touch each of your personal tools in turn in the order that feels right and make a dedication for each to use them wisely for the greatest good and the purest intent.

- You now speak from your heart and from the wisdom of the Goddess a few words, maybe five minutes or more. Just let it flow and know you are blessed.

The consecration

- Bless the cakes and the wine and plunge the athame or, on this occasion, the tip of your wand into the chalice. You would do this as a group after all the initiations.

- Ask that the Goddess and God powers be awakened within you and again promise service and commitment.

- Make your offering of cake and wine to the earth or indoors in your libation bowl.

- Restate your magickal names and that you are a priestess/wise woman or man of the lord and lady, or however you address them.

- Eat and drink and in a group pass round the cakes and wine with blessings on all present.

- Now whether alone or with others, spiral dance and drum/chant to connect with the earth.

- Take your empowered athame from the altar and raise it to the four directions, greeting in turn the Guardian of each and blessing all who live within, above or below their domain, humans, animals, birds, insects, crystals, trees, herbs and flowers.

- Then direct it to the sky, asking the blessings of the moon, sun, stars and planets, and down to the earth, giving thanks to the bounty of the Mother.

- Finally, touch your own heart with the blade, naming your body as the temple of your spirit and promising to revere and care for it.
- In a group, each person would take their athame from the altar and one speak the greetings and the others do the actions.
- End by saying you receive the power of the four directions, the earth and sky in humility and promise to care for the earth, the sky and all its creatures. If you wish, you could substitute a lighted smudge for the athame in greeting the directions.
- Finally, take the new cord from the altar and tie it round your waist, having singed one end in the Goddess candle and the other in the God candle. Say that you bind yourself willingly and joyously in the service of the Goddess and of humankind to the best of your ability, so long as it is right to be.

The closing

- Thank the Guardians and any ancestors and others whom you invited into your circle and then close the four quarters.
- Leave the circle cast and scry using your favourite method by the light of the altar candles or natural light to discover the paths ahead. First, however, raise the scrying bowl or whatever you use to the altar and ask the wisdom and blessings of the Goddess on your insights.
- Afterwards, close the circle or make your final blessing, ending with the words:

  I am a wise man/woman [or you chosen title]. Here ends the rite. Blessings be.

- Now is the time to plant your tree or a flowering herb in the soil to commemorate this occasion. If in a group you can each plant something small.
- Spend time in contemplation or celebration or a mixture of both and ask that your new Guardian may come to you in your dreams.
- It would be good to recycle the old robe material in some way the next day.

Further research

Look at some of the books and websites I suggest and any others you find for ideas on self-initiation.

Further information

Recommended reading

* Andrews, Ted, *Animal Speak*, Llewellyn, 2003
* Palmer, Dawn Jessica, *Animal Wisdom*, Element, 2001
* Shaddaramon, Self, *Initiation for the Solitary Witch Attaining Higher Spirituality through a five degree system*, New Page, 2002
* West, Kate, *The Real Witches' Craft. Magical techniques and guidance for a full year of practising the Craft*, Harper Element, 2005
* Wilby, Emma, *Cunning Folk and Familiar Spirits*, Sussex Academic Press, 2005

Websites

* *Avalonia*
  Good site, with a suggested ritual
  www.avalonia.co.uk/book_of_shadows/self_dedication_explained.htm
* *House Shadow Drake*
  Extensive site on witchcraft traditions
  www.traditionalwithccraft.org/witchcraft/initiation.html
* *Wild Ideas*
  Self-initiation ritual and suggestions
  www.wildideas.net/cathbad/pagan/initiation.html

The End of the Journey, the Beginning of the Adventure

You are already a wise man or woman, a witch, a priest or priestess. Your ceremony is affirmation of the path you have travelled during the past year or maybe much longer. The opening of the doorway from darkness into light or immersion in water and the symbolic rebirth in your initiation is the first step on your continuing lifetime spiritual journey. Today you choose to take your place as part of the universal witchcraft community stretching back through the ages, spanning the oceans, across dimensions and extending through the mists of time into the future. The most important task you are now agreeing to undertake is to carry the old wisdom forward to the next generation.

It is not always easy to convince those impatient for instant results and special effects that there cannot be magickal power without responsibility: that you can't just light the candle and tie the ribbon in an instant spell kit, say the words on the back of the pop-up cardboard altar and, hey presto! the world is at your feet, not to mention a golden coach to take you to the ball.

But even for Cinderella the magick could only last until midnight and as witches we have to answer all kinds of difficult questions about why that should be so and why her pretty glittery frock turned back to rags.

If magick is true, why can't we have what we want?

How come if you can do magick you can't stop my child from dying, bring instant money to stave off repossession of my home now I have lost my job, stop the man who is peddling drugs to my teenager or hex the woman who lures my husband away, leaving me with small children, and who laughs in my face? Why under the threefold law do the terrorist, the dictator or that drug-peddler thrive? We've got to try to answer those questions to understand the limits of magick so we don't make false promises or, on the other hand, make people who come to us for help lose hope.

Being a witch brings you face to face with the seemingly unanswerable and you have to try to find answers to suffering and injustice, offer at least some solutions and try to make a difference through earthly support, as well as though magick. Nor can witches regard the Craft as a passport to riches. *Enough for my needs and a little more* isn't exactly the key to the winning lottery numbers and most of us are better at prosperity spells for others than ourselves.

An' you harm none do as you will, says the Wiccan Rede – or more or less that. That puts a lot of restrictions on zapping villains Harry Potter style. That what you send out comes back three times is some mitigation of unfairness, but sometimes it seems to take so long when you're trying to do a spell to protect a bullied child or to fathom why a lovely person who is sick doesn't get better when they've done good all their lives.

So when you walk through that door of initiation there is the most beautiful light you have ever seen, but it takes you not to fairyland or over the rainbow, but slap back into reality and the dilemmas and challenges you as one of the wise ones have got to try to sort.

Real magick revisited

But for all that, magick is real, magick is valid and sometimes we can move the odd mountain as long as we are willing to pay the Cosmos back as soon as we can, when we are blessed with good results in our spellcasting. Small miracles do happen and, most importantly, magick is most effective when used as an impetus for personal action. The more we help ourselves and can teach others to use magick in that way, the more powerful and effective spells and rituals become. What is more, the greater the number and intensity of positive powers we launch into the cosmos through our magick, the more abundance and good energies are increased. The more those positive cosmic energies are raised, the more we can correspondingly draw down good things into daily life. Then as a result of our increased happiness we in turn generate even more positive energies to swell the cosmic pool of joy and healing.

If every witch in the world focused on peace and abundance for all at the same time there would be a huge explosion of positive power that would flood the energy fields even of indifferent, cynical or malevolent individuals, governments or corporations. We know historically witches working collectively have turned back invasions. If we can organise via the internet and other means, times when everyone works for peace or healing, for example on Earth Day, then we can start to get things moving in the right direction.

The community of witchcraft

You'll know when you meet another witch even in their city suit or work overalls, not because of the pentagram around their neck or because they have a copy of the Witches' Bible sticking out of their bag, but by the connection that is transmitted by an indefinable look in their eyes, a mixture of humour, compassion, optimism, kindness and a belief that the world is a good place and we really can make a difference as individuals. Often when we have a chance to speak, the conversation somehow steers round to magick and suddenly you have a new friend for life. Witchcraft festivals are a good way to make friends and so go along alone if necessary, because you won't stay alone. I am often on my own and incredibly shy, but I always get to meet new people who become friends in a short time, even if we don't meet very often.

Witches don't need a secret handshake or coded words, because wherever you are, you and a fellow witch are instantly on the same wavelength. A smile and deep eye contact whether across a festival café or a crowded city shopping mall tells you that you are members of the world community of wise men and women.

At the end of the day it doesn't matter whether you belong to the Alexandrian tradition, the Gardnerian, to Seax Wicca, a hereditary coven, the Cult of Cassandra (I'm working on that one for my old age!) or have no formal tradition except your own valid accumulated and growing beliefs and ideas about magick. You are a witch in your heart, whether a solitary practitioner or a coven member, part of an informal magickal group or of a family who live by folk magick as your grandma and great-grandma did before you. Maybe you were a witch in a past life and may choose to become one again.

You are a witch, a real, genuine true, 23-carat diamond witch if you open your mind to the old traditions within your spiritual genes that are just a memory away. You are a good witch if you respond in your soul with compassion to the needs of others and try to make your little patch of the world a better place through your magick and your daily actions and words.

The collective well of wisdom

After you have carried out your ceremony, if not before, you will draw information from the well of collective wisdom without even consciously trying. You will start to know magickal correspondences or herb lore without knowing how or why you know them only that they are true. Then you read or hear during a lecture that the information comes from some ancient time and maybe obscure tradition or one whose temples are now buried deep in the sand or whose wisdom is scratched on fast-fading stone tablets. Such seemingly lost knowledge isn't lost at all, but lives on vibrant and echoed in your higher consciousness and can be transmitted in your spells, your teaching and your writing, if you trust it.

Suddenly it all starts to make sense, like the sun bursting through the mists, as seemingly unconnected knowledge, facts and correspondences assume an interconnected pattern. The jigsaw takes shape and even those seemingly insurmountable problems that vex witches about mortality, justice and morality seem suddenly more solvable given goodwill, magick and earthly efforts in equal measure.

Once you have walked through that door in your ceremony, through the darkness into the light, you become one of the custodians of the past with your own key and transmitters, too, of the wisdom of the future with your voice, your wand and your pen. Everything you learn, create in ceremony or recall, adds to the wisdom of witches everywhere.

Rupert Sheldrake, the Cambridge biologist, described how through the principle called morphic resonance one member of a species could learn from the experiences of another unrelated member of that species even a thousand miles away. Nowhere is that more true than of witchcraft.

After I have finished writing, I will burn a candle to send my light and good wishes to you as you read this book. I hope that as you finish the course you will send light on to someone else – and maybe someday some of that amplified light will come bouncing back to me.

Cassandra

INDEX

Major page references are indicated in **bold**

Aborigines 93–96
aether 134
aetts 199–200
    rune aetts 436–443
agricultural rituals 28, 66–67
air (element) 137–139, 328
    making the basis for a whole spell 339
air (Norse element) 155
air dragons 329
air elementals 328–329
absorbing elemental strength 331–333
    and magick 329–331
air spirits 330–331
akasha 134
Akhet 85, **86–88**
Alban Arthuran 66, 78, **82–83,**
    657–659
Alban Eiler 75–76, 241, **639–641**
Alban Elued 80–81, **651–653**
Alban Heruin 77–78, **644–647**
alchemical alphabets 466
alphabets
    alchemical 466
    angelic 466
    Hebrew 32
    Malachim 469–473
    Theban 466, **467–468**
    witches' 466, **467–468**
    see also hieroglyphs; runes

altars 99–100, **157–168**
    choosing indoor altars 158–159
    creating outdoor altars 165–166
    dedicating Egyptian altar
        ritual 172–173
    dedicating indoor altar ritual 161–163
    dedicating Norse altar ritual 175–176
    dedicating outdoor altar ritual 167–168
    Egyptian 171–173
    indoor 158–164
    'inner temple' 163–164
    night altars 169–171
    Norse altars 174–176
    outdoor 164–168
    personal to you 158
    purpose of 157–158
    setting up indoor altars 159–161
    setting up outdoor altars 165–166
amazonite (crystal) 532–533
amber (crystal) 533
American witchcraft trials 44
amethyst (crystal) 533–534
amulets 398, **399–401**
    Ancient Egypt 399
    in early magick 28, 31, 56
    magickal timings 400–401
Anael 582
angel magick 32
angelic alphabets 466
angelite (crystal) 534
angels 574

birth guardian angels 585–589, 594
  Cherubim 592
  Dominions 593
  Powers 593
  Principalities 593
  Seraphim 592
  Thrones 592
  Virtues 593
  see also archangels
anger 15
animal familiars 318, **688–690**
animal power in early magick 31
Ankh, The (symbol) 131
Annwyn, Cauldron of 119
anointing candles 530
Apollo 240
April 197
aquamarine (crystal) 534
Aradia 366
Aradia, gospel of the Witches 46, 260, 366
archangels 32, **289–290, 574–585**, 594
  blessings 591
  days of the week 580–583
  four core **576–579**, 626–628
  hours of the day 589–591
  invoking 289, 291
  rites 583–585
  working with 575–576
archetypal power 31
Arduinna 233
Ariadne 387–388
arm rings 125–126
Artemis 233
Arthurian legends 103, 119
ash magick 348–349
aspergilla 116
astral plane 180
astral travelling 32
astrological candle magick 528–530
athames 104, **106–108**
  ritual functions 107–108
attracting magick 57
August 198

aura 13, 510
  cleansing 284
  higher levels 179
  see also chakras; energy, personal
Australian Aboriginal magick 93–96
autumn equinox 80–81, **651–653**
aventurine (crystal) 535
Awen 503–506

Ba (hieroglyph) 402
Babh 379
bags, charm or spell 412–417
  empowering 415–416
  herbal 570–571
  keeping 416–417
  making 414–415
bags, coven 424
bags, crane 425
bags, Isis bags 412, **423–424**
bags, medicine 422–423
bags, mojo 417–421
  contents 418–419
  making and empowering 420
balance
  A fire and water ritual for balance in your life 89–90
  keeping 21
balancing magick **60–61**, 68, 667
banded agate (crystal) 535
banishing magick 58, **60**
  Three–knot banishing spell 668–669
barley and corn god sacrifice 394–395
base chakra 179–180
baths, ritual 282–283
beads 423
beauty, goddesses of 241
beginners in magick 7, 8, 9–10
belief, power of 51
bell staffs 121
bells 109
Beltane 70, 71, **76–77**, 93, **642–644**
besoms 117
bind runes 443–446

binding magick 58, **59**
birds 328, 329
bird and insect goddesses and gods 234
birth crystals 548
black 523
  and hieroglyphs 463
blessings 285
  angel blessings 591
  power of 284
  protective blessing rituals 286–291
blood sacrifices 52
blue 518
  and hieroglyphs 463
blue calcite (crystal) 536
blue lace agate (crystal) 535–536
blue moons 480
boat (hieroglyph) 402–403
body fluids 19
bolines 117
Book of Shadows 10, **259–267**
  contents 264–266
  creating 261–262
  hand written 262
  online 11, 259, **162**
  origins 259–260
  and secrecy **260**, 262
bottles, witches' 412, **426–428**
bowls 109
Brighid 239, **377–379**
broomsticks 117
brow chakra **182–183**, 601–602
brown 520
Bugady Musun 233
bull gods 387–388

cakes and ale rites 101, **633–634**
calendars 480–483
Camael 76
candles 110
  anointing 530
  astrological magick 528–530
  burnt as offerings 346
  colours of 510

engraving 527
  magick of 527–530
  power of 349–351
  scrying with 614–615
carnelian (crystal) 536–537
Cassiel 82, **582–583**
casting circles 108, **247–251**, 625–626
cauldrons 101, **118–119**
cave magick 26–27
  see also rock art
cedarwood (incense) 336
celebrations and ritual 68
Celtic circling prayer 285
Celtic elements 147–149
Celtic festivals **73–83**, 92–93
Celtic lunar calendar 481
Celtic magick 38–39
Celtic Triskele 148
Celtic Wheel of the Year 73–83
censers 111
ceremonial magick 32, 33
ceremonies *see* rituals
Cernunnos 16, **234, 386**
Cerridwen 238
Cauldron of 118–119
chakras **178–183**, 281, 282
  closing **189**, 281
  and spellcasting 184
chalices 100–101
  chalice and blade rite 633–634
change, gods of 244, **390–393**
chants 9, **293–302**, 492
  creating 296–297
  knot chants 666–668
  revising 298
  rewriting exercise 301
  singing 298–299
  sources of 295
charcoal burning 111
charge of the God 224, 229–231
  Cassandra's charge of the God 230–231
  using in ritual 227
charge of the Goddess 223–228

Cassandra's charge of the Goddess 225–227
using in ritual 227
writing 224–227
charms 398, **401–402**
charm bags 412, **413–417, 570–571**
Creating your wax personalised talisman or
charm 410–411
metal 407–408
natural objects 408–409
spoken 406–407
Cherubim 592
Children of Artemis 17, 24
chime hours 200
Chinese elements 150–154
choirs of angels 592–594
Christianity 16, 17–18
and paganism 41
chrysoprase (crystal) 537
circles, magick 246–253
casting 108, **247–251**, 625–626
cleansing 247–248
doorways in 252–253
measuring 108
physical 249–250
seven directions of 247
size of 248
triple elemental 250–251
uncasting **251–252**, 632
visualising 251
citrine (crystal) 537–538
clairaudience 602–604
clairsentience 604–606
clairvoyance 601–602
clay
pentacles 682–683
symbols 305
cleansing
circles 247–248
crystals 532
personal 282–284
tools 112–113
clear crystal quartz 538
cloud divination 333

collective wisdom 701
colours
of candles 510, **527–530**
colour infused water 360
correspondences 511
of crystals 510
and elements 135
and hieroglyphs 462–464
meanings of 512–523
symbolism 511
use in magick 510–511, 524–525
see also chakras
contagious magick **56**, 57, 68
copal 554
incense 334
cords 110–111
see also knots
corn dollies 56
corn god sacrifice 394–395
court cards (tarot) 314–315
covens 8–9
coven bags 424
and the sun 494–495
crane bags 425
creation and destruction 15
Creative Sisters, The 377–379
crescent moon 205–206
crone/wise woman goddesses 238,
369–370, 375
see also Triple Goddess
crop circles 316
cross–quarter days 65, 69
see also Beltane; Imbolc; Lammas;
Samhain
Crowley, Aleister 32, 33, 47, 50
crown chakra 183
crystal balls 609–610
crystals
birth crystals 548
in charm bags 413–414
cleansing 532
colours of 510
crystal magick 530–532

doorkeeper stones 121–122
empowering 531–532
meanings 532–547
pointed 532
and spellcasting 531–532
curses 20, 22, 60
cyphi 555
incense 336–337

Dark Lord, The 393–394
dark mirrors 617–619
dawn **210–211**, 496–497
day tides 199–200
days of the month 199
days of the week 192–197
and archangels 580–583
December 199
dedication and initiation 690
Dee, John 32, 466
definitions of magick 50–51
*Write and record your personal definition of
magick* 62
deities 232–245
of the eightfold wheel 70
see also gods and goddesses
Demeter 232, 381, 382, 653
destruction and creation 15
Devana 233
devas 317
Devil, The 15–16
Diana 367
Diana Triformis 375
dishes *see* pentacles
divination 432, 607
see also runes; scrying
divine force 220
Djed (hieroglyph)
Djinn 343–344
Dominions (angels) 593
doorkeeper stones 121–122
doorways
in circles 252–253
golden 507–508

dragon's blood 555
incense 337
dragons
air elementals 329
fire elementals 345
drawing down the moon 475–480
Druidry 8, 38–39
crane bags 425
Druid prayer 285
meditation stones 429
nine Awens 503–504
see also under Celtic
drums 122
Dumuzi 394
dusk **211–212**, 498

earth (Chinese element) 153
earth (element) 136–137, 316
earth (Norse element) 155
Earth elementals 316, **318–323**
absorbing elemental strength 322–323
Earth energies 316, 320
Earth goddesses 232, 316
Earth gods 232–233, 392
Earth Mothers 14, 28, **363–365**
see also Gaia; Triple Goddess
Earth spirits 316, **319–323**
eclipse, solar 501–502
ecological preservation 19
Egypt, Ancient
altars 171–173
magick **30–31**, 86, 110, **123–125**,
171–173
magickal symbols 399
magickal tools 123–125
power of names 268–270
see also hieroglyphs
Egyptian Wheel of the Year 85–92
eightfold year 65, 69
see also Wheel of the Year
elemental beings 317, 321
elemental guardians 626–628
elemental spirits 321

elemental thought forms 318
elementals 317–318
  see also individual elementals
elements 134–142
  Celtic tradition 147–149
  Chinese 150–154
  in magick 135–142
  Norse 154–156
  in traditional magick 134
  triple elemental circles 250–251
  Walking the four elements 143–144
  Weaving the elements 144–145
  western elemental system 134–135
  see also air; earth; fire; water
Eleusinian mysteries 382, 641, 653
Elhaz (symbol) 131
elves 330–331
emotions 50, 51
empowering
  crystals 531–532
  symbols 186
  tools 112–114
energy
  Three–knot chant for energy 667–668
  A water ritual to bring new energies into your
    life 87–88
energy, personal 178
  and colours 510
  and spellcasting 184–185
  see also chakras
energy field 13
Enochian magick 32
equinoxes 65
  see also Mabon; Ostara
Esbats 28, 476
essential oils
  anointing candles 530
  see also fragrances
ethics, code of 13, 18–21, 699–700
everyday life and magick 10
evil
  and witchcraft 14–15
  eye 20

exchange in magick 52–53
Eye of Horus (symbol) 131

fairies
  earth elementals 331
  fire elementals 344
familiars 318, 688–690
fate, gods and goddesses of 244
feathers 331–332
February 197
Feng Shui 151
fertility
  Aboriginal mythology 94–95
  of crops 28–29
  dual energy images 98
  goddesses of 241
  Mothers 28–29
  rituals 28
  runes 444–445
  symbols 27–28
festivals 636
  adapting timing 65, 636
  fire festivals 65
  see also Wheel of the Year
Fierce Sisters, The 379
fire
  Celtic festivals 65
  in Egyptian magick 88–92
  A fire ritual for personal power 91–92
  gods and goddesses 239–240
  in magick history 29–30
  in nature 341–342
  offerings 345–346, 347–348
  and water fusion of power 348
fire (Chinese element) 152
fire (element) 139–140, 341
  making the basis for a whole
    spell 351–352
fire (Norse element) 155
fire dragons 345
fire elementals 341, 342–353
  absorbing elemental strength 346–349
  and magick 343–345

fire essences 344

fire nature spirits 344

fire spirits 343–345

fires, ritual 342, 346

flowers
  goddesses 235
  meanings 551–567

folk history 26

folk magick 8, 36, 54

formal magick 29–30, 620
  see also rituals

Fortune, Dion 33, 303

four elements *see* elements

fragrances 569
  and clairsentience 605–606
  herbal spell and charm bags 570–571
  herbs and their meanings 551–567
  infusions 572–573
  working with 567–568
  see also incense

frankincense 557
  incense 337

Frazer, James 46, 55

free will 22, 59, 60

Freyja 241

Freyr 232, **386–387, 393**

Friday 196

Frigg 242

frog (hieroglyph) 403

full moon 204, 206, **475–476, 480**

Furies, The 377

Gabriel 83, **290, 579**

Gaia 14, **232, 316, 364–365**

Gardner, Gerald 44–45, 46, 47, 260

Geb 89, **232, 321, 392–393**

genies 344

gibbous moon 206

giving back 21

gnomes 321–322

goat gods 388–389

God, The 14, **384**
  charge of 224, 229–231

and Wheel of the Year 71

wild god, invoking 396–397

young god 385–390
  see also Goddess; gods and goddesses

God King, The 392

God of the Grain 29

Goddess, The 13–14, 220
  charge of 223–228
  creating your Goddess form 228
  many faces of 363
  as mother of all 363–365
  secret goddess 381–383
  talking to 221–223
  union with the God 29
  and Wheel of the Year 71
  in witchcraft 365–371
  see also gods and goddesses; Triple
    Goddess

gods and goddesses 232–245, 384–397
  bird and insect goddesses and gods 234
  bull gods 387–388
  crone/wise woman goddesses 238,
    369–370
  Earth God 392
  Egyptian 30–31, 86–87, 89
  of fate, justice and wisdom 244
  finding your goddess 372–373
  flower goddesses 235
  goat gods 388–389
  Grain Goddess and Gods 28, 66, 649
  Green Man 232–233, **389–390**
  Horned God, The 15, 16, **385–389**
  of the hunt 233–234
  identifying with 221
  of love, beauty, magick and fertility 241
  in magick 220–228
  Moon goddesses 236
  Moon gods 237
  Norse **125–128**, 154–155
  sea and water gods and goddesses 243
  sky gods and goddesses 237–238, 392
  sun and fire gods and goddesses 239–240
  talking to 221–223

trickster gods/gods of change 244, **390–393**

weather deities 235

in witchcraft 365–371

women's and mother goddesses 242

see also deities

gold 521–522

Golden Bough 46

Golden Dawn 32, **33**

golden doorways 507–508

good and evil 14–15

Goronwy 70

Grail, The **100–101**, 104, 118

Grain Goddess and Gods 28, 66, 649

green 516–517

and hieroglyphs 463

Green Man 232–233, **389–390**

Gregorian chants 603

grey 521

grounding 189

growing season *see* Peret

guardian angels 574, **585–589**, 594,
628–629

zodiacal correspondences 585–589

guardian stones 121–122

Halloween 655

hammers 126

Hammer of Thor 107, 126, **436**

Hapy 86

harm 18

harming none rule **19**, 59

harvest 29, 37, 67

see also Lughnassadh; Mabon; Shemu

Hathor

mirror magick 615–616

seven daughters of 662

*Seven–knot Hathor love know
ritual* 669–670

healing and magick 31

healing Caduceus symbol 130

heart (hieroglyph) 405

heart chakra 181–182

Hebrew magick 31–32

Hecate 369–370

Triple Hecate 376

Heka 293

Heket 87

Hel 238

Helios 240

hematite (crystal) 538–539

herbs 550, 567, 569

infusions 572–573

meanings of 551–567

scrying with 611–612

spell and charm bags 570–571

Hermes Trismesgistos 31

Hermetic tradition 31

Herne the Hunter 234

hexagram (symbol) 29–130

hexes 20

hieroglyphs 402–406, **451–465**

and colours 462–464

determinatives 461–462

and the English alphabet 452–458

and magick 453–454

magick names and spells 461

working with 452

writing 458–460

higher power 221

see also goddess, The

Hinduism 13–14

homeopathic magick 55–56

Horned God, The 15, 16, **385–389**

lords of the hunt 29, 234, 386

symbol 130

horns 127

Horus 86, 90, **234**

hours of the day

and archangels 589–591

planetary 216–218

human body fluids 19

hunt, gods and goddesses of 29,
233–234, 386

hunter–gatherers 66

Hymn to Innana 30

ice (Norse element) 154
images 304–305
Imbolc 69, 71, **73–74, 637–639**
incense **333–338, 568**
    choosing for rituals 334–335
    and cleansing 284
    making 569–570
    offerings 334
    power of 333–334
    Silent incense ritual 335–336
    types 336–338
incense sticks 568
    and fire element 347
influencing others 18–19
infusions 572–573
initiation 690
ink and water scrying 613
Innana 30, 394
internet resources 11, 259, **262**
inundation *see* Akhet
invocations 222–223
Isis 30, 31, **87, 89,** 90, **236, 367–369,**
    662
    bags 412, **423–424**
    buckle of Isis (hieroglyph) 405
    power of 269–270
    Triple Isis 375

Jack o'the Green 390
jade (crystal) 539
January 197
Jarapiri 94
Jesus Christ 15, 29, 70
    see also Holy Grail
jet (crystal) 539
jewellery 283
jinns 344
July 198
June 198
Jung, Carl Gustav 135
Jupiter (god) 237
Jupiter (planet) 214–215

Kabbalah 31
    and angels 574
    Kabbalistic cross 286–287
Kali 370–371
Key of Solomon 32
Khnum 89
knives, Norse 128
    see also athames; bolines
knots 661–673
    chants 666–668
    knot cords 662–663
    ladders 662
    Nine–knot chant for success at work 672
    Seven–knot Hathor love know
        ritual 669–670
    storing and releasing magick 665–666
    Three–knot banishing spell 668–669
    Three–knot chant for energy 667–668
    Three nine–knot spells 670–672
    tying 110–111, 666
    using in magick 664–665
Kunapipi 94, 95

ladder (hieroglyph) 403–404
ladders 662
lake women 357
Lammas 67, 71, **79–80, 648–651**
lances *see* wands
land and earth (Celtic element) 148
lapis lazuli (crystal) 540
lavender 560
    incense 337
Law of Asha 30
Leland, Geoffrey 46, 366
ley lines 67, 254, 319, 320
Lindow man 52
Litha *see* Alban Heruin
lodestones 414
Loki 391
long barrows **67,** 147, 504
Long Man of Wilmington 120
Lords of the Hunt 29, 234, 386

lorelei 356
love
  goddesses of 241
  Seven–knot Hathor love know
    ritual 669–670
Lucifer 16
Lugh 70, 74, **240, 395,** 651
Lughnassadh 67, 71, **79–80, 648–651**
lunar calendars 480–483
  creating 488
lunar energies 69

Mabon 80–81, **651–653**
Macha 379–380
Magi 29, 50
magick 54–55
  angel magick 32
  attracting magick 56–57
  Australian Aboriginal 93–96
  balancing **60–61,** 68, 667
  banishing magick 58, **60,** 668–669
  binding magick 58, **59**
  cave magick 26–27
  Celtic 38–39
  ceremonial 32, 33
  chanting 294–295
  contagious **56,** 57, 68
  definitions of 50–51, 62
  Egyptian **30–31,** 86, 110, **123–125,**
    171–173
  Enochian 32
  and everyday life 9
  exchange in 51–53
  folk magick 8, 36, 54
  formal 29–30
  Hebrew 31–32
  Hermetic tradition 31
  homeopathic 55–56
  misconceptions of 16–17
  modern 46–47
  names 31, **268–280**
  natural 29
  polarity magick 93–94

positive 20
protective 58, **281–292**
and religion 17, 30
ritual 32, 33
rules of 18–21
Scandinavian 39–41, 257
of the seasons 37–38, **65–68**
Solomonic 32
sound magick 93
spontaneous versus structured 53–54
sun magick 208–212
sympathetic 55
see also witchcraft; witches
maiden goddess 374
major arcana 309–313
Malachim alphabet 469–473
malachite (crystal) 540
mantras 294
March 197
Mars (planet) 213–214
Mati Syra–Zemlya 232
May 198
May Day 76
  see also Beltane
medicine bags 422–423
meditation stones 429
menat (hieroglyph) 404
mer people 356–357
Mercury (planet) 214
metal (Chinese element) 153
metal charms 407–408
meteorites 342–343
Michael 77, 211, **290, 578–579**
midnight 212, 499
  Drawing down the sun at midnight 501,
    502–503
Midsummer Solstice 66 **77–78,**
  644–647
  special sun ritual 507–508
Midwinter Solstice 66, 78, **82–83,**
  657–659
Min 91
mind powers 596

ministering Angels 593

minor arcana 313

Minotaur 387–388

mirrors, scrying with 615–619

modern life and witchcraft 16–17

mojo bags 417–421

Monday 193–194

months of the year 197–199

Moon, The 213, **475–489**

  correspondences 202

  drawing down the moon 475–480

  gods and goddesses 236–237

  months 481–483

  phases of 205–208

  phases of in magick 203–204

  and scrying 614–615

  and seasonal magick 66

  symbols on magickal tools 128

  times 202–208

  void of course 207

  see also eightfold year

Moon Mother, The 28

moon water 359

moonstone (crystal) 541

Morphic resonance 54, 66, 701

Morrigu, The 379

moss agate (crystal) 541

Mother Goddess 316, 374, 242

  statuettes 27–28

  Triple Mother Goddesses 380–381

multicultural Wheel of the Year 85–97

museums 36

music for chants 298–299

myrrh 562

incense 337

mystic squares 253–257

mythology

  Aboriginal 94–95

  and the Goddess 14

  Scandinavian 40, 154–155

  see also gods and goddesses

naiads 355

names, magickal 31, **268–280**

  creating 270–276

  Creating a power name talisman 278–279

  and numerology 271–276

  power of 268–269

  ritual to create 270–271

  secrecy of 268, 269

  using 277–278

natural magick 29

natural symbols 305–306

natural world

  and magick 8

  sounds of 604

nature spirits

  earth 319

  fire 344

Naudhiz (symbol) 131

needs

  enough for your needs and a little
    more 20–21

Nefer (hieroglyph) 404

Nefertum 89

negative attraction 58

Nemainn 380

Neopaganism 45

Nephthys 91

nereids 355

Nerthus 232

New Age movement 33

new moon 205

night altars 169–171

night rainbow ritual 170–171

noon 211, 497

Norns, The 376

Norse altars 174–176

Norse elements 154–156

  Ritual using the Norse elements 156

Norse seasons 93

Norse tools **125–128**, 174–175

Norse witches 40–41

November 199

numbers

  and magickal names 271–273

meanings of 273–276
number squares 278–279
tarot cards 314
Nut 237

obsidian (crystal) 542
snowflake obsidian 545
October 198–199
Odin 40–41, **237**, 655
   spear of Odin 104
   triple horn symbol 127
offerings 52
oils
   anointing candles 530
   scrying with oil and water 612
Oimelc 69, 71, **73–74, 637–639**
orange (colour) 514–515
orange (fragrance) 563
Order of the Golden Dawn 32, **33**
orris root (incense) 337
Osiris 87, 89, 90, **232, 395**, 463
Ostara **75–76**, 241, **639–641**
ouroboros (symbol) 130

Pagan Federation, The 24
Pan 16, **234, 388**
Parvati 242
patchouli 563
   incense 338
pentacles 101–103
   magickal significance of 102–103
   making 681–684
pentagrams 101–102
   banishing Earth pentagram 129
   banishing pentagram ritual 287
   invoking earth pentagram 129
   symbol used on magickal tools 129
people, images of 304–305
Peret 85, **88–90**
persecution of witches 42–44
pink 519–520
planetary hours 216–217
   calculating 217–218

planets 212–216
polarities 58, 94
polarity magick 93–94
pomanders 409
positive emotions 51
positive magick 20
   see also binding magick
power
   animals 31, 318
   archetypal 31
   of belief 51
   of blessings 284–285
   of candles 349–351
   A fire ritual for personal power 91–92
   of the Goddess and God 223–228
   grounding 189
   of incense 333–334
   of names 268–269
   psychic 51
   raising 108, **186–188**
   releasing 108, **188–189**, 630–631,
      667
   of symbols 303–315
   of words 293
   of writing 306–307, 431
Powers (angels) 593
prayer sticks 332
prayers
   blessings 285
   to gods and goddesses 222–223
priests and priestesses *see* wise men and
   wise women
Principalities (angels) 593
protective magick 58, **281–292**
   blessing rituals 286–291
   use of athames 108
   see also binding magick
psychic attack 20
psychic defence 20
psychic development 595–606
psychic powers 51
psychic protection 58, **281–292**
psychic sensing *see* clairsentience

psychic shields 58, **284**
psychokinesis 27, 54, **596–598**
  developing 597–598
psychology of spells 177–178
psychometry 600–601
Puck 388–389
purification of yourself 222
purple 518–519
purple fluorite (crystal) 542–543

quarter days 65
quarters, closing 631–632
quarters, opening 626–628
quartz crystals 532
  clear crystal quartz 538
   quartz 543–544
  rutilated quartz 544
  smoky quartz 544

Ra 86, 90, **91, 240, 269**, 615
Raguel 73
rain
  To bring the rains 96–97
  To stop the rains 97
  water 360
Raphael 75, 210, **290, 577–578**
Raziel 32, 106, **574–575**
red 510–511, **513–514**
  and hieroglyphs 464
red jasper (crystal) 543
reincarnation 263–264
relationships, ending 60
religion and magick 17, 30
resins 569
Rismuch 80
ritual baths 282–283
ritual magick, origins 32, 33
ritual offerings 52
rituals 53, **620–635**
  beginning 624–625
  body of 630
  casting the circle 625–626
  and celebrations 68

defining the purpose 629–630
development in early magick 27, 32
fertility 28–29
inviting in the wise ones 628–629
opening the quarters 626–628
planning 621–624
releasing the power 630–631
returning the energies 631
ritual year 621
  and seasons 67–68
uncasting the circle 632
robes, magickal 283
Robin Hood 390
rock art and magick 94–95
roots 414
rose petals 564
  incense 338
rose quartz (crystal) 543–544
rules of magick 18–21
runes 107, 306, **431–450**
  aetts 436–443
  alphabetical correspondences 433–435
  bind runes 443–446
  casting 449
  dedication 447
  fertility rune 444–445
  interpreting 449–450
  making 448
  understanding 432–433
  use in magick 432
  use on magickal tools 128
rutilated quartz (crystal) 544

sabbats 65
Sachiel 79, **581**
sacral chakra 180
sacred water, making 107
sacrifices, ritual 19, **52**
St Bridget 74
salamanders **343–344**, 348
Salem witchcraft trials 44
salt 109
  baths 282–283

magick of 324—325
Protective, health and abundance rituals using salt 325
Samael 580–581
Samhain 70, 71, **81–82**, 93, **654–656**
sandalwood 565
   incense 338
Sanders, Alex 47
Satis 87
Saturday 196–197
Saturn (planet) 215–216
Scandinavian magick 39–41
   grid of nine squares 257
   see also under Norse
scarab (hieroglyph) 404
scrying 595, **607–608**
   crystal balls 609–610
   herbs 611–612
   mirrors 615–619
   oil and water 612
   water 611–615
   water and ink 613
   water and light 614–615
   water and wax 613–614
sea and water (Celtic element) 148
sea and water gods and goddesses 243
seasons
   Making your mark on the seasons 96–97
   Norse 93
   wet and dry 93
seasonal magick 37–38
   Australian Aboriginal 93–96
   history 65–68
   and rituals 67–68
   see also Wheel of the Year
seax 128
secrecy
   and Books of Shadows **260**, 262
   and names 268, 269
secret goddess 381–383
Sekhmet 91, **239**
self–empowerment 54
September 198

Seraphim 592
Set 391
Shemu 85, **90–92**
Shen (hieroglyph) 405
silver 522–523
singing chants 298–299
Sisters of Fate 376–380
sistrums 124–125
   making 684–685
sky and air (Celtic element) 148
sky gods and goddesses 237–238, 392
smoky quartz (crystal) 544
smudging 284
snow water 360
snowflake obsidian (crystal) 545
Sobek 87
sodalite (crystal) 545
soil and magick 323–324
solar cross 158
solar eclipse magick 501–502
solar energies 69
solar festivals 65, 69
   see also individual festivals
solar plexus chakra 181
solar time 209
Solomon 32, 344
   Solomon's Seal 129–130
solstices 65
   see also Midsummer Solstice; Midwinter Solstice
sound
   magick 93
   natural world 604
   sacred 294
   see also clairaudience
spears
   Norse 127
   see also wands
spell bags 412, **413–417, 570–571**
spellcasting 177–191
   benefits to self 184
   and crystals 531–532
   effects on others 18–19

five stages of 185–189
and personal energy 184–185
spells 53
adapting 218–219
and chakras 184–185
Creating a nature spell 190
defining purpose of 185–186
and energy sources 178
how they work 177–178
and increased awareness 178
psychology of 177–178
timings 192–201
writing 306–307
spices *see* fragrances
spirals (symbols) 130
spirit 134
spirit guides 26, 181, 628–629
see also angel guardians; witch guardians
spontaneous magick 53–54
squares, mystic 253–258
grid of nine 257
squares, number
Creating a power name talisman 278–279
staffs 120–121
making or buying 680–681
stangs 121
star water 359–360
stone circles 319, 320, 507, 645
Stonehenge 645
stones
making Druidic meditation stones 429
with holes 408–409
structured magick 53–54
success
Nine–knot chant for success at work 672
suits (tarot cards) 313
Summer Solstice *see* Midsummer Solstice
Sun, The
Cassandra's hymn to the sun 495–496
ceremonies 492–494
connecting with 208
correspondences 209
and the coven 494–495

dark sun 501–509
Drawing down the power of the sun goddess or god 490–500
Drawing down the sun at midnight 501, **502–503**
eclipses 501–502
Egyptian ceremonies 496
gods and goddesses 239–240
in magick 208–212, 213
measuring 210
at midnight 501, **502–503**
and moon energies combined 208–209
scrying with 614–615
special sun ritual 507–508
symbol used on tools 128
and time 209–210
sun water 359
Sunday 193
Sweden, witchcraft trials 44
swords 103–104
sylphs 329–330
symbols
attracting magick 57
balancing magick 60–61
banishing magick 60
binding magick 59
collecting 307
contagious magick 56
empowering in spells 186
fertility 27–28
homeopathic magick 55–56
how they work 303–304
natural 305–306
power of 303–308
preserving the power of 308
tarot cards 309–315
use on tools 128–131
using in spells 185–189
see also individual symbols
sympathetic magick 55

Taliesin 118–119
talismans 399, **401**

cave art 27
Creating a power name talisman 278–279
Creating your wax personalised talisman or charm 410–411
in early magick 28, 31
tarot cards 309–315
Tauret 87
telepathic communication 51
telepathy 54–55, **598–600**
Teresa of Avila 285
Theban alphabet 466, **467–468**
third eye *see* **182–183**, 601–602
Thor 107, **125–126, 235**
Hammer of Thor 107, 126, 436
Thoth 30, 31, **91**
three realms 147–149
ritual 148–149
Three Sisters 376–380
Threefold Law 20
throat chakra 182
Thrones (angels) 592
thuribles 111
Thursday 195
Tibetan singing bowls 109
tiger's eye (crystal) 546
time
measurement 607
and the sun 209–210
timings, magickal 192–201
making amulets 400–401
Titans 369
Tjet (hieroglyph) 405
tools **99–115**
altar tools 99–110
ancient Egyptian **123–125**, 171–172
cleansing ceremony 112–113
empowering ceremony 113–114
inscribing ceremony 132
making 99, **674–686**
non–altar 116–131
Norse **125–128**, 174–175
ritual 32
symbols used on 128–131

tree agate (crystal) 546
triangles, sacred symbols 129–130
trickster gods 244, **390–393**
Triple Goddess 69–70, 74, **374–383**
maiden, mother and crone 374–376
symbol on magickal tools 128, 130
Three Sisters 376–380
Triple Mother Goddesses 380–381
Triple Spiral symbol 130
see also Goddess, The
Triple Horn of Odin 127
Tuesday 194
turquoise (colour) 517
turquoise (crystal) 547

UFOs 319
uncasting circles 251–252, 632
undines 355–356
Uranus (God) 14, **364–365**
Uriel 290, 576–577

Valiente, Doreen 260
Valkyries 234
Venus (goddess) 241
Venus (planet) 215
Vikings 39–41
see also under Norse
Virtues (angels) 593
visualisation 54
visualising the circle of light 251
What does magick mean to you? 11–12
volcanoes 341–342
vulture (hieroglyph) 406

Waite, A. E. 32
Walpurgis Night 76, 643
see also Beltane
wands 104–106
Egyptian 123–124, 679–680
empowering 106
making 675–678
using 105–106
waning moon 204, 207

watchtowers 317, 626–628, 631–632
water
    colour infused water 360
    creatures living in 355
    crystal waters 532
    in Egyptian magick 86–90
    enhancing the power of 358–359
    and fire fusion of power 348
    Making empowered and protective waters
        359–360
    moon water 359
    sacred 107
    scrying with 611–615
    sea and water gods and goddesses 243
    snow water 360
    star water 359–360
    sun water 359
    using for healing, empowerment and
        rituals 357–358
    A water ritual to bring new energies into your
        life 87–88
weather water 360
water (Chinese element) 154
water (element) 141–142, 354
    making the focus for a whole spell 361
water (Norse element) 155
water elementals 354, **355**
water spirits 354–355, **356–357**
wax
    images 304–305
    pentacles 683–684
    scrying with 613–614
    see also candles
waxing moon **203–204**, 205, 206
weather deities 235
weather water 360
wedja (hieroglyph) 406
Wednesday 194–195
wells 354, **358**
Wheel of the Year 29, 37, 39, **64–72**
    Creating your Wheel of the Year 84
    Celtic 73–83
    deities of 70

Egyptian 85–92
    festivals of 73–83
    God and Goddess of 71
    multicultural 85–97
    Plan your personal Wheel of the Year 72
    structure 65
    three–spoke 85–92
    two–spoke 92–93
    see also seasonal magick
white 512–513
    and hieroglyphs 464
Wicca, birth of 45
Wiccan cross 288–289
Wiccan Rede **18–21**, 45, 700
    exploring 22–23
wild god, invoking 396–397
winds 332–333
Winter Solstice see Midwinter Solstice
wisdom
    ancient 25–26
    collective 701
    gods and goddesses of 244
    receiving 223
wise ancestors 628–629
    Making a place of the wise ancestors 48
wise men 7, 8
wise women 7, 8
    in medieval villages 39, 41–42
wishes
    Three nine–knot spells 670–672
witch bottles 412, **426–428**
witch guardians **26**, 50, 121, 180
    Finding your witch guardian 34–36
Witch hammer, The 42–43
witch hunts 42–44
Witch's Rune 300
witchcraft
    and Christianity 17–18
    community 700–701
    and evil 14–15
    and the Devil 15–16
    history 25–47
    in modern–day life 16–17

witches
    beginners 7, 8, 9–10
    commitment ceremonies 687, **691–697**
    dedication and initiation 690
    definition of 13, 45
    groups 8–9
    hedge witches 45
    Making a place of the wise ancestors 48
    Norse 40–41
    persecution in history **42–44**,
        259–260
    personal ethics 22–23
    and reincarnation 263–264
    and secrecy **260**, 262, 268, 269
    solitary 8, 9, 22–23, 45
    see also names, magickal
witches' alphabet 466, **467–468**
witches' mirrors 617–619

women
    and early magick 27–28, 41–42
    women's and mother goddesses 242
    wood (Chinese element) 151–152
    words, power of 293
    writing, power of 306–307, 431

yang and yin 150
yellow 515–516
    and hieroglyphs 464
yellow jasper (crystal) 547
Yule 66, 78, **82–83, 657–659**

Zeus 238, 364
zodiac 29
    birth crystals 548
    birth guardian angels 585–589
    and candle magick 528–530
    and moon spells 484
Zoroaster 29–30